Lecture Notes in Computer Scie

T0238811

Commenced Publication in 1973
Founding and Former Series Editors:
Gerhard Goos, Juris Hartmanis, and Jan van Leeuwen

Editorial Board

Gilles Barthe   Cédric Fournet (Eds.)

Trustworthy Global Computing

Third Symposium, TGC 2007
Sophia-Antipolis, France, November 5-6, 2007
Revised Selected Papers

 Springer

Volume Editors

Gilles Barthe
INRIA Sophia-Antipolis Méditerranée
2004 route des lucioles - BP 93, 06902 Sophia Antipolis Cedex, France
E-mail: Gilles.Barthe@inria.fr

Cédric Fournet
Microsoft Research Ltd.
7 J J Thomson Avenue, Cambridge CB3 0FB, UK
E-mail: fournet@microsoft.com

Library of Congress Control Number: 2008922366

CR Subject Classification (1998): C.2.4, D.1.3, D.2, D.4.6, F.2.1-2, D.3, F.3

LNCS Sublibrary: SL 1 – Theoretical Computer Science and General Issues

ISSN   0302-9743
ISBN   3-540-78662-7 Springer Berlin Heidelberg New York
ISBN   978-3-540-78662-7 Springer Berlin Heidelberg New York

Springer is a part of Springer Science+Business Media

springer.com

© Springer-Verlag Berlin Heidelberg 2008

Typesetting: Camera-ready by author, data conversion by Scientific Publishing Services, Chennai, India
Printed on acid-free paper   SPIN: 12241507   06/3180   5 4 3 2 1 0

Preface

This volume contains the post-proceedings of the third edition of the International Symposium on Trustworthy Global Computing (TGC 2007), held in Sophia-Antipolis, France, November 5–6, 2007, and tutorial papers of the following Workshop on the Interplay of Programming Languages and Cryptography, held in Sophia Antipolis, November 7, 2007.

The Symposium on Trustworthy Global Computing is an international annual venue dedicated to safe and reliable computation in global computers. It focuses on providing tools and frameworks for constructing well-behaved applications and for reasoning about their behavior and properties in models of computation that incorporate code and data mobility over distributed networks with highly dynamic topologies and heterogeneous devices.

This volume starts with an invited paper from Martin Hofmann. It then includes the revised versions of the 19 contributed papers; these versions take into account both the referee's reports and the discussions that took place during the symposium. The Program Committee selected 19 papers from 48 submissions. Every submission was reviewed by at least three members of the Program Committee. In addition, the Program Committee sought the opinions of additional referees, selected because of their expertise on particular topics. We are grateful to Andrei Voronkov for his EasyChair system that helped us to manage these discussions. We would like to thank the authors who submitted papers to the conference, the members of the Program Committee, and the additional reviewers for their excellent work. We would also like to thank the invited speakers to TGC 2007, Andrew D. Gordon, Martin Hofmann, and Jeff Magee.

The proceedings also include three tutorial papers. These papers were presented at the Workshop on the Interplay of Programming Languages and Cryptography, organized by Ricardo Corin (INRIA, Rocquencourt) and Tamara Rezk (INRIA, Sophia-Antipolis).

We gratefully acknowledge support from INRIA Sophia-Antipolis, Microsoft Research, and the MSR-INRIA Joint Centre, as well as the European Global Computing Initiative through the FET program.

November 2007

Gilles Barthe
Cédric Fournet

Organization

Steering Committee

Gilles Barthe (INRIA)
Rocco De Nicola (University of Florence)
Christos Kaklamanis (University of Patras)
Ugo Montanari (University of Pisa)
Davide Sangiorgi (University of Bologna)
Don Sannella (University of Edinburgh)
Vladimiro Sassone (University of Southampton)
Martin Wirsing (University of Munich)

Program Committee

Gilles Barthe (INRIA)
Roberto Bruni (University of Pisa)
Luis Caires (Universidade Nova de Lisboa)
Bruno Crispo (University of Trento)
Silvano Dal Zilio (CNRS)
Rocco De Nicola (University of Florence)
Cédric Fournet (Microsoft Research)
Manuel Hermenegildo (T.U. of Madrid - UPM)
Alan Jeffrey (Bell Labs - Alcatel Lucent)
Christos Kaklamanis (University of Patras)
Cosimo Laneve (University of Bologna)
Uwe Nestmann (TU Berlin)
Dave Sands (Chalmers University of Technology of Göteborg)
Vladimiro Sassone (University of Southampton)
Ian Stark (University of Edinburgh)
Alan Schmitt (INRIA)
Paul G. Spirakis (University of Patras and RACTI)
Éric Tanter (Universidad de Chile)
Nobuko Yoshida (Imperial College London)

Referees

Lucia Acciai
Peter Barron
Moritz Y. Becker
Martin Berger

Michele Boreale
Johannes Borgström
Didier Le Botlan
Maria Grazia Buscemi

Marco Carbone

Manuel Carro

Amadeo Casas

Roberto Cascella

Mariano Ceccato

Ricardo Corin

William Delobel

Simon Gay

Roberta Gori

Daniel Hedin

Kohei Honda

Fabrice Huet

Samuel Hym

Romain Janvier

Alberto Lluch Lafuente

Ivan Lanese

Cosimo Laneve

Diego Latella

Serguei Lenglet

Vasiliki Liagkou

Michael Lienhardt

Sam Lindley

Michele Loreti

Carbone Marco

Francisco Martins

Mieke Massink

Manuel Mazzara

Mario Mendez-Lojo

Edison Mera

Leonardo Gaetano Mezzina

Cristopher Moore

Matthieu Morel

Stijn Mostinckx

Sebastian Nanz

Jorge Navas

Rocco De Nicola

Carlo Nocentini

Jose Pacheco

Luca Padovani

Giuseppe Persiano

David Pichardie

Antonio Ravara

Tamara Rezk

Cesar Sanchez

Ioannis Stamatiou

Daniele Strollo

Josef Svenningsson

Daniele Varacca

Andres Vignaga

Elena Zucca

Sponsoring Institutions

Microsoft Research, Cambridge, UK

MSR-INRIA Joint Centre, Orsay, France

INRIA, Sophia-Antipolis, France

Table of Contents

Trustworthy Global Computing

Invited Papers

Accepted Papers

Tutorial Papers

Elimination of Ghost Variables in Program Logics

Martin Hofmann[1] and Mariela Pavlova[2]

[1] Institut für Informatik LMU München, Germany
[2] Trusted Labs, Sophia-Antipolis, France
hofmann@ifi.lmu.de, Mariela.Pavlova@trusted-labs.fr

Abstract. Ghost variables are assignable variables that appear in program annotations but do not correspond to physical entities. They are used to facilitate specification and verification, e.g., by using a ghost variable to count the number of iterations of a loop, and also to express extra-functional behaviours. In this paper we give a formal model of ghost variables and show how they can be eliminated from specifications and proofs in a compositional and automatic way. Thus, with the results of this paper ghost variables can be seen as a specification pattern rather than a primitive notion.

1 Introduction

With the fast development of programming systems, the requirements for software quality also become more complex. In reply to this, the techniques for program verification also evolve. This is the case also for modern specification languages which must support a variety of features in order to be expressive enough to deal with such complex program properties. A typical example is JML (short for Java Modeling Language), a design by contract specification language tailored to Java programs. JML has proved its utility in several industrial case studies [1,2]. Other examples are ESC/Java [3], the Larch methodology [4] and Spec# [5]. JML syntax is very close to the syntax of Java. JML has also other specification constructs which do not have a counterpart in the Java language. While program logics and specification languages help in the development of correct code they have also been proposed as a vehicle for *proof-carrying code* [6,7,8,9] where clients are willing to run code supplied by untrusted and possibly malicious code producers provided the code comes equipped with a certificate in the form of a logical proof that certain security policies are respected. In this case, the underlying logical formalism must have a very solid semantic basis so as to prevent inadvertent or malicious exploitation. On the one hand, the logic must be shown sound with respect to some well-defined semantics; on the other hand, the meaning of specifications must be as clear as possible so as to minimise the risk of formally correct proofs which nevertheless establish not quite the intuitively intended property. This calls for a rigorous assessment of all the features employed in a specification language; in this paper we do this for JML's *ghost variables*.

G. Barthe and C. Fournet (Eds.): TGC 2007, LNCS 4912, pp. 1–20, 2008.

Coq development. All definitions, theorems, proofs have been carried out within the Coq theorem prover and are available for download at www.tcs.ifi.lmu.de/~mhofmann/ghostcoq.tgz.

2 Ghost Variables and Their Use

In brief, a ghost variable is an assignable variable that does not appear in the executable code but only in assertions and specifications. Accordingly, annotated code is allowed to contain ghost statements that assign into ghost variables. These ghost statements are not actually executed but specifications and assertions involving ghost variables are understood "as if" the ghost statements were executed whenever reached. Note that ghost variables should not interfere with the values of normal program variables or the control flow of a program.

Ghost variables appear to ease proof automation in automatic theorem provers like Simplify as they instantiate existential quantification by pointing the object which satisfies the otherwise existentially quantified proposition. On the other hand, they are intuitive and thus, helpful in the specification process.

2.1 Ghost Variables in Internal Assertions

First, they can be used for an internal method annotation in order to facilitate the program verification process. For instance, in JML ghost variables can be used in an assertion to refer to the value of a program variable at some particular program point different from the point where the assertion is declared and must hold. Thus, we can use a ghost variable to express that a program variable is not changed by a loop execution by assigning to it prior to the loop or in order to count the number of loop iterations. Such use of ghost variables usually makes them appear in intra-method assertions like loop invariants or assertions at a particular program point but does not introduce them in the contract of a method (i.e. the pre- and postcondition). For illustration, we consider an example which doubles the value of the variable x and stores it in the variable y:

```
//@ensures  2*\old(x) = y
y=0;
//@ghost int z;
//@set  z = 0;
//@loop_invariant  2*z = y && z = \old(x) - x
while  (x > 0) {
    x = x - 1;
    y = y + 2;
    //@set  z = z + 1;}
```

The desired property of this code fragment is introduced by the keyword ensures and states that y has accumulated the double of the initial value of x, i.e. \old(x). In the specification, we have used the ghost variable z. We may notice that z is declared in Java comments as is the case for any kind of JML specification. Its value at the beginning of every iteration corresponds to the number of loop iterations done so far. Thus, before the loop, z is initialised to be 0 and at the end of the loop body, it is incremented. Note that z does not appear in the postcondition, i.e., the end-to-end specification of the program fragment. Its purely ancillary role is to facilitate the verification process by allowing the loop invariant to refer to the number of iterations even though no physical variable counts them.

2.2   Expressing Extra-Functional Code Properties

Secondly, ghost variables may be used to express extra-functional properties about program behavior. In such cases, ghost variables may become part of the method contract. For example, they may serve to model the memory consumption of a program. To illustrate this, let us consider a fragment of a Java class with two ghost variables - MEM which counts the number of allocated heap cells and MAX which models the maximal amount of heap space that can be allocated by the program:

```
//@ public static ghost int MEM;
//@ public static final ghost int MAX;

//@ requires MEM + size(A) <= MAX
//@ ensures   MEM <= MAX
public void m () {
  A a = new A ()
  //@ set MEM = MEM + size (A)}
```

The postcondition asserts that MEM is bounded by MAX which ensures bounded memory allocation provided that MEM accurately tracks the number of allocations made. In the example this is ensured by the assignment to MEM.

We notice that this relationship between the value of the ghost variable MEM and the actual memory consumption of the method is implicit in the annotation policy, i.e., lies in the fact that MEM is incremented precisely when memory is being allocated and nowhere else and not modified in any other way either.

Therefore, ghost variables are particularly suitable when the code annotation is completely transparent, for example, for software auditing performed interactively over the source code, i.e. in the process where a code producer verifies if the written code respects their initial intentions. In such situations the good intuitions that ghost variables provide as opposed, perhaps, to more functional or abstract ways of specification are fully brought to bear.

Ghost variables have also been used to indicate when class invariants are required to hold and may be relied upon [10] and as a means to enforce a particular order in which API methods should be invoked [11].

3   Problems with Ghost Variables

In this section we describe why we feel that ghost variables as currently used and modelled might be harmful in a proof carrying code scenario where formal proofs are provided as certificates by untrusted and possibly even malicious code producers.

3.1   Semantics of Ghost Variables

Usually, program semantics is expressed as a transition between states where states represent the values related to program variables. For the case of JML, verification tools like ESC/Java [3] and Jack [12] treat ghost variables as ordinary program variables. While this works in order to generate verification conditions and justify proof rules, it is not entirely satisfactory if we treat program semantics as primary and program verification as a means to an end. To appreciate this point notice that the formal operational semantics of a language, e.g. Java Bytecode, can in principle not be proven adequate. One can compare it to other formalisations of the semantics, e.g. as a virtual machine, but adequacy of the last formalised semantics in such a chain of translations always remains an unprovable axiom. For this reason, we feel that program semantics should be as simple as possible and certainly not be modelled to suit a particular verification methodology. Its primary aim should be to make the correspondence with the real world as evident as possible. Thus, we find that one should give meaning to ghost variables without altering the operational semantics of the language not even by adding non-existent variables to its memory model.

One may argue that one could prove a semantics adequate by formally relating it to assembly language level formalizations of hardware architectures. As argued above this only shifts the "semantic gap" somewhere else. What remains unproven in that case is that the assembly language level formalization does indeed adequately reflect what's going on in the hardware and also that the assumed translation of bytecode to assembly code is what is really done by the compiler and the JVM implementation.

3.2   Modelling Extra-Functional Properties

There is a second problem with ghost variables that shows up only when they are used to track extra-functional program properties like memory consumption above, which is to do with the fact that the intended as opposed to the formal meaning of a contract then is contingent on respecting a particular code annotation policy. For the sake of a concrete example, suppose that someone advertises a Java card game to be run on a mobile phone and claims that it definitely runs within 10M of memory by providing a formal proof that its main-method satisfies the postcondition

```
ensures MEM <= 10485760
```

Unfortunately, such a formal proof only guarantees that the ghost variable MEM has a value $\leq 10M$ after the execution of the program; the fact that it relates to memory allocation remains unproved. Thus, n order to be really sure that the program really does not use more than 10M the recipient would have to carefully study the code to make sure that indeed the ghost variable MEM has been appropriately incremented at every allocation site and not been tempered with anywhere else. Not only does this place an awkward burden on code recipients; it also opens to door to all kinds of exploits by malicious code producers based on somehow hiding assignments to MEM in obcure library functions or similar.

One could argue that this could be fixed by decreeing that a "certificate" of the resource property in question comprises not only the formal proof of the contract but also a successful run of some automatic analysis which checks that ghost assignments are inserted next to all memory allocating instructions and only there.

Note, however, that arguing that such a policy does capture the intended resource property is again part of the *semantic gap* outside the realm of formal verification and must be left to human inspection and ultimately belief. In situations where we assume the existence of malicious code producers who try to fool the code consumer with faked certificates we would prefer to reduce resorting to such non-rigorous methods to a bare minimum. Of course, if we are interested in extra-functional code properties we have to at some point formally define what the observable extra-functional effects of a program are, such as memory usage, time consumptions, consumption of other resources, etc. However, we argue that this formalisation should be done openly by a trusted body of experts, and carefully argued by means of examples, test cases, etc. In brief, it is a procedure that should not be done over and over again for each verification tool or method.

We therefore argue that once we have a program semantics and program logic that can speak about extra-functional prperties it will no longer be necessary to make reference to ghost variables in contracts so that we are thus brought back to essentially the first usage of ghost variables, namely as an auxiliary device employed to facilitate a verification.

Before continuing, we emphasize again that there is nothing wrong with ghost variables in a verification tool or formalism. It is only in the scenario of proof-carrying code where we intend to use proofs in formalised program logic as unforgeable certificates that our discussion applies and our results are of value.

4   Contributions of This Paper

In this paper we demonstrate that ghost variables can be eliminated from formal proofs in a program logic in such a way that on the one hand the same outside contracts will be proved and on the other hand the intuitive ease that ghost variables afford is retained.

We do this by showing that proofs in a program logic with ghost variables can be translated automatically and compositionally into proofs of the same specifications in a logic that does not use ghost variables. In other words, ghost variables become a conservative extension of ordinary program logics.

In order to focus on salient aspects we study the problem of ghost variables using first a simple, unstructured while language specified by a big-step operational semantics and reasoned about in a VDM-style program logic using I/O-relations as assertions. The proof rules of the program logic are such that whenever $C : P$ is provable then whenever S, T are initial, respectively final states of a terminating run of program C then $P(S, T)$ holds.

4.1 Elimination of Ghost Variables

We then consider programs C_g annotated with assignments to ghost variables and introduce ad-hoc proof rules for deducing statements of the form $C_g : P_g$ where, now, P_g is a relations between pairs of states: (initial state, initial ghost state) and (final state, final ghost state). The proof rules are motivated by the intuitive meaning of ghost variables but are not formally validated against any kind of operational semantics of ghost variables. Instead, our first result shows that if we have a derivation of $C_g : P_g$ then we can *effectively* find a derivation of $C : P$ where C is the program C_g with all ghost instructions removed and where $P(S, T) \iff \forall S_g. \exists T_g. P_g((S, S_g), (T, T_g))$. In particular, when $P_g((S, S_g), (T, T_g)) \iff Q(S, T)$ for some I/O-relation Q then $P \iff Q$. This models the case where ghost variables do not appear in the outside contract, but possible in internal assertions, e.g., as invariants in invocations of the proof rule for while-loops. The qualification *"effective"* of the announced proof transformation means that the transformation is by induction on proofs and does not require inventing of new invariants, assertions, mathematical proofs of side condition or similar, and is thus fully automatic. Without this extra qualification a result like the one we announced could be trivially true by appealing to a completeness result for the program logic.

4.2 Extension to Extra-Functional Properties

We then extend our approach to encompass extra-functional properties. In order to model these we extend our language by *external procedures* that have no effect on the store but do cause an event to occur that is visible from the outside. Formally, we assume a set *Extern* of external functions and decree that for $f \in Extern$ and e an integer expression we can form the command $f(e)$ which has the same effect as *Skip* but causes the *event* (f, n) to occur where n is the current value of expression e. Thus, an event is an element of $Event := Extern \times \mathbf{Z}$.

Now that programs can cause observable effects already during their execution we can no longer semantically identify all nonterminating programs as is typically done by big-step operational semantics. Instead we define for each program C as relation $\xrightarrow{C}$ where $S \xrightarrow{C, ev} S'$ means that when we start program C in initial state S then during its execution there is a point at which we have reached state S' and up to that point the events $\boldsymbol{ev} \in Event^*$ have occurred.

We then consider a program logic that in addition to VDM-style assertions (which now, of course, may also mention the trace of events occurred) also has a judgement $C : I$ with the intention that whenever $S \xrightarrow{C, ev} S'$ then $I(S, ev)$ will hold. The rules for the definition of this judgement have premises referring to the usual assertions.

In this extension of the program logic we can thus assert extra-functional properties without using ghost variables. We show that, again, ghost variables can be eliminated from proofs of specifications that do not themselves mention ghost variables.

Suppose now that we have a proof that program C satisifies the invariant "MEM = \old(MEM)" where MEM is a ghost variable purportedly counting the number of memory allocations made. As argued above such a proof ought to be accompanied by a formal argument explaining that the ghost variable MEM really does reflect the number allocations made. In our resource-enhanced logic this could be formalised as a proof of the invariant MEM = $mem(ev)$ where $mem(ev)$ is the number of allocation events in execution trace tr. Combining the two proofs then yields a proof of the invariant $mem(ev) = 0$ to which elimination of ghost variables applies.

5 Language and Program Logic

In this section we define a simple programming language and a VDM style program logic as a vehicle for a formalisation of our results. The language has neither local variables nor objects, yet the salient features of our modelling of ghost variables can be sufficiently well illustrated therein without introducing unnecessary clutter.

5.1 Simple Programming Language

We consider a simple programming language with assignment, conditional, loop, sequence, and skip statements:

Inductive $stmt$: $Type$:=
| $Assign$: $var \rightarrow expr \rightarrow stmt$
| If : $expr \rightarrow stmt \rightarrow stmt \rightarrow stmt$
| $While$: $expr \rightarrow stmt \rightarrow stmt$
| $Sseq$: $stmt \rightarrow stmt \rightarrow stmt$
| $Skip$: $stmt$.

Here and in the rest of the paper, we use a Coq syntax for introducing definitions. The Coq code above is an inductive type with several constructors corresponding to the different statements of the language. This definition thus corresponds to the following more common notation:

$stmt$:=
| $Assign$ (var $expr$)
| If ($expr$ $stmt$ $stmt$)
. . .

We elide the syntax of arithmetic expressions. Values in our language are integers. Our formal Coq development comprises recursive methods; we omit them here for the sake of simplicity. We give a standard big-step operational semantics which characterises the terminating executions of program statements. It is defined as a relation between initial and final states of statement execution where states are mappings from variables to values:

$exec$: $state \rightarrow stmt \rightarrow state \rightarrow Prop$

The inductive definition of $exec$ is given in the Appendix.

5.2 Logic for a Simple Language

The partial correctness logic is formulated in a VDM style [13]. This differs from the perhaps more common Hoare style rules, where assertions are predicates on the current state; in VDM, program assertions are functions of the initial and final state of a program statement:

Definition *assertion* := *state* → *state* → *Prop.*

This choice avoids the use of auxiliary variables which is necessary in Hoare logic used for relating the values of variables in different states, see [14]. The logic is encoded in Coq as an inductive predicate with one constructor for each proof rule, see Appendix:

Inductive *RULET*: *stmt* → *assertion* → *Prop*

The soundness theorem is standard and establishes that a derivation over program and judgement implies that every execution of the program satisfies the judgement:

Proposition 1 (Soundness of partial logic)
∀ *(st: stmt) (s1 s2 : state),*
exec s1 st s2 →∀ *(post : assertion), RULET st post* → *post s1 s2.*

6   Introducing Ghost Variables

We now consider an extension of the simple language with ghost variables. To that end, we assume a set of ghost variables *gVar*   disjoint from the set of program variables *var.*

The language, formalised as an inductive type *Gstmt* (see Appendix) then has the same constructs as the original language (*Stmt*) plus a new construct, *GAssign*, allowing one to assign to ghost variables. Ghost variables are not allowed to appear in guards of loops or case distinctions nor may they be written into ordinary variables so as not to influence the flow of control in any way.

Properties of programs with ghost variables should certainly talk about the values of ghost variables. Thus, assertions with ghost variables ("ghost assertions" for short) *Gassertion* are mappings from the initial and final program states and also from the initial and final ghost states to a truth value:

Definition *Gassertion* := *state* → *gState* → *state* → *gState* → *Prop.*

Now we define inductively a logic for ghost assertions:

Inductive *GRULET*: *Gstmt* → *Gassertion* → *Prop*

The rules for this logic are quite the same as the rules for the standard simple language except that those are defined for assertions with ghost variables. Consider e.g. the assignment rule which differs from the ordinary assignment rule only in that ghost states are threaded through and required not to change.

GAssignRule: $\forall\ x\ e\ (post\ :\ Gassertion),$
$(\forall\ (s1\ s2\ :\ state)\ (g1\ g2:\ gState),$
$g1\ =\ g2\ \rightarrow\ s2\ =\ update\ s1\ x\ (eval\_expr\ s1\ e)\ \rightarrow\ post\ s1\ g1\ s2\ g2)\ \rightarrow$
$GRULET\ (GAssign\ x\ e)\ post$

The only substantial difference between the logic for standard simple language and its ghost extension is the rule for ghost assignment (which does not have an analogue in the standard logic):

GSetRule $:\ \forall\ x\ (e\ :\ gExpr)\ (post\ :\ Gassertion),$
$(\forall\ (s1\ s2\ :\ state\ )\ (g1\ g2:\ gState),$
$\quad g2\ =\ gUpdate\ g1\ x\ (gEval\_expr\ s1\ g1\ e)\ \rightarrow\ s1\ =\ s2\ \rightarrow$
$\quad post\ s1\ g1\ s2\ g2)\ \rightarrow\ GRULET\ (GSet\ x\ e)\ post.$

We do not prove the soundness of this logic w.r.t. an operational semantics instrumented with ghost variables. As we pointed out in the introductory part ghost variables lack a physical meaning and thus, should not be present in the program semantics. Actually, the relation between the ghost and standard logic presented in the following justifies the ghost logic w.r.t. standard operational semantics *exec* presented in the Appendix.

6.1   Relation between Ghost and Standard Logic

In the sequel we use a function *transform* : *Gstmt* $\rightarrow$ *Stmt* that returns the underlying standard program by replacing all ghost assignments with skips. Next, with each ghost assertion ψ (of type *Gassertion*) we associate a standard assertion *transform*(ψ) (of type *assertion*) by

$$transform(\psi) := \lambda\sigma_0, \sigma_1.\forall\sigma_0^g, \exists\sigma_1^g,\ \psi\ \sigma_0\ \sigma_0^g\ \sigma_1\ \sigma_1^g$$

Notice that if ψ does not mention ghost variables then *transform*(ψ) is equivalent to ψ itself. The formal statement about the relation of the two logical systems then says that a proof in the ghost logic (*GRULET*) that a statement *stmt* of the ghost language meets the ghost assertion ψ can be transformed into a proof in the standard logic (*RULET*) that the statement *transform*(*stmt*) meets the assertion *transform*(ψ):

Theorem 1 (Elimination of ghosts)
$\forall\ (gst:\ Gstmt)\ (Gpost:\ Gassertion),$
let st := transform gst in
let post:= (fun s1 s2 $\Rightarrow \forall\ (sg1:\ gState),\exists\ sg2:gState,\ Gpost\ s1\ sg1\ s2\ sg2)\ in$
$GRULET\ gst\ Gpost\ \rightarrow\ RULET\ st\ (fun\ s1\ s2\ \Rightarrow\ post\ s1\ s2).$

The proof of this statement is done by induction over the the ghost logical rules (*GRULET*). The curious part of this result is that the respective proof in the standard logic uses the same loop invariants with the respective quantifications (universal for the values in the initial state and existential for the values in the final state) over the ghost variables. Moreover, the established relation between the ghost and standard logic proposes an algorithm for transformation of "ghost" specifications into standard specification constructs without ghost variables. Since the proof is conducted by induction over proof rules it contains an algorithm that effectively performs the transformation on the level of proofs.

Returning back to our example which is actually provable with the program logic *GRULET*, the respective program and annotation provable in the logic *RULET* are the following:

```
//@ensures  y = 2*\old(x)

y=0;

//@loop_invariant \exists z, y = 2 * z && x = \old(x) - z
while (x > 0) {
    x = x - 1;
    y = y + 2;
}
```

The new specification does not only quantify the loop invariant over the ghost variable, but the ghost variable has been completely removed from it. Of course, it would have been possible to use such existentially quantified invariant in the first place or even cleverly guess the logically equivalent invariant y=2*(x−\old(x)). Many people find this confusing and cumbersome and prefer to use ghost variables. Our result shows that this is perfectly rigorous and can be understood as a shorthand comparable, e.g., to the use of named variables as opposed to combinators.

We remark that if a specification does not contain ghost variables but its proof does then that same specfication is provable in the ordinary program logic using the above correspondence followed by an instance of the consequence rule thus establishing conservativity of ghost variables.

Corollary 1 (Conservativity of ghosts). $\forall$ *(s: Gstmt) (post : assertion),*
GRULETstmt (fun (s1:state)(g1:gState)(s2:state)(g2:gState) $\Rightarrow$ post s1 s2)$\rightarrow$
RULET(transform stmt) post.

Remark on terminology. What we (and the JML community) call ghost variables is in other situations known as *auxiliary variables*, in particular in the context of Jones' rely-guarantee methodology and also in Reynolds' standard reference [15]. There, the term *ghost parameter* is reserved for what we call auxiliary variables, namely universally quantified parameters used to fix old values of variables. In a Hoare-style logic such auxiliary variables (in our sense) are crucial to express that certain program variables are not modified. In our VDM-style version where assertions have explicit access to pre-states such auxiliary variables or ghost parameters in Reynolds' sense are not needed as pointed out by Kleymann [14] and thus not considered in this paper.

It is on the other hand not possible to use ghost variables to get rid of explicit access to pre-states (or auxiliary variables when using Hoare-style logic). Of course, one can use a ghost variable to store the old value of some variable, but then we cannot — in the absence of \old that is — stipulate in the contract that this ghost variable remains itself unmodified.

7   Ghost Variables for Extra-Functional Properties

So far, we have seen the meaning of ghost variables w.r.t. a standard partial correctness. Such formulation describes the functional relation between input/output. In the following sections we show how to extend our results to reasoning about extra-functional properties such as "a program should not allocate more than X memory cells", "a program should not open nested transactions", "a program should not open more than X number of files" etc. Indeed, the practical interest of being able to reason over such extra-functional properties is evident, especially for critical applications tailored to PDAs or smart cards [16,11] or in mobile code scenarios.

An important new feature brought about here is that one can no longer semantically identify all non-terminating programs which we address by axiomatising reachable states and adding invariants to specifications as explained in the Introduction. Formally, we specify the semantics of reachable states of the thus extended language with the following inductive predicate. Recall that we assume a set *event* modelling observable events, e.g., calls to API methods.

Inductive *reach*: *state* → *stmt* → *list event* → *state* → *Prop*

The proposition $reach(\sigma_0, stmt, evs, \sigma_1)$ means that the execution of *stmt* started in state σ_0 reaches the state σ_1 and produces the list of events *evs*. The definition of the predicate *reach* relies on the notion of terminating executions which is defined with the following predicate:

Inductive *t_exec*: *state* → *stmt* → *list event* → *state* → *Prop*

The predicate *t_exec* is defined in the usual big step style but this time keeps track not only of the initial and final state but also of the list of events produced during the execution. The defining clauses for both predicates *reach* and *t_exec* are given in the Appendix. These two definitions delineate the behaviour of extra-functional properties of programs. It is they that must be "openly reviewd by a trusted body experts" so as to ensure that they adequately model the physical behaviour of programs.

Next, we define a logic that allows us to reason about and certify properties of this extra-functional behaviour. The format of the logic relies on relations between pre- and post states for terminating programs and *invariants* delineating the behaviour of possibly nonterminating programs.

Definition *invariant* := *state* → *list event* → *Prop*.

The logic which allows to reason over trace properties is defined in Coq as the inductive type $RULE^R$(see Appendix). The trace logic uses the logic for partial correctness $RULE^T$ presented in the previous Section 6 but which is suitably modified to deal with event traces. In particular, the assertions that $RULE^T$ manipulates now depend not only on the initial and final state but also on the trace of events produced during execution:

Definition *assertion* := *state* → *list event* → *state* → *Prop*.

The soundness statement of the logic requires that if satisfaction of an invariant by a statement is derivable in *RULER* then every reachable state of the execution of that statement satisfies the invariant:

Proposition 2 (Soundness of trace logic). $\forall$ *stmt (s1 s2 : state) events,*
   (reach s1 stmt events s2) $\rightarrow \forall$ *inv, RULER stmt inv* $\rightarrow$ *inv s1 events .*

The proof of that lemma is done by induction over *RULER*. Note that because *RULER* uses the logic *RULET* for partial correctness its soundness proof exploits the soundness of *RULET*.

7.1   Program Logic for Trace Properties and Ghost Variables

The logic for trace properties tailored to a language with ghost variables is analogous to the logic for trace properties for a standard language presented in the previous subsection. The only difference is that the ghost trace logic manipulates assertions with ghost variables and the assertion for trace properties talk about the initial and current values of ghost variables. Thus, the signature of ghost trace invariants is as follows:

   Definition *Ginvariant* := *state* $\rightarrow$ *gState* $\rightarrow$ *list event* $\rightarrow$ *gState* $\rightarrow$ *Prop.*

   Definition *Gassertion* := *state* $\rightarrow$ *gState* $\rightarrow$ *list event* $\rightarrow$ *state* $\rightarrow$ *gState* $\rightarrow$ *Prop*

We now have the following relationship allowing us to effectively eliminate all reference to ghost variables from a proof in the trace logic.

Theorem 2 (Elimination of ghosts from trace logic). $\forall$ *(gstmt:Gstmt)* *(ginv: Ginvariant),*
      let stmt := transform gstmt in
      let inv := (fun s1 event $\Rightarrow \forall$ *g1,* $\exists$ *g2, ginv s1 g1 event g2) in*
      RULERG gstmt ginv $\rightarrow$ *RULER stmt inv.*

7.2   Example Application

In the example of a mobile phone application purportedly using at most 10M of memory we would insist on the invariant

   meminv aState evs = *mem evs* ≤ 10485760

where *mem : list event* $\rightarrow$ *nat* is a Coq function extracting the number of allocations from a list of events.
   Suppose now that someone has already established the following ghost invariant for the program enriched with assignments to a ghost variable *MEM* purportedly tracking memory allocations thus expressing that at all times the ghost variable *MEM* is at most 10M.

   gmeminv aState aGState evs aGState = *aGState.MEM* ≤ 10485760

If indeed the program has been appropriately decorated with assignments to *MEM* at allocation sites and *MEM* has not been tampered with elsewhere then one can automatically produce proof of the invariant

gcorrinv aState aGState evs aGState = aGState.MEM = mem evs

Thus, we obtain a proof of the combined invariant

ginv aState aGState evs aGState = gcorrinv aState aGState evs aGState ∧ *gmeminv aState aGState evs aGState*

Applying the above lemma relating standard and ghost logic we obtain a standard invariant from which *meminv* readily follows.

8 Ghost Variables for Object Invariants

In object oriented languages like Java, it is useful to talk about an object invariant, i.e. a property that must hold in all visible states of an object and on which other objects may rely. For instance, an invariant of objects of class representing a list data structure is that the field length should be always greater or equal 0. Intuitively, the visible states for an object are the initial and final state of every method in the program, see [17] and the object invariant is usually a relation between the components of the object, i.e. the instance fields of the object. In particular, this means that the invariant of an object can be broken during the execution of a method of this object. In order to verify that an object invariant holds it must be proven to hold at the borders of every method in the program, i.e. it is desugared as part of the pre and postcondition of every method in the program. This implies that an object invariant must be "revealed" to all classes in the program and yields the problem of representation exposure. To remedy this, in [10] Barnett et al. describe a modular and sound verification scheme for object invariants based on ghost variables. To do so, a boolean ghost variable *valid* is attached to every object *o*. The correctness of the methodology relies on the following invariant property INV^1 in every execution state:

$$INV = \text{If } o.valid \text{ is true then the property } o.I \text{ holds} \qquad (1)$$

Now, the clients of an object *o* can be informed about the validity of *o.I* just by revealing to them the value of the ghost field *o.valid* and avoiding thus representation exposure. In order to enforce this invariant, the specification language is extended with two more constructs - *o.pack* and *o.unpack* which basically set the object state variable *o.valid* and thus mark the region in the program where the object invariant can be broken or not. We have shown that a proof in such verification scheme can be translated in a standard programming logic and in the following, we sketch this.

---

[1] We focus here on the first part of the article where the authors consider that an object invariant may talk only about the fields of the object.

Let us consider without losing the generality of the problem that we have a simple imperative program provided with an invariant I and a ghost logic formalised in Coq with the inductive type *GHRULE* (see Appendix) based on the principle described in [10]. Because we limit ourselves to a simple language *INV* will look rather like this:

$$INV = \text{If } valid \text{ is true then the property } I \text{ holds} \qquad (2)$$

The rule for assignment should establish that if the invariant *INV* holds in the prestate of the assignment then it will hold after the assignment and the rule will look like this in the Coq system:

Inductive *GHRULE INV* :=
| *GHAssignRule*: ∀ x e (*pre*: *Gpreassertion*)(*post*: *Gassertion*),
   (∀ ($s1$ $s2$: *state*) ($g1$ $g2$: *gState*), *pre* $s1$ $g1$ →*INV* $s1$ $g1$ →
   $g1 = g2$ → $s2 = update$ $s1$ x (*eval_expr* $s1$ e) →
   INV $s2$ $g2$ ∧ *post* $s1$ $g1$ $s2$ $g2$) → *GHRULE INV* *pre* (*GAssign* x e) *post*.

No proof obligations pertaining to invariants arise in the other rules; see e.g. the rule *GHWhileRule* in Appendix C. However, at all times the invariant can be invoked as formalised by rule *GHInvRule*. This system thus formalises the reasoning scheme proposed in [10].

We have formalised in Coq how a proof in such a verification scheme can be transformed in a proof over a language without ghost variables. The key lemma establishes that a proof in a logic which supports the invariant relation (2) can be transformed into a proof in a partial VDM logic with ghost variables which establishes that the invariant I is preserved:

Theorem 3 (Invariants). ∀ *gstmt pre post INV*,
   GHRULE INV pre gstmt post →
   GRULETgstmt (**fun** $s1$ $g1$ $s2$ $g2$ ⇒ *pre* $s1$ $g1$ ∧ *INV* $s1$ $g1$ →
         post $s1$ $g1$ $s2$ $g2$ ∧ *INV* $s2$ $g2$).

The lemma is proved by induction over *GHRULE*. Combined with the result described in Section 6, we can conclude that we can transform a proof in a logic with invariants into a standard one.

9   Conclusion and Further Work

We have given a rigorous semantics of ghost variables in terms of a VDM-style program logic without altering in any way the operational semantics of the language which, as we have argued, is a source of vulnerability for proof-carrying code architectures since it escapes formal validation. We have also argued that ghost variables can be avoided in end-to-end specifications of extra-functional properties provided the program logic is given the ability to speak about traces of observable events.

Dynamic logic also offers some of the features that we propose: asserting that some extra-functional property holds throughout the execution [18] and the use

of existential quantification in situations where ghost variables might appear
[19]. The fact that proofs involving ghost variables (of terminating and non-
terminating programs) can always and automatically be translated into proofs
without ghost variables appears here for the first time and is the main technical
contribution of this paper. We found our approach to be very robust and did
not experience obstacles with the inclusion of recursive methods. We also find
that translation into a standard program logic is in general a useful method for
giving meaning to the fancier features of specification languages.

Although orthogonal to the idea of transformation of ghost proofs, our work
raises the question if high level specification languages like JML should use
ghost variables to model extrafunctional properties. An application of our result
can be the extension of JML with special non assignable constructs to denote
extrafunctional properties which will benefit of a clear semantics and sound
verification framework described in the present article.

In this article we have not covered the use of ghost variables in specification and verification of shared-variable concurrency. Indeed, formalisms such as
Owicki-Gries [20] are incomplete without ghost variables. We found that this is
due to the fact that in the standard formulation of, e.g., Owicki-Gries, given access to the entire state of the system which includes local variables and program
counters of all processes. If such access is provided, ghost variables can, again,
be eliminated using the methods from this paper. It is, however, questionable
whether assertions should be allowed to mention the global state; indeed, we find
that the real issue behind the phenomena around ghost variables in concurrency
is the question of how one should specify a stateful component without revealing
its internal implementation. We leave a detailed investigation of these questions
for future work.

Acknowledgement. We acknowledge support by the EU integrated project MO-
BIUS IST 15905.

References

1. Cataño, N., Huisman, M.: Formal specification of Gemplus' electronic purse case
   study using ESC/Java. In: Eriksson, L.-H., Lindsay, P.A. (eds.) FME 2002. LNCS,
   vol. 2391, pp. 272–289. Springer, Heidelberg (2002)
2. Jacobs, B., Marché, C., Rauch, N.: Formal verification of a commercial smart
   card applet with multiple tools. In: Rattray, C., Maharaj, S., Shankland, C. (eds.)
   AMAST 2004. LNCS, vol. 3116, Springer, Heidelberg (2004)
3. Flanagan, C., Leino, K.R.M., Lillibridge, M., Nelson, G., Saxe, J.B., Stata, R.: Extended static checking for java. In: Proceeding of the ACM SIGPLAN 2002 Conference on Programming language design and implementation, Berlin, Germany,
   pp. 234–245. ACM Press, New York (2002)
4. Guttag, J.V., Horning, J.J. (eds.): Larch: Languages and Tools for Formal Specification. In: Garland, S.J., Jones, K.D., Modet, A., Wing, J.M. (eds.) Texts and
   Monographs in Computer Science, Springer, Heidelberg (1993)
5. Barnett, M., Leino, K., Schulte, W.: The Spec# programming system: An overview.
   In: Barthe, G., Burdy, L., Huisman, M., Lanet, J.-L., Muntean, T. (eds.) CASSIS
   2004. LNCS, vol. 3362, pp. 151–171. Springer, Heidelberg (2005)

6. Necula, G.C.: Proof-carrying code. In: Proceedings of the 24th ACM SIGPLAN-SIGACT Symposium on Principles of Programming Langauges (POPL 1997), Paris, pp. 106–119 (1997)
7. Appel, A.W.: Foundational proof-carrying code. In: Proc. IEEE Symp. Logic in Computer Science (LICS 2001) (2001)
8. Aspinall, D., Gilmore, S., Hofmann, M., Sannella, D., Stark, I.: Mobile resource guarantees for smart devices. In: Barthe, G., Burdy, L., Huisman, M., Lanet, J.-L., Muntean, T. (eds.) CASSIS 2004. LNCS, vol. 3362, pp. 1–26. Springer, Heidelberg (2005)
9. Barthe, G., Beringer, L., Crégut, P., Grégoire, B., Hofmann, M., Müller, P., Poll, E., Puebla, G., Stark, I., Vétillard, E.: Mobius: Mobility, ubiquity, security. objectives and progress report. In: Montanari, U., Sannella, D., Bruni, R. (eds.) TGC 2006. LNCS, vol. 4661, Springer, Heidelberg (2007)
10. Barnett, M., Deline, R., Fähndrich, M., Rustan, K.R.M., Schulte, W.: Verification of object-oriented programs with invariants. Journal of Object Technology 3(6), 27–56 (2004)
11. Pavlova, M., Barthe, G., Burdy, L., Huisman, M., Lanet, J.L.: Enforcing high-level security properties for applets. In: Paradinas, P., Quisquater, J.J. (eds.) Proceedings of CARDIS 2004, Toulouse, France, Kluwer Academic Publishers, Dordrecht (2004)
12. Burdy, L., Requet, A., Lanet, J.L.: Java applet correctness: A developer-oriented approach. In: Araki, K., Gnesi, S., Mandrioli, D. (eds.) FME 2003. LNCS, vol. 2805, pp. 422–439. Springer, Heidelberg (2003)
13. Jones, C.: Systematic Software Development Using VDM. Prentice Hall, Englewood Cliffs (1990)
14. Kleymann, T.: Hoare logic and auxiliary variables. Formal Aspects of Computing 11(5), 541–566 (1999)
15. Reynolds, J.C.: The craft of programming. Prentice Hall (1981); Out of print. Available as PDF from John Reynolds' home page
16. Beckert, B., Mostowski, W.: A program logic for handling java card's transaction mechanism. In: Pezzé, M. (ed.) ETAPS 2003 and FASE 2003. LNCS, vol. 2621, pp. 246–260. Springer, Heidelberg (2003)
17. Leavens, G.T., et al.: Jml reference manual
18. Beckert, B., Schlager, S.: A sequent calculus for first-order dynamic logic with trace modalities. LNCS, vol. 2083, p. 626 (2001)
19. Beckert, B., Hähnle, R., Schmitt, P.H. (eds.): Verification of Object-Oriented Software: The KeY Approach. In: Beckert, B., Hähnle, R., Schmitt, P.H. (eds.) Verification of Object-Oriented Software. LNCS (LNAI), vol. 4334, Springer, Heidelberg (2007)
20. Owicki, S.S., Gries, D.: An axiomatic proof technique for parallel programs i. Acta Inf. 6, 319–340 (1976)

A   Functional Behaviours

A.1   Big Step Operational Semantics for a Simple Language

```
Inductive exec_stmt: state → stmt → state → Prop :=
  | ExecAssign: ∀ s x e,
      exec_stmt s (Assign x e)(update s x (eval_expr s e))
  | ExecIf_true: ∀ s1 s2 e stmtT stmtF,
```

$eval\_expr\ s1\ e \neq 0 \rightarrow exec\_stmt\ s1\ stmtT\ s2 \rightarrow$
$exec\_stmt\ s1\ (If\ e\ stmtT\ stmtF)\ s2$
$|\ ExecIf\_false:\ \forall\ s1\ s2\ e\ stmtT\ stmtF,$
$eval\_expr\ s1\ e = 0 \rightarrow exec\_stmt\ s1\ stmtF\ s2 \rightarrow$
$exec\_stmt\ s1\ (If\ e\ stmtT\ stmtF)\ s2$
$|\ ExecWhile\_true:\ \forall\ s1\ s2\ s3\ e\ stmt,$
$eval\_expr\ s1\ e \neq 0 \rightarrow exec\_stmt\ s1\ stmt\ s2 \rightarrow$
$exec\_stmt\ s2\ (While\ e\ stmt)\ s3 \rightarrow$
$exec\_stmt\ s1\ (While\ e\ stmt)\ s3$
$|\ ExecWhile\_false:\ \forall\ s1\ e\ stmt,$
$eval\_expr\ s1\ e = 0 \rightarrow exec\_stmt\ s1\ (While\ e\ stmt)\ s1$
$|\ ExecSseq:\ \forall\ s1\ s2\ s3\ i\ stmt,$
$exec\_stmt\ s1\ i\ s2 \rightarrow exec\_stmt\ s2\ stmt\ s3 \rightarrow$
$exec\_stmt\ s1\ (Sseq\ i\ stmt)\ s3$
$|\ ExecSkip:\ \forall\ s,\ exec\_stmt\ s\ Skip\ s.$

A.2   Logic for Partial Correctness

Inductive $RULET$: $stmt \rightarrow assertion \rightarrow Prop$:=
$|\ AssignRule:\forall\ x\ e\ (post:\ assertion),$
$(\forall\ (s1\ s2:\ state),\ s2 = update\ s1\ x\ (eval\_expr\ s1\ e) \rightarrow post\ s1\ s2) \rightarrow$
$RULET\ (Assign\ x\ e)\ post$
$|\ IfRule:\forall\ e\ (stmtT\ stmtF:\ stmt\ )\ (post1\ post2\ post:\ assertion),$
$(\forall\ (s1\ s2:\ state),$
$(eval\_expr\ s1\ e \neq 0 \rightarrow post1\ s1\ s2) \rightarrow$
$(eval\_expr\ s1\ e = 0 \rightarrow post2\ s1\ s2) \rightarrow post\ s1\ s2) \rightarrow$
$RULET\ stmtT\ post1 \rightarrow RULET\ stmtF\ post2 \rightarrow$
$RULET\ (If\ e\ stmtT\ stmtF)\ post$
$|\ WhileRule:\forall\ (st:\ stmt)(post\ b\ post1:\ assertion)\ e,$
$(\forall\ s1\ s2,\ eval\_expr\ s2\ e = 0 \rightarrow post1\ s1\ s2 \rightarrow post\ s1\ s2) \rightarrow$
$(\forall\ s\ p\ t,\ eval\_expr\ s\ e \neq 0 \rightarrow b\ s\ p \rightarrow post1\ p\ t \rightarrow post1\ s\ t) \rightarrow$
$(\forall\ s,\ eval\_expr\ s\ e = 0 \rightarrow post1\ s\ s) \rightarrow$
$RULET\ st\ b \rightarrow RULET\ (While\ e\ st)\ post$
$|\ SeqRule:\forall\ (stmt1\ stmt2:\ stmt\ )\ (post1\ post2\ post:\ assertion),$
$(\forall\ s1\ s2,(\exists\ p,\ post1\ s1\ p \wedge post2\ p\ s2) \rightarrow post\ s1\ s2) \rightarrow$
$RULET\ stmt1\ post1 \rightarrow RULET\ stmt2\ post2 \rightarrow$
$RULET\ (Sseq\ stmt1\ stmt2)\ post$
$|\ SkipRule:\forall\ (post:\ assertion),$
$(\forall\ (s1\ s2:\ state),\ s1 = s2 \rightarrow post\ s1\ s2) \rightarrow RULET\ Skip\ post.$

A.3   Syntax of Language with Ghost Variables

Inductive $Gstmt$: $Type$:=
$|\ GAssign:\ var \rightarrow expr \rightarrow Gstmt$
$|\ GIf:\ expr \rightarrow Gstmt \rightarrow Gstmt \rightarrow Gstmt$
$|\ GWhile:\ expr \rightarrow Gstmt \rightarrow Gstmt$
$|\ GSseq:\ Gstmt \rightarrow Gstmt \rightarrow Gstmt$
$|\ GSkip:\ Gstmt$
$|\ GSet:\ gVar \rightarrow gExpr \rightarrow Gstmt.$

B   Extra-Functional Behaviours with Traces

B.1   Semantics of Terminating Executions in the Presence of Traces

Inductive $t\_exec\ (P:\ program)(B:\ body)$: $state \rightarrow stmt \rightarrow list\ event \rightarrow state \rightarrow Prop$:=
$|\ ExecAssign:\ \forall\ s\ x\ e,$
$t\_exec\ P\ B\ s\ (Assign\ x\ e)\ nil\ (update\ s\ x\ (eval\_expr\ s\ e))$
$|\ ExecIf\_true:\ \forall\ s1\ s2\ e\ stmtT\ stmtF\ eventsT,$
$eval\_expr\ s1\ e \neq 0 \rightarrow t\_exec\ P\ B\ s1\ stmtT\ eventsT\ s2 \rightarrow$
$t\_exec\ P\ B\ s1\ (If\ e\ stmtT\ stmtF)\ eventsT\ s2$

| ExecIf_false: ∀ s1 s2 e stmtT stmtF eventsF,
    eval_expr s1 e = 0 → t_exec P B s1 stmtF eventsF s2 →
    t_exec P B s1 (If e stmtT stmtF) eventsF s2
| ExecWhile_true: ∀ s1 s2 s3 e stmt eventsI eventsC,
    eval_expr s1 e ≠ 0 →
    t_exec P B s1 stmt eventsI s2 → t_exec P B s2 (While e stmt) eventsC s3 →
    t_exec P B s1 (While e stmt)(app eventsI eventsC) s3
| ExecWhile_false: ∀ s1 e stmt,
    eval_expr s1 e = 0 → t_exec P B s1 (While e stmt) nil s1
| ExecSseq: ∀ s1 s2 s3 stmt1 stmt2 events1 events2,
    t_exec P B s1 stmt1 events1 s2 → t_exec P B s2 stmt2 events2 s3 →
    t_exec P B s1 (Sseq stmt1 stmt2)(app events1 events2) s3
| ExecSkip: ∀ s, t_exec P B s Skip nil s
| ExecSignal: ∀ s event, t_exec P B s (Signal event)(event::nil)s.

B.2 Semantics of Reachable States in the Presence of Traces

Inductive reach: state → stmt → list event → state → Prop :=
| ReachAssign: ∀ s x e,
    reach s (Assign x e) nil (update s x (eval_expr s e))
| ReachIf_true: ∀ s1 s2 e stmtT stmtF eventsT ,
    eval_expr s1 e ≠ 0 → reach s1 stmtT eventsT s2 →
    reach s1 (If e stmtT stmtF) eventsT s2
| ReachIf_false: ∀ s1 s2 e stmtT stmtF eventsF,
    eval_expr s1 e = 0 → reach s1 stmtF eventsF s2 →
    reach s1 (If e stmtT stmtF) eventsF s2
| ReachWhile_false: ∀ s1 e stmt,
    eval_expr s1 e = 0 → reach s1 (While e stmt) nil s1
| ReachWhile_true1 : ∀ s1 s2 e stmt eventsB,
    eval_expr s1 e ≠ 0 → reach s1 stmt eventsB s2 →
    reach s1 (While e stmt) eventsB s2
| ReachWhile_true2: ∀ s1 s2 s3 e stmt eventsB eventsW,
    eval_expr s1 e ≠ 0 → t_exec s1 stmt eventsB s2 →
    reach s2 (While e stmt) eventsW s3 →
    reach s1 (While e stmt)(eventsB::eventsW) s3
| ReachSseq1: ∀ s1 s2 stmt1 stmt2 events1,
    reach s1 stmt1 events1 s2 → reach s1 (Sseq stmt1 stmt2) events1 s2
| ReachSseq2: ∀ s1 s2 s3 stmt1 stmt2 events1 events2,
    t_exec s1 stmt1 events1 s2 →
    reach s2 stmt2 events2 s3 → reach s1 (Sseq stmt1 stmt2) (events1::events2) s3
| ReachSkip: ∀ s, reach s Skip nil s
| ReachRefl : ∀ s stmt, reach P B s stmt nil s
| ReachSignal: ∀ s event, reach s (Signal event) (event::nil) s.

B.3 Logic for Partial Correctness in the Presence of Traces for the Extended Language

Inductive RULET : stmt → assertion → Prop :=
| AssignRule : ∀ x e (post : assertion) ,
    (∀ (s1 s2: state), s2 = update s1 x (eval_expr s1 e) → post s1 nil s2) →
    RULET (Assign x e) post
| IfRule : ∀ e (stmtT stmtF: stmt)(post1 post2 post : assertion) ,
    (∀ (s1 s2: state) event,
      ((eval_expr s1 e ≠ 0)) → post1 s1 event s2) ∧
      (eval_expr s1 e = 0 → post2 s1 event s2) → post s1 event s2) →
    RULET stmtT post1 →RULET stmtF post2 →
    RULET (If e stmtT stmtF) post
| WhileRule : ∀ (st : stmt) (post post1 posti : assertion) e,
    (∀ s1 s2 event, post1 s1 event s2 ∧ eval_expr s2 e = 0→
      post s1 event s2) →
    (∀ s p t event1 event2, eval_expr s e ≠ 0 → posti s event1 p →
      post1 p event2 t → post1 s (app event1 event2) t) →

$(\forall \ s, \ eval\_expr \ s \ e = 0 \rightarrow post1 \ s \ nil \ s \ ) \rightarrow$
$RULET \ st \ posti \rightarrow RULET \ (While \ e \ st) \ post$
$| \ SeqRule: \forall \ (stmt1 \ stmt2: \ stmt \ ) \ (\ post1 \ post2 \ post: \ assertion),$
$(\forall \ s1 \ s2 \ event1 \ event2, \ (\exists \ p \ , post1 \ s1 \ event1 \ p \wedge post2 \ p \ event2 \ s2) \rightarrow$
$\quad post \ s1 \ (app \ event1 \ event2) \ s2) \rightarrow$
$RULET \ stmt1 \ post1 \rightarrow RULET \ stmt2 \ post2 \rightarrow$
$RULET \ (Sseq \ stmt1 \ stmt2) \ post$
$| \ SkipRule: \forall \ (post: \ assertion),$
$(\forall \ (s1 \ s2: \ state), \ s1 = s2 \rightarrow post \ s1 \ nil \ s2) \rightarrow RULET \ Skip \ post$
$| \ SignalRule : \forall \ (post: \ assertion) \ event,$
$(\forall \ s1 \ s2 \ event, \ s1 = s2 \rightarrow post \ s1 \ (event :: nil) \ s2) \rightarrow RULET \ (Signal \ event) \ post.$

B.4   Logic for Trace Properties for the Extended Language

Inductive $RULER: \ stmt \rightarrow invariant \rightarrow \text{Prop} :=$
$| \ AssignRuleR: \forall \ x \ e \ (post: \ invariant),$
$(\forall \ (s1: \ state) \ l, \ l = nil \rightarrow post \ s1 \ l) \rightarrow RULER \ (Assign \ x \ e) \ post$
$| \ IfRuleR: \forall \ e \ stmtT \ stmtF \ (post1 \ post2 \ post: \ invariant),$
$(\forall \ (\ s1: \ state) \ event,$
$((not \ eval\_expr \ s1 \ e = 0) \rightarrow post1 \ s1 \ event) \rightarrow$
$(eval\_expr \ s1 \ e = 0 \rightarrow post2 \ s1 \ event) \rightarrow post \ s1 \ event) \rightarrow$
$(\forall \ (s1: \ state) \ event, \ event = nil \rightarrow post \ s1 \ event) \rightarrow$
$RULER \ stmtT \ post1 \rightarrow RULER \ stmtF \ post2 \rightarrow$
$RULER \ (If \ e \ stmtT \ stmtF) \ post$
$| \ WhileRuleR: \forall \ (st: \ stmt)(post \ post1: \ invariant) \ e \ (inv: \ assertion),$
$(\forall \ s1 \ event, \ post1 \ s1 \ event \rightarrow post \ s1 \ event) \rightarrow$
$(\forall \ (s1: \ state) \ l, \ l = nil \rightarrow post1 \ s1 \ l) \rightarrow$
$(\forall \ s, \ eval\_expr \ s \ e = 0 \rightarrow post1 \ s \ nil) \rightarrow$
$RULER \ st \ post1 \rightarrow RULET \ st \ inv \rightarrow$
$(\forall \ s1 \ s2 \ e1 \ e2, \ (inv \ s1 \ e1 \ s2 \rightarrow eval\_expr \ s1 \ e \neq 0 \rightarrow$
$\quad post1 \ s2 \ e2 \rightarrow post1 \ s1 \ (app \ e1 \ e2)) \ ) \ ) \rightarrow$
$RULER \ (While \ e \ st) \ post$
$| \ SeqRuleR: \forall \ (stmt1 \ stmt2: \ stmt)(post \ post1 \ postRst2: \ invariant)$
$(postT: \ assertion),$
$(\forall \ s1 \ e, \ post1 \ s1 \ e \rightarrow post \ s1 \ e) \rightarrow$
$(\forall \ s1 \ s2 \ e1 \ e2, \ postT \ s1 \ e1 \ s2 \rightarrow postRst2 \ s2 \ e2 \rightarrow$
$\quad post1 \ s1 \ (app \ e1 \ e2 \ )) \rightarrow$
$RULER \ stmt1 \ post1 \rightarrow RULET \ stmt1 \ postT \rightarrow$
$RULER \ stmt2 \ postRst2 \rightarrow (\forall \ (s1: \ state) \ l, \ l{=}nil \rightarrow post \ s1 \ l) \rightarrow$
$RULER \ (Sseq \ stmt1 \ stmt2) \ post$
$| \ SkipRuleR: \forall \ (post: \ invariant),$
$(\forall \ (s1: \ state) \ l, \ l = nil \rightarrow post \ s1 \ l) \rightarrow RULER \ Skip \ post$
$| \ SignalRuleR: \forall \ (post: \ invariant) \ event,$
$(\forall \ s1 \ l, \ l = nil \rightarrow post \ s1 \ (event::l)) \rightarrow$
$(\forall \ s1 \ l, \ l = nil \rightarrow post \ s1 \ l) \rightarrow RULER \ (Signal \ event) \ post.$

C   Logic for Dealing with Invariants

Inductive $GHRULE(I: \ Invariant): \ Gpreassertion \rightarrow Gstmt \rightarrow Gassertion \rightarrow \text{Prop} :=$
$| \ GHAssignRule: \forall \ x \ e \ (pre: \ Gpreassertion)(post: \ Gassertion),$
$(\forall \ (s1 \ s2 : \ state)(g1 \ g2: \ gState), \ pre \ s1 \ g1 \rightarrow I \ s1 \ g1 \rightarrow$
$g1 = g2 \rightarrow s2 = update \ s1 \ x \ (eval\_expr \ s1 \ e) \rightarrow I \ s2 \ g2 \wedge post \ s1 \ g1 \ s2 \ g2) \rightarrow$
iiiiiii ·mine $GHRULE \ I \ pre \ (GAssign \ x \ e) \ post$
======= $GHRULE \ I \ pre \ (GAssign \ x \ e) \ post$
ذذذذذذ ·r240 $| \ GHIfRule: \forall \ e \ (stmtT \ stmtF: \ Gstmt)(pre \ pre1 \ pre2: \ Gpreassertion)$
$(post1 \ post2 \ post: \ Gassertion),$
$(\forall \ s \ gs, \ pre \ s \ gs \rightarrow pre1 \ s \ gs) \rightarrow (\forall \ s \ gs, \ pre \ s \ gs \rightarrow pre2 \ s \ gs) \rightarrow$
$(\forall \ (s1 \ s2 : \ state \ ) \ (g1 \ g2: \ gState),$
$(not \ (eval\_expr \ s1 \ e = 0) \rightarrow post1 \ s1 \ g1 \ s2 \ g2) \wedge$
$(eval\_expr \ s1 \ e = 0 \rightarrow post2 \ s1 \ g1 \ s2 \ g2) \rightarrow post \ s1 \ g1 \ s2 \ g2) \rightarrow$
$GHRULE \ I \ pre1 \ stmtT \ post1 \rightarrow$
$GHRULE \ I \ pre2 \ stmtF \ post2 \rightarrow$
$GHRULE \ I \ pre \ (GIf \ e \ stmtT \ stmtF) \ post$

| $GHWhileRule$: $\forall$ $(stmt: Gstmt)(pre\ inv: Gpreassertion)$
   $(post1\ post : Gassertion)\ e$,
   $(\forall\ s\ gs,\ pre\ s\ gs \rightarrow inv\ s\ gs) \rightarrow$
   $(\forall\ (s1\ s2: state)(g1\ g2: gState),\ post1\ s1\ g1\ s2\ g2 \rightarrow post\ s1\ g1\ s2\ g2\ ) \rightarrow$
   $(\forall\ (s1\ s2: state)(g1\ g2: gState),$
     $((inv\ s1\ g1 \rightarrow inv\ s2\ g2) \wedge eval\_expr\ s2\ e = 0 \rightarrow post1\ s1\ g1\ s2\ g2)) \rightarrow$
   $GHRULE\ I$ (fun $s1\ g1 \Rightarrow eval\_expr\ s1\ e \neq 0$) $stmt$
                (fun $s1\ g1\ s2\ g2 \Rightarrow inv\ s1\ g1 \rightarrow inv\ s2\ g2) \rightarrow$
  $GHRULE\ I\ pre\ (GWhile\ e\ stmt)\ post$
| $GHSeqRule$: $\forall$ $(stmt1\ stmt2: Gstmt)(pre\ pre1\ pre2 : Gpreassertion)$
   $(post1\ post2\ post: Gassertion)$,
   $(\forall\ s\ gs,\ pre\ s\ gs \rightarrow pre1\ s\ gs) \rightarrow$
   $(\forall\ s1\ s2\ g1\ g2, (\exists\ p, \exists\ gp,\ post1\ s1\ g1\ p\ gp \wedge post2\ p\ gp\ s2\ g2) \rightarrow$
   $post\ s1\ g1\ s2\ g2\ ) \rightarrow$
   $GHRULE\ I\ pre1\ stmt1$ (fun $s1\ g1\ s2\ g2 \Rightarrow pre2\ s2\ g2 \wedge post1\ s1\ g1\ s2\ g2\ ) \rightarrow$
   $GHRULE\ I\ pre2\ stmt2\ post2 \rightarrow$
   $GHRULE\ I\ pre\ (GSseq\ stmt1\ stmt2)\ post$
| $GHSkipRule$: $\forall$ $(pre\ pre1: Gpreassertion)(post1\ post: Gassertion)$,
   $(\forall\ s\ gs,\ pre\ s\ gs \rightarrow pre1\ s\ gs) \rightarrow$
   $(\forall\ (s1\ s2: state)(g1\ g2: gState),\ post1\ s1\ g1\ s2\ g2 \rightarrow post\ s1\ g1\ s2\ g2\ ) \rightarrow$
   $(\forall\ (s1\ s2: state)(g1\ g2: gState),\ g1 = g2 \wedge s1 = s2 \rightarrow post\ s1\ g1\ s2\ g2\ ) \rightarrow$
   $GHRULE\ I\ pre\ GSkip\ post$
| $GHSetRule$: $\forall$ x $(e: gExpr)(pre: Gpreassertion)(post: Gassertion)$,
   $(\forall\ (s1\ s2: state)(g1\ g2: gState),\ pre\ s1\ g1 \rightarrow$
     $g2 = gUpdate\ g1\ x\ (gEval\_expr\ s1\ g1\ e) \wedge s1 = s2 \rightarrow I\ s2\ g2 \wedge post\ s1\ g1\ s2\ g2\ ) \rightarrow$
   $GHRULE\ I\ pre\ (GSet\ x\ e)\ post$
| $GHInvRule$: $\forall$ $stmt$ $(pre : Gpreassertion)\ (post : Gassertion)$,
   $GHRULE\ I$ (fun $s1\ g1 \Rightarrow I\ s1\ g1 \wedge pre\ s1\ g1$) $stmt\ post \rightarrow$
   $GHRULE\ I\ pre\ stmt\ post$.

Web Service Composition: From Analysis to Autonomy

Jeff Magee

Imperial College, London

Abstract. The talk addresses the benefits, costs and research issues involved in taking a rigorous approach to the engineering of web services. In the first part of the talk, we present a way of developing web services in which model checking is used to verify that service compositions are verified against formally specified design goals. In the second part of the talk, we outline an approach to using formally specified goals in developing autonomous or self-managed compositions. The presentation will include some short demonstrations of the tools we are using. The talk is based on work in London Software Systems a grouping that includes academics at Imperial College London (the speaker, Jeff Kramer, Howard Foster and Sebastian Uchitel) and at University College London (Wolfgang Emmerich, Anthony Finkelstein and David Rosenblum).

G. Barthe and C. Fournet (Eds.): TGC 2007, LNCS 4912, p. 21, 2008.

Service Combinators for
Farming Virtual Machines

Karthikeyan Bhargavan[1], Andrew D. Gordon[1], and Iman Narasamdya[2]

[1] Microsoft Research
[2] University of Manchester

Abstract. Management is one of the main expenses of running the server farms that implement enterprise services, and operator errors can be costly. Our goal is to develop type-safe programming mechanisms for combining and managing enterprise services, and we achieve this goal in the particular setting of farms of virtual machines. We assume each server is service-oriented, in the sense that the services it provides, and the external services it depends upon, are explicitly described in metadata. We describe the design, implementation, and formal semantics of a library of combinators whose types record and respect server metadata. We describe a series of programming examples run on our implementation, based on existing server code for order processing, a typical data centre workload.

G. Barthe and C. Fournet (Eds.): TGC 2007, LNCS 4912, p. 22, 2008.

Combining a Verification Condition Generator for a Bytecode Language with Static Analyses[*]

Benjamin Grégoire[1] and Jorge Luis Sacchini[1,2]

[1] INRIA Sophia Antipolis - Méditerranée, France
[2] FCEIA, Univesidad Nacional de Rosario, Argentina
{Benjamin.Gregoire,Jorge-Luis.Sacchini}@sophia.inria.fr

Abstract. In Proof-Carrying Code, the verification condition generator (VCgen) generates a set of formulas whose validity implies that the code satisfies the consumer policy. Applying a VCgen to a bytecode language with exceptions (such as Java bytecode) can result in a large number of proof obligations, due to the amount of branching instructions. We present a VCgen for Java bytecode that uses static analyses to reduce the number of proof obligations. As a result, the task of producing a proof is simpler, and the subsequent proof terms smaller. We formalize the VCgen as a deep embedding in Coq and prove soundness with respect to the Bicolano formalization of the Java bytecode semantics.

1 Introduction

Proof-Carrying Code (PCC) [8] has been developed as a framework to guarantee safety in mobile scenarios. The code that is to be executed by a consumer needs to be accompanied with a proof (certificate) that it satisfies a required safety policy. The consumer checks that the certificate corresponds with a proof of safety of the code. Once the certificate is checked, the code can be safely executed. The task of generating such certificate, which can be a complex task depending on the safety policy, is delegated to the producer. The task of the consumer reduces to checking the certificate, which is in general much simpler.

A verification condition generator (VCgen) is used to generate the proof obligations that will ensure that the code satisfies the given safety policy. The VCgen is usually applied to annotated bytecode. It ensures, no matter which path in the control flow graph of the code is taken at runtime, that the safety policy is satisfied. Programs written in bytecode languages such as Java, that includes objects creation, dynamic method calls, and exception mechanism, have a high degree of branching code, due to the instructions that can throw runtime exceptions.

---

[*] This work was funded in part by the Sixth Framework programme of the European Community under the MOBIUS project FP6-015905. This paper reflects only the authors views and the Community is not liable for any use that may be made of the information contained therein.

G. Barthe and C. Fournet (Eds.): TGC 2007, LNCS 4912, pp. 23–40, 2008.

Consider the following excerpt of Java bytecode:

$$pc_1 \quad \texttt{istore } x$$
$$pc_2 \quad \texttt{getfield } f$$
$$pc_3 \quad \ldots$$

A VCgen (denoted by VC) generates two proof obligations for the program point pc_2:

$$lv(x) \neq \text{null} \Rightarrow VC(pc_3)$$
$$\wedge \ lv(x) = \text{null} \Rightarrow VC(pc_{\text{exc}}),$$

where lv access the local variable array, and pc_{exc} is the program point corresponding to the exception handler. For every instruction that can throw a runtime exception, the VCgen returns two proof obligations: one corresponding to normal execution, and another corresponding to exceptional execution. Usually a program contains many of these instructions, which results in an explosion in the number of proof obligations.

The use of static analyses, such as null-pointer analysis, can ensure that the reference above is non-null and, therefore, it is not necessary to generate a proof obligation for the exceptional execution. In such case, the VCgen will generate the following condition:

$$lv(x) \neq \text{null} \Rightarrow VC(pc_3) \ .$$

Static analyses can provide the required information to reduce many proof obligations that are generated from instructions that may throw exceptions, as in the example above.

We show, in Sect. 3, a way to combine a VCgen with static analyses, to reduce the control flow graph of the program, and hence, the number of proof obligations. We will exemplify the approach using a simple null-pointer analysis, and sketch the proof of soundness of the VCgen.

We have formalized the VCgen as a deep embedding in Coq based on the Bicolano formalization of the Java bytecode semantics, which is described in Sect. 2.

The certificates for our VCgen need to include, besides the proofs of safety, the information collected from the static analyses. We discuss the generation and checking of these certificates in Sect. 4.

2   Preliminaries

We will base our development on the Bicolano formalization [10]. Bicolano is a formalization in Coq of the Java Virtual Machine (JVM), which includes object creation, virtual methods, exception handling, and arrays. We will describe only a small and reduced fragment of the formalization, needed for our purposes.

A program consists of a set of classes, each containing a set of fields and methods. A method is composed by a body (sequence of instructions) and a specification (this component will be described later, when describing the VCgen). The instructions considered in this paper are: getfield *FieldId*, putfield *FieldId*, iload $\mathbb{Z}$, istore $\mathbb{Z}$, invokevirtual *Method*, athrow *ClassName*, ireturn.

For each method m, PC_m denotes the set of program points corresponding to the instructions of m. Most of our definitions refer to a single method, therefore, for simplicity, we will omit the reference to the method when is clear from the context. *State* denotes the type of program states; each s : *State* is a triple, $s = (h, os, l)$, where h is the heap, os is the operand stack, and l is the local variables. The type of values is defined as *Value* = *Int* + *Loc*, where *Int* is the type of integers, and *Loc* the type of reference values. The operand stack is modeled by a list, *Stack* = *list Value*. The local variables are modeled by a function *LocalVar* = $\mathbb{Z} \rightarrow$ *Value*. The heap is modeled by an abstract data type, *Heap*, with operations for creating objects (*newObj*) and accessing their fields (*get*, *update*). The type of *initial states* for a method is *State$_i$* = *Heap* × *LocalVar*, and the type of *final states* is *State$_r$* = *Heap* × *ReturnVal*, where *ReturnVal* = *Value* + *Loc*, representing normal termination of a method with a value, or abnormal termination with the location of an exception object. *Exc* is the type of possible exceptions (e.g. NullPointer, ArrayBound, . . .).

Operational Semantics. The operational semantics is defined only for well-typed programs, so we will assume that all programs considered are well-typed.

The semantics is defined by two relations $\longrightarrow$: *Method* $\rightarrow$ *PC* × *State* $\rightarrow$ *PC* × *State* $\rightarrow$ *Prop* and $\downarrow$: *Method* $\rightarrow$ *PC* × *State* $\rightarrow$ *State$_r$* $\rightarrow$ *Prop*, where $m \vdash (pc, s) \longrightarrow (pc', s')$ represents execution of one instruction in a method, and $m \vdash (pc, s) \downarrow s'$ represents execution of one instruction that reaches a final state. We will write $\longrightarrow^*$ to mean the reflexive, transitive closure of $\longrightarrow$, and $\downarrow^*$ to mean the relation $\longrightarrow^* \circ \downarrow$ (i.e., many steps of $\longrightarrow$ followed by one step of $\downarrow$).

To make the presentation clearer, we define two auxiliary relations: $\rightarrow_{\text{JVM}}$: *Method* $\rightarrow$ *PC* × *State* $\rightarrow$ *Exc* $\rightarrow$ *Prop* and $\rightarrow_{\text{EXC}}$: *Method* $\rightarrow$ *PC* × *State* $\rightarrow$ *Heap* × *Loc* $\rightarrow$ *Prop*, where $m \vdash (pc, s) \rightarrow_{\text{JVM}} e$ indicates that executing the instruction at pc in state s results in the JVM exception e being thrown (e.g., the exception NullPointer is thrown when accessing a null reference), and $m \vdash (pc, s) \rightarrow_{\text{EXC}} (h, loc)$ indicates that the exception pointed by loc in heap h was thrown when executing the instruction at pc in state s, and we need to look for an exception handler. To search for the handler code corresponding to an exception, we have a function *excHandler* : *Method* $\rightarrow$ *PC* × *Heap* × *Loc* $\rightarrow$ *PC* + $\perp$, that returns $\perp$ when no handler is found in the current method.

Figure 1 shows a few rules of the big-step operational semantics. The function *instructionAt* returns the instruction corresponding to a given program point. The function initArgs : *Value* × *list Value* $\rightarrow$ *LocalVar* builds the initial local variables for a method call, where the first argument is a reference to the object, and the second argument is the list of arguments of the method. The infix operators :: and ++ represent the cons function for lists and the concatenation of lists, respectively.

In the rules for the instruction invokevirtual, there is the implicit assumption that the length of *args* is the same as the number of arguments of the method m'. The first rule for invokevirtual corresponds to the case where the

$$\frac{instructionAt(pc) = \text{athrow} \qquad loc \neq \text{null}}{(pc, (h, loc :: os, l)) \rightarrow_{\text{EXC}}(h, loc)}$$

$$\frac{instructionAt(pc) = \text{athrow} \qquad loc = \text{null}}{(pc, (h, loc :: os, l)) \rightarrow_{\text{JVM}}\text{NullPointer}}$$

$$\frac{instructionAt(pc) = \text{getfield } f \qquad get(h, loc, f) = v \qquad loc \neq \text{null}}{(pc, (h, loc :: os, l)) \longrightarrow (pc + 1, (h, v :: os, l))}$$

$$\frac{instructionAt(pc) = \text{getfield } f \qquad loc = \text{null}}{(pc, (h, loc :: os, l)) \rightarrow_{\text{JVM}}\text{NullPointer}}$$

$$\frac{instructionAt(pc) = \text{putfield } f \qquad update(h, (loc, f), v) = h' \qquad loc \neq \text{null}}{(pc, (h, v :: loc :: os, l)) \longrightarrow (pc + 1, (h', os, l))}$$

$$\frac{instructionAt(pc) = \text{iload } x \qquad l(x) = v}{(pc, (h, os, l)) \longrightarrow (pc + 1, (h, v :: os, l))} \qquad \frac{instructionAt(pc) = \text{ireturn}}{(pc, (h, v :: os, l)) \downarrow (h, v)}$$

$$\frac{instructionAt(pc) = \text{istore } x \qquad l\,[x \mapsto v] = l'}{(pc, (h, v :: os, l)) \longrightarrow (pc + 1, (h, os, l'))}$$

$$\frac{instructionAt(pc) = \text{invokevirtual } m' \qquad}{l' = \text{initArgs}(loc, args) \qquad loc \neq \text{null} \qquad m' \vdash (pc_0, (h, [], l')) \downarrow^*(h', v)}{(pc, (h, args ++ loc :: os, l)) \longrightarrow (pc + 1, (h', v :: os, l))}$$

$$\frac{instructionAt(pc) = \text{invokevirtual } m'}{l' = \text{initArgs}(loc, args) \qquad loc \neq \text{null} \qquad m' \vdash (pc_0, (h, [], l')) \downarrow^*(h', loc')}{(pc, (h, args ++ loc :: os, l)) \rightarrow_{\text{EXC}}(h', loc')}$$

$$\frac{instructionAt(pc) = \text{invokevirtual } m' \qquad loc = \text{null}}{(pc, (h, args ++ loc :: os, l)) \rightarrow_{\text{JVM}}\text{NullPointer}}$$

$$\frac{(pc, (h, os, l)) \rightarrow_{\text{JVM}} e \qquad (h', loc) = newObj(h, e)}{(pc, (h, os, l)) \rightarrow_{\text{EXC}}(h', loc)}$$

$$\frac{(pc, (h, os, l)) \rightarrow_{\text{EXC}}(h', loc) \qquad excHandler(pc, h', loc) = pc'}{(pc, (h, os, l)) \longrightarrow (pc', (h', loc :: [], l))}$$

$$\frac{(pc, (h, os, l)) \rightarrow_{\text{EXC}}(h', loc) \qquad excHandler(pc, h', loc) = \bot}{(pc, (h, os, l)) \downarrow (h', loc)}$$

Fig. 1. Operational semantics (excerpt)

called method returns successfully a value, the second one corresponds to the case where the called method throws an exception (so we need to find a handler in the current method), and the third one corresponds to the case where the object is null.

The control flow graph of method m, denoted $\mathcal{G}_m$ is the set of edges (pairs of program points) (pc, pc') such that the program can go from pc to pc' in one step. This means, for instance, that instructions like getfield and putfield have an edge to the null-pointer exception handler (if there is one), and instructions `athrow` and `invokevirtual` have edges to all handlers in their range, since we cannot (statically) determine which exceptions will be thrown.

VCgen. We consider a deep embedding of the VCgen in Coq. As shown in [13], deep embeddings have several advantages over shallow embeddings, such as, smaller proof terms, and the possibility to manipulate the generated proof obligation (e.g. by structural analysis).

The language for expressing assertions, Assrt, used by the VCgen is the following (excerpt):

$$
\begin{aligned}
\text{Assrt} ::= \ & \text{Assrt} \underline{\wedge} \text{Assrt} \mid \text{Assrt} \underline{\vee} \text{Assrt} \mid \underline{\neg}\text{Assrt} \mid \text{Assrt} \underline{\Rightarrow} \text{Assrt} \\
& \mid \ \text{V } CompOp \text{ V} \dots \quad (\text{* assertions *}) \\
\text{V} ::= \ & \text{Lv } \mathbb{Z} \mid \text{Hget H V } FieldId \mid \text{St } \mathbb{Z} \mid \text{Vvar } Value \mid \text{Old V} \mid \text{result} \\
& \mid \ \text{null} \mid \text{V } BinOp \text{ V} \dots \quad (\text{* values *}) \\
\text{H} ::= \ & \text{Hupd H V } FieldId \text{ V} \mid \text{Hvar } Heap \mid \text{CurrHeap} \quad (\text{* heap *}) \\
\text{S}_i ::= \ & \text{H} \times (\mathbb{Z} \to \text{V}) \quad (\text{* initial states *}) \\
\text{S} ::= \ & \text{H} \times (\mathbb{Z} \to \text{V}) \times (\mathbb{Z} \to \text{V}) \quad (\text{* local states *}) \\
\text{S}_r ::= \ & \text{H} \times \text{V} \quad (\text{* final states *}) \\
BinOp ::= \ & \underline{+} \mid \underline{-} \dots \quad CompOp ::= \underline{=} \mid \underline{\neq} \mid \underline{\leq} \mid \underline{\leq} \dots
\end{aligned}
$$

In Assrt we have the usual logical operators ($\underline{\wedge}, \underline{\vee}, \underline{\Rightarrow}, \dots$), including equality and comparison. The operators are underlined to differentiate them from the operators of Coq. The type of values, V, allows to access the local variables (Lv), the stack (St), the heap (Hget(h, loc, f) access the field f of object loc in h), values in the initial state of a method (Old), the result of a method (result), and permits to express binary operations between values. The heap, represented by H, allows to update values (Hupd(h, loc, f, v) updates the field f of object loc with the value v), and access to the current heap (CurrHeap). Note that using Vvar and Hvar we can define a *lift* function that takes a *State* (resp. *State$_i$*, *State$_r$*) and returns a S (resp. S$_i$, S$_r$), so we will consider an element $s : State$ as having also type S (and similarly with *State$_i$* and *State$_r$*).

The specification of a method is a tuple, $\mathcal{S}_m = (Pre, Post_{Nrml}, Post_{Exc}, A)$, where $Pre :$ Assrt is the precondition; $Post_{Nrml}, Post_{Exc} :$ Assrt are the postconditions corresponding to normal termination, and abnormal termination (due to an uncaught exception), respectively; and $A : PC \mapsto$ Assrt is a partial mapping called the *annotation table* containing assertions that are used by the VCgen to construct the proof obligations. We assume that all cycles in the control flow graph contain at least one annotated point.

The precondition states properties of the initial state, the postcondition relates the initial state with the final state, and the annotations relate the initial state with the local state. We also assume a well-formedness condition for specifications: accesses to the local variables or to the stack are in bound, only the postconditions can refer to result, expressions are well-typed, and preconditions do not use the Old construct.

The VCgen is based on weakest precondition calculus, defined by two mutually recursive functions: $\text{wp}_{\text{instr}} : Method \to PC \to \text{Assertion}$, and $\text{wp}_{\text{annot}} : Method \to PC \to \text{Assertion}$, where Assertion $= $ S$_i \to$ S $\to$ Assrt.

$\text{wp}_{\text{instr}}(pc)$ computes the weakest precondition (WP) corresponding to the instruction at pc, while $\text{wp}_{\text{annot}}(pc)$ returns the annotation of pc, or calls $\text{wp}_{\text{instr}}(pc)$ if pc is not annotated. To simplify the presentation, we define the functions $\text{wp}_{\text{JVM}} : Method \rightarrow PC \rightarrow State_i \rightarrow Heap \times LocalVar \rightarrow Exc \rightarrow Assrt$, and $\text{wp}_{\text{EXC}} : Method \rightarrow PC \rightarrow State_i \rightarrow Heap \times LocalVar \rightarrow Loc \rightarrow Assrt$, that roughly corresponds to relations $\rightarrow_{\text{JVM}}$ and $\rightarrow_{\text{EXC}}$, and returns the WP when an exception is thrown. They look for the exception handler and return the WP of the first point of the handler, or return the postcondition corresponding to abnormal termination if no handler is found in the method.

The general form of $\text{wp}_{\text{instr}}(pc)$ contains a conjunction for each branch of $\mathcal{G}$:

$$\text{wp}_{\text{instr}}(pc, s_0, s) = \bigwedge_{(pc, pc') \in \mathcal{G}} C_{(pc, pc')}(s) \Rrightarrow P_{(pc, pc')}(\text{wp}_{\text{annot}}(pc'), s_0, s), \qquad (1)$$

where $C_{(pc, pc')}(s)$ is a necessary condition that needs to be satisfied in order for the program to go from pc to pc' in one step, and $P_{(pc, pc')}(\text{wp}_{\text{annot}}(pc'), s_0, s)$ is a predicate transformer that updates s in correspondence with the instruction at pc and applies it to $\text{wp}_{\text{annot}}(pc')$. To compute $\text{wp}_{\text{instr}}(pc, s_0, s)$ we proceed by case analysis on the instruction at pc, and state s. We show a few cases in Fig. 2. For readability, we change the first parameter, pc, for the corresponding instruction. For instance, the condition $C_{(pc, pc')}$ for the instructions getfield and putfield is that the top of the stack contains a null or non-null value depending on the branch. For iload and ireturn, the condition is simply <u>true</u>.

The function wp_{annot} is defined as follows:

$$\text{wp}_{\text{annot}}(pc, s_0, s) = \begin{cases} \text{subst}(s_0, s, A(pc)) & \text{if } pc \in \text{dom}(A), \\ \text{wp}_{\text{instr}}(pc, s_0, s) & \text{otherwise}. \end{cases}$$

The function $\text{subst} : S_i \rightarrow S \rightarrow Assrt \rightarrow Assrt$, performs a substitution on an expression; $\text{subst}(s_0, (h, os, lv), a)$ traverses a replacing CurrHeap by h, St n by $os(n)$, and Lv x by $lv(x)$. The values protected by Old are substituted using the initial state. The function $\text{subst}_{\text{Post}} : S_i \rightarrow S_r \rightarrow Assrt \rightarrow Assrt$ does the same as subst, but also replacing result.

We need an interpretation function, $\text{interp} : Assrt \rightarrow State_i \rightarrow State \rightarrow Prop$ to transform an expression into a Coq proposition. $\text{interp}(a, s_0, s)$ traverses a replacing the constructors for the corresponding functions in the Bicolano formalization, and replacing the references to the state with the values in s and s_0. The function $\text{interp}_{\text{Post}} : Assrt \rightarrow State_i \rightarrow State_r \rightarrow Prop$ is the same as interp except that it also replaces result. This function are defined for well-formed specifications, returning an undefined value otherwise.

We say an assertion $a : Assrt$ is valid in state s and initial state s_0, and write it $s_0, s \models a$, if $\text{interp}(a, s_0, s)$ is valid in Coq. Similarly with $\text{interp}_{\text{Post}}$. We say an assertion $a : Assertion$ is valid in state s and initial state s_0, and write it $s_0, s \models a$, if $(s_0, s \models a(s_i, s))$, where $s_i = (\text{CurrHeap}, \lambda x.\text{Lv}\, x)$ and $s = (\text{CurrHeap}, \lambda x.\text{St}\, x, \lambda x.\text{Lv}\, x)$. We will write $\models a$ to mean $\forall s_0, s, (s_0, s \models a)$.

The following definition states the proof obligations needed to verify that a method complies with its specification.

$$\text{wp}_{\text{instr}}(\textbf{athrow } f, s_0, (h, loc :: os, l)) =$$
$$loc \neq \text{null} \Rrightarrow \text{wp}_{\text{EXC}}(pc, s_0, (h, l), loc)$$
$$\wedge \, loc \equiv \text{null} \Rrightarrow \text{wp}_{\text{JVM}}(pc, s_0, (h, l), \texttt{NullPointer})$$

$$\text{wp}_{\text{instr}}(\textbf{getfield } f, s_0, (h, loc :: os, l)) =$$
$$loc \neq \text{null} \Rrightarrow \text{wp}_{\text{annot}}(pc + 1, s_0, (h, \mathsf{Hget}(h, loc, f) :: os, l))$$
$$\wedge \, loc \equiv \text{null} \Rrightarrow \text{wp}_{\text{JVM}}(pc, s_0, (h, l), \texttt{NullPointer})$$

$$\text{wp}_{\text{instr}}(\textbf{iload } x, s_0, (h, os, l)) = \text{wp}_{\text{annot}}(pc + 1, s_0, (h, l(x) :: os, l))$$

$$\text{wp}_{\text{instr}}(\textbf{ireturn}, s_0, (h, v :: os, l)) = \mathsf{subst}_{\text{Post}}(s_0, (h, v), Post_{Nrml})$$

$$\text{wp}_{\text{instr}}(\textbf{istore } x, s_0, (h, v :: os, l)) = \text{wp}_{\text{annot}}(pc + 1, s_0, (h, os, l\,[x \mapsto v]))$$

$$\text{wp}_{\text{instr}}(\textbf{putfield } f, s_0, (h, v :: loc :: os, l)) =$$
$$loc \neq \text{null} \Rrightarrow \text{wp}_{\text{annot}}(pc + 1, s_0, (\mathsf{Hupd}(h, loc, f, v), os, l))$$
$$\wedge \, loc \equiv \text{null} \Rrightarrow \text{wp}_{\text{JVM}}(pc, s_0, (h, l), \texttt{NullPointer})$$

$$\text{wp}_{\text{instr}}(\textbf{invokevirtual } m, s_0, (h, args +\!+ loc :: os, l) =$$
$$loc \neq \text{null} \Rrightarrow \left(\begin{array}{l} \mathsf{subst}((h, li), (h, [], li), Pre(m)) \\ \wedge \text{ PostNormal} \\ \wedge \text{ PostExc} \end{array} \right)$$
$$\wedge \, loc \equiv \text{null} \Rrightarrow \text{wp}_{\text{JVM}}(pc, s_0, (h, l), \texttt{NullPointer})$$

$$li = \text{initArgs}(loc, args)$$
$$\text{PostNormal} = \left\{ \begin{array}{l} \forall\, r, \forall\, h', \mathsf{subst}_{\text{Post}}((h, li), (h', r), Post_{Nrml}(m)) \Rrightarrow \\ \text{wp}_{\text{annot}}(pc + 1, s_0, (h', r :: os, l)) \end{array} \right.$$
$$\text{PostExc} = \left\{ \begin{array}{l} \forall\, loc' \; \forall\, h', \mathsf{subst}_{\text{Post}}((h, li), (h', loc'), Post_{Exc}(m)) \Rrightarrow \\ \text{wp}_{\text{EXC}}(pc, s_0, (h, l), loc') \end{array} \right.$$

Fig. 2. Weakest precondition for instructions (excerpt)

Definition 1. *Given a program p and a method m,* certifiedMethod(m) *stands for the following proposition:*

$$\forall s_0, (s_0, \overline{s_0} \models Pre(m) \Rrightarrow \text{wp}_{\text{annot}}(pc_0, \mathsf{s_i}, \mathsf{s}))$$
$$\wedge \bigwedge_{pc \in \text{dom}(A)} \forall s_0 \; s, (s_0, s \models A(pc) \Rrightarrow \text{wp}_{\text{instr}}(pc, \mathsf{s_i}, \mathsf{s})),$$

where $\overline{s_0} = (h, [], l)$ if $s_0 = (h, l)$, i.e. $\overline{s_0}$ is the state obtained by extending the initial state s_0 with an empty operand stack.

To verify a method, we need to check that the precondition implies the WP of the first instruction, and for each annotated point pc, the annotation implies the WP of the instruction at pc.

The soundness is proved with respect to the operational semantics.

Theorem 1 (Soundness of the VCgen). *Let p be a program and m a method. Assume we have a proof of* certifiedMethod(m'), *for all methods m' in the program, and a state (pc, s) such that $s_0, s \models \mathrm{wp}_{\mathrm{annot}}(m, pc)$. Then the following holds:*

- *if $(pc, s) \longrightarrow (pc', s')$, then $s_0, s' \models \mathrm{wp}_{\mathrm{annot}}(m, pc')$,*
- *if $(pc, s) \downarrow (h, r)$, with $r \in$ Value, then $s_0, (h, r) \models Post_{Nrml}(m)$,*
- *if $(pc, s) \downarrow (h, loc)$, with $loc \in$ Loc, then $s_0, (h, loc) \models Post_{Exc}(m)$.*

The proof is divided in the following lemmas.

Lemma 1. *If $(pc, s) \longrightarrow (pc', s')$, then $s \models C_{(pc, pc')}(s)$.*

Lemma 2. *If $(pc, s) \longrightarrow (pc', s')$, where instructionAt($pc$) $\neq$ invokevirtual, and $s_0, s \models \mathrm{wp}_{\mathrm{instr}}(m, pc)$, then $s_0, s' \models \mathrm{wp}_{\mathrm{annot}}(m, pc')$.*

Proof. By case analysis on the current instruction, using Lemma 1.

Lemma 3. *If we have a proof of* certifiedMethod(m), *and $s_0, s \models \mathrm{wp}_{\mathrm{annot}}(m, pc)$, then $s_0, s \models \mathrm{wp}_{\mathrm{instr}}(m, pc)$.*

Proof. If pc is not annotated it is trivial, since $\mathrm{wp}_{\mathrm{annot}}(m, pc)$ is the same as $\mathrm{wp}_{\mathrm{instr}}(m, pc)$. Otherwise, we have $\mathrm{wp}_{\mathrm{annot}}(m, pc, s_0, s) = \mathrm{subst}(s_0, s, A(pc))$, and we conclude using the fact that we have a proof of certifiedMethod(m). □

Lemma 4. *Let p be a program and m a method. Assume we have a proof of* certifiedMethod(m'), *for all methods m' in the program, and a state (pc, s) such that $s_0, s \models \mathrm{wp}_{\mathrm{annot}}(m, pc)$. Then the following holds:*

- *if $(pc, s) \hookrightarrow (pc', s')$, then $s_0, s' \models \mathrm{wp}_{\mathrm{annot}}(m, pc')$,*
- *if $(pc, s) \hookrightarrow (h, r)$, with $r \in$ Value, then $s_0, (h, r) \models Post_{Nrml}(m)$,*
- *if $(pc, s) \hookrightarrow (h, loc)$, with $loc \in$ Loc, then $s_0, (h, loc) \models Post_{Exc}(m)$,*

where the relation $\hookrightarrow$: Method $\rightarrow PC \times State \rightarrow PC \times State + State_r \rightarrow Prop$ is defined in Fig. 3.

Proof. The proof proceeds by induction in the relation $\hookrightarrow$. The relation *call* : Method $\rightarrow PC \times State \rightarrow State_r \rightarrow$ Method $\rightarrow PC \times State \rightarrow PC \times State + State_r \rightarrow Prop$ determines the connection between the states of execution when calling a method. If $call(m, (pc, s), r, m', (pc_0(m'), s'), t)$ is valid, then it means that in method m, *instructionAt*(pc) = invokevirtual m', $(pc_0(m'), s')$ is the initial state of execution in m' (i.e. it has an empty operand stack and the local

$$\frac{}{(pc, s) \hookrightarrow (pc, s)} \qquad \frac{(pc, s) \downarrow r}{(pc, s) \hookrightarrow r} \qquad \frac{instructionAt(pc) \neq \texttt{invokevirtual} \qquad (pc, s) \longrightarrow (pc', s') \qquad (pc', s') \hookrightarrow t}{(pc, s) \hookrightarrow t}$$

$$\frac{m' \vdash (pc_0(m'), s') \hookrightarrow (h, loc) \qquad call(m, (pc, s), (h, loc), m', (pc_0(m'), s'), (h, loc))}{m \vdash (pc, s) \hookrightarrow (h, loc)}$$

$$\frac{m' \vdash (pc_0(m'), s') \hookrightarrow r}{m \vdash (pc'', s'') \hookrightarrow t \qquad call(m, (pc, s), r, m', (pc_0(m'), s'), (pc'', s''))}{m \vdash (pc, s) \hookrightarrow t}$$

Fig. 3. Alternative big-step relation

variables are built from the arguments in the stack of s), and if r is the final state in m', then t is the next state of execution in m. If t is a final state, then it means that m' has thrown an exception that is uncaught in m. If t is a normal state, it means that, either m' has returned successfully (and the return value of r is in the top of the stack of t), or that has thrown an exception that was caught in m (and t contains the location of the exception handler). Note that *call* does not enforce any relation between the initial state s' and the final state r in m', which will be enforced by $\hookrightarrow$.

The relation $\hookrightarrow$ gives us the right induction principle for the `invokevirtual` instruction that was not addressed in Lemma 2.   □

Finally, using Lemma 4 we can prove Theorem 1, by proving that the relation $\hookrightarrow$ is equivalent to the reflexive, transitive closure of the operational semantics.

3   Reducing Proof Obligations

In this section, we show a way to use static analysis to reduce the number of proof obligations generated by the VCgen described in the previous section. Roughly, the analysis is applied to the program, and the results are given to the VCgen. The VCgen can use this information to remove the proof obligations corresponding to paths in the code that cannot be taken at runtime. For example, if a null-pointer analysis can prove the absence of null-pointer exceptions, then the VCgen does not generate proof obligations corresponding to null-pointer exception handlers.

3.1   Preliminary Definitions

We consider a fixed program p and a method m with specification S. pc_0 denotes the first instruction. We will make a small modification to the control flow graph and the semantics. To the set of program points we add two nodes: pc_N that represents normal termination, and pc_E that represents abnormal termination. The control flow graph $\mathcal{G}$ is augmented with edges of the form (pc, pc_N) for each pc that corresponds to a `ireturn` instruction, and (pc, pc_E) for each pc that corresponds to an instruction that can throw an exception that is not caught in m

(this includes `athrow` and `invokevirtual`). We make a small modification to the rules of the operational semantics. We change the relation $\downarrow$, so that, instead of $(pc, s)\downarrow(h, v)$ we have $(pc, s)\longrightarrow(pc_N, (h, v :: [], lv))$, and instead of $(pc, s)\downarrow(h, loc)$ we have $(pc, s)\longrightarrow(pc_E, (h, loc :: [], lv))$. The state considered at the nodes pc_N and pc_E consist of a heap, an operand stack with just one element (the return value, or location of the exception object, respectively), and undefined local variables (since a return state does not contain a local variable array).

Definition 2. *A static analysis $\mathcal{A}$ is a tuple (D, t, I, f), where*

- *$D = (D, \sqsubseteq, \bot, \top, \sqcap, \sqcup)$ is a complete lattice that denotes the domain of the analysis,*
- *$t : \mathcal{G} \to (D \to D)$ is the transfer function, such that for each $(pc, pc') \in \mathcal{G}$, $t_{(pc, pc')}$ is a monotone function in D,*
- *$I : PC \to D$ is the initial value, and*
- *$f \in \{\uparrow, \downarrow\}$ denotes the direction of the analysis. If $f = \uparrow$ we say the analysis is* backward, *and if $f = \downarrow$ we say is* forward.

Definition 3. *A solution (or* table*) for a forward analysis $\mathcal{A} = (D, t, I, \downarrow)$ is a function $S : PC \to D$, such that $I(pc_0) \sqsubseteq S(pc_0)$, and*

$$\forall pc \in PC, \bigsqcup_{(pc', pc) \in \mathcal{G}} t_{(pc', pc)}(S(pc')) \sqsubseteq S(pc) \ .$$

A solution (or table*) for a backward analysis $\mathcal{A} = (D, t, I, \uparrow)$ is a function $S : PC \to D$, such that $S(pc_N) \sqsubseteq I(pc_N)$, $S(pc_E) \sqsubseteq I(pc_E)$, and*

$$\forall pc \in PC, S(pc) \sqsubseteq \bigsqcap_{(pc, pc') \in \mathcal{G}} t_{(pc, pc')}(S(pc')) \ .$$

To find a solution for a given analysis, one needs to find a post-fixpoint to a specific function defined using the transfer function. We will not delve in this, see, e.g., [9] for more details.

To illustrate the combination of analysis and the VCgen, we will define a simple null-pointer analysis. We use a technique described in [3,12] for defining domains for bytecode analysis, where the values stored in the stack are related to their meaning.

Example 1. The null-pointer analysis $\mathcal{A}_{NP} = (D_{NP}, t_{NP}, I_{NP}, \downarrow)$ is defined as follows. The domain D_{NP} represents the operand stack and the local variables, and is defined by:

$$\begin{aligned} D_{NP} &= (list \ E)_\bot^\top \times (\mathbb{Z} \to NP), \\ NP &= \{null, nonnull\}_\bot^\top, \\ E &::= const \ NP \mid localvar \ \mathbb{Z} \ . \end{aligned}$$

The transfer functions, $t_{NP(pc, pc')}(d)$ is defined by case analysis in the instruction at pc and in d. Some of the rules are:

- if $instructionAt(pc) = $ `getfield`

$$t_{\text{NP}(pc,pc+1)}(e :: s, l) = (const \top :: s, [\![e = nonnull]\!](l)),$$
$$t_{\text{NP}(pc,pc_{exc})}(e :: s, l) = (const\ nonnull :: [], [\![e = null]\!](l));$$

- if $instructionAt(pc) = $ `ireturn`, $t_{\text{NP}(pc,pc_N)}(v :: s, l) = (v :: s, l);$
- if $instructionAt(pc) = $ `invokevirtual`,

$$t_{\text{NP}(pc,pc+1)}(args ++ loc :: s, l) = (const \top :: s, [\![e = nonnull]\!](l)),$$
$$t_{\text{NP}(pc,pc_E)}(args ++ loc :: s, l) = (const\ nonnull :: [], l);$$

- if $instructionAt(pc) = $ `iload`, $t_{\text{NP}(pc,pc+1)}(s, l) = (localvar\ x :: s, l).$

Given $e : E$, the expression $[\![e]\!](l) : NP$ evaluates e using the map l. Given $e : E$, $n : NP$, and $l : \mathbb{Z} \to NP$, the expression $[\![e = n]\!](l) : \mathbb{Z} \to NP$ is a mapping that updates l using the fact that $e = n$. Note the way this expression is used for the `getfield` instruction: in the transfer for normal execution we can update the local variables, knowing that the reference is non-null, and for exceptional execution, we know the reference is null. The second rule for `invokevirtual` indicates that it may throw an uncaught exception.

Another example of a static analysis is provided by the weakest precondition defined for the VCgen.

Example 2. The weakest precondition can be viewed as a backward analysis (see [7]), $\mathcal{A}_{\text{WP}} = (D_{\text{WP}}, t_{\text{WP}}, I_{\text{WP}}, \uparrow)$, where $D_{\text{WP}} = \text{Assertion}$. We have

$$d_1 \sqsubseteq d_2 = (\models d_1 \Rrightarrow d_2),$$

and $\top$, $\bot$, $\sqcap$, $\sqcup$ correspond with $\underline{\text{true}}$, $\underline{\text{false}}$, $\underline{\wedge}$, $\underline{\vee}$, respectively.

The transfer function is defined by:

$$t_{\text{WP}(pc,pc')}(e) = \lambda s_0.\lambda s.C_{(pc,pc')}(s) \Rrightarrow P_{(pc,pc')}(e, s_0, s),$$

and finally the initial value $I_{\text{WP}}(pc_N) = \lambda s_0.\lambda s.\text{subst}_{\text{Post}}(Post_{Nrml}, s_0, s)$ and $I_{\text{WP}}(pc_E) = \lambda s_0.\lambda s.\text{subst}_{\text{Post}}(Post_{Exc}, s_0, s).$

The function wp_{annot} computes a solution for this analysis. To check that is in fact a solution, we need to prove that for all pc,

$$\text{wp}_{\text{annot}}(pc) \sqsubseteq \bigwedge_{(pc,pc') \in \mathcal{G}} t_{\text{WP}(pc,pc')}(\text{wp}_{\text{annot}}(pc')) =$$

$$\lambda s_0.\lambda s. \bigwedge_{(pc,pc') \in \mathcal{G}} C_{(pc,pc')}(s) \Rrightarrow P_{(pc,pc')}(\text{wp}_{\text{annot}}(pc'), s_0, s) = \text{wp}_{\text{instr}}(pc) \ .$$

Note that this is stated in Lemma 3.

A static analysis simulates the execution of a program in its domain. To prove that an analysis is sound, we need to prove that a step in the operational semantics, correspond to a transfer function in the domain. We define a *correctness relation* that relates states, with the elements of the domain of the analysis.

Definition 4. *A correctness relation for an analysis* $\mathcal{A} = (D, t, I, f)$ *is a relation* $\vdash \subseteq State \times D$, *such that the following holds:*

- *for all* $d_1, d_2 \in D$, *if* $s \vdash d_1$ *and* $d_1 \sqsubseteq d_2$, *then* $s \vdash d_2$, *and*
- *if* $(\forall d \in D' \subseteq D, s \vdash d)$, *then* $s \vdash (\bigsqcap D')$.

The relation $s \vdash d$ should be read as: d is a safe approximation of s.

Definition 5. *A static analysis* $\mathcal{A} = (D, t, I, f)$ *with correctness relation* $\vdash$, *is* sound *if for every solution* S, *the following holds:* $(pc, s) \longrightarrow (pc', s')$ *and* $s \vdash S(pc)$, *implies* $s' \vdash S(pc')$.

The usual way to prove that an analysis is sound is to prove that the transfer functions preserve the semantics. For a forward analysis, this means that if $(pc, s) \longrightarrow (pc', s')$ and $s \vdash d$, then $s' \vdash t_{(pc, pc')}(d)$. For a backward analysis, the transfer functions preserve the semantics if $(pc, s) \longrightarrow (pc', s')$ and $s \vdash t_{(pc, pc')}(d)$ implies $s' \vdash d$.

If we prove for a given analysis that the transfers functions preserve the semantics, then the soundness of the analysis follows from the properties of the correctness relation, and the definition of a solution.

Continuing with the examples, we define a correctness relation for the null-pointer analysis and the weakest precondition.

Example 3. For the analysis defined in Example 1, we define a correctness relation, $\vdash_{\mathsf{NP}}$, by translating the elements of D_{NP} to Assrt, and using the validity relation of Assrt. First, we define the function $tr : V \times NP \rightarrow$ Assrt, where $tr(e, \bot) = \underline{\mathsf{false}}$, $tr(e, \top) = \underline{\mathsf{true}}$, $tr(e, null) = (e \doteq \mathsf{null})$, and $tr(e, nonnull) = (e \neq \mathsf{null})$.

This function is extended to $\overline{tr} : D_{\mathsf{NP}} \rightarrow$ Assrt. For example, $\overline{tr}(localvar\ 0 ::$ $[], [0 \mapsto nonnull, 1 \mapsto \top]) = tr(\mathsf{St}\,0, nonnull) \wedge tr(\mathsf{Lv}\,0, nonnull) \wedge tr(\mathsf{Lv}\,1, \top)$.

The correctness relation is defined as $(s \vdash_{\mathsf{NP}} d) = (s \models \overline{tr}(d))$ (note that we do not need an initial state). It can be shown that the transfer functions for this analysis preserve the semantics, and therefore, that the analysis is sound.

Example 4. A correctness relation for the analysis defined in Example 2 is:

$$(s_0, s \vdash_{\mathsf{WP}} d) = (s_0, s \models d) \ .$$

This definition depends on a fixed initial state s_0. Note that the soundness of this analysis is stated in Theorem 1.

3.2   Combining a Static Analysis with the VCgen

We show how the VCgen can use the results of the analysis to reduce the proof obligations. The main idea is to use the solution of the analysis as a parameter for the VCgen. When computing the function wp_{instr} at a particular point pc, we can use the information given by the analysis at pc to remove some branch.

Assume we have an analysis $\mathcal{A} = (D, t, I, f)$ with correctness relation $\vdash$, and a solution $S : PC \rightarrow D$. Further, assume we have a function $\gamma : D \rightarrow \mathsf{Assrt}$ that translates the results of the analysis to assertions in the VCgen language that reference to the local state, with the following property: if $s \vdash d$, then $s \models \gamma(d)$.

We redefine the function $\mathrm{wp}_{\mathsf{instr}}$. The general form is now

$$\mathrm{wp}_{\mathsf{instr}}(pc, s_0, s) = \bigwedge_{(pc, pc') \in \mathcal{G}} F_{(pc, pc')}(s_0, s), \tag{2}$$

where the F is defined as

$$F_{(pc, pc')}(s_0, s) = \begin{cases} \underline{\mathsf{true}} & \text{if} \models \mathsf{subst}(s, \gamma(S(pc))) \Rightarrow \neg C_{(pc, pc')}(s), \\ WP(pc, pc', s_0, s) & \text{otherwise,} \end{cases}$$

and $WP(pc, pc', s_0, s) = (C_{(pc, pc')}(s) \Rightarrow P_{(pc, pc')}(\mathrm{wp}_{\mathsf{annot}}(pc'), s_0, s))$.

Intuitively, if we can infer $\neg C_{(pc, pc')}(s)$ from $S(pc)$, then the path going from pc to pc' cannot be taken at runtime, since taking this path would imply that the condition $C_{(pc, pc')}(s)$ is valid. In that case, the proof obligation corresponding to this branch can be removed, replacing it by $\underline{\mathsf{true}}$.

The condition $\models \mathsf{subst}(s, \gamma(S(pc))) \Rightarrow \neg C_{(pc, pc')}(s)$ may not be decidable; in that case we have to replace it with a decidable test, $test(S(pc), C_{(pc, pc')}(s))$, that is a sound approximation, i.e. if $test(S(pc), C_{(pc, pc')}(s))$, it implies that $\models \mathsf{subst}(s, \gamma(S(pc))) \Rightarrow \neg C_{(pc, pc')}(s)$.

The definition of F depends on the domain of the analysis, so we will illustrate with the null-pointer analysis defined above.

Example 5. To remove proof obligations using the null-pointer analysis, we look on the instructions that could generate a null-pointer exception. For instance, let us take `getfield`. If $instructionAt(pc) = \texttt{getfield}$, and $S(pc) = (e :: s, l)$, then $F_{(pc, pc_{\mathsf{exc}})}$ is defined by:

$$F_{(pc, pc_{\mathsf{exc}})}(s_0, s) = \begin{cases} \underline{\mathsf{true}} & \text{if } [\![e]\!](l) = nonnull, \\ WP(pc, pc_{\mathsf{exc}}, s_0, s) & \text{otherwise;} \end{cases}$$

This says that if the analysis guarantees that the top of the stack will contain a non-null pointer, then we do not need to check the branch corresponding to the null-pointer exception handler. In the same way, we can remove the proof obligation corresponding to normal execution if the analysis guarantees that the pointer is null.

A similar definition applies to other instructions such as `putfield`, and `invokevirtual`, i.e. all instructions that take a pointer parameter from the stack, and throw a `NullPointer` if the pointer is null.

3.3   Combining Static Analyses and Specifications

The VCgen presented above generates fewer proof obligations by using static analysis to reduce the control flow graph. However, there are situations where the analysis cannot ensure enough information to make some reduction possible. Consider the following excerpt of Java bytecode:

pc_1 $\quad \ldots$ $\hspace{4cm}$ $A(pc_1) = \mathsf{Lv}\, x \neq \mathsf{null} \,\wedge\, \ldots$

$\ldots$

pc_2 $\quad$ iload x

pc_3 $\quad$ getfield f

Assume that the local variable x does not change between pc_1 and pc_2, and that the annotation table contains the assertion that x is not null at pc_1. Therefore, at pc_3, the getfield instruction is accessing a non-null pointer. If the analysis is not able to ensure this, then the VCgen will generate two proof obligations. The one corresponding to exceptional execution is proved by contradiction using the assertion at pc_1. If there is more that one access to x such as the one at pc_3, the VCgen will generate two proof obligations for each access.

In this section, we propose a way to transfer the assertions contained in the specification to the domain of the analysis, so that the analysis can produce more accurate results. In the example above, if the information contained in $A(pc_1)$ is transferred, the analysis can propagate it to point pc_3, where it can ensure that the object accessed is non-null. Then, only one proof obligation would have been generated.

We will assume an annotated method m with specification S and an analysis $\mathcal{A} = (D, t, I, f)$. In order to translate the assertions contained in the specification to the domain of the analysis, we assume a function $\alpha : \mathsf{Assrt} \to D$, with the following property: $s_0, s \models e \Rightarrow s \vdash \alpha(e)$.

We extend the annotation table A into a total function $\overline{A} : PC \to \mathsf{Assrt}$, where we complete with the value $\underline{\mathbf{true}}$ the elements that are not in the domain.

We redefine the meaning of a solution for the analysis, to use the specification. To differentiate from the previous definition, we call this *combined solution*, and refer to the previous as *simple solution*.

Definition 6. *A* combined solution *(or* combined table*) for a forward analysis $\mathcal{A} = (D, t, I, \downarrow)$ is a function $S : PC \to D$, such that $I(pc_0) \sqcap \alpha(Pre) \sqsubseteq S(pc_0)$ and*

$$\forall pc \in PC, \bigsqcup_{(pc,pc') \in \mathcal{G}} t_{(pc,pc')}(S(pc) \sqcap \alpha(\overline{A}(pc))) \sqsubseteq S(pc') \ .$$

A combined solution *(or* combined table*) for a backward analysis $\mathcal{A} = (D, t, I, \uparrow)$ is a function $A : PC \to D$, such that $S(pc_N) \sqcap \alpha(Post_{Nrml}) \sqsubseteq I(pc_N)$, $S(pc_E) \sqcap \alpha(Post_{Exc}) \sqsubseteq I(pc_E)$ and*

$$\forall pc \in PC, \alpha(\overline{A}(pc)) \sqcap S(pc) \sqsubseteq \bigsqcap_{(pc,pc') \in \mathcal{G}} t_{(pc,pc')}(S(pc')) \ .$$

Note that, since transfer functions and the meet operator ($\sqcap$) are monotone, any simple solution for the analysis is also a combined solution. To find combined solutions, we can use the same methods used to find simple solutions.

Again, we will exemplify the approach using the null-pointer analysis.

Example 6. To define the function α for the analysis $\mathcal{A}_{\mathsf{NP}}$, we first define the function $split :$ Assrt $\rightarrow$ *list* Assrt such that $split(e_1 \wedge e_2) = split(e_1) \mathbin{++} split(e_2)$, and $split(e) = e$ if e is not of the form $e_1 \wedge e_2$.

Then α is defined as: $\alpha(e) = filter(split(e))$, where *filter* looks in the list produced by *split* for expressions of the form $\mathsf{St}\,k = \mathsf{null}$, $\mathsf{St}\,k \neq \mathsf{null}$, $\mathsf{Lv}\,k = \mathsf{null}$, $\mathsf{Lv}\,k \neq \mathsf{null}$, or their symmetric, and translate them to the domain D_{NP}. For instance, $\alpha(\mathsf{Lv}\,0 \neq \mathsf{null} \wedge \mathsf{null} = \mathsf{St}\,1) = (const \top :: const\ null :: [], [0 \mapsto nonnull])$.

Soundness of the VCgen Revisited. Now we focus on the proof of soundness for the VCgen described in this section. We assume an analysis $\mathcal{A}$ with correctness relation $\vdash$ and a combined solution S. Stated in the terms defined in this section, to prove the soundness of the VCgen we need to prove:

$$(pc, s) \longrightarrow (pc', s') \wedge (s_0, s \vdash_{\mathsf{WP}} \mathrm{wp}_{\mathsf{annot}}(pc)) \Rightarrow (s_0, s' \vdash_{\mathsf{WP}} \mathrm{wp}_{\mathsf{annot}}(pc')) \ . \quad (3)$$

However, since the WP of an instruction depends on the combined solution for the analysis, and the solution depends on the validity of the specification, to prove (3) we have to prove the following:

$$(pc, s) \longrightarrow (pc', s') \wedge (s_0, s \vdash_{\mathsf{WP}} \mathrm{wp}_{\mathsf{annot}}(pc)) \wedge (s \vdash S(pc)) \Rightarrow$$
$$(s_0, s' \vdash_{\mathsf{WP}} \mathrm{wp}_{\mathsf{annot}}(pc')) \wedge (s' \vdash S(pc')) \ . \quad (4)$$

The proof of (4) is divided in two parts. We need to prove that for all $(pc, s) \longrightarrow (pc', s')$ we have:

$$(s \vdash S(pc)) \wedge (s_0, s \vdash_{\mathsf{WP}} \overline{A}(pc)) \Rightarrow (s' \vdash S(pc')), \quad (5)$$

$$(s \vdash S(pc)) \wedge (s_0, s \vdash_{\mathsf{WP}} \mathrm{wp}_{\mathsf{annot}}(pc)) \Rightarrow (s_0, s' \vdash_{\mathsf{WP}} \mathrm{wp}_{\mathsf{annot}}(pc')) \ . \quad (6)$$

Equation (5) states that the analysis is sound (for combined solutions) as-suming that the specification is verified. The proof is similar to the soundness proof for simple solutions. We first prove that the transfer functions preserve the semantics (this does not depend on any type of solution), and then conclude using properties of the correctness, and monotony of the transfer function and meet ($\sqcap$) and join ($\sqcup$) operators.

Equation (6) states that the VCgen is sound assuming that the analysis is sound. The proof follows the lines of Theorem 1, however, in this case we cannot prove that $(pc, s) \longrightarrow (pc', s')$ and $s_0, s \models \mathrm{wp}_{\mathsf{instr}}(pc)$ implies

$$P_{(pc, pc')}(\mathrm{wp}_{\mathsf{annot}}(pc'), s_0, s)),$$

since the proof obligation corresponding to the branch (pc, pc') may have been removed (changed to <u>true</u>) because of $S(pc)$. However, in that case, we can prove that $s \models \neg C_{(pc, pc')}(s)$. On the other hand, from Lemma 1 we know that $s \models C_{(pc, pc')}(s)$, therefore we have a contradiction and the result follows.

4   Certificate Generation and Checking

In the typical PCC architecture, the producer runs the VCgen on the annotated code. This generates proof obligations, whose proof provides the certificate that is packaged along with the code and sent to the consumer.

For the VCgen described in the previous section, this framework largely applies. The difference lies in the generation of proof obligations. The analyses are performed on the code, using the specification of the methods. For this stage, any fixpoint algorithm can be used to generate the results of the analysis. The algorithm itself does not need to be verified, since we can check that the results given are correct.

The results of these analyses are then given to the VCgen, that returns the proof obligations. These can be proven by automatic methods or in a proof assistant (Coq in our case). The certificate given to the consumer consists on the proofs obtained and the results of the analysis.

Checking the certificate, on the consumer side, consists of three stages. First, the results of the analyses are checked. This involves a simple procedure that can be done very efficiently in one pass through the code [2]. Second, once the results are checked, they are given to the VCgen that generates the proof obligations. Third, the proofs given as part of the certificate are checked to correspond with the obligations generated by the VCgen. If all the checking goes well, the code can be safely executed.

5   Related Work

The use of abstract interpretation as a tool to verify safety policies in PCC has been proposed by Albert, Puebla and Hermenegildo in their *Abstraction-Carrying Code* (ACC) framework [2], where abstract interpretation is used to represent safety policies. The abstraction of a program is the certificate sent to the consumer alongside the code. We do not use analysis to express safety policies, but to reduce the control flow graph of a program. In [1], Albert et al. develop a technique to compress certificates for ACC. The main idea is to remove redundant information that can be easily reconstructed in one pass through the code. Their work can be readily applied to our case for compressing the results of the analyses.

Another compression technique is presented by Besson, Jensen and Pichardie in [3]. They develop an extensible PCC framework based on abstract interpretation. The compression is done through a set of commands that allows the reconstruction of the solution from partial information. Using these commands, different strategies for reconstruction can be encoded and adapted to each particular program. This can also be directly applied to our case.

Nipkow et al. developed the VeryPCC framework in Isabelle/HOL. They define a generic VCgen that can be instantiated with different programming languages, safety logics and safety policies. In [12], Wildmoser, Chaieb and Nipkow use trusted and untrusted analyses to verify a safety policy incrementally. A

VCgen is used to verify the results of the untrusted analyses, using the results of the trusted analyses as hypothesis.

Proof-producing program analysis (PPPA) [5,11] is a technique to generate Hoare-logic proof derivations from program analyses solutions. The advantage of this approach is that the consumer does not need to have a special procedure to check the results of the analysis. On the other hand, the size of the proofs (even if small compared with the program) can be bigger than using compression techniques mentioned above. Nevertheless, it should be possible to use PPPA techniques in our approach to combine the results of the analysis and the proof terms, into a proof term that ensures both properties.

6   Conclusions and Future Work

We have presented a technique based on static analysis to reduce the number of proof obligations generated by a VCgen for Java bytecode, by reducing the control flow graph of a program. The reduction and simplification of the proof obligations have the advantage that leaves the developer with fewer goals left to prove, which as a consequence, generate smaller proof term that can be more rapidly checked. We have exemplified the approach with a simple null-pointer analysis. We have chosen this type of analysis, because many instructions in the JVM can throw null-pointer exceptions, which allows for large reductions in the proof obligations. A recent study by Chalin and James [6] shows that in 2/3 of the cases, reference variables are meant to be non-null (based on design intent).

We have formalized in Coq the VCgen described in Sect. 2 including the proof of soundness (Theorem 1).[1] We plan to complete the formalization (null-pointer analysis and combination), and apply other type of analyses to our approach. Obvious candidates are interval analysis used for array-bound checking and escaping-exception analysis.

The VCgen does not use the complete solution of the analysis to reduce proof obligations. Removing unused parts could help to further compress the certificates. A good starting point should be [4].

Acknowledgments. We would like to thank David Pichardie for his insightful suggestions and for the help he provided with the formalization in Coq.

References

1. Albert, E., Arenas-Sánchez, P., Puebla, G., Hermenegildo, M.V.: Reduced certificates for abstraction-carrying code. In: Etalle, S., Truszczyński, M. (eds.) ICLP 2006. LNCS, vol. 4079, pp. 163–178. Springer, Heidelberg (2006)
2. Albert, E., Puebla, G., Hermenegildo, M.V.: Abstraction-carrying code. In: Baader, F., Voronkov, A. (eds.) LPAR 2004. LNCS (LNAI), vol. 3452, pp. 380–397. Springer, Heidelberg (2005)

---

[1] Available online at http://www-sop.inria.fr/everest/personnel/Benjamin.Gregoire/Code/Certified_vcgen.tgz

3. Besson, F., Jensen, T.P., Pichardie, D.: Proof-carrying code from certified abstract interpretation and fixpoint compression. Theor. Comput. Sci. 364(3), 273–291 (2006)
4. Besson, F., Jensen, T.P., Turpin, T.: Small witnesses for abstract interpretation-based proofs. In: De Nicola, R. (ed.) ESOP 2007. LNCS, vol. 4421, pp. 268–283. Springer, Heidelberg (2007)
5. Chaieb, A.: Proof-producing program analysis. In: Barkaoui, K., Cavalcanti, A., Cerone, A. (eds.) ICTAC 2006. LNCS, vol. 4281, pp. 287–301. Springer, Heidelberg (2006)
6. Chalin, P., James, P.: Non-null references by default in java: Alleviating the nullity annotation burden. In: Ernst, E. (ed.) ECOOP 2007. LNCS, vol. 4609, Springer, Heidelberg (2007)
7. Cousot, P., Cousot, R.: Systematic design of program analysis frameworks. In: POPL, pp. 269–282 (1979)
8. Necula, G.C.: Proof-carrying code. In: POPL, pp. 106–119 (1997)
9. Nielson, F., Nielson, H.R., Hankin, C.: Principles of Program Analysis. Springer-Verlag New York, Inc., Secaucus, NJ, USA (1999)
10. Pichardie, D.: Bicolano – Byte Code Language in Coq (2006), http://mobius.inia.fr/bicolano
11. Seo, S., Yang, H., Yi, K.: Automatic construction of hoare proofs from abstract interpretation results. In: Ohori, A. (ed.) APLAS 2003. LNCS, vol. 2895, pp. 230–245. Springer, Heidelberg (2003)
12. Wildmoser, M., Chaieb, A., Nipkow, T.: Bytecode analysis for proof carrying code. Electr. Notes Theor. Comput. Sci. 141(1), 19–34 (2005)
13. Wildmoser, M., Nipkow, T.: Certifying machine code safety: Shallow versus deep embedding. In: Slind, K., Bunker, A., Gopalakrishnan, G.C. (eds.) TPHOLs 2004. LNCS, vol. 3223, pp. 305–320. Springer, Heidelberg (2004)

Extracting Control from Data: User Interfaces of MIDP Applications

Pierre Crégut*

France Télécom - Recherche & Développement

Abstract. A midlet is a small Java program using the MIDP library that can be executed on a mobile phone. Midlets are developed by software houses and traded on portals often run by operators. Midlets can access powerful APIs, sometimes silently, especially if they are digitally signed by operators and can cause harm to the end-user assets.

We formalize the notion of *navigation graph*, an abstraction of the behaviour of the graphical user interface of the midlet augmented with security relevant information and we describe an algorithm to extract automatically such a graph from the bytecode of a midlet. Most of the structure of a graph is described by data structures built by the application, not by the static structure of the code.

1 Introduction

A midlet is a small Java program that can be executed on a mobile phone. As the set of libraries necessary to execute those applications, the MIDP profile [9], is available on over 1.2 billion phones worldwide, it is the most portable way to add applications to a mobile phone.

Midlets are usually developed by independent software houses and traded on WAP portals operated by other companies, notably mobile operators. Mobile operators can also sign midlets they trust to give them access to more powerful and more dangerous APIs on the customer handset, or to reduce the number of security alert screens popped up during normal operation.

Mobile operators are facing the responsibility of certifying software without having the source code. We have already developed a tool to analyse the critical calls a midlet may perform [6], we try now to characterize the context of those calls, and typically, which events on which screen may trigger the dangerous actions.

We present a way to extract automatically a graph representing the structure of the graphical user interface of a midlet from its code using static analysis. The nodes are abstractions of the contents of the display. The edges of the

---

* This work was funded in part by the Sixth Framework programme of the European Community under the MOBIUS project FP6-015905. This paper reflects only the author's views and the Community is not liable for any use that may be made of the information contained therein.

G. Barthe and C. Fournet (Eds.): TGC 2007, LNCS 4912, pp. 41–56, 2008.

graph represent potential transitions between screen contents and can be annotated with the most dangerous actions that may be performed during the transition.

This case study is an instance of a more generic problem: how to deal with application frameworks that introduce an overlay of control structures described by objects built dynamically by the program. We use program points as an abstraction for different kind of control structures and live data and we use relational algebra to compose elementary relations between data structures, obtained with static analysis techniques.

The paper is organized as follows. Section 2.1 presents the MIDP library as a combination of small application frameworks. Section 3 presents an axiomatized semantics of the user interface library and combines it with a standard description of the operational semantics of the virtual machine executing the application specific code. Navigation graphs that describe a set of authorized behaviours and the notion of compliance with a navigation graph are defined in Sect. 4. Section 5 lists possible uses and extensions for navigation graphs. An algorithm to extract a navigation graph from a midlet is given in Sect. 6. The last section concludes with new research directions.

2   MIDP

2.1   Application Frameworks

Application frameworks are pervasive in modern object oriented programming. An application framework can be defined informally as a library of collaborating classes used to build a specific part of an application (e.g. concurrency, persistence, user interface). From a syntactic point of view, it structures the source code as it defines where some parts of the control must be implemented. The framework also acts as a real meta-language for the system: an important part of the behaviour of the application is not specified by the control statements in the code any more but are now described by live data structures built with the primitive components provided by the library and interpreted by the application framework.

The system is partly under the control of the framework engine that successively calls callbacks defined in the application code depending on interactions with the environment, its internal state and the framework data defined by the application. Proving a temporal property of a global execution of the program requires understanding the structure of these data because they control the possible sequences of callback calls.

2.2   A Java Variant for Mobile Phones

MIDP [9] is a set of libraries on top of a CLDC [10] compliant runtime environment. CLDC is a simple variant of JAVA that fits in the hardware constraints of mobile phones. Compared to JavaSE, it also offers better sand-boxing properties: reflection, dynamic code downloading and direct access to C extensions by application code (JNI) are not available.

MIDP offers an interface to the most commonly available resources on mobile handsets: the user interface with a set of high level widgets and a canvas object for direct access to the screen, a small database system for persistence called RMS and a framework to open network connections where all connections are described by a URL. MIDP also offers a framework to access various multimedia players and to record video or audio clips.

Handling the midlet life-cycle, managing the user interface, launching threads, controlling the evolution of RMS or using the player API to access a multimedia content are simple instances of the application framework pattern in the MIDP profile. We will limit our study to user interfaces.

2.3   MIDP User Interface

Object-oriented User Interface. GUI libraries are typical examples of application frameworks and user interfaces are coded as objects representing displayed elements such as screens, forms, buttons, etc. Those objects build a *model* of the interface from which some of them are selected at a given point and represent the current *view*. *Control* defines how to react to a user interaction (the keyboard) and modifies the view or the model: a generic part is in the scheduler implemented in the framework, the application specific part is defined in callbacks.

User Interface in MIDP. The high-level GUI in MIDP follows this model.[1] The interface is built as a set of screen contents objects (`Screen`[2]). Each screen belongs to a specialized subclass that defines its behaviour (list of items (`List`), alert screens (`Alert`), forms (`Form`), user editable text (`TextBox`)). Forms may contain subcomponents such as labels (`StringItem`), sliders (`Gauge`), fields for user input (`TextField`) etc.

There is a single `Display` object that represents the current handset screen. To change what is displayed on the screen, the display object is associated to a description of the current visible contents, a `Screen` object, with the method `<Display> void setCurrent(Screen)` Each screen can contain soft buttons usually associated to the top buttons on the phone keyboard. Each soft button is represented by a `Command` object. `<Screen> void addCommand(Command)` adds a command to a screen. The behaviour associated to buttons is defined in an object called a `CommandListener` object that contains a single callback. The method `<Screen>void setCommandListener(CommmandListener)` associates a listener to a screen and not directly to a button. When a button is pressed, the callback `<CommandListener>void commandAction(Screen,CommandAction)` is executed with the current contents of the display and the `Command` object representing the button pressed given as arguments. A similar mechanism exists for selectable elements in a form.

---

[1] `Canvas` objects are not considered here but the same principles apply as long as one does not try to analyse the contents of the canvas.

[2] Package names in class names are omitted (usually `javax.microedition.lcdui`) to keep names short.

3   An Axiomatized Semantics of MIDP User Interface

To be able to formalize the algorithm, we need a formalization of the behaviour of the midlet. We will give an operational semantics of the execution of the midlet application code, but we will keep the execution of the MIDP runtime abstract. Both executions will be kept separate and will cooperate (synchronously) through events. This framework could be extended to handle other MIDP libraries (media players, database event handlers, etc.).

We will use the following notations:

1. $[X]$ denotes finite sequences over X. $x : s$ denotes the sequence obtained by shifting s and adding x as its head (standard cons operation on lists).
2. $\wp(X)$ is the set of subsets of X. $X \times Y$ is the cartesian product of X and Y. $X \to Y$ is the function space with domain X and range Y.
3. ϵ is an overloaded symbol representing an undefined value but should not be confused with $\bot$ used for domains. _ is used as a place-holder.
4. If t is a tuple $(t_1, \ldots, t_n)$ $t \sharp i$ denotes the element t_i (as in Standard ML). We will also introduce the record notation $t.\mathsf{lab}$ where lab is a label as a more readable shorthand notation for $t \sharp i$ for some well-identified index i.

Operational Semantics of a JVM. The operational semantics of the Java virtual machine (JVM) used is a simplified version of Bicolano semantics [14]. For the sake of simplicity, exception handlers and the thread stack are not represented [3].

Let C be a set of methods addresses. L is the set of program points. A program point l is a pair of a method address (written $l.\mathsf{meth}$ and an integer (written $l.\mathsf{instr}$) representing the instruction index in the method or a special element, coded as ϵ, that denotes there is no more code to execute.

$L = (C \times \mathbb{N}) \cup \{\epsilon\}$. The function $next : L \to L$ computes the next instruction address after its argument. We will also write $l_1 \mapsto l_2$ if there is a valid transition of the machine from program point l_1 to program point l_2.

A program P is defined by a tuple $(CN, \prec, cl, code)$. CN denotes the set of class names ordered by the subtype relation $\prec$. Classes are characterized by the methods they define: $meth : CN \times SS \to C$ where SS are local unique field or method identifiers (sub-signatures taking types into account to handle overloading). $MN = CN \times SS$ is the set of methods or fields names (elements written $mn = (mn.\mathsf{class}, mn.\mathsf{sig})$) Finally $code : L \to I$ is a partial function defining the code of methods where I is the set of instructions. $\mathsf{newOf} : L \to CN$ is a partial function which associates to a location l a class-name cn if $code(l) = \mathsf{new}\ cn$.

Let A be an infinite set of object addresses. A value $v \in V$ is coded as either an object address in A or a primitive value in PR ($V = A \cup PR$). An object $o \in O$ is defined as a pair $(cn, f) \in CN \times (SS \to V)$ where $o.\mathsf{class} = cn$ defines

---

[3] Exceptions and threads are handled by the tool but with limitations for threads as explained in Sect. 6.6.

the class of the object and $o.\text{def} = f$ is a partial function defining the value of each field.

A state of the virtual machine is coded as a triple: $(h, f, fs) \in H \times F \times [F])$. The heap h is defined as a function from addresses to object representation: $H = A \rightarrow O$. The current frame f codes the current address, and the operand and local variables stacks: $F = L \times [V] \times [V]$. Finally the last element of the JVM state is a frame stack.

m° and d° are some special addresses coding the addresses of respectively the current midlet and the unique display object.

Some transitions in application code interacting with the user interface scheduler in the MIDP code may have side effects e. The syntax for a subset of effects, using ML style syntax for named sum types, is the following:

$$E = CR(A, L) \mid D(A) \mid ACL(A, A) \mid ACO(A, A) \mid EV(A, A, A) \mid DG(\mathcal{D})$$

CR denotes a creation of an object, D, a change of current screen, ACL, an association between a command listener and a screen, ACO, an association of a command and a screen, EV, a user event involving a screen, a command and a listener and DG a dangerous event ($\mathcal{D}$ is left unspecified).

A transition is written $st \xrightarrow{e} st'$. Let $st = (h, (pc, s, l), f)$ be the current state and $st' = (h, (next(pc), s', l), f)$ be its successor. The rules generating effects are the following:

1. If $code(pc) = \mathsf{invokevirtual}(m)$ and m is one of the following primitives, then there is a side effect:
   (a) $m = \mathsf{setCurrent}$ and $s = d : sc : s_0$ then $s' = s_0$ and $e = D(sc)$ (d is the address of the Display object and is always d°).
   (b) $m = \mathsf{setCommandListener}$ and $s = sc : cl : s_0$ then $s' = s_0$ and $e = ACL(sc, cl)$.
   (c) $m = \mathsf{addCommand}$ and $s = sc : co : s_0$ then $s' = s_0$ and $e = ACO(sc, co)$.
2. If $code(pc) = \mathsf{new}(cn)$ then $s' = a : s$ with a fresh and if $cn \prec \mathsf{Command}$ of $cn \prec \mathsf{Screen}$ or $cn \prec \mathsf{CommandListener}$ then $e = CR(a, pc)$.
3. If $pc = \epsilon$ then there exists $(cl, sc, co) \in A \times A \times A$ such that $e = EV(cl, sc, co)$ and $pc' = (c', 0)$ where $c' = meth(h(cl).\mathsf{class}, \mathsf{commandAction})$ and $s' = sc : co : s$. This definition is non deterministic, the valid choices of the triple are defined by the GUI state presented below.

Graphical User Interface (GUI). The axiomatic model defined in this section has been built from the official MIDP specification [9]. A state of the GUI $g \in G$ is coded as a four tuple: $(ge, sc, aco, acl) \in \wp((\mathcal{()}A \times L) \times A \times \wp(A \times A) \times \wp(A \times A)$. ge (notation $g.\mathsf{genv}$) is the graphical environment and defines all the available objects. sc (notation $g.\mathsf{screen}$)is the current display. aco (notation $g.\mathsf{coms}$) is a relation describing the set of commands associated to a given screen. Each element in aco is a pair of addresses (sc, co) such that, if h is a heap structure as defined above, $h(sc)$ is a screen object and $h(co)$ is a command object. This requirement will be formalized in theorem 1. acl (notation $g.\mathsf{list}$)is a relation describing the set of command listeners associated to a given screen. Each element in acl is a pair of addresses (sc, cl) such that $h(sc)$ is a screen object and $h(cl)$ is a command listener object.

As the JVM state, the GUI state evolves and uses the same set of effects.

$$(ge, sc, aco, acl) \xrightarrow{CR(a,l)} (ge \cup \{(a,l)\}, sc, aco, acl)$$

$$(ge, sc, aco, acl) \xrightarrow{D(sc')} (ge, sc', aco, acl)$$

$$(ge, sc, aco, acl) \xrightarrow{ACO(sc,co)} (ge, sc, aco \cup \{(sc, co)\}, acl)$$

$$(ge, sc, aco, acl) \xrightarrow{ACL(sc,cl)} (ge, sc, aco, acl \cup \{(sc, co)\})$$

$$(ge, sc, aco, acl) \xrightarrow{EV(cl,sc,co)} (ge, sc, aco, acl) \text{ if } (sc, co) \in aco \text{ and } (sc, cl) \in acl$$

$$(ge, sc, aco, acl) \xrightarrow{DG(d)} (ge, sc, aco, acl)$$

Execution Traces. The following rules define the combined evolution of the JVM and the GUI machines as:

$$\frac{st \xrightarrow{e} st' \quad g \xrightarrow{e} g'}{(st, g) \xrightarrow{e} (st', g')} \qquad \frac{st \longrightarrow st'}{(st, g) \longrightarrow (st', g)}$$

As a convention, we will associate a null effect ϵ to steps without effect. An execution trace is a sequence $(st_i, g_i, e_i)_i$ verifying $(st_i, g_i) \xrightarrow{e_i} (st_{i+1}, g_{i+1})$ and $g_0 = (\emptyset, \epsilon, \emptyset, \emptyset)$ and st_0 is a correct initial state. It records the states of the virtual machine and of the user interface but also the effects exchanged between them. We will often use only one of the projections: $(st_i, e_i)_i$ or $(g_i, e_i)_i$ giving a view of the execution from either the JVM side or from the GUI side.

$(st_i)_i$ (resp. $(g_i)_i$) is *well-formed* if and only if there exists $(g_i)_i$ (resp.$(st_i)_i$) and $(e_i)_i$ such that $(st_i, g_i, e_i)_i$ is an execution trace. A GUI or JVM state is *well-formed* if and only if it is an element of a well-formed sequence.

Theorem 1. *Let $(g_i)_i$ be a well-formed sequence and $g = g_i$ an element:*

$$\{a \mid \exists x. \, (a, x) \in (g.\mathsf{coms} \cup g.\mathsf{list})\} \subset \{a \mid \exists l. \, (a, l) \in g.\mathsf{genv} \wedge \mathsf{newOf}(l) \prec \mathsf{Screen}\}$$

$$\{a \mid \exists x. \, (x, a) \in g.\mathsf{coms}\} \subset \{a \mid \exists l. \, (a, l) \in g.\mathsf{genv} \wedge \mathsf{newOf}(l) \prec \mathsf{Command}\}$$

$$\{a \mid \exists x. \, (x, a) \in g.\mathsf{list}\} \subset \{a \mid \exists l. \, (a, l) \in g.\mathsf{genv} \wedge \mathsf{newOf}(l) \prec \mathsf{CommandListener}\}$$

By induction on i. The property is in fact a property of the heap (existence of the object) and of the correct typing of actions generating events.

Theorem 2. *Let $(st_i)_i$ be a well-formed sequence. $st_i = (\_, (\epsilon, \_, \_), \_)$ and $st_{i+1} = (\_, (pc, (cl : sc : co : \_), \_), \_)$ implies there exists $k < i$ and $l < i$ such that $st_k = (\_, (pc_k, sc : co : \_, \_), \_)$ and $code(pc_k) = \mathsf{invokevirtual(addCommand)}$ $st_l = (\_, (pc_l, sc : cl : \_, \_), \_)$ and $code(pc_l) = \mathsf{invokevirtual(setCommandListener)}$*

We use the fact that a command or a listener is registered in the GUI state only if there has been an associated event. The corresponding steps in the JVM trace are the one we are looking for.

4   Navigation Graphs

Definition 1. *A navigation graph* $(N, T, ext, I_N, I_T, I_D)$ *is an oriented multi-graph where* N *is an abstract set of nodes,* T *is a set of transitions,* $ext : T \rightarrow N \times N$ *describes the source and target of a transition and* I_N *and* I_T *are the interpretation function* $I_N : N \rightarrow G \rightarrow \wp(A)$ *and* $I_T : T \rightarrow G \rightarrow \wp(A)$. *They satisfy:*

$$\forall n, g.\ I_N(n)(g) \subset \{a \mid \exists x.(a, x) \in g.\mathsf{coms} \cup g.\mathsf{list}\}$$

$$\forall t, g.\ I_T(t)(g) \subset \{a \mid \exists x.(x, a) \in g.\mathsf{coms}\}$$

$I_D : T \rightarrow \wp(\mathcal{D})$ *is an optional interpretation for critical operations allowed during the transition.*

Nodes represent sets of displayable screens and transitions are labelled with sets of events. Interpretation functions are defined with respect to a GUI state and should be viewed as predicates defining which nodes or transitions of the state are compliant.

Navigation graphs only describe safety properties and are a specialization of security automata [15] in the context of user interfaces.

Compliance of a Midlet with Respect to a Navigation Graph. An execution trace (g_i, e_i) *complies with* NG if and only if there exists sequences $(ns_i)_i$, $(ev_i)_i$ and $(n_i)_i$ $(t_i)_i$ such that:

$$\forall i.\ ext(t_i) = (n_i, n_{i+1})$$

$$\forall i.\ ns_i \leq ev_i < ns_{i+1}$$

$$\forall i.\ (\exists SC.\ e_i = EV(sc, co, cl)) \Leftrightarrow (\exists k.\ i = ev_k)$$

$$\forall i.\ \exists SC.\ \forall k.\ ns_i \leq k < ns_{i+1} \Rightarrow g_k.\mathsf{screen} = SC \wedge SC \in I_N(g_i)(n_i)$$

$$\forall i.\ e_{ev_i} = EV(sc, co, cl) \Rightarrow co \in I(g_i)(t_i)$$

$$\forall k \in [ns_i..ns_{i+1}].\ ev_k = DG(d) \Rightarrow d \in I_D(t_i)$$

(ns_i) extracts a sub-sequence of states where a screen change occurs (or in fact may occur). (ev_i) is the sub-sequence of the trace where a user event is taken into account. $(n_i, t_i)_i$ describes the path followed in the graph.

A midlet *complies with* a navigation graph, if and only if for all well-formed execution trace of the midlet, the GUI projection of the trace complies with the navigation graph.

Although this paper only considers the extraction of GUI graph for MIDP applications, this definition is somewhat independent of the virtual machine technology as long as a notion of effect generating trace can be defined for it.

5   Use of Navigation Graphs

We present four potential use for navigation graphs. The first two are currently the main use of the tool presented in the previous section. The last two are more prospective and use navigation graphs to complement other analyses.

5.1   MIDP Security Principles

Actions performed by midlet could have been launched manually by the user. The underlying principle of MIDP security policy is to ask the end-user if he authorizes each use of a dangerous API.

This security scheme has several drawbacks. The main short-coming of the dynamic security policy is the risk of social engineering attacks. One reason is the lack of knowledge by the end-user of what the midlet will perform in the future. Another is that the number of security screens can affect the end-user watchfulness: he may not notice small changes in displayed parameters such as a small change in a phone number that transforms a regular call into an overcharged one.

Two mechanisms have been designed to avoid an overwhelming number of security screens:

1. One can tune the level of granularity of security screens between one warning screen for the first use (e.g. taking pictures) to one screen per method call for critical APIs (sending an SMS).
2. A trusted authority (usually the mobile operator) can sign the midlet. A signed midlet will open less security screens and will perform more operations silently (operator midlet even completely turn off the dynamic enforcement of the security policy).

Unfortunately, midlet signature only shifts the burden of checking the innocuousness of a midlet from the end-user when he use it to the trusted authority prior to any use but it does not provide any clue for deciding which midlets should be signed. Static analysis provides elements to solve this problem:

1. Calls to dangerous methods can be identified (with devirtualization techniques).
2. Their parameters can be approximated to evaluate their real risk [6].
3. The number of calls in a given user interaction can be bounded to check that there is no dangerous loop repeating a charged action.
4. Finally, the analysis presented here can identify the context of the call.

As an example of the usefulness of the last step, a lot of games send the highest score back to a centralized server as a single SMS. This is considered as an acceptable usage. But sending an SMS each time a game step is performed would not be acceptable. To distinguish those two uses it is necessary to have an overview of the user interface underlying automaton with transitions annotated with the dangerous calls they perform.

5.2   Other Uses

Supporting documentation for evaluation teams: JavaVerified[4] requires that developers provide a schema of the different screens of a submitted

---

[4] The main test program for MIDP applications supported by SUN, phone manufacturers and operators.

application (see page 8 of [16]). It is mainly used as a kind of lean specification that guides testing. These drawings are similar to the concept of screen mock-up used to design an application [4]. A navigation graph is a formal version of such drawings and can be used to estimate the coverage of a test campaign.

Temporal properties of midlets: Resource analysis such as permission checking [3] may require a precise knowledge of the potential sequences of user events to trim impossible execution paths that would violate the resource constraints if they existed. The knowledge on the global control flow embedded in navigation graphs is then mandatory to check such properties.

Identification of data sources: navigation graph can be used to isolate fields in forms where sensitive information can be typed in by the user and relate them with the method calls in the code that will extract this information from the user interface and put it in program variables. Information flow algorithms [2] can then be used to check that the uses of those data comply with the established security policy.

6   Extraction of a Navigation Graph

We present an algorithm to extract a compliant navigation graph from the byte-code of an application. Navigation graphs can also be generated independently and one can check that a midlet complies with a given[5].

6.1   Pointer Analysis

Points-to analysis [1,7] relates each location where a pointer is used to the locations in the program where the structure pointed by the pointer at that program point may have been allocated. Points-to analysis is a basic technique used in more complex analysis such as class analysis or escape analysis. In this section, we will use it to abstract sets of live objects by the set of instructions that allocated the memory space they use.

Points-to analysis can be viewed as the result of an analysis where the collecting semantics records the potential value of each object and where the abstraction used for each object is the location where this object has been declared.

In Java, pointers are variables containing object reference and pointer analysis can be viewed as a function from program points and variables to sets of program points. Variables may be static or instance fields, array cells (usually coalesced to a single cell by most analysis), local variables or operand on the stack (arguments and return value at the level of source code).

$pp_i : L \rightarrow \wp(L)$ is the partial function that associates to a program point an upper approximation of the set of program points that may have allocated ("new" opcodes) the contents of the ith operand on the operand stack when this program point is executed.

---

[5] This path is explored in project MOBIUS following ideas from [8].

$pp_i^m : L \rightarrow \wp(L)$ is the function that coincides with pp_i when the instruction at that point is invokevirtual m' with $m \prec m'$ (ie. m.class $\prec$ m'.class and m.sig $= m'$.sig), and is undefined otherwise.

Class analysis can be implemented as a points-to analysis of the base object of the virtual invocation combined newOf.

The call graph of an application is defined as a function $cg : MN \rightarrow \wp(C \times MN)$ where $(l', mn') \in cg(mn)$ iff:

$$l'.\text{meth} = meth(mn) \wedge \exists l, cn.\ l \in pp_0^{(cn, mn'.\text{sig})}(l') \wedge \text{newOf}(l) = mn'.\text{class}$$

mn'.class $\prec$ cn because the program is well-typed. Each pair contains the index of a call instruction and the name of the method called. Static virtual call resolution may yield several pairs with the same index.

$cg^*(mn)$ as the smallest set satisfying:

$$cg(mn) \subset cg^*(mn) \qquad \forall l', mn'.\ (l', mn') \in cg^*(mn) \Rightarrow cg(mn') \in cg^*(mn)$$

6.2   Relational Algebra Notations

A function $f : A \rightarrow B$ can be viewed as a binary relation on $A \times B$ defined as $\{(x, y) \mid y = f(x)\}$. $r_1 \bowtie_{I/J} r_2$ denotes the join of two relations r_1 and r_2 on respectively the set of columns I and J. $\bowtie$ is used as a left-associative operator.

$$r_1 \bowtie_{i_1,\dots i_p / j_1,\dots j_p} r_2 =$$
$$\{(x\sharp 1, \dots x\sharp n, y\sharp 1, \dots y\sharp m) \mid x \in r_1 \wedge y \in r_2 \wedge \forall k.\ x\sharp i_k = y\sharp j_k\}$$

The projection operator $p_{i_1,\dots,i_n}$ defines the projection of a relation as:

$$\pi_{i_1,\dots,i_m}(r) = \{(x\sharp i_1 \dots x\sharp i_m) \mid x \in r\}$$

6.3   Compound Dependencies

The potential command listener association relation is defined as:

$$pcl = \pi_{24}(pp_0^{\text{setCommandListener}} \bowtie_{1/1} pp_1^{\text{setCommandListener}})$$

and the potential command association relation as:

$$pco = \pi_{24}(pp_0^{\text{addCommand}} \bowtie_{1/1} pp_1^{\text{setCommandListener}})$$

Those relations link screen abstractions to respectively CommandListener abstractions and Command abstractions. As an example, if at program point pp a call to setCommandListener binds a screen declared at sc to a command listener declared at cl, then

$$pcl = \pi_{24}(\{(pp, sc), \dots\} \bowtie_{1/1} \{(pp, cl), \dots\}) = \pi_{1,3}\{(pp, sc, pp, cl)\} = \{(sc, cl), \dots\}$$

$getAction : L \rightarrow C$ is a function that associates to an abstraction of a CommandListener object the code of the callback it contains.

$$getAction(l) = cl(\text{newOf}(l), \texttt{commandAction})$$

The set of displays potentially directly set by a method at address c is defined as $dirDispSet(cn, m) = \{pp_1^{\texttt{setDisplay}}(c, i) \mid i \in \mathbb{N}\}$. The definition is extended to the set of displays potentially set by a method $m \in C$:

$$DispSet(m) = \bigcup_{m' \in cg^*(m)} DirDispSet(m')$$

We define the set of nodes N^P as: $\{l \in L \mid \texttt{newOf}(l) \prec \texttt{Screen}\}$ and the set of transitions $T^P \subset L \times L \times L$ as:

$$T^P = \pi_{1,2,8}(pco \bowtie_{1/1} pcl \bowtie_{4/1} getAction \bowtie_{6/1} DispSet)$$

As an example, a screen declared at program point sc is associated to a command declared at co and command listener declared at cl. This object is of class C whose definition contains a commandAction method at address m. Calling m may lead to the execution of pp that invokes setCurrent and may take as argument a screen object declared at program point sc'. Then

$$T^P = \pi_{1,2,8}(\{(sc, co), \ldots\} \bowtie_{1/1} \{(sc, cl), \ldots\} \bowtie_{4/1} \{(cl, m) \ldots\} \bowtie_{6/1} \{(m, sc') \ldots\})$$
$$= \pi_{1,2,8}(sc, co, sc, cl, cl, m, m, sc') = (sc, co, sc')$$

The auxiliary functions are defined as:

$$ext^P((sc, co, sc')) = (sc, sc')$$
$$I_N^P(n)(g) = \{a \mid (a, n) \in g.\texttt{genv}\}$$
$$I_T^P((sc, co, sc'))(g) = \{a \mid (a, co) \in g.\texttt{com}\}$$

Theorem 3. *P complies with* $(N^P, T^P, ext^P, I_N^P, I_T^P)$.

The proof is done by induction on the size of the execution traces. Theorem 2 is important to establish that some important events have occurred before a user event is registered in the trace. Then the correctness of pco and pcl as abstractions of those events helps to conclude.

6.4   Path Selection Algorithm

The graph obtained so far is only a very crude upper-approximation of the midlet behaviour as its construction ignores the control flow of the midlet. We remove transitions corresponding to invalid execution paths in the code of callbacks, using approximations on the value of the arguments of commandAction.

In the previous definition of T, the original definition of $DispSet$ is replaced with a four tuple relation $DispSet_2$ over $C \times A \times A \times A$. An element $(c, next, old, co)$ states that the callback identified by its address c executed when coming from a screen old with the button corresponding to co pressed can result in a screen change to display $next$.

$$T_2^P = \pi_{1,2,8}(pco \bowtie_{1/1} pcl \bowtie_{4/1} getAction \bowtie_{6,1,2/1,3,4} DispSet_2)$$

VT is a simple forward data flow analysis that computes an upper approximation of valid transitions that is more precise than the initial value. The aim of this section is to show the existence of such a function rather than building a state of the art analysis. We use a classical dataflow analysis framework (see [13] for example).

The elements of our analysis domain are sets of abstract states $\mathcal{F} = \wp(\mathcal{S})$. Each abstract state is represented as a pair $g * f \in \mathcal{S}$ where f is an abstract representation of the current frame and g is the collected information on the potential GUI state.

$(\mathcal{F}, \cup)$ is a complete lattice and satisfies the ascending chain condition as the cardinal of $\mathcal{S}$ is finite. Transfer functions t_l will be chosen as monotone. The analysis is classically defined by the set of equations:

$$VT(c,0) = s_0 \qquad VT(l) = \bigcup_{l' \mapsto l} t'_l(VT(l'))$$

The analysis is inter-procedural but in this simple version, no information is kept in f between calls. So this amounts to consider the cumulative effect of all the methods in the transitive closure of the call-graph associated to l when the instruction at l is an invoke instruction in the potential sequential orders.

$$DispSet_2 = \{(c,n,o,b) \mid \exists g * f \in VT(\epsilon).\ g.\mathsf{screen} = n \wedge (o,b) \in g.\mathsf{pot}\} \cup$$
$$\{(c,o,o,b) \mid \exists g * f \in VT(\epsilon).\ g.\mathsf{screen} = \epsilon \wedge (o,b) \in g.\mathsf{pot}\}$$

An element g is a pair $(g.\mathsf{screen}, g.\mathsf{pot}) \in (L \cup \epsilon) \times \wp(L \times L)$. $g.\mathsf{screen}$ is the next screen and ϵ denotes no screen change. $g.\mathsf{pot}$ is the set of potential value for the arguments of the callback that may lead to this program point. pot values are ordered by $\supset$. The most precise element is the empty set.

The goal of f is to track the initial arguments to extract new constraints when a test is performed on those arguments. f is a pair in $[\mathcal{A}] \times [\mathcal{A}]$ representing the abstraction of the operand stack and the locals. The abstract domain $\mathcal{A}$ states that a frame variable is either one of the initial arguments, or anything else[6]

$$\mathcal{A} = \{\alpha_1, \alpha_2, \bot\}$$

The stacks are bounded by construction (it is a property of preverified bytecode). The initial value at the entry point is $s_0 = g_0 * f_0$:

$$g_0 = (\epsilon, \{(x,y) \in L \times L \mid \mathsf{newOf}(x) \prec \mathsf{Screen} \wedge \mathsf{newOf}(y) \prec \mathsf{Command}\})$$

$$f_0 = ([\alpha_0, \alpha_1], [\bot, \ldots \bot])$$

---

[6] The implementation also approximate the value of some string labels (e.g. command names) associated to them. Those labels are usually immutable.

We do not detail the transfer functions and just give examples of the most significant ones. Transfer function $t_l : S \rightarrow S$ are defined on individual states and must be extended to sets of states by taking the union of the results for all the elements of the argument set:

$$code(l) = \mathsf{ifeq} \wedge op = \alpha_i :\, op' \Rightarrow$$
$$t_l^T((sc, pot) * (op, loc)) = \{((sc, \{a \mid a \in pot \wedge a \sharp i \in pp_2(l)\}) * (op', loc)\}$$
$$code(l) = \mathsf{virtualinvoke} \ \mathtt{setCurrent} \Rightarrow$$
$$t_l((sc, pot) * (\_ op, loc)) = \{(sc, pot) * (op, loc) \mid sc \in pp_1(l)\}$$

The transfer functions are clearly monotone.

Theorem 4. P *complies with* $(N^P, T_2^P, ext^P, I_N^P, I_T^P)$.

6.5 Adding Critical Actions

The previous analysis is modified to record information on which dangerous actions can be performed in callbacks. A method call is dangerous iff the method called $m \in MN$ belongs to a predefined set $Crit$ of dangerous MIDP APIs.

We state $\mathcal{D} = L$ and modify VT to add a field containing subsets of $\mathcal{D}$ to g which is now an element of $(g.\mathsf{screen}, g.\mathsf{pot}, g.\mathsf{crit}) \in (L \cup \epsilon) \times \wp(L \times L) \times \wp(L)$.

$$code(l) = \mathsf{virtualinvoke} \ m \wedge m \in Crit \Rightarrow$$
$$t_l((sc, pot, dg) * (\_ : \ldots : \_ : op, loc)) = \{(sc, pot, dg \cup \{l\}) * (op, loc)\}$$

This new field is propagated in the definition of transitions:

$$DispSet_3 =$$
$$\{(c, n, o, b, d) \mid \exists g * f \in VT(\epsilon). \ g.\mathsf{screen} = n \wedge (o, b) \in g.\mathsf{pot} \wedge d = g.\mathsf{crit}\} \cup$$
$$\{(c, o, o, b, d) \mid \exists g * f \in VT(\epsilon). \ g.\mathsf{screen} = \epsilon \wedge (o, b) \in g.\mathsf{pot} \wedge d = g.\mathsf{crit}\}$$

$$T_3^P = \pi_{1,2,12,8}(pco \bowtie_{1/1} pcl \bowtie_{4/1} getAction \bowtie_{6,1,2/1,3,4} DispSet_3)$$

The MIDP standard requires that the scheduler for events is called only when the previous action has been treated and the callback has returned. There is no guarantee that intermediate screens are displayed. This is also why it is safe to accumulate all the actions performed on the execution path, they will be performed, if ever, before the user interface is reactive again.

6.6 Implementation and Assessment

A prototype of the algorithm has been implemented on top of our analyser MATOS [6]. Soot libraries [17,12] provide a simplified representation of code, the points-to analysis, the class hierarchy, the complete call graph, the control-flow graph of each method, and a framework for data-flow analysis.

Modularity in the composition of basic links is important as the actual specification of MIDP is in fact more complex than the fragment used here: 32 callbacks

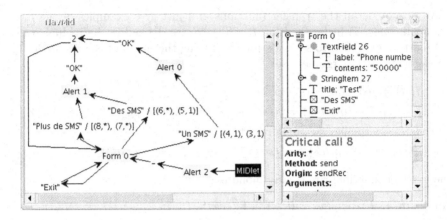

Fig. 1. A navigation graph of a simple midlet

(see Sect 8.1.2 of [9]) have been identified only for the UI and not all of them follow exactly the same pattern. Threads and callbacks for the midlet life cycle must also be handled.

Figure 1 shows the navigation graph of a simple midlet in the prototype. Edge labels are the command names. Numbers refer to the critical actions performed and whether they are executed in a loop (arity *) or not (arity 1). This analysis is done for each call to a critical action using a variant of the algorithm developed by Inria Lande team and described in [5].

Using this drawing, a reviewer can check that dangerous actions such as sending SMS are linked with well-identified commands and are not triggered each time a button is pressed and the most dangerous transition is clearly identified.

Screen labels identify their class. The node labelled MIDlet is the entry point and the edge corresponds to the constructor and the `MIDlet.start` method. Small yellow nodes are just intermediate nodes. The top window on the right describes the subcomponents and attributes of each screen. The bottom window describes the critical actions.

Because the points-to analysis is control-flow insensitive, our analysis is correct even in a multi-threaded context. Moreover our level of abstraction guarantees that the result is correct for every handsets although there are many different implementations with various interpretation of the MIDP standard (known as device fragmentation).

The tool represents threads as separate automata triggered by the main UI but we need a finer specification than a two states automaton: at least, a treatment of synchronization events is required for the handling of the "worker-thread" programming pattern [11].

The result of the analysis is a correct but uninformative graph if the path followed to react to an event in the midlet is not defined by the arguments of the `commandAction` callback. Based on experiments conducted with midlets available on `midlet.org`, a lot of midlets follow the right pattern. Moreover operators can easily dictate it as a rule developers must follow if they want a cheap and almost automatic validation of their code. On the other hand, it is difficult to give informative result for UI relying only on the low-level `Canvas` object.

7 Conclusion

The extraction of navigation graphs is split in a set of generic local static analysis and a more algebraic framework based on relational algebra to combine results using program points as common abstractions. The second part is specific to the applicative field. This separation of concerns is important to keep the analysis adaptable and scalable with respect to the complexity of the execution environment.

Modern application frameworks introduce complex programming patterns in mundane applications, but their initial goal is to hide the complexity of the execution platform to the developer and they can also hide it to reviewers if we stay at the right level of abstraction. We expect that the promising results for GUI can be generalized to more complex frameworks (component frameworks for example).

Finally, the semantics of navigation graphs and of the GUI behaviour presented in Sect. 3 and 4 contributes to the security of mobile applications by providing a formal specification of the part of their behaviour related to security sensitive operations.

Acknowledgements. Cuihtlauac Alvarado provided many inputs during the definition of navigation graphs and comments on early version of this paper. Jeffry Christiandy developed substantial parts of the first prototype of the tool.

References

1. Andersen, L.O.: Program Analysis and Specialization for the C Programming Language. PhD thesis, University of Copenhagen, DIKU report 94/19 (1994)
2. Bernardeschi, C., De Francesco, N., Lettieri, G., Martini, L.: Checking secure information flow in java bytecode by code transformation and standard bytecode verification. Software: Practice and Experience 34(13), 1225–1255 (2004)
3. Besson, F., Dufay, G., Jensen, T.: A formal model of access control for mobile interactive devices. In: Gollmann, D., Meier, J., Sabelfeld, A. (eds.) ESORICS 2006. LNCS, vol. 4189, pp. 110–126. Springer, Heidelberg (2006)
4. Bloch, C., Wagner, A.: MIDP Style Guide for the Java 2 Platform, Micro Edition. The Java Series. Addison-Wesley, Reading (2003)
5. Cachera, D., Jensen, T., Pichardie, D., o Schneider, G.: Certified memory usage analysis. In: Fitzgerald, J.S., Hayes, I.J., Tarlecki, A. (eds.) FM 2005. LNCS, vol. 3582, pp. 91–106. Springer, Heidelberg (2005)
6. Crégut, P., Alvarado, C.: Improving the security of downloadable Java applications with static analysis. In: BYTECODE. ENTCS, vol. 141, Elsevier, Amsterdam (2005)

7. Emami, M., Ghiya, R., Hendren, L.J.: Context-sensitive interprocedural points-to analysis in the presence of function pointers. In: PLDI 1994: Proceedings of the ACM SIGPLAN 1994 conference on Programming language design and implementation, pp. 242–256. ACM Press, New York, NY, USA (1994)
8. Hubbers, E., Oostdijk, M.: Generating JML specifications from UML state diagrams. In: Forum on specification and Design Languages, University of Frankfurt, pp. 263–273 (2003), Proceedings appeared as CD-Rom with ISSN 1636-9874
9. JSR 118 Expert Group. Mobile information device profile MIDP, version 2.1. Java specification request, Java Community Process (November 2006), Revised and clarified version of MIDP 2.0 (released in 2001)
10. JSR 30 Expert Group. Connected limited device configuration CLDC, version 1.0. Java specification request, Java Community Process (2000)
11. Lea, D.: Concurrent Proamming in Java Second Edition. Prentice-Hall, Englewood Cliffs (1999)
12. Lhoták, O., Hendren, L.: Scaling Java points-to analysis using Spark. In: Hedin, G. (ed.) CC 2003. LNCS, vol. 2622, pp. 153–169. Springer, Heidelberg (2003)
13. Nielson, F., Nielson, H.R., Hankin, C.L.: Principles of Program Analysis. Springer, Heidelberg (1999)
14. Pichardie, D.: Bicolano – Byte Code Language in Coq (2006), http://mobius.inia.fr/bicolano
15. Schneider, F.B.: Enforceable security policies. ACM Trans. Inf. Syst. Secur. 3(1), 30–50 (2000)
16. Unified Testing Initiative. Unified testing criteria for Java technology-based applications for mobile devices. Technical report, Sun Microsystems, Motorola, Nokia, Siemens, Sony Ericsson, Version 2.1 (May 2006)
17. Vallée-Rai, R., Hendren, L., Sundaresan, V., Lam, P., Gagnon, E., Co, P.: Soot - A java optimization framework. In: Proceedings of CASCON 1999, pp. 125–135 (1999)

Extending Operational Semantics of the Java Bytecode*

Patryk Czarnik and Aleksy Schubert

Institute of Informatics
University of Warsaw
ul. Banacha 2
02-097 Warsaw
Poland

Abstract. A proof-carrying code infrastructure can ensure safety of global computers. Such an infrastructure requires sound and complete semantics of the global computing platform. Bicolano is an operational semantics of the major part of the Java bytecode language. We present here two extension frameworks for the semantics and discuss their different features. Both frameworks are made in a modular fashion. The first one, so called horizontal, allows to extend states with additional information that traces a running program behaviour (e.g. memory consumption). The second one, so called vertical, additionally allows an extension to supplement the behaviour specified in the original semantics. A comparison of these frameworks is presented. In particular, we prove that the horizontal framework can be simulated by the vertical one and show an example of an extension which cannot be realised in the horizontal one, but can be realised in the vertical one. However, extensions in the horizontal framework are less memory consuming and conceptually simpler. In this light, the choice of the framework to use should depend on a particular application.

1 Introduction

The existence of widely deployable global computing framework requires the presence of mechanisms to guarantee the safety of users' assets even though the executed software is obtained through insecure means. The proof-carrying code (PCC) [Nec97] is a powerful concept that allows to verify the properties of the programs in the executable form and in this way ensure their safety independently of the path the code travelled through. A PCC system which is able to guarantee complicated features of programs should be based on the foundational

---

* This work was partly supported by Polish government grant 177/6.PR UE/2006/7 and Information Society Technologies programme of the European Commission FET project IST-2005-015905 MOBIUS. This paper reflects only authors' views and the Community is not liable for any use that may be made of the information contained therein.

G. Barthe and C. Fournet (Eds.): TGC 2007, LNCS 4912, pp. 57–72, 2008.

PCC introduced by Appel and Felty [AF00]. In this case, the verification is possible as the semantics of the programs can be expressed in a logical formalism. The formulae in such a formalism express the desired properties of programs.

One of the possibilities to provide a framework of the foundational proof-carrying code for the Java platform is to formalise the semantics of the Java Virtual Machine (JVM) and the Java bytecode language in a proof checker. The logic of the proof checker can be then used as a formalism to express the program properties. One of the existing JVM formalisations is Bicolano [Pic06]. It is a formalisation of JVM in the Coq proof assistant [Coq04, BC04] which covers considerable subset of the bytecode instructions (72 out of 142) and handles the aspects such as existence of multiple classes, inheritance, method invocation and exceptions [Con06]. This approach is not comfortable as far as the verification of meta-properties of JVM is concerned since every proof of such a property is quite tedious. However, Bicolano was designed to serve as a possible element of a PCC architecture for mobile devices in which the program properties are expressed in the Coq logic and the certificates are Coq proof scripts. In this light, the semantics should rather explicitly formalise all the instructions than to provide their abstraction like in the work by Klein and Nipkow [KN06]. This approach allows to directly translate the bytecode programs into Coq values while the program properties and proofs are expressed directly within the Coq format. This allows to provide a strong trusted computing base which relies on the Coq typechecker (which is relatively small), Bicolano, and a small set of simple utilities to translate the bytecode program representation to a Coq based one.

The current version of Bicolano covers a set of JVM features which enables certification of a wide range of programs. Still, it is not easy to reason about properties which are of interest for various bytecode programs even when programs running on the restricted CLDC/MIDP mobile platform [Sun03] are only concerned. The existing formalisation is in certain ways idealised, for instance the available heap memory or method stack are unlimited. Moreover, it is not easy to express properties in terms of the actual program runs e.g. it is not straightforward to trace the memory usage throughout the program runs. In this light, it is very likely that Bicolano semantics will have to be adjusted in certain ways to accommodate better the particular verification needs.

Extending semantics with additional features is not straightforward. The reliability of Bicolano semantics was checked in two ways. First, the semantics was developed by one group of people in two flavours: small step and big step, and the big step semantics was proved to be sound with regard to the small step one. Thanks to this effort the semantics gained a good deal of reliability as it is difficult to make the same mistake twice. Second, a separate group of people checked that the code of Bicolano indeed obeys the descriptions in the JVM specification [LY99]. This independent review process increased further the reliability of the informally written Sun specification and the formalisation in Coq. It must be noted that the size of the formalisation and soundness proofs is considerable (over 11 thousand lines) as for the trusted code base. Therefore, the changes to Bicolano formalisation must be done with significant caution. In order to guarantee that the additions do not destroy the already achieved guarantees we tried not to modify the existing Bicolano sources, but rather used the Coq modules mechanism [Chr04] to supplement the existing definitions (this was not possible for big step formalisation). This also led us to define two different kinds of extension frameworks for Bicolano semantics: *the horizontal extension framework* and *the vertical extension framework*. The former allows to augment the state of the computation with an additional field where an information which describes some abstract property of the state may be accumulated along a program run while the latter allows to change the behaviour of semantical steps. Someone who wants to extend Bicolano can take either the simpler framework (the horizontal one) with less overhead and the confidence that the original semantics is left intact or the more complicated one (the vertical one) when its use is unavoidable. We use the term *extension framework* to describe one of the two (horizontal and vertical) general frameworks we provide, while the term *extension* is used for particular semantics extensions, e.g. the memory extension that supports heap memory tracking.

The horizontal extension framework is an extension framework the primary goal of which is to provide a natural basis for reasoning about the traces of the bytecode program runs. The idea of the framework is based on the concept of the types with effects (see e.g. the overview by Nielson and Nielson [NN99]). In this scheme, an original typing discipline can be augmented with an additional property called effect. Each function signature, except from the usual typing information concerning the arguments and the result, comes equipped with an information which abstract effect the execution of the function has on the executing environment (e.g. which variables are assigned [Tof90], what is the memory consumption [TT97], what are the I/O operations, what are the traces of the invoked methods, etc.). In an extreme case, the effect can contain the full history of a computation that is run by a particular piece of code (see e.g. [SS04]). Consequently, this framework can naturally serve as a way to express and specify the properties of program runs. At the same time, this framework is not suitable for extending the behaviour of the semantics since the collecting of the effects is defined so that it is impossible to affect the state manipulated by the program instructions.

The vertical extension framework is an extension framework the primary goal of which is to provide a natural basis for introducing additional behaviours that were omitted from the original semantics. We assume that the additions are incremental in their nature—they usually concern a limited number of instructions (for instance in order to add the memory counting we have to modify the `new` and `newarray` instructions only). Consequently, we assume also that in most cases the original Bicolano semantics is sufficient. These postulates led us to a design in which we retain the original state and admit additional state components which allow to formalise the supplementary behaviours that cannot be expressed in terms of the original heap and stack (e.g. when the heap and stack have limited size, when the multithreaded runs must be considered etc.).

Furthermore, we refer to the original semantics to obtain the state transformation as in the original Bicolano (together with the previous extensions) or to modify the transformation when needed. This arrangement is different from other approaches to the modular semantics such as the modular monadic semantics [LH96] or action semantics [Mos92] since the other frameworks assume that the original semantics is right from the beginning designed to be extended in one of them. These modular semantics express the programming language concepts in terms of atomic operations that are inherent to their construction. Adoption of the approaches would make necessary to rewrite the existing formalisation and this is in our case a very costly operation.

In order to demonstrate the usability of the extensions, we provided a few extensions in both of the frameworks. In particular, we developed in both frameworks an extension that counts the instructions executed in a run of a program and an extension that tracks the memory usage in a run of this kind. Throughout this paper, we use the memory usage tracking extension as an example which illustrates the concepts and the design of the extension frameworks.

Both extension frameworks are formalised in case of the small step semantics. However, the horizontal extension framework is formalised in big step semantic flavour as well. The choice to formalise the small step semantics results from the fact that certain extensions are very difficult to formalise by means of the big step semantics. This concerns, in particular, the extension with the multithreaded execution or the extension which formalises the non-deterministic errors of the virtual machine. Still, we decided to formalise the horizontal framework in the big step flavour as this kind of semantics is required in order to provide the basis for extension of the MOBIUS base logic.

Overview. The paper is organised as follows. Section 2 presents Bicolano architecture and the details of the semantics which are further used in the rest of the paper. Section 3 presents the horizontal extension framework and Section 4 presents the vertical extension framework. In Section 5 we present the comparison of the frameworks and we conclude in Section 6.

2   Preliminaries

In this section we present an overview of Bicolano necessary to understand the details of the formalisation of the extension frameworks we propose.

2.1   Bicolano Architecture

Bicolano consists of three main parts. They are presented as grey rectangles on Figure 1. The *implementation* part contains implementations of signatures specified in the axiomatic base and our extension does not refer to that part at all. We present below the *axiomatic base* and the *semantics* in more detail as they are directly used by our extension frameworks.

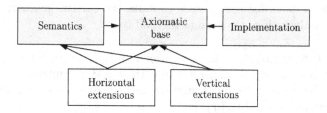

Fig. 1. The relation of the extension frameworks (white boxes) to main parts of Bicolano (grey boxes)

Axiomatic Base. The axiomatic base of Bicolano defines the basic terms used in the formalisation, in particular terms specific for the JVM and bytecode programs. The extension frameworks directly refer to module signatures PROGRAM and SEMANTIC_DOMAIN.

The PROGRAM signature provides the abstract syntax of Java bytecode programs in Coq. Most of the definitions here take up the form of abstract types and are equipped with operations and axioms specifying their properties. The definitions describe, among others, class and method names, the program counter (instruction addressing), local variable indices. They let decompose a given program into classes, a class into methods and a method into subsequent instructions.

The JVM instructions are declared as an inductive type definition. Many JVM instructions were parametrised and in some cases one constructor in Bicolano represents many JVM instructions (e.g. If_icmp, parametrised with a comparison operator, represents many conditional jump JVM instructions).

The SEMANTIC_DOMAIN signature defines the domain of the semantics, that is the values needed to describe a state of a running JVM. As in PROGRAM, many values are declared as abstract types supplied with operations and axioms. Among these values there are types that model local variables, arrays of local variables, the heap and locations. More complex structures are defined via inductive type definitions. These structures include:

- values of JVM primitive types,
- operand stack (a list of values),
- frames (normal or exceptional),
- call stack (a list of normal frames),
- the whole state (normal or exceptional).

A normal state is of the form St h (Fr m pc s l) sf where h is a heap, and sf is a call stack. Fr m pc os l is the current frame composed of the current method m, the current program point pc, the local variables array l, and the operand stack s. An exceptional state is of the form StE h (FrE m pc loc l) sf where all elements are similar as before except the location loc representing the location of the exception object. Exceptional states appear when an exception is thrown but not yet managed by the exception handler mechanism.

It is worth to underline that a state contains the current instruction address and, indirectly through m, the current method code.

Operational Semantics. The operational semantics is provided in two flavours: as the small step semantics and as the big step semantics.

The main objective for the small step semantics is to be as close to the original JVM specification as possible. In principle, one step of the semantics corresponds to the execution of a single JVM instruction, as described in the JVM specification [LY99]. This pattern is violated in case an exception is thrown but not caught within the currently executed method. When this happens a semantical step which exceptionally exits the method has no corresponding instruction.

The step relation has the type Program → State.t → State.t → Prop. It holds for a program p and states st1 and st2 if and only if st1 and st2 are consecutive states when the program p is run.

It is worth stressing that for a given state st1, there may be no state st2 such that step holds. A relation of this type can also be non-deterministic (when many states are in relation with st1), however in the current version of Bicolano (without multithreading and error handling) it is not the case.

The big step semantics was provided for two main reasons: as a kind of internal verification of the semantics formalisation and for the use in the MOBIUS base logic.

The big step semantics defines several kinds of states and steps used in different cases: IntraNormalState and NormalStep, IntraExceptionState and ExceptionStep, InitCallState and CallStep, ReturnState and ReturnStep. Beside these steps, defined as the basic ones, there are several transitive closures defined, with the most general Reachable at the end.

This formalisation of the semantics is more complicated and does not allow to easily formalise certain behaviours (e.g. the interleaving of multiple threads). Moreover, the management of the multitude of states and steps may be difficult.

3   The Horizontal Extension Framework

The primary motivation for this extension framework was to enable an easy way of tracing the resource usage in the actual runs of programs. This is achieved here by adding Coq definitions which parametrise the steps with the additional effect component that allows to trace runs of programs.

The addition of the effect information to the Bicolano semantics enables the possibility to extend the MOBIUS base logic [BH06] with primitives to reason about the resource consumption of programs. This is possible as the framework was developed in the big step flavour as well.

3.1   How to Use the Framework?

Small Step Semantics. In order to exploit the extension framework one has to define a Coq module for the following module type:

```
Module Type SS_EFFECT.
  Declare Module Dom: SEMANTIC_DOMAIN.
  Import Dom Prog.
  Parameter ACT: Set.
  Parameter bookkeepSmall: Program → State.t → State.t →
                                     ACT → ACT.
End SS_EFFECT.
```

The parameter ACT (short for ACtion Trace) determines which information is collected along a run of a bytecode program. It keeps track of the actions we are interested in that were executed in the program in question. An arbitrary type can be assigned to it, depending on the actual need. In case of the memory extension, the parameter may be instantiated to the natural numbers nat.

The parameter bookkeepSmall is a function the arguments of which are in sequence

- an abstract program identifier,
- a state before the execution of the current instruction,
- a state after the execution of the current instruction,
- the value of ACT before the execution of the current instruction.

The bookkeepSmall returns the resulting value of ACT. The role of the function is to specify the effect on ACT values depending on changes in the ordinary Bicolano state. Note that a state contains the program counter, so the instruction to be invoked is known.

In case of the memory extension, bookkeepSmall returns a new value of the memory counter. The instruction to be invoked is determined based on the state before the step which enables the update of the memory consumption for the allocation instructions new and newarray.

Big Step Semantics. In order to exploit the extension framework in case of the big step semantics, one has to provide definitions for a module type BS_EFFECT the idea of which is the same as in the case of the small step semantics, but instead of a single bookkeepSmall one has to define many bookkeeping parameters, one for each of the basic kinds of steps:

- bookkeepNormal (for normal internal steps),
- bookkeepException (for exception steps),
- bookkeepCall (for method call steps),
- bookkeepReturn (for return steps).

The bookkeeping functions should be used to specify the changes in the ACT part of the state that happen in a semantics step. Their types are similar to the type of bookkeepSmall. For example the type of bookkeepException is as follows:

```
Parameter bookkeepException: Program → Method →
    _IntraNormalState → _IntraExceptionState → ACT → ACT.
```

Note that the returned value of ACT depends not only on the program, but also on the method in which the program is executed, the state before the execution of an instruction (_IntraNormalState) and the state after the execution of the instruction (_IntraExceptionState; note that the resulting state is exceptional).

In order to define the extension which traces the memory usage, one has to again instantiate ACT with nat and define all the bookkeeping functions above. However, only bookkeepNormal and bookkeepException should do non-trivial work as the allocation may occur only in case of the normal allocation instructions or in case of runtime errors.

3.2   The Realisation of the Framework

Small Step. In case of the small step semantics there was no need to change the existing Coq code. The new definitions were placed in new files. The main part of the framework is a functor that takes two parameters: an effect (an instance of the SS_EFFECT signature) and an implementation of the ordinary small step semantics. The functor defines the EffState module which encapsulates the old State combined with the action traces in ACT (from SS_EFFECT).

The functor also defines the step relation which takes into account the bookkeeping. The definition of the step looks as follows:

```
Inductive step (p:Program): EffState.t → EffState.t → Prop :=
| ESS_ : ∀ s t S T, SmallStep.step p s t →
           T = bookkeepSmall p s t S →
           step p (s,S) (t,T).
```

SmallStep.step is the step of the original Bicolano semantics. In order to check if the new step relation holds, we have to check whether the original relation takes place and compute the value of the bookkeeping function (bookkeepSmall). Then the original states (s and t) are combined with the ACT effects (S and T, respectively) to form the values of the new state type EffState.t.

Big Step. In case of the big step semantics we made changes in the existing Bicolano code. This was caused by module dependencies and the need to provide accompanying definitions and lemmas for the changed semantics which were deeply interwoven in the existing semantics.

The type of the state was extended with the ACT component while the original state types was renamed by adding the underscore _ as a prefix. For example the old IntraNormalState is now _IntraNormalState while the current IntraNormalState is defined to be _IntraNormalState * ACT.

The reformulation of the semantics is very similar to the one of the small step semantics. Here is an example of a redefined step:

```
Inductive ExceptionStep(p:Program):
      Method → IntraNormalState → IntraExceptionState → Prop :=
| EES_ : ∀ m s t S T, _ExceptionStep p m s t →
           T = bookkeepException p m s t S →
           ExceptionStep p m (s,S) (t,T).
```

This new `ExceptionStep` first checks if the original exceptional step relation holds (`_ExceptionStep`) then it generates the result of the bookkeeping (using `bookkeepException`) to finally establish the required `ExceptionStep` relation.

Additionally several definitions and lemmas existing for the original semantics were updated so that they now concern the new states and steps. The definitions and lemmas are used by the current version of the MOBIUS base logic.

We would like to point out here that the way the semantics is designed the bookkeeping functions cannot influence the original Bicolano state. They can only influence the `ACT` values.

4   The Vertical Extension Framework

This extension framework is build as an aggregation of the extensions. Each of the extensions can add supplementary behaviour to the existing semantics and the extensions may be combined in a stack-based fashion. The general idea of the stack of extensions is presented on Figure 2.

The bottom of the extension stack is the Bicolano semantics. We refer to the semantics as the *bottom semantics*. Another kind of semantics which we take into account here is the semantics just below the currently extended one. This semantics aggregates all the behaviours starting from the bottom semantics till the last already defined one. The semantics just below the currently defined one is called the *support semantics*. Each semantics in extensions between the bottom semantics and support semantics, excluding the former and including the latter, is called *intermediate semantics*.

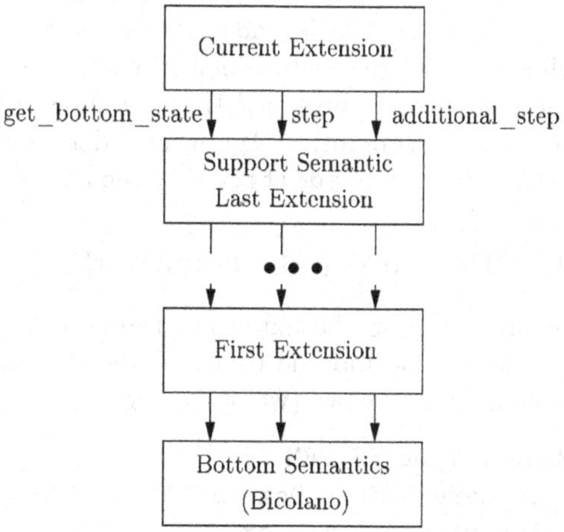

We assume that each extension may define behaviour which cannot

Fig. 2. The schema of the vertical extension framework

be easily modelled with the use of the original Bicolano state definition. For instance the memory usage extension requires an additional field: the current size of the allocated memory (the maximum size is a parameter of the module). That is why, along with the semantics extensions, we define state extensions. The state on which the program operates in the bottom semantics is called the *bottom state*. The *support state* is the state that corresponds to the support semantics.

As Figure 2 suggests, the subsequent extensions are composed with the help of three relations: `step`, `get_bottom_state`, and `additional_step`. The most important relation is the `step` relation which determines the behaviour of the small semantical steps. This relation takes into account the behaviours described in all the extensions below the current one and the one defined by the current extension. It is worth mentioning that the extensions may influence the bottom state. Also, the semantical steps in the extensions below may influence the step in the current extension (e.g. in case the current extension traces the memory usage, the intermediate extensions may allocate silently in the bottom semantics some objects and this must be taken into account by the memory tracing extension).

We assume that the current extension is constructed in such a way that the extension developers understand Bicolano semantics, but have limited understanding of the intermediate extensions. That is why, we allow to directly refer to Bicolano state with the help of `get_bottom_state`. This relation describes how to strip off all the state information which is defined by the intermediate extensions and obtain the component of the state which is directly operated by the bottom semantics. Certain extensions may have the bottom semantics undefined (e.g. an extension which supplements the semantics with a kind of error that is absent from the original formalisation) or have many possible bottom states (e.g. an extension which formalises garbage collection). Therefore, we decided to formalise `get_bottom_state` as a relation rather than as a function.

At last, the relation `additional_step` complements `get_bottom_state` and allows to recognise which behaviour is added by the intermediate extensions and the current one, provided that we know how the state is modified by a step in the bottom semantics. Again, in order to achieve a more general framework we decided to define `additional_step` as a relation.

4.1   How to Use the Framework?

In order to use the extension framework in a particular situation, one has to provide a Coq module that realises the module type `SS_SEM`. The module type is defined as follows (we omit axioms):

```
Module Type SS_SEM.
    Declare Module Dom: SEMANTIC_DOMAIN.
    Import Dom Dom.Prog.
    Parameter state_t : Type.
    Definition bottom_state_t := State.t.
    Parameter get_bottom_state: state_t → bottom_state_t → Prop.
    Parameter step: Program → state_t → state_t → Prop.
    Parameter additional_step: Program →
        state_t → bottom_state_t → state_t → Prop.
End SS_SEM.
```

It declares the module Dom which contains the semantic domain over which the state is build. The extended state is defined as `state_t` while the state component, which is defined and manipulated with the use of the original Bicolano semantics, is accessible through `get_bottom_state`. The signature defines also a shorthand for the type of the bottom state as `bottom_state_t`.

State. The type representing states will usually be the support state type extended with additional fields, depending on the actual needs.

The `state_t` type in case of the memory extension is just a product of the support state and an integer component. The component keeps track of the memory usage. In order to define `get_bottom_state`, we have to just project the state to the support state component and then use `get_bottom_state` in the support semantics to obtain the required relation.

Step. The parameter `step` is *the* semantics provided by the given module. It relates the subsequent steps of the semantics in such a way that `step p st1 st2` holds when in the extended semantics there is a possible step in the program `p` from the state `st1` to the state `st2`.

In case of the memory extension, the `step` relation must, as in the horizontal case, count the amount of used memory. To achieve this the relation must check if the instruction to be invoked allocates memory. This can be determined based on the state before the step with the help of `get_bottom_state`. When the size of the heap memory would exceed the maximum allowed size, the extension changes the bottom semantics behaviour so that the `OutOfMemoryError` error is thrown. This, however, must take into account the `additional_step` of the support semantics as described below.

Additional step. The relation `additional_step p st1 bst st2` in an extension SEM connects the state `st1` in SEM with the state `bst` from the bottom semantics and `st2` again in SEM where all these states are interpreted in a program `p`. It holds when `st2` is the state in SEM that takes into account a hypothetical move from the bottom part of `st1` to `bst`. In the simplest situation, the bottom part of `st2` is just `bst`. However, this is not obligatory.

The `additional_step` relation is provided for use by a potential extension built above the current one. Consider a case when SEM2 extends (is above) SEM1, we describe now how it can exploit `additional_step` from SEM1. The semantics of SEM2 may want to supplement the original behaviour with a new transformation. It knows the state `st1` from SEM1 before the current step and knows how to transform the bottom part of `st1` for its own purposes. Let the result of the transformation be `bst`. Now, it can use `additional_step` to find out how SEM1 reacts to this transformation and obtain `st2`.

Let us illustrate this with an example. Suppose, SEM2 is the memory extension. When a JVM instruction `new` is invoked and there is enough memory, we simply refer to `step` in the support semantics and change only the memory field in the state. However, if SEM2 introduces an additional state transformation we can ask SEM1 to take it into account using `additional_step` from a support semantics SEM1. For instance in the memory extension we can have the following case:

```
| step_new_OutOfMemory: ∀ ..., current_ins sust1 (New c) → ...
  (* size is the amount of the object being created *)
  ch + size > max_heap_size →
  (* h' − heap after creation of the exception (stored in loc') *)
```

```
Support.get_bottom_state sust1 (St h (Fr m pc s l) sf) →
Support.additional_step p sust1
   (StE h' (FrE m pc loc' l) sf) sust2 →
      step_mem p (mem_state sust1 ch)
                (mem_state sust2 (ch + esize))
```

When there is too little memory, the memory extension should raise an exception which is indicated in the state (StE h' (FrE m pc loc' l) sf). We can now ask additional_step in the support semantics SEM1 to react to a change from sust1 to this exceptional state. In this way, we can obtain sust2 which can either accept that exception or change it in its own way.

On the other hand when the memory extension plays the role of the support semantics, its additional_step may be used by the extension above. The additional_step relation can be defined in such a way that it checks if an additional JVM exception is being thrown in a step from the extension above. If so, it counts the size of the exception object and either adds the size to the memory counter or throws OutOfMemoryError. In other cases the memory counter is unchanged. In this way, the memory extension overrides the exception about to be thrown by the semantics above.

Axioms. The additional_step relation should be compatible with the step relation on the same pairs of states. Therefore the SS_SEM signature declares the axiom:

```
Axiom add_step_step_compat: ∀ ..., step p st1 st2 →
   get_bottom_state st2 bost2 → additional_step p st1 bost2 st2.
```

This axiom says that for a given pair of states st1 and st2 if the relation step holds, then additional_step should also hold for the pair and the projection of st2 to the bottom state type. All extensions should provide a proof of this property.

4.2   The Realisation of the Framework

The semantics modules form a stack. At the bottom, there is always the bottom semantics. The actual extensions must be provided as a functor that takes the support semantics as its parameter and returns the resulting semantics of the extension. Therefore, a typical extension module header looks as follows:

```
Module SemExtension (SupportSem: SS_SEM) <: SS_SEM.
```

The module BottomSem is the bottom extension module. It has the mentioned above SS_SEM module type and provides its instantiation with the primary Bicolano semantics. The type state_t is defined here to be the state in the module type SEMANTIC_DOMAIN used in Bicolano. The relation get_bottom_state is defined here as the identity on the state from SEMANTIC_DOMAIN. The state relation is defined to be the small step relation of the original Bicolano as this is the basic semantical step. The relation additional_step is just the identity on the state type as this extension does not add any additional behaviour to the original semantics.

5   The Frameworks Compared

The relation between the frameworks. The vertical framework is strictly more expressive than the horizontal one. In particular, it allows to define a memory tracking extension which is able to throw the OutOfMemoryError in case the memory limit is exceeded. This kind of behaviour is impossible to model with the help of the horizontal framework as the bookkeeping functions do not modify the state. However, an important property of the horizontal extension is that it does not change the semantics—every step of the extended semantics has a corresponding step in the Bicolano semantics and vice-versa. This property can be expressed in the vertical framework, but at additional cost of defining and proving the following lemmas:

```
Lemma support_step_implies_step:
 ∀ p t s', SupportSem.step p (get_support_state t) s' →
   ∃ t': state_t, step p t t' ∧(get_support_state t') = s'.
Lemma step_implies_support_step:
 ∀ p t t', step p t t' →
   SupportSem.step p (get_support_state t) (get_support_state t').
```

The properties hold in particular for an extension that counts the number of executed instructions and for the EffectExtension which simulates the horizontal extension framework. This holds as the extensions do not change the original behaviour. However, the proofs require additional assumption on the intermediate states stack:

```
  Parameter fget_bottom_state: SupportState.state_t →
                          bottom_state_t.
  Axiom get_bottom_state_ok:
   ∀ sust bost, SupportState.get_bottom_state sust bost ↔
               fget_bottom_state sust = bost.
```

The axiom get_bottom_state_ok says that the projection to the bottom state is a function. The assumption holds for the bottom (not extended) state and is preserved by the mentioned other extensions.

Another interesting property of the extensions that do not change the state concerns additional_step:

```
  Lemma additional_step_proj: ∀ ...,
    additional_step p st1 bost2 st2 → get_bottom_state st2 bost2.
```

This property says that the bottom state of the result of the additional step is exactly the same as the one proposed as a transformation from the bottom state of st1 to bost2.

As expected, these properties do not hold for extensions which change the behaviour, in particular for the memory extension we presented in the paper.

Except from these properties, we also provided a functor EffectExtension that allows to realise any extension in the horizontal extension framework by means of our vertical one. We additionally proved in Coq a theorem which expresses that the original horizontal framework is equivalent to the one defined in terms of the vertical one.

```
Theorem EffectExtensionEquiv:
  ∀ p st1 st2, EffSmallStep.step p st1 st2 ↔
               EffectSem.step p st1 st2.
```

In this theorem, `EffSmallStep` is the result of the application of the horizontal extension framework to any effect while `EffectSem` is the result of the application of `EffectExtension` to the same effect. This theorem says that each step in the horizontal extension framework implies an analogous step in the extension in the vertical framework and vice-versa.

The cost of the vertical framework. When talking about the cost of a framework we can distinguish two points of view: extension developer's one and code consumer's one. The cost for an extension developer can be roughly measured as the size of the extension source code. Such a comparison shows that the vertical framework is much more expensive. For instance the memory extension in the vertical framework has 204 lines while in the horizontal extension framework only 50 lines. In this case one could argue that the vertical version describes richer behaviour and this is the reason of the size increase, but the extension that counts instructions, which indeed does not add any supplementary behaviour, has 173 lines in case of the vertical framework while only 26 lines in case of the horizontal one. Moreover, defining the `bookkeepSmall` function is conceptually simpler than defining the `step` and `additional_step` relations when one wants to affect only the extended part of the state. A code consumer pays attention to the size of the certificates attached to the code and the certificates include compiled Bicolano extensions. The size of compiled extensions in the vertical and the horizontal frameworks are, respectively, 181 KB and 148 KB for the memory extension, 158 KB and 135 KB for the instruction counting extension. As we can see, the difference is not so explicit as in the source code, but again the vertical framework seems to be more expensive. In this light, the vertical framework should be rather used to supplement the original semantics with an additional behaviour which is necessary to be modelled while the horizontal one in all the extensions which only trace the history of program runs.

6   Conclusions

We showed two frameworks for extending an existing semantics definition without making any changes in the existing code, in case of the small step semantics, and with very limited changes preserving all previously existing properties in case of the big step semantics in the horizontal framework.

The horizontal framework guarantees the preservation of the original semantics behaviour while the vertical framework allows to change it. The need of changing the behaviour may arise in particular when one needs a semantics in which the lack of resources should trigger an error, which was omitted from the original Bicolano semantics.

We presented here a comparison of the frameworks—the vertical framework is strictly more expressive than the horizontal one. In particular, we proved in Coq that the horizontal framework can be simulated by the vertical one. Moreover, the memory extension can throw the OutOfMemoryError only in case of the vertical framework.

However, taking into account that the horizontal framework is less memory-consuming and that the bookkeeping functions are simpler to devise than the step relation, the choice of the framework to use should rely on a particular application.

Acknowledgements. We would like to thank Lennart Beringer, Jacek Chrząszcz, Martin Hofmann, and David Pichardie for discussions concerning the two extension frameworks.

References

[AF00]   Appel, A.W., Felty, A.P.: A semantic model of types and machine instructions for proof-carrying code. In: Principles of Programming Languages. Association of Computing Machinery Press (2000)

[BC04]   Bertot, Y., Castéran, P.: Interactive Theorem Proving and Program Development. Coq'Art: The Calculus of Inductive Constructions. In: Texts in Theoretical Computer Science, Springer, Heidelberg (2004)

[BH06]   Beringer, L., Hofmann, M.: A bytecode logic for JML and types. In: Kobayashi, N. (ed.) APLAS 2006. LNCS, vol. 4279, pp. 389–405. Springer, Heidelberg (2006)

[Chr04]   Chrząszcz, J.: Modules in Type Theory with Generative Definitions. PhD thesis, Warsaw University and University of Paris-Sud (January 2004)

[Con06]   Mobius Consortium. Deliverable 3.1: Bytecode specification language and program logic (2006), http://mobius.inria.fr

[Coq04]   Coq development team. The Coq proof assistant reference manual V8.0. Technical Report 255, INRIA, France, mars (2004), http://coq.inria.fr/doc/main.html

[KN06]   Klein, G., Nipkow, T.: A machine-checked model for a Java-like language, virtual machine and compiler. ACM Transactions on Programming Languages and Systems 28(4), 619–695 (2006)

[LH96]   Liang, S., Hudak, P.: Modular Denotational Semantics for Compiler Construction. In: Riis Nielson, H. (ed.) ESOP 1996. LNCS, vol. 1058, pp. 219–234. Springer, Heidelberg (1996)

[LY99]   Lindholm, T., Yellin, F.: The Java^{TM} Virtual Machine Specification, 2nd edn. Sun Microsystems, Inc. (1999), http://java.sun.com/docs/books/vmspec/

[Mos92]   Mosses, P.D.: Action Semantics. Cambridge Tracts in Theoretical Computer Science, vol. 26. Cambridge University Press, Cambridge (1992)

[Nec97]   Necula, G.C.: Proof-carrying code. In: Principles of Programming Languages, pp. 106–119. Association of Computing Machinery Press, New York, NY, USA (1997)

[NN99]   Nielson, F., Nielson, H.R.: Type and effect systems. In: Olderog, E.-R., Steffen, B. (eds.) Correct System Design. LNCS, vol. 1710, pp. 114–136. Springer, Heidelberg (1999)

[Pic06]   Pichardie, D.: Bicolano – Byte Code Language in Coq (2006), http://mobius.inia.fr/bicolano

[SS04]   Skalka, C., Smith, S.F.: History effects and verification. In: Chin, W.-N. (ed.) APLAS 2004. LNCS, vol. 3302, pp. 107–128. Springer, Heidelberg (2004)

[Sun03]   Sun Microsystems Inc., 4150 Network Circle, Santa Clara, California 95054. Connected Limited Device Configuration. Specification Version 1.1. Java^{TM} 2 Platform, Micro Edition (J2ME^{TM}) (March 2003), http://jcp.org/aboutJava/communityprocess/final/jsr139/index.html

[Tof90]   Tofte, M.: Type Inference for Polymorphic References. Information and Computation 89(1), 1–34 (1990)

[TT97]   Tofte, M., Talpin, J.-P.: Region-Based Memory Management. IC 132(2), 109–176 (1997)

Relational Analysis for Delivery of Services[*]

Flemming Nielson, Hanne Riis Nielson, Jörg Bauer,
Christoffer Rosenkilde Nielsen, and Henrik Pilegaard

Informatics and Mathematical Modelling, Technical University of Denmark
Kongens Lyngby, Denmark
{nielson,hrn,joba,crn,hepi}@imm.dtu.dk

Abstract. Many techniques exist for statically computing properties of
the evolution of processes expressed in process algebras. Static analysis
has shown how to obtain useful results that can both be checked and
computed in polynomial time. In this paper we develop a static analysis in relational form which substantially improves the precision of the
results obtained while being able to deal with the full generality of the
syntax of processes. The analysis reveals a feasible complexity for practical examples and gives rise to a fast prototype. We use this prototype to
automatically prove the correct delivery of messages for the implementation of an accident service, which is based on multiplexed communication,
a crucial feature of global computing applications.

1   Introduction

Process algebras facilitate abstract models of a number of features of concurrent
and distributed computation. Many use the notion of channel to provide end-to-
end guarantees ensuring secure communications taking place. A prime example
is the π-calculus [10] where channels can be freely created and guarantee that a
message sent along the channel can only be received by a process listening on
that channel. Indeed, processes not having access to the channel cannot observe
or influence any properties of the values being sent along the channel. Hence
end-to-end guarantees of proper delivery of messages is almost automatic.

Moving closer to the actual implementation level there is no direct counterpart
of the notion of channels as used in the π-calculus although symmetric cryptosystems can be used to encode some of their properties. Practical techniques often
include limiting the number of channels used and instead use multiplexing of
several communications over a fixed set of channels. It is then a requirement
on the transporting processes that they correctly implement the intended end-
to-end communication. In this paper we use a running example, a version of
the accident service taken from the automotive case study of the SENSORIA
EU-project, where this problem arises.

This paper shows how to use static analysis for demonstrating that the service requests of the system are correctly distributed by the multiplexer process.

---

[*] This work has been partially sponsored by the project SENSORIA, IST-2005-016004.

G. Barthe and C. Fournet (Eds.): TGC 2007, LNCS 4912, pp. 73–89, 2008.

It turns out that so-called independent attribute analyses [11], as developed in e.g. [1], are unable to deliver the guarantees needed. A static analysis for multiplexing must be *relational*, that is, it must be able to capture precisely the dependence between various names. As an example, if a process contains output operations $a\langle b, b\rangle$ and $a\langle c, c\rangle$ then the analysis must be able to show the absence of the output operations $a\langle b, c\rangle$ and $a\langle c, b\rangle$.

There are strong relational analyses around to prove multiplexing correct, most successful among them the abstract interpretations of Venet [16] and Feret [5]. In contrast to our proposed analyses, they are even able to distinguish different recursive instances of a process.

However, where our analysis is presented for standard π-calculus (with pattern matching) with the standard reduction semantics based on congruence, the analyses of [16,5] rely on heavily customised versions of the language that include input-guarded replication, an instrumented semantics and explicit substitution environments. Thus, these customisations enable strong analyses, but are of disadvantage in the context of global computing where many calculi emerge, for instance [8] and [3], that all use the standard constructs of classical π, in particular congruence and reduction semantics. In contrast, our analysis, being based on these standards, can be easily transferred to new emerging languages, while [16,5] would need to be completely re-designed. Beyond re-usability, which is of utmost importance for global computing, our proposal is implemented and enjoys a correctness result in terms of a subject reduction result, which is the standard proof technique. In contrast, [16,5] settle for a very general soundness result of their abstract interpretation.

Our contribution is thus the development of a relational analysis that can be specified almost as naturally as the simpler (and in fact too simple) independent attribute analyses [1], that is easily extendable to new, emerging global computing calculi, because it relies on standard syntax, semantics, and proof technique. Indeed, our correctness results relies on the invariance of a correctness predicate under subject reduction, where the correctness predicate takes care of the implicit substitutions that need to be made very explicit—and hence deviating from standard reduction semantics—in the approaches of Venet [16] and Feret [5]. The analysis is implemented, and provides results that are sufficiently precise to validate our running example. While the worst case complexity is (necessarily) exponential we show that for realistic programs, e.g. for our running example, we are polynomial in solving the associated constraints. We should also point out that, due to our use of Alternation-free Least Fixed Point Logic (ALFP), the time needed for computing the best solution is asymptotically equal to the time needed for validating a solution (unlike approaches where validation is polynomial time but inference is nondeterministic polynomial time, the latter being exponential in practice).

Outline. We continue by presenting our running example, an accident service from the automotive case study of the SENSORIA EU-project. In Section 2, we present syntax and semantics of $p\pi$, our extension of the π-calculus with pattern

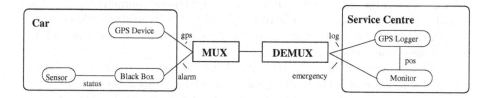

Fig. 1. The overall architecture of the accident service

matching. The analysis itself is specified in Section 3, while its properties are reported in Section 4. Section 5 concludes.

1.1 The Accident Service

A typical service-centred application is the *accident service*. The overall architecture of this service is depicted in Figure 1. In order to subscribe to this service, a car needs to be equipped with a GPS device and a black box. The black box frequently polls internal sensors for abnormal events. In such a case, it will start sending alarm messages containing the car's and the driver's identity. The service centre has two objectives: It logs the GPS data received from the car and monitors whether any alarm occurs. In that case, it gets the location of the car and the identity of its driver from the GPS logger and sends an SOS message to a rescue service (not modelled here). The somewhat intricate specification of the logger ensures that the most recently sent position is actually attached to the SOS.

Table 1. The pπ specification of the accident service. The process P_{acc} is the parallel composition of the components stated here.

GPS device: $!\ (\nu loc)\ \mathsf{gps}\langle car_i, loc \rangle^1$
Sensor: $!\ (\mathsf{status}\langle car_i, \mathsf{ok}\rangle^2 + \mathsf{status}\langle car_i, \mathsf{crit}\rangle^3)$
Black Box: $!\ \mathsf{status}(car_i; x)^4.[x = \mathsf{crit}]^5.\,!\ \mathsf{alarm}\langle car_i, driver_i \rangle^6$

GPS Logger: $(\nu k)(!\ k(;\ )^7.\mathsf{log}(;y_{car},y_{pos})^8.$
$\qquad\qquad\qquad (\mathsf{pos}(y_{car};\ )^9.\mathsf{pos}\langle y_{car}, y_{pos}\rangle^{10}.k\langle\rangle^{11} + k\langle\rangle^{12})$
$\qquad\qquad\ \ \mid k\langle\rangle^{13})$
Monitor: $!\ \mathsf{emergency}(;z_{car}, z_d)^{14}.\mathsf{pos}\langle z_{car}\rangle^{15}.\mathsf{pos}(z_{car}; z_{pos})^{16}.\mathsf{SOS}\langle z_{car}, z_{pos}, z_d\rangle^{17}$

Mux: $\qquad\ !\ \mathsf{gps}(;z_{car}, z_{pos})^{18}.\mathsf{wifi}\langle\mathsf{log}, z_{car}, z_{pos}\rangle^{19}$
$\qquad\qquad \mid\ !\ \mathsf{alarm}(;z_{car}, z_d)^{20}.\mathsf{wifi}\langle\mathsf{emergency}, z_{car}, z_d\rangle^{21}$
Demux: $\qquad !\ \mathsf{wifi}(;z_1, z_2, z_3)^{22}.z_1\langle z_2, z_3\rangle^{23}$

All messages between the car and the service centre are communicated over a *multiplexed, wireless channel*— a feature typical of service oriented architectures. The multiplexer takes care of distributing messages correctly while providing optimal use of bandwidth.

We use a polyadic π-calculus, pπ, extended with pattern matching in input prefixes (as in [2]) in order to write down the accident service formally (Table 1). For analysis purposes, action prefixes are annotated with *labels*. The usual precedence rules—parallelisation < summation < prefix, restriction, replication—hold for pπ as well. An input prefix $x(\bar{y}; \bar{u})$, receives a tuple $\bar{z}$ over channel x if the first $|\bar{y}|$ elements of $\bar{z}$ equal $\bar{y}$, thus binding the remaining elements to $\bar{u}$. The complete syntax and semantics are presented in Section 2. Our analysis presented in Section 3 will be able to find out that the MUX distributes messages correctly, that is, messages over the emergency channel will contain car and driver identity information only, whereas messages sent over the log channel will always contain car identities and position information.

2   The pπ-Calculus

2.1   Syntax

The syntax of the π-calculus extended with pattern matching, pπ, can be seen in Table 2. As in the π-calculus we have *channels* that facilitate synchronous name passing communication. We use *names* picked from the denumerable set Name to denote channels and we shall use the notation n, m, p for elements of this set. Similarly, we shall assume a denumerable set Var of *variables* and let u, v range over this set. When necessary, we shall use x, y, z to range over the disjoint union Name $\cup$ Var. However, as we shall see below names and variables are *bound* in different manners. The calculus is polyadic and we shall use bars to denote polyadic entities, e.g. $\bar{n}, \bar{u}, \bar{x}$ etc.

The intuition behind the set of primitives is as follows: The inactive or *terminal process*, 0, denotes the end of a process, a point from where no further progress can be made. The *parallel composition* construct, $P_1 \mid P_2$, represents the

Table 2. Processes; P

$P ::=$	0	Terminated Process
$\mid$	$!P$	Replication
$\mid$	$P_1 \mid P_2$	Parallel
$\mid$	$P_1 + P_2$	Choice
$\mid$	$(\nu n)P$	Restriction
$\mid$	$[x = y]^\ell P$	Match
$\mid$	$x\langle \bar{y} \rangle^\ell.P$	Output
$\mid$	$x(\bar{y}; \bar{u})^\ell.P$	Input

process that is a concurrent composition of two processes P_1 and P_2. The *choice construct*, $P_1 + P_2$, is used to model non-deterministic behaviour. The *replication construct*, $!P$, describes a process that is the parallel composition of as many occurrences of P as necessary; in the scope of name passing this is adequate for expressing recursive behaviour. The *name restriction* construct, $(\nu n)P$, binds a name, n, that may be used freely in P, but is not free in $(\nu n)P$, i.e. the scope of n is restricted to P. The guarded process, $[x = y]P$, has a simple 'if-then' behaviour - the execution of P can only commence if x and y denote the same name. The polyadic *output prefix* construct, $x\langle \bar{y} \rangle.P$, represents a process that desires to engage, as sender, in a synchronous exchange of information on the channel denoted by x and then proceed as described by P. However, the output can be completed only if a concurrent subprocess is simultaneously willing to participate, as receiver, in a *matching* communication on the same channel. The polyadic *input prefix* construct, $x(\bar{y}; \bar{u}).P$, represents a process that desires to engage, as receiver, in a synchronous exchange of information on the channel denoted by x and then proceed as P. The input can complete if:

1. a concurrent subprocess is simultaneously willing to engage, as sender, in a communication on the same channel, and
2. the output offered by this remote process *matches* the expectations expressed by the input pattern, i.e. the output and input vectors are both of length $|\bar{y}| + |\bar{u}|$ and they agree on the names in the first $|\bar{y}|$ positions.

If these conditions are satisfied the communication can commence binding each *variable* in $\bar{u}$ to the *name* mentioned in the corresponding position of the output vector.

Syntactic conventions. As customary for the π-calculus we shall abstain from writing the terminal 0 at the end of example processes. Furthermore, we shall assume that well-formed programs do not contain free variables. However, for the convenience of writing examples we do allow free names. We use $\star \in \{|, +\}$ for brevity when parallel composition and choice are treated in the same way.

Label Annotations. To aid expressing the analysis in Section 3 we shall annotate the actions of the processes with *labels* $\ell \in \mathbf{Lab}$ as in $x\langle \bar{y} \rangle^\ell$, $x(\bar{y}; \bar{u})^\ell$ and $[x = y]^\ell$. For simplicity we shall assume that the labels are *unique* in the process $P_\star$ to be analysed. The labels play no role whatsoever in the semantics; they only serve as pointers into the syntax.

2.2   Semantics

We now give an operational semantics of the pπ calculus based on a *structural congruence*, $\equiv$, and a *reduction relation*, $\rightarrow$. This is a semantics in the style of Milner's reaction relation [9] for the original π-calculus. The resulting semantics clearly expresses an intuitive understanding of concurrency and interaction. The processes of pπ are grouped into congruence classes by the structural congruence relation, which is defined in Table 3. This definition ensures that the members

Table 3. Structural congruence, $P \equiv Q$, is the smallest congruence relation on processes satisfying the axioms above. We use $\star \in \{|, +\}$ for brevity.

(NAM1) $(\nu n)(\nu m)P \equiv (\nu m)(\nu n)P$ (NAM2) $(\nu n)0 \equiv 0$
(NAM3) $(\nu n)(P \mid Q) \equiv (\nu n)P \mid Q$ if $n \notin \mathsf{fn}(Q)$
(ASSOC) $(P \star Q) \star R \equiv P \star (Q \star R)$ (COM) $P \star Q \equiv Q \star P$
(NIL) $P \mid 0 \equiv P$ (REP) $!P \equiv P \mid !P$
(AEQ) $P \equiv_\alpha Q \Rightarrow P \equiv Q$

Table 4. Disciplined α-equivalence; $P \equiv_\alpha Q$

(ALPHA) $(\nu n)P \equiv_\alpha (\nu m)P[m/n]$ if $m \notin \mathsf{fn}(P) \wedge \lfloor n \rfloor = \lfloor m \rfloor$

of each class are congruent up to trivial syntactic restructuring. In the definition - and the following - we use $\mathsf{fn}(P)$ and $\mathsf{fv}(P)$ to denote the free names and free variables of the process P, respectively.

As usual the congruence includes α-equivalence (Table 4) - asserting that processes are equivalent if they differ only in their choice of bound names. However, as we distinguish between names and variables and shall never substitute a variable for a name or variable we choose to define α-equivalence only for names. Also, we write $P[^m/_n]$ to denote the process that is as P except that every free occurrence of name n is replaced by name m; the notion of substitution is formally defined in Table 5. Finally, we use the notion of *canonical names* ($\lfloor n \rfloor$ as motivated and defined below) and demand that α-equivalence only holds when the bound names have the same canonical name.

In the definition of substitution over a name restriction, α-renaming is used to avoid name capture. This means that constants do not have representations that are stable under evaluation. However, syntactically unstable entities are not suitable for carrying static analysis information. Therefore we associate each constant n with a stable canonical name $\lfloor n \rfloor$ and demand that α-renaming be *disciplined*, such that canonical names are preserved, even when the syntactical representations change. Technically, the canonicalisation of names partitions the name-space into equivalence classes. Each canonical name uniquely identifies the defining syntactic occurrence giving rise to the associated class. Then α-renaming (Rule (SRES) of Table 5) demands that new names be picked from appropriate classes.

The reductions of processes are given by the binary *reduction relation*, which is defined inductively as the least binary relation described by the axioms and rules of Table 6.

When the reduction relation holds between a pair of processes, written $P \rightarrow P'$, it means that P can evolve into P' by a single input/output reduction (COM)

Table 5. Substitution; $P[^m/_z]$

(SNIL)	$0[^m/_z]$	$= 0$
(SREP)	$(!P)[^m/_z]$	$= !P[^m/_z]$
(SPAR)	$(P_1 \star P_2)[^m/_z]$	$= P_1[^m/_z] \star P_2[^m/_z]$

$$(\text{SRES}) \quad ((\nu n)P)[^m/_z] \ = \ \begin{cases} (\nu n)P & \text{if } z = n \\ (\nu n')(P[^{n'}/_n][^m/_z]) & \text{if } z \neq n \wedge m = n \wedge \\ & n' \notin \mathsf{fn}(P) \wedge \lfloor n \rfloor = \lfloor n' \rfloor \\ (\nu n)P[^m/_z] & \text{otherwise} \end{cases}$$

(SMATCH)	$([x = y]P)[^m/_z]$	$= [x[^m/_z] = y[^m/_z]]P[^m/_z]$
(SOUT)	$(x\langle \bar{y} \rangle.P)[^m/_z]$	$= x[^m/_z]\langle \bar{y}[^m/_z] \rangle.P[^m/_z]$

$$(\text{SIN}) \quad (x(\bar{y};\bar{u}).P)[^m/_z] = \begin{cases} x[^m/_z](\bar{y}[^m/_z];\bar{u}).P & \text{if } z \in \{\bar{u}\} \\ x[^m/_z](\bar{y}[^m/_z];\bar{u}).P[^m/_z] & \text{otherwise} \end{cases}$$

Table 6. Reduction Semantics; $P \to P'$

$$(\text{MATCH}) \quad [n = n]P \to P \qquad (\text{PAR}) \quad \frac{P \to P'}{P \mid Q \to P' \mid Q} \qquad (\text{CHO}) \quad \frac{P \to P'}{P + Q \to P'}$$

$$(\text{COM}) \quad m\langle n_1, \ldots, n_k \rangle.P \mid m(n_1, \ldots, n_j; u_{j+1}, \ldots, u_k).Q \to$$
$$P \mid Q[^{n_{j+1}}/_{u_{j+1}}] \cdots [^{n_k}/_{u_k}]$$

$$(\text{VAR}) \quad \frac{P \equiv Q \quad Q \to Q' \quad Q' \equiv P'}{P \to P'} \qquad (\text{RES}) \quad \frac{P \to P'}{(\nu n)P \to (\nu n)P'}$$

or a successful guard (MATCH) within some subprocess of P. The rule (COM) requires radices to be on a certain normal form and the rule (VAR) allows the use of the structural congruence for obtaining this form. The remaining rules, (PAR) and (RES), simply propagate reductions across parallel composition and name restrictions respectively, while (CHO) lets one process in a summation proceed.

3   Relational Analysis

We set the stage for the analysis by defining some auxiliary information. First, a *label environment* L is defined as a mapping

$$\mathsf{L} : \mathbf{Lab} \hookrightarrow \mathbf{Var}^*$$

that to each label ℓ associates a sequence $\bar{u}$ of variables that have been introduced *before* this point in the process. More formally, we shall take $\mathsf{L} = \mathcal{L}_\epsilon[\![P_\star]\!]$ where $\mathcal{L}_{\bar{u}}$ (for $\bar{u} \in \mathbf{Var}^*$) is defined in Table 7. Here we write $\uplus$ for joining two mappings with disjoint domains and $[\,]$ for the mapping with empty domain. The notation

Table 7. Label environment

$$\mathcal{L}_{\bar{u}}[\![P_1 \star P_2]\!] = \mathcal{L}_{\bar{u}}[\![P_1]\!] \uplus \mathcal{L}_{\bar{u}}[\![P_2]\!] \qquad\qquad \mathcal{L}_{\bar{u}}[\![!P]\!] = \mathcal{L}_{\bar{u}}[\![P]\!]$$
$$\mathcal{L}_{\bar{u}}[\![(\nu n)P]\!] = \mathcal{L}_{\bar{u}}[\![P]\!] \qquad\qquad\qquad \mathcal{L}_{\bar{u}}[\![0]\!] = [\,]$$
$$\mathcal{L}_{\bar{u}}[\![x\langle\bar{y}\rangle^\ell.P]\!] = \mathcal{L}_{\bar{u}}[\![P]\!][\ell \mapsto \bar{u}] \qquad \mathcal{L}_{\bar{u}}[\![x(\bar{y};\bar{v})^\ell.P]\!] = \mathcal{L}_{\bar{u}\bar{v}}[\![P]\!][\ell \mapsto \bar{u}]$$
$$\mathcal{L}_{\bar{u}}[\![[x = y]^\ell P]\!] = \mathcal{L}_{\bar{u}}[\![P]\!][\ell \mapsto \bar{u}]$$

Table 8. Flow information; $\mathcal{F}[\![P]\!]$

$$\mathcal{F}[\![P_1 \star P_2]\!] = \text{let } (F_1, E_1) = \mathcal{F}[\![P_1]\!]$$
$$(F_2, E_2) = \mathcal{F}[\![P_2]\!]$$
$$\text{in } (F_1 \uplus F_2, E_1 \cup E_2)$$
$$\mathcal{F}[\![!P]\!] = \mathcal{F}[\![P]\!]$$
$$\mathcal{F}[\![(\nu n)P]\!] = \mathcal{F}[\![P]\!]$$
$$\mathcal{F}[\![0]\!] = ([\,], \emptyset)$$
$$\mathcal{F}[\![x\langle y_1, \ldots, y_k\rangle^\ell.P]\!] = \text{let } (F, E) = \mathcal{F}[\![P]\!]$$
$$\text{in } (F[\ell \mapsto E], \{\ell\})$$
$$\mathcal{F}[\![x(y_1, \ldots, y_j; u_{j+1}, \ldots, u_k)^\ell.P]\!] = \text{let } (F, E) = \mathcal{F}[\![P]\!]$$
$$\text{in } (F[\ell \mapsto E], \{\ell\})$$
$$\mathcal{F}[\![[x = y]^\ell P]\!] = \text{let } (F, E) = \mathcal{F}[\![P]\!]$$
$$\text{in } (F[\ell \mapsto E], \{\ell\})$$

$\bar{u}\bar{v}$ stands for the concatenation of $\bar{u}$ and $\bar{v}$. We will use the notation $\langle x_1, \ldots, x_r \rangle$ to write down vectors.

In the analysis we shall also need a representation of the *flow of control* in the process $P_\star$ of interest. We shall represent this by a *flow mapping* F that to each label ℓ associates the set of labels that will become *exposed* once the action labelled ℓ has been executed; thus

$$\mathsf{F} : \mathbf{Lab} \hookrightarrow \mathcal{P}(\mathbf{Lab})$$

The function $\mathcal{F}$ defined in Table 8 will for each process P define such a mapping together with the set of *exposed labels* of the process itself and we shall define $(\mathsf{F}, \mathsf{E}) = \mathcal{F}[\![P_\star]\!]$.

Example 1. The annotated running example, P_{acc}, was given in Table 1. Using the functions $\mathcal{L}$ and $\mathcal{F}$ we obtain $\mathsf{E} = \{1, 2, 3, 4, 7, 13, 14, 18, 20, 22\}$ and the following samples for flow F and label environment L.

ℓ	1	4	8	14	15	16	17
F.ℓ	$\emptyset$	$\{5\}$	$\{9, 12\}$	$\{15\}$	$\{16\}$	$\{17\}$	$\emptyset$
L.ℓ	ϵ	ϵ	ϵ	ϵ	$\langle z_{car}, z_d \rangle$	$\langle z_{car}, z_d \rangle$	$\langle z_{car}, z_d, z_{pos} \rangle$

3.1   Analysis Domains

The *abstract environments* $\hat{R}$ of the analysis will, given a label ℓ, return a set of sequences of names; the structure of these sequences will equal that of $L.\ell$ and will determine the potential values of the variables. Thus we shall take:

$$\hat{R} : \textbf{Lab} \to \mathcal{P}(\textbf{Name}^*)$$

Note that this is exactly the point, where the analysis becomes relational. We record sets of tuples of names, which are received at the same time, rather than tuples of sets as it would be the case for an independent attribute analysis.

If $\hat{R}.\ell = \emptyset$ it means that the program point ℓ is not reachable; if $\hat{R}.\ell = \{\epsilon\}$ it means that no variables are bound at that program point.

We use the following auxiliary function to determine the potential values of a variable u at the label ℓ: $\Pi_{u@L.\ell}(\bar{w})$, where $\bar{w}$ has the same length as $L.\ell$ and $u \in \{L.\ell\}$. We shall use $\bar{w}$ to denote elements of $\hat{R}.\ell$, that is, vectors of names. In the cases where more than one occurrence of u occurs in $L.\ell$ we always select the rightmost—corresponding to the most recently bound one.

Given an element $\bar{w} \in \hat{R}.\ell$ we can now determine the *value* $\Pi_{x@L.\ell}(\bar{w})$ of x. We have two cases depending on whether x is a name or a variable:

$$\Pi_{n@L.\ell}(\bar{w}) = n \quad \text{(for } n \text{ being a name)}$$
$$\Pi_{u@L.\ell}(\bar{w}) = n_s \text{ where } \bar{w} = \langle n_1, \ldots, n_r \rangle, \ L.\ell = \langle u_1, \ldots, u_r \rangle$$
$$\text{and } s = \max\{i \mid u_i = u\}$$

This operation is extended to sets R of sequences of names and to sequences $\bar{x}$ of names and variables as in $\Pi_{\bar{x}@L.\ell}(R)$.

3.2   The Relational Analysis

The *judgements* of the analysis have the form $\hat{R}, \hat{K} \vdash_{L,F} P$ where L, F and $\hat{R}$ are as above and

$$\hat{K} \subseteq \textbf{Name} \times \textbf{Name}^*$$

records the tuples that potentially are communicated over the channels. Table 9 defines the judgements. Intuitively, they define, whether a given pair $\hat{R}, \hat{K}$ is a valid analysis result. Hence, Table 9 specifies a set of solutions. As discussed in Section 4.2, we are interested in and able to compute the most precise one.

The rules (RPAR), (RREP) and (RRES) are straightforward as they only require that the subprocesses can be analysed using the same analysis information. The rule (RNIL) expresses that any analysis information will be correct for 0.

In the rule (ROUT) we write X for the set of sequences of names that take part in the communication; this set is obtained by extracting the names corresponding to $xy_1 \ldots y_k$ from $\hat{R}.\ell$ using $L.\ell$ as expressed by $\Pi_{x\bar{y}@L.\ell}(\hat{R}.\ell)$. The condition $X \subseteq \hat{K}$ ensures that the output is recorded in $\hat{K}$ and the premise of the rule expresses a reachability test in that the analysis information is only required to be valid for the continuation if something might be communicated over the

Table 9. Relational Analysis; $\hat{R}, \hat{K} \vdash_{\mathsf{L,F}} P$

(RPAR) $\dfrac{\hat{R}, \hat{K} \vdash_{\mathsf{L,F}} P_1 \quad \hat{R}, \hat{K} \vdash_{\mathsf{L,F}} P_2}{\hat{R}, \hat{K} \vdash_{\mathsf{L,F}} P_1 \star P_2}$	(RREP) $\dfrac{\hat{R}, \hat{K} \vdash_{\mathsf{L,F}} P}{\hat{R}, \hat{K} \vdash_{\mathsf{L,F}} !P}$

(RRES) $\dfrac{\hat{R}, \hat{K} \vdash_{\mathsf{L,F}} P}{\hat{R}, \hat{K} \vdash_{\mathsf{L,F}} (\nu n)P}$ (RNIL) $\hat{R}, \hat{K} \vdash_{\mathsf{L,F}} 0$

(ROUT) $\dfrac{X \neq \emptyset \Rightarrow \hat{R}, \hat{K} \vdash_{\mathsf{L,F}} P}{\hat{R}, \hat{K} \vdash_{\mathsf{L,F}} x\langle \bar{y} \rangle^{\ell}.P}$ if $X \subseteq \hat{K} \wedge \forall \ell' \in \mathsf{F}.\ell : X \neq \emptyset \Rightarrow \hat{R}.\ell \subseteq \hat{R}.\ell'$
where $X = \Pi_{x\bar{y}@\mathsf{L}.\ell}(\hat{R}.\ell)$

(RIN) $\dfrac{X \neq \emptyset \Rightarrow \hat{R}, \hat{K} \vdash_{\mathsf{L,F}} P}{\hat{R}, \hat{K} \vdash_{\mathsf{L,F}} x(\bar{y}; \bar{u})^{\ell}.P}$

if $\forall \ell' \in \mathsf{F}.\ell : X \subseteq \hat{R}.\ell'$
where $X = \{\bar{w}\bar{p} \mid \bar{w} \in \hat{R}.\ell \wedge \bar{m} = \Pi_{x\bar{y}@\mathsf{L}.\ell}(\bar{w}) \wedge \bar{m}\bar{p} \in \hat{K} \ \wedge \ |\bar{p}| = |\bar{u}|\}$

(RMATCH) $\dfrac{X \neq \emptyset \Rightarrow \hat{R}, \hat{K} \vdash_{\mathsf{L,F}} P}{\hat{R}, \hat{K} \vdash_{\mathsf{L,F}} [x = y]^{\ell}P}$ if $\forall \ell' \in \mathsf{F}.\ell : X \subseteq \hat{R}.\ell'$
where $X = \{\bar{w} \in \hat{R}.\ell \mid \Pi_{x@\mathsf{L}.\ell}(\bar{w}) = \Pi_{y@\mathsf{L}.\ell}(\bar{w})\}$

channel. Finally, the side condition $\forall \ell' \in \mathsf{F}.\ell : \hat{R}.\ell \subseteq \hat{R}.\ell'$ requires that the information of $\hat{R}.\ell$ flows to all the program points that follow directly after ℓ.

In the rule (RIN) we use the set X to capture how the environment $\hat{R}.\ell$ is extended to contain the bindings of the new variables $\bar{u}$. The set is constructed by first selecting those sequences $\bar{m}\bar{p}$ from $\hat{K}$ that match the potential values of x and $\bar{y}$ in some $\bar{w}$ of $\hat{R}.\ell$ and then extending those $\bar{w}$ sequences with $\bar{p}$. The sequences X constructed in this way will then be the possible environments at all the program points that follow directly after ℓ. Note that the continuation P is only analysed if X is non-empty, that is if there actually are some sequences in $\hat{K}$ that satisfy the conditions expressed in the definition of X.

Finally, in the rule (RMATCH) the set X is defined to be those sequences from $\hat{R}.\ell$ that agree on the values of x and y as obtained using the positions obtained from $\mathsf{L}.\ell$. Only these sequences are required to be recorded as possible environments in the program points that follow directly after ℓ and the continuation P will only be analysed if X is non-empty, that is, when the test might indeed be passed.

Example 2. For the running example P_{acc} the following choice of $\hat{R}$ and $\hat{K}$ satisfies $\hat{R}, \hat{K} \vdash_{\mathsf{L,F}} P_{\mathrm{acc}}$ (and is indeed the most precise solution). Note that this results holds for an arbitrary but fixed number $n > 0$ of identically defined cars.

$\hat{K} = \{ \ \langle \mathsf{pos}, \mathsf{car}_i, \mathsf{loc} \rangle, \langle \mathsf{emergency}, \mathsf{car}_i, \mathsf{driver} \rangle, \langle \mathsf{log}, \mathsf{car}_i, \mathsf{loc} \rangle, \langle \mathsf{alarm}, \mathsf{car}_i, \mathsf{driver} \rangle,$
$\qquad \langle \mathsf{status}, \mathsf{car}_i, \mathsf{crit} \rangle, \langle \mathsf{status}, \mathsf{car}_i, \mathsf{ok} \rangle, \langle \mathsf{gps}, \mathsf{car}_i, \mathsf{loc} \rangle, \langle \mathsf{k} \rangle, \langle \mathsf{pos}, \mathsf{car} \rangle,$
$\qquad \langle \mathsf{SOS}, \mathsf{car}_i, \mathsf{loc}, \mathsf{driver} \rangle, \langle \mathsf{wifi}, \mathsf{emergency}, \mathsf{car}_i, \mathsf{driver} \rangle, \langle \mathsf{wifi}, \mathsf{log}, \mathsf{car}_i, \mathsf{loc} \rangle$
$\qquad \mid i = 1, .., n\}$

$\hat{\mathsf{R}}.5$: $\{\langle \mathsf{ok}\rangle, \langle \mathsf{crit}\rangle\}$ $\hat{\mathsf{R}}.6$: $\{\langle \mathsf{crit}\rangle\}$ $\hat{\mathsf{R}}.9$: $\{\langle \mathsf{car}_i, \mathsf{loc}\rangle\}$ $\hat{\mathsf{R}}.10$: $\{\langle \mathsf{car}_i, \mathsf{loc}\rangle\}$
$\hat{\mathsf{R}}.11$: $\{\langle \mathsf{car}_i, \mathsf{loc}\rangle\}$ $\hat{\mathsf{R}}.12$: $\{\langle \mathsf{car}_i, \mathsf{loc}\rangle\}$ $\hat{\mathsf{R}}.15$: $\{\langle \mathsf{car}_i, \mathsf{driver}\rangle\}$
$\hat{\mathsf{R}}.16$: $\{\langle \mathsf{car}_i, \mathsf{driver}\rangle\}$ $\hat{\mathsf{R}}.17$: $\{\langle \mathsf{car}_i, \mathsf{driver}, \mathsf{loc}\rangle\}$ $\hat{\mathsf{R}}.19$: $\{\langle \mathsf{car}_i, \mathsf{loc}\rangle\}$
$\hat{\mathsf{R}}.21$: $\{\langle \mathsf{car}_i, \mathsf{driver}\rangle\}$ $\hat{\mathsf{R}}.23$: $\{\langle \mathsf{log}, \mathsf{car}_i, \mathsf{loc}\rangle, \langle \mathsf{emergency}, \mathsf{car}_i, \mathsf{driver}\rangle\}$

For all labels $\ell \in \{1, 2, 3, 4, 7, 8, 13, 14, 18, 20, 22\}$ we take $\hat{\mathsf{R}}.\ell = \{\epsilon\}$. For brevity, we left out the condition $i = 1, .., n$, when stating the $\hat{\mathsf{R}}.\ell$ sets.

As stated in the introduction, we see from $\hat{\mathsf{K}}$ that only car and driver identity are communicated over the emergency channel and that messages sent over log only contain car and position information. Moreover, information from different cars is not mixed up. This can be inferred regardless of the number of cars involved, which would be impossible given a non-relational analysis. If we changed the specification of the black box to *separately* send car and driver information, then our analysis would detect the (real) error, that car and driver information from different cars may be mixed up in the multiplexer.

4 Properties of the Analysis

4.1 Correctness

The correctness of the analysis is formulated in terms of a *correctness predicate* which is shown invariant under subject reduction in Theorem 1. In contrast, mere analysability is not preserved under subject reduction (c.f. Appendix A). The correctness predicate is defined in Definition 1 and relates a process syntactically to the process initially analysed thus taking care of the implicit substitutions prevalent in standard reduction semantics.

In the following we will use small Greek letters to denote input, output, and match prefixes. Moreover, we shall assume that $P_\star$ is a uniquely labelled process, and we shall fix $\mathsf{L} = \mathcal{L}_\epsilon[\![P_\star]\!]$ and $(\mathsf{F}, \mathsf{E}) = \mathcal{F}[\![P_\star]\!]$ as information derived from $P_\star$. Additionally, assume a subexpression $\alpha^\ell.P'$ of $P_\star$, an analysis result $\hat{\mathsf{R}}, \hat{\mathsf{K}} \vdash_{\mathsf{L},\mathsf{F}} P_\star$ and an element $\bar{w} \in \hat{\mathsf{R}}.\ell$. We define the instantiation of $\alpha^\ell.P'$ with $\bar{w}$, written $\alpha^\ell.P'[\bar{w}]$ to be the process[1]

$$\alpha^\ell.P'[\Pi_{u_r @\mathsf{L}.\ell}(\bar{w})/u_r] \cdots [\Pi_{u_1 @\mathsf{L}.\ell}(\bar{w})/u_1]$$

where $u_1, \ldots, u_r$ are the variables in $\mathsf{L}.\ell$. We define the correctness predicate for a process Q as follows.

Definition 1 (Correctness Predicate). *Correctness predicate* $\hat{\mathsf{R}}, \hat{\mathsf{K}} \models^{P_\star} Q$ *holds if and only if:*

1. $\hat{\mathsf{R}}, \hat{\mathsf{K}} \vdash_{\mathsf{L},\mathsf{F}} P_\star$

---

[1] The instantiation applies the cumulative effect of all implicit substitutions $[\Pi_{u_r @\mathsf{L}.\ell}(\bar{w})/u_r] \cdots [\Pi_{u_1 @\mathsf{L}.\ell}(\bar{w})/u_1]$ that have taken place during reduction—hence unlike the approaches of Venet [16] and Feret [5] we do not need to modify the standard reduction semantics to use explicit substitutions (nor to rely on a customised version of the semantics).

2. $\forall \ell \in \mathsf{E} : \epsilon \in \hat{\mathsf{R}}.\ell$
3. For all $\beta^\ell.Q'$ exposed in Q, there exists a subexpression $\alpha^\ell.P'$ of $P_\star$ and a $\bar{w} \in \hat{\mathsf{R}}.\ell$, such that $\hat{\mathsf{R}}, \hat{\mathsf{K}} \vdash_{\mathsf{L,F}} \alpha^\ell.P'$ and $\alpha^\ell.P'[\bar{w}] \equiv \beta^\ell.Q'$.

First, we observe some auxiliary properties, whose proofs are omitted. Note that conditions (1) and (2) of Definition 1 imply (3) when reasoning about $P_\star$.

Lemma 1 (Initial Process). *For all processes $P_\star$ with* L, F, *and* E *as above we have: If $\hat{\mathsf{R}}, \hat{\mathsf{K}} \vdash_{\mathsf{L,F}} P_\star$ and $\epsilon \in \hat{\mathsf{R}}.\ell$ for all $\ell \in \mathsf{E}$, then $\hat{\mathsf{R}}, \hat{\mathsf{K}} \models^{P_\star} P_\star$.*

Together with Theorem 1, which states the invariance of the correctness predicate under the reduction relation, this lemma can be used to show that any process derived from the initial process $P_\star$ by the transitive closure of the reduction relation is structurally congruent to a subprocess P' of $P_\star$, where each variable of P' is substituted by one name predicted by the analysis. This constitutes the *correctness of our relational analysis*.

Before getting to the correctness theorem, we state some lemmas about exposed subexpressions with respect to structural congruence and valid analysis results.

Lemma 2. *Let $P \equiv Q$ be two processes. For all $\alpha^\ell.P'$ exposed in P, there exists a $\beta^\ell.Q'$ exposed in Q such that $\alpha^\ell.P' \equiv \beta^\ell.Q'$.*

Lemma 3. *If $\alpha^\ell.P'$ is exposed in P and $\hat{\mathsf{R}}, \hat{\mathsf{K}} \vdash_{\mathsf{L,F}} P$, then $\hat{\mathsf{R}}, \hat{\mathsf{K}} \vdash_{\mathsf{L,F}} \alpha^\ell.P'$.*

The validity of the correctness predicate is invariant under structural congruence as formalised by the following lemma.

Lemma 4. *Let $P_\star$, Q, and R be processes. If $Q \equiv R$ and $\hat{\mathsf{R}}, \hat{\mathsf{K}} \models^{P_\star} Q$, then $\hat{\mathsf{R}}, \hat{\mathsf{K}} \models^{P_\star} R$.*

Proof. Let $\gamma^\ell.R'$ be exposed in R. As $Q \equiv R$, there exists $\beta^\ell.Q'$ exposed in Q. As $\hat{\mathsf{R}}, \hat{\mathsf{K}} \models^{P_\star} Q$, we know that there exists a $\alpha^\ell.P'$ subexpression of $P_\star$ and a $\bar{w} \in \hat{\mathsf{R}}.\ell$ such that $\hat{\mathsf{R}}, \hat{\mathsf{K}} \vdash_{\mathsf{L,F}} \alpha^\ell.P'$ and $\alpha^\ell.P'[\bar{w}] \equiv \beta^\ell.Q'$. By transitivity of $\equiv$, we obtain $\alpha^\ell.P'[\bar{w}] \equiv \gamma^\ell.R'$ and thus $\hat{\mathsf{R}}, \hat{\mathsf{K}} \models^{P_\star} R$. This concludes the proof of Lemma 4.

The validity of the correctness predicate is preserved under reduction as formalised by the following theorem.

Theorem 1 (Subject Reduction). *Let $P_\star$ be a process. If $Q \to R$ and $\hat{\mathsf{R}}, \hat{\mathsf{K}} \models^{P_\star} Q$ then $\hat{\mathsf{R}}, \hat{\mathsf{K}} \models^{P_\star} R$.*

Proof. The proof is by induction on the inference of $Q \to R$. First consider the rule (COM)

$$m\langle \bar{n}\bar{p} \rangle^{\ell_0}.Q_0 \mid m(\bar{n}; \bar{u})^{\ell_1}.Q_1 \to Q_0 \mid Q_1[\bar{p}/\bar{u}]$$

and assume that there exists $\alpha_0^{\ell_0}.P_0$, $\alpha_1^{\ell_1}.P_1$ subprocesses of $P_\star$ as well as $\bar{w}_i \in \hat{\mathsf{R}}.\ell_i$ for $i = 0, 1$ such that

$$\hat{\mathsf{R}}, \hat{\mathsf{K}} \vdash_{\mathsf{L,F}} \alpha_0^{\ell_0}.P_0 \tag{1}$$

$$\hat{R}, \hat{K} \vdash_{\mathsf{L},\mathsf{F}} \alpha_1^{\ell_1}.P_1 \tag{2}$$

$$(\alpha_0^{l_0}.P_0)[\bar{w}_0] \equiv m\langle \bar{n}\bar{p}\rangle^{\ell_0}.Q_0 \tag{3}$$

$$(\alpha_1^{l_1}.P_1)[\bar{w}_1] \equiv m(\bar{n}; \bar{u})^{\ell_1}.Q_1 \tag{4}$$

We need to prove that for all $\beta^\ell.Q'$ exposed in $Q_0 \mid Q_1[\bar{p}/\bar{u}]$, there exists a $\alpha^\ell.P'$ subexpression of $P_\star$ and a $\bar{w} \in \hat{R}.\ell$, such that (a) $\hat{R}, \hat{K} \vdash_{\mathsf{L},\mathsf{F}} \alpha^\ell.P'$ and (b) $\alpha^\ell.P'[\bar{w}] \equiv \beta^\ell.Q'$.

Case 1. Let $\beta^\ell.Q'$ be exposed in Q_0 and let $\alpha_0^{l_0} = x_0\langle \bar{y}_0 \bar{z}_0\rangle$. By the definition of F, we get

$$\ell \in \mathsf{F}.\ell_0 \tag{5}$$

From (3) we obtain $\Pi_{x_0 \bar{y}_0 \bar{z}_0 @ \mathsf{L}.\ell_0}(\bar{w}_0) = m\bar{n}\bar{p}$. Together with (1), the definition of (ROUT), and (5) this yields:

$$m\bar{n}\bar{p} \in \hat{K} \tag{6}$$

$$\hat{R}, \hat{K} \vdash_{\mathsf{L},\mathsf{F}} P_0 \tag{7}$$

$$\bar{w}_0 \in \hat{R}.\ell \tag{8}$$

Choose $\bar{w} = \bar{w}_0$. Requirement (a) is then proven using (7) with Lemma 3. Requirement (b) follows from (3), (8) using Lemma 2.

Case 2. Let $\beta^\ell.Q'$ be exposed in $Q_1[\bar{p}/\bar{u}]$ and let $\alpha_1^{l_1} = x_1(\bar{y}_1; \bar{u})^{\ell_1}$. Let $\beta^\ell.Q'$ be exposed in $Q_1[\bar{p}/\bar{u}]$ implying

$$\ell \in \mathsf{F}.\ell_1 \tag{9}$$

From (4) we obtain $\Pi_{x_1 \bar{y}_1 @ \mathsf{L}.\ell_1}(\bar{w}_1) = m\bar{n}$. Using this fact together with (9) and (6) we can apply rule (RIN) and obtain:

$$\bar{w}_1 \bar{p} \in \hat{R}.\ell \tag{10}$$

$$\hat{R}, \hat{K} \vdash_{\mathsf{L},\mathsf{F}} P_1 \tag{11}$$

We choose $\bar{w} = \bar{w}_1 \bar{p}$ which adheres to requirement (b) by (10). Requirement (a) is clear using Lemma 3 and (11). For requirement (b), we deduce $P_1[\bar{w}_1] \equiv Q_1$ from (4). By the definition of F, we obtain $\mathsf{L}.\ell = (\mathsf{L}.\ell_1)\bar{u}$. Together with the definition of instantiating an expression with an analysis result we get $P_1[\bar{w}] \equiv Q_1[\bar{p}/\bar{u}]$. An application of Lemma 2 to this concludes the proof of the case for (COM).

We shall now consider the application of the rule (MATCH), that is,

$$[n = n]^{\ell_0}.Q_0 \rightarrow Q_0$$

We know that there exists $[x_0 = y_0]^{\ell_0}.P_0$ subexpression of $P_\star$ and $\bar{w}_0 \in \hat{R}.\ell_0$ such that

$$\hat{R}, \hat{K} \vdash_{\mathsf{L},\mathsf{F}} [x_0 = y_0]^{\ell_0}.P_0 \tag{12}$$

$$([x_0 = y_0]^{\ell_0}.P_0)[\bar{w}_0] \equiv [n = n]^{\ell_0}.Q_0 \tag{13}$$

Let $\beta^\ell.Q'$ be exposed in Q_0. We need to show that there exists a $\bar{w} \in \hat{R}.\ell$ and a subexpression $\alpha^\ell.P'$ of $P_\star$ such that (c) $\hat{R}, \hat{K} \vdash_{L,F} \alpha^\ell.P'$ and (d) $(\alpha^\ell.P')[\bar{w}] \equiv \beta^\ell.Q'$. As $\beta^\ell.Q'$ is exposed in Q_0, we deduce

$$\ell \in F.\ell_0 \tag{14}$$

By (13), we may deduce

$$\Pi_{x_0 @ \ell_0}(\bar{w}_0) = \Pi_{y_0 @ \ell_0}(\bar{w}_0) \tag{15}$$
$$P_0[\bar{w}_0] \equiv Q_0 \tag{16}$$

We can apply rule (RMATCH) with (15), (14), and (12) to obtain $\bar{w}_0 \in \hat{R}.\ell$ and $\hat{R}, \hat{K} \vdash_{L,F} P_0$. If we choose $\bar{w} = \bar{w}_0$, we obtain (c) and (d) from $\hat{R}, \hat{K} \vdash_{L,F} P_0$ and (16) using Lemma 3 and Lemma 2.

The result for an application of (VAR) is an immediate consequence of the induction hypothesis and Lemma 4. Let us now consider rule (PAR), that is,

$$\frac{Q \to Q'}{Q \mid R \to Q' \mid R}$$

and assume $\hat{R}, \hat{K} \models^{P_\star} Q \mid R$. Obviously, this implies $\hat{R}, \hat{K} \models^{P_\star} Q$ and $\hat{R}, \hat{K} \models^{P_\star} R$ separately. By the induction hypothesis, we obtain $\hat{R}, \hat{K} \models^{P_\star} Q'$ and hence $\hat{R}, \hat{K} \models^{P_\star} Q' \mid R$. This argumentation can be applied analogously to rule (RES), because the exposed expressions of $(\nu n)Q$ are just those of Q. Also, the case (CHO) is completely analogous. This concludes the proof of Theorem 1.

4.2   Implementation

We have implemented our relational analysis in the Succinct Solver [13], which is able to efficiently compute the stable model of an expressive fragment of predicate logic. From the analysis specification for a program $P_\star$, we generate a clause $\varphi_{P_\star}$ such that $\hat{R}, \hat{K} \vdash_{L,F} P_\star$ if and only if $\vdash \varphi_{P_\star}$. Each model of the clause corresponds to an analysis solution. The generated clauses belong to the class of Alternation-free Least Fixpoint Logic (ALFP) described in [15]. Proposition 1 of [15] states that the set of all solutions of an ALFP clause always has a least element corresponding to the least analysis result we aim for. The Succinct Solver computes this least solution.

Example 3. Consider the specification of the Black Box in Table 1:

$$! \, \text{status}(\text{car}_i; x)^4.[x = \text{crit}]^5. \, ! \, \text{alarm}\langle \text{car}_i \rangle^6$$

The clause generated for this excerpt according to rules (RIN), (RMATCH) and (ROUT) will essentially look as follows:

$$\exists u.\hat{K}(\text{status}, \text{car}_i, u) \Rightarrow ($$
$$(\forall u.\hat{K}(\text{status}, \text{car}_i, u) \Rightarrow \hat{R}.5(u)) \wedge$$
$$\exists u'.(\hat{R}.5(u') \wedge u' = \text{crit}) \Rightarrow ($$
$$(\forall u'.\hat{R}.5(u) \wedge u' = \text{crit} \Rightarrow \hat{R}.6(u')) \wedge$$
$$\hat{K}(\text{alarm}, \text{car}_i)))$$

Each (canonical) name corresponds to a constant in the clause. For each label ℓ in the program there is a $|\,\mathsf{L}.\ell\,|$-ary relation $\hat{\mathsf{R}}.\ell$. Furthermore, for each message length m, there is an $m + 1$-ary relation $\hat{\mathsf{K}}$. The existential parts of the clause take care of the various reachability conditions of the form $X \neq \emptyset$, whereas the universal parts take care of letting the information gathered in X flow to the right places. As an aid to readability we have assumed that $\hat{\mathsf{R}}.4 = \{\epsilon\}$ thus not generated any formula involving $\hat{\mathsf{R}}.4$.

4.3   Complexity

There are mainly three quantities determining the complexity of solving the ALFP clause that is generated for a program $P_\star$. First, the size n of $P_\star$; second, the maximal nesting depth of variables bounded by $m = \max_{\ell \in \mathbf{Lab}} |\,\mathsf{L}.\ell\,|$; third, the length of messages bounded by $k = \max_{x\langle \bar{y} \rangle \in P_\star} |\,\bar{y}\,|$. Quantities m and k determine the maximal arity of relations, whereas n bounds the size of the universe over which the clause is evaluated. The maximal nesting depth of quantifiers is bounded by m. Altogether, we can apply Proposition 1 of [14], which itself makes use of the algorithm presented in [4], to obtain a complexity bound of $\mathcal{O}(n^{3+k+m})$ for solving the clause generated from $P_\star$.

This complexity may be exponential in the worst-case. However, the worst-case is only realised for programs, where the number of sequenced input prefixes (each one binding new variables) and/or the arity of sent tuples grows linearly with the program. In contrast, we may observe that for typical programs, where processes often consist of reception-processing-reply, m and k may be considered constants rendering the complexity polynomial in the size of the program (with a rather large exponent, though). For the running example and other examples of similar size, the least solution to the analysis problem could be computed in less than a second.

5   Conclusion

The proper modelling of services for global computing necessitates the ability to model services in process algebras without using primitives (like the dynamic creation of very flexible channels as in the π-calculus) that have no direct counterpart in actual systems. We used a running example based on a multiplexing device part of the accident service used in the automotive case study of the SEN-SORIA EU-project. This increases the difficulty of validating that the models enjoy the desired properties and at the same time calls for the use of automatic analysis techniques to deal with the scalability issues of "realistic" models.

In this paper we have developed a new relational analysis for a π-calculus extended with pattern matching. The core benefit of a relational analysis (in contrast to an independent attribute analysis) is that sets of tuples of names being received at the same time are tracked (in contrast to tuples of sets). If a process contains output operations $a\langle b, b \rangle$ and $a\langle c, c \rangle$ then a relational analysis is able to show the absence of the output operations $a\langle b, c \rangle$ and $a\langle c, b \rangle$—while an independent attribute analysis is not.

We have shown that semantic correctness amounts to the invariance of a correctness predicate under subject reduction. Furthermore, we have shown that the analysis has polynomial time complexity on realistic programs. We have used the analysis to validate the correct delivery of services in our running example.

In future work we plan to transfer the analysis technology to the richer set of process calculi being developed in the SENSORIA EU-project for describing the behaviour of services. Examples are likely to include variations of the constructs presented in [8,6,3] and [7]. For that work, we will benefit from the fact that we rely on full standard syntax and reduction semantics of π, on which [8,6,3,7] are all based. We also plan to investigate the feasibility of using annotations to indicate which binding occurrences demand a relational treatment. This could lead to developing a mixed independent-attribute and relational analysis. The advantage of such an analysis would be that essentially cubic-time [12] methods for independent-attribute analyses could be used except for those cases where a truly relational analysis (of higher time complexity) is needed. Finally, we plan to incorporate techniques that can tell distinct recursive instances, e.g. several cars having an accident at the same time, apart, i.e., allow the analysis to find out that the SOS messages contain the correct position of each car (and not the position of another car).

Acknowledgements. The design of the pπ calculus was part of a group effort by the following members of the Language Based Technology research group at their retreat in Schloss Dagstuhl: C. R. Nielsen, F. Nielson, H. Pilegaard, C. Probst, H. Riis Nielson, T. Tolstrup, and Y. Zhang.

References

1. Bodei, C., Degano, P., Nielson, F., Nielson, H.R.: Static analysis for the π-calculus with applications to security. Information and Computation 168, 68–92 (2001)
2. Bodei, C., Buchholtz, M., Degano, P., Nielson, F., Nielson, H.R.: Static validation of security protocols. J. Comput. Secur. 13(3), 347–390 (2005)
3. Boreale, M., Bruni, R., Caires, L., De Nicola, R., Lanese, I., Loreti, M., Martins, F., Montanari, U., Ravara, A., Sangiorgi, D., Vasconcelos, V., Zavattaro, G.: SCC: A Service Centered Calculus. In: Bravetti, M., Núñez, M., Zavattaro, G. (eds.) WS-FM 2006. LNCS, vol. 4184, pp. 38–57. Springer, Heidelberg (2006)
4. Dowling, W.F., Gallier, J.H.: Linear-time algorithms for testing the satisfiability of propositional horn formulae. J. Log. Program. 1(3), 267–284 (1984)
5. Feret, J.: Dependency analysis of mobile systems. In: Le Métayer, D. (ed.) ESOP 2002 and ETAPS 2002. LNCS, vol. 2305, pp. 314–330. Springer, Heidelberg (2002)
6. Guidi, C., Lucchi, R., Gorrieri, R., Busi, N., Zavattaro, G.: A calculus for service oriented computing. In: Dan, A., Lamersdorf, W. (eds.) ICSOC 2006. LNCS, vol. 4294, pp. 327–338. Springer, Heidelberg (2006)
7. Hansen, R.R., Probst, C.W., Nielson, F.: Sandboxing in myklaim. In: Availability, Reliability and Security (ARES), pp. 174–181. IEEE Computer Society, Los Alamitos (2006)
8. Lapadula, A., Pugliese, R., Tiezzi, F.: A calculus for orchestration of web services. In: De Nicola, R. (ed.) ESOP 2007. LNCS, vol. 4421, Springer, Heidelberg (2007)

9. Milner, R.: The polyadic pi-calculus: A tutorial. In: Bauer, F.L., Brauer, W., Schwichtenberg, H. (eds.) Logic and Algebra of Specification, pp. 203–246. Springer, Heidelberg (1993)
10. Milner, R.: Communicating and Mobile Systems: The Pi-Calculus. Cambridge University Press, Cambridge (1999)
11. Nielson, F., Nielson, H.R., Hankin, C.L.: Principles of Program Analysis. Springer, Heidelberg (1999) (second printing, 2005)
12. Nielson, F., Nielson, H.R., Seidl, H.: Cryptographic analysis in cubic time. Electronic Notes of Theoretical Computer Science 62, 7–23 (2002)
13. Nielson, F., Nielson, H.R., Sun, H., Buchholtz, M., Hansen, R.R., Pilegaard, H., Seidl, H.: The Succinct Solver Suite. In: Jensen, K., Podelski, A. (eds.) TACAS 2004. LNCS, vol. 2988, pp. 251–265. Springer, Heidelberg (2004)
14. Nielson, F., Seidl, H.: Control-flow analysis in cubic time. In: Sands, D. (ed.) ESOP 2001 and ETAPS 2001. LNCS, vol. 2028, pp. 252–268. Springer, Heidelberg (2001)
15. Nielson, F., Seidl, H., Nielson, H.R.: A succinct solver for ALFP. Nord. J. Comput. 9(4), 335–372 (2002)
16. Venet, A.: Automatic determination of communication topologies in mobile systems. In: Levi, G. (ed.) SAS 1998. LNCS, vol. 1503, pp. 152–167. Springer, Heidelberg (1998)

A   Analysability and Subject Reduction

We have shown the correctness of our analysis in terms of a subject reduction result in Theorem 1. In order to obtain invariance under subject reduction, a correctness predicate needed to take care of the implicit substitution prevalent in standard reduction semantics. This is indeed necessary, because mere analysability is *not preserved* by subject reduction:

Proposition 1. *If $P \to Q$ and $\hat{R}, \hat{K} \vdash_{L,F} P$ then $\hat{R}, \hat{K} \vdash_{L,F} Q$ does not hold necessarily.*

To see this consider the following excerpt from our running example presented in Table 1. The following computation step of the operational semantics is due to an application of rule (COM) describing the reception of a critical message by the black box process.

$$ \ldots \mid \mathsf{status}(car_i; x)^4.[x = \mathsf{crit}]^5. \; ! \; \mathsf{alarm}\langle car_i \rangle^6 \; \to \; [\mathsf{crit} = \mathsf{crit}]^5. \; ! \; \mathsf{alarm}\langle car_i \rangle^6 $$

As shown above in Example 2, an acceptable analysis result $(\hat{R}, \hat{K})$ for the process before the application of (COM) comprises $\hat{R}.5 = \{\langle \mathsf{ok} \rangle, \langle \mathsf{crit} \rangle\}$ and $\hat{R}.6 = \{\langle \mathsf{crit} \rangle\}$. However, we can now observe that this *cannot* be part of an acceptable analysis result for the derived process. The clause for matching, (RMATCH), will require $\hat{R}.5 \subseteq \hat{R}.6$ since the test will hold for all the bindings of the variables of $\hat{R}.5$. But this does not hold and hence we cannot have a subject reduction result of the form suggested above.

The stronger correctness predicate of Definition 1 does hold for the derived process:

$$ \hat{R}, \hat{K} \models^{P_{acc}} [\mathsf{crit} = \mathsf{crit}]^5. \; ! \; \mathsf{alarm}\langle car_i \rangle^6 $$

This is proven by choosing $\bar{w} \in \hat{R}.5$ of Definition 1 to be $\langle \mathsf{crit} \rangle$.

Logical Networks: Towards Foundations for Programmable Overlay Networks and Overlay Computing Systems

Luigi Liquori and Michel Cosnard

INRIA, France
{Luigi.Liquori,Michel.Cosnard}@inria.fr

Abstract. We propose and discuss foundations for *programmable overlay networks* and *overlay computing systems*. Such overlays are built over a large number of distributed *computational individuals*, virtually organized in *colonies*, and ruled by a leader (*broker*) who is elected or imposed by system administrators. Every individual asks the broker to log in the colony by declaring the resources that can be offered (with variable guarantees). Once logged in, an individual can ask the broker for other resources. Colonies can recursively be considered as *evolved individuals* who can log in an outermost colony governed by another (super)-broker. Communications and routing intra-colonies goes through a broker-2-broker PKI-based negotiation. Every broker routes intra- and inter- *service requests* by filtering its *resource routing table*, and then by forwarding the request first inside its colony, and second outside, via the proper super-broker (thus applying an *endogenous-first-estrogen-last* strategy). Theoretically, queries are formulæ in first-order logic equipped with a small program used to *orchestrate* and *synchronize* atomic formulæ. When the client individual receives notification of all (or part of) the requested resources, then the real resource exchange is performed directly by the server(s) individuals, without any further mediation of the broker, in a pure peer-to-peer fashion. The proposed overlay promotes an *intermittent* participation in the colony, since peers can appear, disappear, and organize themselves dynamically. This implies that the routing process may lead to *failures*, because some individuals have quit, or are temporarily unavailable, or they were logged out *manu militari* by the broker due to their poor performance or greediness. We design, validate through simulation, and implement these foundations in a programmable overlay computer system, called Arigatoni.

"Computer is moving on the edge of the Network..."

[Jan Bosch, Nokia Labs, Keynote ARCS, LNCS 4415, 2007]

1 Introduction

The explosive growth of the Internet gives rise to the possibility of designing large *overlay networks* and *virtual organizations* consisting of Internet-connected

G. Barthe and C. Fournet (Eds.): TGC 2007, LNCS 4912, pp. 90–107, 2008.

computers units, able to provide a rich functionality of services that makes use of aggregated computational power, storage, information resources, etc. We would like to start this paper with the standard definition of *Computer System* (we emphasize some text using underline).

Definition 1 (Computer System)
A computer system is composed by a computer hardware and a computer software.

- *A Computer Hardware is the physical part of a computer, including the digital circuitry, as distinguished from the computer software that executes within the hardware. The hardware of a computer is infrequently changed, in comparison with software and data.*
- *A Computer Software is composed by three parts, namely, system software, program software, and application software.*
  - *The System Software helps run the computer hardware and computer system. Examples are operating systems (OS), device drivers, diagnostic tools, servers, windowing systems...*
  - *The Program Software usually provides tools to assist a programmer in writing computer programs and software using different programming languages. Examples are text editors, compilers, interpreters, linkers, debuggers for general purpose languages...*
  - *The Application Software allows end users to accomplish one or more specific (non computer related) tasks industrial automation, business software, educational software, medical software, databases, computer games...*

Starting from the previous basic skeleton definition, we elaborate our vision of what an *Overlay Computer System* is. The reader can focus on the tiny but crucial differences between the above and below definitions.

Definition 2 (Overlay Computer System)
An overlay computer system is composed by an overlay computer hardware and an overlay computer software.

- *An Overlay Computer Hardware is the physical part of an overlay computer, including the digital circuitry, as distinguished from the overlay computer software that executes within the hardware. The hardware of an overlay computer changes frequently and it is distributed in space and in time. Hardware is organized in a network of collaborative computing individuals connected via* IP *or ad-hoc networks; hardware must be negotiated before being used.*
- *An Overlay Computer Software is composed by three parts, namely, overlay system software, overlay program software, and overlay application software.*
  - *The Overlay System Software helps run the overlay computer hardware and overlay computer system. Examples are network middlewares playing as a distributed operating systems(dOS), resource discovery protocols, virtual intermittent protocols, security protocols, reputation protocols...*
  - *The Overlay Program Software usually provides tools to assist a programmer in writing overlay computer programs and software using different overlay programming languages. Examples are compilers, interpreters, linkers, debuggers for workflow-, coordination-, and query-languages.*

- *The Overlay Application Software allows end users to accomplish one or more specific (non-computer related) tasks industrial automation, business software, educational software, medical software, databases, and computer games... Those class of applications deals with computational power (Grid), file and storage retrieval (P2P), web services (Web2.0), band-services (VoIP), computation migrations...*

The Arigatoni overlay network computer, designed and developed since 2006 at INRIA, is a structured multi-layer overlay network which provides resource discovery with variable guarantees in a virtual organization where peers can appear, disappear, and organize themselves dynamically. Arigatoni is mainly concerned with how and where resources are declared and discovered in the overlay, allowing agent computers to make secure use of agent aggregated computational power, storage, information resources etc. We anticipate, in a nutshell, the key functional units of Arigatoni (discussed in details later on).

- An *Agent Computer (AC)* is the basic computational entity of the overlay: it is typically a device, like a PDA, a laptop, a PC, or smaller devices, connected through IP or other *ad hoc* communication protocols in different fashions (wired, wireless, etc.).
- An *Agent Broker (AB)* is devoted to (un)subscribing ACs, to receiving service queries from clients, to contacting and negotiating with potential servers, to authenticating clients and servers, and to routing requests. An AB is the leader of the colony of the ACs and of the sub-colonies that is manages. Intra-colony communication is initiated through the leader AB, while inter-colonies communication is initiated through a chain of (PKI-based) AB-2-AB message exchanges. The rationale ensuring scalability is that every request is handled first inside its colony, and then forwarded through the proper super-leader (thus applying an *endogenous-first-estrogen-last* strategy). In both cases, when a client AC receives an acknowledgment of a service request from the direct leader AB, then the AC is served directly by the server(s), *i.e.* without a further mediation of the AB, in a pure P2P fashion. Logically, an AC can be seen as a *collapsed colony*, or a *broker managing itself*.
- An *Agent Router (AR)* is the basic unit close to ACs and ABs that is devoted to sending and receiving packets of the resource discovery and the virtual intermittent protocols (see below) and to forwarding the "payload" to the units which are connected with this router. The connection AB-AR-AC is ensured via a suitable API.

The total decoupling between peers in *space* (peers do not know other peers' locations), *time* (peers do not participate in the interaction at the same time), *synchronization* (peers can issue service requests and do something else, or may be doing something else when being asked for services), and *encapsulation* (peers do not know each other) are key features of Arigatoni's scalability.

Summarizing, the main challenges in Arigatoni lie in the management of an overlay network with a dynamic topology, the routing of queries, and the discovery of resources in the overlay. In particular, resource discovery is a non-trivial problem for large distributed systems featuring a discontinuous amount of resources offered by agent computers and their intermittent participation in the overlay. For more technical details on the Arigatoni overlay network, the interested reader can have a look on [CLC07b, CCL06, CLC07a, CCL08].

Therefore, the main contributions of this paper are:

- to provide adequate notions and definitions of a programmable overlay network computer;
- on the basis of these definitions, to propose a precise architecture of a programmable network computer;
- to provide insight of the architecture by putting emphasis on technical problems, security, social, implementations, and related issues;
- to summarize and collect previous efforts by the authors on Arigatoni into one reference paper easy to read.

1.1 Virtual Organizations

Computational units in Arigatoni are organized in *Colonies*. A colony is a simple virtual organization composed by exactly one *leader*, offering some broker-like services, and some set of *individuals*. Individuals are agent computers, or sub-colonies. Every colony has *exactly* one leader and at least one individual (the leader itself), and a colony contains only individuals.

Agent computers communicate by first registering to the colony and then by asking and offering services. The leader agent broker analyzes service requests/responses, coming from its own colony or arriving from a surrounding colony, and routes requests/responses to other individuals. Individuals get in touch with each other without any further intervention from the system, in a P2P fashion. Peers' coordination is achieved by a simple program written in an orchestration/business language *à la* BPEL [IBM], or JOpera [Pau].

Symmetrically, the leader of a colony can arbitrarily unregister an individual from its colony, *e.g.*, because of its bad performance when dealing with some requests or because of its high number of "embarrassing" requests for the colony. This strategy, reminiscent of the Roman *do ut des*, is nowadays called, in Game Theory, Rapoport's *tit-for-tat* strategy [Rap63] of cooperation based on reciprocity. Tit-for-tat is commonly used in economics, social sciences, and it has been implemented by a computer program as a winning strategy in a chess-play challenge against humans (see also the well known *prisoner dilemma*). In computer science, the tit-for-tat strategy is the stability (*i.e.* balanced uploads and downloads) policy of the Bittorrent P2P protocol [Bit].

Once an agent computer has issued a request for some services, the system finds some agent computers (or, recursively, some sub-colonies) that can offer the resources needed, and communicates their identities to the (client) agent computer as soon as they are found.

The model also offers some mechanisms to dynamically adapt to *dynamic topology changes* of the overlay network, by allowing an individual (agent computer or sub-colony) to login/logout in/from a colony. This essentially means that the process of routing request/responses may lead to failure, because some individuals logged out or because they are temporarily unavailable (recall that individuals are not slaves). This may also lead to temporary denials of service or, more drastically, to the complete "delogging" of an individual from a given colony in the case where the former does not provide enough services to the latter.

Trees vs. graphs: a conflict without a cause. In the first versions of Arigatoni, the network topology was tree- or forest-based. But since AC are not slaves, multiple registrations are in principle possible and unavoidable. This weaves the network topology to a *dynamic graph*. As an immediate consequence, Arigatoni's protocols deal with multiple registrations of the same individual in different colonies, with the natural consequence of resource overbooking, routing table update loops, and resource discovery loops (when a resource request comes back to the individual that generates the request itself), see [LC07].

As an example of resource overbooking, suppose an AC registers to two colonies, by declaring and offering the same resource S twice, *i.e.* once for each colony. This phenomenon is well known in the telecommunications industry, such as in the "frame-relay" world. For the record, overbooking in telecommunications means that a telephone company has sold access to too many customers which basically flood the telephone company lines, resulting in an inability for some customers to use what they purchased. Other examples of overbooking can be found in the domain of transportation and hotel reservations.

1.2   User Application Independence, Parametricity, Universality

Dealing only with resource discovery has one important advantage: the complete generality and independence of any offered and requested resource. Thus, Arigatoni can fit with various scenarios in the agent computing arena, from classical P2P applications, like file- or band-sharing, to more sophisticated Grid applications, like remote and distributed big (and small) computations, until possible, futuristic *migration computations*, *i.e.* transfer of a non completed local run in another agent computer, the latter being useful in case of catastrophic scenarios, like fire, terrorist attack, earthquake, etc., in the vein of agent programming languages *à la* Obliq [Car95] or Telescript [Whi94]. We could envisage at least the following scenarios to be a tight fit for our model (list not exhaustive):

- Ask for computational power (*i.e.* the Grid);
- Ask for memory space (*i.e.* distributed storage);
- Ask for bandwidth (*i.e.* VoIP);
- Ask for a distributed file retrieving (*i.e.* standard P2P applications);
- Ask for a (possibly) distributed web service (*i.e.* query *à la* Google or any service available via web-oriented protocols);
- Orchestration of a distributed execution of an algorithm;
- Ask for a computation migration (*i.e.* transfer one partial run in another agent computer, saving the partial results;

- Ask for a *human computer interaction* (the human playing the role of an individual);
- ...

Thus, Arigatoni is *parametric* or *universal* in the sense of universal Turing machine, or *generic* as the von Neumann computer architecture. In one sentence: "Arigatoni is the first fully programmable overlay network computer".

2   Functional Units and Protocols in Arigatoni

2.1   Functional Units

*The Agent Computer (*AC*).* This unit can be, *e.g.*, a cheap computer device composed by a small RAM-ROM-HD memory capacity, a modest CPU, a ≤ 40 keystrokes keyboard (or touchscreen), a tiny screen (≤ 4 inch), an IP or *ad hoc* connection (via DHCP, BLUETOOTH, WIFI, WIMAX...), an USB port, and very few programs installed inside (one simple editor, one or two compilers, a mail client, a mini browser...)[1]. Of course an AC can be a supercomputer, or an high performance PC-cluster, a large database server, an high performance visualizer (*e.g.* connected to a virtual reality center), or any particular resource provider, even a *smart-dust*. The operating system (if any) installed in the AC is not important. The computer should be able to work in *local mode* for all the tasks that it could do locally, or in *global mode*, by first registering itself to one or many colonies of the overlay, and then by asking and serving global requests via the colony leaders. In a nutshell, the tasks of an AC are:

- Discover the address of one or many ABs, playing as colony leaders, upon its arrival in a "connected area";
- Register on one or many ABs, so entering *de facto* the Arigatoni's virtual organization;
- Ask and offer some services to others ACs, via the leaders ABs;
- Connect directly with others AC in a P2P fashion, and offer/receive some services. Note that an AC can also be a resource provider. This symmetry is one of the key features of Arigatoni. For security reasons, we assume that all AC come with their proper PKI certificate.

*The Agent Broker (*AB*).* This unit can be, *e.g.*, a computer device made by an high speed CPU, an IP or *ad hoc* connection (via DHCP, BLUETOOTH, WIFI, WIMAX...), an high speed hard-disk with a *resource routing table* to route queries, and an efficient program to match and filter the routing table. The computer should be able to work in *global mode*, by first registering itself in the overlay and then receiving, filtering and dispatching global requests through the network. The tasks of an AB are:

---

[1] Our favorite device actually is the Internet terminal Nokia N810 [Nok].

- Discover the address of another *super*-AB, representing the *super-leader* of the *super-colony*, where the AB colony is embedded. We assume that every AB comes with its proper PKI certificate. The policy to accept or refuse the registration of an individual with a different PKI is left open to the level of security requested by the colony;
- Register/unregister the proper colony on the *leader* AB which manages the super-colony;
- Register/unregister clients and servants AC in its colony, and update the internal resource routing table, accordingly;
- Receive the request of service of the client AC;
- Discover the resources that satisfy an AC request in its local colony, according to its resource routing table;
- Delegate the request to an AB leader of the direct super-colony in case the resource cannot be satisfied in its proper colony. Prior to this, it must register itself (and byproduct its colony) to another super-colony;
- Perform a combination of the above last two actions;
- Deal with all PKI intra- and inter-colony policies;
- Notify, after a fixed *timeout period*, or when all individuals failed to satisfy the delegated request, to the AC client the *denial of service* requested by the AC client;
- Send all the information necessary to make the AC client able to communicate with the AC servants. This notification is encoded using the resource discovery protocol. (Finally, the AC client will directly talk with the ACs servants).

The Agent Router (AR). This unit implements all the low-level overlay network routines, providing access to the underlay network. In a nutshell, an AR is a shared library dynamically linked with an AC or an AB. The AR is devoted to the following tasks:

- Upon the initial start-up of an AC (resp. AB) it helps to register the unit with one or many AB that it knows or discovers;
- Checks the well-formedness and forwards packets of the two Arigatoni's protocols across the overlay toward their destinations;

2.2   The Resource Discovery Protocol (RDP)

Kind of resource discovery. The are mostly three mechanisms of resource discovery in Arigatoni, namely:

- The process of an AB to find and negotiate resources to serve an AC request in its own colony;
- The process of an AC (resp. AB) to discover an AB, upon physical/logical insertion in a colony;

The first discovery is processed by the resource discovery protocol, while the second is processed out of the Arigatoni overlay, using well known network technologies like DHCP [AD97], DNS [GVE00], BLUETOOTH, WIFI, WIMAX...

The current RDP protocol version allows the request for *multiple services* and *service conjunctions*. Adding service conjunctions allows an AC to offer several services at the same time. Multiple services requests can be also asked to an AB; each service is processed sequentially and independently of others. As an example of multiple instances, an AC may ask for three CPUs, *or* one chunk of 10GB of HD, *or* one gcc compiler. As an example of a service conjunction, an AC may ask for another AC offering *at the same time* one CPUs, *and* one chunk of 1GB of RAM, *and* one chunk of 10GB of HD, *and* one gcc compiler. If a request succeeds, then, using a simple orchestration language, the AC client can use all resources offered by the servers ACs.

The RDP protocol proceeds as follows: suppose an AC X registers – using the intermittent protocol VIP presented below – to an AB and declares its availability to offer a service S, while another AC Y, already registered, issues a request for a service S'. Then, the AB looks in its *routing table* and *filters* S' against S. If there exists a solution to this filter equation, then X can provide a resource to Y. For example, the resource S = [CPU=Intel, Time≤10sec] filters against S' = [CPU=Intel, Time≥5sec], with attribute values Intel and Time between 5 and 10 seconds.

2.3   Inside Routing Tables for Resource Discovery

Each AB maintains a *routing table* T locating the *services* that are registered in its colony. The table is updated according to the *dynamic registration and unregistration* of ACs in the overlay; thus, each AB maintains a partition of the data space. When an AC asks for a resource (service request), then the query is *filtered* against the routing tables of the ABs where the query is arrived and the AC is registered; in case of a *filter-failure*, the ABs forward the query to their direct super-ABs. Any answer of the query must follow the reverse path.

Thus, resource look-up overhead reduces when a query is satisfied in the current colony. Most structured overlays guarantee look-up operations that are logarithmic in the number of nodes. To improve routing performance, caching and replication of data and search paths can be adopted. Replication also improves load balancing, fault tolerance, and the durability of data items.

Every AC registers in the colony with a *tuple* of (services,instances), like $SREG:[(S_i, n_i)]^{i=1\ldots h}$, and asks for a another tuple of (service,instances), like $SREQ:[(S_j, n_j)]^{j=1\ldots k}$. Each service is looked-up sequentially and independently of others, by wrapping a unitary resource discovery inside a for-loop:

for each $j = 1 \ldots k$ **do** −find service S$_j$− **end foreach**

An atomic service request may also have the shape $SREQ:[((\bigwedge_{i=1\ldots n} S_i), m)]$, *i.e.* the system is no longer asked to find m occurrences of a single service, but rather m occurrences of a conjunction of n services. That is, the system has to look for m distinct ACs, each AC being able to provide all the services in $\bigwedge_{i=1\ldots n} S_i$.

For a given resource S, one entry in the routing table has the form $T[S] = [(P_j, m_j)]^{j=1\ldots k}$, where $(P_j)^{j=1\ldots k}$ are the addresses of the *direct children in the*

AB*'s colony*, and $(m_j)^{j=1\ldots k}$ are the instances of S available at P_j. Intuitively and for an atomic service request SREQ:$[(S, n)]$, the most economic resource discovery routing steps performed by an AB are:

1. Look in the table $\mathcal{T}$ for all *distinct* q ACs able to provide S in the local AB's colony;
2. If $n \leq q$, then search n resources first inside the current colony (and, recursively, in sub-colonies), and finally delegate to the AB's super-leaders all the denied resources.
3. If $n \geq q$, then search q resources inside the colony (and, recursively, in sub-colonies), and finally delegate all the $n-q$ remaining instances to the AB's super-leader.

Pragmatically speaking this strategy, reminiscent of the object-oriented "method-lookup algorithm", pushes always first queries on the leafs of the overlay in order to avoid, if possible, routing bottlenecks.

An AC receiving a service request first chooses the services that it accepts or denies to serve; then, it generates a SRESP message containing the lists of accepted or rejected services, and finally sends it to its AB. The response messages are then propagated back in the overlay, following the reverse path.

2.4   The Virtual Intermittent Protocol (VIP)

Peers' participation in Arigatoni's colonies is managed by the *Virtual Intermittent Protocol (*VIP*)*; the protocol deals with the *dynamic topology* of the overlay, by allowing individuals to login/logout to/from a colony (using the SREG message). Due to this high node churn, the routing process may lead to *failures*, because some individuals have logged out, or because they are temporarily unavailable, or because they have logged out *manu militari* by the broker for their poor performance or greediness. In the VIP protocol, there are two ways an individual can register to an AB (sensible to its physical position in the network topology), the latter being not enforced in Arigatoni:

1. Registration of an individual to an AB belonging to the same *current administrative domain*;
2. Registration, via *tunneling*, of an individual to another AB belonging to a *different administrative domain*.

If both registrations apply, then the individual is working *de facto* both in local mode *in the current administrative domain*, and in global mode *in another administrative domain*. Symmetrically, an individual can unregister according to the following simple rules *"d'étiquette"*:

– Unregistration of an individual is allowed only when there are no pending services demanded or requested to the leader AB of the colony: individual must always wait for an answer of the AB or for a direct connection of the AC requesting or offering the promised service, or wait for an internal timeout (the time-frame must be negotiated with the AB);

- (As a corollary of the above) an AB cannot unregister from its own colony, *i.e.* it cannot discharge itself. However, for fault tolerance purposes, an AB can be faulty. In that case, the ACs unregister one after the other and the colony disappear;
- Once an AC has been disconnected from a colony, it can physically migrate in another colony belonging to any other administrative domain;
- Selfish nodes in P2P networks, called "free riders", that only utilize other peers' resources without providing any contribution in return, can be fired by a leader; if the leader of a colony finds that an individual ratio of fairness is too small ($\leq \epsilon$, for a given ϵ), it can arbitrarily decide to fire that individual without notice. Here, the VIP protocol also checks that the individual has no pending services to offer, or that the timeout of some promised services has expired, the latter case means that the free rider promised some services but finally did not provide any service at all (not trustfulness).

In both cases of node (un)registration, a *service update* SUPD message will be flooded in the brokers' network in order to keep resource tables as much updated as possible; thus, high node churn leads to message overhead in the overlay.

2.5   Inside Routing Tables for Intermittent Participation

As said before, routing tables denoting the set of resources are stored in AB's. An individual (AC or AB representing a sub-colony) registers to a colony with a tuple of (services,instances), like in SREG:$[(S_i, n_i)]^{i=1...h}$. If a broker AB accepts an individual in its colony, then it sends a service update, written SUPD:$[(S_i, n_i)]^{i=1...h}$, to its direct super-broker AB' in order to communicate the availability of the new resources in its colony, by an update of the routing table T' of AB'. This message is then propagated from broker to broker until the root (if any) of the multi-layer overlay is reached. This means a high node churn forces routing tables to be *faulty* until all service updates are properly propagated. As such, service registration in an overlay network computer is an activity that must be taken seriously into account [CLC07b].

The first Arigatoni network topology was tree-based. In [LC07], the authors make a significant step by moving from a tree-based network topology to a more general graph-based one. As an immediate consequence of this move, the Arigatoni VIP protocol must be reconsidered in order to take into accounts routing loops when updating routing tables.

3   Social Model, Security, Trust and Implementation Issues

3.1   The Social Model Underneath Arigatoni

The Arigatoni overlay network computer defines mechanisms for devices to inter-operate by offering services, in a way that is reminiscent to Rapoport's *tit-for-tat* strategy of co-operation based on reciprocity. This way to understand common behavior of virtual organizations has some theoretical basis on Game Theory [Rap63]. Classical results from game theory are based on the assumption that a shared amount of resources is available, and then users have an incentive to collaborate. The very first design of Arigatoni forced each AC to register to only one AB, but the architecture can be smoothly scaled up to a more general topology where each AC may simultaneously be registered to several AB, and where a *colony* is just one possible *social scheme*.

This means that Arigatoni fits with motivations and cooperation behavior of different communities. It tries to be *policy neutral*, leaving policy choices for each node at the implementation or configuration level, or at the community or organization level. Policy domains can overlap (one node can define itself as belonging "much" to colony *foo* and "a little bit" to colony *bar*). This denotes a decentralized non-exclusive policy model.

One question can arise: who is Arigatoni designed for? We believe the overlay is flexible enough to serve a mix of different "social structures" and "end-users":

- Independent end-user connecting through his ISP or migrating from hot-spot to hot-spot;
- Cooperative communities of disseminated individuals;
- More regulated or hierarchical communities (maybe a better picture of a corporate network);
- Cooperative or competitive resource providers and resource brokers.

The Arigatoni overlay network computer is suitable to support various extended trust models. Moreover, reputation score could be expanded to a multi-dimensional value, for example adding a score for the *quality of the service* offered by an individual. Moreover, Arigatoni encourages cooperation and enables gratuitous resource offering. But it may also suit for business extensions, *e.g.*:

- An individual can sell resource usage, creating a resource business;
- An AB can sell a resource discovery service, creating a brokering business (*"I point you to the best resources, more quickly than anyone else"*).

The Arigatoni overlay network computer is suitable of a number of service extensions: among others, *e.g.*:

- How to create and call third party services for on-line payment of services;
- How to exchange digital cash for payment of services;
- How to negotiate service conditions between client and servant, including price and quality of service.

The one-to-many nature of the RDP protocol service request (SREQ) are of particular interest in this case.

Another possible Arigatoni extension may define how to join a third party auction server. Candidate servants for a SREQ would contact the auction server and make their bid. The trusted auction server chooses the elected candidate and service conditions based on auction terms. The individual client would then contact the auction server and get this information. Those extensions may take advantage of the RDP optional fields [BCLV06], for example, to transmit location and parameter information to call a third party system.

3.2 Trust, Security, and Implementation Issues

In order to work securely, the Arigatoni overlay network computer needs to be able to offer the following guarantees to its components:

- The communication between two individuals must be secured;
- The role played by a node (*i.e.* client AC, servant AC or AB) must be certified by a third party trusted by the nodes which have to communicate with this particular node. A way to implement those constraints is to use PKI certificates. A *Certification Authority* delivers certificates, and couples of private and public keys for ACs and ABs which attest of their distinctive roles. The whole mechanisms involved by a PKI is out of the scope of this paper, but good use of PKIs and an implementation compliant with RFC2743 [Lin00] can provide all the necessary security, namely the trustfulness on the identity of the peers, and the trustfulness of all the transmitted data, *i.e.* secrecy, authenticity, and integrity.
- In addition to PKIs, a more "liquid" trust model could be built, based on *reputation mechanisms* [WV03]. Reputation represents the amount of trust an individual in the overlay has in another individual based on its partial view. In a nutshell:
  - Each individual maintains a reputation score for each individual it knows;
  - Each individual maintains a reputation score for each resource it serves;
  - Exchanges between individuals update dynamically each other's scores;
  - Conflict between two or many individuals are resolved by the brokers leaders of the colonies to which individuals belong;
  - The computation of the reputation score (a trust metrics) and the way individuals exchange scores is left free to each single implementation.

A last word on implementation issues of the Arigatoni overlay network computer: it is well known that two technical barriers are commonly used to block transmission over IP network in overlays, namely:

- *Firewalls* to drop UDP flows (usually considered as suspects);
- NAT techniques to mask to the outside world the real IP addresses of inside hosts; a NAT equipment changes the IP source address when a packet *goes to* outside, and it changes the IP destination address when a packet *comes from* outside.

The usage of these mechanisms is very frequent on the Internet, and barriers exist to prevent connections between *inside* and *outside* nodes in the Arigatoni overlay. RFC3489 [RWHM03] can be used to overcome such obstacles.

4 Related Work, Applications, and Conclusions

4.1 Discussion on Overlay Topologies

Many technologies, algorithms, and protocols have been proposed recently for resource discovery . Some of them focus on Grid or P2P oriented applications, but none of those targets the full generality as the Arigatoni overlay network computer does. Indeed, Arigatoni deals with generic resource discovery for building an overlay network of ABs and ACs, structured in a virtual organization of variable topology, with clear distinct roles between leader ABs and individuals.

In an overlay network, any message is routed through the full overlay; as such, the topology adopted in the overlay strongly affects routing protocols and their complexity. The overlay is built on top of the physical one, and, thus, two neighbor nodes in the overlay network may be many links apart in the physical network. The first Arigatoni network topology was a dynamic *hierarchical n-layer tree*, but a recent work raise Arigatoni to a graph topology [LC07].

To implement resource look-up, structured overlays map (key of) data item to nodes (our ABs). Hence, the mapping is usually done through hashing the key space of the data item to the id in the node space. In the literature, *e.g.* [AEO06], there are essentially the following types of overlays: structured (tree, ring, or grid), unstructured (graphs), hybrid overlays (a combination of the two above), and multi-layer (or n-layer) overlays.

Arigatoni falls mostly in the category of multi-layer. In a nutshell, in a n-layer overlay network, the responsibility assigned to individuals differs (think of the different roles between ABs and ACs), since super-peers (ABs) serve as a server for a subset of all peers. Ordinary peers (ACs) submit queries to their super-peers and receive results from it. Super-peers are also connected to each others; they route messages over the overlay network, submit, delegate, and answer queries on behalf of their sub-peers. This structure is replicated *recursively*, creating a *n-layer topology*, where peers become super-peers with decreasing responsibilities. The possibility of having a graph of super-peers complicates routing, registration protocols and resource table update.

Typical issues in n-layer overlays are the size of each colony (load balancing of the colony), and the internal coherence of the resources offered and requested by each colony (homogeneity of the colony). Typical bottlenecks of n-layers are reliability, service availability (related to few points of failure), and load balancing. Classical solutions to cope with these problems are adding redundancy at the broker-layer. Historically, the most related tree topologies are BATON [JV05] and P-GRID [Abe01], whereas the closest n-layer topologies are the one of CANON [GKGM04] and CORAL [FM03].

- (BATON) is a balanced binary tree that features a left and a right routing table, both contained in each node (denoted by a single logical id). Nodes may join or leave the network at any time, provided the tree remains balanced. The node receiving a join can forward the join towards a node which has less children or which is a leaf node. This implies that an AC can become an AB. Leaving the network is constrained to not breaking the balanced tree unless finding a substitute. As such, load balancing can be costly.
- (P-GRID) is a distributed dynamic binary search tree, such that the search space is partitioned between peers. The salient feature of P-GRID is the separation of concerns between id and its position in the network. All peers maintain a partial routing table of the search space, that is *negotiated*

beteen the closest peers. Multiple peers can be responsible for the same path, resulting in non uniqueness of routing and robustness under peer failure.

- (CANON) is a multi-layer overlay where routing is based on a hierarchical *distributed hash tables* (DHT). As in Arigatoni, the search space is partitioned into *domains*; in contrast, routing inside a domain is DHT-based, and topology is static.
- (CORAL) is another hierarchical DHT. The search space is partitioned into three *clusters*, based on latency; a regional cluster, a continental cluster and a planet-wide cluster. It also comes with algorithm for self-organizing, merging and splitting clusters, to ensure acceptable diameters.

4.2 Discussion on Closest Technologies

The GLOBUS toolkit [Glo], is an open-source set of technology, protocols and middleware, used for building Grid applications (sharing computing power, distributed databases, etc.). The toolkit includes stand-alone software for security, information infrastructure, resource management, data management, communication, fault detection, and portability. The analogies with the Arigatoni overlay network computer are in the *Community Scheduler Framework* component and the *Web Service Grid Resource Allocation and Management*, concerning the resource discovery, and the *Teleoperations Control Protocol* concerning the way units cooperate (in analogy with the RDP protocol and with orchestration languages). Hovever, GLOBUS does not target the full generality of the Arigatoni overlay network computer, that, thanks to its generic resource discovery, is suitable for pervasive, ubiquitous overlay computations in addition to pure Grid-oriented applications.

Promoted by Sun, the JXTA [JXT] technology is a set of open peer-to-peer protocols enabling device to communicate, collaborate and share resources. After a peer discovery process, any peer can interact directly with other peers. Hence, the overlay network of peers induced by the JXTA technology is flat. Moreover, the main concern of Arigatoni is the design of protocols for generic resource discovery and intermittent participation, while the main concern of the JXTA technology is to offer some tools to implement a P2P model. In addition, Arigatoni focuses on the evolution/devolution of colonies, while JXTA technology allows peers to communicate using an already existing overlay network of peers. Further, Arigatoni's aim is the dynamicity of the overlay network, while JXTA's is the freedom of connectivity between peers. Finally, JXTA-peers come with their proper JXTA-id (logical JXTA peers addressing), while Arigatoni relies on the more conventional IP addresses.

Publish/subscribe (pub/sub) [EFGK03] is a communication paradigm for asynchronous dissemination of information. Consumers subscribe to the system (typically called the *Notification Service*) to specify the type of information that they are interested in. Producers publish data to the system. The notification service disseminates the data to all (if possible) the consumers that are interested in receiving it, according to the data and the interests declared by the consumers. Many pub/sub systems have been developed recently, such as XNET

[CF04], SIENA [CRW01] or GRYPHON [BCM$^+$99]. Banavar *et al.*, in [Hei01], propose to adapt the SIENA publish/subscribe system to achieve GNUTELLA-like resource discovery. Their work resembles ours in the sense that Arigatoni is also inspired by the pub/sub paradigm. However, resource discovery in pub/sub is achieved by publishing queries to the notification service. In contrast, Arigatoni implements its own resource discovery algorithm, especially designed for generic and scalable resource look-up.

Worthy also to notice the OSGi technology [OSG], a component integration platform with a service-oriented architecture and life cycle capabilities that enable dynamic delivery of services. These capabilities greatly increase the value of a wide range of computers and devices that use the Java platform. The OSGi specifications provide a platform for an universal middleware.

4.3   Challenges

We envision a long term meta-application and a medium-term specific-application.

Challenge 1: From Large-Scale Computing Machines to Large-Scale Overlay Network Computing Machines

This challenge is inspired by the seminal talk by John von Neumann, given in May 1946, "Principles of Large-Scale Computing Machines", reprinted in [vN88]. At that time, "large-scale" meant the ENIAC computer, *i.e.*, 17,468 vacuum tubes, 7,200 crystal diodes, 1,500 relays, 70,000 resistors, 10,000 capacitors, 5 million joint, 30 short tons, 2.4m x 0.9m x 30m, stored in a 167 m^2 room, and 150 kW to operate. Today, thanks to the Moore's law and to the Internet, "large scale" means "planetary scale", *i.e.* the computer hardware is distributed in space and in time and must be negotiated before being used. The authors think that the main inspirations of our Arigatoni overlay network computer are still contained in that historical paper.

As such, we plan to design and implement a *pervasive, programmable, overlay network computer, i.e.* a colony of communicating computer individuals that exchange resources and services with various guarantees, execute sequential or parallel algorithms on one or more computer individuals, or perform tasks written in a workflow&dataflow language. An *overlay program* will be a combination of an overlay network connectivity dealing with virtual organizations and a computation of an algorithm resulting of the *summa* of all algorithms running on different computer individuals, and the coordination of all computer individuals using an *ad hoc* language. The metalanguage used to program the overlay network computer is often called (terminology often overlaps), *workflow- dataflow- orchestration- composition- metaprogramming- language*. We could better call such metalanguage a *distributed assembler*, since there is a strong similarity with machine code. As examples, the pseudo machine code instruction *à la* Backus [Bac54] move R0 R1 can be "refreshed" as

```
move dataR0 from ipR0:portR0 to ipR1:portR1
```

(where of course latency is an non-trivial issue), and the pseudo machine code instruction op R0 R1 R2 can be recasted as

```
op on ipR0 with
      ipR0:portR0:dataR0 and
      ipR1:portR1:dataR1 and stockin
      ipR2:portR2:dataR2
```

Challenge 2: Developing a Vehicular Infrastructure

We plan to develop algorithmic methods and adapt Arigatoni protocols for building an *ad hoc* vehicular network infrastructure, called Ariwheels [Ari]. That network must enable efficient and transparent access to the resources of on-board and roadside nodes. Commercial services and access to public information will be available to vehicles transiting in specific areas where such information is broadcast by roadside wireless gateways or by other vehicles. Data retrieved can be stored on the on-board vehicle computer; then, they can be used and rebroadcast at a later time without the need of persistent connectivity. We envision that these new features will offer innovative functions and services, such as:

- Distribution, from infrastructure to vehicles (I2V), and among vehicles (V2V), of safety and/or traffic-related information;
- Collection, from vehicles to infrastructures (V2I), of datas useful to perform traffic management operations;
- Information exchange between private vehicles and public transportation systems (buses, vehicles, road side equipments, etc.) to support and, thus, foster inter-modality in urban areas;
- Distribution of real-time information to enable dynamic navigation services.

4.4   Conclusions and Future Work

The design of our programmable overlay network computer is far to be complete. We are working on a more complete mathematical study of our system, based on more elaborate statistical and stochastic models and realistic assumptions [NCL07], as well as the possibility to include hierarchical DHT in addition to the routing tables. We have already implemented an efficient simulator to validate our design choice [Log]. We are currently working on the implementation of a real client to be deployed on a real size experiments and platforms, like, *e.g.* PLANETLAB, and GRID5000 [Gri]. We hope that Arigatoni could represent a step toward a natural integration of different scenarios under the common paradigm of Overlay and Pervasive Computing (see the *Grand UK Challenges* [Cha], or the new INRIA strategic plan [INR]).

Acknowledgment. The authors would warmly like to thank Didier Benza and Marc Vesin on all issues related to trust, security and social networks, and Philippe Nain for its invaluable comments and interactions on the Arigatoni performance model. This work is supported by Aeolus IST-015964.

References

[Abe01]   Aberer, K.: P-Grid: A Self-Organizing Access Structure for P2P Information Systems. In: Batini, C., Giunchiglia, F., Giorgini, P., Mecella, M. (eds.) CoopIS 2001. LNCS, vol. 2172, pp. 179–194. Springer, Heidelberg (2001)

[AD97]   Alexander, S., Droms, R.: RFC2132, DHCP Options and BOOTP Vendor Extensions. Technical report, IETF (1997)

[AEO06]   AEOLUS. Deliverable D2.1.1: Resource Discovery: State of the Art Survey and Algorithmic Solutions (2006)

[Ari]   Ariwheels. Arigatoni on wheels, http://www-sop.inria.fr/mascotte/ Luigi.Liquori/ARIGATONI/Ariwheels.htm

[Bac54]   Backus, J.W.: The IBM 701 Speedcoding System. J. ACM 1(1), 4–6 (1954)

[BCLV06]   Benza, D., Cosnard, M., Liquori, L., Vesin, M.: Arigatoni: Overlaying Internet via Low Level Network Protocols. In: JVA, John Vincent Atanasoff International Symposium on Modern Computing, pp. 82–91. IEEE, Los Alamitos (2006)

[BCM$^+$99]   Banavar, G., Chandra, T., Mukherjee, B., Nagarajarao, J., Strom, R.E., Sturman, D.C.: An efficient multicast protocol for content-based publish-subscribe systems. In: Proc. of ICDCS (1999)

[Bit]   BitTorrent, Inc., http://www.bittorrent.com/

[Car95]   Cardelli, L.: A language with distributed scope. Computing Systems 8(1), 27–59 (1995)

[CCL06]   Chand, R., Cosnard, M., Liquori, L.: Resource Discovery in the Arigatoni Overlay Network. In: I2CS, International Workshop on Innovative Internet Community Systems. LNCS, Springer, Heidelberg (2006)

[CCL08]   Chand, R., Cosnard, M., Liquori, L.: Powerful resource discovery for Arigatoni overlay network. Future Generation Computer Systems 24(1), 31–38 (2008)

[CF04]   Chand, R., Felber, P.: XNet: A Reliable Content-Based Publish/Subscribe System. In: Proc. of SRDS: Symposium on Reliable Distributed Systems (2004)

[Cha]   Grand UK Challenge. Global Computing and Pervasive Computing, http://www-dse.doc.ic.ac.uk/Projects/UbiNet/GC/

[CLC07a]   Chand, R., Liquori, L., Cosnard, M.: Improving Resource Discovery in the Arigatoni Overlay Network. In: Lukowicz, P., Thiele, L., Tröster, G. (eds.) ARCS 2007. LNCS, vol. 4415, pp. 98–111. Springer, Heidelberg (2007)

[CLC07b]   Cosnard, M., Liquori, L., Chand, R.: Virtual Organizations in Arigatoni. DCM, International Workshop on Development in Computational Models 171(3) (2007)

[CRW01]   Carzaniga, A., Rosenblum, D.S., Wolf, A.L.: Design and Evaluation of a Wide-Area Event Notification Service. ACM TOCS 19(3) (2001)

[EFGK03]   Eugster, P.T., Felber, P., Guerraoui, R., Kermarrec, A.M.: The Many Faces of Publish/Subscribe. Computing Survey 35(2), 114–131 (2003)

[FM03]   Freedman, M.J., Mazières, D.: Sloppy Hashing and Self-Organizing Clusters. In: Kaashoek, M.F., Stoica, I. (eds.) IPTPS 2003. LNCS, vol. 2735, pp. 45–55. Springer, Heidelberg (2003)

[GKGM04]   Ganesan, P., Krishna, P., Garcia-Molina, H.: Canon in G-major: Design-
            ing DHTS with Hierarchical Structure. In: Proc. of ICDCS, pp. 263–272.
            IEEE, Los Alamitos (2004)
[Glo]   Globus Alliance, http://www.globus.org/
[Gri]   Grid 5000 Consortium, http://www.grid5000.org
[GVE00]   Gulbrandsen, A., Vixie, P., Esibov, L.: RFC2782, A DNS RR for speci-
            fying the location of services (DNS SRV). Technical report, IETF (2000)
[Hei01]   Heimbigner, D.: Adapting publish/subscribe middleware to achieve
            gnutella-like functionality. In: Vaudenay, S., Youssef, A.M. (eds.) SAC
            2001. LNCS, vol. 2259, pp. 176–181. Springer, Heidelberg (2001)
[IBM]   IBM. Business Process Execution Language, http://www.ibm.com/
            developerworks/library/specification/ws-bpel/
[INR]   INRIA. Strategic Plan 2008-2012 (to appear)
[JV05]   Jagadish, H.V., Ooiand, B.C., Vu, Q.H.: BATON: A Balanced Tree
            Structure for Peer-to-Peer Networks. In: Proc. of VLDB, pp. 661–672.
            ACM, New York (2005)
[JXT]   JXTA Community, http://www.jxta.org/
[LC07]   Liquori, L., Cosnard, M.: Weaving Arigatoni with a Graph Topology. In:
            ADVCOMP, International Conference on Advanced Engineering Com-
            puting and Applications in Sciences, IEEE Computer Society Press, Los
            Alamitos (2007)
[Lin00]   Linn, J.: RFC 2743, Generic Security Service Application Program In-
            terface Version 2, Update 1. Technical report, IETF (2000)
[Log]   LogNet. Arigamulator, http://www-sop.inria.fr/mascotte/Luigi.
            Liquori/ARIGATONI/index.html
[NCL07]   Nain, P., Casetti, C., Liquori, L.: A Stochastic Model of an Arigatoni
            Overlay Computer. Research report, Politecnico di Torino (2007)
[Nok]   Nokia. N810 Internet Terminal
[OSG]   OSGi Alliance. Open Services Gateway Initiative,
            http://www.osgi.org/
[Pau]   Pautasso, C.: JOpera: Process Support for more than Web Services,
            http://www.jopera.org/
[Rap63]   Rapoport, A.: Mathematical models of social interaction. In: Handbook
            of Mathematical Psychology, vol. II, pp. 493–579. John Wiley and Sons,
            Chichester (1963)
[RWHM03]   Rosenberg, J., Weinberger, J., Huitema, C., Mahy, R.: RFC3489, STUN
            - Simple Traversal of User Datagram Protocol (UDP) Through Network
            Address Translators (NATs). Technical report, IETF (2003)
[vN88]   von Neumann, J.: The Principles of Large-Scale Computing Machines.
            IEEE Ann. Hist. Comput. 10(4), 243–256 (1988)
[Whi94]   White, J.E.: Telescript Technology: The Foundation for the Electronic
            Marketplace. White Paper. General Magic, Inc. (1994)
[WV03]   Wang, Y., Vassileva, J.: Trust and Reputation Model in Peer-to-Peer
            Networks. In: Proc. of Peer-to-Peer Computing, IEEE Computer Soci-
            ety, Los Alamitos (2003)

Type-Safe Distributed Programming with ML5*

Tom Murphy VII, Karl Crary, and Robert Harper

Department of Computer Science
Carnegie Mellon University
Pittsburgh, PA, USA
{tom7,crary,rwh}@cs.cmu.edu

Abstract. We present ML5, a high level programming language for spatially distributed computing. The language, a variant of ML, allows an entire distributed application to be developed and reasoned about as a unified program. The language supports transparent mobility of any kind of code or data, but its type system, based on modal logic, statically excludes programs that use mobile resources unsafely. The ML5 compiler produces code for all of the hosts that may be involved in the computation. These hosts may be heterogeneous, with different resources and even different architectures. Currently, our compiler and runtime are specialized to the particular case of web programming: a distributed computation with two sites, the web browser and the web server.

1   Introduction

ML5 is a high-level programming language for distributed computing. The language is designed particularly for those programs that are spatially distributed; where parts of the program must run in physically or logically distinct places. Typically such programs must be distributed because of local resources (such as databases or consoles for interacting with a user) that can only be accessed at those places. ML5's type system permits the programmer to describe the available local resources, and then excludes all programs that use them unsafely.

Distributed applications are often developed by writing a set of programs, one for each host, that communicate via a protocol on network sockets. In contrast, ML5 allows an entire distributed application to be developed as a unified program. This has several benefits: The application may share rich, higher-order data structures, including abstract types, between different hosts. It can even maintain references to arbitrary remote resources, as long as those resources are not *used* remotely. More importantly, the program can be reasoned about as a single semantic entity. Reasoning about the behavior of a set of programs communicating via a network can be awkward, particularly when the programs are written in different languages. ML5's dynamic semantics is a straightforward extension of ML's. The compiler can type check the code to statically verify that certain kinds of runtime failure are impossible. ML5's type system is based on

---

* The ConCert Project is supported by the National Science Foundation under grant ITR/SY+SI 0121633: "Language Technology for Trustless Software Dissemination."

G. Barthe and C. Fournet (Eds.): TGC 2007, LNCS 4912, pp. 108–123, 2008.

modal logic, a kind of logic that permits simultaneous reasoning from multiple perspectives. This logical basis means that the features for distributed computing integrate naturally into ML's type system, retaining (for example) type inference.

From the source program the compiler produces code for all of the hosts that may be involved in the computation. These hosts may be heterogeneous, with different sets of available resources and even different architectures.

ML5 is the subject of Murphy's Ph.D. thesis and is still in development—the language does not incorporate some desirable features such as a module system or high-level database integration. Some planned features (such as mutual exclusion) are not yet implemented in the compiler. However, the implementation works well enough to run useful demo applications, which are available online. Our current prototype is specialized to the particular case of web programming: a heterogeneous distributed computation with exactly two sites, the web browser and web server.

We will begin with a brief review of the modal logic IS5 and the particular formulation we use for ML5 (Section 2). We then present ML5's core features using web programming as a source of examples (Section 3). The remainder of the paper discusses the interesting facets of how ML5 is implemented: our marshaling strategy based on type representations and the complications of typed closure conversion in a modal setting (Section 4.1), and the particulars of producing distributed applications for web browsers (Section 4.2). We conclude with a discussion of related, ongoing, and future work (Section 6).

2 Modal Logic IS5

IS5 is a modal logic with the ability to reason about truth from multiple simultaneous perspectives, which are called "possible worlds." These possible worlds arise from contingent assumptions that differ from world to world. In our application of modal logic to distributed computing, the logical worlds correspond to the hosts involved in a computation, and the contingent assumptions to the local resources particular to these hosts.

Various related logics are distinguished by the way in which the possible worlds can access one another; IS5 is a simple degenerate case where every pair of worlds can access one another. Of the several ways to define a modal logic, we find an explicit worlds formulation [18] to be most suitable for our type system [13]. This formulation uses a judgment $\Gamma \vdash A @ \mathrm{w}$ which states that under the assumptions in Γ, the proposition A is true at the world w. Γ holds assumptions of the form $B @ \mathrm{w}'$ (positing B is true at w'), and ω (assuming the existence of a world ω). World expressions w include only these bound world variables ω and world constants, written $\mathbf{w}$. We can only use an assumption $A @ \mathrm{w}$ to conclude that fact at the same world. The standard connectives from intuitionistic logic are expressed by attaching "$@ \mathrm{w}$" everywhere; for instance, implication is

$$\frac{\Gamma, A @ \mathrm{w} \vdash B @ \mathrm{w}}{\Gamma \vdash A \supset B @ \mathrm{w}} \supset\text{-I} \qquad \frac{\Gamma \vdash A \supset B @ \mathrm{w} \quad \Gamma \vdash A @ \mathrm{w}}{\Gamma \vdash B @ \mathrm{w}} \supset\text{-E}$$

Modal logic often focuses on two connectives, $\Box A$ and $\Diamond B$ ("*A* is true in all worlds;" "*B* is true in some world"). We find that an explicit worlds formulation gives us the ability to define $\Box$ and $\Diamond$ in terms of finer connectives. The most important of these is the **at** modality (following Jia [7]), which internalizes the @ judgment into a proposition. It is defined by

$$\frac{\Gamma \vdash A@\text{w}}{\Gamma \vdash A\,\text{at}\,\text{w}@\text{w}'}\;\text{at-I} \qquad \frac{\Gamma \vdash A\,\text{at}\,\text{w}'@\text{w} \quad \Gamma, A@\text{w}' \vdash C@\text{w}}{\Gamma \vdash C@\text{w}}\;\text{at-E}$$

A modal logic where propositions can mention worlds is known as a "hybrid logic" [5]; contrary to its name we find the connective to be central to our logic. For instance, $\Box A$ is definable as $\forall \omega. A\,\text{at}\,\omega$. Typed closure conversion (Section 4.1) makes heavy use of the **at** modality. In contrast, we do not use the $\Box$ or $\Diamond$ connectives in any of our examples.

The final feature of our logic that distinguishes it from other formulations of S5 is our perspective-shifting rule **get**. This rule allows for reasoning at a world w_1 to be nested within reasoning at a world w_2.

$$\frac{\Gamma \vdash A@\text{w}' \quad A\,\text{mobile}}{\Gamma \vdash A@\text{w}}\;\text{get}$$

This rule would be nonsense for arbitrary A: all worlds would then conclude exactly the same facts. The judgment **mobile** that restricts this rule to certain propositions is better explained in terms of the values of the programming language that characterize those propositions, so we leave that for Section 3. As examples, $A\,\text{at}\,\text{w}$ is mobile for any A, and $A \supset B$ is never mobile.

The **get** rule exists for the benefit of the dynamic semantics. It allows us to isolate all of the communication between hosts into this one rule, ensuring that the other rules avoid any "action at a distance" [13]. For example, without **get**, the **at-E** rule would have to allow the proof of $A\,\text{at}\,w'$ to come from an arbitrary third world. With our decomposition, if we want to use a proof from another world, we explicitly move it first.

Our decompositions preserve the meaning of the logic while allowing for a more natural programming language and implementation. In the next section we describe this programming language.

3   ML5

ML5's syntax and semantics are based on core Standard ML [8]. The largest difference is that ML5's typing judgment is stratified by world, like the truth judgment of IS5. Here, a world is a place in which a computation might run. We type check an expression M using the judgment $\Gamma \vdash M : A@\text{w}$, which means that under variable bindings Γ, the expression M has type A in the world w. It is best to think of the judgment $M{:}A@\text{w}$ as meaning that M is *for* w, rather than *at* w. Although M can only be evaluated at w, at runtime it may be moved around between worlds and placed in data structures at other worlds. World expressions can be either variables ω or constants **w**. Every program must begin execution somewhere; in ML5 this world is the constant **home**. The entire program is therefore also typechecked starting at **home**.

An ML5 program begins by describing what it knows about the universe. This includes the declaration of world constants and the local resources available to them. Here is a working example:[1]

```
extern javascript world home
extern val alert : string -> unit @ home
do alert [Hello, home!]
```

This first line is unnecessary (because the constant **home** is already provided by the compiler) but serves to show how worlds can be declared. The *world-kind* **javascript** dictates that this world (which will be the web browser) runs JavaScript [4] code; this is used only by the backend when generating code for the hosts involved in a program. We can support other worldkinds by implementing a code generator and runtime for them; currently, we support **javascript** and **bytecode** (Section 4.2). The declaration **extern val** asserts the existence of a local resource, in this case, a function called **alert**. The compiled program will expect to find a symbol called **alert** at the world **home**, and a program variable **alert** is bound in the code that follows. It is also possible to declare external abstract types, and global resources (Section 3.1). (Note that although we declare what we know about the universe statically, this does not preclude us from learning about resources dynamically, as long as we can give ML types to the resource discovery facilities.) The **do** declaration evaluates an expression for effect, in this case calling the **alert** function on the supplied string constant. This application type checks because all of these declarations are checked at the world **home**; if **alert** were declared to be at a different world **server** we would not be able to call it without first traveling to the server.

To write distributed programs we also need dynamic tokens with which to refer to worlds. A token for the world w has type w **addr**, and can be thought of as the address of that world. A world can compute its own address with the `localhost()` expression, whose typing rule appears in Figure 1. Typically, a program also expects to know the addresses of other worlds when it begins and imports them with **extern val**. We use an address by traveling to the world it indicates, using the **get** construct. For example, here is a program that involves two worlds, the web browser and server:

```
extern bytecode world server
extern val server : server addr @ home
extern val version : unit -> string @ server
extern val alert : string -> unit @ home
do alert (from server
          get version ())
```

---

[1] Our examples omit the required syntax for wrapping declarations as compilation units, since the implementation currently only supports a single compilation unit.

$$\frac{}{\Gamma \vdash \texttt{localhost}() : \texttt{w addr @w}} \qquad \frac{A \text{ mobile} \quad \Gamma \vdash M : \texttt{w}' \, \texttt{addr @w} \quad \Gamma \vdash N : A@\texttt{w}'}{\Gamma \vdash \texttt{from } M \texttt{ get } N : A@\texttt{w}}$$

$$\frac{\Gamma, \omega' \vdash v : A@\omega'}{\Gamma \vdash \texttt{sham } \omega'.v : \mathbf{8}_{\omega'} A@\texttt{w}} \quad \frac{A \text{ mobile} \quad \Gamma \vdash M : A@\texttt{w}}{\Gamma \vdash \texttt{put } u = M \overset{\texttt{w}}{\rightsquigarrow} u{\sim}A} \quad \frac{\Gamma \vdash M : \mathbf{8}_{\omega} A@\texttt{w}}{\Gamma \vdash \texttt{valid } u = M \overset{\texttt{w}}{\rightsquigarrow} u{\sim}\omega.A}$$

$$\frac{}{\Gamma, x{:}A@\texttt{w}, \Gamma' \vdash x : A@\texttt{w}} \quad \frac{}{\Gamma, u{\sim}\omega.A, \Gamma' \vdash u : [^{\texttt{w}}\!/_{\omega}]A@\texttt{w}} \quad \frac{\Gamma \vdash v : A@\texttt{w}}{\Gamma \vdash \texttt{hold } v : A \texttt{ at w}@\texttt{w}'}$$

$$\frac{\Gamma \vdash d \overset{\texttt{w}}{\rightsquigarrow} \Gamma' \quad \Gamma, \Gamma' \vdash M : C@\texttt{w}}{\Gamma \vdash \texttt{let } d \texttt{ in } M : C@\texttt{w}} \qquad \frac{\Gamma \vdash M : A \texttt{ at w}'@\texttt{w}}{\Gamma \vdash \texttt{drop } x = M \overset{\texttt{w}}{\rightsquigarrow} x{:}A@\texttt{w}'}$$

Fig. 1. Some rules from the ML5 internal language, which have been simplified for presentation purposes. The judgment $\Gamma \vdash d \overset{\texttt{w}}{\rightsquigarrow} \Gamma'$ states that the declaration d, checked at w, produces new hypotheses Γ'.

$$\frac{}{\mathbf{8}A \text{ mobile}} \qquad \frac{}{A \texttt{ at w mobile}} \qquad \frac{b \in \{\texttt{string}, \texttt{int}, \ldots\}}{b \text{ mobile}} \qquad \frac{\alpha \text{ mobile}}{\alpha \text{ mobile}}$$

$$\frac{}{\texttt{w addr mobile}} \qquad \frac{A \text{ mobile} \quad B \text{ mobile}}{A \times B \text{ mobile}} \qquad \frac{A \text{ mobile} \quad B \text{ mobile}}{A + B \text{ mobile}} \qquad \frac{\overset{\cdot}{A} \text{ mobile}}{\mu\alpha.A \text{ mobile}}$$

$$\frac{A \text{ mobile}}{\forall \alpha.A \text{ mobile}} \qquad \frac{A \text{ mobile}}{\forall \omega.A \text{ mobile}}$$

Fig. 2. Definition of the mobile judgment. Not all types are mobile: local resources like arrays and file descriptors are not, nor are function types or abstract types.

This program asserts the existence of a world **server** with a function that returns its version. On the home world, we display an alert whose argument is a subexpression (the call to **version**) that is evaluated at the server. The typing rule for **get** appears in Figure 1; it takes the address of a remote world and an expression well-typed at that world. The type of the expression must be mobile (Figure 2). A type is mobile if *all* values of that type are portable among worlds. **string** is mobile, so this code is well-typed. Function types are not mobile, because for example it would not make sense to move the function **version**—a resource local to **server**—to the world **home**. Even though not *all* functions are mobile, we will be able to demonstrate the mobility of particular functions with the **8** modality, which is discussed in the next section.

3.1 Validity

It turns out that a large fraction of the code and data in a distributed application is not particular to any one world. We say that such values are "valid" and introduce a new kind of hypothesis for valid values. It takes the form $u{\sim}\omega.A$, meaning that the variable u is bound to a valid value which has type A at any world. The world variable ω is bound within A and is instantiated with the world(s) at which u is used. This variable is rarely needed, so we write $u{\sim}A$ when it does not occur in A. Valid hypotheses appear in Γ like the other hypotheses.

Note that we cannot achieve this same effect by adding new types or using polymorphism. For example, if we had a function f that we want to be able to use anywhere, we cannot simply bind it as f : $\forall\omega.$int $\supset$ int@ω. This judgment is ill-formed because the scope of the quantifier does not include @ω, which is part of the *judgment*, not the *type*.

One way to introduce a valid hypothesis is with the put declaration. The code put x = 2 + 3 binds a valid variable $x{\sim}$int. The typing rule for put appears in Figure 1; it requires that the type of the expression be mobile. Unlike get, put does not cause any communication to occur; it simply binds the variable such that it can be used in any world. There can also be global resources that are known to be available at all worlds. For example, extern val server ~ server addr declares that the address of the server is globally available.

The ⌘ modality (pronounced "shamrock") is the internalization of the validity judgment as a type. A value of type ⌘A is a value that can be used at any world at type A. It is introduced by checking that a value is well-typed at a hypothetical world about which nothing else is known (Figure 1). This hypothetical world can in general appear in the type; when it does, we write ⌘$_\omega A$. Elimination of the ⌘ modality with the valid declaration produces a valid hypothesis. Our treatment of validity and the ⌘ modality are inspired by Park's ⊡ modality [14]. Note that the body of a sham (and also hold) must be a value. ML5 has several constructs that are syntactically restricted to values; in these positions we would not be able to safely evaluate an expression because it is typed at some other world.

The ⌘ modality is useful because it analyzes a *particular value* for portability (compare the mobile judgment, which is judgment on types). Therefore it can be used to demonstrate the portability of a function value. For example, the ML5 expression sham (fn x => x + 1) has type {}(int -> int). ({} is the ASCII syntax for ⌘.) Because ⌘A is mobile for any A, we can now get this wrapped function or place it inside other mobile data structures.

The programmer does not usually need to use the ⌘ modality manually, because type inference will automatically generalize declarations to be valid when possible. This is described in the next section.

3.2 Polymorphism and Type Inference

Like Standard ML, ML5 supports Hindley-Milner style type inference. When the right hand side of a val declaration is a value (this includes any fun declaration), the compiler will generalize the free type variables to produce a polymorphic binding. ML5 also infers and generalizes worlds in the same manner. For instance,

```
val f = fn a => from a get 1234
```

produces a polymorphic binding of f at type $\forall\omega.(\omega$ addr $\supset$ int$)$. In ML5 world variables also appear in the judgment (the @w part), which is not in scope of the $\forall$ type operator and so cannot be generalized this way. If this world is unconstrained, the declaration is generalized to produce a valid binding by introducing and immediately eliminating the ⌘ modality. The above code elaborates into

```
valid f = sham (allw w. fn (a : w addr) => from a get 1234)
```

which binds $f{\sim}\forall\omega.(\omega\ \text{addr} \supset \text{int})$.

Validity inference allows declarations of library code (such as the ML Basis library) to precede the program and then be used as desired, without the need to explicitly move the code between worlds or instantiate it. Thus, when not using the distributed features of the language, ML5 looks just like ML, and type inference generally assigns the same (valid) types that the code would have there.

3.3   Web Features

The current ML5 prototype is specialized to web programming, and has a few features that are specific to this domain. Let us look at a tiny application that illustrates these. This program will make use of a simple persistent database on the server that associates string values with string keys. It will allow us to modify those keys, and will asynchronously show the value of the key whenever it is modified (in this or any other session). We begin by importing libraries and declaring the worlds and addresses.

```
import "std.mlh"
import "dom.mlh"
import "trivialdb.mlh"
extern bytecode world server
extern val home ~ home addr
extern val server ~ server addr
```

The Document Object Model (DOM) is JavaScript's interface to the web page [6]. It allows the reading and setting of properties of the page's elements, and the creation of new elements. The dom.mlh library provides a simple interface to the DOM. The trivialdb.mlh library provides access to the persistent database. Both consist mainly of extern declarations.

```
put k = [tdb-test]
fun getkey () =
    let val v = from server get trivialdb.read k
    in  dom.setstring (dom.getbyid [showbox], [innerHTML], v) end
fun setkey () =
    let put s = dom.getstring (dom.getbyid [inbox], [value])
    in  from server get trivialdb.update (k, s) end
```

The valid variable k holds the name of the key we're concerned with (ML5 string constants are written with square brackets; see below). The function getkey fetches the current value of the key from the server. It then finds the DOM element with id *showbox* and sets its HTML contents to be the value of the key. The function setkey reads the value of the DOM element *inbox* (a text input box), travels to the server and sets that as the value of the key. Both functions have type unit -> unit @ home.

```
do dom.setstring (dom.getbyid [page], [innerHTML],
                  [[k]'s value: <div id="showbox"> </div> <br />
                  <input type="text" id="inbox" /> <br />
                  <div onclick="[say setkey ()]"
                       style="cursor:pointer">set key</div> ])
do from server
   get trivialdb.addhook (k, cont (fn () => from home get getkey ()))
```

We then create the web page that the functions above interact with. We do
this by updating the element called *page* (provided by the ML5 runtime) with an
HTML string. This string contains the elements *showbox* and *inbox* referenced
by name above. There are two things to note here: One is ML5's syntax for
strings, which uses square brackets. Within a string, square brackets allow an
ML5 expression of type `string` to be embedded (it may contain further strings,
etc.). The other is the `say` keyword. It takes an ML5 expression (here `setkey`
`()`) and, at runtime, returns a JavaScript expression (as a string) that when run
will evaluate that expression.[2] In this example we set the `onclick` property of
the `<div>` so that it triggers `setkey ()` when the user clicks it. Finally, we add
a hook on the key that travels to the client and calls `getkey` whenever the key
is changed. The hook is expected to be a first-class continuation; `cont` is a valid
function from the standard library of type `(unit -> unit) -> unit cont`.

When this program is compiled, it produces a JavaScript source file to run on
the client, and a bytecode file to run on the server. To run the application, the
user visits a URL on the web server, which creates a new session and returns
the JavaScript code along with the runtime to his web browser. The server also
launches an instance of its code. The program runs until the client leaves the
web page, at which point the session is destroyed on the server. This example
and others, including a chat server, Wiki and spreadsheet, can be run online at
http://tom7.org/ml5/.

Having given a tour of the language, we now describe how it is implemented.

4   Implementation

The ML5 implementation consists of a CPS-based type directed compiler, a
simple web server, and two runtimes: one for the client and one for the server.
For reasons of space we concentrate on only the most interesting aspects of these,
which tend to arise as a result of ML5's modal typing judgment.

We first discuss our strategy for marshaling, which pervasively affects the way
we compile. We then discuss the phases of compilation in the same order they
occur in the compiler. We finish with a brief discussion of the runtime system.

Marshaling. The design of ML5 maintains a conceptual separation between marshaling and mobility. Marshaling is an implementation technique used to represent

---

[2] We can not provide any type guarantees about JavaScript once it is in string form.
An improvement would be to use a richer language for embedded XML documents
(like Links; see Section 6) so that we can type check them, and then to have `say`
return a JavaScript function object rather than a string.

values in a form suitable for transmission over the network. Mobility is a semantic quality of values determined at the language level. In ML5, any well-typed value can be marshaled, but only some values are mobile. We are able to make this distinction because of the modal typing judgment: when a value of type $A@w_1$ is marshaled and then unmarshaled at w_2, it still has type $A@w_1$ and therefore cannot be consumed at w_2. The notion of mobility allows us to coerce some values of type $A@w_1$ to $A@w_2$.

In order to marshal and unmarshal values, we need dynamic information about their types and worlds. For example, to compile a polymorphic function, we might need to generate code that marshals a value of an arbitrary type. To do this uniformly, the low-level `marshal` primitive takes a value (of type A) and a representation of its type. The type of the dynamic representation of A is A `rep`. (We also have w `wrep`, the type of a representation of the world w.) The `marshal` primitive analyzes the type representation in order to know how to create marshaled bytes from the value. Recursively, the behavior of marshal is guided by both the type and world of the value. Because `marshal` is a primitive—not user-defined code—we do not need to support general type analysis constructs like typecase.

To make sure that we have the appropriate type representation available when we invoke `marshal`, we establish an invariant in the compiler that whenever a type variable α is in scope, so is a valid variable with type α `rep`. Similarly, for every world variable ω in scope, there will be a valid variable with type ω `wrep`. Once we have generated all of the uses of these representations, we discard the invariant and can optimize away any type representations that are not needed.

4.1 Compiler

After the program is elaborated into the intermediate language (IL), the first step is to CPS convert it. CPS conversion is central to the implementation of threads and tail recursion in JavaScript, because JavaScript does not have any native thread support or tail call support, and has an extremely limited call stack. We give a sample of the CPS language in Figure 3. CPS conversion of most constructs is standard [1]; IL expressions are converted to CPS expressions via a function convert, which is itself continuation-based. In addition to the IL expression argument, it takes a (meta-level) function $\mathcal{K}$ that produces a CPS expression from a CPS value (the result value of M). It may be illuminating to see the case for `get`:

$$\text{convert } (\texttt{from } M_{a'} \texttt{ get } M_r)\ \mathcal{K} = \text{convert } M_{a'}\ \mathcal{K}_1$$
$$\text{where } \mathcal{K}_1(v_{a'}) = \texttt{let } a = \texttt{localhost() in}$$
$$\texttt{put } u_a = a \texttt{ in}$$
$$\texttt{go}[v_{a'}] \text{ convert } M_r\ \mathcal{K}_r$$
$$\text{where } \mathcal{K}_r(v_r) = \texttt{put } u_r = v_r \texttt{ in}$$
$$\texttt{go}[u_a]\ \mathcal{K}(u_r)$$

We first convert $M_{a'}$, the address of the destination, and then compute our own address and make it valid so that we can use it at our destination to return. We

values $v ::= x \mid u \mid \textbf{sham } \omega.v \mid \lambda x.c \mid v_1\langle \overline{w}; \overline{A}; \overline{v}\rangle \mid \Lambda\langle\overline{\omega}; \overline{\alpha}; \overline{x:A}\rangle.v \mid$
$\qquad\qquad \textbf{wrepfor } w \mid \textbf{repfor } A$

conts $c ::= \textbf{halt} \mid \textbf{go}[v]c \mid \textbf{letsham } u = v \textbf{ in } c \mid \textbf{leta } x = v \textbf{ in } c \mid \textbf{call } v_f \ v_a$

$$\frac{}{\Gamma \vdash \textbf{wrepfor } w : w \textbf{ wrep} @ w'} \qquad \frac{\Gamma, \overline{\omega}, \overline{\alpha}, \overline{x:A} \vdash v : B @ w}{\Gamma \vdash \Lambda\langle\overline{\omega}; \overline{\alpha}; \overline{x:A}\rangle.v : \langle\overline{\omega}; \overline{\alpha}; \overline{A}\rangle.B @ w}$$

$$\frac{}{\Gamma \vdash \textbf{repfor } A : A \textbf{ rep} @ w} \qquad \frac{\Gamma \vdash v_f : \langle\overline{\omega}; \overline{\alpha}; \overline{A}\rangle.B @ w_0 \quad \Gamma \vdash \overline{v} : \overline{A @ w_0}}{\Gamma \vdash v_f\langle \overline{w}; \overline{C}; \overline{v}\rangle : [\overline{w}/\omega][\overline{C}/\alpha]B @ w_0}$$

$$\frac{\Gamma \vdash v : A @ w'}{\Gamma \vdash \textbf{hold } v : A \textbf{ at } w' @ w} \quad \frac{}{\Gamma, x:A @ w, \Gamma' \vdash x : A @ w} \quad \frac{}{\Gamma, u{\sim}\omega.A, \Gamma' \vdash u : [^w/_\omega]A @ w}$$

$$\frac{\Gamma \vdash v_a : w' \textbf{ addr } @ w \quad \Gamma \vdash c @ w'}{\Gamma \vdash \textbf{go}[v_a]c @ w} \quad \frac{A \textbf{ cmobile} \quad \Gamma \vdash v : A @ w \quad \Gamma, u{\sim}A \vdash c @ w}{\Gamma \vdash \textbf{put } u = v \textbf{ in } c @ w}$$

$$\frac{\Gamma \vdash v : \boxtimes_\omega A @ w \quad \Gamma, u{\sim}\omega.A \vdash c @ w}{\Gamma \vdash \textbf{letsham } u = v \textbf{ in } c @ w} \quad \frac{\Gamma \vdash v : A \textbf{ at } w' @ w \quad \Gamma, x:A @ w' \vdash c @ w}{\Gamma \vdash \textbf{leta } x = v \textbf{ in } c @ w}$$

Fig. 3. Some of the CPS language. The judgment $\Gamma \vdash v : A @ w$ checks that the value v has type A at w. Continuation expressions c are checked with the judgment $\Gamma \vdash e @ w$; they do not return and so do not have any type. The judgment cmobile is analogous to the IL judgment mobile, but for CPS types. In an abuse of notation, we use an overbar to indicate a vector of values, vector of typing judgments, or simultaneous substitutions.

then go to the destination, evaluate the body M_r, and make it valid so that we can use it when we return. To return, we go back to the original world.

The CPS abstract syntax is implemented in the compiler using a "wizard" interface [10], where binding and substitution are implemented behind an abstraction boundary rather than exposing a concrete SML datatype and relying on compiler passes to respect its binding structure. This interface guarantees that every time a binder is "opened," the client code sees a new freshly alpha-varied variable. In our experience this is successful in eliminating alpha-conversion bugs, a major source of mistakes in compilers we have written previously.

Because the compiler is type-directed, all of the transformations are defined over typing derivations rather than the raw syntax. In order to recover these derivations (particularly, the types of bound variables) each transformation must essentially also be a type checker. We do not want to repeat the code to type check and rebuild every construct in every pass. Instead, we define an identity pass that uses open recursion, and then write each transformation by supplying only the cases that it actually cares about. This does have some drawbacks (for instance, we lose some useful exhaustiveness checking usually performed by the SML compiler), but it drastically reduces the amount of duplicated code that must be maintained in parallel.

Representation Insertion. The first such pass establishes the representation invariant mentioned above. A number of constructs must be transformed: constructs that bind type or world variables must be augmented to additionally take representations, and uses must provide them. The CPS language uses a "fat lambda" (written $\Lambda\langle\overline{\omega};\overline{\alpha};\overline{x:A}\rangle.v$) for values that take world, type, and value arguments. It is converted by adding an additional value argument (of type $\omega\,\mathtt{wrep}$ or $\alpha\,\mathtt{rep}$) for each world and type argument. As examples, the value $\Lambda\langle\omega_1,\omega_2;\alpha;x{:}\mathtt{int}\rangle.x$ converts to

$$\Lambda\langle\omega_1,\omega_2;\alpha;x_1{:}\omega_1\,\mathtt{wrep},x_2{:}\omega_2\,\mathtt{wrep},x_3{:}\alpha\,\mathtt{rep},x{:}\mathtt{int}\rangle.x$$

and the application $y\langle\mathbf{home},\omega_3;(\mathtt{int}\times\alpha);0\rangle$ converts to

$$y\langle\mathbf{home},\omega_3;(\mathtt{int}\times\alpha);\mathtt{wrepfor}\,\mathbf{home},\mathtt{wrepfor}\,\omega_3,\mathtt{repfor}\,(\mathtt{int}\times\alpha),0\rangle.$$

The value $\mathtt{repfor}\,A$ is a placeholder for the representation of A. It is only a placeholder because it may contain free type variables. In a later phase, $\mathtt{repfor}$ is replaced with a concrete representation, and the free type variables become free valid variables.

We also perform a similar translation for the $\mathtt{sham}\,\omega.v$ and $\mathtt{letsham}$ constructs. For the introduction form, we lambda-abstract the required world representation. We do not change the elimination site, which binds a valid variable that can be used at many different worlds. Instead, at each use we apply the variable to the representation of the world at which it is used.

In this phase we also insist that every $\mathtt{extern}$ $\mathtt{type}$ declaration is accompanied by a $\mathtt{extern}$ $\mathtt{val}$ declaration for a valid representation of that type.

Closure Conversion. Closure conversion implements higher-order, nested functions by transforming them to closed functions that take an explicit environment. The environment must contain all of the free variables of the function. Closure conversion is interesting in the ML5 implementation because a function may have free variables typed at several different worlds, or that are valid.

To closure convert a lambda, we compute the free variables of its typing derivation. This consists of world, type, and value variables. After closure conversion the lambda must be closed to all dynamic variables, including the representations of types and worlds. This means that in order to maintain our type representation invariant, the set of free variables must additionally include a valid representation variable for any occurring world or type variable. Ultimately, the free variables $x_i{:}A_i\,@\,\mathsf{w}_i$ are the actually occurring free variables, and the free valid variables $u_i{\sim}\omega.B_i$ come from three sources: (1) actually occurring valid variables; (2) the world representation variable $u_{\omega_k}{\sim}\omega_k\,\mathtt{wrep}$ for any free world variable ω_k; (3) the type representation variable $u_{\alpha_l}{\sim}\alpha_l\,\mathtt{rep}$ for any free type variable α_l.

The environment will consist of a tuple containing the values of all of the free variables. Some of these values are typed at other worlds, so they need to be encapsulated with the $\mathtt{at}$ modality. We must preserve the validity of the valid ones using ⅋. The environment and its type are thus

$$(\text{hold } x_1, \ldots, \text{ sham } \omega.u_1, \ldots) : (A_1 \text{ at } \mathsf{w}_1, \ldots, \text{⅋}_\omega.B_1, \ldots)$$

Inside the body of the converted function we rebind these variables using leta and letsham on components of the tuple. As usual [9], the pair of the closed lambda and its environment are packed into an existential, so that all function types are converted independently of the instance's free variable set. Since unpacking an existential binds a type variable, we must also include a type representation inside each existential package so that we can maintain our invariant.

The design of closure conversion is what originally informed our addition of the at and ⅋ modalities to ML5. A general lesson can be derived: In order to type closure conversion, the language must have constructs to internalize as types any judgments that appear as (dynamic) hypotheses. The elimination forms must be able to restore these hypotheses from the internalized values.

In addition to closure converting the regular λ construct, we must convert Λ since it takes value arguments. We closure convert the body of go as well, since we send that continuation as a marshaled value to the remote host.

After closure conversion we will never need to insert another repfor, so a pass replaces these with the actual values that form the runtime representations of types and worlds. We then discard our representation invariant and can optimize away unused representations.

Hoisting. A separate process of hoisting pulls closed lambdas out of the program and assigns them global labels. The hoisted code must be abstracted over all of its free type and world variables, but these are now purely static. Hoisted code can either be fixed to a specific world (when it is typed at a world constant), or it can be generic in its world (when it is typed at a world variable). When we generate code for each world in the back-end, we produce code for those labels that are known to be at that world, and also for any label generic in its world. Any other label is omitted—it will not be invoked here and we might not even be able to generate the code if it makes use of resources particular to its true world. The form of code generated for each world depends on the declared worldkind (Section 3); currently we assume that we know statically the architectures of the hosts involved.

4.2   Runtime

The runtime system is responsible for providing communication between the server and client. It also contains the implementation of marshaling and threads.

When the web server returns a compiled ML5 program for the client, it begins a session of the program that runs on the server as well. This session contains a queue of server threads and a marshaling table (see below). Via the go construct, threads can transfer control from client to server or vice versa. A client thread transfers control to the server by making an HTTP request whose body is a marshaled continuation for the server to execute. Starting a thread on the client is trickier: For security reasons JavaScript cannot accept incoming network connections. Instead, the client is responsible for maintaining a devoted connection to the server, fetching a URL and asynchronously waiting on that request. When the server wishes to start a thread on the client, it sends a response; the client begins that thread and reinstates the connection. (This mode of interaction is now fairly standard in web applications.)

With type representations available, marshaling is a straightforward matter. One interesting aspect is how we use the representations of worlds; as we marshal, we recursively keep track of the world of the value (for instance, as we descend into a value of type A at w_2, we record w_2). We can then specialize the marshaled representation of a value based on where it comes from. This is how we can marshal local resources: A JavaScript DOM handle is represented natively at home, but when we marshal it, we place it into a local table and marshal the index into that table. At any other world, the handle is represented and marshaled as this index. When it arrives back at home, we know to reconstitute the actual handle by looking it up in the table. Other than the fact that we must be able to marshal any well-formed value, there is nothing special about the language or implementation that limits the range of marshaling strategies we could adopt.

5   Theory

We have formalized several of the calculi on which ML5 is based in Twelf [16] and proved properties about them. For example, we prove that ML5 without the validity judgment is equivalent to Intuitionistic S5, and that ML5's dynamic semantics is type safe. In addition, we have formalized a few of the first stages of compilation, including CPS and closure conversion. (These languages are somewhat simplified; for example we omit recursion and type representations.) For these we prove that every well-typed program can be converted, and that the resulting program is well-typed. All of the proofs are machine checkable. Some of the proofs appear in Murphy's thesis proposal [11] and the remainder will appear in his dissertation.

6   Related and Future Work

Related Work. ML5 is in a class of new web programming languages that Wadler deems "tierless," that is, they allow the development of applications that normally span several tiers (database, server logic, client scripts) in a uniform language. Links [3] is such a programming language. Functions may be annotated as "client" or "server," and Links allows calls between client and server code. However, their type system does no more to indicate what code and data can be safely mobile, and marshaling can fail at runtime. On the other hand, Links has many features (such as a facility for embedding and checking XML documents and database queries) that make typeful web programming easier. It additionally supports a mode of page-oriented application where all of the session state is stored on the client, as marshaled data inside of hyperlinks and forms. In contrast, ML5 only supports AJAX style web applications (*i.e.*, a single page that the user never leaves), because our computational model requires that the server be able to contact the client at any time.

Hop [17] is another tierless web programming language, using Scheme as the unifying language. Hop has constructs for embedding a client side expression within a server expression and vice-versa, analogous to get in ML5 (but specific to the two-world case). The chief difference is simply that Hop is untyped, and thus subject to dynamic failures.

Our modal calculus is closely related to λ_{rpc}, a hybrid variant of IS5 by Jia and Walker [7]. They give their dynamic semantics in a process calculus style. Our chief innovation over λ_{rpc} is the use of the mobile judgment and the get construct to enable a simple call-by-value semantics compatible with existing compilation technology for ML. Moreover, we have developed such an implementation. Others have used modal logic for distributed computing as well; for a complete discussion see our previous papers on Lambda 5 [13] and C5 [12], as well as Murphy's thesis proposal [11] and dissertation.

Future Work. There is much potential for future work on ML5 and related languages. In the short term, we wish to develop larger applications and implement the language support necessary to do so. This will probably include support for structured databases and mutual exclusion between threads. We will need to improve the performance of the compiler, particularly by implementing optimizations that undo our simplistic closure conversion (for instance, when all calls are direct) and type representation passing (when the representations are not used). There is also some opportunity for optimizations particular to the ML5 primitives (such as when a get is from a world to itself).

A more serious performance issue is resource leaks caused by mobile data structures. Garbage that is purely local is collected by the server and JavaScript collectors, but once a local resource is marshaled by inserting it in a table and sending that index remotely, we can never reclaim it. Web programming systems typically deal with this by assuming that sessions are short-lived, but it would be preferable to allow for long-running programs through some form of distributed garbage collection [15].

Our type theory naturally supports an arbitrary number of worlds, and most of the compiler does, as well. Adding the ability for a program to access many different servers would just be a matter of adding runtime support for it. Unfortunately, JavaScript's security model prevents outgoing connections to any server other than the one that originally sent the JavaScript code. To get around this, we would need to build an overlay network where the original server acts as a proxy for the others. Supporting multiple *clients* in the same application instance is trickier still. This is mainly because we consider the thread of control to begin on the (one) client; it would instead need to start on the server, which would then need to be able to discover new connecting clients at runtime.

Another concern is security. JavaScript code intended to run on the client is actually under the complete control of an attacker. He can inspect its source and cause it to behave arbitrarily, and invoke any continuation on the server for which he is able to craft acceptable arguments. This is true of any distributed system where some hosts are controlled by attackers, and the programmer must defend against this by not trusting (and explicitly checking) data and code it receives from the client. In some ways this problem is exacerbated in ML5: The process of compilation from the high-level language is not fully abstract, in that it introduces the possibility for more behaviors in the presence of an attacker than can be explained at the source level. For example, depending on how closure conversion and optimizations are performed, a client may be able to modify a marshaled closure in order to swap the values of two of the server's variables! We believe a solution to this problem would take the form of an "attack semantics" provided by the language and implemented by the compiler through a series of countermeasures. The semantics would describe the range of behaviors that a program might have in the presence of an attacker, so that the programmer can ensure that these behaviors do not include security breaches on the server. (The client will always be able to format his own hard drive, if he desires.) One example of such a semantics is the Swift web programming language [2], where data are annotated with information flow policies that guide how the program is compiled. (This language is somewhat different from ML5 in that the assignment of code to hosts is performed implicitly by the compiler, via program partitioning.) In any case, such properties are inherently in terms of the principals (places) involved in the computation, and therefore we believe that our type system and semantics is an important first step in being able express and prove properties of programs in the presence of an attacker, and to develop mechanisms for building secure programs.

Conclusion. We have presented ML5, a new programming language for distributed computing. ML5's current prototype is specialized to web programming, a domain for which its programming model is well suited—it joins a collection of other languages with similar design goals and principles. Many of the ideas from these languages are compatible with all three systems. ML5's main contribution to this is its type system, which permits the programmer to describe local resources and prevent unsafe access to them. Being based on logic, the type system is elegant and is compatible with the design of ML-like languages, including polymorphic type inference.

References

1. Appel, A.: Compiling With Continuations. Cambridge University Press, Cambridge (1992)
2. Chong, S., Liu, J., Myers, A.C., Qi, X., Vikram, K., Zheng, L., Zheng, X.: Secure web applications via automatic partitioning. In: 21st ACM Symposium on Operating Systems Principles (SOSP), October 2007 (2007)
3. Cooper, E., Lindley, S., Wadler, P., Yallop, J.: Links: Web programming without tiers. In: de Boer, et al. (eds.) FMCO 2006. LNCS, vol. 4709, pp. 266–296. Springer, Heidelberg (2007)

4. ECMAScript language specification. Technical Report ECMA-262 (1999)
5. Hybrid logics bibliography (2005), http://hylo.loria.fr/content/papers.php
6. W3C DOM IG. Document object model (2005), http://w3c.org/DOM/
7. Jia, L., Walker, D.: Modal proofs as distributed programs (extended abstract). In: European Symposium on Programming (2004)
8. Milner, R., Tofte, M., Harper, R., MacQueen, D.: The Definition of Standard ML (Revised). MIT Press, Cambridge, Massachusetts (1997)
9. Morrisett, G., Walker, D., Crary, K., Glew, N.: From System F to typed assembly language. ACM Transactions on Programming Languages and Systems 21(3), 527–568 (1999)
10. Murphy VII, T.: The wizard of TILT: Efficient(?), convenient and abstract type representations. Technical Report CMU-CS-02-120, Carnegie Mellon School of Computer Science (2002)
11. Murphy VII., T.: Modal types for mobile code (thesis proposal). Technical Report CMU-CS-06-112, Carnegie Mellon, Pittsburgh, Pennsylvania, USA (2006)
12. Murphy VII, T., Crary, K., Harper, R.: Distributed control flow with classical modal logic. In: Ong, L. (ed.) CSL 2005. LNCS, vol. 3634, Springer, Heidelberg (2005)
13. Murphy VII, T., Crary, K., Harper, R., Pfenning, F.: A symmetric modal lambda calculus for distributed computing. In: Proceedings of the 19th IEEE Symposium on Logic in Computer Science (LICS 2004), IEEE Computer Society Press, Los Alamitos (2004)
14. Park, S.: A modal language for the safety of mobile values. In: Fourth ASIAN Symposium on Programming Languages and Systems, November 2006 (2006)
15. Plainfossé, D., Shapiro, M.: A survey of distributed collection techniques. Technical report, BROADCAST (1994)
16. Schürmann, C., Pfenning, F.: A coverage checking algorithm for LF. In: Basin, D., Wolff, B. (eds.) TPHOLs 2003. LNCS, vol. 2758, pp. 120–135. Springer, Heidelberg (2003)
17. Serrano, M., Gallesio, E., Loitsch, F.: HOP, a language for programming the Web 2.0. In: Proceedings of the First Dynamic Languages Symposium (2006)
18. Simpson, A.: The Proof Theory and Semantics of Intuitionistic Modal Logic. PhD thesis, University of Edinburgh (1994)

Transactional Service Level Agreement*

Maria Grazia Buscemi and Hernán Melgratti

IMT, Lucca Institute for Advanced Studies, Italy
m.buscemi@imtlucca.it, h.melgratti@imtlucca.it

Abstract. Several models based on process calculi have addressed the definition of linguistic primitives for handling long running transactions and Service Level Agreement (SLA) in service oriented applications. Nevertheless, the approaches appeared in the literature deal with these aspects as independent features. We claim that transactional mechanisms are relevant for programming multi-step SLA negotiations and, hence, it is worth investigating the interplay among such formal approaches. In this paper we propose a process calculus, the *committed cc-pi*, that combines two proposals: (i) cc-pi calculus accounting for SLA negotiation and (ii) cJoin as a model of long running transactions. We provide both a small- and a big-step operational semantics of committed cc-pi as labelled transition systems, and we prove a correspondence result.

1 Introduction

Service Oriented Computing (SOC) is an emerging paradigm in distributed computing. Services are autonomous computational entities that can be described, published, and dynamically discovered for developing distributed, interoperable applications. Along with functional properties, services may expose non-functional properties including Quality of Service (QoS), cost, and adherence to standards. Non-functional parameters play an important role in service discovery and binding as, e.g., multiple services able to fulfill the same user request (because they provide the same functionality) can still be differentiated according to their non-functional properties. Service Level Agreements (SLAs) capture the mutual responsibilities of the provider of a service and of its client with respect to non-functional properties, with emphasis on QoS values.

The terms and conditions appearing in a SLA contract can be negotiated among the contracting parties prior to service execution. In the simplest case, one of the two parties exposes a contract template that the other party must fill in with values in a given range; in case of failure, no agreement is reached and a new negotiation must be initiated. However, in general, arbitrary complex scenarios involving distributed transactions may occur: (i) third parties may take part to or just exert some influence on a negotiation, (ii) negotiations can be nested, (iii) if a commit cannot be achieved, compensation mechanisms may be activated, e.g. clients may relax their own SLA requirements and providers may add further service guarantees until an agreement is reached.

Several approaches have appeared in the literature for specifying and enforcing SLA contracts [14,10,7,2] and for modelling and analysing long running transactions in the

---

* Research supported by the FET-GC II Project IST-2005-16004 SENSORIA and by the Italian FIRB Project TOCAI.IT.

G. Barthe and C. Fournet (Eds.): TGC 2007, LNCS 4912, pp. 124–139, 2008.

context of name passing calculi [5,11,4]. However, such theories treat these two issues as independent features. By contrast, we claim that transactions can be conveniently employed for programming SLA negotiation scenarios. In this paper, we propose the *committed cc-pi calculus (committed cc-pi)*, a language for specifying SLAs that also features coordination primitives tailored to multi-party negotiations. More specifically, committed cc-pi extends cc-pi [7] with the transactional mechanism of cJoin[5] for handling commits and aborts of negotiations along with possible activations of compensations. We remind that, unlike compensatable flows [8,6], the approaches in [5,11,4] rely on a notion of compensation that is essentially an exception handling mechanism.

The cc-pi calculus [7] is a simple model for SLA contracts inspired by two basic programming paradigms: name-passing calculi (see e.g. [12]) and concurrent constraint programming [13]. More in detail, cc-pi combines synchronous communication and a restriction operation *à la* process calculi with operations for creating, removing and making logical checks on constraints. The constraint systems employed in cc-pi are based on the *c-semiring* structures [3], which are able to model networks of constraints for defining constraint satisfaction problems and to express fuzzy, hierarchical, or probabilistic values.

cJoin [5] is an extension of the Join calculus [9] with primitives for distributed nested commits. The two key operations of cJoin are: the "abort with compensation", to stop a negotiation and activate a compensating process; and the "commit", to store a partial agreement among the parties before moving to the next negotiation phase.

Before introducing committed cc-pi, we single out the transactional primitives of cJoin and add them to the pi-calculus. This intermediate step highlights the interplay of compensating transactions with a channel-based interaction mechanism that is different from Join and it is intended to make the treatment of constraints easier to understand.

Synopsis. In §2 we highlight the main features of cc-pi, and in §3 we briefly recall cJoin and we present a transactional extension of the pi-calculus inspired by cJoin. In §4 we introduce the committed cc-pi calculus by giving its syntax and operational semantics in terms of labelled transition system and we show some examples of modelling transactional SLA negotiations. In §5 we define a big-step semantics of committed cc-pi and we prove a correspondence result.

2   Constrained-Based SLA Negotations

The cc-pi calculus integrates the Pi-F calculus [15] with a constraint handling mechanism. The Pi-F calculus is a variant of the pi-calculus whose synchronisation mechanism is global and, instead of binding formal names to actual names, it yields an *explicit fusion*, i.e., a simple constraint expressing the equalities of the transmitted parameters. cc-pi extends Pi-F by generalising explicit fusions to arbitrary constraints and by adding primitives like `tell` and `ask`, which are inspired by the constraint-based computing paradigms. We defer a technical treatment of the syntax and semantics of the cc-pi to §4, where we will give a formal presentation of an extended version of cc-pi including transactional features. Here, we simply overview the main principles of the calculus.

Underlying constraint system. The cc-pi calculus is parametric with respect to *named constraints*, which are meant to model different SLA domains. Consequently, it is not necessary to develop ad hoc primitives for each different kind of SLA to be modelled. A named constraint c is defined in terms of c-semiring structures and comes equipped with a notion of *support* supp(c) that specifies the set of "relevant" names of c, i.e. the names that are affected by c. The notation $c(x,y)$ indicates that supp(c) = $\{x,y\}$. In this work, we leave such underlying theory implicit and we refer the interested reader to [7,3]. For our purposes, we simply assume usual notions of entailment relation ($\vdash$), of combination of constraints ($\times$) and of consistency predicate (see e.g. [13]). Moreover, we will only consider *crisp* constraints (instead of the more general *soft* constraints), i.e. we will assume a constraint system leading to solutions consisting of a set of tuples of legal domain values. As an example the constraint $c(x,y) = (7 \leq x \leq 9) \times (15 \leq y \leq 18)$ specifies that the names x and y can only assume domain values in the range $[7,\ldots,9]$ and $[15,\ldots,18]$. Assuming a constraint $d(x,y) = (6 \leq x \leq 8) \times (17 \leq y \leq 19)$, the result of combining c and d is the intersection of their respective possible values, i.e. the constraint $e(x,y) = c(x,y) \times d(x,y) = (7 \leq x \leq 8) \times (17 \leq y \leq 18)$. We say a constraint to be inconsistent when it has no tuples, and we write 0 for the inconsistent constraint.

In cc-pi, the parties involved in a negotiation are modelled as communicating processes and the SLA guarantees and requirements are expressed as constraints that can be generated either by a single process or as a result of the synchronisation of two processes. Moreover, the restriction operator of the cc-pi calculus can limit the scope of names thus allowing for local stores of constraints, which may become global after a synchronisation. A single process $P = \texttt{tell}\ c.Q$ can place a constraint c corresponding to a certain requirement/guarantee and then evolve to process Q. Alternatively, two processes $P = \overline{p}\langle \tilde{x} \rangle.P'$ and $Q = p\langle \tilde{y} \rangle.Q'$ that are running in parallel ($P\,|\,Q$) can synchronise with each other on the port p by performing the output action $\overline{p}\langle \tilde{x} \rangle$ and the input action $p\langle \tilde{y} \rangle$, respectively, where $\tilde{x}$ and $\tilde{y}$ stand for sequences of names. Such a synchronisation creates a constraint induced by the identification of the communicated parameters $\tilde{x}$ and $\tilde{y}$, if the store of constraints obtained by adding this new constraint is consistent, otherwise the system has to wait that a process removes some constraint (action $\texttt{retract}\ c$).

Example 1. Consider a user that is looking for a web hosting solution with certain guarantees about the supplied bandwidth and cost. We assume the client and the provider to communicate over channel r the information about the requested bandwidth, and over channel p the information about the price of the service. The constant rb stands for the minimal bandwidth accepted by the client, while ob represents the maximal bandwidth offered by the provider. Moreover, the provider fixes the price uc as the cost for any unit of bandwidth, and the client the maximal cost c it is intended to pay for the service. Then, the whole system can be modelled by the following two processes: one describing the behaviour of the client $\mathsf{Client}_{rb,c}(r,p)$ and the other the provider $\mathsf{Provider}_{ob,uc}(r,p)$.

$$\mathsf{Client}_{rb,c}(r,p) \equiv (bw)(cost)(\texttt{tell}\ (bw \geq \mathsf{rb}).\overline{r}\langle bw \rangle.\texttt{tell}\ (cost \leq \mathsf{c}).p\langle cost \rangle)$$

$$\mathsf{Provider}_{ob,uc}(r,p) \equiv (bw')(cost')(\texttt{tell}\ (bw' \leq \mathsf{ob}).r\langle bw' \rangle.\texttt{tell}\ (bw' * \mathsf{uc} = cost').$$
$$\overline{p}\langle cost' \rangle)$$

The client starts by fixing the constraint about the minimal requested bandwidth, then it contacts the provider by communicating on channel r and, after that, it fixes the maximal cost it can afford and synchronises on p. The provider behaves similarly, by fixing an upper bound ob on the offered bandwidth, accepting a request from the client over r and, then, fixing the cost of the service and synchronising with the client.

Consider the following system composed of a client and two providers.

$$S \equiv (r)(p)\text{Client}_{4\text{Gb},\$100} \mid \text{Provider}_{6\text{Gb},\$20} \mid \text{Provider}_{3\text{Gb},\$15}$$

The client requests at least 4 Gigabytes (Gb), while one provider offers at most 6Gb and the other 3Gb. As expected, after each party has placed its own constraint on the required/offered bandwidth, the client can synchronize only with the first provider (the interaction with the second one is not possible since the constraints $bw \geq 4\text{Gb}$, $bw' \leq 3\text{Gb}$, $bw = bw'$ are inconsistent). As a next step, the first provider and the client fix the constraints about the cost of the service, the synchronisation over p takes place, and the negotiation succeeds. The released constraints are the agreed parameters of the contract. If we consider a domain of integer solutions, the contract is either the solution $bw = bw' = 4\text{Gb}$ and $cost = cost' = \$80$, or $bw = bw' = 5\text{Gb}$ and $cost = cost' = \$100$. Note that tell prefixes handle local stores of constraints, while synchronisations allow to identify variables belonging to different stores, thus yielding a global store.

3   Compensating Transactions

cJoin is a process calculus that provides programming primitives for handling transactions among interacting processes. The communication primitives of cJoin are inherited from the Join calculus [9], which is a process calculus with asynchronous name-passing communication, while the transactional mechanism is based on compensations, i.e., partial execution of transactions are recovered by executing user-defined programs instead of providing automatic roll-back. So, in addition to the usual primitives of Join, cJoin provides a new kind of terms of the form $[P : Q]$, denoting a process P that is required to execute until completion. In case P cannot successfully complete, i.e., when P reaches the special process **abort**, the corresponding compensation Q is executed.

The main idea in cJoin is that transaction boundaries are not permeable to ordinary messages, so that a transactional process $[P : Q]$ can only compute locally. However, a limited form of interaction is allowed with other transactional processes: in this case, after the interaction, the transactional processes become part of the same larger transaction, and hence all parties should reach the same agreed outcome, i.e., if some party commits (resp. aborts) then all of them commit (resp. aborts).

Rather than providing the formal definition of cJoin, below we focus on its transactional primitives. To this purpose, we present *committed pi*, an extension of the pi-calculus with the transaction mechanism introduced in cJoin. This choice aims to show the interplay of compensating transactions with the channel-based process communication of pi-calculus (and of cc-pi), thus making the transactional extension of cc-pi presented in §4 more straightforward.

3.1 From Cjoin to committed pi

Assume an infinite, countable set of names $\mathcal{N}$, ranged over by $a,b,x,y,z,\ldots$ and a set of process identifiers, ranged over by D. The syntax of committed pi processes is given in Figure 1(a). As in the pi-calculus, a process is either the inert process $\mathbf{0}$, the parallel composition $P|P'$ of two processes, a guarded choice $\Sigma_i\alpha_i.P_i$ where $\alpha_i.P_i$ is either (i) an agent $x(\tilde{y}).P$ that accepts a message on channel x and then continues as P, (ii) the synchronous emission of a message $\bar{x}\langle\tilde{y}\rangle$ with continuation P, or (iii) the internal choice $\tau.P$. The process $(\nu x)P$ defines the private channel x. A defining equation for a process identifier D is of the form $D(\tilde{x}) \stackrel{\text{def}}{=} P$ where the free names of P are included in $\tilde{x}$. Then, for any process $D(\tilde{y})$ we require $|\tilde{x}| = |\tilde{y}|$. In addition, committed pi provides two primitives for handling transactions: $[P:Q]$ for defining a transactional process P with compensation Q, and **abort** for indicating an aborted transaction.

We write $(\nu x_1\ldots x_n)P$ as an abbreviation for $(\nu x_1)\ldots(\nu x_n)P$. When $\tilde{x}=x_1\ldots x_n$ and $n=0$, $(\nu\tilde{x})P$ stands for P. We abbreviate $\bar{z}\langle\tilde{y}\rangle.\mathbf{0}$ by $\bar{z}\langle\tilde{y}\rangle$ and we write M for a process consisting only on sent messages, i.e. $M=\overline{x_1}\langle\tilde{y_1}\rangle|\ldots|\overline{x_n}\langle\tilde{y_n}\rangle$. M is $\mathbf{0}$ when $n=0$. The reduction semantics is the least relation satisfying the rules in Figure 1(c) (modulo the the usual structural equivalence rules in Figure 1(b)). Free and bound names (written $fn(P)$ and $bn(P)$) are defined as usual.

Rules (COMM), (TAU), (PAR), and (RES) are the standard ones for the synchronous pi-calculus. Rule (TRANS) describes the internal computations of a transactional process, in which the compensation Q is kept frozen. Rule (TR-COMP) handles the case of a transaction that aborts, which causes the remaining part of the transactional process to be removed and the associated compensation Q to be activated. Instead, rule (COMMIT) defines the behaviour of a transaction that commits. A transaction commits when it produces a set of output messages M, each of them followed by $\mathbf{0}$, i.e., there are no remaining computation inside the transaction. At this point, all produced messages M are released and the associated compensation is discarded. Last rule (TR-COMM) describes the interaction among two transactions. In particular, when one transactional process sends a message that is received by another transactional process both transactional scopes are merged into a larger one containing the remaining parts of the original transactions and its compensation is the parallel composition of the original ones.

Example 2. Consider the typical scenario in which a user books a room through a hotel reservation service. The ideal protocol can be sketched as below.

$$C \equiv \overline{request}\langle data\rangle.offer(price).\overline{accept}\langle cc\rangle$$
$$H \equiv request(details).\overline{offer}\langle rate\rangle.accept(card)$$

The client starts by sending a booking request to the hotel, which answers it with a rate offer. After receiving the offer, the client accepts it. Nevertheless, there are several situations in which parties may be forced/inclined not to complete the execution of the protocol (e.g., the hotel has no available rooms for the requested day, or the client does not obtain convenient rates).

$$\text{Client} \equiv [\overline{request}\langle data\rangle.offer(price).(\overline{accept}\langle cc\rangle + \tau.\mathbf{abort}) : alt(h).Q]$$
$$\text{Hotel} \equiv [request(details).(\overline{offer}\langle rate\rangle.accept(card) + \tau.\mathbf{abort}) : \overline{alt}\langle hotel\rangle]$$

$$P ::= \mathbf{0} \mid P|P \mid \Sigma_i \alpha_i.P_i \mid (\nu x)P \mid D(\tilde{y}) \mid [P:Q] \mid \mathbf{abort}$$
$$\alpha ::= x(\tilde{y}) \mid \bar{x}\langle \tilde{y} \rangle \mid \tau$$

(a) Syntax

$$P \mid \mathbf{0} \equiv P$$
$$P \mid Q \equiv Q \mid P$$
$$(P \mid Q) \mid R \equiv P \mid (Q \mid R)$$
$$P + Q \equiv Q + P$$
$$(\nu x)\mathbf{0} \equiv \mathbf{0}$$

$$P \equiv Q \qquad if \ P \equiv_\alpha Q$$
$$(\nu x)(\nu y)P \equiv (\nu y)(\nu x)P$$
$$(\nu x)P \mid Q \equiv (\nu x)(P|Q) \ \ if \ x \notin fn(Q)$$
$$(P+Q)+R \equiv P + (Q+R)$$
$$D(\tilde{y}) \equiv P\{\tilde{y}/\tilde{x}\} \ \ if \ D(\tilde{x}) \overset{def}{=} P$$

(b) Structural equivalence

(COMM)
$$x(\tilde{y}).P + P' \mid \bar{x}\langle \tilde{z} \rangle.Q + Q' \ \rightarrow \ P\{\tilde{z}/\tilde{y}\} | Q$$

(TAU)
$$\tau.P + Q \ \rightarrow \ P$$

(PAR)
$$\frac{P \rightarrow P'}{P|Q \rightarrow P'|Q}$$

(RES)
$$\frac{P \rightarrow P'}{(\nu x)P \rightarrow (\nu x)P'}$$

(TRANS)
$$\frac{P \rightarrow P'}{[P:Q] \rightarrow [P':Q]}$$

(TR-COMP)
$$[\mathbf{abort}|P:Q] \ \rightarrow \ Q$$

(COMMIT)
$$[M:Q] \ \rightarrow \ M$$

(TR-COMM)
$$[(\nu\tilde{x})y(\tilde{v}).P_1 + R_1 \mid P'_1 : Q_1] \mid [(\nu\tilde{z})\bar{y}\langle\tilde{w}\rangle.P_2 + R_2 \mid P'_2 : Q_2] \rightarrow [(\nu\tilde{x}\tilde{z})P_1\{\tilde{w}/\tilde{v}\} \mid P'_1 \mid P_2 \mid P'_2 : Q_1 \mid Q_2]$$
$$if \ y \notin \tilde{x} \cup \tilde{z} \ and \ \tilde{x} \cap fn(P_2|P'_2) = \emptyset \ and \ \tilde{z} \cap fn(P_1|P'_1) = \emptyset$$

(c) Reduction Semantics

Fig. 1. Syntax and Semantics of the committed pi calculus

The above protocol allows the client to abort the transaction after receiving an offer (for instance when the offer does not satisfy her expectations). Alternatively, the hotel may abort after receiving a request (for instance when no rooms are available). We illustrate the use of compensations by making the component Hotel to generate the single message $\overline{alt}\langle hotel \rangle$ to provide the client with an alternative hotel to contact. The compensation of Client is a process that receives a message on the port alt and then behaves like Q, which stands for the process that contacts the alternative hotel h.

The process Client|Hotel behaves in committed pi as follows. When both transactions communicate through the port *request* for the first time they are merged in a unique larger transaction, whose transactional process and compensation correspond respectively to the parallel composition of the residuals of the original transactions and to the parallel composition of the original compensations, as shown below

$$\text{Client|Hotel} \rightarrow [offer(price).(\overline{accept}\langle cc \rangle + \tau.\mathbf{abort})$$
$$\mid (\overline{offer}\langle rate \rangle.accept(card) + \tau.\mathbf{abort}) : alt(h).Q \mid \overline{alt}\langle hotel \rangle]$$

From this moment the system may evolve as usual. Assuming the hotel sends an offer and the client replies with a confirmation, the system commits the transaction as follows

$$\rightarrow [(\overline{accept}\langle cc \rangle + \tau.\mathbf{abort}) \mid accept(card) : alt(h).Q \mid \overline{alt}\langle hotel \rangle]$$
$$\rightarrow [\mathbf{0} : alt(h).Q \mid \overline{alt}\langle hotel \rangle]$$
$$\rightarrow \mathbf{0}$$

Otherwise, if we assume that the client refuses the offer then the system evolves as follows and activates the compensation of both parties.

$$\rightarrow [(\overline{accept}\langle cc \rangle + \tau.\mathbf{abort}) \mid accept(card) : alt(h).Q \mid \overline{alt}\langle hotel \rangle]$$
$$\rightarrow alt(h).Q \mid \overline{alt}\langle hotel \rangle$$

4   Committed cc-pi

In this section we enrich cc-pi with the transactional mechanism described above. Before introducing the extended calculus, we show an example that motivates the addition of compensating transactions for modelling SLA negotiations.

Example 3. Consider the system shown in Example 1. Suppose that the client is intended to pay a maximal cost $60 instead of $100. The new system is as follows.

$$S' \equiv (r)(p)\mathsf{Client}_{4\mathsf{Gb},\$60} \mid \mathsf{Provider}_{6\mathsf{Gb},\$20} \mid \mathsf{Provider}_{3\mathsf{Gb},\$15}$$

The evolution of S' is as in the original system until the first provider and the client place their own constraints on the cost (as before the client cannot synchronise with the other provider). Then, the negotiation between the client and the first provider fails, because the constraints $cost \leq c$, $bw' \leq ob$ and $cost = cost'$ are inconsistent, and the system is stuck. Later in §4.3, we will see how to model this scenario using the transactional mechanism of committed cc-pi.

4.1   Syntax

The syntax of committed cc-pi processes is specified in Figure 2(a). Assume the infinite set of names $\mathcal{N}$, ranged over by $x, y, z, \ldots$ and a set of process identifiers, ranged over by D. We let c range over the set of constraints of an arbitrary named c-semiring C.

The syntax of the calculus is the same as for the cc-pi except for the inclusion of a transactional primitive which is inspired by committed pi. The τ prefix stands for a silent action, output $\overline{x}\langle \tilde{y} \rangle$ and input $x\langle \tilde{y} \rangle$ are complementary prefixes used for communications. Unlike other calculi, the input prefix is not binding, hence input and output operations are fully symmetric and the synchronisation of two complementary prefixes $x\langle \tilde{y} \rangle$ and $\overline{x}\langle \tilde{z} \rangle$, rather than binding $\tilde{y}$ to $\tilde{z}$, yields the name fusion $\tilde{y} = \tilde{z}$. Prefix $\mathtt{tell}\ c$ generates a constraint c and puts it in parallel with the other constraints, if the resulting parallel composition of constraints is consistent; $\mathtt{tell}\ c$ aborts otherwise. Prefix $\mathtt{ask}\ c$ is enabled if c is entailed by the set of constraints in parallel. Prefix $\mathtt{retract}\ c$ removes a constraint c, if c is present. *Unconstrained processes* U are essentially processes that can only contain constraints c in prefixes $\mathtt{tell}\ c$, $\mathtt{ask}\ c$, and $\mathtt{retract}\ c$. As usual, $\mathbf{0}$ stands for the inert process and $U \mid U$ for the parallel composition. $\sum_i \pi_i.U_i$ denotes a mixed choice in which some guarded unconstrained process U_i is chosen when the corresponding guard π_i is enabled. Restriction $(x)U$ makes the name x local in U. A defining equation for a process $D(\tilde{y})$ is of the form $D(\tilde{x}) \stackrel{\mathrm{def}}{=} U$ where $|\tilde{x}| = |\tilde{y}|$ and the free names of U must be included in $\tilde{x}$. The transaction primitive $[P : Q].U$ defines a

Prefixes	$\pi ::= \tau \mid \bar{x}\langle \tilde{y}\rangle \mid x\langle \tilde{y}\rangle \mid \texttt{tell } c \mid \texttt{ask } c \mid \texttt{retract } c$
Unconstrained Processes	$U ::= \mathbf{0} \mid U|U \mid \Sigma_i \pi_i.U_i \mid (x)U \mid D(\tilde{y}) \mid [P:Q].U$
Constrained Processes	$P ::= U \mid c \mid P|P \mid (x)P$

(a) Syntax

$$P|\mathbf{0} \equiv P \qquad\qquad P+Q \equiv Q+P \qquad\qquad (x)(y)P \equiv (y)(x)P$$

$$P|Q \equiv Q|P \qquad (P+Q)+R \equiv P+(Q+R) \qquad P|(x)Q \equiv (x)(P|Q) \text{ if } x \notin \mathrm{fn}(P)$$

$$(P|Q)|R \equiv P|(Q|R) \qquad\qquad D(\tilde{y}) \equiv U\{\tilde{y}/\tilde{x}\} \text{ if } D(\tilde{x}) \stackrel{\mathrm{def}}{=} U \qquad (x)\mathbf{0} \equiv \mathbf{0}$$

$$[(x)P:Q].U \equiv (x)[P:Q].U \quad \text{if } x \notin \mathrm{fn}(Q,U)$$

(b) Structural equivalence

(TAU)

$$C|\tau.U \stackrel{\tau}{\rightarrow} C|U$$

(OUT)

$$C|\bar{x}\langle \tilde{y}\rangle.U \stackrel{\bar{x}\langle \tilde{y}\rangle}{\longrightarrow} C|U$$

(INP)

$$C|x\langle \tilde{y}\rangle.U \stackrel{x\langle \tilde{y}\rangle}{\longrightarrow} C|U$$

(TELL)

$$C|\texttt{tell } c.U \stackrel{\tau}{\rightarrow} C|c|U \text{ if } C|c \text{ consistent}$$

(ABT-TELL)

$$C|\texttt{tell } c.U \stackrel{\texttt{abr}}{\longrightarrow} \mathbf{0} \text{ if } C|c \text{ not consistent}$$

(ASK)

$$C|\texttt{ask } c.U \stackrel{\tau}{\rightarrow} C|U \quad \text{if } C \vdash c$$

(RETRACT)

$$C|\texttt{retract } c.U \stackrel{\tau}{\rightarrow} (C-c)|U$$

(COMM)

$$\frac{C|U \stackrel{x\langle \tilde{y}\rangle}{\longrightarrow} C|U' \quad C|V \stackrel{\bar{z}\langle \tilde{w}\rangle}{\longrightarrow} C|V'}{C|U|V \stackrel{\tau}{\rightarrow} C|\tilde{y}=\tilde{w}|U'|V'} \quad \text{if } |\tilde{y}| = |\tilde{w}| \text{ and } C|\tilde{y}=\tilde{w} \text{ consistent and } C \vdash x=z$$

(ABT-COMM)

$$\frac{C|U \stackrel{x\langle \tilde{y}\rangle}{\longrightarrow} P \quad C|V \stackrel{\bar{z}\langle \tilde{w}\rangle}{\longrightarrow} Q}{C|U|V \stackrel{\texttt{abr}}{\longrightarrow} \mathbf{0}} \quad \text{if } |\tilde{y}| = |\tilde{w}| \text{ and } C|\tilde{y}=\tilde{w} \text{ not consistent and } C \vdash x=z$$

(PAR)

$$\frac{P \stackrel{\alpha}{\rightarrow} P' \quad \alpha \neq \texttt{abr}}{P|U \stackrel{\alpha}{\rightarrow} P'|U}$$

(ABT-PAR)

$$\frac{P \stackrel{\texttt{abr}}{\longrightarrow} \mathbf{0}}{P|Q \stackrel{\texttt{abr}}{\longrightarrow} \mathbf{0}}$$

(SUM)

$$\frac{C|\pi_i.U_i \stackrel{\alpha}{\rightarrow} U'}{C|\Sigma \pi_i.U_i \stackrel{\alpha}{\rightarrow} U'}$$

(RES)

$$\frac{P \stackrel{\tau}{\rightarrow} P'}{(x)P \stackrel{\tau}{\rightarrow} (x)P'}$$

(TRANS)

$$\frac{P \stackrel{\tau}{\rightarrow} P'}{[P:Q].U \stackrel{\tau}{\rightarrow} [P':Q].U}$$

(TR-COMP)

$$\frac{P \stackrel{\texttt{abr}}{\longrightarrow} P'}{[P:Q].U \stackrel{\tau}{\rightarrow} Q}$$

(TR-COMMIT)

$$[C:Q].U \stackrel{\tau}{\rightarrow} C|U$$

(TR-PAR)

$$\frac{[P:Q].U \stackrel{\tau}{\rightarrow} P'}{C|[P:Q].U \stackrel{\tau}{\rightarrow} C|P'}$$

(TR-COMM)

$$\frac{C_1|U_1 \stackrel{\bar{x}\langle \tilde{y}\rangle}{\longrightarrow} R_1 \quad C_2|U_2 \stackrel{z\langle \tilde{w}\rangle}{\longrightarrow} R_2 \quad |\tilde{y}| = |\tilde{w}| \text{ and } C|C_1|C_2|\tilde{y}=\tilde{w} \text{ consistent and } C|C_1|C_2 \vdash x=z}{C|[C_1|U_1:Q_1].V_1|[C_2|U_2:Q_2].V_2 \stackrel{\tau}{\rightarrow} C|[R_1|R_2|\tilde{y}=\tilde{w}:Q_1|Q_2].(V_1|V_2)}$$

(c) Labelled Semantics

Fig. 2. Syntax and Small-Step Semantics of the committed cc-pi calculus

transactional process P which evolves to U in case of a commit, while otherwise activates the compensation Q. *Constrained processes* P are defined like unconstrained processes U but for the fact that P may have constraints c in parallel with processes. We simply write processes to refer to constrained processes.

4.2 Operational Semantics

The *structural equivalence* relation $\equiv$ is defined as the least equivalence over processes closed with respect to α-conversion and satisfying the rules in Figure 2(b). Note that the notion of *free names* fn(P) of a process P is extended to handle constraints by stating that the set of free names of a constraint c is the support supp(c) of c. The structural axioms can be applied for reducing every process P into a normal form $(\tilde{x})(C|U)$, where C is a parallel composition of constraints and U can only contain restrictions under prefixes, i.e. $U \not\equiv (\tilde{y})U'$.

Well-formedness. Let $Ch \subseteq \mathcal{N}$ be a set of *channel names* that can only be fused among each other and let chn(P) be the set of channel names occurring free in P. P is *well-formed* if there exists a process $Q \equiv P$ such that every occurrence of transaction in Q has the form $(x_1,\ldots,x_n)[P':Q'].U$, where $(\text{fn}(P',Q') \setminus \text{chn}(P',Q')) \subseteq \{x_1,\ldots,x_n\}$. For example, $P \equiv (x)(\texttt{tell}\,(x=z)\,|\,(w)[\bar{y}\langle w\rangle.\mathbf{0}:Q].U)$ is well-formed, but $R \equiv (x)(\texttt{tell}\,(x=y))\,|\,[\bar{y}\langle x\rangle.\mathbf{0}:Q].U)$ is not. Hereafter, we assume all processes to be well-formed.

Let $A = \{\tau, \bar{x}\langle\tilde{y}\rangle, x\langle\tilde{y}\rangle, \texttt{abr}\,|\,x, y_i \in \mathcal{N}\text{ for }\tilde{y} = \langle y_1,\ldots,y_n\rangle\,\}$ be a set of labels and let α range over A. The labelled transition semantics of processes (taken up to structural equivalence $\equiv$) is the smallest relation $P \xrightarrow{\alpha} Q$, defined by the inference rules in Figure 2(c), where: C stands for the parallel composition of constraints $c_1\,|\,\ldots\,|\,c_n$; C *consistent* means $(c_1 \times \ldots \times c_n) \neq 0$; $C \vdash c$ if $(c_1 \times \ldots \times c_n) \vdash c$; $C-c$ stands for $c_1\,|\,\ldots\,|\,c_{i-1}\,|\,c_{i+1}\,|\,\ldots\,|\,c_n$ if $c = c_i$ for some i, while $C-c = C$ otherwise.

The choice of giving a labelled transition semantics rather than a reduction semantics is stylistic and not relevant for our treatment. After this remark, the rules in Figure 2(c) essentially include the original rules of cc-pi plus the rules concerning the transactional mechanism. Roughly, the idea behind this operational semantics is to proceed as follows. First, rearranging processes into the normal form $(x_1)\ldots(x_n)(C|U)$ by applying the structural axioms. Next, applying the rules (TELL), (ASK), (RETRACT) for primitives on constraints and the rule (OUT), (INP), possibly (SUM) and (COMM) for synchronising processes. Finally, closing with respect to parallel composition and restriction ((PAR), (RES)). More in detail, rule (TELL) states that if $C|c$ is consistent then a process can place c in parallel with C, the process aborts otherwise. Rule (ASK) specifies that a process starting with an ask c prefix evolves to its continuation when c is entailed by C and it is stuck otherwise. By rule (RETRACT) a process can remove c if c is one of the syntactic constraints of C. In rules (COMM), we write $\tilde{y} = \tilde{w}$ to denote the parallel composition of fusions $y_1 = w_1\,|\,\ldots\,|\,y_n = w_n$. Intuitively, two processes $\bar{x}\langle\tilde{y}\rangle.P$ and $z\langle\tilde{w}\rangle.Q$ can synchronise when the equality of the names x and z is entailed by C and the parallel composition $C\,|\,\tilde{y} = \tilde{w}$ is consistent. Note that it is legal to treat name equalities as constraints c over C, because named c-semirings contain fusions. Rule (PAR) allows for the closure with respect to unconstrained processes in parallel. This rule disallows computations that consider only partial stores of constraints and, consequently, it makes necessary to add the parallel composition of constraints C in several operational rules, such as (TAU) and (SUM), even though this might seem superfluous. The remaining rules deal with transactions. Rules (TRANS), (TR-COMP), (COMMIT), and (TR-COMM) serve the same purpose as the homologous rules of the committed pi. Note that the well-formedness assumption ensures that C, C_1 and C_2 can only share channel names. Rules (ABT-TELL) and (ABT-COMM) force an abort in case a process tries to place a constraint that is not consistent with the parallel composition of constraints C. Rules (ABT-PAR) extends the effect of an abort to the sibling processes. Unlike rule (PAR), rule (TR-PAR) allows closure with respect to constraints running in parallel. Note that such composition is legal in virtue of the well-formedness assumption which ensures $\text{fn}(C) \cap fn(P,Q) = \emptyset$.

4.3 Example: A Transactional SLA

We now model in committed cc-pi the scenario depicted in Example 1. The client and the server can be sketched as follows.

$$\text{Client}_{rb,c}(r,p) \equiv (bw)(cost)[\texttt{tell } (bw \geq rb).\bar{r}\langle bw \rangle.\texttt{tell } (cost \leq c).p\langle cost \rangle.\mathbf{0}:Q].$$
$$U(bw,cost)$$

$$\text{Provider}_{ob,uc}(r,p) \equiv (bw')(cost')[\texttt{tell } (bw' \leq ob).r\langle bw' \rangle.$$
$$\texttt{tell } (bw' * uc = cost').\bar{p}\langle cost' \rangle.\mathbf{0} : Q'].U'(bw',cost')$$

The specification above is the same as the one given in Example 1 using cc-pi, apart from the fact that here the sequences of actions taken by each party are within a transactional scope and that they include compensating processes Q and Q'. Assume the following system composed of a client and two providers.

$$S \equiv (r)(p)\text{Client}_{4Gb,\$100} \mid \text{Provider}_{6Gb,\$20} \mid \text{Provider}_{3Gb,\$15}$$

By executing the `tell` prefixes in all transactions we obtain the following derivation (we abbreviate $U(bw,cost)$ and $U'(bw',cost')$ with U and U' respectively).

$$S \xrightarrow{\tau}^* (r)(p)(bw)(cost)[bw \geq 4Gb \mid \bar{r}\langle bw \rangle.\texttt{tell } (cost \leq \$100).p\langle cost \rangle.\mathbf{0} : Q].U$$
$$\mid (bw')(cost')[bw' \leq 6Gb \mid r\langle bw' \rangle.\texttt{tell } (bw' * \$20 = cost').\bar{p}\langle cost' \rangle.\mathbf{0}:Q'].U'$$
$$\mid (bw')(cost')[bw' \leq 3Gb \mid r\langle bw' \rangle.\texttt{tell } (bw' * \$15 = cost').\bar{p}\langle cost' \rangle.\mathbf{0}:Q'].U'$$

As in the non-transactional case, the client can synchronise only with the first provider. Hence, the only possible reduction is

$$\xrightarrow{\tau} (r)(p)(bw)(cost)(bw')(cost')$$
$$[bw \geq 4Gb \mid bw = bw' \mid bw' \leq 6Gb$$
$$\mid \texttt{tell } (cost \leq \$100).p\langle cost \rangle.\mathbf{0} \mid \texttt{tell } (bw' * \$20 = cost').\bar{p}\langle cost' \rangle.\mathbf{0}:Q|Q'].(U|U')$$
$$\mid (bw')(cost')[bw' \leq 3Gb \mid r\langle bw' \rangle.\texttt{tell } (bw' * \$15 = cost').\bar{p}\langle cost' \rangle.\mathbf{0} : Q'].U'$$

Next, the provider and the client fix their constraints on the cost of the service, the communication over p takes place, and the transaction can commit:

$$\xrightarrow{\tau}{}^{*} (r)(p)(bw)(cost)(bw')(cost')$$
$$bw \geq 4\text{Gb} \mid bw = bw' \mid bw' \leq 6\text{Gb} \mid bw' * \$20 = cost' \mid cost \leq \$100 \mid U \mid U'$$
$$\mid (bw')(cost')[bw' \leq 3\text{Gb} \mid r\langle bw'\rangle.\texttt{tell}\ (bw' * \$15 = cost').\overline{p}\langle cost'\rangle.0 : Q'].U'$$

Consider now the variant shown in Example 3 in which the client is $\text{Client}_{4\text{Gb},\$60}$ instead of $\text{Client}_{4\text{Gb},\$100}$. In this case, the system may evolve as before until the client and the provider fix the constraint about variables $cost$ and $cost'$. Afterwards, when they synchronise on p, the transaction aborts since the constraints are now not consistent. In such case the compensations Q and Q' are activated. Note that the precise definition of the compensations may dictate the strategy followed by each participant during the negotiation. For instance, for the client the compensation could be $\text{Client}_{rb,c+\$10}$. That is it may offer to pay more for the requested bandwidth, or alternatively $\text{Client}_{rb-1\text{Gb},c}$ to request less bandwidth by offering the same price. Similarly, the provider may fix its own negotiation strategy.

5   Big-Step Operational Semantics

In this section we introduce an alternative definition for the semantics of committed cc-pi, which allows us to reason about transactional computations at different levels of abstraction. In particular, the big-step semantics is intended to single out the computations of a system that are not transient, or in other words, the states containing no running transactions. Therefore, the big-step semantics provides a description of the possible evolution of a system through stable states. Processes associated to stable states of the system are said *stable processes*. Formally, a process P is *stable* if $P \not\equiv (\tilde{x})[P_1 : Q_1].U_1 \mid P_2$, i.e. P does not contain active transactions. We remark that our definition of stable process is intentionally not preserved by weak bisimulation. In case such property is required, an alternative characterization of stable process could be given by slightly adapting the original semantics in order to make the beginning of transaction executions observable.

A committed cc-pi process P is a *shallow process* if every subterm of the form $[P' : Q']$ occurs under a prefix τ. Moreover, we require U shallow for any definition $D(\tilde{x}) \stackrel{\text{def}}{=} U$. The main idea behind shallow processes is that of syntactically distinguish transactional terms that have not been activated yet (i.e., those occurring after τ prefixes) from those that are already active (i.e., non stable processes). For instance, the process $\tau.[U : U']$ denotes a transaction that has not been activated, while the term $[U : U']$ stands for a transaction that is in execution.

Hereafter we assume all processes to be shallow. Moreover, we let P_S and U_S range over *stable* processes and *stable unconstrained* processes, respectively. We remark that any process P can be straightforwardly rewritten as a shallow process by adding τ prefixes before any transactions, without changing the meaning of the program.

The big-step or high-level semantics of processes is the smallest relation $P \stackrel{\tau}{\Rightarrow} Q$ induced by the rules in Figure 3. Most rules are analogous to the small-step semantics.

(TAU)
$$C \mid \tau.U \xrightarrow{\tau} C \mid U$$

(OUT)
$$C \mid \overline{x}\langle \widetilde{y} \rangle.U \xrightarrow{\overline{x}\langle \widetilde{y} \rangle} C \mid U$$

(INP)
$$C \mid x\langle \widetilde{y} \rangle.U \xrightarrow{x\langle \widetilde{y} \rangle} C \mid U$$

(TELL)
$$C \mid \mathtt{tell}\ c.U \xrightarrow{\tau} C \mid c \mid U \ \text{ if } C \mid c \text{ consistent}$$

(ABT-TELL)
$$C \mid \mathtt{tell}\ c.U \xrightarrow{\mathtt{abr}} \mathbf{0} \ \text{ if } C \mid c \text{ not consistent}$$

(ASK)
$$C \mid \mathtt{ask}\ c.U \xrightarrow{\tau} C \mid U \ \text{ if } C \vdash c$$

(RETRACT)
$$C \mid \mathtt{retract}\ c.U \xrightarrow{\tau} (C - c) \mid U$$

(COMM)
$$\frac{C \mid U \xrightarrow{x\langle \widetilde{y} \rangle} C \mid U' \quad C \mid V \xrightarrow{\overline{z}\langle \widetilde{w} \rangle} C \mid V' \quad \text{if } |\widetilde{y}| = |\widetilde{w}| \text{ and } C \mid \widetilde{y} = \widetilde{w} \text{ consistent and } C \vdash x = z}{C \mid U \mid V \xrightarrow{\tau} C \mid \widetilde{y} = \widetilde{w} \mid U' \mid V'}$$

(ABT-COMM)
$$\frac{C \mid U \xrightarrow{x\langle \widetilde{y} \rangle} P \quad C \mid V \xrightarrow{\overline{z}\langle \widetilde{w} \rangle} Q \quad \text{if } |\widetilde{y}| = |\widetilde{w}| \text{ and } C \mid \widetilde{y} = \widetilde{w} \text{ not consistent and } C \vdash x = z}{C \mid U \mid V \xrightarrow{\mathtt{abr}} \mathbf{0}}$$

(PAR)
$$\frac{P \xrightarrow{\alpha} P' \quad \alpha \neq \mathtt{abr}}{P \mid U \xrightarrow{\alpha} P' \mid U}$$

(ABT-PAR)
$$\frac{P \xrightarrow{\mathtt{abr}} \mathbf{0}}{P \mid Q \xrightarrow{\mathtt{abr}} \mathbf{0}}$$

(SUM)
$$\frac{C \mid \pi_i.U_i \xrightarrow{\alpha} U'}{C \mid \sum \pi_i.U_i \xrightarrow{\alpha} U'}$$

(RES)
$$\frac{P \xrightarrow{\tau} P'}{(x)P \xrightarrow{\tau} (x)P'}$$

(TRANS')
$$\frac{P_S \xRightarrow{\tau} P_S'}{[P_S : Q_S].U_S \xrightarrow{\tau} [P_S' : Q_S].U_S}$$

(TR-COMP)
$$\frac{P \xrightarrow{\mathtt{abr}} P'}{[P : Q].U \xrightarrow{\tau} Q}$$

(TR-COMMIT)
$$[C : Q].U \xrightarrow{\tau} C \mid U$$

(TR-PAR)
$$\frac{[P : Q].U \xrightarrow{\tau} P'}{C \mid [P : Q].U \xrightarrow{\tau} C \mid P'}$$

(TR-COMM')
$$\frac{C_1 \mid U_{S_1} \xrightarrow{\overline{x}\langle \widetilde{y} \rangle} R_{S_1} \quad C_2 \mid U_{S_2} \xrightarrow{z\langle \widetilde{w} \rangle} R_{S_2} \quad |\widetilde{y}| = |\widetilde{w}| \text{ and } C \mid C_1 \mid C_2 \mid \widetilde{y} = \widetilde{w} \text{ consistent and } C \mid C_1 \mid C_2 \vdash x = z}{C \mid [C_1 \mid U_{S_1} : Q_{S_1}].V_1 \mid [C_2 \mid U_{S_2} : Q_{S_2}].V_2 \xrightarrow{\tau} C \mid [R_{S_1} \mid R_{S_2} \mid \widetilde{y} = \widetilde{w} : Q_{S_1} \mid Q_{S_2}].(V_1 \mid V_2)}$$

(SEQ)
$$\frac{P \xrightarrow{\tau} P' \quad P' \xrightarrow{\tau} P''}{P \xrightarrow{\tau} P''}$$

(UP)
$$\frac{P_S \xrightarrow{\tau} P_S'}{P_S \xRightarrow{\tau} P_S'}$$

Fig. 3. Big step semantics

The only rules that have been redefined are (TRANS) and (TR-COMM). In particular, the new (TR-COMM') allows the merge of transactions only when the synchronising processes U_{S_1} and U_{S_2} are stable. Similarly, rule (TRANS') requires internal reductions to be high-level steps, i.e., reductions from stable processes to stable processes. Hence, the reduction $[P_S : Q_S].U_S \xrightarrow{\tau} [P_S' : Q_S].U_S$ is not a high-level step, since it does not relate stable processes. In addition, rule (SEQ) stands for the sequential composition of low-level steps, and rule (UP) states that a low-level step is a high-level step when the involved processes are stable.

Example 4. We show the big-step reductions for the example given in Section 4.3. In particular, we consider the shallow version of the processes $\mathsf{Client}_{rb,c}$ and $\mathsf{Provider}_{ob,uc}$ (i.e., by adding the prefixes τ before transactional scopes). For instance, the following system

$$S' \equiv (r)(p)\mathsf{Client}_{4Gb,\$100} \mid \mathsf{Provider}_{6Gb,\$20} \mid \mathsf{Provider}_{5Gb,\$30}$$

has the following two big-step reductions

$$S' \overset{\tau}{\Rightarrow} (r)(p)(bw)(cost)(bw')(cost')$$
$$bw \geq 4Gb \mid bw = bw' \mid bw' \leq 6Gb \mid bw' * \$20 = cost' \mid cost \leq \$100 \mid U \mid U'$$
$$\mid \mathsf{Provider}_{5Gb,\$30}$$

and

$$S' \overset{\tau}{\Rightarrow} (r)(p)(bw)(cost)(bw')(cost') Q \mid Q' \mid \mathsf{Provider}_{6Gb,\$20}$$

The first one describes the successful negotiation between the provider $\mathsf{Provider}_{6Gb,\$20}$ and the client, while the the second one describes the failed negotiation between the client and $\mathsf{Provider}_{5Gb,\$30}$.

The remaining of this section is devoted to show that the small- and the big-step semantics coincide for shallow processes. Next propositions are auxiliary results that will be used for proving the main theorem.

Proposition 1. *If $P_S \overset{\alpha}{\rightarrow} P$ and $\alpha = x\langle \tilde{y} \rangle, \bar{x}\langle \tilde{y} \rangle$, then P is stable.*

Proof. By rule induction (using the fact that transactions occur only under τ prefixes in shallow processes).

The following result assures that a derivation from a stable process P_S that reduces to a non stable process, which is able to perform an input, an output, or an abort action, can be rewritten as a computation that executes the respective action first, and then starts all the transactions.

Proposition 2. *Let P_S be a stable process. If $P_S \overset{\tau}{\rightarrow}{}^* (\tilde{x})R_S|T$ and $R_S \overset{\alpha}{\rightarrow} R'$ for $\alpha = y\langle \tilde{z} \rangle, \bar{y}\langle \tilde{z} \rangle, \mathsf{abr}$, then, there exists a stable process T_S s.t. $P_S \overset{\tau}{\rightarrow}{}^* (\tilde{x})R_S|T_S \overset{\alpha}{\rightarrow} (\tilde{x})R'|T_S \overset{\tau}{\rightarrow}{}^* (\tilde{x})R'|T$.*

Proof (sketch). Proof follows by induction on the length of the derivation $P_S \overset{\tau}{\rightarrow}{}^n (\tilde{x})R_S|T$. The base case ($n = 0$) is immediate by considering $T_S \equiv T$ (note that $P_S \equiv (\tilde{x})R_S|T$ and, hence, T is stable). Inductive step follows by considering $P_S \overset{\tau}{\rightarrow} P$. There are two main possibilities: if P is stable, then the proof is immediate by inductive hypothesis. If P is not stable, the only possibility for $P_S \overset{\tau}{\rightarrow} P$ is $P_S \equiv (\tilde{z})\tau.[Q : Q'].U|O_S$ (by shallowness, transactions occur only under τ prefixes). Consequently, $P \equiv (\tilde{z})[Q : Q'].U|O_S$. There are three possibilities: (i) when $O_S \overset{\tau}{\rightarrow}{}^* \overset{\alpha}{\rightarrow} O'_S$, then the proof follows by using inductive hypothesis; (ii) when $[Q : Q'].U \overset{\tau}{\rightarrow}{}^* \overset{\alpha}{\rightarrow} O$, then α occurs after the commit of the transaction and $U \overset{\tau}{\rightarrow}{}^* \overset{\alpha}{\rightarrow} O$, it follows by inductive hypothesis (since U is stable); (iii) $[Q : Q'].U|O_S \overset{\tau}{\rightarrow}{}^* \overset{\alpha}{\rightarrow} O$ by applying at least once rule (TR-COMM). Also in this case α may occur only after the commit of all joint transactions, which releases only stable processes. Hence, the proof follows by inductive hypothesis.

Next proposition assures that all the possible states reached by the execution of a pair of transactions that have no active subtransactions can be obtained by computations that never merge transactions containing subtransactions.

Proposition 3. *For any two shallow non nested transactions* $[P_{S_1} : Q].U$ *and* $[P_{S_2} : Q'].U'$, *the following holds*

$$C|[P_{S_1} : Q].U|[P_{S_2} : Q'].U' \xrightarrow{\tau}{}^* C|[P_1 : Q].U|[P_2 : Q'].U' \xrightarrow{\tau} C|[P : Q|Q'].(U|U')$$

implies

$$C|[P_{S_1} : Q].U|[P_{S_2} : Q'].U' \overset{\tau}{\rightarrowtail}{}^* C|[P'_{S_1} : Q].U|[P'_{S_2} : Q'].U' \overset{\tau}{\rightarrowtail} C|[P_S : Q|Q'].(U|U') \overset{\tau}{\rightarrowtail}{}^*$$
$$C|[P : Q|Q'].(U|U')$$

Proof (sketch). The reduction step $C|[P_1 : Q].U|[P_2 : Q'].U' \xrightarrow{\tau} C|[P : Q|Q'].(U|U')$ implies that $\exists x, z$ s.t. $P_1 \xrightarrow{x\langle \tilde{y} \rangle} P'_1$, $P_2 \xrightarrow{\bar{z}\langle \tilde{w} \rangle} P'_2$, $C \vdash x = z$, and $P = P'_1 | P'_2 | \tilde{y} = \tilde{w}$. Note that $P_1 \xrightarrow{x\langle \tilde{y} \rangle} P'_1$ implies $P_1 \equiv (\tilde{v}) R_{S_1} | T_1$ and $R_{S_1} \xrightarrow{x\langle \tilde{y} \rangle} R'_{S_1}$. By Proposition 2, there exists a stable process P'_{S_1} s.t. $P_{S_1} \xrightarrow{\tau}{}^* P'_{S_1} \xrightarrow{x\langle \tilde{y} \rangle} P''_1 \xrightarrow{\tau}{}^* P'_1$. By Proposition 1, P''_1 is stable. Similarly, for P_{S_2}. Hence, both transactions can be merged, obtaining $C|[(\tilde{v}) P''_1 | P''_2 | \tilde{y} = \tilde{w} : Q|Q'].(U|U')$. Note $P''_1 | P''_2$ is stable and therefore the proof follows by taking $P_S \equiv (\tilde{v}) P''_1 | P''_2 | \tilde{y} = \tilde{w}$.

Lemma 1. $P_S \xrightarrow{\tau}{}^+ P'_S$ *implies* $P_S \overset{\tau}{\rightarrowtail} P'_S$.

Proof (sketch). Follows by induction on the length of the derivation $P_S \xrightarrow{\tau}{}^n P'_S$. Base case ($n = 1$) is immediate by rule analysis. Inductive step ($n = k$) considers $P_S \xrightarrow{\tau} P \xrightarrow{\tau}{}^k P'_S$. If P is stable, the proof is completed by applying inductive hypothesis. Otherwise, the only possibility is $P \equiv (\tilde{x})[Q_S : Q'_S].U_S | P_{S_1}$ and $P_S \overset{\tau}{\rightarrowtail} P$ (proved by structural induction over P_S). Since $P \xrightarrow{\tau}{}^k P'_S$, there are three possibilities for completing the computation:

1. The transaction commits by itself, then $Q_S \xrightarrow{\tau}{}^* (\tilde{y})C$. By inductive hypothesis $Q_S \overset{\tau}{\rightarrowtail} (\tilde{y})C$. By rule (UP) $Q_S \overset{\tau}{\Rightarrow} (\tilde{y})C$, by (TRANS') $[Q_S : Q'_S].U_S \overset{\tau}{\rightarrowtail} [(\tilde{y})C : Q'_S].U_S$, by (COMMIT) $[(\tilde{y})C : Q'_S].U_S \overset{\tau}{\rightarrowtail} (\tilde{y})C|U_S$, by (TR-PAR) and (PAR) $[Q_S : Q'_S].U_S | P_{S_1} \overset{\tau}{\rightarrowtail} (\tilde{y})C|U_S|P_{S_1}$, and finally by (RES) $(\tilde{x})[Q_S : Q'_S].U_S|P_{S_1} \overset{\tau}{\rightarrowtail} (\tilde{x})(\tilde{y})C|U_S|P_{S_1}$. The proof is completed by inductive hypothesis on $(\tilde{x})(\tilde{y})C|U_S|P_{S_1} \overset{\tau}{\rightarrowtail} P'_S$ and rule (STEP).

2. The transaction aborts by itself, then $Q_S \xrightarrow{\tau}{}^* Q \overset{abr}{\Rightarrow} Q'$. Then, by Proposition 2 there exists Q'' and Q''' stable s.t. $Q_S \xrightarrow{\tau}{}^* Q'' \overset{abr}{\Rightarrow} Q'''$. By, inductive hypothesis $Q_S \overset{\tau}{\rightarrowtail} Q''$. By (TRANS') $[Q_S : Q'_S].U_S \overset{\tau}{\rightarrowtail} [Q'' : Q'_S].U_S$. By structural induction we can prove that $Q'' \overset{abr}{\Rightarrow} Q'''$ implies $Q'' \overset{\tau}{\rightarrowtail} Q'''$, and then by (TR-COMP) $[Q'' : Q'_S].U_S \overset{\tau}{\rightarrowtail} Q'_S$. The proof is completed as in the previous case.

3. The transaction merges with some transaction activated by P_{S_1}. The proof follows by using repeatedly Proposition 3 for proving that merge of transactions can be done with non nested transactions, and inductive hypothesis for proving that reductions inside transactions from stable to stable processes correspond to $\rightarrowtail$ reductions.

Theorem 1. $P_S \xrightarrow{\tau}^+ P'_S$ implies $P_S \xRightarrow{\tau} P'_S$.

Lemma 2. $P \rightarrowtail^{\tau} P'$ implies $P \xrightarrow{\tau}^+ P'$.

Proof (sketch). Proof follows by rule induction. Rules (TAU), (TELL), (ASK), (RETRACT), are immediate. Cases (PAR), (SUM), (RES), (TR-PAR) follows by inductive hypothesis. Cases (COMM) and (TR-COMM) follow by proving using rule induction that $P \xrightarrow{\alpha} P'$ for $\alpha = x\langle \tilde{y} \rangle, \bar{x}\langle \tilde{y} \rangle$ implies $P \xrightarrow{\alpha} P'$. If the last applied rule is (TRANS), then $P \equiv [P_S : Q_S].U_S$. Consequently, the proof has the following shape:

$$\frac{\dfrac{P_S \xrightarrow{\tau}{}^{\rightarrowtail} P'_S}{P_S \xRightarrow{\tau} P'_S} \ (\text{UP})}{[P_S : Q_S].U_S \xrightarrow{\tau}{}^{\rightarrowtail} [P_S : Q_S].U_S} \ (\text{TRANS})$$

By inductive hypothesis on $P_S \rightarrowtail^{\tau} P'_S$ we have that $P_S \xrightarrow{\tau}^+ P'_S$. Then, it can be proved by induction on the length of the derivation that $P_S \xrightarrow{\tau}^+ P'_S$ implies $[P_S : Q_S].U_S \xrightarrow{\tau}^+ [P'_S : Q_S].U_S$

Theorem 2. $P \xRightarrow{\tau} P'$ implies $P \xrightarrow{\tau}^+ P'$.

Theorem 3. $P \xRightarrow{\tau} P'$ iff $P \xrightarrow{\tau}^+ P'$.

Proof. Immediate by Theorems 1 and 2.

6 Concluding Remarks

We have presented a constraint-based model of transactional SLAs. In our language, the mutual responsibilities of service providers and clients are expressed in terms of constraints, which are placed by each party during the negotiation. If the combination of such constraints is consistent, then they form the SLA contract. On the contrary, if the negotiation fails, each party can activate a programmable compensation aimed e.g. at relaxing client requirements or increasing service guarantees.

The proposed approach seems promising for studying more complex negotiation scenarios that, for instance, include third parties applications or feature arbitrarily nested transactions. We also plan to investigate different compensation mechanisms in which, e.g., the constraints placed until the failure are not discarded when the transaction aborts and allowing the compensating process to take advantage of them. Similarly, it would be interesting to consider an optimistic approach to transactions along the lines of [1]. This could be achieved by relaxing the well-formedness assumption and by allowing global constraints to be copied inside transactional scopes upon transaction activation.

Acknowledgments. We thank Roberto Bruni and Ugo Montanari for fruitful discussions.

References

1. Acciai, L., Boreale, M., dal Zilio, S.: A concurrent calculus with atomic transactions. In: De Nicola, R. (ed.) ESOP 2007. LNCS, vol. 4421, Springer, Heidelberg (2007)
2. Bacciu, D., Botta, A., Melgratti, H.: A fuzzy approach for negotiating quality of services. In: Montanari, U., Sannella, D., Bruni, R. (eds.) TGC 2007. LNCS, vol. 4661, Springer, Heidelberg (2007)
3. Bistarelli, S., Montanari, U., Rossi, F.: Semiring-based constraint satisfaction and optimization. Journal of the ACM 44(2), 201–236 (1997)
4. Bocchi, L., Laneve, C., Zavattaro, G.: A calculus for long-running transactions. In: Najm, E., Nestmann, U., Stevens, P. (eds.) FMOODS 2003. LNCS, vol. 2884, pp. 124–138. Springer, Heidelberg (2003)
5. Bruni, R., Melgratti, H., Montanari, U.: Nested commits for mobile calculi: extending Join. In: Proc. of the 3rd IFIP-TCS 2004, 3rd IFIP Intl. Conference on Theoretical Computer Science, pp. 569–582. Kluwer Academic Publishers, Dordrecht (2004)
6. Bruni, R., Melgratti, H., Montanari, U.: Theoretical foundations for compensations in flow composition languages. In: POPL 2005: Proceedings of the 32nd ACM SIGPLAN-SIGACT Symposium on Principles of Programming Languages, pp. 209–220. ACM Press, New York (2005)
7. Buscemi, M.G., Montanari, U.: Cc-pi: A constraint-based language for specifying service level agreements. In: De Nicola, R. (ed.) ESOP 2007. LNCS, vol. 4421, Springer, Heidelberg (2007)
8. Butler, M., Hoare, T., Ferreira, C.: A trace semantics for long-running transactions. In: Abdallah, A.E., Jones, C.B., Sanders, J.W. (eds.) Communicating Sequential Processes. LNCS, vol. 3525, pp. 133–150. Springer, Heidelberg (2005)
9. Fournet, C., Gonthier, G.: The reflexive chemical abstract machine and the Join calculus. In: Proc. of 23rd Annual ACM SIGPLAN - SIGACT Symposium on Principles of Programming Languages (POPL 1996), pp. 372–385. ACM Press, New York (1996)
10. Keller, A., Ludwig, H.: The WSLA framework: Specifying and monitoring service level agreements for web services. Jour. Net. and Sys. Manag. 11(1), 57–81 (2003)
11. Laneve, C., Zavattaro, G.: Foundations of web transactions. In: Sassone, V. (ed.) FOSSACS 2005. LNCS, vol. 3441, pp. 282–298. Springer, Heidelberg (2005)
12. Milner, R., Parrow, J., Walker, J.: A calculus of mobile processes, I and II. Inform. and Comput. 100(1), 1–77 (1992)
13. Saraswat, V., Rinard, M.: Concurrent constraint programming. In: Proc. of the 17th Symposium on Principles of programming languages (POPL 1990), ACM Press, New York (1990)
14. Skene, J., Lamanna, D., Emmerich, W.: Precise service level agreements. In: Proc. of the 26th International Conference on Software Engineering (ICSE 2004) (2004)
15. Wischik, L., Gardner, P.: Explicit fusions. Theoret. Comput. Sci. 340(3), 606–630 (2005)

On the Complexity of Termination Inference for Processes*

Romain Demangeon[1], Daniel Hirschkoff[1], Naoki Kobayashi[2],
and Davide Sangiorgi[3]

[1] ENS Lyon, CNRS, INRIA, UCBL, UMR 5668, France
[2] Tohoku University, Japan
[3] Università di Bologna, Italy

Abstract. We study type systems for termination in the π-calculus from the point of view of type inference. We analyse four systems by Deng and Sangiorgi. We show that inference can be done in polynomial time for two of these, but that this is not the case for the two most expressive systems. To remedy this, we study two modifications of these type systems that allow us to recover a polynomial type inference.

1 Introduction

Termination of concurrent systems is an important property. Even if some concurrent systems, like servers, are designed to offer continuously some interaction, subsystems are often expected to terminate. Typical examples include guaranteeing that interaction with a resource will eventually end (in order to avoid denial of service situations), insuring that the participants in a transaction will reach an agreement, or relying on termination to guarantee other properties (such as, e.g., lock freedom [3,9]). Such example applications are important for distributed frameworks exploiting various forms of mobility. Being able to assert termination for (part of) a system whose topology can change dynamically is challenging. It can be particularly useful if the method includes some form of automation.

In this paper, we focus on the π-calculus, a model of mobile computing based on name passing, and revisit the work by Deng and Sangiorgi [4] from the point of view of type inference. As we explain below, this can in particular be useful in relation with the work on TyPiCal reported in [9]. [4] introduces four type systems for the π-calculus with replicated inputs, which we will call System 1, 2, 3 and 4, in short S1, S2, S3 and S4. These systems have an increasing expressiveness, in the sense that every process typable in S_i is typable in S_{i+1}. The main idea behind these systems is to associate an integer *level* to each name, and to enforce that, for each replicated process, the computation that 'fires' the

---

* This work has been supported by the french ANR project "ARASSIA — Modularité Dynamique Fiable", by the EC project "SENSORIA" and Italian MIUR Project n. 2005015785 "Logical Foundations of Distributed Systems and Mobile Code".

G. Barthe and C. Fournet (Eds.): TGC 2007, LNCS 4912, pp. 140–155, 2008.

replication has a bigger weight than the computation which is triggered by this firing step.

In system S1, the point of view is that a term of the form $!a(\widetilde{x}).P$ is triggered by offering an output on a. Hence, the weight of P (which is defined as the total weight of outputs that occur in P without occurring under a replication) has to be strictly smaller than the weight of the output on a, i.e., the level associated to a. Weights are compared lexicographically, which entails that several outputs can occur in P, provided they all happen on names whose level is strictly smaller than the level associated to a.

We show (Sec. 2) that type inference for S1 can be done in polynomial time w.r.t. the size of the process being type checked. This entails that S2, a mild adaptation of S1, enjoys the same property. S2 adds to S1 the possibility to analyse the values being communicated on channels, when these are first order. Provided we have a polynomial time procedure to handle constraints about first order expressions, type inference for S2 is polynomial.

We then move to more expressive type systems from [4]. In system S3, replicated processes are written $!\kappa.P$, where κ is a maximal sequence of input prefixes (i.e., P is not an input process). To typecheck such a process, the weight of outputs in P must be smaller than the total weight of κ (weights are computed as vectors of weights for any level, and vectors are compared lexicographically). System S4 extends S3 with the possibility to use a partial order between names in order to typecheck replications whenever the weight of κ and the weight of the continuation P are equal. For instance, even if a and b have the same level, process $P_0 = !p.a.(\overline{p} \mid \overline{b})$ can be typed provided a dominates b in the partial order (here $\kappa = p.a$).

Our first main result is to show that for systems S3 and S4, the type inference problem is NP complete. Our proof relies on a reduction from 3SAT. More precisely, we prove that an instance of 3SAT determines a CCS process such that the existence of a typing derivation for the induced process is equivalent to the existence of a solution of the original instance of 3SAT.

To remedy the NP-completeness of S3 and S4, we propose two type systems. In the first type system, called S3', we renounce the lexicographic ordering on levels, and simply add the weight (that is, the level) associated to each name to compute the weights of κ and P. We establish that for this system, type inference amounts to solve linear programming on rational numbers without constants, which can be done in polynomial time. We moreover show that system S3' is strictly more expressive than S3. This constitutes the second main contribution of this paper.

The main improvement of system S4 w.r.t. S3 in terms of expressiveness is the possibility to type replicated processes in which the triggered continuation has the same weight as the outputs needed to trigger it, such as process P_0 above. In system S4', we retain the partial order ingredient inherent to S4, and simplify type checking for replicated inputs. We show soundness of S4' (every typable process terminates), and describe a sound and complete inference procedure for it. We prove that the type inference problem is polynomial for system S4', and illustrate the expressiveness of S4' by revisiting an example from [4] that cannot be directly typed in that system. The definition and analysis of S4' is the third main contribution we present in this paper.

Related Work. There are many works on type systems for the π-calculus. In addition to [4], type systems to ensure termination of π-calculus processes have been studied in [11,13]. In these works, the technique of logical relations is used to isolate a class of terminating processes.

After the seminal work of [6] for Milner's sorts, several studies of type inference in the π-calculus have been conducted, addressing richer type systems or variants of the calculus, such as [12,5,7]. To our knowledge, type systems for termination in the π-calculus have not been studied from the perspective of type inference so far.

Our results are connected with the work on the TyPiCal tool [8], which implements various type-based analyses of π-calculus processes. Other recent developments on the question of termination are presented in [9]. The focus is different: [9] extends the termination type systems to guarantee a stronger property called robust termination. Robust termination is then used to insure lock-freedom (which means that certain communications will eventually succeed). The present work can be useful for refining the verification proposed in [9].

Another relevant reference is the work on Terminator [1], and its recent extension to prove thread termination [2]. While the general objectives are similar to ours, the approaches are technically rather different. [2] deals with a fixed number of threads (without dynamic thread creation), and proves termination by detecting some variance of states, while in this paper, we deal with programs that create threads and channels dynamically.

Paper outline. In Sec. 2, we introduce the π-calculus and recall the type systems from [4]. Sec. 3 is devoted to the complexity of type inference for these systems. We present two systems for which type inference is polynomial: S3' in Sec. 4, and S4' in Sec. 5. Final remarks are given in Sec. 6.

2   Processes and Type Systems

We let $a, b, c, \ldots, p, q, \ldots, x, y, z$ range over an infinite set of *names*. Processes, ranged over using $P, Q, \ldots$, are defined by the following syntax:

$$P \quad ::= \quad \mathbf{0} \mid (\boldsymbol{\nu} c)\, P \mid P_1 | P_2 \mid a(\widetilde{x}).P \mid !a(\widetilde{x}).P \mid \overline{a}\langle \widetilde{n} \rangle.P \mid P_1 + P_2 \ .$$

The constructs of input, replicated input and restriction are binding; we shall often use $x, y, z, \ldots$ for *variables* – names bound by input – and c for *channels* – names bound by restriction. a is called the *subject* of the prefixes in the grammar above. We shall sometimes extend the calculus with first-order values (integers, booleans, ...). This kind of extension is standard (the reader can refer e.g. to [4]), and we shall use it implicitly when necessary. We let $\mathsf{os}(P)$ stand for the *multiset* of subjects of outputs that occur in P and do not occur under a replication. Similarly, $\mathbf{rs}(P)$ stands for the multiset of names that are restricted in P and such that the restriction does not occur under a replication.

The standard operational semantics of the calculus is omitted. The reduction relation is written $P \longrightarrow P'$.

Type systems. We recall here briefly the definitions of systems S1 to S4. We refer to [4] for detailed explanations and motivating examples accompanying the definitions. To remain close to [4], we give a presentation of the type systems à la Church: each name has a given type a priori, and hence we could also omit mentioning the typing context (ranged over using Γ) in the typing rules. [9] proposes a version à la Curry of these type systems. We keep typing contexts in typing rules in order to ease reading. All systems assign *levels* to names: a typing hypothesis has the form $a : \#^k \widetilde{T}$, to specify that name a transmits tuples of type $\widetilde{T}$, and that the level of a is k, which we write $\mathtt{lvl}(a) = k$ (k is a natural number).

System S1. Below are the typing rules for S1. With respect to simple types, the differences worth mentioning are that level information decorates types, and that the rule for replicated inputs is adapted to control termination.

$$\frac{\Gamma(a) = \#^k \widetilde{x} \quad \Gamma \vdash P}{\Gamma \vdash a(\widetilde{x}).P} \qquad \frac{\Gamma(a) = \#^k \widetilde{T} \quad \Gamma(\widetilde{p}) = \widetilde{T} \quad \Gamma \vdash P}{\Gamma \vdash \overline{a}\langle \widetilde{p} \rangle.P}$$

$$\frac{\Gamma \vdash P_1 \quad \Gamma \vdash P_2}{\Gamma \vdash P_1 | P_2} \qquad \frac{\Gamma \vdash P_1 \quad \Gamma \vdash P_2}{\Gamma \vdash P_1 + P_2} \qquad \frac{}{\Gamma \vdash \mathbf{0}} \qquad \frac{\Gamma \vdash P}{\Gamma \vdash (\nu a)\, P}$$

$$\frac{\Gamma(a) = \#^k \widetilde{x} \quad \Gamma \vdash a(\widetilde{x}).P \quad \forall n \in \mathbf{os}(P).\, \mathtt{lvl}(n) < k}{\Gamma \vdash !a(\widetilde{x}).P}$$

As explained in the introduction, the control on replications consists in verifying that all names in $\mathbf{os}(P)$ (the multiset of subjects of outputs that occur in P without being guarded by a replication) have a level strictly smaller than $\mathtt{lvl}(a)$.

System S2. System S2 is of minor interest for the purposes of this paper, because type inference can be done almost as for system S1. The only typing rule that differs w.r.t. S1 is the rule for replication:

$$\frac{\Gamma \vdash a(\widetilde{x}).P \quad \forall \overline{b}\langle \widetilde{v} \rangle \in \mathbf{out}(P).\, \overline{b}\langle \widetilde{v} \rangle \lhd a(\widetilde{x})}{\Gamma \vdash !a(\widetilde{x}).P}$$

$\overline{b}\langle \widetilde{v} \rangle \lhd a(\widetilde{x})$ holds if either $\mathtt{lvl}(b) < \mathtt{lvl}(a)$, or $\mathtt{lvl}(b) = \mathtt{lvl}(a)$ and $\widetilde{v}, \widetilde{x}$ are tuples of first-order expressions that can be compared according to some well-founded order. For instance, this is the case if $\widetilde{x} = \langle x_1, x_2 \rangle$, $\widetilde{v} = \langle x_1 - 1, x_2 + 2 \rangle$, and if tuples of expressions are compared lexicographically (the x_is are natural numbers, and we suppose we can prove $x_1 > 0$).

S2 makes it possible to allow outputs on a in a term of the form $!a(\widetilde{x}).P$: a process like $!a(x).\texttt{if } x > 0 \texttt{ then } \overline{a}\langle x - 1\rangle \texttt{ else } \overline{b}\langle x\rangle$ is typable in S2 provided $\texttt{lvl}(b) < \texttt{lvl}(a)$ (x is a natural number), despite the emission on a.

System S3. The typing rule for replication in S3 is:

$$\frac{\Gamma \vdash \kappa.P \qquad \operatorname{wt}(\kappa) \succ \operatorname{wt}(P)}{\Gamma \vdash !\kappa.P}$$

κ is a maximal sequence of input prefixes (i.e., in $\kappa.P$, P is not an input). The meaning of condition $\operatorname{wt}(\kappa) \succ \operatorname{wt}(P)$ is the following: $\operatorname{wt}(\kappa)$ is defined as a vector of natural numbers $(I_k, \ldots, I_1)$, where I_j is equal to the number of occurrences of names at level j occurring in subject position in κ (k is the level of biggest weight). Similarly, $\operatorname{wt}(P)$ is $(O_k, \ldots, O_1)$, and O_j is the number of occurrences of names at level j in $\operatorname{os}(P)$. Relation $\succ$ is defined as the lexicographical comparison of the weight vectors. For instance, $!p.q.(\overline{p} \mid \overline{p})$ is well-typed if $\texttt{lvl}(p) = 1$, $\texttt{lvl}(q) = 2$ (the vectors corresponding to κ and P are $(1, 1)$ and $(0, 2)$ respectively).

In [4], S3 additionally imposes that the name being used as last input subject in κ should be *asynchronous*, that is, no continuation can appear after outputs on this name. This constraint, which is present mostly for technical reasons in [4], can actually be removed, and the proof of soundness can be adapted rather easily — we therefore omit it here.

System S4. The typing judgement for S4 is of the form $\Gamma \vdash_{\mathcal{R}} P$, where $\mathcal{R}$ is a strict partial order on the free names of P. Only names having the same simple type can be compared using $\mathcal{R}$.

The syntax of types is extended to include partial order information. If S is a set of pairs of natural numbers, $p : \#_S^k \widetilde{T}$ specifies that p is of level k, carries a tuple of names of type $\widetilde{T}$, and imposes that whenever $(k, l) \in S$, (i) the kth and lth components of $\widetilde{T}$ exist and have the same simple type; and (ii) for any tuple of names emitted on p, the kth component of the tuple must dominate the lth component according to the partial order. For instance, if $p : \#_{\{(2,3)\}}^k \langle T_1, T_2, T_2 \rangle$ and if the process contains a subterm of the form $\overline{p}\langle u, v, w\rangle.\mathbf{0}$, where u, v, w are free names, then typability imposes that v and w have type T_2 and $v\mathcal{R}w$. Checking this kind of constraints is enforced by the typing rule for outputs. The typing rules for restriction and input are modified w.r.t. S3 in order to extend $\mathcal{R}$ appropriately in the premise (see [4]).

Intuitively, the role of $\mathcal{R}$ is to insure termination in replicated processes for which $\operatorname{wt}(\kappa) = \operatorname{wt}(P)$. In such situations, there is a risk to generate infinite computations by extending relation $\mathcal{R}$ via newly created names. S4 therefore imposes a form of control over restricted names. An occurrence of a restriction is *unguarded* if it does not occur under an input or output prefix. *RN* stands for the set of names n such that if n appears in prefix subject position, then the continuation process has no unguarded restrictions.

In S4, the condition of S3 in the rule for replication is replaced with $\kappa :\succ P$. $\kappa :\succ P$ holds iff either (i) wt$(\kappa) \succ$ wt(P) (as in S3), or (ii) wt$(\kappa) =$ wt(P), $\kappa \widehat{\mathcal{R}_\kappa} P$ and the last input subject of κ belongs to RN. For the needs of this paper, we can avoid entering the technical details of the definition of $\widehat{\mathcal{R}_\kappa}$, as we shall use a simplified version of this relation in S4' (and, in analysing the complexity of S4, we shall not resort to (ii) above). Let us just say that this relation is based on a multiset extension of the order $\mathcal{R}$ on free names.

The problem of type inference. In the sequel, we shall always implicitly consider a process P, from which we want to infer an explicitly typed process, where inputs and restrictions are decorated with type information. We suppose that P obeys the Barendregt convention, i.e., all its bound names are pairwise distinct and distinct from all the free names of P. Typing constraints between (bound or free) names of P will be generated regardless of scope – we will of course then take scope into account to assert whether a process is typable.

We shall say that a type inference procedure is *polynomial* to mean that it can be executed in polynomial time w.r.t. the size of P. We shall sometimes simply call a type system 'polynomial' to mean that it admits a polynomial time inference procedure.

Type inference for simple types is standard (see, e.g., [12]), and can be done in polynomial time. In the remainder of the paper, we shall implicitly assume that each process we want to type admits a simple typing, and we will concentrate on the question of finding annotations (levels, and, possibly, partial order information) that allow us to ensure typability for the systems we study.

3 Type Inference for Deng and Sangiorgi's Type Systems

3.1 Inference for Systems S1 and S2 Is in P

Proposition 1. *Type inference for system S1 is polynomial.*

Proof. We adapt the standard type inference procedure for simple types [12]. We associate to each type a *level variable*. Based on the typing rules, we can generate a set C of constraints consisting of unification constraints on types and inequality constraints (of the form $l_1 < l_2$) on level variables, such that C is satisfiable if and only if P is typable, and the size of C is linear in the size of P. Using the standard unification algorithm, we can transform C into a set C' of inequality constraints on level variables in polynomial time. The satisfiability of C' is equivalent to the acyclicity of the graph induced from C', which can again be checked in polynomial time. Thus, the type inference problem for S1 is polynomial. □

We can adapt this proof to derive a similar result for S2: whenever we find a cycle in the graph, if the cycle only contain names carrying first-order values, instead of failing, we invoke $\lhd$ to check for typability (otherwise, we fail).

Proposition 2. *Suppose we are given relation $\lhd$ together with a procedure to decide $\lhd$ in polynomial time. Then type inference for S2 is polynomial.*

3.2   Hardness of Systems S3 and S4

Theorem 3. *The type inference problem for system S3 is NP-complete.*

Proof. Let z be the number of names occurring in P. The problem is in NP because trying one of the z^z different ways of distributing names into z levels can be done in polynomial time w.r.t. the size of the process and the number of names. It is easy to prove that no more than z levels are required.

We now show that we can reduce 3SAT to the problem of finding a mapping of levels. We consider an instance $\mathcal{I}$ of 3SAT: we have n clauses $(C_i)_{i \leq n}$ of three literals each, $C_i = l_i^1, l_i^2, l_i^3$. Literals are possibly negated propositional variables taken from a set $V = \{v_1, \ldots, v_m\}$. The problem is to find a mapping from V to $\{True, False\}$ such that, in each clause, at least one literal is set to True.

All names we use to build the processes below will be CCS names. We fix a name true. To each variable $v_k \in V$, we associate two names x_k and x_k', and define the process

$$P_k \stackrel{\text{def}}{=} \ !\text{true.true.}\overline{x_k}.\overline{x_k'} \ | \ !x_k.x_k'.\overline{\text{true}} \ .$$

We then consider a clause $C_i = \{l_i^1, l_i^2, l_i^3\}$ from $\mathcal{I}$. For $j \in \{1, 2, 3\}$ we let $n_i^j = x_k$ if l_i^j is v_k, and $n_i^j = x_k'$ if l_i^j is $\neg v_k$. We then define the process

$$Q_i \stackrel{\text{def}}{=} \ !n_i^1.n_i^2.n_i^3.\overline{\text{true}} \ .$$

We call $\mathcal{I}_t$ the problem of finding a typing derivation in S3 for the process $P \stackrel{\text{def}}{=} P_1 | \ldots | P_m | Q_1 | \ldots | Q_n$. Note that the construction of P is polynomial in the size of $\mathcal{I}$.

We now analyse the constraints induced by the processes we have defined. The level associated to name true is noted t.

– The constraint associated to $!\text{true.true.}\overline{x_k}.\overline{x_k'}$ is equivalent to

$$\bigl(t \geq \text{lvl}(x_k) \wedge t \geq \text{lvl}(x_k')\bigr) \ \wedge \ \bigl(t > \text{lvl}(x_k) \vee t > \text{lvl}(x_k')\bigr) \ .$$

The constraint associated to $!x_k.x_k'.\overline{\text{true}}$ is equivalent to

$$t \leq \text{lvl}(x_k) \ \vee \ t \leq \text{lvl}(x_k') \ .$$

Hence, the constraint determined by P_k is equivalent to

$$\bigl(\text{lvl}(x_k) = t \wedge \text{lvl}(x_k') < t\bigr) \ \vee \ \bigl(\text{lvl}(x_k') = t \wedge \text{lvl}(x_k) < t\bigr) \ . \quad (1)$$

– The constraint associated to $!n_{i_1}.n_{i_2}.n_{i_3}.\overline{\text{true}}$ is equivalent to

$$t \leq \text{lvl}(n_i^1) \ \vee \ t \leq \text{lvl}(n_i^2) \ \vee \ t \leq \text{lvl}(n_i^3) \ . \quad (2)$$

We now prove that '$\mathcal{I}_t$ has a solution' is equivalent to '$\mathcal{I}$ has a solution'.

First, if $\mathcal{I}$ has a solution $S : V \rightarrow \{True, False\}$ then fix $t = 2$, and set $\mathtt{lvl}(x_k) = 2, \mathtt{lvl}(x'_k) = 1$ if v_k is set to True, and $\mathtt{lvl}(x_k) = 1, \mathtt{lvl}(x'_k) = 2$ otherwise. We check easily that condition (1) is satisfied; condition (2) also holds because S is a solution of $\mathcal{I}$.

Conversely, if $\mathcal{I}_t$ has a solution, then we deduce a boolean mapping for the literals in the original 3SAT problem. Since constraint (1) is satisfied, we can set v_k to True if $\mathtt{lvl}(x_k) = t$, and False otherwise. We thus have that v_k is set to True iff $\mathtt{lvl}(x_k) = t$, iff $\mathtt{lvl}(x'_k) < t$. Hence, because constraint (2) is satisfied, we have that in each clause C_i, at least one of the literals is set to True, which shows that we have a solution to $\mathcal{I}$.   □

This proof can be easily adapted to establish the same result for S4: the idea is to 'disable' the use of the partial order, e.g. by adopting a different type for true. We thus get:

Corollary 4. *The type inference problem for System S4 is NP-complete.*

The cause of NP-difficulty. The crux in the proof of Thm. 3 is to use the 'κ component' of S3 to introduce a form of choice: to type process $!a.a'.P$, we cannot know a priori, for $b \in \mathtt{os}(P)$, whether to set $\mathtt{lvl}(a) \geq \mathtt{lvl}(b)$ or $\mathtt{lvl}(a') \geq \mathtt{lvl}(b)$. Intuitively, we exploit this to encode the possibility for booleans to have two values, as well as the choice of the literal being set to True in a clause. By removing the κ component from S3, we get system S1, which is polynomial.

However, it appears that NP-completeness is not due only to κ: indeed, it is possible to define a polynomial restriction of S3 where the choice related to the κ component is present. Let us call S3" the type system obtained from S3 by imposing *distinctness of levels*: two names can have the same level only if in the inference process, their types are unified when resolving the unification constraints. Note that this is more demanding than simply having the same simple type: in process $\bar{p} \mid \bar{q}$, names p and q have the same simple type, but, since their types are not unified during inference, they must be given different levels in system S3".

Although typing a process of the form $!a(x).a'(y, z).P$ seems to introduce the same kind of choice as in S3, it can be shown that type inference is polynomial in S3". Intuitively, the reason for this is that there exists a level variable, say α, such that for every constraint on weight vectors of the shape $\mathtt{wt}(\kappa) \succ \mathtt{wt}(P)$ induced along type inference, the cardinal of α in $\mathtt{wt}(P)$ is not greater than the cardinal in $\mathtt{wt}(\kappa)$. It can be shown that if no such α exists, then the process is not typable.

This gives a strategy to compute a level assignment for names, and do so in polynomial time: assign the maximum level to α, and consider a weight vector constraint $\mathtt{wt}(\kappa) \succ \mathtt{wt}(P)$: if there are as many αs in $\mathtt{wt}(\kappa)$ as in $\mathtt{wt}(P)$, replace the constraint with the equivalent constraint where the αs are removed. Otherwise, the number of αs strictly decreases, which means that we can simply remove this constraint. We thus obtain an equivalent, smaller problem, and we can iterate this reasoning (if there are no more constraints to satisfy, we pick a random assignment for the remaining levels).

System S3" retains the lexicographical comparison and the κ component from S3, but is polynomial. By Prop. 7 below, since S3" is a restriction of S3, it is less expressive than S3'. In some sense, S3" 'respects the identity of names': while in S3' levels are added, and we rely on algebraic calculations on natural numbers, only comparisons between levels are used in S3"; this means that, intuitively, we cannot trade a name a for one or several names whose role in the given process is completely unrelated to the role of a.

4   Summing the Levels Assigned to Names

We now study system S3', in which we renounce the lexicographical comparison between names through levels, and instead add levels to compute the weight of κ and P in a term of the form $!\kappa.P$.

Definition 5 (System S3'). *We let* $\mathrm{subj}(\kappa)$ *stand for the multiset of names occurring in subject position in* κ.

System S3' is defined by the same rules as system S3, except that the condition for the replication rule is $\Sigma_{n\in\mathrm{subj}(\kappa)}\mathtt{lvl}(n) > \Sigma_{n\in\mathrm{os}(P)}\mathtt{lvl}(n)$ *(for all* n, $\mathtt{lvl}(n)$ *is a natural number).*

Note that $\mathrm{subj}(\kappa)$ and $\mathrm{os}(P)$ are *multisets*, so that the weight of names having multiple occurrences is counted several times.

Soundness of S3' can be established by adapting the proof for S3 in [4]:

Proposition 6. *System S3' ensures termination.*

Proposition 7. *System S3' is strictly more expressive than S3.*

Proof. We first show that S3' is at least as expressive as S3. We consider a process of the form $P_0 = !\kappa.P$, that can be typed in S3 (κ is a maximal input prefix). We write $(I_k, \ldots, I_1)$ and $(O_k, \ldots, O_1)$ for the vectors of levels associated to κ and $\mathrm{os}(P)$ respectively (the I_js are natural numbers, and I_j is the number of subject occurrences of names of level j in κ — and similarly for the O_js). We fix an integer b such that $\forall j \in [1\ldots k].|O_j - I_j| < b$, and build a S3' typing context for P_0 by assigning level $b^{L(n)}$ to name n, where $L(n)$ denotes the level of n according to the S3-typing of P_0.

Let us show that this induces a correct typing for P_0 in S3'. Because P_0 is typed in S3, there exists u such that $I_k = O_k, I_{k-1} = O_{k-1}, \ldots, I_{u+1} = O_{u+1}$ and $I_u > O_u + 1$. We compute the difference of weights between κ in P according to S3': $\mathrm{wt}(\kappa) - \mathrm{wt}(P) = \Sigma_{1\leq j\leq k}(I_j - O_j)b^j \geq b^u + \Sigma_{1\leq j<u}(I_j - O_j)b^j$. The latter quantity is strictly positive by definition of b, which shows that P_0 is S3'-typable.

We can generalise this reasoning by remarking that an arbitrary process Q has a finite number of replications, which allows us to fix a b which is suitable for all replicated subterms of Q.

To show that there are processes which can be typed by system S3' but not by S3, consider $P_1 \stackrel{\text{def}}{=} !a.\bar{b} \mid !b.b.\bar{a}$. P_1 is ill-typed according to S3: the first subterm imposes $\text{lvl}(a) > \text{lvl}(b)$, and the vectors associated to the second subterm are hence of the form $(0, 2)$ and $(1, 0)$, and we do not have $(0, 2) \succ (1, 0)$. By setting $\text{lvl}(a) = 3$ and $\text{lvl}(b) = 2$, we can check that P_1 is typable for S3'.   □

Theorem 8. *Type inference for system S3' is polynomial.*

Proof. By inspecting the process to be typed, type inference amounts to find a solution to a system of inequalities of the form $\Sigma_j a_{i,j}.u_j > 0$, where the $a_{i,j}$s are integers and the solution is the vector of the u_js, which are natural numbers. This system has a solution if and only if the system consisting of the inequalities $\Sigma_j a_{i,j}.u_j \geq 1$ has one. We resort to linear programming in rationals to solve the latter problem (we can choose to minimise $\Sigma_j u_j$), which can be done in polynomial time. Because of the shape of inequalities generated by the typing problem (there are no constant factors), there exists a rational number solution to the inequalities if and only if there exists an integer solution.   □

5   Exploiting Partial Orders on Names

5.1   System S4': Definition and Properties

System S4 from [4] is built on top of S3, and improves its expressiveness by allowing the use of partial orders. To define S4', we restrict ourselves to the partial order component of S4, and do not analyse sequences of input prefixes (κ) as in S3: in a term of the form $!a(\tilde{x}).P$, name a must dominate every name in $\text{os}(P)$, either because it is of higher level, or via the partial order relation.

We now introduce S4'. Let $\mathcal{R}$ be a relation on names, $\mathcal{S}$ a relation on natural numbers, and $\tilde{x}$ a tuple of names. We define two operators $/$ and $*$ as follows:

$$\mathcal{R} / \tilde{x} = \begin{cases} \emptyset & \text{if } n(\mathcal{R}) \cap \tilde{x} = \emptyset \\ \{(i, j) \mid x_i \mathcal{R} x_j\} & \text{if } n(\mathcal{R}) \subseteq \tilde{x} \\ \text{undefined} & \text{otherwise} \end{cases} \qquad \begin{array}{c} \mathcal{S} * \tilde{x} = \{(x_i, x_j) \mid i \mathcal{S} j\} \\ \text{if } \max(n(\mathcal{S})) \leq |\tilde{x}| \end{array}$$

Above, $n(\mathcal{R}) = \{a. \exists b. a\mathcal{R}b \vee b\mathcal{R}a\}$, $n(\mathcal{S}) = \{i. \exists j. i\mathcal{S}j \vee j\mathcal{S}i\}$, and $|\tilde{x}|$ denotes the number of names in $\tilde{x}$. We also define
$$\mathcal{R} \Downarrow_{\tilde{x}} = \{(a, b) \mid a, b \notin \tilde{x} \text{ and } a\mathcal{R}c_1\mathcal{R} \cdots \mathcal{R}c_n\mathcal{R}b \text{ for some } \tilde{c} \subseteq \tilde{x} \text{ and } n \geq 0\}.$$

The typing rules for S4' are given on Fig. 1. Again, although the type system is defined à la Church, we mention the typing context to ease readability. When writing a judgement of the form $\Gamma \vdash_{\mathcal{R}} P$, we implicitly require that $\mathcal{R}$ does not contain a cycle. Note that w.r.t. system S4 in [4], we relax the constraint that $\mathcal{R}$ should only relate names having the same simple type.

As explained above (Sec. 2), given a name a, $\mathcal{S}$ captures the relation between types communicated along a: to typecheck an emission of names $\tilde{x}$ on a, we compute $\mathcal{S} * \tilde{x}$, which is the order on names in $\tilde{x}$ induced from $\mathcal{S}$ by their index position in $\tilde{x}$. Conversely, $\mathcal{R} / \tilde{x}$ is the '$\mathcal{S}$' one can extract from a relation $\mathcal{R}$ by focusing on a tuple of names $\tilde{x}$.

$$\Gamma \vdash_{\mathcal{R}} 0 \qquad \frac{\Gamma \vdash_{\mathcal{R}_1} P \qquad \Gamma \vdash_{\mathcal{R}_2} Q}{\Gamma \vdash_{\mathcal{R}_1 + \mathcal{R}_2} P | Q} \qquad \frac{\Gamma \vdash_{\mathcal{R}_1} P \qquad \Gamma \vdash_{\mathcal{R}_2} Q}{\Gamma \vdash_{\mathcal{R}_1 + \mathcal{R}_2} P + Q}$$

$$\frac{\Gamma(a) = \sharp_{\mathcal{S}}^n \Gamma(\widetilde{x}) \qquad \Gamma \vdash_{\mathcal{R}} P \qquad \mathcal{S} \supseteq \mathcal{R} / \widetilde{x}}{\Gamma \vdash_{\mathcal{R} \downarrow_{\widetilde{x}}} a(\widetilde{x}).P}$$

$$\frac{\Gamma(a) = \sharp_{\mathcal{S}}^n \Gamma(\widetilde{v}) \qquad \Gamma \vdash_{\mathcal{R}} P \qquad \mathcal{R} \supseteq \mathcal{S} * \widetilde{v}}{\Gamma \vdash_{\mathcal{R}} \overline{a}\langle \widetilde{v} \rangle.P} \qquad\qquad \frac{\Gamma(c) = \sharp_{\mathcal{S}}^n \widetilde{T} \qquad \Gamma \vdash_{\mathcal{R}} P}{\Gamma \vdash_{\mathcal{R} \downarrow_c} (\nu c) P}$$

$$\frac{\Gamma(a) = \sharp_{\mathcal{S}}^n \Gamma(\widetilde{x}) \qquad \Gamma \vdash_{\mathcal{R}} P \qquad \mathcal{S} \supseteq \mathcal{R} / \widetilde{x} \qquad \Gamma \vdash_{\mathcal{R}} a :\succ (\mathsf{os}(P), \mathsf{rs}(P))}{\Gamma \vdash_{\mathcal{R} \downarrow_{\widetilde{x}}} !a(\widetilde{x}).P}$$

$$\frac{\Gamma \vdash_{\mathcal{R}'} P \qquad \mathcal{R}' \subseteq \mathcal{R}}{\Gamma \vdash_{\mathcal{R}} P}$$

Fig. 1. System S4': Typing Rules

In the rule for replication, $\Gamma \vdash_{\mathcal{R}} a :\succ (N_1, N_2)$ holds if either of the following conditions holds:

(i) $\forall v \in N_1.\mathtt{lvl}(v) < \mathtt{lvl}(a) \wedge \forall v \in N_2.\mathtt{lvl}(v) \leq \mathtt{lvl}(a)$
(ii) $\forall v \in N_2.\mathtt{lvl}(v) < \mathtt{lvl}(a)$
$\wedge \exists b \in N_1.\mathtt{lvl}(b) = \mathtt{lvl}(a) \wedge a\mathcal{R}b \wedge \forall v \in N_1 - \{b\}.\mathtt{lvl}(v) < \mathtt{lvl}(a).$

(notice that N_1 is a multiset).

The last rule in Fig. 1 is optional; it does not change typability, but makes the correspondence with the constraint generation algorithm more clear. Accordingly, in the rules for parallel composition and choice, we could mention the same relation $\mathcal{R}$ in both premises and in the conclusion — the version of the rules we present is closer to the type inference procedure (see Sec. 5.2).

Notice that the partial order can be used for *at most one output* in the continuation process to typecheck a replication. Indeed, by omitting this constraint in case (ii) above, we could typecheck the following divergent process:

$$P_2 \stackrel{\mathrm{def}}{=} !p(a, b, c, d).(!a.\overline{c}.\overline{d} \mid !b.(\nu e, f)\overline{p}\langle c, d, e, f \rangle) \mid \overline{p}\langle u, v, w, t \rangle.(\overline{u} \mid \overline{v}),$$

by setting $a\mathcal{R}c$ and $a\mathcal{R}d$. In P_2, the subterm replicated at b makes a recursive call to p with two new fresh names; the subterm replicated at a is typed using the partial order twice, and the outputs it triggers feed the loop (a similar example can be constructed to show that we must also forbid using $\mathcal{R}$ twice with the same pair of names).

Proposition 9. *System S4' ensures termination.*

Proof. We suppose that there exists a process P admitting a diverging sequence $\mathcal{D}: P = P_1 \longrightarrow P_2 \longrightarrow P_3 \longrightarrow \ldots$, and that P is well-typed according to S4'. Let k be the maximum level assigned to names in the typing of P.

We call I the set of integers i such that the reduction step from P_i to P_{i+1} is obtained by triggering a replicated input whose subject is of level k. We let $S_i \overset{\text{def}}{=} \{n \in \mathsf{os}(P_i). \mathtt{lvl}(n) = k\}$ (S_i is a multiset).

We remark that the size of S_i cannot grow. Indeed, if the reduction from P_i to P_{i+1} does not trigger a replicated input, this obviously holds. If on the contrary the reduction does, there are two cases: either $i \notin I$, and by maximality of k, no output at level k can be unleashed by triggering an input at level strictly smaller than k; or $i \in I$, and there are two cases again. If the replicated input has been typed using clause (i) of the definition of $:\succ$, then S_{i+1} has one element less than S_i. If clause (ii) has been used, then S_{i+1} has been obtained from S_i by removing an element a and replacing it with b, with $a\mathcal{R}b$ (by abuse of notation, we write this $S_i\mathcal{R}S_{i+1}$).

Let us now show that I is finite. The above reasoning implies that I contains only a finite number of reductions corresponding to a replicated input that has been typed using clause (i). Hence there exists an index after which all reductions of $\mathcal{D}$ on a name of level k involve a replicated input typed using clause (ii). We observe that between two such reductions, no name of level k can be created, and none can be created either by such a reduction. This means that we have an infinite sequence $S_j\mathcal{R}S_{j+1}\mathcal{R}\ldots$ (using the notation introduced above): this is impossible, as $\mathcal{R}$ is acyclic, and the support of $\mathcal{R}$ at level k cannot grow.

Since I is finite, $\mathcal{D}$ has a suffix such that the resulting infinite sequence does not contain any reduction involving a replicated input at a name of level k. We can reason as above for $k-1$, and finally obtain a contradiction.   □

5.2   Type Inference for S4'

We now present the type inference procedure for S4', which has two phases: in the first part, we generate constraints, that are solved in the second part.

Constraint generation algorithm. The rules of Fig. 2 define the constraint generation phase of type inference. The output of this procedure is a pair (r, C) where r is a relation variable and C consists of:

- unification constraints $T_1 = T_2$
- order constraints $\Gamma \vdash_r a :\succ (N_1, N_2)$
- relation constraints $r \supseteq \mathcal{R}$, where $\mathcal{R}$ is made of relation variables, pairs of names, operations such as $+$, $*$, $\Downarrow$, and $/$.

The size of C is polynomial in the size of the process. Note that relation variables range over relations between names, or between integers (when they correspond to '$\mathcal{S}$' components). They are hence 'intrinsically typed', as is the case for operators $*$ and $/$.

The following lemma can be proved easily. (Here, by solution of C, we mean an assignment of type variables to valid types, level variables to levels, and relation variables to strict partial orders that satisfy all the constraints in C).

$$\texttt{Tinf}(\Gamma, 0) = (r, \emptyset) \ (r \ \text{fresh})$$
$$\texttt{Tinf}(\Gamma, a(\widetilde{x}).P) =$$
$$\quad \texttt{let} \ (r, C_1) = \texttt{Tinf}(\Gamma, P)$$
$$\quad\quad\quad C_2 = \{\Gamma(a) = \natural_{r_1}^l \Gamma(\widetilde{x})\} \ (l, r_1 \ \text{fresh})$$
$$\quad \texttt{in} \ (r_2, C_1 \cup C_2 \cup \{r_1 \supseteq r \ / \ \widetilde{x}, r_2 \supseteq r \Downarrow_{\widetilde{x}}\}) \ (r_2 \ \text{fresh})$$
$$\texttt{Tinf}(\Gamma, !a(\widetilde{x}).P) =$$
$$\quad \texttt{let} \ (r, C_1) = \texttt{Tinf}(\Gamma, P)$$
$$\quad\quad\quad C_2 = \{\Gamma(a) = \natural_{r_1}^l \Gamma(\widetilde{x})\} \ (l, r_1 \ \text{fresh})$$
$$\quad\quad\quad C_3 = \{r_1 \supseteq r \ / \ \widetilde{x}, r_2 \supseteq r \Downarrow_{\widetilde{x}}\} \ (r_2 \ \text{fresh})$$
$$\quad \texttt{in} \ (r_2, C_1 \cup C_2 \cup C_3 \cup \{\Gamma \vdash_r a :\succ (\texttt{os}(P), \texttt{rs}(P))\}))$$
$$\texttt{Tinf}(\Gamma, \overline{a}\langle \widetilde{v} \rangle.P) =$$
$$\quad \texttt{let} \ (r, C_1) = \texttt{Tinf}(\Gamma, P)$$
$$\quad\quad\quad C_2 = \{\Gamma(a) = \natural_{r_1}^l \Gamma(\widetilde{v})\} \ (l, r_1 \ \text{fresh})$$
$$\quad \texttt{in} \ (r, C_1 \cup C_2 \cup \{r \supseteq r_1 * \widetilde{v}\})$$
$$\texttt{Tinf}(\Gamma, (\nu c)P) =$$
$$\quad \texttt{let} \ (r_1, C) = \texttt{Tinf}(\Gamma, P)$$
$$\quad \texttt{in} \ (r, C \cup \{r \supseteq r_1 \Downarrow_c\}) \ (r \ \text{fresh})$$
$$\texttt{Tinf}(\Gamma, P_1 | P_2) =$$
$$\quad \texttt{let} \ (r_1, C_1) = \texttt{Tinf}(\Gamma, P_1)$$
$$\quad\quad\quad (r_2, C_2) = \texttt{Tinf}(\Gamma, P_2)$$
$$\quad \texttt{in} \ (r, C_1 \cup C_2 \cup \{r \supseteq r_1 + r_2\}) \ (r \ \text{fresh})$$
$$\texttt{Tinf}(\Gamma, P_1 + P_2) = \texttt{Tinf}(\Gamma, P_1 | P_2)$$

Fig. 2. Constraint Generation

Lemma 10 *Let* $\{v_1, \ldots, v_n\}$ *be the set of all the names occurring in* P, *and* $\Gamma = v_1 : \alpha_1, \ldots, v_n : \alpha_n$. *If* $\texttt{Tinf}(\Gamma, P) = (r, C)$, *then* θ *is a solution of* C *if and only if* $\theta\Gamma \vdash_{\theta r} P$.

Constraint solving. Constraints are solved through several constraint transformation steps, that we now describe.

- Step 1: By solving the unification constraints in C, we obtain a set C_1 of order constraints and relation constraints.
- Step 2: Eliminate level variables
  For each order constraint $\Gamma \vdash_r a :\succ (N_1, N_2)$, generate necessary conditions

$$\{\texttt{lvl}(v) \leq \texttt{lvl}(a) \mid v \in N_1 \cup N_2\}.$$

Thus, we obtain a set of level constraints $C_2 = \{l_1 \leq l'_1, \ldots, l_k \leq l'_k\}$. Compute a solution of C_2 that is *optimal* in the sense that whenever possible, different levels are assigned to different level variables. (That can be computed as follows. Construct a directed graph G whose node set is $\{l_1, l'_1, \ldots, l_k, l'_k\}$, and whose edge set is $\{(l_i, l'_i)\}$. Compute strongly connected components of G, and unify all the level variables in the same component. Then, perform a topological sort on the strongly connected components, and assign a level to each component.) Then, substitute the solution for each $\Gamma \vdash_r a :\succ (N_1, N_2)$.

- Step 3: Eliminate order constraints $\Gamma \vdash_r a :\succ (N_1, N_2)$
  $\Gamma \vdash_r a :\succ (N_1, N_2)$ can be reduced as follows. Check whether $\forall v \in N_1.\mathtt{lvl}(v) < \mathtt{lvl}(a)$ holds. If so, then just remove the constraint. Otherwise, check that for only one $b \in N_1$, $\mathtt{lvl}(b) = \mathtt{lvl}(a)$ holds, and that $\forall v \in N_2.\mathtt{lvl}(v) < \mathtt{lvl}(a)$ holds. If this is the case, replace $\Gamma \vdash_r a :\succ (N_1, N_2)$ with $r \supseteq \{(a, b)\}$. Otherwise, report that the constraints are unsatisfiable.
- Step 4: Solve relation constraints:
  We are now left with a set of relation constraints:

$$\{r_1 \supseteq f_1(r_1, \ldots, r_k), \ldots r_k \supseteq f_k(r_1, \ldots, r_k)\} \ .$$

(We assume here that $\{r_1, \ldots, r_k\}$ contains all the relation variables introduced by $\mathtt{Tinf}$; otherwise add a trivial constraint $r \supseteq r$.) Here, $f_1, \ldots, f_k$ are monotonic functions on relations (in particular, $\mathcal{R} \Downarrow_{\tilde{x}}$ is monotonic if we treat 'undefined' as the biggest element). Thus, we can obtain the least solution in a standard manner [10].

Finally, we check that the transitive closure of the solution for each relation variable r is irreflexive. When this is the case, we have a level assignment and a definition of partial orders (between free names, and to decorate types) which are sufficient to deduce a typing derivation for the process being analysed.

Comments about the constraint solving procedure. Step 1 in the procedure above is standard. In Step 2, each order constraint of the form $\Gamma \vdash_r a :\succ (N_1, N_2)$ generates a set of necessary inequalities between level variables. Cycles in the graph that is constructed in this step correspond to level variables that are necessarily identified. The purpose of Step 3 is to get rid of order constraints by determining whether each corresponding subterm is typed using clause (i) or clause (ii) of the definition of $:\succ$. If all inequalities corresponding to the order constraint are satisfied in a strict sense by the level assignment, by clause (i), there is nothing to do. When this is not the case, we necessarily rely on clause (ii): we check that the corresponding hypotheses are satisfied, and generate a relation constraint. Relation constraints are handled in Step 4.

It can be remarked that type inference gives priority to clause (i) to type replicated terms. For instance, consider process $P_3 = \overline{p}\langle a, b\rangle \mid p(x, y)!x.\overline{y}$. Type inference assigns a type of the form $\#^1\langle\#^2 T, \#^1 T'\rangle$ to p. Alternatively, we can choose to set $p : \#^1_{\{(1,2)\}}\langle\#^1 T, \#^1 T'\rangle$, i.e., use clause (ii). By construction, Step 2 assigns different levels whenever possible, and hence chooses the former typing.

Theorem 11. *The type inference procedure for S4' is sound and complete w.r.t. the typing rules, and runs in polynomial time.*

Soundness and completeness follow from Lemma 10 and the fact that each of the above steps preserves the satisfiability of constraints. For the complexity result, $\mathtt{Tinf}$ runs in polynomial time and generates constraints of polynomial size. In turn, each step of the constraint solving part runs in time polynomial in the size of the constraints.

6 Conclusion

We have studied the complexity of type inference for the type systems of [4], and shown how the NP complete type systems can be simplified in order to get a polynomial type inference procedure.

A question that remains to be addressed is how to enrich system S3' with the possibility to use partial orders, in order to get closer to systems S4 or S4' in terms of expressiveness. In S4, the partial order can be used when the vector of weights remains the same, while in S4' the vector of weights can even increase when the partial order is used. How to adapt S4 or S4' to a system where weights are summed (as natural numbers) is not clear to us at the moment.

A natural extension of this work is to experiment with the results we have presented. TyPiCal already implements a type inference algorithm for a type system obtained by combining systems S1 to S4, as reported in [9]. The parts of this combined type system that are related to S3 and S4 are treated using a heuristic, incomplete, polynomial algorithm, because of the NP-completeness result we have shown in Sec. 3. It is left for future work to implement S3' and S4' discussed in the paper. For that purpose, a main remaining issue is how to integrate S3' and S4' with S2. As hinted above, our results could also be useful for the developments presented in [9].

Acknowledgements. We thank Alain Darte for his help in finding the reduction used for Thm. 3.

References

1. The Terminator Project: proof tools for termination and liveness (2007), http://research.microsoft.com/terminator/
2. Cook, B., Podelski, A., Rybalchenko, A.: Proving Thread Termination. In: Proc. of PLDI 2007, pp. 320–330. ACM Press, New York (2007)
3. Cook, B., Gotsman, A., Podelski, A., Rybalchenko, A., Vardi, M.Y.: Proving that programs eventually do something good, pp. 265–276 (2007)
4. Deng, Y., Sangiorgi, D.: Ensuring Termination by Typability. Information and Computation 204(7), 1045–1082 (2006)
5. Fournet, C., Laneve, C., Maranget, L., Rémy, D.: Implicit Typing à la ML for the Join-Calculus. In: Mazurkiewicz, A., Winkowski, J. (eds.) CONCUR 1997. LNCS, vol. 1243, pp. 196–212. Springer, Heidelberg (1997)
6. Gay, S.J.: A Sort Inference Algorithm for the Polyadic Pi-Calculus. In: Proc. of POPL 1993, pp. 429–438. ACM Press, New York (1993)
7. Igarashi, A., Kobayashi, N.: Type Reconstruction for Linear Pi-Calculus with I/O Subtyping. Information and Computation 161(1), 1–44 (2000)
8. Kobayashi, N.: TyPiCal: Type-based static analyzer for the Pi-Calculus (2007), http://www.kb.ecei.tohoku.ac.jp/~koba/typical/
9. Kobayashi, N., Sangiorgi, D.: From Deadlock-Freedom and Termination to Lock-Freedom (submitted 2007)

10. Rehof, J., Mogensen, T.: Tractable Constraints in Finite Semilattices. Science of Computer Programming 35(2), 191–221 (1999)
11. Sangiorgi, D.: Termination of Processes. Mathematical Structures in Computer Science 16(1), 1–39 (2006)
12. Vasconcelos, V.T., Honda, K.: Principal Typing Schemes in a Polyadic pi-Calculus. In: Best, E. (ed.) CONCUR 1993. LNCS, vol. 715, pp. 524–538. Springer, Heidelberg (1993)
13. Yoshida, N., Berger, M., Honda, K.: Strong Normalisation in the Pi-Calculus. Information and Computation 191(2), 145–202 (2004)

A Practical Approach for Establishing Trust Relationships between Remote Platforms Using Trusted Computing

Kurt Dietrich, Martin Pirker, Tobias Vejda, Ronald Toegl, Thomas Winkler, and Peter Lipp

Institute for Applied Information Processing and Communications (IAIK), Graz University of Technology, Inffeldgasse 16a, A–8010 Graz, Austria {kdietrich,mpirker,tvejda,rtoegl,plipp}@iaik.tugraz.at, thomas.winkler@uni-klu.ac.at

Abstract. Over the past years, many different approaches and concepts in order to increase computer security have been presented. One of the most promising of these concepts is *Trusted Computing* which offers various services and functionalities like reporting and verifying the integrity and the configuration of a platform (attestation). The idea of reporting a platform's state and configuration to a challenger opens new and innovative ways of establishing trust relationships between entities. However, common applications are not aware of Trusted Computing facilities and are therefore not able to utilise Trusted Computing services at the moment. Hence, this article proposes an architecture that enables arbitrary applications to perform remote platform attestation, allowing them to establish trust based on their current configuration. The architecture's components discussed in this article are also essential parts of the OpenTC proof-of-concept prototype. It demonstrates applications and techniques of the Trusted Computing Group's proposed attestation mechanism in the area of personal electronic transactions.

1 Introduction

Trusted Computing (TC) is constantly gaining ground in industry and the public perception of Trusted Computing is starting to improve [6]. A central role is played by the Trusted Computing Group (TCG) [18] which is specifying the core components, namely the Trusted Platform Modules (TPM) and surrounding software architectures like the TCG Software Stack (TSS) [15]. Based on these components, security and trust related services like *remote attestation*, *sealing* or *binding* are defined.

Hence, in the first contribution the question how trust relationships between remote platforms can be established by using TC is addressed. The approach presented in this paper allows to establish trusted communication channels by means of the TCG's specified remote attestation. The approach introduces a so-called *attestation proxy* that is placed in front of the actual application and performs a mutual platform attestation of the two communication parties. The

G. Barthe and C. Fournet (Eds.): TGC 2007, LNCS 4912, pp. 156–168, 2008.

actual communication channel is only established if the attestation succeeded. This approach allows legacy applications to benefit from attested communication channels without the need to modify the application code.

As the proof-of-concept implementation is done in Java, the second contribution deals with the problem how TC concepts can be integrated into virtual machine based runtime environments such as Java^{TM}. Questions to be answered are how to measure loaded class and jar files, how to deal with external resources or how to handle calls to native code.

The basis for all TC related services is the TPM. The TPM is a hardware chip providing essential functionality for a TC enabled system like a RSA engine, a true random number generator or mechanisms to securely store and report the state of a system. While TPMs are produced and shipped by a variety of manufacturers, important software components like the trusted software stack are not widely available yet. The presented IAIK TSS for the Java Platform (jTSS [14]) provides TC services to applications and manages the communication with the TPM. The jTSS provides the foundations for the two main contributions of this work.

1.1 Related Work

The idea of remote attestation has been pursued by various research groups. Hence, many different approaches discussing this research area have been published. The most important are introduced in the following paragraphs.

The concept of *Property-Based Attestation* (PBA) [11] provides an alternative to the attestation mechanisms specified by the TCG henceforth called *binary attestation*. A Trusted Third Party (TTP) translates the actual system configuration into a set of properties and issues certificates for those properties. During the attestation process a (remote) verifier can decide whether or not the platform security properties meet the requirements of the respective use case. In literature, using TTPs for certification of properties is called *delegation*. This scenario avoids several (undesired) drawbacks of binary attestation. For instance, presenting the concrete system configuration to a verifier is not desirable from a privacy perspective and management of all possible configurations is a difficult task.

Alternatively, *Semantic Remote Attestation* (SRA) [12] uses language-based techniques to attest high level properties of an application. The proposal is based on the Java Virtual Machine (JVM) environment which is attested by binary attestation itself. The JVM can enforce a security policy on the running code based on data flow control and taint propagation mechanisms. Hence, this approach is a hybrid approach between binary attestation and attesting properties.

Moreover, the Trusted Computing Group - as the leading group for TC specifications - has published a concept for trusted network access also known as Trusted Network Connect (TNC) [22]. TNC enforces a policy based access and integrity control by measuring the state and configuration of a platform according to specified policies. Furthermore, TNC introduces the concept of isolation. Platforms that cannot be attested correctly are *isolated*. This means that they are not allowed to access the network unless they can successfully report that their integrity has been restored (remediation). The usage of a TPM is optional in order to make this technology available on a variety of platforms. Nevertheless, if a TPM is present it is used for extended integrity checking and binding of access credentials to the platform.

Other approaches focus on improving established protocols like SSL. The main problem these approaches deal with is that there is no linkage between the attestation information (i.e. the signed quote and the AIK certificate) and the SSL authentication information. Stumpf et al. [21] discuss a concept for a robust integrity reporting protocol by combining it with a key agreement protocol. The same problem is addressed by Sailer et al. [20]. In their paper a solution for linking SSL tunnel endpoints to attestation information by adding the SSL public key to the event log and PCRs is discussed. Furthermore, they introduce a new certificate type, the so-called platform property certificate that links an AIK to a SSL private key. Binding the keys with the certificate should prevent the misuse of a compromised SSL key.

1.2   Outline of the Paper

The remainder of this paper is organised as follows: Section 2 gives details about the overall architecture. Section 2.1 describes the attestation proxy and illustrates the use of the concept of remote attestation to establish and validate trusted relationships between two entities. Section 2.2 presents an outline of the IAIK jTSS, discussing the overall structure as well as implementation concepts. Section 2.3 deals with aspects of adapting the Java virtual machine to be fully integrated into TC environments. Section 2.4 explains the link between TPM based keys and public key infrastructure concepts. Finally, Section 3 concludes the paper.

2   The Proof of Concept Architecture

In this section, the overall architecture and actions of the proposed approach are briefly discussed. As shown in Figure 1 the architecture includes a proxy that provides an attestation service to applications, a trusted software stack (jTSS) and the trusted Java VM. The integrity of all components of the architecture is measured as defined by [23] in order to establish a chain-of-trust starting from the platform's BIOS up to the proxy service (see Figure 1). However, in order to build the full chain, the architecture requires further components. These components include a core-root-of-trust for measurement (CRTM)[1] that is included in the BIOS, a trusted boot loader (e.g. Trusted Grub [19]) and a trusted operating system. They are out of scope for this implementation and are therefore not discussed in this paper. Nevertheless, the architecture assumes that the platform performs an authenticated boot as defined by [18].

---

[1] Modern computer systems use a dynamic-root-of-trust for measurement (DRTM).

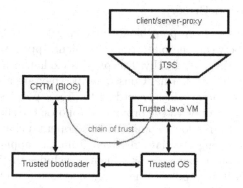

Fig. 1. Attestation Service Architecture and *Chain-of-Trust*

The scenario depicted in Figure 2 is as follows: A client application wants to establish a connection to a server based service. The application could be a web-browser or any application that requires a network connection[2]. However, the application is only allowed to connect if the trust state of the client and the server meet specified requirements that are defined by policies. The trust state in the context of TC is derived from the software components that are running on a platform and the hardware the platform is equipped with. Consequently, the policies include certain sets of allowed hardware and software configurations.

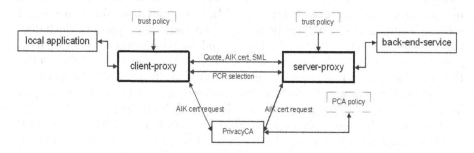

Fig. 2. Attestation Process Scenario

The platform state has to be reported to the remote platform which is then verified by it. To allow this, the presented architecture is embedded in the context of a trusted computing enhanced Public Key Infrastructure (PKI).

Each component of the proposed approach is discussed in detail in the following sub-sections.

---

[2] The scenario focused on within OpenTC uses a web browser as application and a bank server as back-end service, nevertheless the architecture can be used with any arbitrary application and service.

2.1   The Attestation Proxy

The attestation-proxies are responsible for attesting the platforms and routing the network traffic between the platforms, the client application and the back-end service (Figure 2). Additionally, the proxies exchange measurement- and attestation values of the platforms. Consequently, they are also responsible for validating the measurement values according to preset policies.

The platform attestation with the proxy is as follows: the client-proxy receives a connection request from a local application and opens a channel to the server-proxy. Prior to forwarding the data received from the application, the proxy initiates the attestation sequence. This sequence includes the following steps:

Depending on the proxy policy, the proxy may use a previously generated attested identity key (AIK) or may create a new one. Reusing of the AIK from a previous proxy connection saves the time for creating a new one. However this potentially lowers the level of privacy. When a new identity key is created in the TPM, the key has to be attested by a Privacy CA which issues a corresponding AIK certificate. The key is then used to sign the content of the PCR register.

The state of the system is reflected in the Platform Configuration Registers (PCR) of a TPM. The client-proxy proves to the server-proxy that the system is running in a desired trusted configuration by running the special TPM "quote" operation. It reports the content of a selected set of PCR registers and signs this information with an identity key.

As shown in Figure 2 the proxy sends the following items: the quote blob, the AIK certificate and the Stored Measurement Log (SML). The verification component of the proxy is now able to determine the state of the remote platform by evaluating the quote blob and the SML. The SML contains a list of all software components that have been loaded on the remote platform including their hashes. By recalculating the hashes and comparing them with the hash from the quote blob, the proxy has evidence of the remote platforms state. Furthermore, the signature on the quote blob is verified with the help of the included AIK certificate. If required, the Privacy CA is contacted for additional data (i.e. CRLs, OCSP requests) for verification of the certificate itself.

Only after all attestation steps have been successfully completed and both platforms have validated and accepted each other's state and configuration the connection between the application and the back-end service is permitted.

The attestation process in the depicted scenario is done in both directions. Other scenarios might require only the server or the client to be attested.

In order to access TC services and the TPM, the proxy relies on the trusted Java stack. It provides TC services to application like the proxy and manages the communication with the TPM. The trusted Java stack is discussed in the following section.

2.2   The Trusted Software Stack

The TCG not only specifies TPM hardware but also defines an accompanying software infrastructure called the TCG Software Stack (TSS) [15]. The stack

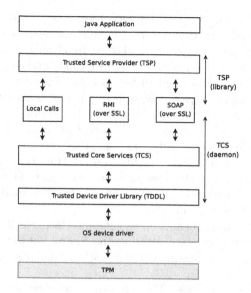

Fig. 3. Overview of jTSS Stack Layered Architecture

consists of different modules: the Trusted Service Provider, the Trusted Core Services and the Trusted Device Driver Library. The exact requirements of these modules can be found in [15]. A Java specific discussion is provided in the next sections.

Architecture. The TCG chose a layered architecture, which specifies interfaces in the C programming language, thus allowing applications to access the Trusted Computing functionality in a standard way. At the time of writing, several implementations for specific operating systems are available [2] or under development [5]. Up to now, aside from the TrouSerS TSS stack [9], the here presented IAIK TSS for the Java Platform (jTSS) is the only TCG software stack available as open source. All other known implementations are proprietary meaning that they only support TPMs from specific manufacturers .

The architecture presented in this paper allows operating system independence by providing the TC functionality within the Java programming language. At the same time, different TPM implementations, including a software based emulator, are supported. Thus actual platform-independent trusted services can be built on top of the presented TCG Software Stack for the Java Platform (jTSS). In contrast to other projects [7] that implement only sub-sets of the functionality, this stack closely follows the specification and includes both, high and low level APIs as proposed by the TCG. The different layers of the stack architecture are presented in Figure 3 and discussed in the following paragraphs.

The application level Trusted Service Provider. Java applications can access Trusted Computing functionality by using a derivate of the Trusted Service

Provider (TSP) interface. By providing an object oriented interface, the application developer is relieved from internal handle and memory management. A context object serves as entry point to all other functionality such as TPM specific commands, policy and key handling, data hashing and encryption and PCR composition. In addition, command authorisation and validation is provided and user owned cryptographic keys can be held in a per-user persistent storage.

Each application has an instance of the TSP library running on its own. This TSP communicates with the underlying Trusted Core Services (TCS). Different means of communication are possible. For small set-ups and for testing, a local binding using standard java function calls is used. However, the TCS may also run on another machine. In this case, Java Remote Method Invocation (RMI) may be used. Here, the communication between the two modules can be protected with Secure Socket Layers (SSL).

In addition to this implementation specific interface, the TSS standard also calls for an alternative interface utilising the Simple Object Access Protocol (SOAP) [16], which is implementation and platform independent.

The Trusted Core Services. The Trusted Core Services (TCS) are implemented as a system service, with a single instance for a TPM. By ensuring proper synchronisation, it is designed to handle requests from multiple TSPs. Among the main functionalities implemented in the TCS are key management, key cache management, TPM command generation and communication mechanisms.

Since the hardware resources of the TPM are limited, the loading, eviction and swapping of keys and authorisation sessions needs to be managed. Keys can be permanently stored in and retrieved from the system persistent storage using globally unique UUIDs [13]. With these mechanisms, complex key hierarchies can be defined, allowing to implement domain (i.e. enterprise) wide policies. The TCS event manager handles the SML, where PCR extension operations are tracked. For low level access, commands and data are assembled.

Low Level Integration. The TCS communicate with the TPM via the TSS Device Driver Library (TDDL). For hardware access, the Java objects need to be mapped to the standardized C-structures. Primitive data types need to be converted as well, considering the byte order of the host platform. These structures are then processed as byte streams. Since all commands and data are sent as such plain byte streams, this allows for an OS and hardware-independent implementation.

In the Linux operating system, hardware-vendor specific driver modules and a generic driver are integrated in recent kernel releases. The TPM can be accessed through the /dev/tpm device. With Microsoft Windows Vista, a generic system driver for version 1.2 TPMs is supplied. With the so called Trusted Base Services (TBS) [8], basic functionality like resetting or taking ownership is provided and TSS implementations can be supported. To integrate this Windows interface in the Java environment, a small native C helper library is accessed via the Java

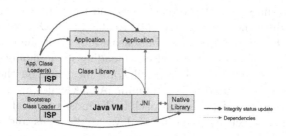

Fig. 4. Transitive trustmodel for the Java VM

Native Interface (JNI). The already pre-assembled byte stream is passed on as a command to the TPM via the TBS, and the response stream is returned to the Java interface.

2.3   The Trusted Java Virtual Machine

All currently proposed attestation mechanisms rely on integrity measurement of the software stack running on a platform. This holds also true for all forms of property-based attestation. In our work, we extended the trust chain to the Java VM as shown in Figure 4. We describe the additions to the Java VM in this section starting with trusted class loading.

Trusted Class Loading. Dynamic class loading is a feature of the Java VM specification. Classes are loaded during run time from any location pointed to by the class path. The class loaders form a tree structure to enable a delegation model. A class loader can delegate the loading of classes to a parent classloader and, if the loading fails, try to locate and load classes for itself. The root of the tree is the so-called bootstrap (or primordial) class loader. The loaded classes are assigned to so-called *protection domains* which prevent leakage of information between trusted code and application-specific code. Note that the term *trusted code* in this case merely refers to the class library shipped with the Java VM. However, this separation between different classes can be exploited for the functionality of our Trusted Java VM as well. The security mechanisms of the Java VM rely on the activation of the *security manager* which is enabled by default in our implementation.

The proposed approach extends class loading by measurement of executable contents which is, in the case of the Java environment, restricted to class files. Before the actual bytecode is present in the VM, the files are hashed and a PCR is extended. For the case of a secure boot functionality, the VM has the ability to terminate execution if a class file is not previously known. A special case for class loading is the reflection API of the Java language. Using qualified names, the application designer can dynamically load classes. For trusted class loading, this has no impact as those classes are loaded through the usual class loading mechanism and are measured as well.

JAR-files contain a collection of class files and their measurement offers the possibility to reduce the *PCR extend* calls to the TPM. Our experiments with the measurement architecture show that measurement of single class files can significantly affect the performance of class loading if the number of class files of the application grows large. If JAR-files are measured on the other hand, this overhead can be reduced to a minimum. As JAR-files are a usual way to distribute Java applications, this approach is the most practical one.

Other files that affect the security of Java applications and the Java VM itself are configuration files such as the Java security policy. For measurement, configuration files (and hence the subsequent configuration) are equal if and only if their hashes are equal. However, innumerous possibilities of formatting leading to the same configuration exist. As this provides no robust means to determine security, we decided to skip their measurement altogether.

Java Native Interface. The Java Native Interface (JNI) allows the application designer to use programming languages such as C/C++ or assembly to interact with Java applications. The interface is two-way, which means that the native code can also access Java objects, i.e. create, inspect and update them, call Java methods, catch and throw exceptions, load classes and obtain class information. Whereas there are applications where this proves to be useful, from a security perspective native libraries pose potential threats.

IBM designed an integrity measurement architecture on a Linux environment [1]. In their design, they intercept a set of system calls where files (executables, libraries, etc.) are loaded and measured into a PCR. Hence, as the VM loads the libraries dynamically, this measurement architecture would take care of the measurement and we can omit further discussion of this issue.

An alternative view on the problem is taken from an application perspective. A native library is part of the application it is used by. Hence, despite some restrictions, it might still be useful to include loaded libraries in the measurement. If there is also a measurement hook on OS level, one has to take care that the measurement is not taken twice. The general problem with this approach lies in the fact that loading of shared libraries on a Linux/GNU like environment can be followed by loading further shared libraries which is taken care of by the operating system. From the perspective of the VM, these libraries cannot be measured.

Components. In this section we give a component level description of our Java VM design. To keep the design simple and the code changes to the class loader as small as possible, we chose to implement a single interface for interaction with the measurement architecture which is called *Integrity Service Provider* (ISP). It manages the integrity measurement and provides methods necessary to enforce the integrity measurement policy. The *Measurement Agent* (MA) offers an interface to measure data that is crucial for the state of the platform. For the Java VM this would be class- and JAR-files. The *Verification Agent* (VA) performs the task of verifying the measurements taken by the MA against reference values. The *Storage Manager* class abstracts operations necessary to load and store Reference Integrity Measurements (RIMs) from a location.

In general, the storage of RIMs is a non-trivial task. Two possibilities have been proposed so far: storage inside a shielded location and the usage of RIM certificates. If the Java VM running on a device is using only a restricted number of applications the storage inside a shielded location is possible. On a general purpose computer the number of RIMs may become large which could introduce storage problems. A more practical solution would be to use cryptographic means to ensure the integrity and authenticity of RIMs which then can be kept on any type of storage [17].

Usage Model for PCRs. The Integrity Measurement Architecture (IMA) proposed by IBM [1] is attached to the Linux kernel. If we compare it to our Trusted Java VM the operating system has more power to manage measurements. Obviously, the operating system never gets unloaded and hence the data structures introduced in IMA can hold links to already measured files. If a file is opened a second time, IMA hashes it and compares this hash to the value in its data structures. If the hashes are equal, everything is fine and no PCR is extended. If the hashes differ, the number of PCR is extended with the new hash value. This allows IMA to only report a file twice if it is really necessary and changes (malicious or not) of files are detected.

This mechanism cannot be adapted to the VM measurement architecture for the obvious reason that, if the VM terminates, the data structures get reset and the measurement history is no longer available.

Those facts impose several restrictions on the architecture. At first, there need to be separate registers for extending the virtual machine itself, and the applications that run on this VM. Otherwise it will not be possible to seal any Java application to this VM configuration. If we suppose the operating system takes care of the measurement of the VM, it can also detect changes in the executable and core libraries of the VM as outlined in the IMA approach. Furthermore, as files are usually not measured twice, the value in the PCR for the VM represents a unique value to which applications can be sealed to.

2.4   Trusted PKI Support

The proposed approach strongly relies on a public key infrastructure. Hence, this section discusses the components required for establishing a trusted PKI.

A trusted PKI or *trusted computing enhanced public key infrastructure* is a framework enabling authentication, confidentiality and integrity services by using public key cryptography with support of trusted computing technology. It assists entities of (public) networks to establish levels of trust and/or secure communication channels. In the following two paragraphs we describe the trust enabling components required for our architecture.

Attested (Trusted) Identity. The TPM Endorsement Key (EK) uniquely identifies a TPM and hence a specific platform. Therefore, the privacy of a user is at risk if the EK would be used directly for transactions. As a countermeasure, the TCG introduced Attestation Identity Keys (AIKs) and associated AIK certificates (standard X.509 Public Key Certificates that include private extensions defined by TCG[17]), which cannot be backtracked directly to a specific platform. Still, they contain sufficient proof that the Trusted Computing supported hardware is hosting the certified key.

A trusted identity comprises two data objects: a non-migratable identity keypair hosted by a TPM and an associated certificate proving that the keypair belongs to a valid TPM, vouched for by a Privacy CA entity.

An identity key can only be used to operate upon data created by the TPM itself and not for signing arbitrary data.

Privacy CA. As depicted in Figure 2, the certification of AIKs is done by a dedicated and trusted third party, the so-called *Privacy CA* (PCA). A PCA is a CA with the requirement of hiding the platform specific EK credential. In order to obtain an AIK certificate, a specific protocol between trusted platform and Privacy CA takes place: The TPM creates a request package containing identity public key, AIK certificate label and platform specific certificates. The Privacy CA checks the included information and if all pieces conform to the CA policy, an AIK certificate is issued. The response is encrypted so that only the TPM indicated in the request can extract the AIK certificate.

The mode of operation of a Privacy CA is regulated by policy. It clearly describes how the relationship between EK certificates and the issued AIK certificates is managed. The policy options for a Privacy CA cover the spectrum from "remember everything" to "know enough for the specific operation, forget everything after completion of operation". Thus, the usage of a specific Privacy CA is scenario dependent and has to consider the intended level of privacy. In a restricted deployment scenario the Privacy CA - as a central authority - issues and validates AIK certificates only from well-known clients. This requires an initial registration step of each client's EK certificate.

3   Conclusion

This paper proposes an architecture for enhancing arbitrary applications with Trusted Computing functionality. With this architecture, legacy applications can now benefit from Trusted Computing services - in this special scenario from remote attestation - without being modified. Furthermore, they are now able to derive a trust state based on the remote platforms software configuration. In order to demonstrate the feasibility of the approach a proof-of-concept prototype has been developed by implementing the architecture.

Moreover, by adapting a Java Virtual Machine, we showed that it is possible to create a chain-of-trust starting from the BIOS up to a virtualised execution environment like Java. The adapted Java VM allows user applications to execute in a trusted environment. By integrating measurement mechanisms directly into the run time environment, high flexibility for these applications can be maintained, even within tight security requirements when building a trustworthy system.

Acknowledgements. The efforts at IAIK to integrate TC technology into the Java programming language are part of OpenTC project funded by the EU as part of FP-6, contract no. 027635. The projects aims at providing an open source TC framework with a special focus on the Linux operating system platform. Started as an open source project, the results can be inspected by everybody thus adding towards the trustworthiness of Trusted Computing solutions.

References

1. Sailer, R., Zhang, X., Jaeger, T., van Doorn, L.: Design and Implementation of a TCG-based Integrity Measurement Architecture. In: Proceedings of the 13th USENIX Security Symposium, pp. 223–238 (2004)
2. NTRU Cryptosystems, Inc. NTRU Core TCG Software Stack (CTSS) (2005), http://www.ntru.com/products/tcg_ss.htm
3. Stallman, R.: Can You Trust Your Computer (2007), http://www.gnu.org/philosophy/can-you-trust.html
4. Schneier, B.: Who Owns Your Computer (2007), http://www.schneier.com/blog/archives/2006/05/who_owns_your_c.html
5. Baek, K.-Y., Ingersoll, W., Rotondo, S.A.: OpenSolaris Project: Trusted Platform Module Support (2007), http://www.opensolaris.org/os/project/tpm/
6. Kay, R.L.: Trusted Computing is Real and it's Here (2007), https://www.trustedcomputinggroup.org/news/Industry_Data/ Endpoint_Technologies_Associates_TCG_report_Jan_29_2007.pdf
7. Sarmenta, L., Rhodes, J., Müller, T.: TPM/J Java-based API for the Trusted Platform Module (2007), http://projects.csail.mit.edu/tc/tpmj/
8. Microsoft Developer Network. TPM Base Services (2007), http://msdn2.microsoft.com/en-us/library/aa446796.aspx
9. TrouSerS - An Open-Source TCG Software Stack Implementation (2007), http://trousers.sourceforge.net/
10. Kinney, S.: Trusted Platform Module Basics: Using TPM in Embedded Systems. Elsevier, Burlington, MA, USA (2006)
11. Sadeghi, A.-R., Stüble, C.: Property-based Attestation for Computing Platforms: Caring about Policies, not Mechanisms. In: Proceedings of the New Security Paradigm Workshop (NSPW), pp. 67–77 (2004)
12. Haldar, V., Chandra, D., Franz, M.: Semantic Remote Attestation - Virtual Machine Directed Approach to Trusted Computing. In: Proceedings of the 3rd Virtual Machine Research and Technology Symposium, pp. 29–41 (2004)
13. International Telecommunication Union. Generation and registration of Universally Unique Identifiers (UUIDs) and their use as ASN.1 object identifier components. ITU-T X.667 (2004), http://www.itu.int/ITU-T/studygroups/com17/oid/X.667-E.pdf
14. Pirker, M., Winkler, T., Toegl, R.: Trusted Computing for the Java™Platform (2007), http://trustedjava.sourceforge.net/
15. Trusted Computing Group. TCG Software Stack Specification, Version 1.2 Errata A (2007), https://www.trustedcomputinggroup.org/specs/TSS/
16. W3C. Simple Object Access Protocol (SOAP) 1.1, W3C Note (2000), http://www.w3.org/TR/2000/NOTE-SOAP-20000508/
17. Trusted Computing Group. TCG Infrastructure Specifications (2007), https://www.trustedcomputinggroup.org/specs/IWG

18. Trusted Computing Group (2007), https://www.trustedcomputinggroup.org
19. Selhost, M., Stüble, C.: TrustedGRUB, Version 1.1 (2007),
    http://sourceforge.net/projects/trustedgrub
20. Goldman, K., Perez, R., Sailer, R.: Linking remote attestation to secure tunnel
    endpoints. In: Proceedings of the first ACM workshop on Scalable Trusted Com-
    puting, pp. 21–24 (2006)
21. Stumpf, F., Tafreschi, O., Röder, P., Eckert, C.: A Robust Integrity Reporting
    Protocol for Remote Attestation. In: Second Workshop on Advances in Trusted
    Computing (WATC 2006 Fall) (2006)
22. Trusted Computing Group. Trusted Network Connect (TNC) Specifications (2007),
    https://www.trustedcomputinggroup.org/specs/TNC/
23. Trusted Computing Group. TCG Specification Architecture Overview, Revision
    1.4 (2007), https://www.trustedcomputinggroup.org/groups/
    TCG_1_4_Architecture_Overview.pdf

Access Control Based on Code Identity for Open Distributed Systems

Andrew Cirillo and James Riely*

CTI, DePaul University
{acirillo,jriely}@cs.depaul.edu

Abstract. In computing systems, *trust* is an expectation on the dynamic behavior of an agent; *static analysis* is a collection of techniques for establishing static bounds on the dynamic behavior of an agent. We study the relationship between code identity, static analysis and trust in open distributed systems. Our primary result is a robust safety theorem expressed in terms of a distributed higher-order pi-calculus with code identity and a primitive for remote attestation; types in the language make use of a rich specification language for access control policies.

Keywords: Trusted Computing, Remote Attestation, Access Control, Authorization Logic, Compound Principals, Higher-Order Pi Calculus, Typing.

1   Introduction

Trust is an important concept in computer security. One may think of trust as an expectation on the *behavior* of some agent. We say that an agent is *trusted* if the achievement of a security goal is dependent on the agent behaving in the expected way. An agent is *trustworthy* if it behaves in the expected way in all circumstances.

An effective way to determine that an agent is trustworthy is to establish bounds on its behavior through static analysis of its software components. Many important security-related behavioral properties can be usefully established statically, including memory and type safety, non-interference, compliance with mandatory and discretionary access control policies and adherence to an ad-hoc logical policy specification.

An *open* system is one in which software components are under the control of multiple parties whose interests do not necessarily coincide. The use of static analysis in these systems is more complicated than in *closed* systems, where all components are under the control of a single party.

To discuss the issues involved, we find it useful to distinguish software components according to their relative *roles*. Given a particular unit of code and a statically derivable property, we distinguish four primary roles: the *producer* is the original author of the code; a *host* is a system that executes, or is considering executing, the code; a *certifier* is a third party capable of performing an analysis directly on the code that determines whether the property holds; and a *relying party* is the entity whose safe operation depends on the property holding for the code.

---

* This work was supported by the National Science Foundation under Grant No. 0347542.

G. Barthe and C. Fournet (Eds.): TGC 2007, LNCS 4912, pp. 169–185, 2008.
© Springer-Verlag Berlin Heidelberg 2008

When code is distributed in a compiled format, it may be the case that only the producer, who has the original source, is able to tractably certify many important properties. A host for the compiled code, if it is a relying party, may not able to establish the properties it needs.

This problem is well studied, and at least two solutions have been developed. By distributing the executable as intermediate-level *bytecode*, the analysis may be made tractable; in this case many useful analyses may remain intractable, or at least impractical. With *proof-carrying code* [1] the producer uses a certifying compiler to generate a proof of the desired property that can be checked efficiently by the host; this allows a greater range of analyses, but with the limitation that properties have to be agreed upon in advance.

A second issue arises when the relying party and host systems are physically distinct. For example, a server may hold sensitive data that it is only willing to release to remote clients that are known to be running certifiably safe code. The certification could be done by the client, but on what grounds can the server trust the results? The certification can instead be done by the server, but only if it can authenticate the code running on the client.

In conventional authentication protocols, remote parties authenticate themselves by demonstrating knowledge of a secret. When executables are distributed over public channels, however, embedded secrets are vulnerable to extraction and misuse by attackers so code cannot in general be relied upon to authenticate itself. This problem is addressed in part by *trusted computing*, where a trusted host authenticates the code it is running, and when necessary attests to the identity of the code to remote parties.

Remote code authentication, or *attestation*, is based on measurements of static executables. Therefore, trusted computing platforms only attest to initial states of processes. This makes static analysis particularly important for reasoning in systems using attestation. Code identity is a degenerate example of a static property; more abstract properties can be defined as sets of executables that satisfy the property. Knowing that the executable running on a host satisfies a certain property may allow a relying party to determine something about the dynamic state of the host.

Even weak static properties may be useful in validating trust. For example, knowing that a server has the latest patches applied may ease the mind of an e-commerce client. Similarly, a bounded model checker or test suite may give some assurance of memory safety without proving absolute trustworthiness.

For concreteness, we concentrate here on access control properties established via a type system, leaving the general case to future work. This focus allows us to establish absolute guarantees of trustworthiness and thus to prove a robust safety theorem. We do so in the context of a higher-order π-calculus enhanced with process identity and primitive operations for remote attestation.

The contributions of this paper are twofold. First, we illustrate how the trusted computing paradigm can be used to enforce an access control model based on static properties of code. Second, we demonstrate the importance of higher-order languages in studying policies and protocols that make use of remote attestation.

Organization. In the remainder of this introduction, we provide some intuitions about our formalism and results. In Section 2 we present the syntax and operational semantics of our language. Detailed examples follow in Section 3. Section 4 summarizes the type system and the main safety theorem; details are elided here for lack of space. Related work is discussed in Section 5.

Background: Remote Attestation. Remote attestation is a technique that allows processes to prove their identity to remote systems through the use of a trusted third party that is physically collocated with the process. In the Trusted Computing Group (TCG) specification [2] this comes in the form of a Trusted Platform Module (TPM) – an embedded co-processor that has the ability to measure the integrity of the boot sequence and securely store cryptographic keys. Each TPM is created with a unique keypair and a certificate from a trusted certificate authority.

The TPM serves as the root of trust for a Trusted Software Stack (TSS) [3], which in turn serves a trusted operating system which hosts user programs. As the software stack progresses, a measurement (cryptographic hash) of the next item to be loaded is placed in a secure register before it executes. Upon request, the TPM will produce a signature for the contents of the secure register bank using a private key. An *attestation* is a list of measurements plus a payload, signed by a TPM key.

Measurements of program executables, in this case, serve as a form of code identity. Modifying an executable changes its measurement, so attestation effectively identifies the remote process, and also demonstrates that the software running on the remote system has not been compromised.

We do not, in this paper, attempt to model the underlying protocol of remote attestation using explicit cryptographic primitives [4] nor do we attempt to translate our calculus into a lower level calculus with cryptographic primitives [5]. Instead, we take it for granted that the following capabilities are available and treat attestation as a primitive operation. We assume that executables can be measured in a globally consistent fashion (e.g., using an SHA-1 hash), and that the keys embedded in each TPM are issued by a globally trusted (and trustworthy) certificate authority. We also assume that, when multitasking, trustworthy operating systems enforce strong memory isolation between processes. Attestation protocols [6] are designed to be anonymous, so we do not assume any capability for distinguishing between different instances of a program nor do we assume that any information is available regarding the physical location of a process.[1]

Access Control with Remote Attestation. Remote attestation enables a model of access control in which executables, as identified by their cryptographic hashes, assume the role of principal. In its most basic form, it allows an attesting system to demonstrate to remote parties exactly what executables it has loaded. The remote party may exercise a simple form of access control by choosing to continue interacting with the attesting system only if all of its loaded executables are known and trusted. For example, an online media server may refuse access to clients not running its digital rights management (DRM) software.

While this simple approach may be sufficient in a limited context where only a small number of well-known executables need be trusted, such as in the proprietary DRM

---

[1] While attestations are anonymous in the sense that an individual user or machine cannot be identified, the recipient does get precise information about the software and hardware running on the attesting system that could be considered sensitive. Sadeghi and Stüble [7] cite this as a shortcoming of the TCG specification in their argument for property-based attestation.

example above, it is low-level, inefficient and inflexible. A common criticism [8] of trusted computing cautions that this lack of flexibility could be used by industry leaders to lock out open-source software and products from smaller competitors.

A more robust design is necessary to broaden the applicability of trusted computing, and indeed a number of extensions to the existing specification have already been proposed [7,9,10].

Overview of Our Solution. Modeling systems that operate on static units of executable code is a suitable task for a higher-order π-calculus [11,12,13], where processes can be abstracted and treated as data. Thus, we develop a higher-order π-calculus, dubbed HOπ-rat, enhanced with process identity and primitives for creating and using attestations. Process identity is implemented in the form of *configurations*, which are located processes where location is a representation of the identity (measurement) of the software stack that spawned the process.

Access control in HOπ-rat is based on a notion of principal that is tied to code identity. Static properties of code also play a role. We model these qualities as membership in a *security class*. Security classes are the basis for our access control policies, and a single executable may belong to multiple security classes. Complex principals are specified by a language of compound principals that includes both primitive identities and security classes.

There are two aspects to access control policy. First, read and write authorizations are specified explicitly in type annotations on channels in the form of expressions in the language of compound principals. Second, the sort of trust that a process places in particular identities is represented as a mapping of identities to security classes.

Our security classes are flexible, and can accommodate a wide range of security expectations, however one expectation is distinguished: each participant in a trusted software stack must maintain the expectations of the trusted system as a whole. In particular, they must not do anything to compromise the integrity of an attestation, and they must not leak secret data on insecure channels. We designate this behavior with the security class cert. We also develop a notion of *robust safety* and present a sketch of a type system that ensures robust safety in the presence of arbitrary attackers. We discriminate between typechecked and non-typechecked identities via membership in cert, and refer to typechecked processes as *certified*.

2   The Language

In this section we describe the syntax and operational semantics of the HOπ-rat calculus. We first define a sub-calculus of compound principals that will serve as the basis for access control in our system. We then define the syntax of terms, types, processes and configurations, followed by the operational semantics.

2.1   A Calculus of Compound Principals

To support the creation of sophisticated access control policies, we develop a calculus of compound principals in the style of Abadi et al. [14]. Primitive principals include identities and classes (including the distinguished class cert) drawn from an infinite set

($\mathcal{N}$) of atomic principal names. The principal constant 0 represents the inert process – always trustworthy by virtue of its inertness – and **any** represents an arbitrary process.

Compound principals are constructed using conjunction ($\wedge$), disjunction ($\vee$) and quoting ($|$) operators. Of these, quoting is essential because it is used to represent one process running in the context of another. For example, the principal $tss|myos|widget$ might represent a user application running on an operating system running on a trusted software stack. The other combinators are provided only to add expressiveness to the policy language.

A *policy environment* (Σ) maps identities to classes. For example, $\Sigma(a, \alpha)$ indicates that a is a member of α. Class membership is many-to-many; an identity may be a member of multiple classes, and a class may have multiple members. We write $a \Rightarrow \alpha$ for a policy environment consisting of a single pair.

PRINCIPALS AND POLICY ENVIRONMENTS

$a, b, c \in \mathcal{N}_{id}$ $\alpha - \omega \in \mathcal{N}_{cls}$ (including **cert**)	*identities/classes*
$A, B, C ::= $ **any** $\mid 0 \mid a \mid \alpha \mid A \wedge B \mid A \vee B \mid A|B$	*principals*
$\Sigma, \Phi \subseteq \mathcal{N}_{id} \times \mathcal{N}_{cls}$	*policy environment*

We define a partial order ($\Rightarrow$), ranking principals in terms of trustedness. When $A \Rightarrow B$, A is trusted at least as much as B. Derivations are defined in terms of a policy environment so that $\Sigma \vdash A \Rightarrow B$ if $\Sigma(A, B)$, or $A = 0$, or $B = $ **any**, so that $\wedge, \vee$ are commutative, associative, idempotent, absorptive and distribute over each other, so that $|$ is monotone and idempotent, and so that $\Rightarrow$ is reflexive, transitive and antisymmetric. Thus defined, $\Rightarrow$ forms a distributive lattice with $\wedge, \vee$ as meet and join operators, and **any**, 0 as top and bottom elements. If Σ and Φ are policy environments, we write $\Sigma \vdash \Phi$ if for every a, α such that $\Phi(a, \alpha)$, we have that $\Sigma \vdash a \Rightarrow \alpha$.

Our treatment of compound principals builds on existing work [14,15]. In the interest of minimality, we use only a calculus of principals and do not incorporate a full modal authorization logic, which would include a "says" construct. Existing techniques [16,17,18] for using authorization logics in π-calculi could be applied here as well.

2.2 Syntax

In addition to principals, the main syntactic categories of HOπ-rat are terms, types, processes and configurations. As usual in π, we assume an infinite set ($\mathcal{N}$) of names, but we distinguish channels (n, m) from variables (x, y, z). We use a *local* syntax [19,20,21] in the sense that only output capabilities may be communicated as it is syntactically disallowed to read from a variable.

TERMS

$n, m \in \mathcal{N}_{ch}$ $x, y, z \in \mathcal{N}_{var}$	*channels/variables*
$M, N ::= n \mid x \mid \texttt{unit} \mid (x : T)P \mid (M, N) \mid [M : T] \mid \{M : T @ A\}_*$	*terms*

Terms include channel names, variables, a unit term and process abstractions from higher-order π, pairs, and two novel constructs. The term $[M : T]$, where M is a process abstraction and T is an abstraction type, represents an executable. We assume that the identity of an executable can be taken directly using a well-known measurement algorithm, which we represent as a function (#) taking executable terms to primitive identities. Since otherwise trustworthy programs can sometimes be coerced to misbehave if they are initialized incorrectly, executables include a type annotation to ensure that the identity function takes the type of the program arguments into account.

The term $\{M : T @ A\}_*$ represents an attestation – the payload M tagged with type T and the principal A, where A stands for a list of the measurements of the executables that were running when the attestation was requested.

TYPES

$$S, T ::= \mathsf{Ch}\langle A, B\rangle(T) \mid \mathsf{Wr}\langle A, B\rangle(T) \mid \mathsf{Unit} \mid T \to \langle A\rangle\mathsf{Proc} \mid S \times T \mid \mathsf{Tnt} \mid \mathsf{Un} \mid \mathsf{Prv} \mid \mathsf{Pub}$$

Types include constructs for read/write and write-only channels, unit, abstractions, pairs and four top types. The unit and pair types are standard; we discuss the others below.

Channel types include annotations for specifying policy. For example, the type $\mathsf{Ch}\langle A, B\rangle(T)$ is given to channels that communicate values of type T, and may be used for input by processes authorized at principal B with the expectation that it will only be used for output by processes authorized at principal A. As in Sangiorgi's localized pi [19], we syntactically restrict input to channels, disallowing input on variables. Therefore, channel types may only be used with names. Write types are similar, but only allow output and therefore may be used to type variables.

The security annotations allow for fine-grained specifications of access control policy. For example, a channel annotated with type $\mathsf{Ch}\langle \alpha \wedge \beta, B\rangle(T)$ can only be written on by processes that are members of both α and β. Conversely, $\mathsf{Ch}\langle \alpha \vee \beta, B\rangle(T)$ requires membership in either α or β. Other policies can place restrictions on the software stack, as in $\mathsf{Ch}\langle myos|any, B\rangle(T)$, which permits any process running on the *myos* operating system.

Types for abstractions take the form $S \to \langle A\rangle\mathsf{Proc}$, where S is the type of the argument and A is a security annotation representing a principal that the process may expect to run at (discussed in Section 4). We sometimes write $S \to \mathsf{Proc}$ when the security annotation is not of interest.

Attestations and executables are typed at one of the four top types ($\mathsf{Tnt}, \mathsf{Un}, \mathsf{Prv}, \mathsf{Pub}$) which are used to classify data by secrecy and integrity properties. The top types are used in the kinding judgment mentioned in section 4.

PROCESSES AND CONFIGURATIONS

$$P, Q ::= 0 \mid n?N \mid \mathsf{repeat}\ n?N \mid M!N \mid M\ N \mid \mathsf{new}\ n : T;\ P \mid P \mid Q$$
$$\mid \mathsf{split}\ (x : S, y : T) = M;\ P \mid \mathsf{let}\ x = \mathsf{attest}(M : T);\ P$$
$$\mid \mathsf{check}\ \{x : T\} = M;\ P \mid \mathsf{load}\ M\ \mathsf{as}\ [T]\ N$$
$$\mid \Sigma \mid \mathsf{wr\text{-}scope}\ n\ \mathsf{is}\ A \mid \mathsf{rd\text{-}scope}\ M\ \mathsf{is}\ A$$
$$\mid \mathsf{spoof}\ A; P \mid \mathsf{let}\ \vec{x} = \mathsf{fn}(M);\ P$$
$$G, H ::= 0 \mid A[P] \mid G \mid H \mid \mathsf{new}_A\ n : T;\ G$$

Processes include the usual constructs for HOπ: the inert process; input and replicated input; output; higher-order application, as in $M\ N$, which applies the argument N to the abstraction M; restriction; and parallel composition. The form $\texttt{split}\,(x:S,y:T)=M;\,P$ is used to split a pair into its constituent parts.

The main security extensions are $\texttt{attest}$, $\texttt{check}$ and $\texttt{load}$. The form $\texttt{let}\,x=\texttt{attest}(M:T);\,P$ represents a call to trusted hardware to create a new attested message with payload M and attested type T. The form $\texttt{check}\,\{x:T\}=M;\,P$ tests and conditionally destructs an attestation. The form $\texttt{load}\,M$ as $[T]\,N$ dynamically tests the identity and argument type of an executable prior to running it. The inclusion of Σ in the process language allows processes to carry knowledge about other processes at runtime. The expectations $\texttt{wr-scope}\,n$ is A and $\texttt{rd-scope}\,M$ is A are only used in the definition of runtime error and are discussed further below.

The final two forms are reserved for attackers, and therefore cannot appear in any well-typed term. The form $\texttt{spoof}\,A;P$ allows the process to change its identity and the form $\texttt{let}\,\vec{x}=\texttt{fn}(M);\,P$ extracts the free names of a term.

Configurations (G,H) are composed of processes located at principals (e.g., $A[P]$). Our treatment of configurations is mostly standard for located π-calculi [22,23] with one exception: our locations expand as new code is loaded. For example, we use the compound principal $(a|b|c)$ to represent the sequence of a having loaded b having loaded c.

2.3   Operational Semantics

Evaluation is defined on configurations. We elide the structural equivalence rules which are mostly standard for located calculi [22] (for example "$A[P\mid Q]\equiv A[P]\mid A[Q]$"). The one novelty is the rule, "$\Sigma\mid\Phi\equiv\Sigma,\Phi$", which allows policy environments to be combined.

EVALUATION

$$\text{(R-COMM)}\ \ A[n?M]\mid B[n!N]\longrightarrow A[M\,N]\qquad \text{(R-STRUC)}\ \ \frac{G\equiv G'\quad H'\equiv H\quad G'\longrightarrow H'}{G\longrightarrow H}$$

$$\text{(R-APP)}\ \ A[(x:T)P\,N]\longrightarrow A[P\{x:=N\}]\qquad \text{(R-RES)}\ \ \frac{G\longrightarrow G'}{\texttt{new}\,n:T;\,G\longrightarrow \texttt{new}\,n:T;\,G'}$$

$$\text{(R-ATT)}\ \ A[\texttt{let}\,x=\texttt{attest}(M:T);\,P]\longrightarrow A[P\{x:=\{M:T\,@\,A\}_*\}]\qquad \text{(R-PAR)}\ \ \frac{G\longrightarrow G'}{G\mid H\longrightarrow G'\mid H}$$

$$\text{(R-SPLIT)}\ \ A[\texttt{split}\,(x:S,y:T)=(M,N);\,P]\longrightarrow A[P\{x:=M\}\{y:=N\}]$$

$$\text{(R-CAST)}\ \ \frac{\Sigma\vdash S<:T\quad \Sigma\vdash B\Rightarrow\texttt{cert}}{A[\Sigma]\mid A[\texttt{check}\,\{x:T\}=\{M:S\,@\,B\}_*;\,P]\longrightarrow A[\Sigma]\mid A[P\{x:=M\}]}$$

$$\text{(R-CASTUN)}\ \ A[\texttt{check}\,\{x:\texttt{Tnt}\}=\{M:S\,@\,B\}_*;\,P]\longrightarrow A[P\{x:=M\}]$$

$$\text{(R-LOAD)}\ \ \frac{\Sigma\vdash S<:T\to\langle B\rangle\texttt{Proc}\quad \Sigma\vdash a\Rightarrow\texttt{cert}}{A[\Sigma]\mid A[\texttt{load}\,[M:S]\text{ as }[T\to\langle B\rangle\texttt{Proc}]\,N]\longrightarrow A[\Sigma]\mid (A|a)[M\,N]}\ \ a=\#([M:S])$$

$$\text{(R-LOADUN)}\ \ \frac{\vdash S<:T\to\langle B\rangle\texttt{Proc}\quad \vdash T<:\texttt{Un}\quad b=\#([M:S])}{A[\texttt{load}\,[M:S]\text{ as }[T\to\langle B\rangle\texttt{Proc}]\,N]\longrightarrow (A|b)[M\,N]}$$

$$\text{(R-SPOOF)}\ \ A[\texttt{spoof}\,B;P]\longrightarrow (A|B)[P]$$

$$\text{(R-PEEK)}\ \ \frac{}{A[\texttt{let}\,\vec{x}=\texttt{fn}([M:T]);\,P]\longrightarrow A[P\{\vec{x}:=fn(M)\}]}\ \ \text{if }|\vec{x}|=|fn(M)|$$

The rule for communication (R-COMM) passes a value along a channel in the standard way. When a value is communicated from one identity to another, the resulting process takes on the identity of the receiving process. The rule for splitting pairs (R-SPLIT) is standard.

In the rule for the creation of attestations (R-ATT) a term is tagged with a type and the pair is signed with the identity of the creating process. In the first rule for destruction (R-CAST), the identity of the generating process is recovered and tested against the local policy of the receiving process. The receiver must believe that the generating process is certified before it can trust the contents of the message. If the necessary facts are not present the destructor blocks, so for example these two configurations in parallel will reduce whereas the latter on its own would not.

$$A[b \Rightarrow \mathsf{cert}] \mid A[\mathsf{check}\ \{x : T\} = \{N : T @ b\}_*; P] \longrightarrow A[b \Rightarrow \mathsf{cert}] \mid A[P\{x := N\}]$$

In order to safely unpack $\{N : T @ B\}_*$ one must be able to establish that B is certified, that is that $B \Rightarrow \mathsf{cert}$ holds in the lattice of principals derived from the receiver's local policy. Note that from the idempotency and monotonicity of $\mid$ one can derive $a \mid b \Rightarrow \mathsf{cert}$ if $a \Rightarrow \mathsf{cert}$ and $b \Rightarrow \mathsf{cert}$. The principals used in attestations always have this form, so an attestation will be trusted if each of its component identities are certified. The receiving process need not know of all certified processes, only those with which it interacts, however a process may be unable to unpack a perfectly safe message if any identity in the sequence is unknown.

The second rule for destruction (R-CASTUN) allows a process to skip the dynamic checks if there are no type requirements for the extracted data (the type Tnt is at the top of the subtype hierarchy).

The rule for application (R-APP) converts an abstraction into a running process by substituting the argument for the bound variable. R-LOAD allows parent processes to run abstractions that they have received from untrusted sources after completing two dynamic checks. First, it tests the hash of M for certification. If M is known to be certified, then the type assertion can be trusted. Second, it tests that the asserted type is a subtype of the expected type. If both tests are successful, it extracts the enclosed abstraction and applies it to the argument.

As with attestations a second version (R-LOADUN) allows the dynamic checks to be skipped, in this case if the argument is of a safe type (i.e., contains no secrets). For example, suppose $b = \#([M : T])$. The following process located at A loads M.

$$A[b \Rightarrow \mathsf{cert}] \mid A[\mathtt{load}\ [M : T]\ \mathtt{as}\ [T]\ N] \longrightarrow A[b \Rightarrow \mathsf{cert}] \mid (A \mid b)[M\ N]$$

A's local mapping $(b \Rightarrow \mathsf{cert})$ indicates that $[M : T]$ is known to be certified, which enables the loading. Note that the residual is located at $A \mid b$.

The final two rules are reserved for uncertified systems and are necessary to model realistic attacks on higher-order code. R-SPOOF allows a process to impersonate an arbitrary principal as long as the root is preserved and R-PEEK allows a process to extract the free names of a higher-order term. Spying on, or "debugging," a child process can be modeled using a combination of these operations as follows: the attacker first extracts the free names of an executable, then builds a new executable identical to the original except that all bound names are replaced with names in the attacker's scope, and finally loads the modified executable and spoofs the identity of the original process.

3 Examples

In this section we illustrate the use of HOπ-rat in two detailed examples. Throughout this section we use the following notational conveniences: we elide trivial type annotations, we abbreviate $\text{load}\,M$ as $[\text{Un} \rightarrow \langle 0 \rangle \text{Proc}]\,N$ as $\text{load}\,M\,N$, and we abbreviate $(x : \text{Unit})P$ as $()P$ when $x \notin fn(P)$.

3.1 Example: A Trusted Software Stack

Our first example shows how the integrity of the software stack can be preserved in a trusted system, from the booting of the operating system to the execution of a user application. We start with a simple computer system composed of a BIOS (*BIOS*), disk drive (*DSKDRV*), user interface (*UI*) and operating system (*OS*). The first three components are loaded by hardware, thus they are represented as pre-existing processes. The operating system, however, must be booted from code stored on the disk drive.

We assume that the disk drive is untrusted. (Unencrypted storage devices are easily tampered with while the computer is switched off, so anything loaded from the disk drive must be treated as if it came from a public source.) The process representing the drive listens for file requests on a series of channels, one for each file, and responds by writing the file on the request channel. Some of these files will be executable programs; in particular, a request on the distinguished channel *mbr* (for *master boot record*) will return the operating system kernel code.

$$DSKDRV \triangleq \texttt{repeat}\ mbr?(x)x!OS\ |\ \texttt{repeat}\ f_i?(x)x!FILE_i\ |\ \dots$$

The BIOS is responsible for locating and loading the operating system, which it does by sending a request on *mbr* and loading the returned executable. The BIOS does not need to verify the safety or identity of the executable because the load command stores the hash of the loaded program in the PCR, ensuring that it is reflected in the identity of the resulting process.

$$BIOS \triangleq \texttt{new}\ n;\ mbr!n\ |\ n?(y)\texttt{load}\,y\,\texttt{unit}$$

Let $dskdrv = \#([()DISKDRV])$, $bios = \#([()BIOS])$, and $os = \#([()OS])$. At startup the BIOS process will be located at *bios* and the disk process at *dskdrv*. The boot sequence proceeds as follows.

Booting with Integrity

$$bios\,[\texttt{new}\ n;\ mbr!n\ |\ n?(y)\texttt{load}\,y\,\texttt{unit}]\ |\ dskdrv\,[\texttt{repeat}\ mbr?(x)x![()OS]\ |\ \dots]$$
$$\longrightarrow^4 bios\,[\texttt{load}\,[()OS]\,\texttt{unit}]\ |\ dskdrv\,[\texttt{repeat}\ mbr?(x)x![()OS]\ |\ \dots]$$
$$\longrightarrow^2 (bios|os)\,[OS]\ |\ dskdrv\,[\texttt{repeat}\ mbr?(x)x![()OS]\ |\ \dots]$$

By the end of the boot process, the operating system code is running at the identity *bios|os*. The BIOS code has terminated, but its identity is reflected in the identity of the operating system process. This ensures that a malicious BIOS cannot compromise or impersonate a trusted operating system without detection.

Note that no access control checks are required for the boot process. We consider it to be perfectly acceptable for a trusted system to load untrusted code as long as the identity of that code is recorded. This distinguishes this boot sequence from a *secure boot*, which only executes trusted code.

Once loaded, the operating system code enters a loop listening for requests to start user programs. Requests come in the form of a channel name that corresponds to a file on disk, and an argument term. The operating system fetches the corresponding file from the disk drive and loads it, passing it the argument term.

$$OS \triangleq \texttt{repeat } req?(x)\texttt{split } (f,arg) = x; \texttt{ new } n; \ (f!n \mid n?(y)\texttt{load } y \, arg)$$

The type of the argument term is not checked. If the executable were initialized with an argument of the wrong type it could cause the security of the resulting process to fail, therefore the evaluation rule (R-LOADUN) requires that the executable be annotated to accept arguments of type Un. Any certified executable with such an annotation will have been proven to operate safely with arbitrary arguments.

Now we can consider how the system responds to a user request to run a program. Let *ui* represent part of the user interface hardware (keyboard, mouse, etc.) for some system, and assume that the user has indicated a request to load the program *PROG* by keying in "prog *args*" to the interface.

LOADING A USER PROGRAM

$dskdrv[... \mid \texttt{repeat } prog?(x)x![(z)PROG] \mid ...]$
$\mid (bios|os)[\texttt{repeat } req?(x)\texttt{split } (f,arg) = x; \texttt{new } n; \ (f!n \mid n?(y)\texttt{load } y \, arg)]$
$\mid ui[req!(prog,args)]$

$\longrightarrow^4 dskdrv[... \mid \texttt{repeat } prog?(x)x![(z)PROG] \mid ...]$
$\mid (bios|os)[\texttt{repeat } req?(x)\texttt{split } (f,arg) = x; \texttt{new } n; \ (f!n \mid n?(y)\texttt{load } y \, arg)]$
$\mid (bios|os)[\texttt{load } [(z)PROG] \, args]$

$\longrightarrow^2 dskdrv[... \mid \texttt{repeat } prog?(x)x![(z)PROG] \mid ...]$
$\mid (bios|os)[\texttt{repeat } req?(x)\texttt{split } (f,arg) = x; \texttt{new } n; \ (f!n \mid n?(y)\texttt{load } y \, arg)]$
$\mid (bios|os|prog)[PROG\{z := args\}]$

After several reduction steps, the user program (*PROG*) is running at the identity *bios|os|prog*, and the operating system is back in its original state, awaiting a new command.

A user program can also load another user program through the operating system functionality. The new identity of this program will be *bios|os|newprog*; it does not reflect the identity of the calling program as it would if the calling program had invoked the load command directly. The operating system loop only loads programs that are expecting arbitrary arguments, so there is no chance that a malicious program can use this functionality to misconfigure a trusted program while excluding its own measurement from the identity sequence.

This illustrates an important difference between stand-alone executables started through operating system functionality, as in the example above, and dynamically loaded modules, such as shared libraries and browser plugins. In the former case the operating system is solely responsible for the safe initialization of the code; in the latter, the calling process is relied upon to initialize the new module correctly, therefore its identity is reflected in the identity of the resulting process.

3.2 Example: Secure E-Commerce

In this example, remote attestation is used to facilitate secure communication between a vendor and customer. Each party has different security requirements. In order to complete the transaction the customer has to provide sensitive personal information – a credit card number and delivery address – and therefore requires that the vendor be secure and comply with an electronic privacy policy.

On the other side, because the vendor may have to cover the cost of fraudulent charges, it has an interest in ensuring that the request is coming from an actual user, and not a trojan horse or virus running on the customer's machine. They can accomplish this by requiring that the request come from an actual web browser (as opposed to a script, or other program) and that the browser be free from security holes.

The two main parties are the customer (*cust*) and vendor (*vend*) executables; but there are also the customer (*c_host*) and vendor (*v_host*) hosts. We represent the requirements that the customer has of the vendor with the security class *ok_vend*, and that the vendor has of the customer with *ok_cust*. These properties are established by two independent certifiers, *vendcc* and *custcc*.

The code for the customer certifier (*custcc*) is shown below, the vendor certifier is similar. It listens for requests on a well-known public channel (*getCustIsOk*), and responds with a certificate mapping the *cust* identity to the *ok_cust* security class. Recall that policy environments are part of the process language, so we communicate them as thunked processes. A certificate therefore has the form of a thunked policy environment wrapped in an attestation.

Customer Certifier

```
(...|custcc) [ repeat getCustIsOk?(c)
              let msg = attest(()#(cust) ⇒ ok_cust : Unit → ⟨cert⟩Proc); c!msg ]
```

The location of *custcc* is not important. It is the vendor process that requires the customer certifier, so they could be running on the same host, however the use of an attestation to sign the certificate means that the processes could just as easily be distributed. Trust is placed in the *program* doing the certification, not the physical node running it, so any node equipped with a TPM running the correct software – even the customer node itself – can host a certifier process.

At the start of the protocol, *cust* (1) trusts only the vendor certifier. It first consults a trusted certifier (2-3) and obtains a certificate listing some trustworthy vendors; *vend* (11-13) does the same but for trustworthy customers. The customer then initiates the protocol by creating (5) a partially secure (only the customer can read, but anyone can write) callback channel, wrapping it (6) in an attestation and forwarding it (7) to the vendor on a well-known public channel. At this point the attested message will have the form $\{cch : \text{Wr}\langle any, ok\_cust\rangle(\text{Tnt}) @ c\_host|cust\}_*$. After receiving the message, the vendor performs a dynamic check (15) to ensure that the message is from a trusted source, and that the contents are of the expected type. Succeeding at that, it continues by creating its own secure callback (16), wrapping it in an attestation (17) and sending it back to the customer (18). At this point the parties have established bidirectional secure communications, and the customer data can be sent (10) safely with all security requirements met.

Note that in order for the dynamic checks (3,9,15,13) to pass, the process must explicitly trust the attestors. The trust required to allow the first checks (3,13) to pass is already hard-coded (1,11) in the executables. The trust required for the other checks (9,15) are acquired at runtime from the trusted certifiers.

CUSTOMER AND VENDOR EXECUTABLES

```
(c_host|cust)[
 1| vendcc ⇒ cert | v_host ⇒ cert |
 2| new c; getVendIsOk!c | c?(x : Un)
 3|   check {y : Unit → ⟨cert⟩Proc} = x; x unit |
 4| new address, credit_card : Ch⟨cert, ok_cust⟩(Prv);
 5| new cch : Ch⟨any, ok_cust⟩(Tnt);
 6| let amsg = attest(cch : Wr⟨any, ok_cust⟩(Tnt));
 7| vpub!amsg |
 8| cch?(x : Tnt)
 9|   check {y : Wr⟨ok_cust, ok_vend⟩(Prv)} = x;
10|   y!(address, credit_card) ]

(v_host|vend)[
11| custcc ⇒ cert | c_host ⇒ cert |
12| new c; getCustIsOk!c | c?(x : Un)
13|   check {y : Unit → ⟨cert⟩Proc} = x; x unit |
14| vpub?(x : Un)
15|   check {y : Wr⟨any, ok_cust⟩(Tnt)} = x;
16| new vch : Ch⟨ok_cust, ok_vend⟩(Prv);
17| let vmsg = attest(vch : Wr⟨ok_cust, ok_vend⟩(Prv));
18| y!vmsg
19| vch?(data : Prv)(...continue processing transaction...) ]
```

4   A Type System for Certified Processes

We have developed a type system that ensures that typed processes meet the behavioral requirements for certified processes, even in the presence of arbitrary attackers. For space reasons, most of the details are elided.

We begin by formalizing the requirements as a definition of *robust safety*. Attackers come in two forms: as any software stack running on a system without a TPM, and as an untrusted process running on an otherwise trusted system. Our assumptions about attackers are as liberal as possible. The only requirements are that they be located at an uncertified identity, and that any attestations they possess must be acquired at runtime. In addition, we allow attackers to do the following: (1) if they are of the latter form, they may create attestations that extend the measurement sequence arbitrarily, provided that the measurements up to and including the untrusted process are accurate, (2) they may extract the contents of executables, including any embedded keys, and (3) they may peek at the memory of (i.e., debug) running child processes.

DEFINITION 1 (INITIAL ATTACKER). Let H be a configuration and Σ a policy environment. H is considered a Σ-*initial attacker* if it is of the form $A_1[P_1]\dots A_n[P_n]$ where $(\forall i)\Sigma \nvdash A_i \Rightarrow \mathsf{cert}$, and it has no subterms of the form $\{M : T @ B\}_*$.

Robust Safety. Safety is defined in terms of runtime error. The full system includes shape errors in addition to the access control errors presented here.

RUNTIME ERROR (PARTIAL)

$$
\text{(E-WRSCP)} \quad \frac{}{\Sigma \triangleright A[\mathtt{wr\text{-}scope}\ n\ \mathtt{is}\ C] \mid B[n!N] \xrightarrow{error}} \quad if\ \Sigma \vdash A \Rightarrow \mathsf{cert}\ and\ \Sigma \nvdash B \Rightarrow C
$$

$$
\text{(E-RDSCP)} \quad \frac{}{\Sigma \triangleright A[\mathtt{rd\text{-}scope}\ n\ \mathtt{is}\ C] \mid B[n?N] \xrightarrow{error}} \quad if\ \Sigma \vdash A \Rightarrow \mathsf{cert}\ and\ \Sigma \nvdash B \Rightarrow C
$$

A configuration is in error, for example, if a certified configuration is expecting the write scope of a channel to be restricted to one principal, and the channel is written on by a process located at another principal that does not carry that level of authorization in the lattice of principals.

Robust safety requires that no certified process can lead to a runtime error even in the presence of arbitrary attackers. It is defined relative to a policy environment, so it is perfectly reasonable to have policies that disagree on the safety of a given process. Our main result is that well-typed configurations are robustly safe.

DEFINITION 2 (ROBUST SAFETY). Let G be a configuration and G' a Σ-initial attacker. If $G \mid G' \longrightarrow^* H$ implies that $\Sigma \triangleright H \xrightarrow{error}$ for an arbitrary G' then we say that G is *robustly Σ-safe*.

THEOREM 3 (ROBUST SAFETY). Let G be a configuration, Σ a policy and Γ a global environment. If all of the the type assignments in Γ are of the form $\mathsf{Ch}\langle \mathsf{any}, \mathsf{any}\rangle(\mathsf{Un})$, and $\Sigma;\Gamma \Vdash G$, then G is robustly Σ-safe.

Typing Rules. Types are constrained by kinding rules which prevent secret data from leaking to uncertified processes, or typed data from being read from an uncertified source. Subtyping allows integrity guarantees to be relaxed and write authorization requirements to be constrained. Our development of kinds and subtyping borrows heavily from Jeffrey and Gordon [24] and Haack and Jeffrey [25], and is similar to the system presented in [23].

The rules for terms and processes tag abstractions with the principal that it impersonates. For example, a process that uses a channel reserved for α will type as $\langle\alpha\rangle\mathsf{Proc}$, and one that uses both α and β channels will type as $\langle\alpha\wedge\beta\rangle\mathsf{Proc}$. If M is an abstraction that takes an argument of type T and makes use of α and β channels, it will type as $T \rightarrow \langle\alpha\wedge\beta\rangle\mathsf{Proc}$. Our technique for typing processes and process abstractions is similar to that of Yoshida and Hennessy [26], although our types are less precise than theirs in that we only record the authorizations required rather than the exact channels used.

Rules ensure that processes located at certified principals typecheck at a type compatible with that principal. For example, a process that types at $\langle\alpha\rangle\mathsf{Proc}$ can be located at a principal A only if $\Sigma \vdash A \Rightarrow \alpha$. There are, on the other hand, no constraints on locating processes at uncertified principals.

Consistency requirements for enforceable policies ensure that 1) only typechecked executables are assigned to class cert, and 2) typechecked executables that are assigned to cert are also assigned to other classes they require. For example, suppose M types at $T \rightarrow \langle \alpha \wedge \beta \rangle \mathsf{Proc}$. If a policy assigns #($[M : T \rightarrow \langle \alpha \wedge \beta \rangle \mathsf{Proc}]$) to cert, then it must also assign it to α and β to be considered enforceable.

5   Related Work

This paper expands on our prior work [23] in two ways. First, the use of a higher-order calculus allows us to describe code distribution and loading. Second, the incorporation of security classes and a calculus of principals allow for rich specification of policy.

Abadi [27] outlines a broad range of trusted hardware applications that use remote attestation to convey trust assertions from one process to another. Our work can be seen as a detailed formal study of a specific kind of trust assertion, namely information about the type and access control policy for communicated code.

The NGSCB [28] remote attestation mechanism, and the TCG [29] hardware that underpins it, are more complex than the HOπ-rat remote attestation mechanism. We have omitted much of the complexity in order to focus on the core policy issues. For a logical description of NGSCB's mechanism, see [30]. For a concrete account of implementing NGSCB-like remote attestation on top of TCG hardware see [31].

Haldar, Chandra, and Franz [32,33] use a virtual machine to build a more flexible remote attestation mechanism on top of the primitive remote attestation mechanism that uses hashes of executables. Sadeghi and Stüble [7] observe that systems using remote attestation may be fragile, and discuss a range of options for implementing more flexible remote attestation mechanisms based upon system properties (left unspecified, as the focus is upon implementation strategies). Sandhu and Zhang [9] consider the use of remote attestation to protect disseminated information.

Our formal development builds upon existing work [34,24] with symmetric-key and asymmetric-key cryptographic primitives in pi-calculi. Notably, the kinding system is heavily influenced by the pattern-matching spi-calculus [25]. Our setting is quite different, however. In particular, processes establish their own secure channels and corresponding policies, as opposed to relying upon a mutually-trusted authority to distribute initial keys and policies. In addition, the access control policies used here are not immediately expressible in spi, since processes do not have associated identity. The techniques used to verify authenticity and other properties as in [35,36] should be applicable to HOπ-rat, though we make no attempt to address authenticity or replay attacks here. Finally, our primitive for checking attestations includes an implicit notion of *authorization*, which is made explicit in [25]. Scaling up to explicit authorizations would allow the possibility of enforcing policies that require multiple authorizations for certain actions.

Authorization based on code identity is also used by Wobber et al. in the context of the Singularity operating system [37], as well as in stack inspection [38] and other history-based access control policies [39]. Remote attestation can be used to implement similar policies in a distributed environment, but we leave this for future work.

The HOπ-rat type system allows executables to be typechecked independently and subsequently linked together. Separate compilation and linkability is not a new idea in programming languages, see, for example, [40], but is uncommon in spi-like calculi because there is usually a need to reliably distribute some shared secret or untainted data between separate processes in accordance with a type (policy). Recently Bugliesi, Focardi, and Maffei [41,42] have considered separate typechecking in the context of a spi-like calculus.

We assume that trusted hardware is trustworthy. For accounts of the difficulties involved in creating such trusted hardware, see [43,44] for an attacker's perspective and [45,46] for a defender's perspective. Irvine and Levin [47] provide a warning about placing too much trust in the integrity of COTS.

6 Conclusions

We defined a new extension to the higher-order π-calculus for analyzing protocols that rely on remote attestation. Our system extends our previous work [23] by incorporating higher-order processes and using a logic of principals to specify policy. This development allows parties to establish the identity and integrity of a remote process even if its executable has been exposed to attackers, but also allows us to expand the access control model from one based only on specific executables to one that incorporates abstract properties of code. This is an important advancement over existing capacities because these properties can include static analyses that establish bounds on the dynamic state of a remote host. We also provide a static analysis technique for ensuring robust safety in the presence of arbitrary attackers.

For future work, we are interested in internalizing program analysis, such as trusted compilers, typecheckers or code verifiers. This would allow us to model systems in which analysis tools are applied to programs at an enterprise boundary, then freely communicated and used within the enterprise without further analysis. We believe that such systems are very desirable, in that an enterprise may require that all code to be run in its systems must pass certain requirements. These requirements can be expressed as membership in a HOπ-rat security class. Analysis may be performed once, leading to a certificate (attestation) that the code belongs to the security class. The certificates may be communicated with the code, or independently, and verified through an efficient check of the hash of the code itself. We intend that these certificates be signed by the analysis tool itself, running on trusted hardware, rather than by an entity (such as a corporation) that vouches for the analysis. The use of hashes and rich policy specifications brings us close to being able to reason about such systems; HOπ-rat, as presented here, lacks only the ability to dynamically analyze abstractions.

References

1. Necula, G.C.: Proof-carrying code. In: POPL 1997 (1997)
2. Trusted Computing Group: TCG TPM Specification Version 1.2 (March 2006), http://www.trustedcomputinggroup.org

3. Trusted Computing Group: TCG Software Stack (TSS) Specification Version 1.2 (January 2006), http://www.trustedcomputinggroup.org
4. Abadi, M., Gordon, A.D.: A calculus for cryptographic protocols: The spi calculus. Information and Computation 148(1) (1999)
5. Abadi, M., Fournet, C., Gonthier, G.: Authentication primitives and their compilation. In: POPL, pp. 302–315. ACM Press, New York, NY, USA (2000)
6. Brickell, E., Camenisch, J., Chen, L.: Direct anonymous attestation. In: CCS 2004: Proceedings of the 11th ACM conference on Computer and communications security, pp. 132–145. ACM Press, New York, NY, USA (2004)
7. Sadeghi, A.R., Stüble, C.: Property-based attestation for computing platforms: Caring about properties, not mechanisms. In: New Security Paradigms Workshop (2004)
8. Schoen, S.: Trusted Computing: Promise and Risk. Electronic Frontier Foundation (October 2003), http://www.eff.org/Infrastructure/trusted_computing/20031001_tc.pdf
9. Sandhu, R., Zhang, X.: Peer-to-peer access control architecture using trusted computing technology. In: SACMAT 2005: Proceedings of the tenth ACM symposium on Access control models and technologies, pp. 147–158. ACM Press, New York, NY, USA (2005)
10. Jaeger, T., Sailer, R., Shankar, U.: Prima: policy-reduced integrity measurement architecture. In: SACMAT 2006: Proceedings of the eleventh ACM symposium on Access control models and technologies, pp. 19–28. ACM Press, New York, NY, USA (2006)
11. Sangiorgi, D.: Expressing Mobility in Process Algebras: First-Order and Higher-Order Paradigms. PhD thesis, University of Edinburgh (1993)
12. Thomsen, B.: Plain chocs: A second generation calculus for higher order processes. Acta Informatica 30(1), 1–59 (1993)
13. Milner, R.: Functions as processes. In: Paterson, M. (ed.) ICALP 1990. LNCS, vol. 443, pp. 167–180. Springer, Heidelberg (1990)
14. Abadi, M., Burrows, M., Lampson, B., Plotkin, G.: A calculus for access control in distributed systems. ACM Trans. Program. Lang. Syst. 15(4), 706–734 (1993)
15. Abadi, M., Birrell, A., Wobber, T.: Access control in a world of software diversity. Tenth Workshop on Hot Topics in Operating Systems (HotOS X) (June 2005)
16. Fournet, C., Gordon, A.D., Maffeis, S.: A type discipline for authorization policies. In: ESOP, pp. 141–156 (2005)
17. Fournet, C., Gordon, A., Maffeis, S.: A type discipline for authorization in distributed systems. CSF 00, 31–48 (2007)
18. Cirillo, A., Jagadeesan, R., Pitcher, C., Riely, J.: Do As I SaY! Programmatic Access Control with Explicit Identities. CSF 0, 16–30 (2007)
19. Sangiorgi, D.: Asynchronous process calculi: the first-order and higher-order paradigms (tutorial). Theoretical Computer Science 253, 311–350 (2001)
20. Yoshida, N.: Minimality and separation results on asynchronous mobile processes. In: Sangiorgi, D., de Simone, R. (eds.) CONCUR 1998. LNCS, vol. 1466, p. 131. Springer, Heidelberg (1998)
21. Merro, M.: Locality in the pi-calculus and applications to distributed objects. PhD thesis, Ecole des Mines de Paris (October 2000)
22. Hennessy, M., Riely, J.: Resource access control in systems of mobile agents. Inf. Comput. 173(1), 82–120 (2002)
23. Pitcher, C., Riely, J.: Dynamic policy discovery with remote attestation. In: Aceto, L., Ingólfsdóttir, A. (eds.) FOSSACS 2006. LNCS, vol. 3921, Springer, Heidelberg (2006)
24. Gordon, A.D., Jeffrey, A.S.A.: Types and effects for asymmetric cryptographic protocols. J. Computer Security 12(3/4) (2004)
25. Haack, C., Jeffrey, A.S.A.: Pattern-matching spi-calculus. In: Proc. IFIP WG 1.7 Workshop on Formal Aspects in Security and Trust (2004)

26. Yoshida, N., Hennessy, M.: Assigning types to processes. LICS 00, 334 (2000)
27. Abadi, M.: Trusted computing, trusted third parties, and verified communications. In: SEC 2004: 19th IFIP International Information Security Conference (2004)
28. Peinado, M., Chen, Y., England, P., Manferdelli, J.: NGSCB: A Trusted Open System. Information Security and Privacy 3108/2004, 86–97 (2004)
29. Pearson, S.: Trusted Computing Platforms: TCPA Technology in Context. Prentice-Hall, Englewood Cliffs (2002)
30. Abadi, M., Wobber, T.: A logical account of NGSCB. In: Núñez, M., Maamar, Z., Pelayo, F.L., Pousttchi, K., Rubio, F. (eds.) FORTE 2004. LNCS, vol. 3236, Springer, Heidelberg (2004)
31. Sailer, R., Zhang, X., Jaeger, T., van Doorn, L.: Design and implementation of a TCG-based integrity measurement architecture. In: 13th USENIX Security Symposium (2004)
32. Haldar, V., Chandra, D., Franz, M.: Semantic remote attestation: A virtual machine directed approach to trusted computing. In: USENIX VM (2004)
33. Haldar, V., Franz, M.: Symmetric behavior-based trust: A new paradigm for internet computing. In: New Security Paradigms Workshop (2004)
34. Abadi, M., Blanchet, B.: Secrecy types for asymmetric communication. Theoretical Computer Science 298(3) (2003)
35. Gordon, A.D., Jeffrey, A.S.A.: Authenticity by typing for security protocols. J. Computer Security 11(4) (2003)
36. Fournet, C., Gordon, A., Maffeis, S.: A type discipline for authorization policies. In: Sagiv, M. (ed.) ESOP 2005. LNCS, vol. 3444, Springer, Heidelberg (2005)
37. Wobber, T., Yumerefendi, A., Abadi, M., Birrell, A., Simon, D.R.: Authorizing applications in Singularity. In: EuroSys 2007: Proceedings of the ACM SIGOPS/EuroSys European Conference on Computer Systems 2007, Lisbon, Portugal, pp. 355–368. ACM, New York, NY, USA (2007)
38. Wallach, D.S., Appel, A.W., Felten, E.W.: SAFKASI: a security mechanism for language-based systems. ACM Trans. Softw. Eng. Methodol. 9(4) (2000)
39. Abadi, M., Fournet, C.: Access control based on execution history. In: Proceedings of the 10th Annual Network and Distributed System Security Symposium (2003)
40. Cardelli, L.: Program fragments, linking, and modularization. In: POPL 1997 (1997)
41. Bugliesi, M., Focardi, R., Maffei, M.: Compositional analysis of authentication protocols. In: Schmidt, D. (ed.) ESOP 2004. LNCS, vol. 2986, Springer, Heidelberg (2004)
42. Bugliesi, M., Focardi, R., Maffei, M.: Analysis of typed analyses of authentication protocols. In: CSFW (2005)
43. Anderson, R., Kuhn, M.: Tamper resistance - a cautionary note. In: Second USENIX Workshop on Electronic Commerce Proceedings (1996)
44. Huang, A.: Hacking the Xbox. Xenatera Press (2003)
45. Arbaugh, W.A., Farber, D.J., Smith, J.M.: A secure and reliable bootstrap architecture. In: IEEE Symposium on Security and Privacy (1997)
46. Smith, S., Weingart, S.: Building a high-performance, programmable secure coprocessor. Computer Networks, Special Issue on Computer Network Security 31 (1999)
47. Irvine, C., Levin, T.: A cautionary note regarding the data integrity capacity of certain secure systems. In: Integrity, Internal Control and Security in Information Systems (2002)

Service Oriented Architectural Design[*]

R. Bruni[1], A. Lluch Lafuente[1], U. Montanari[1], and E. Tuosto[2]

[1] Department of Computer Science, University of Pisa
{bruni,lafuente,ugo}@di.unipi.it
[2] Department of Computer Science, University of Leicester
et52@mcs.le.ac.uk

Abstract. We propose *Architectural Design Rewriting* (ADR), an approach to formalise the development and reconfiguration of software architectures based on term-rewriting. An architectural style consists of a set of architectural elements and operations called *productions* which define the well-formed compositions of architectures. Roughly, a term built out of such ingredients constitutes the proof that a design was constructed according to the style, and the value of the term is the constructed software architecture. A main advantage of ADR is that it naturally supports style-preserving reconfigurations. The usefulness of our approach is shown by applying ADR to SRML, an emergent paradigm inspired by the *Service Component Architecture*. We model the complex operation that composes several SRML modules in a single one by means of suitable rewrite rules. Our approach guarantees that the resulting module respects SRML's metamodel.

1 Introduction

Service orientation is becoming a standard paradigm in the development of software applications. The paradigm is centred around the notion of *service*, i.e. a computational entity whose functional and non-functional aspects can be described in a standard document to be advertised in some service registries and made available for discovery. Contrary to traditional applications, service oriented ones are not just statically assembled. Instead, they have the potentialities for allowing dynamic assembly via publication, discovery, selection and binding.

SENSORIA [10] (*Software Engineering for Service-Oriented Overlay Computers*) is a research project that aims to develop a novel and comprehensive approach for engineering service oriented computations. Key issues of SENSORIA concern the early stage and development of service specification, like design and reconfiguration of service-based architectures. In this setting, the configuration of a system consists of the present components and interconnections (i.e. the architecture), together with their current state. Architectural styles can be

[*] This work has been partly supported by the EU within the FETPI Global Computing, project IST-2005-016004 SENSORIA (*Software Engineering for Service-Oriented Overlay Computers*) and by the Italian FIRB Project TOCAI.IT.

applied to reuse existing design patterns and thus facilitate software development. In addition, they offer a further benefit when architectural information is carried over the execution of the system, since one can control whether changes in the system imply changes in the architecture. During run-time, changes in the configuration like dynamic binding require reconfigurations of the architecture. Static reconfiguration of an architecture may also be necessary, e.g. when deploying an existing architecture on a platform it was not originally designed for. Often, the architectural style must be preserved or consistently changed.

In this paper, we propose *Architectural Design Rewriting* (ADR) [5] as a novel formal approach to tackle some of the aforementioned issues of service-oriented software development. A formal metamodel for static and dynamic aspects of the SENSORIA Reference Modelling Language (SRML) [13] is given in order to demonstrate the expressiveness and flexibility of ADR. SRML has been inspired by various formalisms: orchestration languages such as ORC [24], transactional process calculi such as Sagas [6], Web service conversation models [4] and, most notably, IBM's Service Component Architecture (SCA) which has become part of the *Open Service Oriented Application* [25] initiative involving many major industrial partners (IBM, Sun and Oracle, among others). SCA and SRML are complementary approaches. Indeed, SRML is aimed at the definition of mathematical semantics for modules while SCA focuses on implementation.

Though some aspects of architectural reconfiguration can be captured within other type-theoretic frameworks e.g., the calculus of constructions [9], we argue that ADR is very intuitive and more flexible with respect to other approaches. Indeed, ADR gives software architects the possibility to avoid style-preserving reconfigurations when necessary while usually type-theoretic frameworks impose it or require a complex machinery to get around it.

SRML Overview. When designing an architecture, it is desirable to consider the concept of *architectural style* [26], i.e. some set of rules indicating which components can be part of the architecture and how they can be legally interconnected. Traditional architectural styles include client-server and pipelines. Some of such styles have been also defined in the realm of service oriented applications, going from abstract client-server styles [21] to more concrete and complex architectures [2]. The basic ingredients of a style are architectural elements and structural constraints. For instance, the architectural elements of SRML are drawn in Fig. 1 (borrowed from [13]) and include service modules (square boxes), components (rounded boxes), wires (straight lines) and interfaces (concave and convex polygons). This graphical notation is in the line of the traditional boxes-and-lines or component-and-connectors [8] notations and much more inspired by the graphical notation of SCA. The structural constraints, in their turn, require modules to be interconnected via external wires such that one of the require interfaces (EX-R) of a module is connected to the provide interface (EX-P) of another one. Inside a module, components and interfaces are connected via internal wires (IW). An SRML architecture is given at the highest level of abstraction by an *assembly of modules* with possibly some discovered but not bound service modules interconnected via *external wires*. For instance,

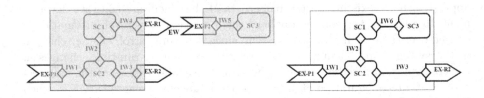

Fig. 1. An SRML diagram before (left) and after (right) composition

Fig. 1 depicts an architecture with a service module (the leftmost square) which requires two additional services to be attached to the external interfaces EX-R1 and EX-R2. The one corresponding to EX-R1 has been discovered and connected via an external wire (EW).

An example of a reconfiguration in SRML is the *composition* of (already discovered) interconnected modules into a single module [12]. SRML provides a mechanism to achieve this static reconfiguration, by means of an algorithm that manipulates SRML specifications. As an example, the assembly of Fig. 1 (left) can be composed into the service module depicted in Fig. 1 (right), where wire IW6 is derived according to certain composition rules. Such reconfigurations require a proof of correctness w.r.t. style preservation.

ADR Overview. ADR [5] is a recent proposal for the style-consistent design and reconfiguration of software architectures, conceived in the spirit of initiatives (e.g. [20]) that promote the conciliation of software architectures and process calculi by means of graphical methods. Although not discussed here, ADR can also represent the normal behaviour of systems (i.e., the evolution of components). For example, a representation of π-calculus [23] based on a graphical encoding [15] is currently under development. ADR offers a unified setting where design development, ordinary execution and reconfiguration are defined on the same foot. The key features of ADR are: (i) rule-based approach; (ii) hierarchical and graphical design; (iii) algebraic presentation; and (iii) inductively-defined reconfigurations. Architectures are suitable modelled by so-called *designs*: a kind of graphs whose items suitably represent the architectural components and their interconnections. Architectures are designed hierarchically by a set of composition operators called *design productions* which enable: (i) top-down design by refinement, (ii) bottom-up typing of actual architectures, and (iii) well-formed composition of architectures. An architectural style is defined as a set of *design productions* such that a design is style-consistent whenever it can be defined by a *design term* which makes use of the corresponding design productions. Reconfiguration and behaviour are given as rewrite rules that are defined over design terms rather than over designs. The main advantages of ADR are that: (i) instead of reasoning on flat architectures (designs), ADR specifications provide a convenient hierarchical structure (design terms), by exploiting the architectural classes introduced by the style, (ii) complex reconfiguration schemes can be

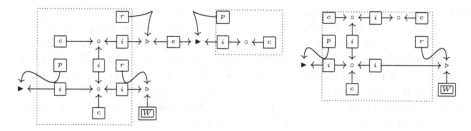

Fig. 2. Two SRML diagrams in the graphical representation of ADR

defined inductively at any level of abstraction, and (iii) style-guarantees during reconfiguration or execution are ensured by construction.

Contribution. Our main goal is to define an ADR-based architectural style to support the development and reconfiguration of SRML diagrams according to the SRML metamodel. We shall define an architectural style given by a vocabulary of architectural elements and a set of operations for the construction of SRML diagrams. More precisely, we build an algebra where the evaluation of a design term is a design representing an SRML diagram. It is worth mentioning that any SRML diagram can be represented by a design. For instance, Fig. 2 depicts ADR designs for the SRML diagrams of Fig. 1: the correspondence is explained in § 3. SRML reconfigurations are then modelled as ADR rewrite rules over the design terms rather than over plain designs, guaranteeing style preservation and, thus, metamodel conformance.

Structure of the Paper. § 2 overviews ADR. § 3 describes an ADR style for SRML. § 4 addresses the problem of reconfiguration of SRML diagrams, focusing on module composition. § 5 summarises our work, draws conclusions and sketches interesting research avenues. For reader's convenience the graphical representation of the most complex reconfiguration rule is included in appendix A.

2   Architectural Design Rewriting

In this section we summarise the key features of ADR. We refer the reader to [5] for a detailed technical presentation. Roughly, ADR adheres to three main principles: (i) architectural designs are modelled by suitable graphs called *designs* and come equipped with their proofs of construction called *design terms*; (ii) architectures are designed hierarchically by a set of composition operations called *productions* out of which design terms are built and architectural styles are basically given by sets of such productions such that an architectural design is compliant with a style if its design term uses the corresponding productions only; (iii) reconfigurations are powerful, expressive, hierarchical and style-consistent rewrite rules defined over design terms instead of designs.

We illustrate the principles of ADR with a simple example where a local network architecture admits two styles where each network hub has respectively two and three degrees of connectivity. Connections between hubs are also driven by the style, so that, for instance, the only legal 2-degree networks are rings.

Principle i), i.e. modelling architectural designs by suitable graphs, has been widely exploited in the literature (e.g. [2,22]). For instance, in the well established component and connector view, software architectures are modelled by graphs of components and connectors. In ADR one can represent such graphs as follows. A component is modelled by a hyperedge whose outgoing tentacles represent the components interface, i.e. its ports. Similarly, a connector is modelled by a hyperedge whose outgoing tentacles represent the connector's interface, i.e. its roles. Attaching a port to a role is done by connecting the respective tentacles to the same node. The main actor of ADR are *designs* (see Definition 2), which are used to model components, connectors and architectural configurations.

The choice of graphs as the domain of our algebra is inherited from the previously mentioned approaches, but it is well justified by the immediate user-friendly visual representation and the expressive power of graphs and their rewritings which have been used for years as a model, not only of software architectures, but of many other things ranging from data structures to process calculi.

Definition 1. *A graph is tuple* $G = \langle V, E, \theta \rangle$ *where* V *is the set of nodes,* E *is the set of edges and* $\theta : E \to V^*$ *is the tentacle function.*

The different classes of edges used in the network example are drawn in Fig. 3 where an explicit numbering or naming of tentacles is avoided in favour of an implicit convention that assumes that the order of tentacles exiting from each edge is given by considering the leftward tentacle as the first one and the remaining tentacles as clockwise ordered.

More generally, we could consider the association of semantic information to graph items. For example, nodes can represent variables taking values over a finite domain and edges can express suitable constraints over them. Another example is the association of theories to nodes and theory morphisms to edges (e.g. a theory of interaction signatures). Then, this additional information can be exploited to drive the development and reconfiguration phases. We shall not give special emphasis to such aspects. However, we shall return to this issue along with the paper suggesting how we could capture semantical aspects of SRML in addition to the structural ones, on which we shall focus.

Principle ii), i.e the hierarchical design of architectures, is also not particularly original in itself [18], but it is here enhanced by a novel algebraic presentation. An architectural style consists of a vocabulary of architectural elements (represented by a type graph), and a set of production rules indicating how they can be legally interconnected. We distinguish two kinds of edges in the type graph: terminals $\mathcal{T}$ and non-terminals $\mathcal{NT}$. Likewise string grammars, terminal edges represent basic, non-refinable, concrete components of the architecture, while non-terminal edges, represent complex, refinable, abstract components.

In the network example we have $\mathcal{T} = \{2\text{hub}, 3\text{hub}\}$ and $\mathcal{NT} = \{2\text{N}, 3\text{N}, \text{NET}\}$. Our graphical notation uses single-framed and double-framed boxes for terminals and non-terminals, respectively (see Fig. 3).

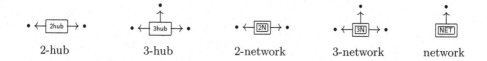

2-hub   3-hub   2-network   3-network   network

Fig. 3. Architectural elements of the network example

In ADR, software architectures are not just specified by graphs. Instead, they are represented by *designs*. A design is a well-formed architecture with a typed interface (represented by a non-terminal edge) and an internal structure (represented by a graph). The interface is an abstract view of the design as a single component, thus hiding the internal representation except for those nodes that are exposed in the interface.

Definition 2. *A design is a triple* $d = \langle L_d, R_d, i_d \rangle$, *where* L_d *is the interface graph consisting a single non-terminal edge (called* interface*) whose tentacles are attached to distinct nodes;* R_d *is the body graph; and* $i_d : V_{L_d} \to V_{R_d}$ *is the total function associating body nodes to interface nodes.*

A design d is *partial* (resp. *concrete*) if R_d contains (resp. does not contain) non-terminal edges. In service-oriented applications dealing with partial designs is natural and essential: the architecture of services is only instantiated when needed after a proper discovery, selection and binding.

Designs are assembled by means of composition operations, called *design productions*.

Definition 3. *A production is a tuple* $p = \langle L_p, R_p, i_p, l_p \rangle$ *where* $\langle L_p, R_p, i_p \rangle$ *is a design with* n_p *occurrences of non-terminal edges in* R_p *that are mapped by the bijection* l_p *on segment* $[1, 2, \ldots, n_p]$.

Each production p has a functional reading $p : A_1 \times A_2 \times \ldots \times A_n \to A_{n_p}$, where $\times$ has precedence on $\to$, A_p is the type of the interface and A_k is the type of the k-th non-terminal edge e_k of R_p (i.e. $e_k = l_p^{-1}(k)$). In fact, p can be considered as the obvious graph pasting that, when applied to a tuple of designs $\langle d_1, d_2, \ldots, d_{n_p} \rangle$ (of types $A_1, A_2, \ldots A_{n_p}$, respectively), returns a design $p(d_1, d_2, \ldots, d_{n_p})$ of type A_p obtained by replacing each non-terminal edge e_k in R_p with the graph R_{d_k} (preserving the correspondence of tentacles).

Our network example uses production $\texttt{link2} = \langle L_{\texttt{link2}}, R_{\texttt{link2}}, i_{\texttt{link2}}, l_{\texttt{link2}} \rangle$ whose functionality is $\texttt{link2} : 2N_1 \times 2N_2 \to 2N$. Intuitively, $\texttt{link2}$ specify an operator of the algebra that arranges two designs of type 2N into a new 2N design. In hyperedge replacement style (see [16] for details) $\texttt{link2}$ can be written as

$$\bullet u_1 \leftarrow\boxed{e{:}2N}\rightarrow \bullet u_2 \quad \rightsquigarrow \quad \bullet u_1 \leftarrow\boxed{e_1{:}2N}\rightarrow \bullet v \leftarrow\boxed{e_2{:}2N}\rightarrow \bullet u_2$$

where the left-hand side graph can be replaced by the right-hand side one. A compact and elegant graphical representation of $\texttt{link2}$ is drawn in Fig. 4 where

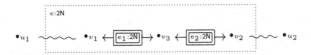

Fig. 4. Graphical representation of production `link2`

the left-hand side (i.e., the interface edge) is represented by the outermost dotted box whose nodes u_1 and u_2 are outside the dotted box. The right-hand side graph of `link2` is depicted in the dotted box and the nodes v_1 and v_2 are exposed in the interface through waved lines. Finally, the order of arguments of each production is implicit: from top to bottom, and left to right if on the same row, e.g. $l_{\text{link2}} = \{e_1 \mapsto 1, e_2 \mapsto 2\}$. In the rest of the paper we will neglect the textual representation of productions as well as the identities graph items in their visual representation. The rest of the productions of our example are depicted in Fig. 5. For example, a 2-network is either a network with just one 2-hub (`basic2`) or the chaining of two 2-networks (`link2`). For 3-degree networks the composition involves three arguments of type 3N. For instance, production `link3` has type $3N \times 3N \times 3N \rightarrow 3N$. Finally, a network is either a 2-network (`net2`) or a 3-network (`net3`), whose interface nodes are merged together. To illustrate the operations associated to productions, consider the term `net2(link2(link2(basic2, basic2), basic2))`. Subterm `link2(basic2, basic2)` evaluates to a 2-network made of two concatenated 2-hubs. Such value is used in the subterm `link2(link2(basic2, basic2), basic2)` to obtain a 2-network made of three 2-hubs. Finally the whole term evaluates to the design on the right of Fig. 6. Similarly, the term `net3(link3(basic3, basic3, basic3))` evaluates to the design on the left of Fig. 6. Instead an expression like `net2(basic3)` is not valid, because types mismatch.

The use of productions offers a mechanism that supports the construction of architectural designs both in a top-down way by refinement of terms and a bottom-up way by composition of terms. A typing mechanism can be used as a reverse engineering method to obtain a design term for a given design.

A crucial benefit of the use of productions regards the concept of *architectural style*, i.e. a certain set of architectural designs considered to be valid or in conformance with some design pattern. In fact, while changes in the architecture are acceptable and even necessary, the architectural style should be preserved in most cases. For instance, in a system with client-server architectural style clients connecting and disconnecting from the server are permitted, while a client connecting to a client is not. Changes in style are also interesting, take for instance, a token ring architecture configuring into a star-shaped one to achieve a most efficient communication. Typical architecture description languages define a style in terms of architectural constraints to be checked after or during the construction of a design. Instead in ADR, an architectural design is defined by a set of productions. Any design term that uses those productions defines an architectural design that is consistent with the corresponding style. As a consequence, no proof of style-consistency is needed. Designs are style-consistent by construction.

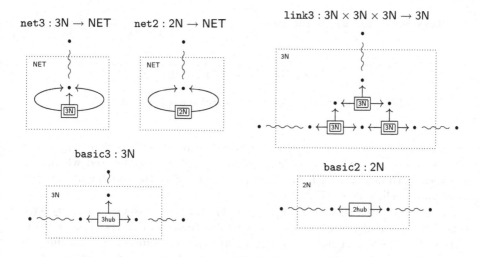

Fig. 5. Design productions of the network example

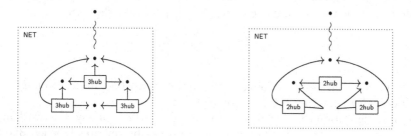

Fig. 6. Two network designs: with three-degrees (left) and two-degrees (right) hubs

We say that a design d is *well-formed* if there is a well-typed design term whose value is d, while we say that d is consistent w.r.t. to a style (or *style-consistent*) if the design term uses design productions of the style. Note that style-conformance implies well-formedness, but the contrary is not true. For instance, one could construct an architecture mixing productions of two different styles. However, for the sake of simplicity we assume that mixing styles is not possible. This is achieved by requiring the set of types used in each pair of styles to be disjoint, in which case the style of a design term is automatically given by its type and thus well-formedness and style-consistency coincide.

Principle iii), i.e. reconfigurations defined over design terms instead of actual architectures, exploits the algebraic presentation of ADR. This enables a straightforward definition of hierarchical and inductive reconfigurations as ordinary term rewriting and conditional SOS rules. The main guarantee offered by ADR is that reconfigurations are style-preserving by construction.

A reconfiguration rule is seen as a rewrite rule $L \rightarrow R$. There is a very simple sufficient condition for enforcing style preservation, namely that both L and R

$$\texttt{basic3to2}: \texttt{basic3} \xrightarrow{\text{3to2}} \texttt{basic2} \qquad \texttt{net3to2}: \frac{x \xrightarrow{\text{3to2}} x'}{\texttt{net3}(x) \longrightarrow \texttt{net2}(x')}$$

$$\texttt{link3to2}: \frac{x_1 \xrightarrow{\text{3to2}} x'_1 \quad x_2 \xrightarrow{\text{3to2}} x'_2 \quad x_3 \xrightarrow{\text{3to2}} x'_3}{\texttt{link3}(x_1, x_2, x_3) \xrightarrow{\text{3to2}} \texttt{link2}(\texttt{link2}(x'_2, x'_1), x'_3)}$$

Fig. 7. Conditional reconfigurations of the network example

are terms of the same type. Then, it is possible to apply the rule in any larger architecture $t(L\eta)$, where η assigns design terms to variables and where t is any term with one hole with the same type as L. After the reconfiguration, the well-typed architecture $t(R\eta)$ is obtained.

For example, the rule $\texttt{link2}(x_1, x_2) \to \texttt{link2}(x_2, x_1)$ where x_1 and x_2 have type 2N, reconfigures any 2N chain by switching the order of its two components.

In case certain local changes in the architecture are subordinated to the corresponding adaptation of the adjacent environment, we can use conditional reconfiguration rules, expressing that a composed architecture can be rewritten only if its sub-components are suitably transformed first. This step makes the formalism very powerful. Simple conditional rewrites take the form:

$$\frac{t_1 \to t'_1 \quad \dots \quad t_n \to t'_n}{L \to R}$$

meaning that, given an assignment η, the architecture $L\eta$ can be reconfigured according to $R\eta$ only if each $t_i\eta$ can be reconfigured to $t'_i\eta$.

The reconfiguration rules needed to downgrade the hubs of any 3-network are defined in Fig. 7. Note that types are not preserved by rewrites labelled 3to2, which change the type from 3N to 2N. But this is not a problem because rules are intended to be applied in appropriate (inductively defined) contexts. This is particularly clear in the rule **net3to2** where the conclusion actually transforms a network into a network: the silent label makes it applicable in any larger context. The rule **link3to2** is graphically represented in Fig. 8. By applying **net3to2** (once), **link3to2** (once) and **basic3to2** (three times), we obtain a style-preserving rewrite from the leftmost design in Fig. 6 to the rightmost one.

For another simple but illustrative example of the ADR modelling of a road assistance scenario we refer the reader to [5].

3   Design of SRML Diagrams

The metamodel of SRML is defined in terms of some class diagrams. Roughly, a *module* is an abstraction of a business entity that can either perform a task (in which case it is called an *activity module*) or provide a service (called a *service module*). Modules consist of *components* and *external interfaces*, possibly linked via *internal wires*. Components abstract the computational aspects of

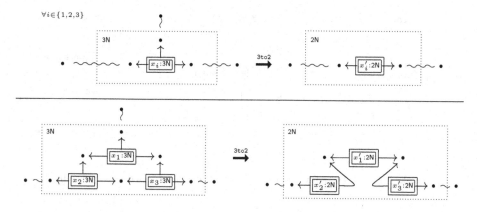

Fig. 8. Graphical representation of rule `link3to2`

modules, while interfaces model the interaction with the external world. There are two kinds of external interfaces: *provide* and *require*. The former are present in service modules and indeed they specify the service provided by modules. Require interfaces, instead, specify the services needed. A needed service can be identified during static- or run-time. The latter being the open-frontier of the service-oriented paradigm, but static binding is interesting too as we shall see.

In this section we define an ADR architectural style that is compliant with the SRML metamodel. The encoding of SRML composition as ADR reconfiguration is deferred until § 4.

3.1   Architectural Elements of SRML

Service components, wires and interfaces are concrete architectural elements that we represent as terminal edges (see Fig. 2, for instance). A service component is represented by an edge of type c with a unique tentacle representing its interaction port attached to a node of type ∘ (a *component port*). Require and provide interfaces are edges of type r and p, respectively, whose tentacles are attached to nodes of type ▷ (*required port*) and ▶ (*provided port*), respectively. Internal and external wires are represented with edges respectively typed by i and e. Internal wires must be attached to a node of type ∘ or ▶ and another node of type ∘ or ▷. This means that the left (resp. right) tentacle of an internal wire cannot be of type ▷ (resp. ▶). External wires are attached to one node of type ▷ via its left tentacle and another one of type ▶ via its right tentacle.

Typing imposes syntactical restrictions not present in the (less-accurate) UML metamodel (e.g., it does not make sense to connect two require interfaces via an internal wire). Further syntactical and semantic aspects are enforced by suitable mechanisms that impose restrictions on the actual use of wires in a diagram. For instance, the ports of components and interfaces and the roles of wires have associated suitable interaction signatures. Then, a component or interface can share a node with an internal wire only if their respective ports and roles have

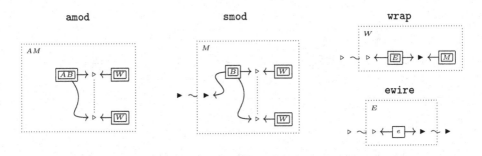

Fig. 9. An activity (left), a service (center) and a wrapped service (right)

the same signature. External wires, instead require both attached signatures to be *compatible* and the behaviour of the required service to be entailed from the provided one. We deal only with the most abstract structural aspects of SRML; insights on aforementioned restrictions are in [13] where suitable models of interaction signatures and service behaviour entailment are fully detailed.

The non-terminal architectural elements of the SRML style are present in the various figures of this section where families of architectural elements are actually represented. In fact, designs and productions are parametrised by the rank of their constituents. For simplicity, our graphical notation abstracts away from ranks and a dotted line between two nodes for representing any number of them. In other words, we overload the name of (ranked) productions and assume the application of production exploits polymorphism in a suitable way.

The presented architectural elements are the basic ingredients to build graphs that represent SRML diagrams such as those in Fig. 2.

3.2 Design Productions for SRML

We follow a top-down presentation of the ADR productions for SRML (from modules to wires and components).

Service and activity Modules. An SRML module consists of a body (to be identified during development) and some wrapped services (to be refined at run-time). Productions smod and amod in Fig. 9 model this structure. For instance, we could have amod(t, x_1, x_2), t being a concrete design of type AB (the complete specification of the body of the activity), while x_1 and x_2 are variables of type W.

Remarkably, the ADR modelling of SRML binding is performed in two steps. First, the selected service is wrapped in the module via an external wire and then the internal wires of both the activity and the service are rearranged to internalise the connection (cf. Section 4). Here, the wrapping step is modelled by production wrap : $E \times M \rightarrow W$ in Fig. 9, that wraps a service module by means of a binding wrapper that connects the require interface port with the interface port provided by the service. The only binding considered here is a single external wire (see production ewire).

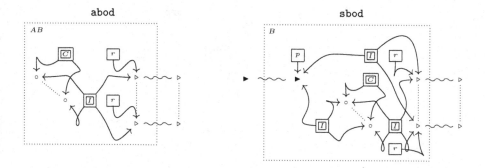

Fig. 10. The body of an activity module (left) and a service module (right)

Module Bodies. The body of a module consists of a collection of service components and interfaces connected via internal wires. The difference between the body of an activity and a service module is that the former does not have a provide interface. In the body of a service module it is convenient to distinguish three collections of internal wires connecting, respectively, the provide interface with the require interfaces, the provide interface with the service components and the service components with the require interfaces. This distinction leads to three arguments of type I, that partition internal wires depending on the types of the ports their tentacles are attached to. Correspondingly, production sbod has type $I \times C \times I \times I \to B$ (see Fig. 10). Production abod is very similar, but requires only a collection of internal wires. Its type is $C \times I \to AB$.

Again, suitable restrictions should be imposed on connecting wires when further aspects are in order. For instance, assume/guarantee relations between a require and a provide interfaces can be given as an entailment of the provide interface from the require one.

Service Components and Internal Wires. Service components are the main computational entities of SRML modules. We define two design productions to construct collections of such, possibly interconnected, service components: comp (of type $\to C$) to create a single component, and comps (of type $C \times C \times I \to C$) to compose two collections of components via internal wires (see Fig. 11).

Productions iwire :$\to I$ and wires : $I \times I \to I$ respectively build a single wire and a collection of wires (out of two collections of wires). Regarding iwire, observe that Fig. 12 actually represents all the productions obtained by attaching the leftward and rightward tentacles of the edge of type i to any of the exposed nodes. Production nowire accounts for empty wire collections.

The ADR designs in Fig. 2 that encode the SRML diagrams in Fig. 1 are well-formed by the design terms m1 = smod(b1, w1, x) and m2 = smod(b2, x), where x is a variable of type W that models the non-discovered service, and:

b1 = sbod(nowire, comps(comp, iwire, comp), iwire, wires(iwire, iwire))
w1 = wrap(ewire, smod(sbod(nowire, comp, iwire, nowire)))
b2 = sbod(nowire, comps(comps(comp, iwire, comp), iwire, comp), iwire, iwire).

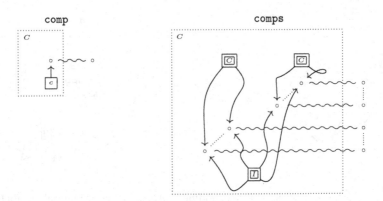

Fig. 11. An interconnection of service components

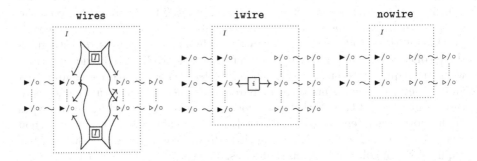

Fig. 12. Internal wires

4   Reconfiguration of SRML Diagrams

Rewriting of architectural designs can be used to define interesting reconfiguration mechanisms in SRML, like turning an assembly of modules into a composite module. The reconfiguration of an assembly into a module is called *composition*. It is typically applied during run-time while needed services are discovered and bound, but it can be applied at static time too, in order to avoid the run-time computational effort required for service discovery, selection and binding in dynamic composition.

The composition operation has already been sketched in § 1, where the assembly of the two modules on the left of Fig. 1 yields the single module on the right. The only external wire EW has been *internalised*: the linked interfaces disappear and the components of both modules that were previously connected via those interfaces and the external wire are now directly connected via internal wires. SRML defines an algorithm that performs the composition by manipulating the involved SRML diagrams. The main idea is that each pair of internal wires connected via an external wire becomes an internal wire. However, no formal proof of compliance w.r.t. SRML's metamodel is provided.

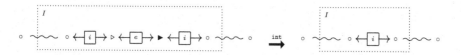

Fig. 13. Base rule that internalises a wires

Here, we encode internalisation of wrapped modules as proper ADR reconfigurations. The corresponding ADR rewrite rules transform a term representing any SRML diagram with a wrapped service into a term representing the diagram where the wrapped service has been internalised. We exploit an auxiliary design production link, which is very simple: it connects two collections of wires via an external wire (see, e.g. its use in Figure 14). Production link was not presented in § 3 because it is not really used to construct SRML diagrams and modules, but just needed in some rule premises to compute the internal wires to be inserted in the module.

The basic rule transforms the indirect connection of two ports into a direct, internal connection (see Fig. 13): $\mathtt{link(iwire, iwire)} \xrightarrow{int} \mathtt{iwire}$.

Recall that we are dealing with the most abstract structural aspects, but SRML imposes further syntactical restriction on these rule as well semantic restrictions in binding services. Indeed, the interaction signature of the internal wire obtained by the rule should be the result of properly combining the interaction signatures of the wires appearing in the left-hand side of the rewrite.

The premises of the second rule (see Fig. 14) require each possible combination of internal wires to be properly internalised. If this is possible separately, then the overall internalisation is performed.

$$\frac{\mathtt{link}(u_1, v_1) \xrightarrow{int} w_1^1 \quad \mathtt{link}(u_1, v_2) \xrightarrow{int} w_1^2 \quad \mathtt{link}(u_2, v_1) \xrightarrow{int} w_2^1 \quad \mathtt{link}(u_2, v_2) \xrightarrow{int} w_2^2}{\mathtt{link}(\mathtt{wires}(u_1, u_2), \mathtt{wires}(v_1, v_2)) \xrightarrow{int} \mathtt{wires}(\mathtt{wires}(w_1^1, w_2^1), \mathtt{wires}(w_1^2, w_2^2))}$$

Once we have presented the rule for internalising wires, we are ready to give the general rule for internalising a wrapped service (see Appendix A for the graphical representation). The rule takes into account the more general form of a design term with a wrapped service to be internalised:

$$\frac{\mathtt{link}(w_3, w_4) \xrightarrow{int} w_3^4 \quad \mathtt{link}(w_2, w_4) \xrightarrow{int} w_2^4 \quad \mathtt{link}(w_3, w_5) \xrightarrow{int} w_3^5 \quad \mathtt{link}(w_2, w_4) \xrightarrow{int} w_2^5}{\begin{array}{l} \mathtt{smod}(\mathtt{sbod}(c_1, w_1, \mathtt{wires}(w_2, w_2'), \mathtt{wires}(w_3, w_3')), \\ \qquad \mathtt{wrap}(\mathtt{smod}(\mathtt{sbod}(c_2, w_5, w_6, w_4), s_{n+1}, \ldots, s_m), s_1, \ldots, s_n)) \\ \longrightarrow \mathtt{smod}(\mathtt{sbod}(\mathtt{comps}(c_1, w_2^5, c_2), \mathtt{wires}(w_1, w_2^4), \mathtt{wires}(\mathtt{wires}(w_2', w_6), w_3^5), \\ \qquad \mathtt{wires}(w_3', w_3^4), s_1, \ldots, s_n, s_{n+1}, \ldots, s_m) \end{array}}$$

As an example of reconfiguration, it can be verified that m1 is reconfigured into m2 (cf. end of § 3 and Fig. 2) in one rewrite step by applying the above rule, where the only required premise is $\mathtt{link(iwire, iwire)} \xrightarrow{int} \mathtt{iwire}$ (which is trivially satisfied).

It is worth noting that the composition rule can be applied in any context thus ensuring well-typedness and style-preservation.

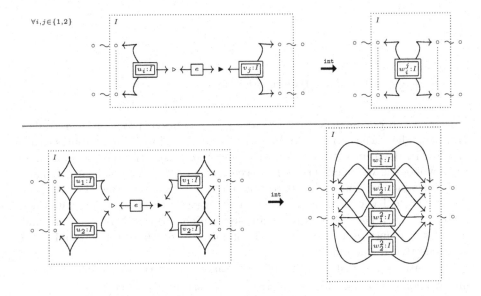

Fig. 14. Rule that internalises a wires: recursive case

5 Conclusion

We have proposed *Architectural Design Rewriting* as a framework for hierarchical style-based reconfigurations of software architectures. The approach is based on algebras of typed graphs with interfaces, yielding a unifying treatment of style-based design and reconfiguration. Its hierarchical and inductive features allows us to compactly represent complex reconfiguration rules. While in other approaches (e.g. [22]) correctness of each reconfiguration rule must be formally proved, in ADR correctness is automatically given by the fact that rewrites act on design terms, rather than on designs. Comparing ADR to architectural description languages, ADR offers a unifying model to represent architectural design, reconfiguration, and ordinary behaviour too. A deeper comparison of ADR against similar approaches can be found in [5].

In this paper we have defined an ADR style to support the design and reconfiguration of service-oriented specifications given in SRML whose choice is justified by the fact that it aims at providing a formal approach to service-oriented modelling that is close to SCA [25]. The model of SRML consists of an ADR-based architectural style that is compliant with the SRML metamodel so that it can suitably define SRML complex reconfigurations with the main benefit they are compliant with the metamodel by construction.

We plan to analyse and eventually enrich our approach to support further issues inherent to the design and management of service-oriented architectures, like the treatment of modes [17] or the semantical information of SRML [14]. In addition we plan to perform a deeper comparative analysis of ADR against similar approaches like process calculi to deal with reconfigurable component based architectures [1], architectural metaprogramming initiatives [3] that promote the unifying treatment of software refactoring, synthesis and development as algebras over programs, and graphical representation of concurrent systems such as those based on process calculi encodings [15], Synchronized Hyperedge Replacement [11], and bigraphs [19]. An implementation of ADR in Maude [7] is also under development.

References

1. Aguirre, N., Maibaum, T.S.E.: Hierarchical temporal specifications of dynamically reconfigurable component based systems. Electr. Notes Theor. Comput. Sci. 108, 69–81 (2004)
2. Baresi, L., Heckel, R., Thöne, S., Varró, D.: Style-based modeling and refinement of service-oriented architectures. Software and Systems Modeling 5(2), 187–207 (2006)
3. Batory, D.S.: Program refactoring, program synthesis, and model-driven development. In: Krishnamurthi, S., Odersky, M. (eds.) CC 2007. LNCS, vol. 4420, pp. 156–171. Springer, Heidelberg (2007)
4. Benatallah, B., Casati, F., Toumani, F.: Web service conversation modeling: A cornerstone for e-business automation. IEEE Internet Computing 8(1), 46–54 (2004)
5. Bruni, R., Lluch Lafuente, A., Montanari, U., Tuosto, E.: Style based reconfigurations of software architectures. Technical Report TR-07-17, Dipartimento di Informatica, Università di Pisa (2007)
6. Bruni, R., Melgratti, H.C., Montanari, U.: Theoretical foundations for compensations in flow composition languages. In: Palsberg, J., Abadi, M. (eds.) POPL, pp. 209–220. ACM, New York (2005)
7. Clavel, M., Durán, F., Eker, S., Lincoln, P., Martí-Oliet, N., Meseguer, J., Talcott, C. (eds.): All About Maude - A High-Performance Logical Framework. LNCS, vol. 4350. Springer, Heidelberg (2007)
8. Clements, P., Garlan, D., Bass, L., Stafford, J., Nord, R., Ivers, J., Little, R.: Documenting Software Architectures: Views and Beyond. Pearson Education (2002)
9. Coquand, T., Huet, G.: The calculus of constructions. Inf. Comput. 76(2-3), 95–120 (1988)
10. FETPI Global Computing project IST-2005-016004 SEnSOria (Software Engineering for Service-Oriented Overlay Computers), http://sensoria.fast.de
11. Ferrari, G.L., Hirsch, D., Lanese, I., Montanari, U., Tuosto, E.: Synchronised hyperedge replacement as a model for service oriented computing. In: de Boer, F.S., Bonsangue, M.M., Graf, S., de Roever, W.-P. (eds.) FMCO 2005. LNCS, vol. 4111, pp. 22–43. Springer, Heidelberg (2006)
12. Fiadeiro, J.L., Lopes, A., Bocchi, L.: Algebraic semantics of service component modules. In: Fiadeiro, J.L., Schobbens, P.-Y. (eds.) WADT 2006. LNCS, vol. 4409, pp. 37–55. Springer, Heidelberg (2007)
13. Fiadeiro, J.L., Lopes, A., Bocchi, L.: A formal approach to service component architecture. In: Bravetti, M., Núñez, M., Zavattaro, G. (eds.) WS-FM 2006. LNCS, vol. 4184, pp. 193–213. Springer, Heidelberg (2006)
14. Fiadeiro, J.L., Schmitt, V.: Structured co-spans: An algebra of interaction protocols. In: Mossakowski, T., Montanari, U., Haveraaen, M. (eds.) CALCO 2007. LNCS, vol. 4624, pp. 194–208. Springer, Heidelberg (2007)

15. Gadducci, F.: Graph rewriting for the π-calculus. Mathematical Structures in Computer Science 17(3), 407–437 (2007)
16. Habel, A.: Hyperedge Replacement: Grammars and Languages. Springer, New York, Secaucus, NJ, USA (1992)
17. Hirsch, D., Kramer, J., Magee, J., Uchitel, S.: Modes for software architectures. In: Gruhn, V., Oquendo, F. (eds.) EWSA 2006. LNCS, vol. 4344, pp. 113–126. Springer, Heidelberg (2006)
18. Hirsch, D., Montanari, U.: Shaped hierarchical architectural design. Electronic Notes on Theoretical Computer Science 109, 97–109 (2004)
19. Jensen, O.H., Milner, R.: Bigraphs and mobile processes. Technical Report 570, Computer Laboratory, University of Cambridge (2003)
20. König, B., Montanari, U., Gardner, P. (eds.): Graph Transformations and Process Algebras for Modeling Distributed and Mobile Systems, June 6-11, 2004, Dagstuhl Seminar Proceedings. vol. 04241, IBFI, Schloss Dagstuhl, Germany (2005)
21. Loulou, I., Kacem, A.H., Jmaiel, M.: Consistent reconfiguration for publish/subscribe architecture styles. In: Proc. of the First International Workshop on Verification and Evaluation of Computer and Communication Systems (VECoS 2007) (2007)
22. Métayer, L.D.: Describing software architecture styles using graph grammars. IEEE Trans. Software Eng. 24(7), 521–533 (1998)
23. Milner, R.: Communicating and Mobile Systems: The π-calculus. Cambridge University Press, Cambridge (1992)
24. Misra, J., Cook, W.: Orchestration computation: A basis for wide area computing. Software and Systems Modeling 6(1), 83–110 (2006)
25. Service Component Architecture, http://osoa.org
26. Shaw, M., Garlan, D.: Software Architectures: Perspectives on an emerging discipline. Prentice-Hall, Englewood Cliffs (1996)

The figure below depicts the left- (top) and right-hand sides of the rule for composing modules. The premises $\mathtt{link}(w_3, w_4) \xrightarrow{\text{int}} w_3^4$, $\mathtt{link}(w_2, w_4) \xrightarrow{\text{int}} w_2^4$, $\mathtt{link}(w_3, w_5) \xrightarrow{\text{int}} w_3^5$ and $\mathtt{link}(w_2, w_4) \xrightarrow{\text{int}} w_2^5$ are neglected from the figure due to space constraints (they are similar to those in Fig. 14).

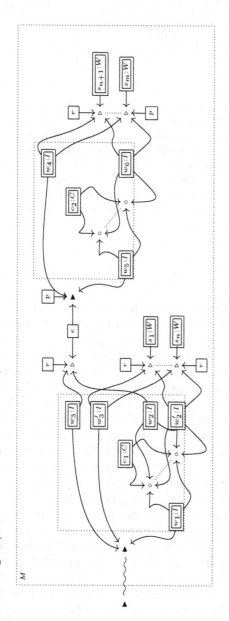

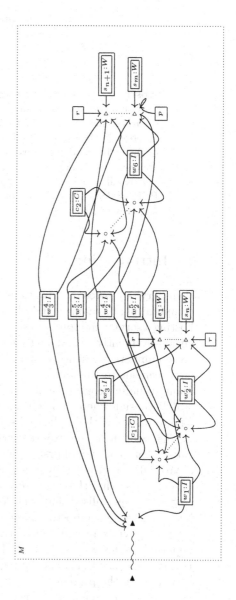

Replicating Web Services for Scalability

Mario Bravetti[1], Stephen Gilmore[2], Claudio Guidi[1], and Mirco Tribastone[2]

[1] University of Bologna
[2] University of Edinburgh

Abstract. Web service instances are often replicated to allow service provision to scale to support larger population sizes of users. However, such systems are difficult to analyse because the scale and complexity inherent in the system itself poses challenges for accurate qualitative or quantitative modelling. We use two process calculi cooperatively in the analysis of an example Web service replicated across many servers. The SOCK calculus is used to model service-oriented aspects closely and the PEPA calculus is used to analyse the performance of the system under increasing load.

1 Introduction

Web Services expose applications on the Internet for open, accessible use. The computational dynamics of such a distribution are that the resources of a server hosting a service endpoint are shared among its many, geographically distributed, clients. Evidently such a single-server design cannot scale to accommodate very large numbers of clients so when scalability is identified as a concern a crucial enhancement to this deployment architecture is to replicate the service across many, usually geographically distributed, servers. This deployment leads to a scalable design where more clients can be accommodated by adding more servers. The resources of the replicated services are federated to serve many clients.

Clients of such a distributed service will usually need to become more complicated because they will first need to discover service endpoints before binding to a particular service instance. Service providers must also register with a registry of services, so that they may later be discovered by the clients. Some services are sufficiently specialised that their locations are known and this knowledge is built into the service composition, and exploited. We consider such a scenario here.

Web Services provide all of the necessary infrastructure for services to be deployed in this way, with formal statements of the service provided, a formal notion of registration with the registry and a procedure for service discovery in registries. In the present paper we are concerned with the analysis of the high-level design of a replicated service, based on measurements of individual service instances and probabilistic estimates of likely bindings chosen by clients.

We are concerned here with using process calculus models to investigate how well a distributed system can balance load in order to provide a scalable service for larger pools of users downloading content over a shared network. The specific

G. Barthe and C. Fournet (Eds.): TGC 2007, LNCS 4912, pp. 204–221, 2008.

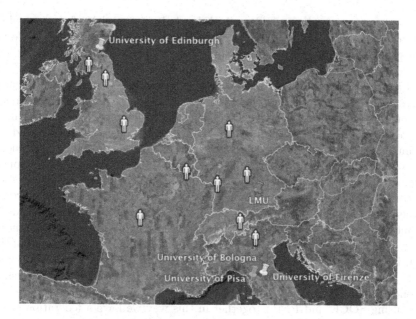

Fig. 1. Both the students and the university sites are geographically distributed. Services are replicated across sites to allow the system to scale to support larger populations of student users.

scenario which we consider as an illustration of this class of systems is a Distributed E-Learning and Course Management System (DCMS) which provides management of courses and degrees offered at several co-operating universities, implemented as a collection of services. The system encompases services to provide e-learning courses which can be shared between universities and services which enable several universities to jointly provide e-learning courses, thus federating resources and providing a wider programme of courses of study than would be found at any of the universities individually. Lightweight federation of resources in this way to form a "virtual university" is exactly the type of interaction envisaged by the architects of the Web Service vision.

One of the difficulties of modelling such a design is capturing behaviour correctly, and assuring oneself and others that this has been achieved. We model the behaviour of the system in the SOCK calculus [1,2]. We have exercised this model using the JOLIE interpreter [3] in order to increase our confidence that the model describes the behaviour which we intended to capture.

Another challenge of this type of work is the well-known state-space explosion problem whereby a formal model of a system to which the algebraic methods and tools of concurrency theory can be applied would be very likely to be resistant to effective formal analysis. State-space explosion arises because the size of the system as a whole is bounded by the product of the individual state-spaces of the components which are composed in parallel. Evidently, this grows very quickly even when the components used are high-level abstact models of services which incorporate only the essential details needed for the modelling study. Due to the state-space explosion problem models might be require either an infeasibly long time to analyse, or an infeasibly large amount of storage.

To address this challenge, and be able to model the scalability problem of interest, we adopt a continuous-space representation of the process algebra model in contrast to the usual discrete-state representation of process algebra models via labelled transition systems. The process algebra used, PEPA, and the continuous-state representation are both due to Hillston [4,5]. The continuous-state representation avoids the requirement to represent each possible state of the system, making this analysis method applicable to systems of vastly greater scale and complexity than those analysable using the explicit, discrete-state representations which are usually based on Continuous-Time Markov Chains (CTMCs). In contrast the continuous-state representation maps the process algebra model to a system of coupled Ordinary Differential Equations (ODEs). Because of this an entirely different arsenal of numerical analysis procedures are available which can efficiently compute valuable analysis results for large-scale systems such as the one considered here.

By using SOCK and PEPA together in this way we have a federation of the resources of the two calculi as a "virtual process calculus" (in the same way that real organisations federate their resources to become a virtual organisation). In the present paper we use this virtual process calculus to model a virtual university.

Structure of this paper. In Section 2 we describe related work. In Section 3 we present the Service Oriented Computing Kernel (SOCK) calculus used in Section 4 to model our example Web Service. Following this we introduce Performance Evaluation Process Algebra (PEPA) in Section 5 which we use to analyse the non-functional aspects of the example in Section 6. We present our conclusions in Section 8.

2   Related Work

There are now many papers where stochastic process calculus models are mapped to Continuous-Time Markov Chains, semi-Markov processes or generalised semi-Markov processes for performance analysis [6,7]. Hillston's method of mapping process calculus models to ordinary differential equations is a more recent development [5] but has already been used to analyse multi-stage job execution on Grid compute clusters [8], peer-to-peer systems [9] and internet-scale spread of computer viruses such as worms [10]. An earlier paper by two of the present authors used Hillston's ODE method to show the failure of a centralised server model for the DCMS e-learning system to scale with increasing load [11]. The present paper is the first to show the potential for ODEs, however they are obtained, to be used as a modelling tool for replicated services as found in the Web Services paradigm.

3   The SOCK Calculus

SOCK (Service Oriented Computing Kernel) [1] is a formal calculus developed for reasoning about the main Service Oriented Computing issues. SOCK is divided into three different calculi which addresses different aspects of service design. The three SOCK calculi are called: *service behaviour calculus, service engine calculus* and *services system calculus*. The first one allows for the design of service behaviours by supplying computation and external communication primitives inspired by Web Services operations and workflow operators (e.g. sequence, parallel and choice). The service engine calculus is built on top of the former and allows for the specification of the service declaration where it is possible to design in an orthogonal way three main features: *execution modality, persistent state* flag and *correlation sets*. The execution modality deals with the possibility of executing a service in a sequential order or in a concurrent one; the persistent state flag allows the designer to declare if each session (of the service engine) has its own independent state or if the state is shared among all the sessions of the same service engine; correlation sets is a mechanism for distinguishing sessions initiated by different invokers by means of the values received within some specified variables. Finally, the services system calculus allows for the composition of service engines into a system.

The term syntax of the calculus includes numerical values and (possibly empty) tuples of variables $x = \langle x_0, x_1, \ldots, x_n \rangle$ and values $v = \langle v_0, v_1, \ldots, v_n \rangle$. The null process is $\mathbf{0}$. Operations are single message ($\mathcal{O}$) or involve two messages ($\mathcal{O}_r$). Outputs can be a signal s, a notification $o@k(x)$ or a solicit-response $o_r@k(x, y)$ where o is an operation in $\mathcal{O}$, o_r in $\mathcal{O}_r$, k the receiver location, x the tuple of variables sent and y the received information. The process term $x := e$ denotes an assignment. $\chi?P : Q$ is the if-then-else process. $P; P$ is sequential composition and $P \mid P$ is parallel. Guarded choice is $P + P$. $\chi \leftrightarrows P$ is guarded iteration. For a complete description the reader is referred to [1].

A brief discussion of the SOCK operators for service engine description and execution is given below:

Persistence. The flags $\times$ and $\bullet$ are used to distinguish persistent and non-persistent state. Where P is a service behaviour then $P_\times$ is equipped with a non-persistent state whereas $P_\bullet$ is equipped with a persistent state.

Guards. The execution of sessions may be guarded by correlation sets. In the term $c \triangleright P_\bullet$ the correlation set c guards the execution of the persistent service P. Correlation sets may be empty ($\emptyset$).

Sessions. $!W$ denotes a concurrent execution of the sessions in W whereas W^* denotes that sessions are executed in sequential order. For example $!(\emptyset \triangleright P_\bullet)$ indicates the concurrent execution of uncorrelated persistent service P.

Engines. A service engine Y is the composition of a service declaration D and an execution environment H, denoted $D[H]$. H represents the actual sessions which are running on the engine coupled with a state $(P, \mathcal{S})$.

Locations. A service engine system E can be a located service engine Y_{LOC} or a parallel composition of them $E \parallel E$.

4   Modelling Behaviour with SOCK

In an e-learning system the teaching material prepared by the teaching staff of each university is made available as *learning objects* which students must obtain by download from the content servers of the universities involved. The learning objects contain electronic versions of course notes and presentation material such as lecture slides. In addition many learning objects contain digital audio or digital video recordings of lecture presentations given by teaching staff. Learning objects are compressed archives of teaching material which vary in size and scale from collections of material for a single lecture in a course to a complete record of an entire lecture course. The lecture presentations of the course are downloaded instead of being streamed because they may require repeated review in order to digest the content.

Universities which host e-learning content are concerned with providing services which ensure good availability of the content and limited download times for the learning objects. Both of these are considered to be important metrics and are addressed in different ways. A high level of availability of the content is ensured by replicating the content distribution services (and the associated learning objects) across the content servers of many of the universities involved. Download times are reduced where possible by binding content requestors at the point of download to the content server which is most likely to be able to serve them well at that time.

The dynamic choice of content server is made using a metric which takes into account the geographical location of the content requestor and the content server, available bandwidth between the hosts, and the current load on the content server. Some of these factors can be known or bounded in advance (e.g. the maximum possible bandwidth between two endpoints) but some values must be obtained at the time that the service is invoked (e.g. the current load on a server).

It might seem that the best choice of server should always be the one which is geographically closest however it is possible that a lightly-loaded server further away from the content requestor might be able to serve them more quickly than a heavily-loaded server which is nearby. When considering home download it is usually the bandwidth to the Internet Service Provider which is the limiting factor on download rate in any case. The metric used by the dynamic discovery service attempts to take location, bandwidth and load factors into account in order to be able to make a good selection of content host for the content requestor.

Below we describe in the SOCK calculus the policy which would be used at the Bologna site to determine the selection of content server. Each of the content servers provides a service getLoad which, when invoked returns the current load on the server as a integer value in the range 0 (no load, available for use) to 100 (fully loaded, unavailable for use). Lower numbers are better. The policy at the Bologna site (UNIBO) compares its own load with the load at Pisa (UPISA), Florence (UNIFI), Munich (LMU) and Edinburgh (UEDIN) before returning the

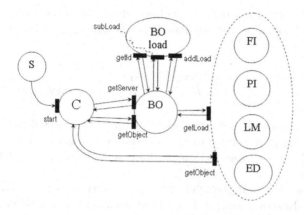

Fig. 2. The configuration of servers and services at the five sites

name of the server to download from. The remote servers are checked in a priority order, with geographically nearer servers being checked before those which are further away. A graphical representation of the system is shown in Figure 2.

4.1   Model in SOCK

In this section we present the SOCK behaviour of the services involved in the system, together with their deployment in terms of SOCK service engines concurrently composed within the process *System*. The names *UNIBO, UPISA, UNIFI, LMU* and *UEDIN* abstractly represent the location of the services provided by the universities of Bologna, Pisa, Firenze, Munich and Edinburgh, respectively. In particular, three behaviours are described: the *clientBehaviour*, the *UniBoBehaviour* and the *ObjServerBehaviour*.

The *clientBehaviour* models the behaviour of a client which sends a request to the service of the University of Bologna by exploiting the Solicit-Response *getServer@UNIBO* and, as a reply, it receives the address of the service to invoke for retrieving the e-learning object it is looking for. If the response message contains a valid address (here we model a fault reply message with the value -1), the client downloads the e-learning object by invoking the *getObject* operation of the service whose location has been stored within the variable *ServerAddress*. Here, we exploit the value *id_value*, assigned to the variable *ObjectID*, for modelling the reference of the object to download and we suppose that all the servers are able to provide the same e-learning objects.

$$clientBehaviour ::= getServer@UNIBO(\langle\rangle, ServerAddress);$$
$$ServerAddress == -1?0 :$$
$$(objectID := id\_value$$
$$; getObject@ServerAddress(objectID, object))$$

The *UniBoBehaviour* models the behaviour of the service provided by the University of Bologna and it supplies two different operations: *getServer* and *getObject*.

$$UniBoBehaviour ::= getServer(\langle\rangle, addr, search)$$
$$+getObject(id, obj, obj := \texttt{retrieve\_obj}(id))$$

The former allows for the individual identification of the downloading service by following a policy that takes into account the load of each server, whereas the latter allows the service user to download an e-learning object directly from the UNIBO service.

It is worth noting that the load of the other servers is retrieved by exploiting the Solicit-Response operation *getLoad* whereas the functions `loadhere()` and `retrieve_obj()` model the internal computations for calculating the actual load of the UniBo server and retrieving the requested object from the internal database of the server, respectively.

$$search ::= load := \texttt{loadhere}(); load < 75?addr := UNIBO$$
$$: getLoad@UNIFI(\langle\rangle, load); load < 60?addr := UNIFI$$
$$: getLoad@UPISA(\langle\rangle, load); load < 60?addr := UPISA$$
$$: getLoad@LMU(\langle\rangle, load); load < 40?addr := LMU$$
$$: getLoad@UEDIN(\langle\rangle, load); load < 20?addr := UEDIN$$
$$: load := \texttt{loadhere}(); load < 95?addr := UNIBO$$
$$: addr := -1$$

Finally, the *ObjServerBehaviour* models the behaviour of each downloading service by providing two different Request-Response operations: *getLoad* and *getObject*. The former allows for the returning of the load of the server whereas the latter provides a means for downloading the requested e-learning object.

$$ObjServerBehaviour ::= getLoad(\langle\rangle, load, load := \texttt{loadhere}())$$
$$+getObject(id, obj, obj := \texttt{retrieve\_obj}(id))$$

As far as the deployment of the services is concerned, below six service engines are composed within a process called *System*.

For the sake of precision, the *client* is not a service because it does not start with a receiving operation thus, its service engine provides only an execution environment, without any declaration, where the service behaviour can be executed once.

The *UniBoServer* is the service engine which executes the *UniBoBehaviour* whereas *UPisaServer*, *UniFiServer*, *LmuServer* and *UEdinServer* are the service engines of the downloading servers which all execute the same behaviour *ObjServerBehaviour* but at different locations.

$$client ::= [clientBehaviour]_{CLIENT}$$

$$UniBoServer ::= !(\emptyset \rhd UniBoBehaviour_\bullet)[\emptyset \rhd (0, \mathcal{S})]_{UNIBO}$$

$$UniFiServer ::= !(\emptyset \rhd ObjServerBehaviour_\bullet)[\emptyset \rhd (0, \mathcal{S})]_{UNIFI}$$

$$UPisaServer ::= !(\emptyset \rhd ObjServerBehaviour_\bullet)[\emptyset \rhd (0, \mathcal{S})]_{UPISA}$$

$$LmuServer ::= !(\emptyset \rhd ObjServerBehaviour_\bullet)[\emptyset \rhd (0, \mathcal{S})]_{LMU}$$

$$UEdinServer ::= !(\emptyset \rhd ObjServerBehaviour_\bullet)[\emptyset \rhd (0, \mathcal{S})]_{UEDIN}$$

$$System ::= client \parallel UniBoServer \parallel UPisaServer \parallel UniFiServer$$
$$\parallel LmuServer \parallel UEdinServer$$

5   The PEPA Stochastic Process Algebra

Systems are represented in PEPA as the composition of *components* which under-take *actions*. In PEPA the actions are assumed to have a duration, or delay. Thus the expression $(\alpha, r).P$ denotes a component which can undertake an α action, at rate r to evolve into a component P. Here $\alpha \in \mathcal{A}$ where $\mathcal{A}$ is the set of action types and $P \in \mathcal{C}$ where $\mathcal{C}$ is the set of component types. The rate r models a delay of variable duration. Delays are samples from an exponential random variable with parameter r, where this parameter is most often constant. In this paper we will make use of *functional rates* [12] which allow the rate at which an activity is performed to depend on the current state of the model. (In Petri nets terms, a "marking-dependent" rate.)

For example, a server might offer its computing resources at a rate which depended on the current state, $(compute, f_{SERVER})$ where the function f_{SERVER} is defined as follows:

$$f_{SERVER} = \begin{cases} 0, \text{ if } Server_{down} \\ \lambda, \text{ if } Server_{up} \end{cases}$$

A full description of the PEPA language can be found in [4]. To briefly sum-marise, PEPA has a small set of combinators, prefix (.), choice ($+$), co-operation ($\bowtie$, when co-operating over a set of activities, or $\parallel$ when there is no co-operation) and hiding (which we will not use here). Because we will be working with large populations of replicated processes we write $P[n]$ to denote n copies of compo-nent P executing in parallel. For example,

$$P[5] \equiv (P \parallel P \parallel P \parallel P \parallel P).$$

The total capacity of a component P to carry out activities of type α is termed the *apparent rate* of α in P, denoted $r_\alpha(P)$. For example, $r_{compute}(Server_{up}[2]) = 2\lambda$, $r_{compute}(Server_{up} \parallel Server_{down}) = \lambda$, and $r_{compute}(Server_{down}[2]) = 0$.

5.1   Relating Markov Chains and ODEs

In performance modelling based on continuous-time Markov chains, measures of system performance are often derived by a calculation which uses the steady-state probability distribution. To help us to compare modelling with ODEs and CTMCs in this section we consider the simpler example of a queue in PEPA.

$$Q_0 \overset{def}{=} (arrive, \lambda).Q_1$$
$$Q_i \overset{def}{=} (arrive, \lambda).Q_{i+1} + (serve, \mu).Q_{i-1} \quad (0 < i < N)$$
$$Q_N \overset{def}{=} (serve, \mu).Q_{N-1}$$

A typical performance measure for a model based on queues is the average queue length, which is computed in different ways, depending on the observations offered by the chosen semantics for the interpretation of the model.

When modelling in the Markovian interpretation we obtain the steady-state probability distribution, π. For a given queue bound, say $N = 8$, the average queue length is computed by weighting the probability of a state (Q_i denotes the state where the queue is of length i) by the number of customers in the queue at that point.

$$a = \sum_{i=0}^{8} i\pi(i)$$

When the state-space of the model grows in size any analysis which is based on an interleaving semantics (as in CTMCs) becomes prohibitively expensive. We turn then to a continuous approximation and solve the *initial value problem* for the ODEs to see how the numbers of each type of component change from initial (known) values at time $t = 0$, as time progresses forwards. We cannot compute the average queue length in the same way as for the CTMC because we do not have the stationary probability distribution. Instead we calculate it by considering a collection of 90 (say) independent queues all of capacity 8. The average queue length at time t is

$$a = \sum_{i=0}^{8} i\frac{[Q_i(t)]}{90}$$

where the term $[Q_i(t)]$ is understood to mean "the number of instances of Q_i at time t". We divide by 90 because that is the number which we have in our collection in this example.

We compute the average queue length numerically using both CTMC-based and ODE-based approaches, up to a specified accuracy of the numerical solution procedures (that is, a specified number of decimal places of accuracy). When we compare these we find good agreement in the results, up to the specified accuracy of the calculation of the solutions (see Figure 3). The solutions are computed using two entirely different numerical procedures. For the Markov chain, Jacobian over-relaxation, and for the differential equations, fifth-order Runge-Kutta with an adaptive step size.

λ	μ	Av. queue length (CTMCs at equilibrium)	Av. queue length (ODEs at $t = 200$)	Difference
1	4	0.333299009029	0.333298753978	2.5×10^{-7}
1	2	0.982387959648	0.982386995556	9.6×10^{-7}
1	1	4.000000000000	4.000000266670	-2.6×10^{-7}
2	1	7.017612040350	7.017613704440	-1.6×10^{-6}
4	1	7.666700990970	7.666701306580	-3.2×10^{-7}

Fig. 3. Solutions computed using CTMCs and ODEs

It is pleasing to have such good agreement in the results but it might be something of a mystery to the reader as to why the agreement is so good. In order to illuminate further the relationship between the CTMC and ODE interpretations we consider a simpler instance of the model above, a single sequential component with only three states defining a two-place queue.

$$Q_0 \stackrel{def}{=} (arrive, \lambda).Q_1$$
$$Q_1 \stackrel{def}{=} (arrive, \lambda).Q_2 + (serve, \mu).Q_0$$
$$Q_2 \stackrel{def}{=} (serve, \mu).Q_1$$

The continuous-time view. This process is at least enough to contain a use of a choice (in Q_1). When interpreted against the operational semantics of Markovian PEPA [4] this generates the following generator matrix for the underlying Markov chain. (By convention this matrix is called $\mathbf{Q}$, but it is not to be confused with our process variables Q_0, Q_1 and Q_2).

$$\mathbf{Q} = \begin{bmatrix} -\lambda & \lambda & 0 \\ \mu & -\lambda - \mu & \lambda \\ 0 & \mu & -\mu \end{bmatrix}.$$

The stationary probability distribution of this Markov chain, $\boldsymbol{\pi}$, is obtained by solving the equation

$$\boldsymbol{\pi}\mathbf{Q} = 0$$

subject to the requirement that the distribution is a good probability distribution (i.e. sums to 1).

$$\sum \boldsymbol{\pi} = 1$$

The symbolic solution of the above set of simultaneous linear equations is

$$\boldsymbol{\pi} = \left[\frac{\mu^2}{\lambda^2 + \mu\lambda + \mu^2}, \frac{\mu\lambda}{\lambda^2 + \mu\lambda + \mu^2}, \frac{\lambda^2}{\lambda^2 + \mu\lambda + \mu^2} \right].$$

The continuous-space view. When interpreted against the ODE semantics of PEPA [5], the above model instead gives rise to the following system of ordinary differential equations.

$$\frac{dQ_0}{dt} = -\lambda Q_0 + \mu Q_1$$
$$\frac{dQ_1}{dt} = \lambda Q_0 - \lambda Q_1 - \mu Q_1 + \mu Q_2$$
$$\frac{dQ_2}{dt} = \lambda Q_1 - \mu Q_2$$

A system of differential equations has a stationary solution, which occurs, as you might expect, when nothing is changing. That is, for our queue:

$$0 = -\lambda Q_0 + \mu Q_1$$
$$0 = \lambda Q_0 - \lambda Q_1 - \mu Q_1 + \mu Q_2$$
$$0 = \lambda Q_1 - \mu Q_2$$

If we re-write the above system of linear equations in vector-matrix form, we find that it is:

$$\mathbf{0} = [Q_0 \quad Q_1 \quad Q_2]\mathbf{Q}$$

If we then solve this initial value problem for the above system of differential equations for initial values of $Q_0 = 1, Q_1 = 0, Q_2 = 0$ then, because of conservation of mass, the equilibrium points will coincide with the steady-state distribution of the CTMC model. Therefore all measures calculated from the steady-state probability distribution (such as average queue length) will coincide. We argued this agreement only by considering one simple example here but a formal correspondence between the two semantic descriptions has been proven by Hillston by reference to Kurtz's theorem.

6   Modelling Performance with PEPA

The distributed system in PEPA is based on the cooperation between a population of clients and instances of server threads at each mirror site. Let m be the number of classes of clients in the system and k the number of mirror sites. In this modelling framework, the distributed system is completely characterised by the following entities:

- *Connection Setup Matrix* $\mathbf{C} \in \mathbb{R}^{+^{m,k}}$, whose element $c_{i,j}$ is the rate at which a class-i client connects to mirror j.
- *End-to-End Available Bandwidth Matrix* $\mathbf{D} \in \mathbb{R}^{+^{m,k}}$, whose element $d_{i,j}$ is the rate at which a class-i client downloads from mirror j.
- *Idle Vector* $\mathbf{t} \in \mathbb{R}^{+^m}$, whose element $r_{idle,i}$ is a class-i client's *thinking time*.
- *Population Vector* $\mathbf{p} \in \mathbb{N}^{+^m}$, whose element p_i is the population of class-i clients.

- *System Deployment Vector* $\mathbf{q} \in \mathbb{N}^{+^k}$, whose element q_j denotes the number of threads available at mirror j.

The model of a client is as follows.

$$
\begin{aligned}
Client_i &\stackrel{def}{=} (connect_1, c_{i,1}).(download_1, d_{i,1}).Idle_i \\
&+ (connect_2, c_{i,2}).(download_2, d_{i,2}).Idle_i \\
&\quad \ldots \\
&+ (connect_k, c_{i,k}).(download_k, d_{i,k}).Idle_i \\
&+ (overload, \top).Client_i \\
Idle_i &\stackrel{def}{=} (idle, r_{idle,i}).Client_i
\end{aligned}
$$

$$(1 \le i \le m)$$

Although the clients attempt connections to all the mirrors, we will model the mirrors in such a way that only one connection is granted as determined by the policy expressed below. For each mirror $Mirror_j, 1 \le j \le m$, we have:

$$
\begin{aligned}
Mirror_j &\stackrel{def}{=} (connect_j, f_j(s)).MirrorUploading_j \\
MirrorUploading_j &\stackrel{def}{=} (download_j, \top).Mirror_j
\end{aligned}
$$

This description features a functional rate for the *connect* action, $f_j(s) : \mathcal{C} \to \{0, \top\}$ where s is a PEPA component denoting the current state of the system. When f_j evaluates to 0, the activity is not enabled by the sequential component. We have determined that in any state at most one such function evaluates to $\top$, i.e.:

$$\forall s, \nexists f_i, f_j : f_i(s) = \top, f_j(s) = \top, j \ne i$$

By defining the functional rates for the *connect* action we encode the load balancer's policy into the model, as we shall see later. Note that no mirror performs any *overload* action. This is accomplished by another sequential component as follows:

$$Overload \stackrel{def}{=} (overload, o(s)).Overload$$

$$o(s) = \begin{cases} \top & f_i(s) = 0, 1 \le i \le m \\ 0 & \text{otherwise} \end{cases}$$

That is, *Overload* is enabled if all the mirrors' functional rates evaluate to 0. This ensures that no state is deadlocked. The initial state of the system is:

$$
\begin{aligned}
&\left(Client_1[p_1] \parallel Client_2[p_2] \parallel \ldots \parallel Client_m[p_m]\right) \\
&\quad \underset{L}{\bowtie} \left(Mirror_1[q_1] \parallel Mirror_2[q_2] \parallel \ldots \parallel Mirror_k[q_k]\right)
\end{aligned}
$$

$$
\begin{aligned}
L = \{&connect_1, connect_2, \ldots connect_k, \\
&download_1, download_2, \ldots download_k, overload\}
\end{aligned}
$$

Let *Loc* be a k-tuple assigning labels to mirrors, so that we can use $Mirror_j$ and $Mirror_{Loc_j}$ interchangeably. We now provide the model using the framework described above. In this case study, let $Loc = $ (UNIBO, UNIFI, UPISA, LMU, UEDIN). In this example, we consider a single class of clients located at UNIBO, i.e. $m = 1$. In the definitions of the functional rates $f_{UNIBO}-f_{UEDIN}$, we use process terms to indicate the number of copies of sequential components that behave as those terms in the system's state. The functional rates are defined thus.

$$f_{UNIBO} = \begin{cases} \top & \text{if } MirrorUploading_{UNIBO} < 75 \\ \top & \text{if } MirrorUploading_{UNIBO} < 95, \\ & MirrorUploading_{UNIFI} \geq 60, \\ & MirrorUploading_{UPISA} \geq 60, \\ & MirrorUploading_{LMU} \geq 40, \\ & MirrorUploading_{UEDIN} \geq 20 \\ 0 & \text{otherwise} \end{cases}$$

$$f_{UNIFI} = \begin{cases} \top & \text{if } MirrorUploading_{UNIBO} \geq 75, \\ & MirrorUploading_{UNIFI} < 60 \\ 0 & \text{otherwise} \end{cases}$$

$$f_{UPISA} = \begin{cases} \top & \text{if } MirrorUploading_{UNIBO} \geq 75, \\ & MirrorUploading_{UNIFI} \geq 60, \\ & MirrorUploading_{UPISA} < 60 \\ 0 & \text{otherwise} \end{cases}$$

$$f_{LMU} = \begin{cases} \top & \text{if } MirrorUploading_{UNIBO} \geq 75, \\ & MirrorUploading_{UNIFI} \geq 60, \\ & MirrorUploading_{UPISA} \geq 60, \\ & MirrorUploading_{LMU} < 40 \\ 0 & \text{otherwise} \end{cases}$$

$$f_{UEDIN} = \begin{cases} \top & \text{if } MirrorUploading_{UNIBO} \geq 75, \\ & MirrorUploading_{UNIFI} \geq 60, \\ & MirrorUploading_{UPISA} \geq 60, \\ & MirrorUploading_{LMU} \geq 40, \\ & MirrorUploading_{UEDIN} < 20 \\ 0 & \text{otherwise} \end{cases}$$

This model can be analysed through the underlying CTMC, stochastic simulation or ODEs. As far as Markovian analysis is concerned, the model allows us to fully take advantage of state space reduction by aggregation [13]. For instance, the state $[Mirror_{\text{UNIBO}} = 74, MirrorUploading_{\text{UNIBO}} = 1]$ aggregates 75 states. However, basic combinatorics suggests that the state space size of the underlying Markov chain, even with aggregation, is at least the product of the maximum number of incoming connections in each site. With this model's parameters, that would mean a Markov chain with over 273 million states, which is at the limit of the state-of-the-art in Markov chain solution technology. On the other hand, the model can be represented by a system of 17 coupled ODEs. This is the mathematical representation that we use to evaluate the performance of this system [5].

In this section we carry out time series analysis which allows us to see how the number of each type of component in the model varies as a function of time. This can provide the modeller with insights into the utilisation of the mirrors in both the transient and the steady state (as time increases and the transient behaviour tends to the equilibrium behaviour). In particular, we studied the impact that the client's behaviour has on such a performance index. The model parameters are as follows. The initial population of clients is 400. The deployment vector is the maximum number of available threads at each site as inferred from the definitions of the functional rates. Connection rate to all the mirror sites is 20.0. Available bandwidth per thread is 1/60 at LMU and UNIFI and 1/30 at UNIBO, UEDIN, and UPISA. We conducted sensitivity analysis of the *idle* activity by solving the system for the following values of r_{idle}: 0.001, 0.01, 0.02, 0.03, 0.04, 0.05 and 0.06. The graphs in Fig. 4 show time-series plots of the number of threads at each site in the 0–400 s time interval for such values of r_{idle}. The results were obtained by running the model through the adaptive step-size 5th-order Dormand Prince solver with default settings in our software tool, the "PEPAto" library [14] (100 data points, 0.001 step size, 1E-4 absolute error, 1E-4 relative error).

We compared the results from the numerical integration of the differential equations against stochastic simulation. Figure 5 shows good agreement between the deterministic trajectory (black line) and four independent runs of Gillespie's stochastic simulation algorithm (grey lines). The plot shows the evolution of the number of active threads at UNIFI for $r_{idle} = 0.01$. Similar fitting has been observed in the other cases under study.

6.1   Commentary on the Results

From these analysis results we are able to see how the load on each server varies as a function of time and see how the speed with which all servers reach saturation varies as a function of variation in idle time. In Figures 4(b)–4(h) we see how the load on the servers is balanced out in response to increasing client demand. In our model increasing client demand is achieved by decreasing client idle time (going from $r_{idle} = 0.001$ to $r_{idle} = 0.06$). At the system initiation all clients stand ready to connect and so the load on the Bologna server (UNIBO) rises rapidly. Thus we are considering here a difficult case for the system, but one which is likely to occur in practice. In systems with large numbers of

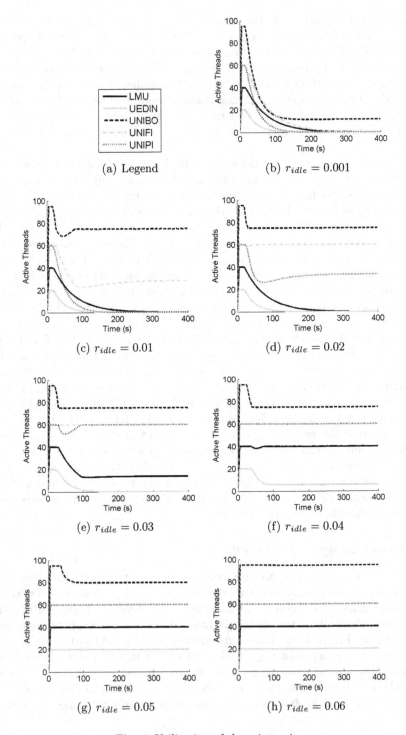

Fig. 4. Utilisation of the mirror sites

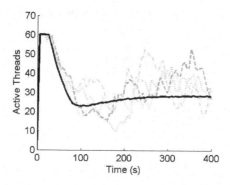

Fig. 5. Comparison between ODE analysis and stochastic simulation of the evolution of the number of active threads at UNIFI for $r_{idle} = 0.01$

clients one often observes the well-known "flashcrowd effect" where large numbers of clients attempt to connect at the system initiation. This phenomenon is widely observed in peer-to-peer systems [9].

When the system is lightly loaded (Figure 4(b)) then after the initial flurry of work we find that from time 200 onwards the Bologna server is processing all requests itself and passing nothing on to the other servers. As the load increases (Figure 4(c) and (d)) we observe that the Bologna server is passing work on to the other servers in Italy (UNIFI and UNIPI). Small increases in load beyond this point cause work to be passed to the further-away Munich server (LMU) until it saturates (Figure 4(f)), and the Edinburgh server similarly (Figure 4(g)). Finally, the Bologna server must bear the remaining load itself (Figure 4(h)). These results show the load-balancing function at work in practice.

7 Software Tools

We used the Jolie interpreter [3] to execute our SOCK language model of the DCMS e-learning system and the PEPA Eclipse Plugin [14] to compile our PEPA model to a system of coupled ODEs and to solve these numerically.

We are interested in the solution of *initial value problems* (IVPs) where the initial quantities of the components of the problem are known and we wish to find out how these change over time. Compared with modelling with CTMCs, modelling with ODEs resembles most strongly transient analysis of CTMCs: there is no implicit assumption that the system reaches steady-state equilibrium and we observe states of the system as time progresses, working forwards from their initial values at time $t = 0$.

ODEs can be solved numerically using solvers which implement the Runge-Kutta method, or Rosenbrock's algorithm, or others. Numerical computing platforms offer high-level support for the solution of ODEs [15]. The PEPA Eclipse Plugin uses an adaptive step-size 5th-order Runge-Kutta solver.

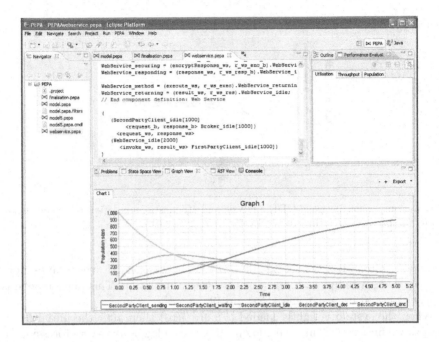

Fig. 6. The PEPA Eclipse Plugin provides a sophisticated modelling environment for quantitative modelling work with the PEPA process algebra. The screenshot above shows the workspace navigator displaying projects and model files on the filesystem together with a syntax-highlighting editor for the PEPA language. Performance results are shown in the performance evaluation view or in the graph view.

8   Conclusions

By federating the resources of the SOCK and PEPA process calculi we have been able to consider our case study of a replicated Web Service from both the functional and the non-functional (performance) perspectives. In a previous study we used analysis of a process calculus model using differential equations [5] to show that an architecture based on a centralised single server would not scale in the way desired [11]. In the present paper we use these methods to show that a replicated design does scale adequately. We have been able to use the continuous-space methods of [5] to analyse a model of a size which would defeat discrete-state analysis. The method is illustrated on the example of an e-learning system here but is generally applicable to analyse the scalability of replicated Web Services.

Acknowledgements. The authors are supported by the EC-funded FET-IST GC2 project number 016004 SENSORIA (Software Engineering for Service-Oriented Overlay Computers). The Jolie interpreter and the example considered here are available for download from http://jolie.sourceforge.net. The authors thank the anonymous reviewers for their insightful remarks which helped us to improve the paper for this version. Thanks to Adam Duguid for many helpful suggestions on model analysis.

References

1. Guidi, C., Lucchi, R., Gorrieri, R., Busi, N., Zavattaro, G.: Sock: A calculus for service oriented computing. In: Dan, A., Lamersdorf, W. (eds.) ICSOC 2006. LNCS, vol. 4294, pp. 327–338. Springer, Heidelberg (2006)
2. Busi, N., Gorrieri, R., Guidi, C., Lucchi, R., Zavattaro, G.: Choreography and orchestration conformance for system design. In: Ciancarini, P., Wiklicky, H. (eds.) COORDINATION 2006. LNCS, vol. 4038, Springer, Heidelberg (2006)
3. Montesi, F., Guidi, C., Lucchi, R., Zavattaro, G.: JOLIE: a Java Orchestration Language Interpreter Engine. In: Proceedings of CoOrd 2006, ENTCS (2006)
4. Hillston, J.: A Compositional Approach to Performance Modelling. Cambridge University Press, Cambridge (1996)
5. Hillston, J.: Fluid flow approximation of PEPA models. In: Proceedings of the Second International Conference on the Quantitative Evaluation of Systems, Torino, Italy, pp. 33–43. IEEE Computer Society Press, Los Alamitos (2005)
6. Holton, D.: A PEPA specification of an industrial production cell. The Computer Journal 38(7), 542–551 (1995)
7. Forneau, J., Kloul, L., Valois, F.: Performance modelling of hierarchical cellular networks using PEPA. Performance Evaluation 50(2–3), 83–99 (2002)
8. Benoit, A., Cole, M., Gilmore, S., Hillston, J.: Enhancing the effective utilisation of Grid clusters by exploiting on-line performability analysis. In: Proceedings of CCGrid workshop on Grid Performability (CCGrid Performability 2005), Cardiff, Wales, IEEE Computer Society Press, Los Alamitos (2005)
9. Duguid, A.: Coping with the parallelism of BitTorrent: Conversion of PEPA to ODEs in dealing with state space explosion. In: Asarin, E., Bouyer, P. (eds.) FORMATS 2006. LNCS, vol. 4202, pp. 156–170. Springer, Heidelberg (2006)
10. Bradley, J., Gilmore, S., Hillston, J.: Analysing distributed Internet worm attacks using continuous state-space approximation of process algebra models. J. Comput. System Sci. (to appear, 2007), doi:10.1016/j.jcss.2007.07.005
11. Gilmore, S., Tribastone, M.: Evaluating the scalability of a web service-based distributed e-learning and course management system. In: Bravetti, M., Núñez, M., Zavattaro, G. (eds.) WS-FM 2006. LNCS, vol. 4184, pp. 156–170. Springer, Heidelberg (2006)
12. Hillston, J., Kloul, L.: An efficient Kronecker representation for PEPA models. In: de Luca, L., Gilmore, S. (eds.) PROBMIV 2001, PAPM-PROBMIV 2001, and PAPM 2001. LNCS, vol. 2165, pp. 120–135. Springer, Heidelberg (2001)
13. Gilmore, S., Hillston, J., Ribaudo, M.: An efficient algorithm for aggregating PEPA models. IEEE Transactions on Software Engineering 27(5), 449–464 (2001)
14. Tribastone, M.: The PEPA Plug-in Project. In: Proceedings of the 4th International Conference on the Quantitative Evaluation of Systems (QEST 2007), pp. 53–54. IEEE Computer Society Press, Los Alamitos (2007)
15. Shampine, L.F., Gladwell, I., Thompson, S.: Solving ODEs with Matlab. Cambridge University Press, Cambridge (2003)

Location-Aware Quality of Service Measurements for Service-Level Agreements

Ashok Argent-Katwala[1], Jeremy Bradley[1], Allan Clark[2], and Stephen Gilmore[2]

[1] Department of Computing, Imperial College, London
[2] LFCS, School of Informatics, University of Edinburgh

Abstract. We add specifications of location-aware measurements to performance models in a compositional fashion, promoting precision in performance measurement design. Using immediate actions to send control signals between measurement components we are able to obtain more accurate measurements from our stochastic models without disturbing their structure. A software tool processes both the model and the measurement specifications to give response time distributions and quantiles, an essential calculation in determining satisfaction of service-level agreements (SLAs).

1 Introduction

Accurate performance analysis is essential to the system design process. A system which does not meet its performance and dependability requirements – crucial parts of its trustworthiness or *performability* [1] – is, in practical terms, as unacceptable as a system which does not meet its correctness requirements. Modern engineered systems are vast and complex and so high-level modelling of these systems is a vital step in determining that they satisfy necessary service-level agreements (SLAs). Our attention here is on the quantitative core of such an SLA, which will typically claim that some percentage of incoming requests will receive a response from the system within a specified time bound.

Computing performance results is a subtle matter. The location of performance measurements in a model can have a dramatic effect on the resulting performance measurement. In this paper, we show how performance measurements, known as *stochastic probes*, can be installed in performance models with increased precision. We show how both the positioning of these probes in the performance model, and the translation of these probes using immediate transitions, improves the reliability of the measurement which results.

Good practice in performance modelling suggests the use of a *compositional approach* [2]. Models are structured by building up co-operations between model components, defining complex models as the composition of smaller sub-models. The leading exemplars of languages supporting compositional performance modelling are *stochastic process algebras* (such as PEPA [2], EMPA [3], the Stochastic π-calculus [4] and SPADES [5]). In these languages *model components* are separate units of functionality which perform stochastically timed activities and can be composed. One way to compose model components P and Q is to require

G. Barthe and C. Fournet (Eds.): TGC 2007, LNCS 4912, pp. 222–239, 2008.

them to co-operate on the activities in the set $\mathcal{K}$, allowing them to proceed independently with any activities not listed in $\mathcal{K}$.

$$P \bowtie_{\mathcal{K}} Q$$

Models can be hierarchically structured in this way. Below, we require P and Q to co-operate on $\mathcal{K}$ as before, and we also require R and S to co-operate on $\mathcal{M}$. Further, we require the composition of P and Q to co-operate with the composition of R and S on any activities in the set $\mathcal{L}$.

$$(P \bowtie_{\mathcal{K}} Q) \bowtie_{\mathcal{L}} (R \bowtie_{\mathcal{M}} S)$$

In process algebras with multi-way synchronisation this hierarchical co-operation over $\mathcal{L}$ can express co-operation between one of P and Q and one of R and S; or three of these components; or even all four (for activities in $\mathcal{K} \cap \mathcal{L} \cap \mathcal{M}$).

Here model components P, Q, R and S represent parts of the system being modelled and activity sets $\mathcal{K}$, $\mathcal{L}$, and $\mathcal{M}$ list the activities performed by these components in co-operation with others. Compositionality facilitates re-use. In our schematic example above P and S might even be instances of the same class of model component (although configured differently by having different partners to co-operate with, and different co-operation sets to operate under).

Given a hierarchically structured model such as this we can define performance measures of interest by adding *measurement components* which seek to expose important activity sequences so that they may be conveniently measured. One use of these would be to compute response time quantiles used in service-level agreements of the form "97.5% of message sends see an acknowledgement within 600 milliseconds."

Such a measurement component is a *stochastic probe* [6] which can be described directly, as model components are, or more conveniently can be generated from a higher-level description language.

$$((P \bowtie_{\mathcal{K}} Q) \bowtie_{\mathcal{L}} (R \bowtie_{\mathcal{M}} S)) \bowtie_{\mathcal{N}} Probe$$

The intention is that a model is not disturbed by the addition of a probe in the sense that all of the activities which could happen previously can still happen, and at the same rate as before. Thus if archiving models and results in an organised store for sharing and re-use [7], models can be stored in a canonical form and measurement components and their associated results can be stored separately from these. The relationship between the model and the probe can also be formally recorded, and made available for later inspection and review.

It is intended that several different probes can be applied to a single model without needing to alter the model and it is even possible that probes are re-used, where a single probe is applied to several different models.

In a modelling language which supports multi-way synchronisation (such as PEPA [2]) probes may observe activities even if those activities are performed by model components in co-operation (for example, an activity from the set $\mathcal{K}$ performed by both P and Q).

As introduced in [6], probes are stateful components which can observe activities, can count, and can change state to remember that an activity has been performed. Using these a modeller can check complex service level agreements such as "97.5% of message sends need two retransmissions or fewer to see an acknowledgement within 600 milliseconds."

However, the position of a probe is that of an external observer. The external observer has a location-ignorant viewpoint. He is unable to distinguish an activity α emanating from P's location from an activity α emanating from S's location. This impedes the expression of many service level agreements which arise naturally. For example, "97.5% of sensor message sends need two retransmissions or fewer to see an acknowledgement from the relay within 600 milliseconds."

In the case where we are interested in the activities of P and not those of S one solution could be to move the probe inside the model so that we can focus on P.

$$(((P \underset{N}{\bowtie} Probe^P) \underset{K}{\bowtie} Q) \underset{L}{\bowtie} (R \underset{M}{\bowtie} S))$$

This would be effective in this case but if instead any of the activities performed by other components (say, S) influence the state of the probe then the probe is at the wrong place in the composed model to observe them. To remedy this we could add another probe to S and have both of these slave probes report to a master which combines their reports appropriately.

$$(((P \underset{N}{\bowtie} Probe^P) \underset{K}{\bowtie} Q) \underset{L}{\bowtie} (R \underset{M}{\bowtie} (S \underset{O}{\bowtie} Probe^S))) \underset{T}{\bowtie} Probe^{Master}$$

The addition of these probes is an automated procedure performed on an input model without probes. The modeller need not see the version of the model expanded by the addition of the measurement components and can consider this just to be an intermediate form produced before state-space derivation (in a manner similar to unfolding a coloured Petri net).

The position of $Probe^P$ allows it to send to the $Probe^{Master}$ the control message "P performed α" on seeing an activity α performed by P. Similarly the position of $Probe^S$ allows it to send to the $Probe^{Master}$ the control message "S performed α" on seeing an activity α performed by S. Model components Q and R could be probed in exactly the same way.

In a purely Markovian process algebra such as PEPA there is a fundamental difficulty with the above design; all activities are timed, and so a rate must be associated with the control messages. The duration of these control messages would then be added to the duration of the model activities occurring in the passage from the start state to the final state. This would interfere with the passage time calculation being made and lead to inaccurate numerical results being produced. We could try to repair this by assigning control messages a rate several orders of magnitude higher than any already in the model but this would not entirely solve the problem because the infinite support of the exponential distribution means that there is a possibility that "fast" control messages are occasionally beaten by "slow" model activities, leading to the master probe being out-of-step with the model description. Even if this problem does not arise the widely-separated values for the rate constants would very likely lead to stiffness problems in the numerical solution of the underlying Markov chain.

We address this problem by using high-priority immediate actions for the control messages (whereas the process algebra model being probed contains only low-priority exponentially timed activities). Instantaneous control messages flow from the slave probes to the master probe, sending the control signal needed without perturbing the passage-time measurement taking place.

The idea of extending high-level Markovian modelling languages with immediate actions is not new. Stochastic Petri nets were extended to Generalised Stochastic Petri nets in [8] by incorporating immediate transitions and distinguishing between tangible and vanishing states. Neither is the use of immediate actions with stochastic process algebras new. The languages EMPA [3], MoDeST [9], SM-PEPA [10] and SPADES [5] all support immediate actions.

The novelty in the present paper is the introduction of immediate actions in a structured way which facilitates the development of a powerful query language for Markovian models which is an extension of the language proposed in [11]. We first present the ideas from the existing query language then show the location-aware extension together with an example. We have implemented the query language in a new software tool.

The query language which we propose for Markovian models can be used as an alternative to logics such as CSL used in the stochastic model-checking approach [12]. One feature which may be of benefit to users is that our query language offers features such as activity counting and location-identification which cannot be expressed directly in a CSL formula. The technology which underpins both styles is the same: transient analysis of a continuous-time Markov chain.

2   Stochastic Probes

In assessing service level agreements it is often convenient to measure from the observation of one of a set of "start" activities to an occurrence of one of a further set of "stop" activities. For example, $(a{:}\mathsf{start} \mid b{:}\mathsf{start}), c{+}, (x{:}\mathsf{stop} \mid y{:}\mathsf{stop})$. From this a master probe is generated with two distinct states for *running* and for *stopped* as described in [6]. The probe begins *stopped* and moves to *running* if it observes any of the start activities. Since the master probe must cooperate with the model over the start and stop activities it must be capable of performing these in both states. ("$(a, \top)$" passively observes the timed activity a.)

$$Probe_{stopped}^{Master} \overset{\mathrm{def}}{=} (a, \top).Probe_{running}^{Master} + (b, \top).Probe_{running}^{Master}$$
$$+ (x, \top).Probe_{stopped}^{Master} + (y, \top).Probe_{stopped}^{Master}$$
$$Probe_{running}^{Master} \overset{\mathrm{def}}{=} (x, \top).Probe_{stopped}^{Master} + (y, \top).Probe_{stopped}^{Master}$$
$$+ (a, \top).Probe_{running}^{Master} + (b, \top).Probe_{running}^{Master}$$

The master probe synchronises with the whole model (including the observation probe) over the start and stop activities but not any other activities which the probe may perform, in our case c.

$$(Model \underset{\{a,b,c,x,y\}}{\bowtie} Probe_1^{Obs}) \underset{\{a,b,x,y\}}{\bowtie} Probe_{stopped}^{Master}$$

The start and stop activities are used as communications from the observation probe to the master probe. Whenever an a or b activity is performed the observation probe signals to the master probe to begin measurement and conversely for stop activities.

This will not work for a location-aware probe. The purpose of applying the probe to only a part of the larger model was that the probe could then ignore any of the "start" or "stop" activities performed by other parts of the model with which the current measurement is unconcerned. Instead of cooperating with the master probes over the "start" activities (a and b) and the "stop" activities (x and y), the probe can instead send immediate control messages (*start* and *stop*) to the master probe to say that the activities of interest have been observed. By using immediate actions as the control messages the observation probe may communicate with the master probe in a private manner which also does not affect the model being observed.

$$Probe_1^{Obs} \overset{def}{=} (a, \top).start.Probe_2^{Obs} + (b, \top).start.Probe_2^{Obs}$$
$$+ (c, \top).Probe_1^{Obs}$$
$$+ (x, \top).Probe_1^{Obs} + (y, \top).Probe_1^{Obs}$$
$$Probe_2^{Obs} \overset{def}{=} (a, \top).Probe_2^{Obs} + (b, \top).Probe_2^{Obs}$$
$$+ (c, \top).Probe_3^{Obs}$$
$$+ (x, \top).Probe_2^{Obs} + (y, \top).Probe_2^{Obs}$$
$$Probe_3^{Obs} \overset{def}{=} (a, \top).Probe_3^{Obs} + (b, \top).Probe_3^{Obs}$$
$$+ (c, \top).Probe_3^{Obs}$$
$$+ (x, \top).stop.Probe_1^{Obs} + (y, \top).stop.Probe_1^{Obs}$$

The master probe is altered so that instead of observing the model (including the observation probe) performing a, b, x and y actions it observes only start and stop communication events.

$$Probe_{stopped}^{Master} \overset{def}{=} start.Probe_{running}^{Master} + stop.Probe_{stopped}^{Master}$$
$$Probe_{running}^{Master} \overset{def}{=} stop.Probe_{stopped}^{Master} + start.Probe_{running}^{Master}$$

The names start and stop are labels in the regular expression syntax of probes. Because these now turn into communication signals, the labels can be generalised to include any names that the user wishes. In this way multiple observation probes may be attached to various portions of the model. Their communication signals are distinct labels so these probes avoid name clashes. Generally a control probe will cooperate over the whole model and interpret all of the communication signals from localised observation probes.

3   Location-Aware Stochastic Probes

This example illustrates the need for location-aware probes. The model is that of a simple client server system. The key point is that there are two indistinguishable servers available to respond to each of the three indistinguishable clients and the problem is correctly matching requests and responses.

$$Client_{idle} \stackrel{\text{def}}{=} (request, \lambda).Client_{waiting}$$
$$Client_{waiting} \stackrel{\text{def}}{=} (response, \top).Client_{idle}$$

$$Server_{idle} \stackrel{\text{def}}{=} (request, \top).Server_{computing}$$
$$Server_{computing} \stackrel{\text{def}}{=} (compute, \pi).Server_{responding}$$
$$Server_{responding} \stackrel{\text{def}}{=} (response, \rho).Server_{idle}$$

$$System \stackrel{\text{def}}{=} Client_{idle}[3] \bowtie_{\mathcal{L}} Server_{idle}[2]$$
$$\text{where } \mathcal{L} = \{request, response\}$$

Suppose one wishes to measure the expected response time, that is the time taken from a particular client making a request to that client receiving a response. A probe component is added to the model which passively observes all *request* and *response* activities flipping between running and stopped states appropriately. The desired measurement can then be taken to be the expected time for the probe component to be in the running state. So for our model a first attempt at a measurement of response time may be to add the probe in this fashion:

$$System \stackrel{\text{def}}{=} (Client_{idle}[3] \bowtie_{\mathcal{L}} Server_{idle}[2]) \bowtie_{\mathcal{L}} Probe \qquad (3.1)$$

This global probe over-estimates the performance of the system because it measures the time from *some* client's request to whenever *either* of the servers responds. In particular it may measure the time between one client's *request* and the *response* which corresponds to an earlier *request* performed by another client.

The reason that the global probe does not work as we would expect it is due to the fact that it cannot distinguish between identical actions performed by separate components. Additionally the probe only observes start actions when it is in the stopped state. For this reason when the model performs more than one start action before a stop action is encountered, the probe will still be running.

Figure 1 depicts the error that the response from $Server[2]$ to $Client[2]$ is paired with the request from $Client[3]$ to $Server[1]$. This measurement error occurs due to the use of a location unaware probe.

To fix this problem, the probe can be location-aware. Instead of cooperating with the entire system, the probe cooperates only with a single *Client* process. Writing ($\|$) to denote cooperation over the empty set the system is:

$$System \stackrel{\text{def}}{=} ((Client_{idle} \bowtie_{\mathcal{L}} Probe) \| Client_{idle}[2]) \bowtie_{\mathcal{L}} Server_{idle}[2] \qquad (3.2)$$

The graph in Figure 2 shows the difference in measurement between the local probe from (3.2) and the global probe from (3.1). The graph plots the measured

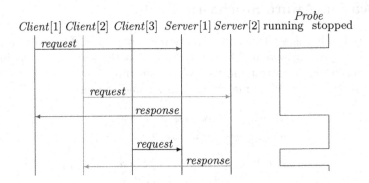

Fig. 1. Diagram showing the trace of a run with a faulty global probe

time since a *request* action against the probability that the probe has cooperated over a *response* action. From this graph the error of the global probe is apparent. The line plotted for the probe is above that of the local probe indicating that the probability of observing a *response* activity is higher.

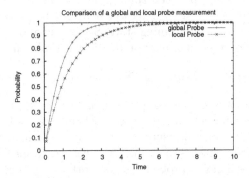

Fig. 2. Graph showing the flawed measurement taken from a global probe versus the true measurement obtained from a local probe

4   Impact on Aggregation

Modelling formalisms founded on Continuous-Time Markov Chains (CTMCs) suffer from the well-known problem of state-space explosion whereby the number of states of the model as a whole may be as large as the product of the number of states of each of the model components. Model *aggregation* [13] battles this state-space growth by exploiting symmetries in the model to reduce the number of states in the state-space. This is done by replacing several *strongly equivalent* states with a canonical representative of them, and adjusting the outgoing rates accordingly. Aggregation based on strong equivalence induces a *lumpable* [14] partition of the state-space which preserves performance measures. The proof of this result appears in [2]. The definition of the strong equivalence relation is also found there.

Aggregation depends on replication of components in that each component C in an array of N copies of C, $C[N]$, is considered to be interchangeable. With a location-aware measurement component we are able to isolate one of these copies and make it no longer interchangeable with the others. An inevitable consequence of this is that aggregation will now be less productive (because there are now effectively only $N-1$ copies of the component, and so symmetries which existed before have now been broken).

In the worst case, isolating a model component in this way may decrease the profit from aggregation to the point where the model is no longer solvable because its memory requirements exceed those of the machine on which the analysis is taking place. We view this as an inescapable cost of the more accurate identification of model components afforded by location-aware measurement components.

5 Communicating Stochastic Probes

This example expands upon the first to show the need for immediate communication between location-aware probes. We wish to analyse the impact of the breakdown of a server on the response time. In order to measure this our model from before is enhanced with the possibility for servers to break down. Once a server has broken down it must be repaired before it can continue to service client requests.

$$Server_{idle} \stackrel{def}{=} (request, \top).Server_{responding}$$
$$+ (break, \kappa).Server_{broken}$$
$$Server_{responding} \stackrel{def}{=} (response, \rho).Server_{idle}$$
$$Server_{broken} \stackrel{def}{=} (repair, \nu).Server_{idle}$$

$$System \stackrel{def}{=} Client_{idle}[3] \underset{\mathcal{L}}{\bowtie} Server_{idle}[2]$$
$$\text{where } \mathcal{L} = \{request, response\}$$

In this example the *Client* processes include a local working activity.

$$Client_{idle} \stackrel{def}{=} (work, \mu).Client_{requesting}$$
$$Client_{requesting} \stackrel{def}{=} (request, \lambda).Client_{waiting}$$
$$Client_{waiting} \stackrel{def}{=} (response, \top).Client_{idle}$$

Suppose we wish to determine the response time if the client is ready to make the request when at least one of the servers is currently broken. One way to do this is to insist that the probe observes the *work* activity from the probed client after observing a *break* activity from one of the servers and without observing a *repair* activity. Note that a *repair* activity may take place after the *work* activity has been observed by the probe and the measurement begun.

We require one probe which is attached to a single client, a further probe which is attached to one of the servers, and a master probe which combines the communication messages from the two local probes.

$$Clients \stackrel{def}{=} ((Client_{idle} \bowtie_{\mathcal{L}} Probe_{stopped}^{Client}) \parallel Client_{idle}[2])$$

$$Servers \stackrel{def}{=} ((Server_{idle} \bowtie_{\mathcal{M}} Probe_{stopped}^{Server}) \parallel Server_{idle})$$

$$System \stackrel{def}{=} ((Clients \bowtie_{\mathcal{L}} Servers) \bowtie_{\mathcal{N}} Probe_{stopped}^{Master})$$

$$\text{where } \mathcal{L} = \{work, response\}$$
$$\mathcal{M} = \{break, repair\}$$
$$\mathcal{N} = \{clientWork, clientRes, in, out\}$$

The local server probe is attached to one of the servers and sends a signal to the master probe whenever the local server breaks down or is repaired.

$$Probe_{stopped}^{Server} \stackrel{def}{=} (break, \top).in.Probe_{broken}^{Server}$$
$$+ (repair, \top).out.Probe_{stopped}^{Server}$$
$$Probe_{broken}^{Server} \stackrel{def}{=} (repair, \top).out.Probe_{stopped}^{Server}$$
$$+ (break, \top).in.Probe_{broken}^{Server}$$

When the local client probe passively observes a *work* activity in one of the clients it sends a communication message to the master probe. Upon observing a *response* activity it sends a message again.

$$Probe_{stopped}^{Client} \stackrel{def}{=} (work, \top).clientWork.Probe_{run}^{Client}$$
$$Probe_{run}^{Client} \stackrel{def}{=} (response, \top).clientRes.Probe_{stopped}^{Client}$$

The master probe then receives the communication from the two local probes and connects together the logic to determine whether or not the measurement should begin. It has three states. In the first state, $Probe_{stopped}^{Master}$, it waits for a communication message indicating that one of the servers is broken. When this occurs it moves on to the second state. In the second state, $Probe_{waiting}^{Master}$, there is at least one server broken hence should the probe local to the client send a message indicating that a measurement may begin (that is, the client has performed a *work* action) then the master probe will indeed begin measurement by entering the third state $Probe_{running}^{Master}$. In this state the only message of interest is one from the client probe to indicate that it has observed a *response* activity which causes the measurement to terminate. Note that it is not the case that every *clientWork* activity will cause measurement to start and neither is it the case that every *clientRes* activity will cause measurement to stop.

$$Probe_{stopped}^{Master} \stackrel{def}{=} in.Probe_{waiting}^{Master}$$
$$+ clientWork.Probe_{stopped}^{Master}$$
$$+ clientRes.Probe_{stopped}^{Master}$$
$$Probe_{waiting}^{Master} \stackrel{def}{=} clientWork.start.Probe_{running}^{Master}$$

$$+ \ out.Probe^{Master}_{stopped}$$
$$+ \ clientRes.Probe^{Master}_{waiting}$$
$$Probe^{Master}_{running} \ \stackrel{\text{def}}{=} \ clientRes.stop.Probe^{Master}_{stopped}$$
$$+ \ out.Probe^{Master}_{running}$$

For the purposes of explanation the probes defined here have been given as though directly written by the user. However in general such probes are specified using a regular expression-like syntax. They are then automatically attached to the model at the appropriate place. To reproduce the full model with the probes attached the following three probe specifications would be given:

1. $Client :: (work : clientWork, response : clientReq)$
2. $Server :: (break : in, repair : out)$
3. $(in, clientWork : start)/out, clientRes : stop$

The first two probes specify a location to which the probe should be attached, *Client* and *Server* respectively. The final probe is the master probe and will be attached to the whole model and hence does not require a location. The syntax $/out$ specifies that the whole of the probe to the left must be observed without observing an *out* signal. Should one occur during the sequence then the probe is reset. We analysed this model with the probes given and with two other configurations. The results are shown in the graph in Figure 3. The line labelled "maybe" is the model analysing from a *clientWork* message to a *clientRes* message regardless of the state of the servers at that time.

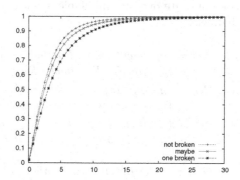

Fig. 3. Graph showing the change of completion of a client's request depending on the state of the servers

6 Worked Example: Wireless Sensor Network

As a worked example, we present a model of a lossy wireless sensor network. The network consists of a set of *SensorBots* which monitor the environment and report key events across the network. The bots both take measurements and route traffic from other bots in the network. In routing traffic either from other bots or itself, a bot has a simple send-acknowledge mechanism for sending traffic to a nearest-receiving bot. If an ack is not received, the bot enters a backoff phase before retrying, and repeats this until an ack is received.

$$
\begin{aligned}
SensorBot \stackrel{\text{def}}{=}\ & (monitor, r_{mon}).SensorBot \\
+\ & (monitorActive, r_{monA}).SensorBotSend \\
+\ & (messageIn, \top).SensorBotRelay \\
+\ & (messageIn, \top).SensorBotProcess \\
SensorBotProcess \stackrel{\text{def}}{=}\ & (ackOut, r_{ack}).(think, r_{think}).SensorBot \\
SensorBotSend \stackrel{\text{def}}{=}\ & (messageOut, r_{msgOut}).SensorBotWait \\
SensorBotWait \stackrel{\text{def}}{=}\ & (ackIn, \top).SensorBot \\
+\ & (timeout, r_{timeout}).SensorBotRetrySend \\
SensorBotRetrySend \stackrel{\text{def}}{=}\ & (backoff, r_{backoff}).SensorBotSend \\
+\ & (giveup, r_{giveup}).SensorBot \\
SensorBotRelay \stackrel{\text{def}}{=}\ & (ackOut, r_{ack}).SensorBotSend
\end{aligned}
$$

Each *SensorBot* is symmetrically described and is either involved in: monitoring events, *SensorBot*; processing a received event notification from another bot, *SensorBotProcess*; sending a message, *SensorBotSend*; waiting for an ack from another bot that received its message, *SensorBotWait*; resending a message after a backoff period, *SensorBotRetrySend*; or relaying a message across the sensor network, *SensorBotRelay*.

The *SensorBots* communicate over an unreliable wireless network that comprises a number of channels:

$$
\begin{aligned}
UnreliableChannel \stackrel{\text{def}}{=}\ & (messageOut, \top).UnreliableChannelMsg \\
+\ & (ackOut, \top).UnreliableChannelAck \\
UnreliableChannelMsg \stackrel{\text{def}}{=}\ & (messageIn, r_{netDelay}).UnreliableChannel \\
+\ & (messageLose, r_{msgLose}).UnreliableChannel \\
UnreliableChannelAck \stackrel{\text{def}}{=}\ & (ackIn, r_{netDelay}).UnreliableChannel \\
+\ & (messageLose, r_{msgLose}).UnreliableChannel
\end{aligned}
$$

A channel can relay a message from one bot to another bot, by picking up a *messageOut* action and transmitting a *messageIn* action to a receiver bot. A similar process transmits acknowledgement messages. What makes this network unreliable is that there is a probability that any given message may be lost, where the probability of loss is determined by:

$$
\frac{r_{msgLose}}{r_{msgLose} + r_{netDelay}}
$$

Finally, the whole sensor network comprises B bots connected by the unreliable wireless network of C channels, as described by;

$$SensorNet \overset{\text{def}}{=} SensorBot[B] \underset{L}{\bowtie} UnreliableChannel[C]$$

where $L = \{ ackIn, ackOut, messageIn, messageOut \}$.

This is a simplistic protocol, where it is for instance possible for one bot to acknowledge the message that another bot received. The system probabilistically guards against this, by incorporating a quick timeout mechanism. If the sending bot does not hear an acknowledgement within a short window, it backs off and retries later. If it does hear an acknowledgement, it assumes that this was the response for its message. Given the power constraints involved in sensor networks, this type of simplistic mechanism is not an unreasonable way to conserve sensor battery-life. If guaranteed message sending is required, then a more sophisticated protocol could be deployed.

6.1   Location Probe Measurements

In this model the measurement in which we may be interested is the length of time a sensor can expect to wait for an acknowledgement. This model is distinct from the earlier "Client–Server" style of model in that each sensor acts as both a "Client" and a "Server". Since in this case the response is the acknowledgement that the message has been routed onwards and the sender can continue its monitoring operations. In the traditional "Client–Server" style of model it is clear that as we increase the number of "Client" components without increasing the number of "Server" components the response-time for each individual "Client" should worsen. In the distributed setting of the sensor net, because each additional "Client" (or *SensorBot*) also becomes a "Server" it is less clear how the addition of *SensorBot* components will affect the response-time for each individual *SensorBot*. With each additional *SensorBot* there is a further "Server" which may respond to the individual measured *SensorBot*. However in addition there is an additional "Client" component which may compete not only for the "Server" components but also for the resource components modelled here by the unreliable network channels.

To measure the response-time for a single *SensorBot* component we wish to measure between occurrences of the activity *messageOut* – the *SensorBot* has sent a message to be delivered – and the activity *ackIn* – the *SensorBot* has received an acknowledgement that the message has been relayed/accepted. To achieve this we cannot attach a global-probe component to the entire model as this will not distinguish the occurrences of *messageOut* activity and the *ackIn* activity performed by separate *SensorBot* components. We therefore attach a probe to a single *SensorBot* component. The probe itself waits for an occurence of the *messageOut* activity to start the measurement and an occurrence of the *ackIn* activity to end it. This is written down in our probe language as:

$$SensorBot :: (messageOut : start, ackIn : stop)$$

Figure 4 shows the cumulative distribution functions for the model as we vary the number of *SensorBot* and *UnreliableChannel* components. These results suggest that increasing the number of *SensorBot* components always improves the response-time. The number of channels may act as a bottleneck in the network and hence increasing the number of channels likewise improves the response-time. Therefore in the "Client–Server" style of model increasing the number of "Servers" is the only way to increase the performance of the system. However in the distributed network increasing either the "peers" or the resources (channels) leads to an improvement in the number of messages relayed.

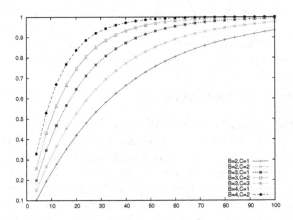

Fig. 4. Graph showing the cdf from 'msgOut' to 'ackIn' for the sensor net model varying the numbers of sensors and channels

7   Design

An extended Markovian process algebra with immediate actions is a step on the way towards the more ambitious goal of an extended process algebra with general distributions. We first explain the relationship between this algebra and immediate actions and then explain the relationship between immediate actions and probes.

7.1   Immediate Actions and SM-PEPA

Semi-Markov PEPA [10] (SM-PEPA), is a version of PEPA that allows general distributions as well as exponential distributions from the standard PEPA model. The syntax for SM-PEPA is given below:

$$P ::= (a^{[n]}, D).P \mid P + P \mid P \underset{L}{\bowtie} P \mid P/L \mid A \tag{7.3}$$

where:

$$D ::= \lambda \mid \omega : L(s) \tag{7.4}$$

where λ is the standard PEPA exponential rate parameter:

$$\lambda \in \mathbb{R}^+ \cup \{r\top \mid r \in \mathbb{Q}, r > 0\}$$

The action a is annotated with a priority $n \in \mathbb{N}$ (where a larger n indicates a higher priority). SM-PEPA introduces a notion of priority-enabling where an action is priority-enabled only if it is enabled in the normal PEPA sense and there are no higher priority actions that are enabled at the same time. The D variable indicates a duration, either an exponential rate or a weighted general distribution. The general distribution is specified in terms of its Laplace transform for numerical convenience. The weights, ω, are used to select probabilistically between concurrently priority-enabled generally-distributed actions.

The use of priorities in activities (action-duration pairs) is restricted so that within a particular priority level, either Markovian activities are available (containing standard PEPA) or generally-distributed activities are. This prevents the simultaneous racing of exponential and generally-distributed distributions. A detailed semantics for SM-PEPA can be found in [10].

The immediate transition model required for use with stochastic probes can be derived from a subset of SM-PEPA; it uses a similar approach as that used in generalised stochastic Petri nets (GSPNs) [15]. For this purpose only two priority levels are required, level 1 for Markovian activities and level 2 for immediate actions. We use the standard PEPA prefix notation $(a, \lambda).P$ to mean $(a^{[1]}, \lambda).P$ in SM-PEPA and the enhanced immediate prefix notation $(a, immediate).P$ to mean $(a^{[2]}, 1 : 1).P$. This gives each immediate transition equal weight (although we avoid simultaneous enabling of immediate actions in our use of probes here). Where user-defined weighting of immediate transitions is useful, $(a, \omega : immediate).P$ is translated to $(a^{[2]}, \omega : 1).P$. The immediate transition aspect is represented by the Laplace transform, $L(s) = 1$.

7.2   Immediate Actions and Probes

In working with immediate actions together with timed activities we need to clarify how these interact. The first design decision to resolve is with respect to the relative priority of actions and activities.

Priority: Immediate actions have priority over timed activities.

It is necessary to impose this requirement, as in GSPNs, so as to avoid potential problems associated with infinite re-enabling of timed and immediate activities. The priorities are obtained from the mapping to SM-PEPA, described earlier.

The second design decision relates to the names of immediate actions and timed activities.

Separation: Actions and activities have different names.

Concretely, we never have (α, r) and α in the same model. Similarly we never find $(\alpha, \top)$ and α in the same model. Co-operation in PEPA is based on the matching of names and so we have the following consequence from this design decision.

Homogeneity: Actions and activities do not co-operate.

That is, from the semantics of SM-PEPA, we disallow co-operation between immediate actions and timed activities. We use different terms for the two kinds of name-matching, saying that components *co-operate* on timed activities and *synchronise* on immediate actions.

We use immediate actions to report on the occurrence of a timed activity. For this reason timed activities must precede immediate actions.

Pursuit: In each model component every immediate action must be preceded by a timed activity.

We consider Markov models with non-deterministic choice not to be well-specified. This concern has been thoroughly studied previously with generalised stochastic Petri nets and stochastic activity nets [16]. Immediate actions have a default *weight* (of 1) thus $\alpha.P + \beta.Q$ expresses a weighted probabilistic choice between performing action α and continuing as P or performing action β and continuing as Q where each of these outcomes is equally likely. Syntactically $\alpha.P + \beta.Q$ is an abbreviation for $(\alpha, immediate).P + (\beta, immediate).Q$ and a 3:2 weighted choice is written as $(\alpha, 3 : immediate).P + (\beta, 2 : immediate).Q$.

Finally, the purpose of immediate actions in this context of stochastic probes is to send control signals between measurement components in the model. For this reason, we disallow individual occurrences of immediate actions; these must form a synchronisation point between measurement components.

Synchronisation: Each immediate action must be performed as a synchronisation event between two (or more) components.

Immediate actions may not be performed by one component individually. Thus, for example, we will never see $(\tau, immediate)$ in a model, because components cannot synchronise on the silent τ action.

It would be possible to avoid the need to use immediate actions, or indeed measurement components entirely, if we altered or rewrote the model to allow a particular passage-time calculation. We are not willing to do this. Customising the model in this way would injure its potential for re-use. Further, making visible at the top level particular start and stop activities at the beginning and end of the passage of interest may require context-sensitive renaming of activities and the introduction of choices between distinguished names, with a corresponding adjustment in the rates at which these activities are performed. Clearly there is great potential for human error here, even assuming that the modeller is willing to customise the model for just the measure of current interest.

Instead of handing the problem of adjusting the model to the modeller, we would rather automate the process to allow instrumentation of the model for location-aware service-level calculations. Introducing immediate actions allows us to do this.

8   Implementation

We have implemented the facility to describe location-aware probes as a companion to the software tool ipc, The Imperial PEPA Compiler [17]. This tool

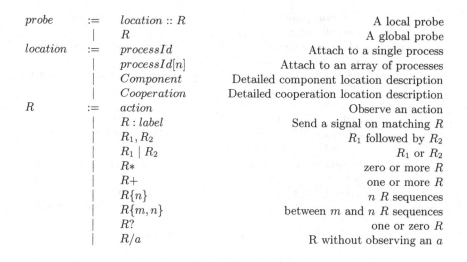

probe	:=	location :: R	A local probe
	|	R	A global probe
location	:=	processId	Attach to a single process
	|	processId[n]	Attach to an array of processes
	|	Component	Detailed component location description
	|	Cooperation	Detailed cooperation location description
R	:=	action	Observe an action
	|	R : label	Send a signal on matching R
	|	R_1, R_2	R_1 followed by R_2
	|	$R_1 \mid R_2$	R_1 or R_2
	|	R*	zero or more R
	|	R+	one or more R
	|	R{n}	n R sequences
	|	R{m,n}	between m and n R sequences
	|	R?	one or zero R
	|	R/a	R without observing an a

Fig. 5. The grammar for probe specification in ipc

generates compiled representations of PEPA models in a form suitable for input to the Hydra response-time analyser, the most recent release of the DNA-maca Markov chain analyser [18]. Although we have concentrated here mostly on passage-time computation, ipc also supports the computation of steady-state, transient and counting measures as described in [11].

The new software tool developed for this work is part of the ipclib suite, a collection of tools for the specification and evaluation of complex performance measures over Markovian process algebra models. These, and other software tools required, can be downloaded from http://www.dcs.ed.ac.uk/pepa.

Probes are defined using a regular-expression-like syntax fully explained in [6]. A probe specification is given by the grammar in Figure 5. The location part specifies where to attach the probe to the model system equation. The *processId* and *processId*[n] terms specify the location of the probe where that uniquely defines the location, otherwise the *Component* and *Cooperation* syntax are defined in Figure 6.

Where there are a number of choices for a given location, we can pick an individual component or cooperation using the syntax in Figure 6, for instance, by its numeric position. For example, the "third component called P" in the following system is underlined:

$$(P \bowtie_{\mathcal{K}} P) \bowtie_{\mathcal{L}} (\underline{P} \bowtie_{\mathcal{M}} P).$$

The "offering" keyword means that the component, or one of its derivatives, offers the action. We can place a probe at the "component offering *go, stop*" to measure the component using some actions the probe expects to see. This lets us use the same measurement description across a range of models.

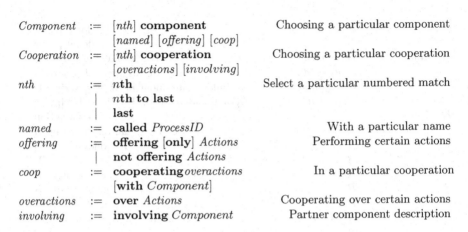

Component	:=	[*nth*] **component** [*named*] [*offering*] [*coop*]	Choosing a particular component
Cooperation	:=	[*nth*] **cooperation** [*overactions*] [*involving*]	Choosing a particular cooperation
nth	:=	**nth**	Select a particular numbered match
	|	**nth to last**	
	|	**last**	
named	:=	**called** *ProcessID*	With a particular name
offering	:=	**offering** [**only**] *Actions*	Performing certain actions
	|	**not offering** *Actions*	
coop	:=	**cooperating** *overactions* [**with** *Component*]	In a particular cooperation
overactions	:=	**over** *Actions*	Cooperating over certain actions
involving	:=	**involving** *Component*	Partner component description

Fig. 6. The grammar for probe placement

We can also distinguish between different instances of a component, based on how it cooperates with its neighbours. For example, the "component called P cooperating over b with component called Q" is underlined: $(P \bowtie_{\{a\}} Q) \bowtie_L (Q \bowtie_{\{b\}} \underline{P})$.

9   Conclusions

By adding location-awareness to probe specifications, we give the performance modeller the flexibility to identify model components within the model for selective instrumentation. We have shown that this can have a marked effect on the results produced when compared with an approach using only a single external observer, as used in previous work. By enhancing the probe translation to use immediate transitions, we can capture the response time of interest exactly with no introduction of error from the measurement activities of the probe.

In adding these features we have found it necessary to increase the expressiveness of the probe specification language. In doing this we have endeavoured to maintain a simple language syntax. The more straightforward the language which can be used to describe service-level agreements, the lower the barrier to entry to their use, allowing practitioners to access sophisticated performance evaluation technology and apply it at low cost. Our efforts here have been to design a concise, yet clear, mechanism for adding measurement components to model components in a way that improves the precision of the measurement specification and the accuracy of the result.

Acknowledgements. Ashok Argent-Katwala and Jeremy Bradley are supported by PerformDB, under EPSRC grant, EP/D054087/1. Allan Clark and Stephen Gilmore are supported by the EU FET-IST Global Computing 2 project SENSORIA ("Software Engineering for Service-Oriented Overlay Computers" (IST-3-016004-IP-09)). The Hydra response-time analyser was developed by Will Knottenbelt and Nick Dingle of Imperial College, London.

References

1. Meyer, J.F.: On evaluating the performability of degradable computing systems. IEEE Transactions on Computers C-29(8), 720–731 (1980)
2. Hillston, J.: A Compositional Approach to Performance Modelling. Cambridge University Press, Cambridge (1996)
3. Bernardo, M., Gorrieri, R.: A tutorial on EMPA: A theory of concurrent processes with non-determinism, priorities, probabilities and time. Theoretical Computer Science 202, 1–54 (1998)
4. Priami, C.: Stochastic π-Calculus. The Computer Journal 38(6), 578–589 (1995)
5. Strulo, B., Harrison, P.G.: Spades – A process algebra for discrete event simulation. J. Logic Computation 10(1), 3–42 (2000)
6. Argent-Katwala, A., Bradley, J.T., Dingle, N.J.: Expressing performance requirements using regular expressions to specify stochastic probes over process algebra models. In: Proceedings of the Fourth International Workshop on Software and Performance, Redwood Shores, California, USA, pp. 49–58. ACM Press, New York (2004)
7. AESOP performance modelling group: PerformDB performance model database, Imperial College London (2007), http://performdb.org
8. Marsan, M.A., Conte, G., Balbo, G.: A class of generalised stochastic Petri nets for the performance evaluation of multiprocessor systems. ACM Transactions on Computer Systems 2(2), 93–122 (1984)
9. D'Argenio, P.R., Hermanns, H., Katoen, J.-P., Klaren, R.: MoDeST – A modelling and description language for stochastic timed systems. In: de Luca, L., Gilmore, S. (eds.) PROBMIV 2001, PAPM-PROBMIV 2001, and PAPM 2001. LNCS, vol. 2165, pp. 87–104. Springer, Heidelberg (2001)
10. Bradley, J.T.: Semi-Markov PEPA: Modelling with generally distributed actions. International Journal of Simulation 6(3-4), 43–51 (2005)
11. Argent-Katwala, A., Bradley, J.T.: Functional performance specification with stochastic probes. In: Horváth, A., Telek, M. (eds.) EPEW 2006. LNCS, vol. 4054, pp. 31–46. Springer, Heidelberg (2006)
12. Kwiatkowska, M., Norman, G., Parker, D.: Stochastic model checking. In: Bernardo, M., Hillston, J. (eds.) SFM 2007. LNCS, vol. 4486, pp. 220–270. Springer, Heidelberg (2007)
13. Gilmore, S., Hillston, J., Ribaudo, M.: An efficient algorithm for aggregating PEPA models. IEEE Transactions on Software Engineering 27(5), 449–464 (2001)
14. Kemeny, J., Snell, J.: Finite Markov Chains. Van Nostrand (1960)
15. Marsan, M.A., Balbo, G., Conte, G., Donatelli, S., Franceschinis, G.: Modelling with Generalized Stochastic Petri Nets. John Wiley, Chichester (1995)
16. Deavours, D.D., Sanders, W.H.: An efficient well-specified check. In: Proceedings of PNPM 1999: the 8th International Workshop on Petri Nets and Performance Models, Zaragoza, Spain, IEEE Computer Society Press, Los Alamitos (1999)
17. Bradley, J., Dingle, N., Gilmore, S., Knottenbelt, W.: Derivation of passage-time densities in PEPA models using ipc: The Imperial PEPA Compiler. In: Kotsis, G. (ed.) Proceedings of the 11th IEEE/ACM International Symposium on Modeling, Analysis and Simulation of Computer and Telecommunications Systems, University of Central Florida, October 2003, pp. 344–351. IEEE Computer Society Press, Los Alamitos (2003)
18. Knottenbelt, W.: Generalised Markovian analysis of timed transition systems. Master's thesis, University of Cape Town (1996)

Multipoint Session Types for a Distributed Calculus

Eduardo Bonelli[1] and Adriana Compagnoni[2]

[1] LIFIA, Fac. de Informática, UNLP, Argentina and CONICET
eduardo@lifia.info.unlp.edu.ar
[2] Stevens Institute of Technology, Hoboken NJ 07030, USA
abc@cs.stevens.edu

Abstract. Session types are a means of statically encoding patterns of interaction between two communicating parties. This paper explores a distributed calculus with session types in which a number of fixed sites interact. The reduction schemes describing the operational semantics satisfy the locality principle: at most one site is involved. Both session engagement and data communication are local and asynchronous. Furthermore, our setting is a natural one in which the novel notion of multipoint session types, sessions in which more than two parties may be involved, can be introduced.

1 Introduction

We study a type based approach to structuring interaction between multiple distributed parties. A natural way of specifying interactions is to describe them in terms of sequences of types of the entities being sent or received. This is the idea behind *session types* [Hon93, HKT94, HVK98]. We develop a theory of session types for a core distributed calculus called DCMS (*distributed calculus with multipoint session types*). Regarding the distributed nature of DCMS we take, as fundamental working hypothesis, that the schemes defining its semantics follow the locality principle [Bou03]: all such schemes should involve at most one site.

In DCMS a *site* is an expression of the form $n[\![e]\!]$ where n is the name of the site and e is a *thread expression*. In order for sites to communicate we assume they share some set of global names which we refer to as *ports* given their similarity in nature to TCP/IP port numbers. Before exchanging information, however, sites must first establish a private channel through such a port. In all extant calculi with session types this is achieved via some variation of the following reduction scheme [HVK98]:

$$\text{request}\, a(k:s)\,\{P\} \mid \text{accept}\, a(k:\bar{s})\,\{Q\} \longrightarrow (\nu k)(P \mid Q)$$

Here a is the aforementioned port and s a *session type* indicating the communication pattern to be followed on the fresh private channel k. For example, s

G. Barthe and C. Fournet (Eds.): TGC 2007, LNCS 4912, pp. 240–256, 2008.

could be !int.!int.?int.*end* if the process to the left of the pipe were connecting to an adding server (the process to the right) that receives two numbers and sends back their sum. The output type !int is read as "send an int" and the input type ?int as "receive an int". The session type $\bar{s}$ is the *dual* of s, in this case reading ?int.?int.!int.*end* and establishes the pattern to be followed by the server at its own endpoint of the channel. Duality guarantees the absence of *communication errors*.

If we assume these primitives are executed at different sites, then the locality principle is seen to fail. We introduce an asynchronous connection mechanism whereby the connection request on a is buffered at the local sites of all the parties participating (as described below) in the session s. A similar treatment is given to language expressions for sending/receiving values and selection/branching. Before providing further details on how asynchronous connection is established, we discuss what form session types take in DCMS.

Session types in DCMS are *multipoint*: a channel has one positive or *master* endpoint and one or more negative or *slave* endpoints. Each input/output or branch/select type (see Sec. 3) in the sequence that makes up a session type is decorated with a label (a site name or site name variable) indicating the referenced site. As an example, consider the system $cl[\![e_1]\!] \parallel atm[\![e_2]\!] \parallel bk[\![e_3]\!]$, adapted from [BCG05], where cl, atm and bk stand for client, ATM and bank, resp. Consider the following session type s for a:

$$?^{cl}\text{int}.\&^{cl}\{$$
$$\text{withdraw}: ?^{cl}\text{int}.!^{bk}\text{int}. \oplus^{bk} \{\text{withdraw}: !^{bk}\text{int}.?^{bk}\text{int}.!^{cl}\text{int}.end,$$
$$\diamond\text{balance}: end\},$$
$$\diamond\text{balance}: !^{bk}\text{int}. \oplus^{bk} \{\text{balance}: ?^{bk}\text{int}.!^{cl}\text{int}.end,$$
$$\diamond\text{withdraw}: end\}$$
$$\}$$

It reflects the pattern from the view of the *atm* and is the type assigned to the master endpoint (the types of the other endpoints are discussed below). The ATM first expects an integer from the client (an id) and then an indication as to whether a withdrawal or a balance request is required. In the case of the former (the latter is described similarly), the amount is expected from the client after which this amount is sent to the bank followed by an indication that the client has requested a withdrawal. Note that the type *end* for **balance** indicates that this branch is not available for selection *here*. Other occurrences of the **balance** branch may have a type different from *end*, however all different uses of this branch should be compatible: any two non-end types should be the same. This encoding of multiple uses of branches in multipoint session types allows a higher degree of expressiveness not readily available in standard (binary) session types without adding new features (cf.[BCG05]): indeed, although this example could be presented using binary session types, it is at a loss in precision (for example, after receiving a withdraw request from the client, the ATM could issue multiple withdrawl requests from the bank without violating the patterns described by the binary session types).

$$\left\langle \begin{array}{cc} !^{bk}\mathrm{int.} \oplus^{bk} \{\mathtt{withdraw} : !^{bk}\mathrm{int.}?^{bk}\mathrm{int.}end, & !^{bk}\mathrm{int.} \oplus^{bk} \{\mathtt{balance} : ?^{bk}\mathrm{int.}end, \\ \diamond\,\mathtt{balance} : end\} & \diamond\,\mathtt{withdraw} : end\} \end{array} \right\rangle$$

$$?^{atm}\mathrm{int.}\&^{atm}\{\mathtt{withdraw} : ?^{atm}\mathrm{int.}!^{atm}\mathrm{int.}end, \\ \diamond\,\mathtt{balance} : !^{atm}\mathrm{int.}end\}$$

Fig. 1. Compatible session types

Returning to the discussion on connecting through ports, recall that the **request** primitive buffers a request on port a at each of the participating sites of the session type s. Each of these sites may agree to participate by issuing an **accept** primitive on a with some session type s'. It should be mentioned that we do not require that all participating sites issue an **accept** before engaging in communication. This reduces the possibility of stuck systems due to the absence or reluctance of a participating site to engage.

Suppose n is one of these participating sites (in our example, apart from atm, they are cl and bk as may be read off from s). In order to guarantee the absence of communication errors, the *part of* s that pertains to n (called the restriction of s to n) should be compared for duality with s'. This requires that all uses of the same branch be compatible, as mentioned above. In our example the restriction of s to bk yields the set of session types in Fig. 1(top) which, if compatible, allows the desired restriction to be obtained (Fig. 1(bottom)). These concepts are precised below.

Finally, the main ingredient in the proof of Communication Safety (Prop. 3) and Subject Reduction (Prop. 1) is the notion of *duality invariant*. As execution progresses session types pending consumption together with the values already sent out and residing in buffers distributed over the system are synthesized into sequences of types and values which we dub *trace types*. Trace types are compared using a binary relation that takes into account the asynchronous nature of communication. Subject Reduction is then formulated as the property that this invariant is upheld during reduction.

Structure of the paper. Sec. 2 introduces the syntax of DCMS together with its operational semantics. Types and typing rules are presented in Sec. 3. Here we also discuss compatibility and duality. Sec. 4 introduces the duality invariant and addresses Subject Reduction and Safety. Finally, we conclude and offer avenues for further research.

2   Syntax and Operational Semantics

2.1   Syntax

The syntax of DCMS is presented in Fig. 2. A *site* $n[\![e]\!]$ has a name n which ranges over a set of site names $m, n, \ldots$ and a *thread expression* e which is said to run at n. A *system* is a set of sites. For simplicity we assume all sites in a system to have different site names. Expressions may be one of the following. An identifier x; a value v (described below); a let expression let $x = e_1$ in e_2 with the usual interpretation; a connection, communication or branching expression. A *connection expression* can be of one of two kinds: request $a(u : s)\{e\}$ or accept $a(u : s, d)\{e\}$. The former requests asynchronously on port a that a new multipoint channel be established for communication following pattern s. The latter accepts such a request and replaces u with its corresponding endpoint and d with the name of the requesting site. A *communication expression* can be either send(u, λ, e) or receive(u, λ). The former sends the value resulting from e over u to location λ, whereas the latter reads from its local buffer u a value expected from λ. A branching expression can either be a select $\langle u, \lambda \rangle \rhd l$ in $\{e\}$ or branch $\langle u, \lambda \rangle \lhd \{l_1 : e_1 \diamond \ldots \diamond l_n : e_n\}$ (abbreviated $\langle u, \lambda \rangle \lhd_{i=1,n} \{l_i = e_i\}$). The former selects a branch by sending (asynchronously) a label over u to site λ. The latter reads a label from its local buffer u to see if λ has selected a branch. In the case that the buffer is empty, execution is blocked until a label is received.

A *value* is the result of a computation. It can be either true, false or null, the null expression. The additional run-time value (shaded in the figure) l is also possible. This value is not part of the user syntax but arises as a consequence of the definition of the operational semantics. Connection request values are discussed in Sec. 2.2. We write $\bar{v}$ (resp. $\bar{r}$) for a sequence of values (resp. connection request values) and ϵ for the empty such sequence. Also, $\bar{v}^R$ is the reverse sequence of $\bar{v}$.

We write FV(e) for the free variables of e. In particular, let binds the declared variable; in both request and accept u is bound in e, in accept d is also bound in s and e. Also, $e_1; e_2$ is shorthand for let $x = e_1$ in e_2 with $x \notin$ FV(e_2). We write $e\{x \mapsto v\}$ for the capture-free substitution of all free occurrences of x in e by v. Expressions are identified modulo renaming of bound variables.

2.2   Operational Semantics

The operational semantics of DCMS is described in terms of a *global buffer*. A global buffer (written h) associates a mapping describing the contents of its local port and local channel buffers to each location. We write h_n for the mapping for site n. A *port buffer* for a, denoted $h_n(a)$, is a sequence of connection request values $k^+@n$. The expression $k^+@n$ in the port buffer indicates the request by a foreign party n to establish a session of type s. A *channel buffer* for $k^p \mathbb{F} m$, denoted $h_n(k^p \mathbb{F} m)$, is a sequence of values received so far from location m via channel k^p.

Reduction schemes are presented in two groups: Fig. 3 presents those for expressions and Fig. 4 those for sites. A request expression adds a request to the buffer for port a at each of the sites participating in session type s. This set of sites is written PARTICIPANTS(s) and simply collects the set of all site names occurring in s. Additionally, a new empty channel buffer is locally created for each of the participating parties in preparation for receiving values from them. Finally, note that k^+ is required to be *locally* fresh in the sense that it has not been used as the master endpoint of a previously established

System	$S ::= n[\![e]\!]$	site
	$\mid\ S \parallel S$	distributed sites
Thread Expression	$e ::= x \mid v \mid \mathsf{let}\ x = e\ \mathsf{in}\ e$	
	$\mid\ \mathsf{request}\ a(u : s)\{e\}$	
	$\mid\ \mathsf{accept}\ a(u : s, d)\{e\}$	
	$\mid\ \mathsf{send}(u, \lambda, e)$	
	$\mid\ \mathsf{receive}(u, \lambda)$	
	$\mid\ \langle u, \lambda \rangle \triangleright l\ \mathsf{in}\ \{e\}$	
	$\mid\ \langle u, \lambda \rangle \triangleleft \{l_1 : e_1 \diamond \ldots \diamond l_n : e_n\}$	
Site Name	$\lambda ::= m \mid n \mid \ldots$	site name
	$\mid\ d$	site variable
Port	$a, b, \ldots$	
Polarity	$p ::= + \mid -$	
(Polarized) Channel	$u ::= k^p$	channel
	$\mid\ x \mid y \mid \ldots$	channel variable
Value	$v ::= \mathsf{true} \mid \mathsf{false} \mid \mathsf{null} \mid l$	
Conn. Request Value	$r ::= k^+ @ n$	
Heap	$h ::= [] \mid h \cdot [(m)(a) \mapsto \overline{r}]$	
	$\mid\ h \cdot [(m)(k^p \mathbb{F} n) \mapsto \overline{v}]$	

Fig. 2. Syntax

connection at that site. We write $h \cdot [(m_i)(a) \mapsto \overline{r}_i]_{i \in 1..o}$ as a shorthand for $h \cdot [(m_1)(a) \mapsto \overline{r}_1] \ldots [(m_o)(a) \mapsto \overline{r}_o]$. Likewise $h \cdot [(n)(k^p \mathbb{F} m_i) \mapsto \epsilon]_{i \in 1..o}$ stands for $h \cdot [(n)(k^p \mathbb{F} m_1) \mapsto \epsilon] \cdot \ldots \cdot [(n)(k^p \mathbb{F} m_o) \mapsto \epsilon]$.

The accept expression requires a pending connection request to be available at its local buffer for port a. It then creates a new local channel buffer for communication with the master endpoint and updates its local port buffer by removing the request. The k^- endpoint is assumed to be locally fresh for otherwise reduction blocks. The asynchronous send expression adds the value v to the local channel buffer of the corresponding endpoint. The result of executing a send expression is null. The receive expression blocks until a value is available at the appropriate local buffer and then reads it. The schemes for select and branch are similar to send and receive except that labels are sent or received rather than arbitrary values (and the appropriate branch is selected). Finally, there are two congruence schemes for reducing in the declaration part of a let expression and inside the last argument of a send expression.

Reduction schemes for sites are standard. Note that, as usual, reduction is modulo structural congruence ($\equiv$) rules.

3 Type System

Typing judgements for thread expressions and sites are $\Gamma; \Sigma \blacktriangleright_n e : t; \Sigma'$ and $\Gamma; \Sigma \blacktriangleright S : \Sigma'$, resp. The *standard environment* Γ maps standard types to

[REQUEST-R]
$$\text{request } a(u:s)\{e\}, h \cdot [(m_i)(a) \mapsto \overline{r}_i]_{i \in 1..k}$$
$$\longrightarrow_n$$
$$e\{u \mapsto k^+\}, h \cdot [(m_i)(a) \mapsto k^+@n \cdot \overline{r}_i]_{i \in 1..k} \cdot [(n)(k^+\mathbb{F}m_i) \mapsto \epsilon]_{i \in 1..k}$$
$$\text{where } \text{PARTICIPANTS}(s) = \{m_1, \ldots, m_k\} \text{ and } k^+ \notin h_n.$$

[ACCEPT-R]
$$\text{accept } a(u:s,d)\{e\}, h \cdot [(n)(a) \mapsto \overline{r} \cdot k^+@m]$$
$$\longrightarrow_n$$
$$e\{u \mapsto k^-\}\{d \mapsto m\}, h \cdot [(n)(a) \mapsto \overline{r}] \cdot [(n)(k^-\mathbb{F}m) \mapsto \epsilon]$$
$$\text{where } k^- \notin h_n.$$

[SEND-R]
$$\text{send}(k^p, m, v), h \cdot [(m)(k^{\overline{p}}\mathbb{F}n) \mapsto \overline{v}]$$
$$\longrightarrow_n$$
$$\text{null}, h \cdot [(m)(k^{\overline{p}}\mathbb{F}n) \mapsto v \cdot \overline{v}]$$

[RCV-R]
$$\text{receive}(k^p, m), h \cdot [(n)(k^p\mathbb{F}m) \mapsto \overline{v} \cdot v]$$
$$\longrightarrow_n$$
$$v, h \cdot [(n)(k^p\mathbb{F}m) \mapsto \overline{v}]$$

[SELECT-R]
$$k^p@m \rhd l_i \text{ in } \{e\}, h \cdot [(m)(k^{\overline{p}}\mathbb{F}n) \mapsto \overline{v}]$$
$$\longrightarrow_n$$
$$e, h \cdot [(m)(k^{\overline{p}}\mathbb{F}n) \mapsto l_i \cdot \overline{v}]$$

[BRANCH-R]
$$k^p@m \lhd \{\diamond_{i=1,n} l_i : e_i\}, h \cdot [(n)(k^p\mathbb{F}m) \mapsto \overline{v} \cdot l_i]$$
$$\longrightarrow_n$$
$$e_i, h \cdot [(n)(k^p\mathbb{F}m) \mapsto \overline{v}]$$

[LET-R]
$$\text{let } x = v \text{ in } e, h$$
$$\longrightarrow_n$$
$$e\{x \mapsto v\}, h$$

[CONGLET-R]
$$\frac{e_1, h \longrightarrow_n e_1', h'}{\text{let } x = e_1 \text{ in } e_2, h \longrightarrow_n \text{let } x = e_1' \text{ in } e_2, h'}$$

[CONGSEND-R]
$$\frac{e, h \longrightarrow_n e', h'}{\text{send}(k^p, m, e), h \longrightarrow_n \text{send}(k^p, m, e'), h'}$$

Fig. 3. Expression Reduction Schemes

term variables and ports and the *session environment* Σ maps located channels (i.e. expressions of the form $k^p@m$) to session types. Fig. 5 defines types and environments. We assume $a \notin \text{DOM}(\Gamma)$, $x \notin \text{DOM}(\Gamma)$ and $u \notin \text{DOM}(\Sigma)$ (i.e. $u@m \notin \text{DOM}(\Sigma)$ for any m). We write $\Sigma\{u \mapsto k^p\}$ for substitution of channel variable u by a channel k^p in environment Σ. Likewise, $\Sigma\{d \mapsto m\}$ stands for substitution of site variable d by a site name m in environment Σ. These notions are standard and hence their definitions omitted.

The aforementioned judgements are defined in terms of *typing rules* (Fig. 7 and 6). We only describe the interesting ones. However, before doing so, we need to provide a precise meaning to the part of a session type that pertains to a specific site. As mentioned, this part can only be computed if different uses of branches are *compatible*. Thus we first make this notion precise (Def. 2).

$$S_1 \parallel S_2 \equiv S_2 \parallel S_1$$
$$S_1 \parallel (S_2 \parallel S_3) \equiv (S_1 \parallel S_2) \parallel S_3$$
$$S_1 \equiv S_2 \Rightarrow S \parallel S_1 \equiv S \parallel S_2$$

$$\text{[Site-R]} \quad \frac{e, h \longrightarrow_n e', h'}{n[\![e]\!], h \longrightarrow n[\![e']\!], h'}$$

$$\text{[Par-R]} \quad \frac{S, h \longrightarrow S', h'}{S \parallel S_1, h \longrightarrow S' \parallel S_1, h'}$$

$$\text{[Str-R]} \quad \frac{S_1' \equiv S_1 \quad S_1, h \longrightarrow S_2, h' \quad S_2 \equiv S_2'}{S_1', h \longrightarrow S_2', h'}$$

Fig. 4. Site Reduction Schemes

Direction $\dagger ::= \ ? \ | \ !$
Partial Session Type $\pi ::= \epsilon \ | \ \dagger^\lambda t.\pi$
$\qquad\qquad\qquad | \ \ \&^\lambda\{l_1 : s, \dots, l_n : s\}$ Standard Env. $\Gamma ::= \epsilon \ | \ \Gamma, a : s \ | \ \Gamma, x : t$
$\qquad\qquad\qquad | \ \ \oplus^\lambda\{l_1 : s, \dots, l_n : s\}$ Channel Env. $\Sigma ::= \epsilon \ | \ \Sigma, u@n : s$
Session Type $s ::= \pi.end$
Standard Type $t ::= \textsf{bool} \ | \ \textsf{cmd} \ | \ s$

Fig. 5. Types

Definition 1 (Compatible Set). *A set of session types $\{s_1, \dots, s_n\}$ is compatible if $s_1 \sqcup s_2 \sqcup \dots \sqcup s_n$ is defined, where $\sqcup$ is the following commutative, associative operation:*

$$s \sqcup s = s$$
$$end \sqcup s = s$$
$$s \sqcup end = s$$
$$\pi.end \sqcup \pi'.end = (\pi \sqcup \pi').end$$

$$\pi \sqcup \pi = \pi$$
$$?^\lambda t.\pi_1 \sqcup \ ?^\lambda t.\pi_2 = \ ?^\lambda t.(\pi_1 \sqcup \pi_2)$$
$$!^\lambda t.\pi_1 \sqcup \ !^\lambda t.\pi_2 = \ !^\lambda t.(\pi_1 \sqcup \pi_2)$$
$$\&^\lambda_{i=1,n}\{l_i : s_i\} \sqcup \&^\lambda_{i=1,n}\{l_i : s_i'\} = \&^\lambda_{i=1,n}\{l_i : s_i \sqcup s_i'\}$$
$$\oplus^\lambda_{i=1,n}\{l_i : s_i\} \sqcup \oplus^\lambda_{i=1,n}\{l_i : s_i'\} = \oplus^\lambda_{i=1,n}\{l_i : s_i \sqcup s_i'\}$$

A session type is compatible when it is compatible from the viewpoint of all participating sites.

Definition 2 (Compatible session type). *A session type s is compatible if for all $m \in \text{Participants}(s)$, $\text{Simplify}(s \downarrow m)$ is compatible, where*

Typing Rules for Values

$$\frac{}{\Gamma; \Sigma \blacktriangleright_n \text{null} : \text{cmd}; \Sigma} \text{[NULL]} \qquad \frac{e \in \{\text{true}, \text{false}\}}{\Gamma; \Sigma \blacktriangleright_n e : \text{bool}; \Sigma} \text{[TRUE/FALSE]}$$

Typing Rules for Sites

$$\frac{\Gamma; \Sigma \blacktriangleright_n e : t; \Sigma'}{\Gamma; \Sigma \blacktriangleright n[\![e]\!] : \Sigma'} \text{[STARTSITE]} \qquad \frac{\Gamma; \Sigma \blacktriangleright S_1 : \Sigma' \quad \Gamma; \Sigma' \blacktriangleright S_2 : \Sigma''}{\Gamma; \Sigma \blacktriangleright S_1 \parallel S_2 : \Sigma''} \text{[PARSITE]}$$

Fig. 6. Typing Rules for Values and Sites

$$(\pi.end) \downarrow m = (\pi \downarrow m).end$$
$$(\dagger^\lambda t.\pi) \downarrow m = \begin{cases} \dagger^\lambda t.(\pi \downarrow m) & \text{if } \lambda = m \\ \pi \downarrow m & \text{otherwise} \end{cases}$$
$$\&^\lambda_{i=1,n}\{l_i : s_i\} \downarrow m = \begin{cases} \&^\lambda_{i=1,n}\{l_i : s_i \downarrow m\} & \text{if } \lambda = m \\ \{s_1 \downarrow m, \ldots, s_n \downarrow m\} & \text{otherwise} \end{cases}$$
$$\oplus^\lambda_{i=1,n}\{l_i : s_i\} \downarrow m = \begin{cases} \oplus^\lambda_{i=1,n}\{l_i : s_i \downarrow m\} & \text{if } \lambda = m \\ \{s_1 \downarrow m, \ldots, s_n \downarrow m\} & \text{otherwise} \end{cases}$$

where SIMPLIFY(_) *rewrites its argument, in all subterms, using the following term rewrite rule until a normal form is reached*[1].

$$\dagger^\lambda t.\{s_1, \ldots, s_n\} \longrightarrow \{\dagger^\lambda t.s_1, \ldots, \dagger^\lambda t.s_n\}$$

Under the assumption of compatibility we can define the *restriction* of a session type s to a site name m, for $m \in \text{PARTICIPANTS}(s)$, as $\sqcup(\text{SIMPLIFY}(s \downarrow m))$ and write $s \restriction m$. Finally, we introduce the notion of dual session types, used to type the accept expression. It is the standard notion that may be found in the extant literature on the subject: session types s and s' are *dual* (or (m, n)-*dual* to be more precise) if the predicate DUAL(s, s') holds:

$$\text{DUAL}(\epsilon, \epsilon) \text{ holds}$$
$$\text{DUAL}(\pi.end, \pi'.end) = \text{DUAL}(\pi, \pi')$$
$$\text{DUAL}(?^n t.\pi, !^m t.\pi') = \text{DUAL}(\pi, \pi')$$
$$\text{DUAL}(!^n t.\pi, ?^m t.\pi') = \text{DUAL}(\pi, \pi')$$
$$\text{DUAL}(\&^n_{i=1,p}\{l_i : s_i\}, \oplus^m_{i=1,p}\{l_i : s'_i\}) = \bigwedge_{i=1,p} \text{DUAL}(s_i, s'_i)$$
$$\text{DUAL}(\oplus^n_{i=1,p}\{l_i : s_i\}, \&^m_{i=1,p}\{l_i : s_i\}) = \bigwedge_{i=1,p} \text{DUAL}(s_i, s'_i)$$

The typing rules for values are standard, as are those for variables and let expressions. Note that the session environment remains unmodified in the case of values and variables given that these expressions themselves do not perform operations involving channels. A request on port a requires the type of a to be

---

[1] Uniqueness of normal forms follows from orthogonality and termination.

$$\frac{}{\Gamma, x : t; \Sigma \blacktriangleright_n x : t; \Sigma} \text{ [VAR]} \qquad \frac{\Gamma; \Sigma \blacktriangleright_n e : t; \Sigma' \quad \Gamma, x : t; \Sigma' \blacktriangleright_n e' : t'; \Sigma''}{\Gamma; \Sigma \blacktriangleright_n \text{ let } x = e \text{ in } e' : t'; \Sigma''} \text{ [LET]}$$

$$\frac{\Gamma, a : s; \Sigma, u@n : s \blacktriangleright_n e : t; \Sigma', u@n : end}{\Gamma, a : s; \Sigma \blacktriangleright_n \text{ request } a(u : s)\{e\} : t; \Sigma'} \text{ [REQUEST]}$$

$$\frac{\text{DUAL}(s \upharpoonright n, s'\{d \mapsto m\}) \quad m \text{ fresh} \quad \Gamma, a : s; \Sigma, u@n : s' \blacktriangleright e : t; \Sigma', u@n : end}{\Gamma, a : s; \Sigma \blacktriangleright_n \text{ accept } a(u : s', d)\{e\} : t; \Sigma'} \text{ [ACCEPT]}$$

$$\frac{\Gamma; \Sigma \blacktriangleright_n e : t; \Sigma', u@n :!^\lambda t.s}{\Gamma; \Sigma \blacktriangleright_n \text{ send}(u, \lambda, e) : cmd; \Sigma', u@n : s} \text{ [SEND]}$$

$$\frac{}{\Gamma; \Sigma, u@n :?^\lambda t.s \blacktriangleright_n \text{ receive}(u, \lambda) : t; \Sigma, u@n : s} \text{ [RECEIVE]}$$

$$\frac{\Gamma; \Sigma, u@n : s_i \blacktriangleright_n e : t; \Sigma'}{\Gamma; \Sigma, u@n : \oplus_{i=1,n}^\lambda \{l_i : s_i\} \blacktriangleright_n \langle u, \lambda \rangle \triangleright l \text{ in } \{e\} : t; \Sigma'} \text{ [SELECT]}$$

$$\frac{\Gamma; \Sigma, u@n : s_i \blacktriangleright_n e_i : t; \Sigma'}{\Gamma; \Sigma, u@n : \&_{i=1,n}^\lambda \{l_i : s_i\} \blacktriangleright_n \langle u, \lambda \rangle \triangleleft \{\diamond_{i=1,n} l_i = e_i\} : t; \Sigma'} \text{ [BRANCH]}$$

Fig. 7. Typing Rules for Expressions

declared globally with some session type s. The session environment is augmented with a new located channel (i.e. expression of the form $u@n$) before typing the body e. The type of the request expression is that of its body. Finally, the located channel is assumed to be completely consumed within this body. A accept also augments the session environment before typing its body, however it uses the declared type s'. A check is performed to verify whether the session type of a restricted to n, the site hosting the accept expression, is dual to s' (prior application of the substitution $\{d \mapsto m\}$). Given that the name of the site requesting the request is unknown, a fresh name is substituted for all occurrences of the site name variable d in s'. A $send(u, \lambda, e)$ expression requires that we first type e. The resulting session environment should include a session type for $u@n$ with a output type expression at the head. The type of e and the one declared in the output type should agree. Also, the label of the output type should agree with the destination declared in the send expression. The remaining typing rules may be understood along similar lines.

We conclude this section with a standard property of type systems also shared by DCMS.

Lemma 1 (Substitution Preserves Typing)

1. $\Gamma; \Sigma_1 \blacktriangleright_n e : t; \Sigma_2$ and $k^p \notin \Sigma_1$ implies $\Gamma; \Sigma_1\{u \mapsto k^p\} \blacktriangleright_n e\{u \mapsto k^p\} : t; \Sigma_2\{u \mapsto k^p\}$.
2. $\Gamma; \Sigma_1 \blacktriangleright_n e : t; \Sigma_2$ and $m \neq n$ implies $\Gamma; \Sigma_1\{d \mapsto m\} \blacktriangleright_n e\{d \mapsto m\} : t; \Sigma_2\{d \mapsto m\}$.

4 Subject Reduction and Safety

This section addresses Subject Reduction (SR) and Safety. The latter states that the type system guarantees the absence of communication errors while the former ensures that reduction preserves this state of affairs. We consider a communication error to be an execution state where a site attempts to read a value from its local buffer with the wrong type. In order to prove the absence of such errors, we must take into consideration how the system evolves during computation. During the course of reduction, values are sent out to local buffers distributed throughout the system. Accordingly, the types of channels are consumed. Therefore, both session types and the contents of buffers must be taken into account in order to determine safety. *Trace types* merge session types and values and are defined by the grammar on the left:

$$
\begin{aligned}
\tau ::= \ & end \\
| \ & \epsilon \\
| \ & \dagger t.\tau \\
| \ & v.\tau \\
| \ & \&_{i=1,n}\{l_i : \tau_i\} \\
| \ & \oplus_{i=1,n}\{l_i : \tau_i\}
\end{aligned}
\qquad
\begin{aligned}
O ::= \ & \square_{n \in \mathbb{N}} \\
| \ & !t.O \\
| \ & v.O \\
| \ & \oplus_{i=1,n}\{l_i : O_i\}
\end{aligned}
$$

The absence of site names in $\dagger$, $\&$ and $\oplus$ allows for a conciser presentation (correspondence between site names is guaranteed by the typing rule for accept). The grammar on the right defines *trace-output contexts*. In an asynchronous setting sending a value is a non-blocking operation and hence trace-output contexts represent the activity that could take place before a blocking operation is executed. An example trace-output context is $O = 3. \oplus \{l_1 : \square_1, l_2 : l_j.\square_2, l_3 : \square_3\}$ (assuming we may send integers): a 3 may be sent followed by one of l_1, l_2, l_3, followed by l_j in the case that l_2 was selected. Note that output-trace contexts may have more than one occurrence of a hole. Holes are indexed with a unique index indicated with a natural number as subscript. We write $O[\tau_1, \ldots, \tau_n]$ or simply $O[\boldsymbol{\tau}]_{k=1,n}$ for the result of filling in holes $\square_1$ to $\square_n$ with τ_1 to τ_n, resp. We often omit the subscript in $O[\boldsymbol{\tau}]_{k=1,n}$ (and write $O[\boldsymbol{\tau}]$) for the sake of readability.

Both trace types and trace-output contexts are used for stating the duality invariant, as motivated above. A further word on notation: $v : t$ is a shorthand for $\emptyset; \emptyset \blacktriangleright_n v : t; \emptyset$, for any n.

Definition 3 (A-Duality of trace types). *The binary relation on trace types called a(synchronous)-duality is defined inductively as follows:*

$$\frac{}{end \bowtie end} \; [\text{END}/\text{END-D}] \qquad\qquad \frac{}{\epsilon \bowtie \epsilon} \; [\epsilon/\epsilon\text{-D}]$$

$$\frac{\sigma \bowtie \tau \quad v : t}{?t.\sigma \bowtie v.\tau} \; [?/v\text{-D}] \qquad\qquad \frac{\sigma \bowtie \tau}{?t.\sigma \bowtie \,!t.\tau} \; [?/!\text{-D}]$$

$$\frac{\sigma \bowtie O[\tau] \quad v : t}{v.\sigma \bowtie O[?t.\tau]} \; [v/?\text{-D}] \qquad\qquad \frac{\sigma \bowtie O[\tau]}{!t.\sigma \bowtie O[?t.\tau]} \; [!/?\text{-D}]$$

$$\frac{\sigma_j \bowtie \tau \quad j \in 1..n}{\&_{i=1,n}\{l_i : \sigma_i\} \bowtie l_j.\tau} \; [\&/l\text{-D}] \qquad \frac{\sigma_i \bowtie \tau_i \quad for\ each\ i \in 1..n}{\&_{i=1,n}\{l_i : \sigma_i\} \bowtie \oplus_{i=1,n}\{l_i : \tau_i\}} \; [\&/\oplus\text{-D}]$$

$$\frac{\sigma \bowtie O[\tau_j]_{k=1,o} \quad j \in 1..n_k}{l_j.\sigma \bowtie O[\&_{i=1,n}\{l_i : \tau_i\}]_{k=1,o}} \; [l/\&\text{-D}]$$

$$\frac{\sigma_i \bowtie O[\tau_i]_{k=1,o} \quad for\ each\ i \in 1..n}{\oplus_{i=1,n}\{l_i : \sigma_i\} \bowtie O[\&_{i=1,n}\{l_i : \tau_i\}]_{k=1,o}} \; [\oplus/\&\text{-D}]$$

If $\sigma \bowtie \tau$, then we say σ is *a-dual* to τ. The intuition behind $\sigma \bowtie \tau$ is that σ is the session type of one endpoint of a session *including* the values this endpoint already sent out and likewise for the other endpoint τ. If they are both *end* or ϵ, then they are said to agree. If σ expects to receive a value of type t, then either it has already been sent ([?/v-D]) or the send operation is next in line according to the session type of τ ([?/!-D]). If σ has sent out a value ([v/?-D]), then τ must be prepared to read but not necessarily immediately. Indeed, first it may send out some other values (represented by the trace-output context O). Note that $O[?t.\tau]_{k=1,o}$ in [v/?-D] and [!/?-D] means $O[?t.\tau_1, \ldots, ?t.\tau_o]$. The remaining rules follow similar arguments.

Let $|s|$ stand for the trace type resulting from erasing all site name information from session type s. Note that dual session types are a-dual, as may be verified by induction on s:

Lemma 2. *Let s, s' be session types. Then* $\text{DUAL}(s, s')$ *implies* $|s| \bowtie |s'|$.

There are, of course, a-dual session types that are not dual. For example, we have $!t.?t'.end \bowtie \,!t'.?t.end$, for any t, t', however for no decoration of site names shall these types become dual. A-duality shares another property of duality, namely symmetry.

Lemma 3 (Symmetry of $\bowtie$)

1. $O[\sigma]_{k=1,o} \bowtie \tau$ *implies*
   (a) $O[?t.\sigma]_{k=1,o} \bowtie v.\tau$, *if* $v : t$.
   (b) $O[?t.\sigma]_{k=1,o} \bowtie !t.\tau$,
   (c) $O[\&_{i=1,n}\{l_i : \rho_i\}]_{k=1,o} \bowtie l_j.\tau$, *where* $\rho_{j_k} = \sigma_k$ *for each* $k \in 1..o$, *if* $j \in 1..n$.
2. $\sigma \bowtie \tau$ *implies* $\tau \bowtie \sigma$.

Proof. The first item is by induction on the structure of O and the second by induction on the derivation of $\sigma \bowtie \tau$ and resorts to the first one.

Some further properties of $\bowtie$ shall be useful. Items (1) and (2) below are used in the proof of Subject Reduction to show that the duality invariant (stated below) is upheld after a send and receive expression has been executed. Items (3) and (4) are required for the case of select and branch. The proof of all items is by induction on the length of $\overline{v}$.

Lemma 4. *1. $\overline{v}.!t.\tau_1 \bowtie \tau_2$ and $v : t$ imply $\overline{v}.v.\tau_1 \bowtie \tau_2$.*
2. $\overline{v}.?t.\tau_1 \bowtie v.\tau_2$ implies $v : t$ and $\overline{v}.\tau_1 \bowtie \tau_2$.
3. $\overline{v}. \oplus_{i=1,n} \{l_1 : \tau_i\} \bowtie \sigma$ and $j \in 1..n$ imply $\overline{v}.l_j.\tau_j \bowtie \sigma$.
4. $\overline{v}.\&_{i=1,n}\{l_i : \tau_i\} \bowtie l_j.\sigma$ implies $j \in 1..n$ and $\overline{v}.\tau_j \bowtie \sigma$.

Let us illustrate the first item with a concrete example. Consider the reduction of the expression $\mathsf{send}(k^p, m, v)$ at site n. The trace type $\overline{v}.!t.\tau_1 \bowtie \tau_2$ will be interpreted as the view of k^p at n as follows:

- $\overline{v}$ is the sequence of values already sent out by n on k^p to m and not consumed, and
- $!t.\tau_1$ is the channel type of k^p at n (with its site names erased).

Assuming this view is a-dual to that of m (represented by τ_2), Lemma 4(1) states that replacing $!t$ by v (the value sent by n on k^p) preserves a-duality.

Definition 4 (Duality Invariant). *A pair of session environment and global buffer satisfy the duality invariant, written $\mathrm{DUALITYINV}(\Sigma; h)$, if $k^+@n : s_n \in \Sigma$ and $k^-@m : s_m \in \Sigma$ implies*

$$\overline{v}^R.|s_n \lceil m| \bowtie \overline{w}^R.|s_m|$$

where $h_n(k^+\mathbb{F}m) = \overline{w}$ and $h_m(k^-\mathbb{F}n) = \overline{v}$.

One final ingredient is required before formulating our main result. Given that request and accept expressions create new communication channels, session environments may grow as reduction proceeds. Therefore, we define $\Sigma \leq \Sigma'$ as the smallest partial order that contains $\Sigma, u@\lambda : end \geq \Sigma$. The following property relating this partial order and typability is seen to hold.

Lemma 5 (Weakening)

1. $\Gamma; \Sigma_1 \blacktriangleright_n e : t; \Sigma_2$ and $\Sigma_1' \geq \Sigma_1$ imply $\Gamma; \Sigma_1' \blacktriangleright_n e : t; \Sigma_2'$, for some $\Sigma_2' \geq \Sigma_2$.
2. $\Gamma; \Sigma_1 \blacktriangleright S : \Sigma_2$ and $\Sigma_1' \geq \Sigma_1$ imply $\Gamma; \Sigma_1' \blacktriangleright S : \Sigma_2'$, for some $\Sigma_2' \geq \Sigma_2$.

Proposition 1 (SR for Expressions). *$\Gamma; \Sigma_1 \blacktriangleright_n e : t; \Sigma_2$ and $\mathrm{DUALITYINV}(\Sigma_1; h)$ and $e, h \longrightarrow_n e', h'$ implies $\Gamma; \Sigma_1' \blacktriangleright_n e' : t; \Sigma_2'$ and $\mathrm{DUALITYINV}(\Sigma_1'; h')$, for some Σ_1' and $\Sigma_2' \geq \Sigma_2$.*

Proof. By induction on the derivation of $e, h \longrightarrow_n e', h'$. We include a sample case, namely that of a [SEND-R] reduction step.

- $e = \mathsf{send}(k^p, m, v)$ and $h = h'' \cdot [(m)(k^{\overline{p}}\mathbb{F}n) \mapsto \overline{v}]$,
- $e' = \mathsf{null}$ and $h' = h'' \cdot [(m)(k^{\overline{p}}\mathbb{F}n) \mapsto v \cdot \overline{v}]$.

From $\Gamma; \Sigma_1 \blacktriangleright_n \mathsf{send}(k^p, m, v) : \mathsf{cmd}; \Sigma_2$ we deduce

1. $\Sigma_1 = \Sigma_{11}, k^p@n : !^m t.s$ and
2. $\Sigma_2 = \Sigma_{11}, k^p@n : s$.

Set $\Sigma'_1 = \Sigma_{11}, k^p@n : s$ and $\Sigma'_2 = \Sigma_2(= \Sigma'_1)$. Then note that

3. $\Gamma; \Sigma_{11}, k^p@n : s \blacktriangleright_n \mathsf{null} : \mathsf{cmd}; \Sigma_{11}, k^p@n : s$ is immediate and also
4. $\textsc{DualityInv}(\Sigma_{11}, k^p@n : s; h')$.

We develop (4). Suppose $p = +$ and $k^-@m : s_m \in \Sigma'_1$. Then also $k^-@m : s_m \in \Sigma_1$ and from $\textsc{DualityInv}(\Sigma_1; h)$:

$$\overline{v}^R.|!^m t.s \upharpoonright m| \bowtie \overline{w}^R.|s_m|$$

where $h_n(k^+\mathbb{F}m) = \overline{w}$. By Lemma 4(1),

$$\overline{v}^R.v.|s \upharpoonright m| \bowtie \overline{w}^R.|s_m|$$

Suppose now that $p = -$ and $k^+@m : s_m \in \Sigma'_1$. Then also $k^+@m : s_m \in \Sigma_1$ and from $\textsc{DualityInv}(\Sigma_1; h)$:

$$\overline{w}^R.|s_m \upharpoonright n| \bowtie \overline{v}^R.|!^m t.s|$$

where $h_n(k^-\mathbb{F}m) = \overline{w}$. We resort to symmetry of $\bowtie$ (Lemma 3), followed by Lemma 4(1), and finally symmetry again.

Prop. 1 holds for sites too. This requires first showing that:

Lemma 6 (Structural Congruence Preserves Typability). $\Gamma; \Sigma_1 \blacktriangleright S : \Sigma_2$ and $S \equiv S'$ implies $\Gamma; \Sigma_1 \blacktriangleright S' : \Sigma_2$.

We can then obtain the desired extension.

Proposition 2 (SR for Sites). $\Gamma; \Sigma_1 \blacktriangleright S : \Sigma_2$ and $\textsc{DualityInv}(\Sigma_1; h)$ and $S, h \longrightarrow S', h'$ implies $\Gamma; \Sigma'_1 \blacktriangleright S' : \Sigma'_2$ and $\textsc{DualityInv}(\Sigma'_1; h')$, for some Σ'_1 and $\Sigma'_2 \geq \Sigma_2$.

Proof. By induction on the derivation of $S, h \longrightarrow S', h'$.

- [SITE-R]. Then $S = n[\![e]\!]$, $S' = n[\![e']\!]$ and $e, h \longrightarrow_n e', h'$. Also, $\Gamma; \Sigma_1 \blacktriangleright_n e : t; \Sigma_2$ for some t. We conclude by resorting to Subject Reduction for Expressions.
- [PAR-R]. Then $S = S_1 \parallel S_2$, $S' = S'_1 \parallel S_2$ and $S_1, h \longrightarrow S'_1, h'$. Also, there exists Σ_3 such that $\Gamma; \Sigma_1 \blacktriangleright S_1 : \Sigma_3$ and $\Gamma; \Sigma_3 \blacktriangleright S_2 : \Sigma_2$. By the IH there exists Σ'_1, Σ'_3 such that $\Sigma'_3 \geq \Sigma_3$ and $\Gamma; \Sigma'_1 \blacktriangleright S_1 : \Sigma'_3$ and $\textsc{DualityInv}(\Sigma'_1; h')$. We conclude by Lemma 5.
- [STR-R]. Then there exist S_1, S_2 such that
  1. $S \equiv S_1$,

2. $S_1, h \longrightarrow S_2, h'$ and
3. $S_2 \equiv S'$.

From Lemma 6, $\Gamma; \Sigma_1 \blacktriangleright S_1 : \Sigma_2$. By IH, there exist Σ_1' and Σ_2' such that

4. $\Sigma_2' \geq \Sigma_2$,
5. $\Gamma; \Sigma_1' \blacktriangleright S_2 : \Sigma_2'$ and
6. DUALITYINV$(\Sigma_1'; h')$.

We conclude from (3) and Lemma 6.

In order to formally state Communication Safety we first introduce the convenient notion of evaluation context E:

$$E ::= \Box \mid \text{let } x = E \text{ in } e \mid \text{send}(k^p, m, E)$$

The hole in an evaluation environment singles out the part of the context where the redex involved in the next reduction step is located. Communication Safety says that if receive is the next expression to be reduced at some site n, then either the value expected has not been sent by the expected party yet and the channel type of this party coincides with the one expected by the receive, or the value is located in n's local buffer and has the expected type. Similarly for a branch expression.

Proposition 3 (Communication Safety). *Suppose* $\Gamma; \Sigma_1 \blacktriangleright_n e : t; \Sigma_2$ *and* DUALITYINV$(\Sigma_1; h)$.

1. *If* $e = E[\text{receive}(k^p, m)]$ *and* $k^{\overline{p}}@m \in \Sigma_1$, *then* $\Sigma_1(k^p@n) = ?^m t.s_n$ *and* $\Sigma_1(k^{\overline{p}}@n) = s_m$, *for some session types* s_n, s_m, *and*

$$\overline{v}^R.|?^m t.s_n \restriction m| \bowtie \overline{w}^R.|s_m|$$

   where $h_n(k^p \mathbb{F}m) = \overline{w}$ *and* $h_m(k^{\overline{p}} \mathbb{F}n) = \overline{v}$, *and one of two cases holds*
   (a) *either* $\overline{w}^R = \epsilon$ *and* $s_m = !^n t.s_m'$, *for some* s_m',
   (b) *or* $\overline{w}^R = w.\overline{w}'$ *and* $w : t$, *for some* w *and* $\overline{w}'$.

2. *If* $e = E[\langle k^p, m \rangle \vartriangleleft_{i=1,o} \{l_i = e_i\}]$ *and* $k^{\overline{p}}@m \in \Sigma_1$, *then* $\Sigma_1(k^p@n) = \&_{i=1,o}^m \{l_i : s_i'\}$ *and* $\Sigma_1(k^{\overline{p}}@n) = s_m$, *for some session types* s_i', s_m, *and*

$$\overline{v}^R.|\&_{i=1,o}^m \{l_i : s_i'\} \restriction m| \bowtie \overline{w}^R.|s_m|$$

   where $h_n(k^p \mathbb{F}m) = \overline{w}$ *and* $h_m(k^{\overline{p}} \mathbb{F}n) = \overline{v}$, *and one of two cases holds*
   (a) *either* $\overline{w}^R = \epsilon$ *and* $s_m = \oplus_{i=1,o}^n \{l_i : s_i'\}$, *for* s_i' *with* $i \in 1..o$,
   (b) *or* $\overline{w}^R = l_j.\overline{w}'$ *and* $j \in 1..o$, *for some* $\overline{w}'$.

The proof is by induction on E and relies on the following lemma:

Lemma 7. 1. $\overline{v}.?t.\sigma_1 \bowtie \overline{w}.\sigma_2$ *implies*
   (a) *either* $\overline{v} = \epsilon$ *and* $\sigma_2 = !t.\sigma_2'$, *for some* σ_2',
   (b) *or* $\overline{w} = w.\overline{w}'$ *and* $w : t$, *for some* $\overline{w}'$.
2. $\overline{v}.\&_{i=1,o} \{l_i : s_i\} \bowtie \overline{w}.\sigma_2$ *implies*
   (a) *either* $\overline{w} = \epsilon$ *and* $\sigma_2 = \oplus_{i=1,o} \{l_i : s_i'\}$, *for* s_i' *with* $i \in 1..o$,
   (b) *or* $\overline{w} = l_j.\overline{w}'$ *and* $j \in 1..o$, *for some* $\overline{w}'$.

5   Related Work

Session types were introduced in work of Honda et al [Hon93, HKT94, HVK98]. Since then it has been studied in various programming language paradigms: π-calculus like [GH99, HG03, GVR03, BCG05, BCG04], mobile ambients [GCDC06], CORBA [VVR03], functional threads [VRG04] and for object-oriented programming [DCYAD05, DCMYD06]. Recent work [YV06] revisits Subject Reduction for session types in view of some subtle issues related with naming.

Dezani-Ciancaglini et al [DCYAD05] present a distributed object-oriented language with session types. Although they also deal with a system of named sites, they use synchronous communication. In later work [DCMYD06] they considered higher-order sessions for roughly the same language and study a progress property. Also, they introduce buffers to model the operational semantics. However, connection is still synchronous and no notion of multipoint session types is studied. The work of Neubauer and Thiemann [NT04] seems to be the first work on session types for asynchronous communication. They consider a functional programming language which, although lacks a notion of multipoint session type nor is distributed, introduces an interesting relation on values similar to a-duality. Session types for asynchronous communication in the setting of operating system services [FAH+06] and object-oriented languages [CDCY07] has also been studied.

In recent [Yos07], independent work Honda, Yoshida and Carbone [HYC08] have developed a similar calculus of *multiparty* asynchronous session types. Interaction between participants is described by means of a "global type", essentially sequences of expressions of the form $p \rightarrow p' : k < U >$ expressing that "participant p sends a message of type U to channel k received by participant p'" (constructs for branching/selection and recursive types are also considered). Thus participants may share any number of channels, in contrast to our more restricted setting where only the master endpoint of a multipoint session type is shared. Since sharing gives rise to conflicts, a causality condition (dubbed "linearity" of global types) is required to ensure that global types are conflict-free. The remaining development is close to the one presented here: our notion of compatible session types corresponds to "coherence" of global types (Def. 4.2. in op. cit.), our duality invariant corresponds to "rollback of a message" (Sec. 5.2. in op. cit.). It should also be mentioned that Honda et al consider, in addition to Communication Safety, a progress property [DCMYD06]: roughly that, under certain conditions, a well-typed process that is ready to communicate shall always do so (Sec. 5.6. in op. cit.). We feel such a property should also hold for DCMS, although the details should be worked out.

6   Conclusions

We have presented a theory of session types for a core distributed calculus called DCMS. Distributed systems are represented as sets of named sites running threads. These sites communicate with each other by either sending/receiving values or selecting/branching on alternative code branches. The type system is built on the notion of session type: sequences of types of the entities being sent or received. The resulting session types are multipoint in the sense that they encode the interaction protocol to be followed by two or more parties. One such party is selected as a master and is the one that initiates a connection; multiple other parties are designated as slaves and each follow their own interaction scheme with the master. All communication expressions in DCMS are asynchronous: its semantics is described in terms of connection and communication buffers local to each site. Correctness of DCMS is proved in the form of a subject reduction theorem. This result consists in showing that a predicate on all buffers and the type assigned to each open connection called *duality invariant* is upheld at all times. This invariant roughly synthesizes run-time types, consisting of sequences of standard types and values, for channels and checks that any two endpoints have asynchronous dual such types. Asynchronous dual types is an extended notion of dual types that takes asynchronicity into account.

In order to bring out the fundamentals of combining session types and distributedness we have reduced our calculus to a minimal core. In particular, we have not included features such as run-time session type creation, sending/receiving session types, delegation of channels or spawning of new threads. This is left to future work. Type checking and inference based on the more lax notion of a-duality and an appropriate notion of subtyping should also be interesting avenues for further work.

Acknowledgements. To Healfdene Goguen and the referees for comments.

References

[BCG04]   Bonelli, E., Compagnoni, A., Gunter, E.: Typechecking safe process synchronization. In: FGUC 2004, ENTCS. Elsevier, Amsterdam (2004)

[BCG05]   Bonelli, E., Compagnoni, A., Gunter, E.: Correspondence assertions for process synchronization in concurrent communications. Journal of Functional Programming, Special issue on Language-Based Security, 15(2) (March 2005)

[Bou03]   Boudol, G.: Mobile calculi based on domains: Core programming model v1. Technical Report Deliverable 1.2.1, MIKADO Global Computing Project IST-2001-32222 (2003)

[CDCY07]   Coppo, M., Dezani-Ciancaglini, M., Yoshida, N.: Asynchronous session types and progress for object-oriented languages. In: Bonsangue, M.M., Johnsen, E.B. (eds.) FMOODS 2007. LNCS, vol. 4468, pp. 1–31. Springer, Heidelberg (2007)

[DCMYD06]   Dezani-Ciancaglini, M., Mostrous, D., Yoshida, N., Drossopoulou, S.: Session types for object-oriented languages. In: Thomas, D. (ed.) ECOOP 2006. LNCS, vol. 4067, pp. 328–352. Springer, Heidelberg (2006)

[DCYAD05]   Dezani-Ciancaglini, M., Yoshida, N., Ahern, A., Drossopoulou, S.: A distributed object-oriented language with session types. In: De Nicola, R., Sangiorgi, D. (eds.) TGC 2005. LNCS, vol. 3705, pp. 299–318. Springer, Heidelberg (2005)

[FAH⁺06]   Fähndrich, M., Aiken, M., Hawblitzel, C., Hodson, O., Hunt, G., Larus, J., Levi, S.: Language support for fast and reliable message-based communication in singularity os. In: Zwaenepoel, W. (ed.) EuroSys 2006. ACM SIGOPS, pp. 177–190. ACM Press, New York (2006)

[GCDC06]   Garralda, P., Compagnoni, A., Dezani-Ciancaglini, M.: BASS: Boxed ambients with safe sessions. In: Maher, M. (ed.) PPDP 2006, pp. 61–72. ACM Press, New York (2006)

[GH99]   Gay, S., Hole, M.: Types and subtypes for client-server interactions. In: Swierstra, S.D. (ed.) ESOP 1999 and ETAPS 1999. LNCS, vol. 1576, pp. 74–90. Springer, Heidelberg (1999)

[GVR03]   Gay, S., Vasconcelos, V., Ravara, A.: Session types for inter-process communication. Technical Report TR-2003-133, Department of Computing Science, University of Glasgow (2003)

[HG03]   Hole, M., Gay, S.: Bounded polymorphism in session types. Technical Report TR-2003-132, Department of Computing Science, University of Glasgow (2003)

[HKT94]   Honda, K., Kubo, M., Takeuchi, K.: An interaction-based language and its typing system. In: Halatsis, C., Philokyprou, G., Maritsas, D., Theodoridis, S. (eds.) PARLE 1994. LNCS, vol. 817, pp. 398–413. Springer, Heidelberg (1994)

[Hon93]   Honda, K.: Types for dyadic interaction. In: Best, E. (ed.) CONCUR 1993. LNCS, vol. 715, pp. 509–523. Springer, Heidelberg (1993)

[HVK98]   Honda, K., Vasconcelos, V., Kubo, M.: Language primitives and type discipline for structured communication-based programming. In: Hankin, C. (ed.) ESOP 1998 and ETAPS 1998. LNCS, vol. 1381, pp. 122–138. Springer, Heidelberg (1998)

[HYC08]   Kohei Honda, Nobuko Yoshida, and Marco Carbone. Multiparty asynchronous session types. In: POPL 2008 (to appear, 2008)

[NT04]   Neubauer, M., Thiemann, P.: Session types for asynchronous communication. Universität Freiburg (2004)

[VRG04]   Vasconcelos, V., Ravara, A., Gay, S.: Session types for functional multithreading. In: Gardner, P., Yoshida, N. (eds.) CONCUR 2004. LNCS, vol. 3170, pp. 497–511. Springer, Heidelberg (2004)

[VVR03]   Antonio Vallecillo, Vasco Vasconcelos, and António Ravara. Typing the behavior of objects and component using session types. ENTCS, 68(3) (2003)

[Yos07]   Yoshida, N.: Personal communication (September 5, 2007)

[YV06]   Yoshida, N., Vasconcelos, V.: Language primitives and type disciplines for structured communication-based programming revisited. In: SecRet 2006, ENTCS. Elsevier, Amsterdam (2006)

On Progress for Structured Communications*

Mariangiola Dezani-Ciancaglini[1], Ugo de'Liguoro[1], and Nobuko Yoshida[2]

[1] Dipartimento di Informatica, Università di Torino
[2] Department of Computing, Imperial College London

Abstract. We propose a new typing system for the π-calculus with sessions, which ensures the progress property, i.e. once a session has been initiated, typable processes will never starve at session channels. In the current literature progress for session types has been guaranteed only in the case of nested sessions, disallowing more than two session channels interfered in a single thread. This was a severe restriction since many structured communications need combinations of sessions. We overcome this restriction by inferring the order of channel usage, but avoiding any tagging of channels and names, neither explicit nor inferred. The simplicity of the typing system essentially relies on the session typing discipline, where sequencing and branching of communications are already structured by types. The resulting typing enjoys a stronger progress property than that one in the literature: it assures that for each well-typed process P which contains an open session there is an irreducible process Q such that the parallel composition $P|Q$ is well-typed too and it always reduces, also in presence of interfered sessions.

1 Introduction

Structuring communication to ensure safe interaction of concurrent systems is a central issue in the theory and practice of concurrent and mobile computing. Communication has indeed evolved into a growing number of complex activities, including several kinds of transactions as well as the offer and fruition of services through a large gamma of systems and networks. In this scenario computation consists in exchanging messages between loosely coupled parties, whose number and identity might also change dynamically. A case in point is delegation of activities to third parties in a client/server interaction, which often occurs transparently to the client.

Existing programming languages and standards, while adding communication primitives and syntactical tools to rule interaction, still leave to the programmer much of the responsibility in guarantying that the sequence of messages is well structured and that e.g. the client of a service will complete all needed transactions without getting into some unwanted state. The lack of structuring principles is also a defect of theoretical calculi such as the π-calculus: the economy of its syntax and semantics is an advantage for the elegance of the theory, but a drawback when controlling and disciplining specific kinds of behaviour.

---
* Work partially supported by EPSRC GR/T04724, GR/T03208, GR/T03215, IST2005-015905 MOBIUS, FP6-2004-510996 Coordination Action TYPES, and MURST PRIN'05 project "Logical Foundations of Distributed Systems and Mobile Code".

G. Barthe and C. Fournet (Eds.): TGC 2007, LNCS 4912, pp. 257–275, 2008.

A solution proposed by [22,12,10,2,9] consists in adding primitives to creat *sessions* to the π-calculus. A session is an abstraction of a series of communications through a private channel between two processes. It is created by a connection over a session channel (we call *shared*), that binds a channel name which, after connection, is substituted by a fresh private name (the *live channel*) in such a way that both privacy and duality are guaranteed, in the sense of the presence of input/output, branching/selection and delegation actions with the same live channel as subject (as it is checked by basic session type systems).

A central motivation for developing sessions and related type systems is to model safe hand-shake communications. In such a context privacy is not the unique desirable property of sessions, whereas compliance should be also guaranteed, namely that any session does not get stuck into some blocking state. To explain this safety issue, let us consider the following simple process with sessions, written in a π-calculus dialect that admits sequential composition (the semicolon):

$$P_1 = a(x).(x!\langle 3 \rangle; x?(z).x!\langle Apple \rangle; P_1')$$

This is a server process that first accepts the session communication through a shared channel a, and then performs a series of communication via the live channel which will replace x: it first outputs an integer, second inputs an integer, then outputs a string, and continue as P_1'. This behaviour is abstracted in the type system of [12] as the session type !int.?int.!string.

A client process intended to interact with the server above will have the following communication pattern:

$$Q_1 = \bar{a}(x).(x?(z).x!\langle 5+z \rangle; x?(z').Q_1')$$

This process requests the session communication through a and then performs the dual actions through x, typed by ?int.!int.?string. Once the session is established, and provided that only the two connected parties interact together, the communication over the live channel replacing x always *proceeds* at least up to the transmission of the string (and to the end of the session if x does not occur in P_1' nor in Q_1'), since their communication patterns are dual and private.

The main limitation of the approach is that two parties are assumed to interact in one session, and that these should not overlap. On the contrary in the case of e.g. Web Services communications [23], we need to establish more than one session between two or even multiple peers. In such a case, the safety is easily destroyed by the interleaving of two or more sessions. The simplest example is as follows:

$$P_2 = a(x).b(y).(x!\langle 3 \rangle; x?(z).y!\langle Apple \rangle; P_2') \quad Q_2 = \bar{a}(x).\bar{b}(y).(y?(z').x?(z'').x!\langle 5 \rangle; Q_2')$$

where the live channels replacing x and y create a circular dependency, causing deadlock. However in the session type systems from the literature, the latter processes are typable since the two sessions, one for x and the other for y, are correctly structured if taken in isolation. Thus progress of communications on live channels cannot be guaranteed when two or more sessions are mixed.

In the present work, we enhance existing session type systems to check progress with respect to live channels belonging to several sessions, while keeping the full session constructions, such as branching/selection, delegation and replication. The calculusis equipped with the construct for *sequencing* by which complex synchronisation behaviours such as joining and forking processes can be modelled. In spite of this extension, we show that a great simplification w.r.t. existing type systems for partial deadlock-freedom is achieved by relativising progress to session structured processes, avoiding any tagging of channels and names, neither explicit nor inferred. Our type system enjoys a progress property tailored to the soundness of session execution: for each well-typed process P which contains live channels there is an irreducible process Q such that the parallel composition $P|Q$ is well-typed too and it always reduces. The main technical difficulties for progress come from the two central features of the π-calculus: one is name hiding and passing, which can stop communications forever, and the other is process replication, which can destroy the bilinearity of communications.

Related work. The present paper moved from the desire to remove the limitations arising from strictly nested sessions in [8,6], where a similar progress property has been established in the case of an object-oriented, class-based language with communication primitives for sessions and with concurrency disciplined by the use of spawning commands. That result has been obtained under the condition that overlapping sessions can only be nested and that the inner sessions have been ended before the outer ones may proceed. Such a restriction is abandoned here; moreover we leave aside any particular paradigm of programming languages, and consider an extension of the full π-calculus with the session primitives of [12].

A tight relation exists with work by Kobayashi and his colleagues on partial deadlock-freedom. We were inspired by [15,17,24,19,18] in considering the relation between channel names induced by their use. However there are both technical and conceptual differences.

First we do not decorate types by multiplicities, namely we do not record levels of capabilities/obligations. Usages e.g. in [19], as well as "types" in the general framework of [14], are far more concrete behavioral descriptions than session types; hence the usages make sense as internal machinery of an automatic testing procedure, not as interfaces or abstract protocols for the user, we are looking for.

Second the structure of session types allows us to get a significant analysis without any form of tagging (neither by the user, nor by the typing system) and by means of a syntax directed type system, where the number of rules only depends on the richness of the language syntax. This is coherent with the aim of using session primitives and session types directly as the basis for programming language design, rather than as a tool to perform some form of static analysis. We leave for a future work to analyse relationships with the encodings of session types into functional and process linear typing systems [11,20].

Paper structure. Section 2 describes the syntax and the reduction rules of our calculus, and Section 3 discusses the type system. The features of well-typed processes are the subject of Section 4. The full definitions and proofs can be found at http://www.di.unito.it/~dezani/dly.pdf.

2   A Calculus for Structured Communications

2.1   Process Syntax

The π-calculus with sessions we consider is an extension of the calculus studied in [12], by means of *sequencing*, which allows to get forks and joins of processes [1]. The syntax is reported in Table 1.

For channels we use names and variables, the latter in place of bound names in accept/request and receive guarded processes. We further distinguish among two sorts of channel names: shared and live. *Shared channels* (called simply "names" in [12]), ranged over by $a, b, \ldots$ are used to open sessions, so that they can be either public or private; *live channels* (the "channels" of [12]), written as $k^p, k_1^q, \ldots$ are instead used only within open sessions, as it becomes clear in the definition of the operational semantics, so that their intended use (enforced by the reduction relation and the type system) is within the scope of the ν operator. The *polarity* $p \in \{+, -\}$ in apices of k^p represents the two end points created by the session initialisation. This notion is originally introduced in [10] to assure subject reduction (see [25] for the detailed discussion).

We write $a(x).P$ and $\bar{a}(x).P$ for the *accept* and *request* primitives of [12]. Instead of the recursive agents, we use *permanent accept*, written $\star a(x).P$, and for shared channels only, to model a server providing for a service to an unbounded number of clients. In case of $a(x).P$, $\star a(x).P$ and $\bar{a}(x).P$ the identifier a represents the public interaction point over which a session may commence. We say that a is the *subject* of the (permanent)

Table 1. Syntax

(Shared Channels)		(Live Channels)	
$c ::= x, y, z$	variable	$\kappa ::= x, y, z$	variable
$\mid a, b$	name	$\mid k^p$	polarised name

(Values)		(Expressions)	
		$e ::= v$	value
$v ::= a$	shared channel name	$\mid x, y, z$	variable
$\mid$ true, false	boolean	$\mid e + e$	sum
$\mid n$	integer	$\mid$ not(e)	not
		$\mid \ldots$	

(Processes)		(Prefixed processes)	
		$T ::= c(x).P$	accept
		$\mid \star c(x).P$	permanent accept
$P ::= \mathbf{0}$	inaction	$\mid \bar{c}(x).P$	request
$\mid T$	prefixed process	$\mid \kappa!\langle e \rangle$	data send
$\mid P \,; Q$	sequencing	$\mid \kappa?(x).P$	data receive
$\mid P \mid Q$	parallel	$\mid \kappa \triangleleft l.P$	selection
$\mid (\nu a)P$	shared channel hiding	$\mid \kappa \triangleright \{l_1 : P_1 [\!] \ldots [\!] l_n : P_n\}$	branching
$\mid (\nu k)P$	live channel hiding	$\mid \kappa!\langle\!\langle \kappa' \rangle\!\rangle$	session send
		$\mid \kappa?(\!(x)\!).P$	session receive
		$\mid$ if e then P else Q	if-then-else

accept/request process. The bound variable x represents the actual channel over which the session communications will take place, to be replaced by a live channel when the session has been opened and the connection established.

Constants and expressions of ground types (booleans and integers) are also added to model data, which are sent and received by means of the prefixes $\kappa!\langle e \rangle$ and $\kappa?(x).P$. We write $\kappa \triangleleft l.P$ for *selection*, which chooses an available branch, and $\kappa \triangleright \{l_1 : P_1 [] \ldots [] l_n : P_n\}$ for *branching*, which offers alternative interaction patterns; these are the same as in [12].

We use $\kappa!\langle\!\langle \kappa' \rangle\!\rangle$ (session send) and $\kappa?(\!(x)\!).P$ (session receive) for throw and catch primitives of [12] respectively. These are called *higher-order session communication primitives* since live channel κ' is passed via live channel κ. This mechanism enables to represent complex but safe delegations without interference by any third party.

In data and session sending, data and session receive, branching and selection, we call the channel κ the *subject* of the prefixed process.

The essential difference with the calculus in [12] is the adding of *sequencing*, written $P \, ; Q$, meaning that P is executed before Q. This syntax allows for complex forms of synchronisation as P can include any parallel composition of arbitrary processes.

The precedence of the operators building processes is (from the strongest) "$\triangleleft, \triangleright, \{\}$", ".", ";" and "| ". Moreover we convene that "." associates to the right. For example, $\kappa \triangleleft l.\kappa?(x).P; Q \,|\, R$ means $((\kappa \triangleleft l.(\kappa?(x).P)); Q) \,|\, R$. We often omit $\mathbf{0}$ and write $(\nu ab)(P)$ for $(\nu a)((\nu b)(P))$, etc. The bindings for channels and variables are standard and we write fn(P), fv(P) and bn(P) for free channels, free variables and bound channels respectively.

We say that the following pairs of prefixed processes are *dual*: $\{a(x).P, \bar{a}(x).Q\}$, $\{\star a(x).P, \bar{a}(x).P\}$, $\{k^p!\langle e \rangle, k^{\bar{p}}?(x).P\}$, $\{k^p \triangleleft l_i.P, k^{\bar{p}} \triangleright \{l_1 : Q_1 [] \ldots [] l_n : Q_n\}\}$ where $i \in \{1,\ldots,n\}$, and $\{k^p!\langle\!\langle \kappa \rangle\!\rangle, k^{\bar{p}}?(\!(x)\!).Q\}$.

2.2   Operational Semantics

We formalise the operational semantics of the calculus by a one-step reduction relation $\longrightarrow$, defined in Table 2, up to the standard structural equivalence $\equiv$ plus the rule $\mathbf{0}; P \equiv P$.

The reduction rules are based on those of the π-calculus with the session primitives [12,10], taking into account the behaviour of sequencing. By the interplay between parallel composition and sequencing it is handy to introduce evaluation contexts.

Evaluation contexts are defined by:

$$\mathcal{E}[\,] := [\,] \mid \mathcal{E}[\,]; P \mid \mathcal{E}[\,] \,|\, P \mid (\nu a)\mathcal{E}[\,] \mid (\nu k)\mathcal{E}[\,]$$

We say that a processes P is a *head subprocess* of a process Q if $Q \equiv \mathcal{E}[P]$ for some evaluation context $\mathcal{E}[\,]$. Examining the reduction rules it is easy to check that all prefixed processes (but in case of if-branching) in head positions reduce only if a dual subprocess is in head position too.

Rules [CON] and [CONR] are session initiation rules where two polarised fresh names are created, then restricted because the leading parts $P\{k^+/x\}$ and $Q\{k^-/y\}$ now share the channel k to start private interactions via k. In rule [CONR], we write

Table 2. Reduction

[CON] $\mathcal{E}_1[a(x).P] \mid \mathcal{E}_2[\bar{a}(y).Q] \rightarrow (\nu k)(\mathcal{E}_1[P\{k^+/x\}] \mid \mathcal{E}_2[Q\{k^-/y\}])$ (k fresh)

[CONR] $\mathcal{E}_1[\star a(x).P] \mid \mathcal{E}_2[\bar{a}(y).Q] \rightarrow (\nu k)(\mathcal{E}_1[P\{k^+/x\} \mid \star a(x).P] \mid \mathcal{E}_2[Q\{k^-/y\}])$

                                                                              (k fresh)

[COMV] $\mathcal{E}_1[k^p!\langle e\rangle] \mid \mathcal{E}_2[k^{\bar{p}}?(x).Q] \rightarrow \mathcal{E}_1[\mathbf{0}] \mid \mathcal{E}_2[Q\{v/x\}]$ $(e \downarrow v)$

[LABEL] $\mathcal{E}_1[k^p \triangleleft l_i.P] \mid \mathcal{E}_2[k^{\bar{p}} \triangleright \{l_1 : Q_1 [\!] \ldots [\!] l_n : Q_n\}] \rightarrow \mathcal{E}_1[P] \mid \mathcal{E}_2[Q_i]$ $(1 \leq i \leq n)$

[COMS] $\mathcal{E}_1[k^p!\langle\!\langle k_1^q \rangle\!\rangle] \mid \mathcal{E}_2[k^{\bar{p}}?(\!(x)\!).Q] \rightarrow Q\{k_1^q/x\} \mid \mathcal{E}_1[\mathbf{0}] \mid \mathcal{E}_2[\mathbf{0}]$ $(k_1 \notin \mathrm{bn}(\mathcal{E}_1[\,]) \,\&$

                                                            $\mathrm{bn}(\mathcal{E}_2[\,]) \cap \mathrm{fn}(Q) = \emptyset)$

[IF1]   **if** e **then** P_1 **else** $P_2 \rightarrow P_1$ $(e \downarrow \mathtt{true})$

[IF2]   **if** e **then** P_1 **else** $P_2 \rightarrow P_2$ $(e \downarrow \mathtt{false})$

[EVAL] $P \rightarrow P' \;\Rightarrow\; \mathcal{E}[P] \rightarrow \mathcal{E}[P']$

[STR] $P \equiv P' \quad P' \rightarrow Q' \quad Q' \equiv Q \;\Rightarrow\; P \rightarrow Q$

---

directly the effect of the replication of the accept/request action, and we do not postulate $\star a(x).P \equiv \star a(x).P \mid a(x).P$: hence replication is triggered only in presence of a dual session request, a property which simplifies the soundness of the typing system.

Rule [COMV] sends data ($e \downarrow v$ means that the expression e evaluates to the value v). Rule [LABEL] selects the i-th branch.

In rule [COMS] the process which receives the live channel is put in parallel with the evaluation contexts. Notice that this does not happen in the other rules. This rule allows for a safe form of delegation: indeed the process that receives the live channel must proceed, even if it is put in a context of overlapping sessions, as it happens e.g. in Example 4.3 of [12] (Fpt server). This is not guaranteed by the "standard" version of the rule below:

$$\mathcal{E}_1[k^p!\langle\!\langle k_1^q \rangle\!\rangle] \mid \mathcal{E}_2[k^{\bar{p}}?(\!(x)\!).Q] \rightarrow \mathcal{E}_1[\mathbf{0}] \mid \mathcal{E}_2[Q\{k_1^q/x\}] \quad (k_1^q \notin \mathrm{bn}(\mathcal{E}_1[\,]))$$

In fact by using this rule the process

$$\bar{a}(x).\bar{b}(y).(y?(\!(z)\!).z!\langle 5\rangle);x?(t).\mathbf{0} \mid a(x').b(y').y'!\langle\!\langle x' \rangle\!\rangle$$

reduces to $(\nu k)(k^-!\langle 5\rangle; k^+?(t).\mathbf{0})$ which is stuck, while its intended meaning should be that $y?(\!(z)\!).z!\langle 5\rangle$ completes and eventually 5 is communicated along k and replaced to t.

Notice that ";" is essential in order to identify which process must be executed in parallel with the contexts. The example above shows that – without the sequencing operator – we would be not able both to preserve progress and to require that a live channel is received before a communication on other live channels is executed. This is necessary e.g. for modelling a real estate agent who wants to be delegated by the owner before showing the house to potential buyers.

Rule [COMS] *subsumes* the channel passing rule named [PASS] in [12], since the standard version of this rule and [PASS] coincide if we ignore the sequencing. All other reduction rules are as usual.

3   Typing System for Progress Communication

The type system discussed in this section is designed to guarantee linearity of live channels, communication error freedom and progress.

3.1 Types

The full syntax of types is given in Table 3. *Partial session types*, ranged over by σ, represent sequences of communications, where ε is the empty communication, and $\sigma_1.\sigma_2$ consists of the communications in σ_1 followed by those in σ_2. We put $\varepsilon.\sigma = \sigma.\varepsilon = \sigma$ and we consider partial session types modulo this equality. The types !t and ?t express respectively the sending and reception of a value of type t. The types !s and ?s represent the exchange of a live channel, and therefore of an active session, with remaining communications determined by the ended session type s.

Table 3. Types

(direction)	$\dagger$ ::=	$!\ \mid\ ?$
(select/branch)	$\ddagger$ ::=	$\oplus\ \mid\ \&$
(partial session type)	σ ::=	$\varepsilon\ \mid\ \dagger t\ \mid\ \dagger s\ \mid\ \sigma.\sigma\ \mid\ \ddagger\{l_1 : \sigma_1, \ldots, l_n : \sigma_n\}$
(ended session type)	s ::=	$\sigma.\text{end}\ \mid\ \ddagger\{l_1 : s_1, \ldots, l_n : s_n\}$
(running session type)	τ ::=	$\sigma\ \mid\ s$
(standard type)	t ::=	$[s]\ \mid\ \text{bool}\ \mid\ \text{int}\ \mid\ \ldots$

The *selection type* $\oplus\{l_1 : \sigma_1, \ldots, l_n : \sigma_n\}$ represents the transmission of a label l_i chosen in the set $\{l_1, \ldots, l_n\}$ followed by the communications described by σ_i. The *branching type* $\&\{l_1 : \sigma_1, \ldots, l_n : \sigma_n\}$ represents the reception of a label l_i chosen in the set $\{l_1, \ldots, l_n\}$ followed by the communications described by σ_i.

An *ended session type* s is a partial session type concatenated either with end or with a selection or branching whose branches in turn are both ended session types. It expresses a sequence of communications with its termination, i.e. no further communications on that channel are allowed at the end.

A *running session type*, τ, ranges over both partial and ended session types.

A *shared session type* [s] is the type of shared channels, and has one or more endpoints, denoted by end. *Standard types* t are either shared session types or ground types.

Each running session type τ has a corresponding *dual*, denoted $\bar{\tau}$, which is obtained as follows:

- $\bar{?} =!\quad \bar{!} =?\quad \overline{\oplus} = \&\quad \overline{\&} = \oplus\quad \bar{\varepsilon} = \varepsilon$
- $\overline{\dagger t} = \bar{\dagger}t\quad \overline{\dagger s} = \bar{\dagger}s\quad \overline{\sigma_1.\sigma_2} = \overline{\sigma_1}.\overline{\sigma_2}\quad \overline{\ddagger\{l_1 : \sigma_1, \ldots, l_n : \sigma_n\}} = \bar{\ddagger}\{l_1 : \overline{\sigma_1}, \ldots, l_n : \overline{\sigma_n}\}$
- $\overline{\sigma.\text{end}} = \bar{\sigma}.\text{end}\quad \overline{\ddagger\{l_1 : s_1, \ldots, l_n : s_n\}} = \bar{\ddagger}\{l_1 : \overline{s_1}, \ldots, l_n : \overline{s_n}\}.$

Note that duality is an involution: $\bar{\bar{\tau}} = \tau$.

3.2 Motivating the Design of the Type System

This subsection discusses the key ideas behind the type system introduced in § 3.4 with some examples, focusing on progress.

Example 3.1 (Circularity of channels). As we explained in the Introduction, the order of session channels should be taken into account. Recall the processes P_2 and Q_2 from the Introduction:

$$P_2 = a(x).b(y).(x!\langle 3\rangle; x?(z).y!\langle Apple\rangle; P_2') \quad Q_2 = \overline{a}(x).\overline{b}(y).(y?(z').x?(z'').x!\langle 5\rangle; Q_2')$$

These processes use the channels bound by a and b in reverse order, hence they lead to a deadlock. This is prevented by the type systems, which allows instead to compose P_2 e.g. with

$$Q_2'' \equiv \overline{a}(x).\overline{b}(y).(x?(z').x!\langle 5\rangle; y?(z'').Q_2')$$

For a similar reason, we prohibit processes which have self-circularity of a shared channel like:

$$P_3 \equiv a(x).a(y).(x!\langle 3\rangle; y!\langle 5\rangle) \mid \overline{a}(z).\overline{a}(t).(t?(t').z?(w).\mathbf{0})$$

which reduces to the deadlock process $(\nu k k_1)(k^+!\langle 3\rangle; k_1^+!\langle 5\rangle \mid k_1^-?(t').k^-?(w).\mathbf{0})$.

On the other hand, we want to allow self-circularity of live channels. Fortunately we can profit of the expressiveness of the session types to simplify our type system: since sequences of communications are *already structured* by types, we do not have to consider the ordering between the same live channels. For example $P_4 \equiv k^p!\langle 3\rangle; k^p?(y).\mathbf{0}$ and $P_5 \equiv a(x).(x!\langle 3\rangle; x?(y).\mathbf{0})$ shall be typable according to our system.

Example 3.2 (Sequencing and live channels). It is a well known constraint for the linearly typed π-calculi to disallow live channels that occur in repeated processes. For example, $P_6 \equiv \star a(x).k^+!\langle 3\rangle$ in parallel with $P_7 \equiv \overline{a}(y).\mathbf{0} \mid \overline{a}(z).\mathbf{0}$ reduces to $P_6 \mid k^+!\langle 3\rangle \mid k^+!\langle 3\rangle$. This can be easily avoided using a standard technique. However, the sequencing operator requires more careful analysis for preserving progress. Let us consider a slightly different process $P_8 \equiv \star a(x).\mathbf{0}; k^+!\langle 3\rangle$ which does *not* destroy linearity, but progress. For example, $P_7 \mid P_8$ reduces to P_8 where the linearity of k^+ is preserved, but $k^+!\langle 3\rangle$ is blocked forever.

Example 3.3 (Bound shared channels). A bound shared channel which does not have a dual to start a session can block the communication on live channels forever, as in $P_9 \equiv (\nu a)(\overline{a}(x).k^+!\langle 3\rangle) \mid k^-?(y).\mathbf{0}$. The problem does not arise if the shared channel a is free, since we can always compose with a dual process, as in $P_{10} \equiv \overline{a}(x).k^+!\langle 3\rangle \mid k^-?(y).\mathbf{0} \mid a(z).\mathbf{0}$.

Example 3.4 (Shared channel passing). Shared channels can be sent only if their dual processes can communicate without waiting other communications to succeed. For example, consider the processes:

$$P_{11} \equiv \overline{a}(t).t!\langle b\rangle \mid a(x).\overline{c}(y).x?(z).\overline{z}(q).q?(w).y?(w').\mathbf{0} \quad P_{12} \equiv c(s).b(r).(s!\langle 3\rangle; r!\langle 4\rangle)$$

Then $P_{11} \mid P_{12}$ reduces to $(\nu k_b k_c)(k_b^+?(w).k_c^+?(t).\mathbf{0} \mid k_c^-!\langle 3\rangle; k_b^-!\langle 4\rangle)$ which is a deadlock. A safe process is the parallel composition of P_{11} and $P_{12}' \equiv c(s).b(r).(r!\langle 4\rangle; s!\langle 3\rangle)$.

Example 3.5 (Session channel passing). Live channels can be sent only if the receiving process does not contain live channels, as shown by the process:

$$P_{13} \equiv a(x).b(y).x!\langle\!\langle y \rangle\!\rangle \mid \overline{a}(t).\overline{b}(z).t?(\!(t')\!).(t'!\langle 3 \rangle; z?(w).\mathbf{0})$$

which reduces to the deadlock process $(\nu k_b)(k_b^+!\langle 3 \rangle; k_b^-?(w).\mathbf{0})$. A similar, but sound process is $P'_{13} \equiv a(x).b(y).x!\langle\!\langle y \rangle\!\rangle \mid \overline{a}(t).\overline{b}(z).(t?(\!(t')\!).t'!\langle 3 \rangle; z?(w).\mathbf{0})$, where $z?(w).\mathbf{0}$ is not in the body of $t?(\!(t')\!)$.

3.3 Typing Judgements

The typing judgements for expressions and processes are of the shape:

$$\Gamma \vdash e : t \qquad \Gamma; S; \mathcal{B} \vdash P : \Delta \,[\!]\, C$$

where we define:

$$\Gamma ::= \emptyset \mid \Gamma, x{:}t \mid \Gamma, a{:}[s] \qquad S ::= \emptyset \mid S, a \qquad \mathcal{B} ::= \emptyset \mid \mathcal{B}, a$$
$$\Delta ::= \emptyset \mid \Delta, \kappa{:}\tau \mid \Delta, \diamond \qquad C ::= \emptyset \mid C, \lambda \mid C, \lambda \prec \lambda'$$

Γ is the *standard environment* which associates variables to types and shared channel names to shared session types; S (resp. $\mathcal{B}$) is the set of *shared channel names* which can be *sent* (resp. *bound*); Δ is the *session environment* which associates live channels to running session types, and it can also contain the special symbol $\diamond$. The session environment Δ represents the open communication protocols of a process; the occurrence of $\diamond$ in Δ is used to prevent that any process sequentially composed with the term to which $\diamond$ has been assigned, might contain any occurrence of free live channels (see the definition of $\Delta \cdot \Delta'$ in Table 5). C is the *channel relation*, which is intended to give information about the ordering in the usage of channels. In C the metavariable λ ranges over shared and live channels. A well-formed channel relation is irreflexive w.r.t. shared channel names, and cannot contain cycles (see the next subsection).

3.4 Type System

Table 4 defines the type system. We omit the typing rules for expressions which are standard and identical with [25]. For typing processes, we use the auxiliary operators defined in Table 5. We list the key points of the typing rules for processes.

Session Initiation. As discussed in the examples, accept/request processes whose subjects are going to be bound or sent require particular care. The most liberal typing rules are *Acc* and *Req* where the shared channel can neither be bound nor sent. The resulting session environment is obtained by erasing the type of the bound channel x and the resulting channel relation is obtained by replacing x by a to prevent the circular ordering between names.

If the shared channel is a permanent accept, or when it can be bound but not sent, we cannot allow live channels in the continuation processes (see Examples 3.2 and 3.3). In rules *AccB*, *ReqB*, and *Acc**, the satisfaction of this condition is enforced by requiring that the session environment of the body process only contains the current channel and by typing the whole process with the session environment $\{\diamond\}$. Notice that session environments containing ◇ cannot be composed with session environments containing channels by the definition of $\Delta \cdot \Delta'$ given in Table 5.

Table 4. Typing Rules

$$\frac{\Gamma \vdash a:[\mathsf{s}] \quad \Gamma;\mathcal{S};\mathcal{B} \vdash P : \Delta, x:\mathsf{s} \,[\!]\, C \quad a \notin \mathcal{S} \cup \mathcal{B}}{\Gamma;\mathcal{S};\mathcal{B} \vdash a(x).P : \Delta \,[\!]\, C\{a/x\}} \; Acc \qquad \frac{\Gamma \vdash a:[\bar{\mathsf{s}}] \quad \Gamma;\mathcal{S};\mathcal{B} \vdash P : \Delta, x:\mathsf{s} \,[\!]\, C \quad a \notin \mathcal{S} \cup \mathcal{B}}{\Gamma;\mathcal{S};\mathcal{B} \vdash \bar{a}(x).P : \Delta \,[\!]\, C\{a/x\}} \; Req$$

$$\frac{\Gamma \vdash a:[\mathsf{s}] \quad \Gamma;\mathcal{S};\mathcal{B} \vdash P : \{x:\mathsf{s}\} \,[\!]\, C \quad a \notin \mathcal{S}}{\Gamma;\mathcal{S};\mathcal{B} \vdash a(x).P : \{\diamond\} \,[\!]\, C\{a/x\}} \; AccB \qquad \frac{\Gamma \vdash a:[\bar{\mathsf{s}}] \quad \Gamma;\mathcal{S};\mathcal{B} \vdash P : \{x:\mathsf{s}\} \,[\!]\, C \quad a \notin \mathcal{S}}{\Gamma;\mathcal{S};\mathcal{B} \vdash \bar{a}(x).P : \{\diamond\} \,[\!]\, C\{a/x\}} \; ReqB$$

$$\frac{\Gamma \vdash a:[\mathsf{s}] \quad \Gamma;\mathcal{S};\mathcal{B} \vdash P : \{x:\mathsf{s}\} \,[\!]\, C \quad a \notin \mathcal{S}}{\Gamma;\mathcal{S};\mathcal{B} \vdash \star a(x).P : \{\diamond\} \,[\!]\, C\{a/x\}} \; Acc^\star \qquad \frac{\Gamma \vdash c:[\mathsf{s}] \quad \Gamma;\mathcal{S};\mathcal{B} \vdash P : \{x:\mathsf{s}\} \,[\!]\, C}{\Gamma;\mathcal{S};\mathcal{B} \vdash \star c(x).P : \{\diamond\} \,[\!]\, C \backslash\backslash x} \; Acc^\star S$$

$$\frac{\Gamma \vdash a:[\mathsf{s}] \quad \Gamma;\mathcal{S};\mathcal{B} \vdash P : \Delta, x:\mathsf{s} \,[\!]\, C \quad a \notin \mathcal{B}}{\Gamma;\mathcal{S};\mathcal{B} \vdash a(x).P : \Delta \,[\!]\, C \backslash\backslash x} \; AccS \qquad \frac{\Gamma \vdash a:[\bar{\mathsf{s}}] \quad \Gamma;\mathcal{S};\mathcal{B} \vdash P : \Delta, x:\mathsf{s} \,[\!]\, C \quad a \notin \mathcal{B}}{\Gamma;\mathcal{S};\mathcal{B} \vdash \bar{a}(x).P : \Delta \,[\!]\, C \backslash\backslash x} \; ReqS$$

$$\frac{\Gamma \vdash c:[\mathsf{s}] \quad \Gamma;\mathcal{S};\mathcal{B} \vdash P : \{x:\mathsf{s}\} \,[\!]\, C}{\Gamma;\mathcal{S};\mathcal{B} \vdash c(x).P : \{\diamond\} \,[\!]\, C \backslash\backslash x} \; AccBS \qquad \frac{\Gamma \vdash c:[\bar{\mathsf{s}}] \quad \Gamma;\mathcal{S};\mathcal{B} \vdash P : \{x:\mathsf{s}\} \,[\!]\, C}{\Gamma;\mathcal{S};\mathcal{B} \vdash \bar{c}(x).P : \{\diamond\} \,[\!]\, C \backslash\backslash x} \; ReqBS$$

$$\frac{\Gamma \vdash e:\mathsf{t} \quad \text{if } e = a \text{ then } a \in \mathcal{S}}{\Gamma;\mathcal{S};\mathcal{B} \vdash \kappa!\langle e \rangle : \{\kappa:!\mathsf{t}\} \,[\!]\, \{\ell(\kappa)\}} \; Snd \qquad \frac{\Gamma, x:\mathsf{t};\mathcal{S};\mathcal{B} \vdash P : \Delta \,[\!]\, C}{\Gamma;\mathcal{S};\mathcal{B} \vdash \kappa?(x).P : \{\kappa:?\mathsf{t}\} \cdot \Delta \,[\!]\, \mathsf{pre}(\{\ell(\kappa)\}, C)} \; Rcv$$

$$\frac{\Gamma;\mathcal{S};\mathcal{B} \vdash P : \Delta, \kappa:\tau_i \,[\!]\, C \quad (1 \le i \le n)}{\Gamma;\mathcal{S};\mathcal{B} \vdash \kappa \triangleleft l_i.P : \Delta, \kappa: \oplus\{l_1 : \tau_1, \ldots, l_n : \tau_n\} \,[\!]\, \mathsf{pre}(\{\ell(\kappa)\}, C)} \; Sel$$

$$\frac{\Gamma;\mathcal{S};\mathcal{B} \vdash P_i : \Delta, \kappa:\tau_i \,[\!]\, C_i \quad (i = 1, \ldots, n)}{\Gamma;\mathcal{S};\mathcal{B} \vdash l_1 : P_1 \,[\!] \ldots [\!]\, l_n : P_n : \Delta, \kappa: \&\{l_1 : \tau_1, \ldots, l_n : \tau_n\} \,[\!]\, \mathsf{pre}(\{\ell(\kappa)\}, \cup_{1 \le i \le n} C_i)} \; Bra$$

$$\frac{\mathsf{s} \ne \varepsilon.\mathsf{end}}{\Gamma;\mathcal{S};\mathcal{B} \vdash \kappa!\langle\!\langle \kappa' \rangle\!\rangle : \{\kappa:!\mathsf{s}, \kappa':\mathsf{s}\} \,[\!]\, \{\ell(\kappa), \ell(\kappa'), \ell(\kappa) \prec \ell(\kappa')\}} \; CSnd$$

$$\frac{\Gamma;\mathcal{S};\mathcal{B} \vdash P : \{x:\mathsf{s}\} \,[\!]\, \{x\} \quad \mathsf{s} \ne \varepsilon.\mathsf{end}}{\Gamma;\mathcal{S};\mathcal{B} \vdash \kappa?(\!(x)\!).P : \{\kappa:?\mathsf{s}\} \,[\!]\, \{\ell(\kappa)\}} \; CRcv \qquad \frac{\Gamma \vdash e:\mathsf{bool} \quad \Gamma;\mathcal{S};\mathcal{B} \vdash P_i : \Delta \,[\!]\, C \quad (i = 1, 2)}{\Gamma;\mathcal{S};\mathcal{B} \vdash \text{if } e \text{ then } P_1 \text{ else } P_2 : \Delta \,[\!]\, C} \; If$$

$$\frac{\Gamma;\mathcal{S};\mathcal{B} \vdash P : \Delta \,[\!]\, C \quad \Gamma;\mathcal{S};\mathcal{B} \vdash Q : \Delta' \,[\!]\, C'}{\Gamma;\mathcal{S};\mathcal{B} \vdash P;Q : \Delta \cdot \Delta' \,[\!]\, \mathsf{pre}(C, C')} \; Seq \qquad \frac{\Gamma;\mathcal{S};\mathcal{B} \vdash P : \Delta \,[\!]\, C \quad \Gamma;\mathcal{S};\mathcal{B} \vdash Q : \Delta' \,[\!]\, C'}{\Gamma;\mathcal{S};\mathcal{B} \vdash P|Q : \Delta \cup \Delta' \,[\!]\, C \cup C'} \; Par$$

$$\frac{\Gamma, a:[\mathsf{s}];\mathcal{S};\mathcal{B} \vdash P : \Delta \,[\!]\, C \quad a \in \mathcal{B}}{\Gamma;\mathcal{S} \setminus a;\mathcal{B} \setminus a \vdash (\nu a)P : \Delta \,[\!]\, C \setminus a} \; HidingS \qquad \frac{\Gamma;\mathcal{S};\mathcal{B} \vdash P : \Delta, k^p:\tau, k^{\bar{p}}:\bar{\tau} \,[\!]\, C}{\Gamma;\mathcal{S};\mathcal{B} \vdash (\nu k)P : \Delta \,[\!]\, C \setminus k} \; HidingL$$

$$\frac{}{\Gamma;\mathcal{S};\mathcal{B} \vdash \mathbf{0} : \emptyset \,[\!]\, \emptyset} \; Inact \qquad \frac{\Gamma;\mathcal{S};\mathcal{B} \vdash P : \Delta \,[\!]\, C \quad \kappa \notin \mathsf{dom}(\Delta)}{\Gamma;\mathcal{S};\mathcal{B} \vdash P : \Delta, \kappa:\varepsilon \,[\!]\, C} \; Weak1 \qquad \frac{\Gamma;\mathcal{S};\mathcal{B} \vdash P : \Delta, \kappa:\varepsilon \,[\!]\, C}{\Gamma;\mathcal{S};\mathcal{B} \vdash P : \Delta, \kappa:\varepsilon.\mathsf{end} \,[\!]\, C} \; Weak2$$

If the shared channel can be sent but it cannot be bound we need to require that all communications on that channel can be executed without requiring other channels to communicate (Examples 3.4). This can be achieved by asking that the channel is minimal in the current channel relation, i.e. using $C \setminus\!\!\setminus x$ (defined in Table 5) in the conclusion. We ask $C \setminus\!\!\setminus x$ to be the channel relation in the conclusion of rules $AccS$, $ReqS$, and $Acc^\star S$, convening that the rules cannot be applied if it is undefined.

Rules $AccBS$ and $ReqBS$ put the above restrictions together, and are used to type shared channels which can be both bound and sent. In rules $Acc^\star S$, $AccBS$ and $ReqBS$ the subject can also be a variable, which will be replaced by a channel name which surely can be sent and possibly can be bound.

Session Communication. These rules add relevant information to session environments and to channel relations. Rule Snd checks that only shared channels in the set S are sent. The resulting session environment is $\{\kappa : t\}$, where κ is the subject of the sent process and t is the type of the sent expression. The resulting channel relation contains the name (without polarity) of the subject, where we define $\ell(\kappa) = k$ if $\kappa = k^p$ and $\ell(\kappa) = \kappa$ otherwise.

Rule Rcv uses the composition operator defined in Table 5 between session environments, which extends that one between running session types. In this way we can prefix by ?t the possible communications on channel κ prescribed by Δ. In the obtained channel relation all channels in C are bigger than $\ell(\kappa)$ by the definition of $\text{pre}(C, C')$ given in Table 5.

In rules Sel and Bra all τ_i are either partial session types or ended session types – this is guaranteed by the syntax of conditional session types (see Table 3).

Table 5. Operators for Types and Environments

Composition for Running Session Types and Session Environments

$$\tau \cdot \tau' = \begin{cases} \tau . \tau' & \text{if } \tau \text{ is a partial session type and } \tau' \text{ is a running session type} \\ \bot & \text{otherwise.} \end{cases}$$

$$\Delta \cdot \Delta' = \begin{cases} \Delta & \text{if } \diamond \in \Delta \text{ and } \Delta' \subseteq \{\diamond\}; \\ \Delta \setminus \Delta' \cup \Delta' \setminus \Delta \cup \{\kappa : \Delta(\kappa) \cdot \Delta'(\kappa) \mid \kappa \in \text{dom}(\Delta) \cap \text{dom}(\Delta')\} \cup \{\diamond \mid \diamond \in \Delta'\} \\ \quad \text{if } \diamond \notin \Delta \text{ and } \forall \kappa \in \text{dom}(\Delta) \cap \text{dom}(\Delta') : \Delta(\kappa) \cdot \Delta'(\kappa) \neq \bot; \\ \bot & \text{otherwise.} \end{cases}$$

Operators for Channel Relations

$$C \setminus \lambda = \{\lambda_1 \prec \lambda_2 \mid \lambda_1 \prec \lambda_2 \in C \ \& \ \lambda_1 \neq \lambda \ \& \ \lambda_2 \neq \lambda\} \cup \{\lambda' \mid \lambda' \in C \ \& \ \lambda' \neq \lambda\}$$

$$C \setminus\!\!\setminus x = \begin{cases} C \setminus x & \text{if } x \text{ is minimal in } C \\ \bot & \text{otherwise.} \end{cases}$$

$$\text{pre}(C, C') = (C \cup C' \cup \{\lambda \prec \lambda' \mid \lambda \in C \ \& \ \lambda' \in C'\})^*$$

where C^* is the transitive closure of C and λ is minimal in C if $\nexists \lambda' \prec \lambda \in C$.

The condition $\tau \neq \varepsilon.\text{end}$ in rules *CSnd* and *CRcv* allows to exchange only live channels which are not consumed, a reasonable requirement for a good programming discipline. Example 3.5 justifies the requirement that x is the only live channel of P.

Compositional and Structural Rules. Rule *Seq* takes into account that all communications in P must be executed before the communications in Q. Instead in rule *Par* the communications in P and Q can be executed in any order, and for this reason we take the unions of session environments and channel relations, with the proviso that $\Delta \cup \Delta'$ is defined only if $\text{dom}(\Delta) \cap \text{dom}(\Delta') = \emptyset$. In the rules for restrictions we use $C \setminus \lambda$ defined in Table 3, while $S \setminus a$ is simply the set S without a and similarly for $\mathcal{B} \setminus a$. The weakening rules are standard and necessary to type branching processes.

We assume that the typing rules are applicable only if *all channel relations in the conclusion of typing rules do not contain cycles and do not relate a shared channel with itself*: such channel relations are said to be well-formed. The first condition disallows a cycle between two names, while the second condition disallows $a \prec a$, but it allows both $k \prec k$ and $x \prec x$ in channel relations. These conditions are justified below through Example 3.1.

3.5   Justifying Examples

We end this section by briefly explaining why the negative examples given in § 3.2 cannot be typed, while the positive ones are typable. For the channel relations, we only write the order of the channels, omitting the set of channels.

Example 3.1: The channel relation of P_2 and Q_2'' is $\{a \prec b\}$, while the channel relation of Q_2 is $\{b \prec a\}$. Therefore $P_2 \mid Q_2$ creates a cyclic relation, which is not well-formed. Hence it is untypable. On the other hand, $P_2 \mid Q_2''$ is typable. Similarly, P_3 is not typable since $\{a \prec a\}$ is not a well-formed channel relation, while P_4 and P_5 are typable since $\{k \prec k\}$ and $\{x \prec x\}$ are well-formed channel relations.

Example 3.2: The process P_6 cannot be typed since Rules $Acc^\star$ and $Acc^\star S$ require the session environment of the body of the repeated accept to contain only x as subject, while the session environment of $k^+!\langle 3 \rangle$ contains k^+ as subject. The process P_8 is untypable since $\star a(x).\mathbf{0}$ must be typed by the session environment $\{\diamond\}$ (see rules $Acc^\star$ and $Acc^\star S$), and we cannot sequentially compose $\{\diamond\}$ with $k^+!\langle 3 \rangle$ by the definition of "." (used in rule *Seq*).

Example 3.3: The argument of Example 3.2 shows that $\overline{a}(x).k^+!\langle 3 \rangle$ cannot be typed by rules *ReqB* and *ReqBS*, hence P_9 is untypable, while P_{10} is typable since we can apply rules *Req* and *ReqS*.

Example 3.4: The process P_{12} cannot be typed by using rules *ReqS* and *ReqBS*, since r is not minimal in its channel relation $\{s \prec r\}$. Instead the process P_{12}' is typable using rules *ReqS* and *ReqBS*.

Example 3.5: The process $t?(\!(t')\!).(t'!\langle 3 \rangle;z?(w).\mathbf{0})$ in P_{13} cannot be typed, since rule *CRcv* requires the session environment of the body of the receive to contain only t' as subject. Rule *CRcv* allows to type $t?(\!(t')\!).t'!\langle 3 \rangle$ instead, hence P_{13}' is typable.

4 Subject Reduction and Progress

This section discusses the features of our type system. It naturally splits into two parts: subject reduction and progress. Proofs are given in outline, by stating the needed lemmas.

4.1 Subject Reduction

The basic property of substitutivity of values and live channels to variables within derivable typing judgments is easily checked by induction on derivations:

Lemma 4.1 (Substitution Lemma)

1. *If* $\Gamma,x:t;\mathcal{S};\mathcal{B} \vdash P : \Delta \,[\!] \, C$ *and* $\Gamma \vdash v:t$, *then* $\Gamma;\mathcal{S};\mathcal{B} \vdash P\{v/x\} : \Delta \,[\!] \, C$.
2. *If* $\Gamma;\mathcal{S};\mathcal{B} \vdash P : \Delta,x:\tau \,[\!] \, C$ *and* k *fresh, then* $\Gamma;\mathcal{S};\mathcal{B} \vdash P\{k^p/x\} : \Delta,k^p:\tau \,[\!] \, C\{k^p/x\}$.

Subject Equivalence, namely the invariance of typing judgments w.r.t. structural equivalence is proved straightforwardly by case analysis of the applied equivalence law.

Lemma 4.2 (Subject Equivalence). *If* $\Gamma;\mathcal{S};\mathcal{B} \vdash P : \Delta \,[\!] \, C$ *and* $P \equiv Q$, *then* $\Gamma;\mathcal{S};\mathcal{B} \vdash Q : \Delta \,[\!] \, C$.

Subject Reduction, namely the invariance of derivable typing judgments w.r.t. reduction, does not hold literally, since session types are shortened by reduction and the channel relation becomes a subrelation of the original one. However a weaker statement, which suffices for the present purposes, can be established modulo inclusion of channel relations and of prefixing of session environments, called below evaluation order.

Definition 4.3 (Inclusion). *The* inclusion between channel relations $C \Subset C'$ *holds if* $\lambda \in C$ *implies* $\lambda \in C'$ *and* $\lambda \prec \lambda' \in C$ *implies* $\lambda \prec \lambda' \in C'$, *for all* λ,λ'.

One might think of an ordering C as a graph (V,E) where V is the set of channels in C, and E is just the relation $\prec$; therefore $C \Subset C'$ holds if and only if C is a subgraph of C'.

The partial order among pairs of session environments defined next reflects the difference between two running session types before and after one step reduction.

Definition 4.4 (Evaluation Order)

1. $\sqsubseteq$ *is defined as the smallest partial order on running session types such that:* $\varepsilon \sqsubseteq \tau$; $\varepsilon.\text{end} \sqsubseteq s$; $\sigma_i \sqsubseteq \ddagger\{l_1 : \sigma_1,\ldots,l_n : \sigma_n\}$; $s_i \sqsubseteq \ddagger\{l_1 : s_1,\ldots,l_n : s_n\}$; *and* $\sigma \sqsubseteq \sigma'$ *implies* $\sigma \cdot \tau \sqsubseteq \sigma' \cdot \tau$.
2. $\sqsubseteq$ *is extended to session environments as follows:* $\Delta \sqsubseteq \Delta'$ *if* $\diamond \in \Delta$ *implies* $\diamond \in \Delta'$; *and* $k^p : \tau \in \Delta$ *implies* $k^p : \tau' \in \Delta'$ *and* $\tau \sqsubseteq \tau'$.

Before stating Subject Reduction, we recall the important notion of balanced session environments [10]. A session environment Δ is *balanced* if $k^p : \tau$ and $k^{\overline{p}} : \tau' \in \Delta$ imply $\tau' = \overline{\tau}$. The need of restricting to balanced session environments is illustrated by the process $k_1^p!\langle\text{true}\rangle \mid k_1^{\overline{p}}?(x).k_2^p!\langle x+1\rangle$, which would be typable by unbalanced session environments, whereas it reduces to $k_2^p!\langle\text{true}+1\rangle$ leading to a run-time error.

Theorem 4.5 (Subject Reduction)

1. *If $\Gamma \vdash e : t$ and $e \downarrow v$, then $\Gamma \vdash v : t$.*
2. *If $\Gamma; \mathcal{S}; \mathcal{B} \vdash P : \Delta \,[\![\, C$, where Δ is balanced, and $P \to Q$, then $\Gamma; \mathcal{S}; \mathcal{B} \vdash Q : \Delta' \,[\![\, C'$, for some Δ', C' such that Δ' is balanced, $\Delta' \sqsubseteq \Delta$ and $C' \Subset C$.*

The main part of the theorem, namely (2), says that after a session has begun the required communications are always executed in the expected order specified by channel orderings $C' \Subset C$ and session environments $\Delta' \sqsubseteq \Delta$.

4.2 Progress

This subsection discusses the main result of this paper, i.e. that typable processes which contain live channels can always execute, unless there are either accept or request head subprocesses with free subjects waiting for the dual processes. We formalise this property as follows:

Definition 4.6 (Progress). *A process P has the* progress *property if $P \to^* P'$ implies that either P' does not contain live channels or $P' \mid Q \to$ for some Q such that $P' \mid Q$ is well-typed and $Q \not\to$.*

A process P has the progress property if it is not blocked, and a process is blocked if it is some "bad" normal form. In our setting this means that some open session is incomplete. This might happen because some internal communication cannot occur and the obstacle cannot be removed either by internal or by external communications, namely by communications relative to other sessions. This is why we do *not* consider any irreducible process as blocked, rather we say that even an irreducible P has the progress property whenever it is able to interact in parallel with some Q such that $P \mid Q$ is well-typed: we ask Q itself to be irreducible to ensure that P actually participates in the reduction step.

The goal of this section is to show that any process representing a state in the running of some well-typed "program", has the progress property. Put together with Subject Reduction, this implies the safety of well-typed programs w.r.t. execution. By analogy with the theory of sequential languages, programs are closed processes; moreover they do not contain live channels, since the latters only appear while running. We call closed typable processes without live channels *initial*.

Definition 4.7 (Initial Processes). *A process P is* initial *if $\Gamma; \mathcal{S}; \mathcal{B} \vdash P : \emptyset \,[\![\, C$ for some Γ not containing variables and some C, with a deduction which does not use rule HidingL.*

Notice that initial processes cannot contain free live channels since the session environment is empty, nor bound live channels since to type them rule *HidingL* is needed.

As in the case of type systems for partial deadlock-freedom, we have first to establish a relation between the ordering in the usage of channels, especially the live ones, and their formal counterpart in our system, namely channel relations. To make this precise we define the auxiliary notion of precedence between prefixed subprocesses.

Definition 4.8 (Precedence). *The* precedence relation *between prefixed processes inside a process is defined by:* T *precedes* T' *in* P *if* P *contains either* $T = C'[T']$ *or* $C[T]; C'[T']$, *where* $C[\,]$, $C'[\,]$ *denote arbitrary contexts.*

The main lemma states that in a process obtained by reducing an initial process a live channel which is minimal in the channel relation can only be preceded by an accept/request on a free channel.

Lemma 4.9. *Let* P_0 *be initial and* $P_0 \to^* (\vec{vak})P$ *and* $\Gamma; S; \mathcal{B} \vdash P : \Delta [\![\, C$ *be derivable and let* T *be a subprocess of* P *with subject* k^p *and let* k *be minimal in* C, *then either* P *contains as head subprocess an accept or request on a free channel, or* P *contains* T *as head subprocess.*

Proof. *(Sketch)* The proof is a consequence of the following properties:

(P1) If P_0 is initial and $P_0 \to^* P$ and T precedes T' in P and k^p is the subject of T, then $k^{\overline{p}}$ cannot be the subject of T'.

(P2) If T precedes T' in a typable P and the subject of T' is a free live channel, then the subject of T is neither an accept/request on a bound channel nor a permanent accept.

(P3) Let P be typable with channel order C and let T precede T' in P. If k^p is the subject of T and k_1^q is the subject of T' and both k and k_1 are free in P, then we have $k \prec k_1 \in C$.

Property (P1) can be shown by induction on reduction.

Property (P2) is guaranteed by the use of $\diamond$ in the type system. If the subject of T' is a free live channel, then the session environment for typing a process which contains T' cannot be empty. By the hypothesis P contains either $T = C[T']$ or $C[T]; C'[T']$. In both cases, if T is an accept/request on a bound channel or a permanent accept, then T must be typed by one of the rules $AccB, ReqB, Acc^*, AccBS, ReqBS, Acc^*S$. These rules prescribe the session environment of the body of T only contains the channel variable bound by T and the session environment of T itself to be $\{\diamond\}$. So if $T = C[T']$ the thesis follows immediately, otherwise it follows from the definition of "$\cdot$" and the typing rule Seq.

For property (P3) notice that by the hypothesis P contains either $T = C[T']$ or $C[T]; C'[T']$. In the former case, since k^p is the subject of T, we know that $k \in C$; similarly, since k_1^q is the subject of T', we know that $k_1 \in C'$, for some C' such that $C = \text{pre}(k, C')$, since $C[T']$ is the conclusion of one rule among Rcv, Sel, Bra (not of $Send$ or $CSend$ because no prefix could occur inside). This implies that $k_1 \prec k \in C$ as desired. The case P contains $C[T]; C'[T']$ is similar and easier.

A key notion in showing progress is the natural correspondence between communication patterns and shapes of session types.

Definition 4.10. *Define* $\propto$ *between prefixed processes and partial/ended session types, as follows:*

$$\kappa!\langle e \rangle \propto !\mathsf{t} \quad \kappa?(x).P \propto ?\mathsf{t}$$
$$\kappa \triangleleft l_i.P \propto \oplus\{l_1 : \sigma_1, \ldots, l_n : \sigma_n\} \quad \kappa \triangleright \{l_1 : P_1 [\![\ldots [\![l_n : P_n\} \propto \&\{l_1 : \sigma_1, \ldots, l_n : \sigma_n\}$$
$$\kappa \triangleleft l_i.P \propto \oplus\{l_1 : \mathsf{s}_1, \ldots, l_n : \mathsf{s}_n\} \quad \kappa \triangleright \{l_1 : P_1 [\![\ldots [\![l_n : P_n\} \propto \&\{l_1 : \mathsf{s}_1, \ldots, l_n : \mathsf{s}_n\}$$
$$\kappa!\langle\!\langle \kappa' \rangle\!\rangle \propto !\mathsf{s} \quad \kappa?(\!(x)\!).P \propto ?\mathsf{s}$$

where $i \in \{1,\ldots,n\}$.

Then, by analysis of deductions using standard generation lemmas, we have:

Lemma 4.11. *If P is typable with a session environment Δ such that $\Delta(k^p) = \tau \notin \{\varepsilon, \varepsilon.\text{end}\}$, then P contains at least one prefix with subject k^p. Moreover if T is the prefix with subject k^p which precedes in P all other prefixes with subject k^p, then either $T \propto \tau$ or $\tau = \sigma.\tau'$ and $T \propto \sigma$.*

Since rule *HidingL* only restricts dual live channels with dual session types, we only get session environments which are balanced if we start from initial processes.

Lemma 4.12. *If P_0 is initial and $P_0 \rightarrow^* (\nu \vec{a}\vec{k})P$, then there exist $\Gamma, S, \mathcal{B}, \Delta, C$ such that $\Gamma; S; \mathcal{B} \vdash P : \Delta \Vert C$ and Δ is balanced.*

We eventually come to the Progress Theorem: for each process P obtained by reducing an initial process if P contains an open session, then there is an irreducible process Q such that the parallel composition $P|Q$ is well-typed too and it always reduces, also in presence of interleaved sessions.

Theorem 4.13 (Progress). *All initial processes have the progress property.*

Proof. Let P_0 be initial and $P_0 \rightarrow^* P$. If P does not contain live channels or $P \rightarrow P'$ there is nothing to prove. No head prefixed process in P is an if-then-else statement: otherwise P would reduce, since P is closed (being P_0 closed) and any closed boolean value is either true or false. If one head prefixed subprocess in P is an accept/request on a free channel a, then a must be in the domain of the standard environment Γ used to type P_0 and P. Let $\Gamma(a) = [s]$ and a head prefixed subprocess in P on a be an accept process. Then we can build Q as a request process on a which offers in the given order all the communications prescribed by $\bar{s}$ according to the relation $\propto$. Notice that if $\bar{s}$ prescribes to send live channels, then the body of Q must contain pairs of accept/request which produce these live channels. We can choose fresh names as subjects of these pairs of accept/request and put them in parallel, the accepts followed by all the communications prescribed by $\bar{s}$. More precisely, first we define in Table 6 the mapping β from a session type and a channel variable to a pair of a process and a session environment. Second we define the mapping α from a session type and a channel variable to a process as follows:

$$\alpha(s,x) = (\nu b_1 \ldots b_n)(b_1(y_1).\ldots.b_n(y_n).\mathsf{p}_1(\beta(s,x)) \,|\, \overline{b_1}(y_1).\alpha(\overline{s_1},y_1) \,|\, \ldots \,|\, \overline{b_n}(y_n).\alpha(\overline{s_n},y_n))$$
$$\text{if } \mathsf{p}_2(\beta(s,x)) = \{y_1:s_1,\ldots,y_n:s_n\} \text{ and } b_1,\ldots,b_n \text{ are fresh.}$$

Let $\Gamma(a) = [s]$: then we can take $Q = \bar{a}(x).\alpha(\bar{s},x)$ if P is an accept on the channel a, or $Q = a(x).\alpha(s,x)$ if P is a request on the channel a. If P_0 is initial then $\Gamma; S; \mathcal{B} \vdash P_0 : \emptyset \Vert C$ for some $\Gamma, S, \mathcal{B}, C$. By Theorem 4.5(2) we get $\Gamma; S; \mathcal{B} \vdash P : \emptyset \Vert C'$ for some $C' \subseteq C$. It is easy to verify by induction on the construction of Q that $\Gamma; S; \mathcal{B} \vdash Q : \Delta \Vert C''$ for some $C'' \subseteq C'$ and Δ, where $\Delta = \emptyset$ if $\mathsf{p}_2(\beta(s,x)) = \emptyset$ and $\Delta = \{\diamond\}$ otherwise. Since $C'' \subseteq C'$ implies that $C' \cup C''$ is well-formed, we conclude $\Gamma; S; \mathcal{B} \vdash P|Q : \Delta \Vert C' \cup C''$.

Otherwise P does not contain as head subprocess an accept or a request on a free shared channel, but P contains live channels. Let $P \equiv (\nu \vec{a}\vec{k})Q$, where $\vec{a}$ includes the set of all shared channels which are subjects of the head prefixed processes in P and $\vec{k}$ is

Table 6. Mapping β

$$\beta(\varepsilon,x) = (\mathbf{0},\emptyset)$$
$$\beta(\varepsilon.\mathtt{end},x) = (\mathbf{0},\emptyset)$$
$$\beta(!\mathtt{bool}.\tau,x) = (x!\langle \mathtt{true}\rangle; p_1(\beta(\tau,x)), p_2(\beta(\tau,x)))$$

...

$$\beta(![s].\tau,x) = ((\nu b)x!\langle b\rangle; p_1(\beta(\tau,x)), p_2(\beta(\tau,x)))\quad b\ \text{fresh}$$
$$\beta(?t.\tau,x) = (x?(y).p_1(\beta(\tau,x)), p_2(\beta(\tau,x)))\quad y\ \text{fresh}$$
$$\beta(!s.\tau,x) = (x!\langle\!\langle y\rangle\!\rangle; p_1(\beta(\tau,x)), p_2(\beta(\tau,x))\cup\{y{:}s\})\quad y\ \text{fresh}$$
$$\beta(?s.\tau,x) = (x?(\!(y)\!).p_1(\beta(\tau,x)), p_2(\beta(\tau,x)))\quad y\ \text{fresh}$$
$$\beta(\oplus\{l_1:\sigma_1,\ldots,l_n:\sigma_n\}.\tau,x) = (x\triangleleft l_1.p_1(\beta(\sigma_1,x)); p_1(\beta(\tau,x)), p_2(\beta(\sigma_1,x))\cup p_2(\beta(\tau,x)))$$
$$\beta(\&\{l_1:\sigma_1,\ldots,l_n:\sigma_n\}.\tau,x) = (x\triangleright\{l_1:p_1(\beta(\sigma_1,x))[\!]\ldots[\!]l_n:p_1(\beta(\sigma_n,x))\}; p_1(\beta(\tau,x)),\Delta)$$
$$\text{where } \Delta = \bigcup_{1\le i\le n} p_2(\beta(\sigma_i,x))\cup p_2(\beta(\tau,x))$$
$$\beta(\oplus\{l_1:s_1,\ldots,l_n:s_n\},x) = (x\triangleleft l_1.p_1(\beta(s_1,x)), p_2(\beta(s_1,x)))$$
$$\beta(\&\{l_1:s_1,\ldots,l_n:s_n\},x) = (x\triangleright\{l_1:p_1(\beta(s_1,x))[\!]\ldots[\!]l_n:p_1(\beta(s_n,x))\},\bigcup_{1\le i\le n} p_2(\beta(s_i,x)))$$

where $(\,,\,)$ is a pair constructor and $p_1(\,)$, $p_2(\,)$ are standard projections.

---

the set of all live channels which occur in P. By Lemma 4.12, we know that $\Gamma;S;\mathcal{B}\vdash Q:\Delta[\!]\,C$ for some $\Gamma,S,\mathcal{B},\Delta$ and C. Let k be a minimal live channel in C. This implies $k^p:\tau\in\Delta$ for some τ such that $\tau\notin\{\varepsilon,\varepsilon.\mathtt{end}\}$. By Lemma 4.12 Δ is balanced and then $k^{\overline{p}}:\overline{\tau}\in\Delta$. By Lemma 4.11 the channels k^p and $k^{\overline{p}}$ must occur in P. By Lemma 4.9 there are two head prefixed processes in P with subjects k^p and its $k^{\overline{p}}$, respectively. Notice that k^p and $k^{\overline{p}}$ have dual types, so that by Lemma 4.11 they are the subject of dual communication actions: it follows that P reduces.

5   Conclusion and Future Works

This paper proposed the first session typing system for the progress property on interleaving sessions, which are not necessarily nested. The resulting typing system ensures a strong progress property for a calculus allowing creation of new names and full concurrency, significantly enlarging the approach taken in [8,6]. In spite of the richness of the calculus, the typing system is based on the intuitive idea of channel causality without additional information on the syntax of the original session types.

For simplicity, we use the replications rather than the recursive agents [12] for representing infinite behaviours. We conjecture that our approach can be smoothly extended to recursive agents and recursive types. Since our typing system uses standard types, it can be easily integrated with subtyping [10], bounded session polymorphism [9] and correspondence assertions [2], guaranteeing the progress through the additional information represented by the sets of sent and bound channels and the channel relations. Challenging extensions are progress guarantees for choreographic (global) communication dependencies [5], combining more powerful means such as cryptography [7,3], refinements [21] and logical approach [4], by which more advanced security properties can be ensured.

The main reason for including the sequencing constructor was to provide a basis for the progress straightforwardly expendable to conventional imperative and Web Service languages [8,5,13]. In our experience of implementations, the sequencing construct is essential in writing optimal code for the branching structures. In particular, for our ongoing work on session types with advanced exception, we require explicit sequencing to model escaping blocks during session communication and resuming an intermediate session.

Without the sequencing constructor our calculus would only be slightly simpler. We could not get rid of the evaluation contexts, since progress requires that the process which receives a live channel is evaluated in parallel with the contexts, as shown in the example at the end of Section 2. For the same reason we need a terminator for the receiving process, role which is played by sequencing in the current calculus. To sum up without the sequencing constructor we would loose expressivity with the only gain of sparing one typing rule.

We plan to extend the current formulation and typing system for preserving the progress property on live channels, and to apply it to the design of a type safe exception handling for Java with session communication [13].

Acknowledgements. We thank Simon Gay, Naoki Kobayashi, Vasco Vasconcelos, the TGC referees and participants for their comments and discussions. The final version of the paper improved due to their suggestions.

References

1. Beaton, J., Weijiland, W.: Process Algebra. Cambridge Tracks in Theoretical Computer Science. In: CUP, vol. 18 (2000)
2. Bonelli, E., Compagnoni, A., Gunter, E.: Correspondence Assertions for Process Synchronization in Concurrent Communications. Journal of Functional Programming 15(2), 219–248 (2005)
3. Briais, S., Nestmann, U.: A Formal Semantics for Protocol Narrations. In: De Nicola, R., Sangiorgi, D. (eds.) TGC 2005. LNCS, vol. 3705, pp. 163–181. Springer, Heidelberg (2005)
4. Caires, L.: Spatial-Behavioral Types, Distributed Services, and Resources.. In: Montanari, U., Sannella, D., Bruni, R. (eds.) TGC 2007. LNCS, vol. 4661, pp. 263–280. Springer, Heidelberg (2007)
5. Carbone, M., Honda, K., Yoshida, N.: Structured Communication-Centred Programming for Web Services. In: De Nicola, R. (ed.) ESOP 2007. LNCS, vol. 4421, pp. 2–17. Springer, Heidelberg (2007)
6. Coppo, M., Dezani-Ciancaglini, M., Yoshida, N.: Asynchronous Session Types and Progress for Object-Oriented Languages. In: Bonsangue, M.M., Johnsen, E.B. (eds.) FMOODS 2007. LNCS, vol. 4468, pp. 1–31. Springer, Heidelberg (2007)
7. Corin, R., Deniélou, P.-M., Fournet, C., Bhargavan, K., Leifer, J.: Secure Implementations for Typed Session Abstractions. In: CSF 2007, pp. 170–186. IEEE Computer Society Press, Los Alamitos (2007)
8. Dezani-Ciancaglini, M., Mostrous, D., Yoshida, N., Drossopoulou, S.: Session Types for Object-Oriented Languages. In: Thomas, D. (ed.) ECOOP 2006. LNCS, vol. 4067, pp. 328–352. Springer, Heidelberg (2006)
9. Gay, S.: Bounded Polymorphism in Session Types. Mathematical Structures in Computer Science (to appear, 2007)

10. Gay, S., Hole, M.: Subtyping for Session Types in the Pi-Calculus. Acta Informatica 42(2/3), 191–225 (2005)
11. Gay, S., Vasconcelos, V.T.: Asynchronous Functional Session Types. TR 2007-251, Department of Computing, University of Glasgow (2007)
12. Honda, K., Vasconcelos, V.T., Kubo, M.: Language Primitives and Type Disciplines for Structured Communication-based Programming. In: Hankin, C. (ed.) ESOP 1998 and ETAPS 1998. LNCS, vol. 1381, pp. 22–138. Springer, Heidelberg (1998)
13. Hu, R., Yoshida, N., Honda, K.: Language and Runtime Implementation of Sessions for Java. In: ICOOOLPS 2007 (2007), http://www.doc.ic.ac.uk/~rh105/sessiondj.html
14. Igarashi, A., Kobayashi, N.: A Generic Type System for the Pi-Calculus. Theoretical Computer Science 311(1-3), 121–163 (2004)
15. Kobayashi, N.: A Partially Deadlock-Free Typed Process Calculus. ACM TOPLAS 20(2), 436–482 (1998)
16. Kobayashi, N.: Type Systems for Concurrent Programs. In: Aichernig, B.K., Maibaum, T.S.E. (eds.) Formal Methods at the Crossroads. From Panacea to Foundational Support. LNCS, vol. 2757, pp. 439–453. Springer, Heidelberg (2003)
17. Kobayashi, N.: A Type System for Lock-Free Processes. Information and Computation 177, 122–159 (2002)
18. Kobayashi, N.: Type-Based Information Flow Analysis for the Pi-Calculus. Acta Informatica 42(4–5), 291–347 (2005)
19. Kobayashi, N.: A New Type System for Deadlock-Free Processes. In: Baier, C., Hermanns, H. (eds.) CONCUR 2006. LNCS, vol. 4137, pp. 233–247. Springer, Heidelberg (2006)
20. Kobayashi, N.: Type Systems for Concurrent Programs. Extended version of [17], Tohoku University (2007)
21. Laneve, C., Padovani, L.: The Must Preorder Revisited: An Algebraic Theory for Web Services Contracts. In: Caires, L., Vasconcelos, V.T. (eds.) CONCUR. LNCS, vol. 4703, pp. 212–225. Springer, Heidelberg (2007)
22. Takeuchi, K., Honda, K., Kubo, M.: An Interaction-based Language and its Typing System. In: Halatsis, C., Philokyprou, G., Maritsas, D., Theodoridis, S. (eds.) PARLE 1994. LNCS, vol. 817, pp. 398–413. Springer, Heidelberg (1994)
23. Web Services Choreography Working Group. Web Services Choreography Description Language, http://www.w3.org/2002/ws/chor/
24. Yoshida, N., Berger, M., Honda, K.: Strong Normalisation in the π-Calculus. Information and Computation 191(2), 145–202 (2004)
25. Yoshida, N., Vasconcelos, V.T.: Language Primitives and Type Disciplines for Structured Communication-based Programming Revisited. In: SecReT 2006. ENTCS, vol. 171, pp. 73–93. Elsevier, Amsterdam (2007)

A Protocol Compiler for Secure Sessions in ML

Ricardo Corin[1,2] and Pierre-Malo Deniélou[1]

[1] MSR-INRIA Joint Centre
[2] University of Twente

Abstract. Distributed applications can be structured using *sessions* that specify flows of messages between roles. We design a small specific language to declare sessions. We then build a compiler, called s2ml, that transforms these declarations down to ML modules securely implementing the sessions. Every run of a well-typed program executing a session through its generated module is guaranteed to follow the session specification, despite any low-level attempt by coalitions of remote peers to deviate from their roles. We detail the inner workings of our compiler, along with our design choices, and illustrate the usage of s2ml with two examples: a simple remote procedure call session, and a complex session for a conference management system.

1 Sessions for Distributed Programming

Programming networked, independent systems is complex: when systems communicate through an untrusted network, and do not trust each other, enforcing security properties is hard. As a first step to simplify this task, programming languages and system libraries offer abstractions for common communication patterns (such as private channels or RPCs). Beyond simple abstractions for communications, distributed applications can often be structured as parties that exchange messages according to some fixed, pre-arranged patterns, called *sessions* (also named contracts, or workflows, or protocols). Sessions simplify distributed programming by specifying the behaviour of each network entity, or *role*: the parties can then resolve most of the programming complexity upfront.

Research on language-based support for sessions is active [5–7, 11, 14, 25, 26, 18]. Several of these works focus on developing type systems which statically ensure compliance to session specifications. There, type safety implies that user code that instantiates a session role always behaves as prescribed in the session. Thus, assuming that every distributed program participating in a session is well-typed, any run of the session follows its specification. There, being well-typed implies that every session participant is benign, and therefore complies with the session specification. Moreover, the network is also assumed to behave as expected, (e.g., delivering messages correctly).

However, in an adversarial setting, remote parties may not be trusted to play their role. Moreover, they may collude to attack compliant participants, and may also control the network, being able to eavesdrop, intercept, and modify en route messages. Hence, defensive implementations also have to monitor one another, in order to prevent any confusion between parallel sessions, to ensure authentication, correlation, and causal dependencies between messages, and to detect any deviation from the assigned roles of

G. Barthe and C. Fournet (Eds.): TGC 2007, LNCS 4912, pp. 276–293, 2008.

a session. Left to the programmer, this task involves delicate low-level coding below session abstractions, which defeats their purpose.

In order to keep sessions being useful and safe abstractions, we consider their secure implementation in terms of cryptographic communication protocols, by developing s2ml. To our knowledge, our compiler s2ml is the first to systematically compile session specifications to tailored cryptographic protocols, providing strong security guarantees beyond simple functional properties.

In ongoing work [8], we explore language-based support for sessions. We design a small language for specifying sessions, and identify a secure implementability condition. We present a formal language extending ML [20, 21] with distributed communication and sessions, designed in a way so that type safety yields functional guarantees: any sent message is expected by its receiver, with matching payload types. Then, we develop the s2ml compiler that translates sessions to cryptographic communication protocols, and formally show, as main result, that programs are shielded from any low-level attempt by coalitions of remote peers to deviate from their roles. In that work, we are most concerned about establishing the correctness of the code generation, and illustrate the approach with a small, simple toy example.

In this paper, we turn to present the details of our implementation. We focus on presenting our compiler s2ml, along with its usage and inner workings. Furthermore, we investigate the applicability and scalability of our approach to more realistic and complex settings through the study of a RPC session and a conference management system (CMS) session example.

Architecture. The basis of our work is a language for sessions with a CCS-like syntax to describe the different roles in a session. The s2ml compiler reads the session declarations, and works as follows: First, it checks correctness and security conditions on every session declaration, using an internal graph-based, global representation of the message flow. Then, it generates an ML module (along with its interface) for each specified session. The interface provides the programmer with the functions and types needed to execute every session role.

We rely on the ML language for several reasons. First, we take advantage of ML's typechecking to ensure functional correctness (i.e., that user code follows the session as prescribed), as opposed to having a dedicated type system as in other session types approaches. Second, our generated session role functions have (usually mutually recursive) types which are driven by user code using a continuation passing style (CPS) which allows for compact session programming. Finally, our generated types and cryptographic protocols heavily use algebraic types and pattern matching to specify and check the different allowed session paths. Our generated code uses the Ocaml syntax[1] and can be run in both Ocaml and F# [23].

Programs using the generated session interfaces can be linked against networking and cryptographic libraries, obtaining executable code. We provide three alternative implementations for these libraries: two concrete implementations using either Ocaml/OpenSSL and F#/Microsoft .NET produce executable code supporting distributed runs; a third, symbolic library implements cryptography using algebraic datatypes and communication via a Pi calculus library, useful for correctness checks and debugging.

---

[1] Although we use Ocaml syntax, our work can easily be adapted to other ML dialects.

Related Work. Session types have been first investigated for process calculi [15, 17, 26], to organize interactions on single channels. Behavioral types [7, 19] support more expressive sessions, typed as CCS processes possibly involving multiple channels. Another type system [4] also combines session types and correspondence assertions [16]. Recent works consider applications of session types to settings such as CORBA [24], a multi-threaded functional language [25], and a distributed object-oriented language [11]. In particular, the Singularity OS [14] explores the usage of typed contracts in operating system design and implementation. In all these works, type systems are used to ensure session compliance within fully trusted systems, excluding the presence of an (active, untyped) attacker. Sessions for Web Services are considered for the WSDL and WS-SecureConversation specification languages (see e.g. [1, 6]); Bhargavan *et al.* [1] verify security guarantees for session establishment and for sequences of SOAP requests and responses. In recent work, Carbone *et al.* [5] also present a language for describing Web interactions from a global viewpoint and describe their end-point projection to local roles. Their approach is similar to our treatment of session graphs and roles in Section 2; however, their descriptions are executable programs, not types. Honda *et al.* [18] subsequently consider multi-party session types and their local projections for the pi-calculus. More generally, distributed languages such as Acute and HashCaml [22, 10, 3] also rely on types to provide general functional guarantees for networked programs, in particular type-safe marshalling and dynamic rebinding to local resources.

Contents. Section 2 presents the session language that serves as input to s2ml, and introduces the examples. Section 3 illustrates the usage of sessions used by programmers to develop secure distributed applications, by coding the roles the RPC and CMS examples. Section 4 presents our security property, called session integrity, along with several threats our implementation needs to guard against. Section 5 focuses on the compiler s2ml: first it describes its inner workings, then it illustrates generated output for examples, and finally, it presents some performance measurements. Section 6 concludes. The project website [9] contains additional information, including a fully functional release of s2ml including the examples presented in this paper.

2   Specifying Sessions

A *session* is a static description of the valid message flows between a fixed set of roles. Every message is of the form $f(v)$, where f is the message descriptor, or label, and v is the payload. The label indicates the intent of the message and serves to disambiguate between messages within a session. Labels are also used as ML type constructors (and are thus expected to start with a capital letter).

We denote the roles of a session by $\mathcal{R} = \{r_0, \ldots, r_{n-1}\}$ where $n \geq 2$. By convention, the first role (r_0) sends the first message, thereby initiating the session. In any state of the session, at most one role may send the next message—initially r_0, then the role that received the last message. The session specifies which labels and target roles may be used for this next message, whereas the selection of a particular message and payload is left to the role implementation.

We define two interconvertible representations for sessions. A session is described either globally, as a graph defining the message flow, or locally, as a process for each role defining the schedule of message sends and receives:

Global graph. The graph describes the session as a whole and is convenient for discussing security properties and the secure implementability condition. Briefly, a session graph consists of nodes representing global states that are annotated with the corresponding active role (the role sending the next message), and edges between nodes labelled with message labels and the types of their payloads.

Local roles. Local role processes are the basis of our implementation: they describe the session from each role's point of view. They thus provide a direct typed interface for programming roles, and constitute our language for sessions.

2.1   A Language for Sessions

Our language for sessions has a CCS-like grammar for expressing local roles processes:

$\tau ::=$	Payload types
$\quad$ unit $\mid$ int $\mid$ string	base types
$p ::=$	Role processes
$\quad !(f_i\!:\!\tau_i\;;\;p_i)_{i<k}$	send
$\quad ?(f_i\!:\!\tau_i\;;\;p_i)_{i<k}$	receive
$\quad \mu\chi.p$	recursion declaration
$\quad \chi$	recursion
$\quad 0$	end
$\Sigma ::=$	Sessions
$\quad (r_i\!:\!T_i = p_i)_{i<n}$	initial role processes

Role processes can perform two communication operations: *send* (!) and *receive* (?). When sending, the process performs an internal choice between the labels f_i for $i = 0, \ldots, k-1$ and then sends a message $f_i(v)$ where the payload v is a value of types τ_i (for convenience, we consider only the basic unit, int and string types which simplify marshalling). Conversely, when receiving, the process accepts a message with any of the receive labels f_i (thus resolving an external choice). The $\mu\chi$ construction sets a recursion point which may be reached by the process χ; this corresponds to cycles in graphs. Finally, 0 represents a completion of the role for the session. On completion, a session role produces a value whose type T_i is specified in the process role $r_i\!:\!T_i = p_i$. For the return type T_i, we accept any ML type.

For convenience, we omit the trailing semicolon and 0 process at ending points. Also, our concrete syntax uses the keyword 'mu' for μ and keywords 'session' and 'role' in front of session and role definitions.

2.2   Example A: Remote Procedure Call

Figure 1 (top) shows a session graph for a simple RPC exchange, in which the client role, called **C**, sends the server role **S** a **Query** message (of payload type string), who answers with a **Response** message (of payload type int). The bottom part of the figure specifies the RPC session in terms of local role processes, using the above grammar.

After naming the session as **Rpc**, the two roles are defined with a return type and their local message flows: the client sends a **Query**, then expects a **Response** and finally returns an int; the server waits for a **Query**, then sends a **Response** and finally returns unit. These three lines are the actual input of our compiler.

session **Rpc** =
    role **client**:int = !**Query**:string; ?**Response**:int
    role **server**:unit = ?**Query**:string; !**Response**:int

Fig. 1. Session graph and Local roles for an RPC (file `rpc.session`)

2.3 Example B: A Conference Management System

We now describe a session for a conference management system. Although this system is rather simplified from a real life implementation, we believe it's significantly large in comparison with other case studies attempted in the session types literature.

Global description. Figure 2 shows the graph of a CMS session. There are three roles: **pc** (the conference organizer), **author**, and **confman** (the submission manager). All messages carry as a payload either a string value (which is used for the call for papers, paper submissions, and so on), or a unit value, when no payload is necessary.

The session proceeds as follows. Initially, the program committee pc sends a call for papers message, **Cfp**, to the prospective author [2]. The author then uploads a draft by sending an **Upload** message to the conference manager confman, who checks whether the draft meets the conference format (e.g., style format or compliance with the size). If the format is invalid, the confman replies to the author with a **BadFormat** message, with an explanation; at this point we have a loop in which the author can fix the draft and try again. Eventually the format is valid, and the confman replies with an **Ok** message. Now the author can submit a paper by sending a **Submit** message to the confman. Alternatively, it can choose to refrain from submitting a paper by sending a **Withdraw** message, which the confman communicates to the pc by sending a **Retract** message. If the author indeed submitted a paper, the confman forwards it to pc, who then will evaluate it. The pc can ask the author to revise the paper, by sending a **ReqRevise** message to the confman which will in turn send a **Revise** message to the author. This phase can loop until eventually the pc reaches a decision, and asks the confman to stop receiving revisions by sending a **Close** message. The confman answers with a **Done** message, and then the pc can notify the result to the author, enclosing possibly reviews for the paper. The notifications are either acceptance of the paper (sending an **Accept** message), or rejection (sending a **Reject** message), or a decision to exceptionally 'shepherd' the

---

[2] Our session specifications exclude broadcast, e.g. assuming here that the **Cfp** is sent to a single author, already chosen by the program committee. We can anyways replicate easily the program committee to start other sessions with other prospective authors.

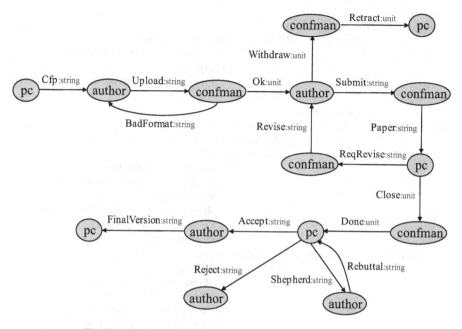

Fig. 2. A Conference Management System (CMS): Global graph

paper (sending a **Shepherd** message), in which the author can support her submission by sending a **Rebuttal**. This can again loop until the pc decides a final verdict, i.e. either accepting or rejecting the paper. In the case of acceptance, the author sends the pc a final version of the paper.

Local processes. Figure 3 presents the counterpart of the CMS graph from Figure 2 in terms of local roles. We illustrate local roles by describing in detail the behaviour of the author role. From the author's point of view, the session starts by receiving a **Cfp** message. A recursion point called **reformat** is created, and then the author checks the paper by sending an **Upload** message. If a **BadFormat** message is received, execution jumps back to the **reformat** point. If an **Ok** message is received, the author sets a recursion point called **submission** and then choose to either send a **Submit** or a **Withdrawal** message. For the latter, execution ends. For the former, another recursion step **discuss** is set, and several messages can be expected: either an **Accept**, in which the author ends by sending a **FinalVersion**, or a **Reject** which also ends execution, or a **Shepherd** message to which the author replies with a **Rebuttal** and then jumps back to **discuss**; finally, a **Revise** message may also be received, in which the author jumps back to **submission**.

3 Programming with Sessions

Once we know how to specify sessions, we are now ready to use them by instantiating the different session roles by actual principals. We start by describing how principals

session **Conf** =
  role **pc**:string = !**Cfp**:string; mu **start**.
                  ?(**Paper**:string; !(**Close**:unit; ?**Done**:unit; mu **discuss**.
                                   !(**Accept**:string; ?**FinalVersion**:string
                                   + **Reject**:string
                                   + **Shepherd**:string; ?**Rebuttal**:string; **discuss**)
                          + **ReqRevise**:string; **start**)
              + **Retract**:unit)
  role **author**:string = ?**Cfp**:string; mu **reformat**. !**Upload**:string;
                          ?(**BadFormat**:string; **reformat**
                        + **Ok**:unit; mu **submission**.
                              !(**Submit**:string; mu **discuss**.
                                  ?(**Accept**:string; !**FinalVersion**:string
                                  + **Reject**:string
                                  + **Shepherd**:string; !**Rebuttal**:string; **discuss**
                                + **Revise**:string; **submission**)
                            + **Withdraw**:unit))
  role **confman**:string = mu **uploading**. ?**Upload**:string;
                    !(**Ok**:unit; mu **waiting**.
                        ?(**Submit**:string; !**Paper**:string;
                        ?(**Close**:unit; !**Done**:unit
                        + **ReqRevise**:string; !**Revise**:string; **waiting**)
                        + **Withdraw**:unit; !**Retract**:unit)
                  + **BadFormat**:string; **uploading**)

Fig. 3. A Conference Management System: Local role processes (file `cms.session`)

are defined. Then we program the simple RPC session from the previous section, and finally we consider the more challenging case of the CMS session.

Principals. Principals are the network entities that instantiate session roles and specify networking information (i.e., IP address and port) and cryptographic credentials (X.509 certificates and private keys), for message delivery and security. Hence, when a programmer wants to initiate or join a session, she must register the principals in a local store used by our implementation. To this end, we provide a library for managing principals called **Prins**, with a **register** function, which when invoked as **register id filename inet port** registers a principal called **id**, whose credentials are in the file **filename**, IP address is **inet** and port is **port**.

For example, the programmer's source code for the CMS example that involves three participants includes the following calls:

```
let _ = Prins.register "alice" "alice.cer" "193.55.250.70" 8765
let _ = Prins.register "bob" "bob.cer" "193.55.250.71" 8765
let _ = Prins.register "charlie" "charlie.cer" "193.55.250.72" 8765
```

Files containing cryptographic credentials have to include an X.509 certificate, plus optionally the corresponding private key. Thus, user code can register both the running principal of a session role by including both keys (which the generated protocol will use to sign and verify messages) and other principals running the session, by registering only their certificates (which are used to verify other principals'signatures).

3.1   Programming an RPC Session

Initially we invoke our compiler with file `rpc.session` from Figure 1. Two files, called `Rpc.ml` and `Rpc.mli`, are created by `s2ml`. The former is the generated module implementing the RPC session, while the latter is its interface:

```
type principal = string
type principals = {client:principal; server:principal}

type result_client = int
type msg0 = Query of (string*msg1) and msg1 = {hResponse:(principals→ int→ result_client)}
val client : principals→ msg0→ result_client

type result_server = unit
type msg3 = {hQuery: (principals→ string→ msg4)} and msg4 = Response of (int*result_server)
val server : principal→ msg3→ result_server
```

The record type principals is used to instantiate roles with principals at runtime. Function **client** runs the session as the client role; when invoked, user code needs to provide:

1. a principals record populating the roles (since the client role is the session initiator, it can choose the session participants); and
2. a continuation (of type msg0) which drives the client role (our programming discipline relies on a CPS style, see below Section 3.2); here, it sends a **Query** message consisting of a payload to be sent (of type string) and a continuation message handler (of type msg1), which processes the answer **Response** message.

The server is symmetric, except that as responder it only needs to choose its identity.

We can easily program this RPC session; here's the code for a client that runs as `alice`, contacts `bob`, as the server, with a **Query** "Number?", and prints the response (we assume the principals registered as described above):

```
open Rpc
... (* register principals *)
let prins = {client = "alice"; server = "bob"}
let answer = client prins (Query("Number?",{hResponse = fun _ i → i}))
let _ = Printf.printf "Answer is %i\n" answer
```

A programmer runs a session (as role client) by calling function **client** providing a record instantiating roles to principals, and a continuation that sends and processes incoming messages. The first message (of type msg0) has to be sent by client, modelled by constructor **Query** which awaits for a payload and a continuation. Since the client then waits for a reply, the programmer has to provide a function handler for each of the possible incoming messages, those functions acting as continuations: here only one continuation is required (since only a **Response** may arrive) and the record has thus only one field labelled **hResponse**. The continuation has to be a function of two arguments: the first is the vector of principals involved in the session and the second is the payload of the corresponding message.

The code for a server ignoring the query content and responding with '42' is shown next. Although this code implements a single instance of a server, it is easy to replicate it, enabling several server instances.

```
open Rpc
... (* register principals *)
let _ = server "bob" {hQuery = fun _ _ → Response(42,())}
```

From the session programmer's point of view, sending a message is as simple as returning a constructed type with the right payload and continuation: **Response**(42,()). Here the continuation is simply unit as the session ends and any value of type **result_server** (which is above defined as unit) will do. All the rest is taken care by the module **Rpc** generated by s2ml, like message formatting, cryptographic signing, and routing.

Finally, in order to obtain an executable, we compile this user code with Rpc.ml and libraries for implementing cryptographic operations (like hashing and signing) and networking using the standard Ocaml compiler. Conveniently, if user code implements a session incorrectly (i.e., not respecting the message flow), then a type error (indicating the incompatible message) is given.

3.2   Session Programming and CMS Example

We run s2ml with the CMS example of Figure 3 on file cms.session. This produces files Conf.ml and Conf.mli. As in the RPC example, the interface Conf.mli contains a specialized principals record plus generated types and functions for each role (here we show only the ones for the author role):

```
type principal = string
type principals = {pc:principal; author:principal; confman:principal}
type msg9 = { hCfp : (principals → string → msg10)}
and msg10 = Upload of (string * msg11)
and msg11 = { hBadFormat : (principals → unit → msg10) ;
              hOk : (principals → unit → msg12)}
and msg12 = Submit of (string * msg13) | Withdraw of (unit * result_author)
and msg13 = { hAccept : (principals → string → result_author) ;
              hReject : (principals → string → result_author) ;
              hShepherd : (principals → string → msg16) ;
              hRevise : (principals → string → msg12)}
and msg16 = Rebuttal of (string * msg13)
val author : principal → msg9 → result_author
```

The principle behind session programming using CPS is that, whenever a message is received by the role, the generated secure implementation calls back the continuation provided by the user and resumes the protocol once user code returns the next message to be sent. Taking advantage of this calling convention, with a separately-typed user-code continuation for each state of each role of the session, we can thus entirely rely on ordinary ML typing to enforce session compliance in user code. The programmer is then free to design the continuations that will be safely executed whenever the chosen role is active. Programming with a session consists then in following the (possibly recursive) generated types by s2ml, by filling in the internal choices and payload handling functions (i.e., the continuations).

4 Session Security

At run time, a session is executed by processes running on hosts connected through an untrusted network. Each process runs on behalf of a principal. In order to state our security property, called session integrity, we first describe the threat model, and then informally discuss session integrity and possible threats to it.

Threat model. We consider a variant of the standard Dolev-Yao threat model [12]: the attacker can control corrupted principals (that may instantiate any of the roles in a session, and do not necessarily run as specified by the session declaration nor use our compiler), and perform network-based attacks: intercept, modify, and send messages on public channels, and perform cryptographic computations. Moreover, the corrupted principals may collude between themselves and the network during an attack. However, the attacker cannot break cryptography, guess secrets belonging to compliant principals, or tamper with communications on private channels.

Session Integrity. We say that a distributed session implementation preserves session integrity if during every run, regardless of the behaviour of the attacker, the process states at compliant principals (which use the generated cryptographic protocols as detailed in the next section) are consistent with a run where all principals seem to comply with all sessions. (This informal notion is made precise in [8]; see also below.)

Session integrity requires that all message sequences exchanged by compliant principals are consistent and comply with the session graph, that is, every time a compliant principal sends or accepts a message in a session run, such a message be allowed by the session graph; conversely, every time a malicious principal tries to derail the session by sending or replaying an incorrect message, this message is silently dropped, or reliably detected as anomalous.

In order for our compiler s2ml to enforce session integrity, it must generate a cryptographic protocol for each compliant principal that can guard against several possible attacks. We illustrate next some of these attempts to break integrity, and how the generated cryptographic protocol prevents them.

Session identifier confusions. Each session instance needs to have a unique session identifier, as otherwise there could be confusions between running sessions. The generated protocols compute a unique session identifier as $s = \mathbf{hash}(D\widetilde{a}N)$, where $D\,\widetilde{a}\,N$ is the tagged concatenation of $D = \mathbf{hash}(\Sigma)$, a digest of the whole session declaration, $\widetilde{a}$, the principals assigned to the session roles; and N, a nonce freshly generated by the initiator. Including D prevents confusions about the specification of the session being executed; including $\widetilde{a}$ prevents confusions about which principal is executing which role; and including N prevents confusion with other running session instances of the same declaration Σ and principal assignment $\widetilde{a}$. Messages sent by our generated cryptographic protocols always include as header the session identifier s, plus, in initial messages, $\widetilde{a}$ and N to allow receivers to recompute s (we assume D is expected and known by receivers). For example, for our CMS example, the generated protocol computes D as the hash of the session declaration from Figure 3, $\widetilde{a} =$ charlie alice bob (indicating that charlie plays the **pc** role, alice the **author** and bob the **confman**), and N is a random nonce.

Message integrity attacks. Whenever a principal playing a role in a session receives a message corresponding to a path executed in the session graph, it needs to ensure every label in the path has been sent by the presumed principal. Otherwise, an attack is possible, where some principal is impersonated by the attacker: for example in Figure 2, a malicious author could send the confman an **Upload** message even though the pc never sent a **Cfp**; if the confman does not check the presence of the pc, session integrity is violated. In order to prevent these attacks, the generated protocols include in messages a series of cryptographic signatures[3]: one signature from the message sender, plus one forwarded signature from each peer involved in the session since the receiver's last message (or the start of the session).

For our CMS example, consider the first time that the confman role gets contacted with an **Upload** message in Figure 2. At that point, the generated protocol needs to check signatures from the principals playing the roles author and pc; for our running session with session identifier as above, an incoming message is accepted by bob as **confman** only if it includes a signature from charlie (as role **pc**) of a **Cfp** message, and another signature from alice (as author) of an **Upload** message. On the other hand, if bob as **confman** is at the same node contacted again (e.g., because bob sent a **BadFormat** message and entered a loop), in the next incoming message bob needs to only check a (new) **Upload** message from alice, and the **Cfp** message needs not be forwarded again, as bob already checked it. The compiler accounts for both situations, and outputs accordingly specifically tailored functions for message generation and verification.

Intra- and Inter-session replays. Message replays can also thwart session integrity. Three situations can happen: (1) a message from one running session can be injected into another running session; (2) an initial message involving a principal can be replayed, trying to re-involve the same principal twice; and (3) a message from one running session can be replayed in the same running session (e.g., messages inside loops, which are particularly vulnerable).

Whilst (1) is directly prevented using a unique session identifier as detailed above, (2) and (3) need special treatment. For the former, like any protocol with responder roles, our generated protocol relies on dynamic anti-replay protection for the messages that may cause principals to join a session, that is, the first messages they may receive in their roles. To prevent such replays, each principal maintains a cache that records pairs of session identifiers and roles for all sessions it has joined so far. For the latter, our generated protocol includes a logical timestamp for messages inside loops, that is incremented at each loop iteration; it thus disambiguates messages occurring in cycles (messages not occurring in loops are not vulnerable, as message labels are assumed to be unique, see below).

Valid Sessions. Not every session encodable using the language of Section 2 makes sense: for example, a role sending a message that is never received is clearly undesirable. Our compiler checks this and other syntactic conditions that a session has to satisfy in order to be implementable (see Section 5). In particular, the compiler checks the absence of 'blind forks', which are in fact a security threat to session

---

[3] Cryptographic (or *digital*) signatures ensure the sender authenticity, as the signing private key of a compliant principal is kept secret.

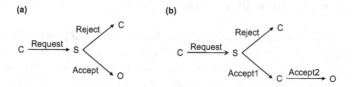

Fig. 4. (a) A session graph with a 'blind fork' and (b) its safe counterpart

integrity. Consider for instance the session of Figure 4(a), where S may send either a **Reject** to C or an **Accept** to O. Unless C and O exchange some information, they cannot prevent a malicious S from sending both messages, thereby breaking the session specification. (In fact, any graph containing the one in Figure 4(a) as subgraph is vulnerable!)

Nevertheless, such vulnerable session graphs can be transformed to equivalent ones without forks, at the cost of inserting additional messages. Figure 4(b) shows a safe counterpart of the vulnerable session of Figure 4(a), in which message **Accept** is split into two, **Accept1** and **Accept2**, and S is obliged to contact C no matter which branch is taken. (The general transformation is not difficult to build [8].)

Proving Session Integrity. The security of automatically-generated cryptographic protocol implementations crucially relies on formal verification. To this end, our language design and prototype implementation build on the approach of Bhargavan *et al.* [2], which narrows the gap between concrete executable code and its verified model. Our generated code depends on libraries for networking, cryptography, and principals, with dual implementations.

A concrete implementation uses standard cryptographic algorithms and networking primitives; the produced code supports distributed execution (we have both Ocaml/OpenSSL and F#/Microsoft .NET implementations). A second, symbolic implementation defines cryptography using algebraic datatypes, in Dolev-Yao style; the produced code supports concurrent execution, and is also our formal model.

In order to formally state and prove session integrity, we develop a high-level semantics that enforces sessions following their specification [8]. Our compiler, in turn, transforms session declarations to modules implementing them. Thus, we have two possible semantics in which user code runs: either a high-level configuration (where sessions execute as prescribed by definition) and a low-level configuration, in which user code executes calling the session-implementation modules. Our main security result (Theorem 1 in [8]), stated in terms of may testing, expresses that any behaviour of a low-level configuration can be simulated by a corresponding high-level configuration. Hence, the cryptographic protocol implementing the session is not letting an adversary gain anything, as *any* possible behaviour of session implementations using our compiler interacting with an adversary (comprising of corrupted principals colluding with the network) can be also reproduced by an adversary that does not interact with session implementations, and is subject to semantics where sessions run as prescribed.

5   Compiling Sessions to Modules

In Section 3 we present the interface generated by s2ml, so that programmers can use sessions. In this section, in turn, we discuss the inner workings of the compiler, i.e., how s2ml generates a cryptographic protocol securely implementing the session, and preventing possible threats to session integrity as detailed in the previous section. Our compiler s2ml works as follows:

1. For each session definition using local roles, it transforms it to a global graph and checks several well-formed and implementability conditions on it. From this graph, it also generates visible sequence messages which are used by the code generation phase.
2. Then, the compiler generates for each session its corresponding cryptographic protocol, and emits both its interface and its code as an ML module.

Checking validity conditions and generating visible sequences. As the session specifications are written in term of local role processes, and since a global view is required, the compiler first tries to generate the graph version of the session. Following the flow of the session (starting from the first role and messages), s2ml verifies that all the sent messages are expected by someone (i.e., are among the messages declared to be possibly received by a different role). Each node of the graph thus corresponds to a given active role and the edges are the messages sent to a different role which, after reception of the message, becomes active.

This conversion checks the correctness and coherence of the session declaration. In particular, we rule out invalid sessions in which messages are sent but not expected, and self-sent messages. We also require that labels are unique: two different edges cannot have the same label. This ensures the intent of each message label is unambiguous: the label uniquely identifies the source and target session states.

As explained in the previous section, branching in itself can lead to a security risk. The minimal condition to avoid this kind of attacks can be formulated in the following way (see [8] for details): For any two paths in the graph starting at the same node and ending with roles r_1 and r_2, we require that if neither r_1 nor r_2 are in the active roles of the two paths (i.e., they don't send any of the messages), then $r_1 = r_2$. Basically, this means that paths that fork and lead to different roles are dangerous. Checking this property is done in the s2ml implementation by a careful look at branching nodes: lists of active roles are recorded on every path starting at these nodes, followed by a comparison that ensures that the roles in different branches are related.

As an additional output, from this global graph s2ml generates the DOT [13] graph of the session graph, which can be used to view the specified session.

Visibility. After checking that the graph is valid and safe, s2ml generates the *visible* sequences, an essential part of the generation of the cryptographic protocol. Briefly, a sequence of labels is visible at a given node in the session graph if it contains only the last label sent by every other role. This notion is used in minimizing the number of signatures checks at runtime in the generated implementation: it relies on the fact that only the latest labels sent by every other role have to be checked to ensure session integrity.

We compute the visible sequences at compile-time to avoid any graph computation at runtime: the runtime signature checks which rely on visible sequences can thus be efficiently performed. For example, in the CMS example of Figure 2, the node in which the confman role is first contacted by an **Upload** message has two visible sequences, **Cfp-Upload** (along the initial path) and just **Upload** (through the cycle).

Generating the session interface and implementation. The main difficulty in the interface generation is to produce the set of recursive types that specify the alternation of constructed messages and continuations required from the user.

The generation of these types is based on four principles: first, an internal choice is translated into an algebraic sum type where message labels are used as constructors and where the constructor expects a correct payload and a continuation corresponding to the role's next expected message; second, an external choice generates a record whose labels are derived from message labels and whose data are functions handlers for the incoming messages (those functions take as arguments the record of principals and the payload of the message); third, mutual recursion reflects a recursive point in the local role description; forth, when ending, the result type is used.

More formally, our algorithm first associate type names to each of the sub-processes of a given role process: the names are of the form **msg**n (below we call this function *name*). The **0** sub-process is a particular case and its associated type name is of the form **result_**rolename.

Then we have the following generating function that is applied successively to all sub-processes:

$$[\![!(f_i : \tau_i \; ; \; p_i)_{i<k}]\!] = \text{and } name(p) = \{ \; | \; f_i \text{ of } (\tau_i * name(p_i)) \}_{i<k}$$
$$[\![?(f_i : \tau_i \; ; \; p_i)_{i<k}]\!] = \text{and } name(p) = \{\{\mathbf{h}f_i : \text{principals} \to \tau_i \to name(p_i); \}_{i<k}\}$$

This generates a collection of potentially mutually recursive types, which explains the default use of the and keyword. A pretty-printing phase then completes the interface generation. As shown in section 3, the result types have the following shape:

```
[...] and msg11 = {
        hBadFormat : (principals → unit → msg10) ; hOk : (principals → unit → msg12)}
        and msg12 =
        | Submit of (string * msg13) | Withdraw of (unit * result_author)
[...]
```

Wired types and messages generation. The low-level handling of messages in the generated protocols is done by a series of specialized types and functions. These functions have also the task of maintaining a local store containing the necessary cryptographic material for the session. Concretely, s2ml generates a family of **sendWired**$label$ functions (one generated function for each message tagged with $label$ of the session) that perform the following operations:

1. build the session id (a digest of the session declaration, principals, and a nonce);
2. build the header (the session id plus the sender and receiver's identities);
3. marshall the payload;
4. create a new signature of the label and logical time;
5. update the local signature store and logical clock;

6. build the message from the header, the label, the payload and the transmitted signatures (whose list is known from the previously computed visibility);
7. send the message on the network

Symmetrically, the receiving sequence of actions done by the family of **receiveWired**n functions (one function for each node n in the graph) is the following:

1. receive the message from the network;
2. unmarshall and decompose into parts (header, label, payload, signatures);
3. check the session id;
4. match the message label against possible incoming messages;
5. check the signatures' correctness (using visibility) and logical time-stamps;
6. update the local signature store and logical clock;
7. check the message against the cache (if it is the first message of a run of the session)

Any check failure will either silently restart the function (to continue listening) or throw an exception. Since initial messages require special treatment (e.g., cache checking), s2ml creates specific versions of the low-level functions (named with the **init** suffix). The types of the **sendWired**$label$ and **receiveWired**n are of the form:

val **sendWired**$label$: **wired**n → state
val **receiveWired**n : state → unit → **wired**n

where the state corresponds to the local cryptographic store, and the **wired**n types are the sum types corresponding to messages that can be received in the state n of the role's process. The internals of the proxy, in charge of enforcing the session flow and user interaction, critically relies on these types.

Proxy functions. The last part of the generated protocol implementation consists on the proxy functions that the user can call from the interface. Their purpose is to follow the flow of sent and received messages as specified by the session and to call back a user-defined continuation at the correct moment.

Concretely, these functions have to be able to handle the users' choices of messages to send and call the appropriate low-level **sendWired**$label$ function. Then they have to listen to incoming messages using the **receiveWired**n functions and, when a message is received, to call back the appropriate field of the user-specified record of continuations.

We illustrate these proxy functions by the **author** function from the CMS example:

```
let author (prin: principal) (user_input : msg9) =
...
and author_msg10 (st:state) : msg11 → result_author = function
  | Upload(x, next) → let newSt = sendWiredUpload host dest (WiredUpload(st, x)) in
    author_msg11 newSt next
and author_msg9_init : msg9 → result_author =
  function handlers →
  let (newSt, r) = receiveWired0_init host prin () in
    match r with
    | WiredCfp (newSt, x) → let next = handlers.hCfp newSt.prins x in
    author_msg10 newSt next
  in
```

Printf.printf "Executing role author with principal %s...\n" **prin;**
author_msg9_init user_input

Initially it calls the function **author_msg9_init** which uses **receiveWired0_init** to receive a first message. It is checked to be a **Cfp** message, and if so, the payload **x** is applied to the user code continuation (**handlers.hCfp**), and then the function **author_msg10** is invoked, which continues the session by sending a **Upload** message.

5.1 Concrete Implementation and Benchmarks

Our concrete implementation links the generated code against concrete cryptographic implementations (as opposed to a symbolic model, used to formally prove security, which uses algebraic datatypes). We provide two variants of concrete libraries: one using Ocaml and wrappers for OpenSSL, and another using F#/Microsoft .NET cryptography. (Unfortunately the two implementations do not yet interoperate, due to incompatibilities among certificates.) The data and cryptographic functions we use are as follows. For cryptography, we use SHA1 for hashing, RSASHA1 for signing, and the standard pseudorandom function for nonce generation. Signing uses certificates in '.key' format for OpenSSL and '.cer' for Microsoft .NET. As for data, we use Base64 for encoding the messages in a communicable format. We use UDP-based communication (although in the future we plan to move to TCP-based communications).

Benchmarks. We executed the CMS example using the Ocaml/OpenSSL concrete implementation in a setting in which every loop is iterated 500 times. This table reports the benchmarks for a Pentium D 3.0 GHz running linux-2.6.17-x86_64:

	No crypto	Signing, not Verifying	Signing, Verifying	Standard OpenSSL
first loop	0.231s	2.79s	2.95s	
second loop	0.468s	5.62s	6.11s	
third loop	0.243s	2.81s	2.98s	
total	0.942s	11.22s	12.04s	8.38s

These results show that most execution time is devoted to cryptography, as expected: the generated code s2ml consists of optimally compact, specialized message handlers. The last column, labelled 'Standard OpenSSL', compares our implementation to the standard OpenSSL 0.9.8e by reporting the time it takes to send 4000 single character messages using the command-line tool from the distribution. Our implementation, that deals with much more complex messages, is comparable in speed.

6   Conclusions

We present a simple language for specifying sessions between roles, and we detail its usage as a secure communication abstraction on top of ML. Our compiler s2ml generates custom cryptographic protocols that guarantee global compliance to the session specification for the principals that use our implementation, with no trust assumptions for the principals that do not.

Whilst in previous work we focus on establishing (theoretical) security guarantees for the generated code of s2ml, here we concentrate on describing the inner workings of the compiler, and explore its applicability to the concrete examples of an RPC exchange and a rather large conference management system. This latter case study is treated smoothly by s2ml, providing confidence for its usability as a concrete tool for structuring and securing distributed programming.

Future Work. We are exploring variants of our design to increase the expressiveness of session specifications: session-scoped data bindings that ensure the same values are passed in a series of messages, as well as more dynamic principal-joining mechanisms, to enable new principals to enter a role subject to agreement among the current principals. (Still, we remind the reader that sessions are at the level of message flow specifications, and user code implementing them can be arbitrary ML code.) We are also interested on providing support for communicating richer payload types, by studying the extension of s2ml with general and secure marshalling.

Acknowledgments. This work benefited from discussions with K. Bhargavan, C. Fournet, J. Leifer, and J-J. Lévy. Special thanks to James Leifer for his insightful comments, and to the anonymous reviewers for their useful suggestions. An earlier version of s2ml was developed while visiting at Microsoft Research Cambridge, UK.

References

1. Bhargavan, K., Corin, R., Fournet, C., Gordon, A.D.: Secure sessions for web services. In: ACM Workshop on Secure Web Services (SWS), pp. 11–22 (October 2004)
2. Bhargavan, K., Fournet, C., Gordon, A.D., Tse, S.: Verified interoperable implementations of security protocols. In: 19th IEEE Computer Security Foundations Workshop (CSFW), July 2006, pp. 139–152 (2006)
3. J. Billings, P. Sewell, M. Shinwell, and R. Strniša. Type-Safe Distributed Programming for OCaml. In: ACM SIGPLAN Workshop on ML, September 2006 (2006)
4. Bonelli, E., Compagnoni, A., Gunter, E.: Correspondence assertions for process synchronization in concurrent communications. In: Brogi, A. (ed.) 1st International Workshop on Foundations of Coordination Languages and Software Architectures (FOCLASA). ENTCS, vol. 97, pp. 175–195. Elsevier, Amsterdam (2004)
5. Carbone, M., Honda, K., Yoshida, N.: Structured communication-centred programming for web services. In: De Nicola, R. (ed.) ESOP 2007. LNCS, vol. 4421, Springer, Heidelberg (2007)
6. Carpineti, S., Laneve, C.: A basic contract language for web services. In: Sestoft, P. (ed.) ESOP 2006. LNCS, vol. 3924, pp. 197–213. Springer, Heidelberg (2006)
7. Chaki, S., Rajamani, S.K., Rehof, J.: Types as models: model checking message-passing programs. In: 29th ACM SIGPLAN-SIGACT symposium on Principles of Programming Languages (POPL), January 2002, pp. 45–57 (2002)
8. Corin, R., Denielou, P.M., Fournet, C., Bhargavan, K., Leifer, J.: Secure implementations for typed session abstractions. In: 20th IEEE Computer Security Foundations Symposium (CSF 2007), Venice, Italy, July 2007, IEEE Computer Society Press, Los Alamitos (to appear, 2007)
9. Corin, R., Dénielou, P.-M., Fournet, C., Bhargavan, K., Leifer, J.: Secure sessions project (2007), http://www.msr-inria.inria.fr/projects/sec/sessions/

10. Deniélou, P.-M., Leifer, J.J.: Abstraction preservation and subtyping in distributed languages. In: 11th International Conference on Functional Programming (ICFP) (2006)
11. Dezani-Ciancaglini, M., Mostrous, D., Yoshida, N., Drossopoulou, S.: Session types for object-oriented languages. In: 20th European Conference for Object-Oriented Languages, July 2006 (2006)
12. Dolev, D., Yao, A.C.: On the security of public key protocols. IEEE Transactions on Information Theory 29(2), 198–208 (1983)
13. Dot, http://www.graphviz.org/
14. Fahndrich, M., Aiken, M., Hawblitzel, C., Hodson, G.H.O., Larus, J.R., Levi, S.: Language support for fast and reliable message-based communication in Singularity OS. In: EUROSYS (2006)
15. Simon, J.: Gay and Malcolm Hole. Types and subtypes for client-server interactions. In: Programming Languages and Systems, 8th European Symposium on Programming (ESOP), pp. 74–90 (1999)
16. Gordon, A.D., Jeffrey, A.: Authenticity by typing for security protocols. Journal of Computer Security 11(4), 451–521 (2003)
17. Honda, K., Vasconcelos, V.T., Kubo, M.: Language primitives and type disciplines for structured communication-based programming. In: Hankin, C. (ed.) ESOP 1998 and ETAPS 1998. LNCS, vol. 1381, pp. 22–138. Springer, Heidelberg (1998)
18. Honda, K., Yoshida, N., Carbone, M.: Multiparty asynchronous session types. In: Proceedings of the 35th ACM SIGPLAN-SIGACT Symposium on Principles of Programming Languages, POPL 2008 (to appear, 2008)
19. Igarashi, A., Kobayashi, N.: A generic type system for the pi-calculus. In: 28th ACM SIGPLAN-SIGACT symposium on Principles of programming languages (POPL), pp. 128–141 (2001)
20. Milner, R., Tofte, M., Harper, R.: The Definition of Standard ML. MIT Press, Cambridge (1990)
21. Objective Caml, http://caml.inria.fr
22. Sewell, P., Leifer, J.J., Wansbrough, K., Nardelli, F.Z., Allen-Williams, M., Habouzit, P., Vafeiadis, V.: Acute: High-level programming language design for distributed computation. In: 10th International Conference on Functional Programming (ICFP), September 2005 (2005)
23. Syme, D.: F# (2005), http://research.microsoft.com/fsharp/
24. Vallecillo, A., Vasconcelos, V.T., Ravara, A.: Typing the behavior of objects and components using session types. In: 1st International Workshop on Foundations of Coordination Languages and Software Architectures (FOCLASA). ENTCS, vol. 68, Elsevier, Amsterdam (2003)
25. Vasco, T.: Vasconcelos, Simon Gay, and António Ravara. Typechecking a multithreaded functional language with session types, TCS 368(1–2), 64–87 (2006)
26. Yoshida, N., Vasconcelos, V.T.: Language primitives and type discipline for structured communication-based programming revisited: Two systems for higher-order session communication. In: 1st International Workshop on Security and Rewriting Techniques, ENTCS (2006)

Application of Dependency Graphs to Security Protocol Analysis

Ilja Tšahhirov[1] and Peeter Laud[2,3]

[1] Tallinn University of Technology
[2] Tartu University
[3] Cybernetica AS

Abstract. We present a computationally sound technique of static analysis for confidentiality in cryptographic protocols. The technique is a combination of the dependency flow graphs presented by Beck and Pingali and our earlier works – we start with the protocol representation as a dependency graph indicating possible flows of data in all possible runs of the protocol and replace the cryptographic operations with constructions which are "obviously secure". Transformations are made in such a way that the semantics of the resulting graph remains computationally indistinguishable from the semantics of the original graph. The transformed graphs are analysed again; the transformations are applied until no more transformations are possible. A protocol is deemed secure if its transformed version is secure; the transformed versions are amenable to a very simple security analysis. The framework is well-suited for producing fully automated (with zero user input) proofs for protocol security.

1 Introduction

A protocol is a convention that enables the connection, communication, and data exchange between several computing entities. A cryptographic protocol is a protocol, which performs some security-related function and applies cryptographic methods. Naturally, the cryptographic protocol is expected to satisfy certain security properties. Examples of those properties could be confidentiality, integrity, and so on. Therefore there is a need for methods for indicating whether the given protocol satisfies the given security property or not. The latter is simpler than the first – having an example of successful attack breaching the property of interest is sufficient to show that the protocol does not satisfy it. Showing that the protocol is secure with respect to certain properties is essentially convincing that no attack (known or unknown) breaching these properties exist.

In this paper we propose a framework for examining the protocol security properties based on the notion of computational indistinguishability, assuming certain properties of cryptographic operations. Currently the framework is used for checking the preservation of confidentiality and integrity properties in protocols. In principle, the framework should be suitable for verifying all properties whose fulfilment can be observed by the protocol participants and/or the adversary — the transformation process does not change the observable properties of protocols.

G. Barthe and C. Fournet (Eds.): TGC 2007, LNCS 4912, pp. 294–311, 2008.

The basis of the analysis – protocol semantics and the set of assumptions on the cryptographic operations we used – is similar to [18,27], while the protocol language is much more powerful, and the analysis methodology is significantly different. Our contribution is the introduction of the support for the replication to the analysed protocols, and using the approach based on the extensive usage of the dependency graphs, similar to those introduced in [26], for the analysis of the protocols' security. The developed framework is suitable for producing the automated, computationally sound proofs for the protocols' security.

This paper has the following structure. After reviewing the previous work in this field in Sec. 2, we go on with defining the protocol representation on which the technique is based in Sec. 3. The criterion for considering the protocol corresponding to a given graph secure is defined in Sec. 4, followed by Sec. 5, where more complex types of the dependency graphs, corresponding to the protocols with replication, are considered. Sec. 6 contains key rules for graph transformation preserving the semantics of the graph. In Sec. 7 we explain how the integrity properties can be verified in our framework.

2   Related Work

The research presented in this paper belongs to a body of work attempting to bridge the gap between the two main approaches for modeling and analyzing the cryptographic protocols — the Dolev-Yao model [15] and the complexity-theory-based approach [28]. The most related, and also a source of inspiration to the work reported in this paper has been the protocol analysis framework by Blanchet [9,10,11]. The difference of our approaches is in the choice of the program (protocol) representation. We believe that the use of dependency graphs instead of a more conventional representation allows our analyser to better focus on the important details of data and control flow. Both frameworks are based on the view of cryptographic proofs as sequences of games [8,18]. In both frameworks, in order to prove a protocol correct, the automated analyser constructs such a sequence where the adversary's advantage diminishes only negligibly from one game to the next one, and where the adversary has obviously no advantage in the final game. Another difference with [9,10,11] is the degree of automation – the analyser from [9,10,11] still requires the human-produced hints on the set and order of transformations to apply for some protocols; the analyser prototype implemented based on our framework does not require any hints.

The work in this area has been started by Abadi and Rogaway [1], who considered the relationship of formal and computational symmetric encryption under passive attacks and provided a procedure to check whether two formal messages have indistinguishable computational semantics. The same primitive and class of attacks have been further considered in [2,23,17,22,3], in these papers the language has been expanded (the constraints have been weakened) and the security definitions have been clarified. Further on, the active attacks with the range of cryptographic primitives were considered in [13,16,21] (based on the translation of protocol traces from the computational to the formal model) and

[19,5] (based on the application of the universally composable [12,25] crypto-graphic library [4]).

Another body of research the present work is based on is the static analysis on the intermediate program representations. We use the protocol representation close to [26]. Unlike some of the frameworks based on protocol rewriting – [18,27], the protocol transformations we perform do not produce several sub-protocols which are to be analyzed separately; the representation chosen is capable of hold-ing all the possible information flows and execution variants, therefore having better potential for analyzing the replication and data flows between different protocol runs.

3   Dependency Graphs

The analysis is performed over a dependency graph, representing the protocol inputs, outputs, operations performed during the execution of the protocol, and the data flows between them. Dependency graph is one possible representation of a protocol. It is universal – every protocol that can be specified in a WHILE-style language [24] can be represented by a dependency graph as well.

The dependency graph is a directed graph defined by a set of *operations* (vertices) and *dependencies* (edges). The operation is an equation with the left side consisting of a dependency (acting as a short-term name for the result of the operation), and the right side being the application of an operator to zero or more dependencies. Each operation is uniquely identified by its label from the *Lab* (set of operation labels). An operation is a *source* for the dependency on the left side of the equation and a *sink* for dependencies listed on the right side. A dependency has exactly one source but can have many sinks.

An operation, in general, is a deterministic computation from its inputs to the output. Some of the operations (e.g. encryption) use randomness in computation, but this randomness is taken as a data dependency, and the operation itself is still deterministic. The following operations can occur in the dependency graph: Constants ($i \in \mathbb{N}$, *true*, *false*, *error*), asymmetric encryption (*keypair*, *pubkey*, *pubenc*, *pubdec*), symmetric encryption (*symkey*, *symenc*, *symdec*), tupling and projecting ($tuple_m$, $proj_i^m$), conversion of random coins to numeric form (*nonce*), boolean operations (and_m, or_m), condition check (*isok*, *iseq*), and selection of one of the values (*mux*). Most operations' names give the general idea on what they do; additional details on some of the operations are provided throughout the article. Operations and_m, or_m, and $tuple_m$ are actually families of opera-tions; each instance in the family having m arguments (for instance, and_2 is a conjunction of two dependencies). The operations not falling into this model are:

- *rs* — returns random coins, *secret* — returns the (also randomly generated) secret message. Let $Lab_* \subseteq Lab$ be the set of labels of all such operations; let $Lab_\bullet \subseteq Lab$ be the set of labels of all "normal" operations (i.e. those labels that are not included in $Lab_\leftarrow$ (introduced below) and Lab_*).
- *send*. The only output operation, making the information available to the adversary, is *send*. It has two dependencies – control dependency and the

value to be sent to the network. If the control dependency is *true*, the adversary learns the value of the other dependency. There can be no outgoing dependencies from *send*-nodes. Let $Lab_\rightarrow \subseteq Lab_\bullet$ be the labels of all *send*-operations.

— *receive*, *req* - return values set by adversary. *receive* denotes the reception of a message from the network (which is assumed to be under adversarial control). *req*-nodes are flags associated with *send*-nodes; they can be set by the adversary when it wants these *send*-nodes to produce a message. Let $Lab_\leftarrow \subseteq Lab$ be the set of labels of all such operations.

According to the way treated by operations, the dependencies (arguments) can be divided into two groups — data and control dependencies. Data dependency provides the operation with the argument required to perform the computation (for example, encryption key for the encryption operation). Control dependency indicates whether the operation is to be performed or not. The control dependency of an operation is *true* if it is necessary and possible to perform it. Necessity follows from the adversary's choice to evaluate the public output (i.e. set *req* for the corresponding *send* operation to *true*), or from necessity to evaluate an operation dependent from the given (all such chains terminate with *req*). Possibility to evaluate an operation follows from the possibility to evaluate each operation the current operation is dependent on. For operations having no data dependencies it is always possible to evaluate them (so the control dependency is just the necessity); for operations having one or more data dependencies, the control dependency is a conjunction of necessity to evaluate the current operation and possibility to evaluate each operation the current operation is dependent on. The *if ... then ...* construction introduces additional control dependency from the result of the evaluation of the condition to each operation under the *then* branch.

For example, let *pubkey*(*keypair*), *secret*(), *rs*(), and *pubenc*(*key*, *text*, *random*) be the operations returning public key, secret message, random coins, and encrypting the text using the key and random input, respectively. Let *if*(*condition*, *statement*) be the conditional execution construction. The dependencies for the program fragment $x := pubkey(\ldots); y := secret(); if(a = b, z := rs(); w := pubenc(x, y, z));$ are illustrated in Fig. 1. The operation label is shown in the right part of the node. Data dependencies are drawn as solid lines, control dependencies – as dashed lines. Control dependency of the *pubenc* and *rs* operations specify that (among other conditions) the condition checked in *if* has to be *true* in order for the operation to be executed. Circles represent the nodes of the dependency graph connected to the fragment in question. In the following we present the dependency graphs or their fragments as listings of nodes of the form $Operation^l(l_1 \ldots l_m)$. Here l is the label (identity) of the current node, *Operation* is the operation performed in this node and $l_1, \ldots, l_m$ are the labels of the nodes that are the dependencies of the current node l — that produce the values consumed at the node l.

Note that some information on the execution order, not essential to the analysis, is lost. For instance, based on the data dependencies there's no difference

in which order the operations with labels 1 and 2 are computed; in the original
program, however, these 3 values are computed in a particular order. The evaluation of the operations on the graph could be made in any possible order, as
long as the constraints defined by the control dependencies are met. Due to the
properties of the graph evaluation semantics, every such evaluation will stop at
the same point and give the same final result.

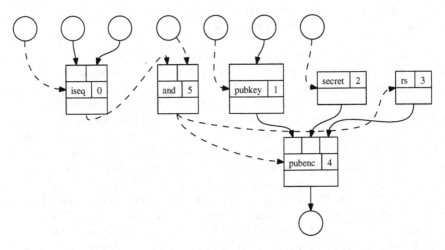

Fig. 1. Dependency graphs

The semantics of the dependency graphs are defined as follows. Let Σ be the
set of bit strings the computations are performed on. Let $\Sigma_\perp$ be the $\Sigma \cup \{\perp\}$.
Let $\leq_\Sigma$ be the order on the $\Sigma_\perp$, defined as $\forall x \in \Sigma_\perp . \perp \leq_\Sigma x$, and everything
else is incomparable. Let $\mathbb{B} = \{true, false\}$, ordered by $false \leq_\mathbb{B} true$. Let Lab be
the set of labels.

The configuration is the state of the computation on a graph. It assigns the
values to all dependencies (including the adversary's view), adversarial inputs,
and random coin tosses. Formally, it has the type:

$$Configuration : ((Lab_\bullet \to \Sigma_\perp \cup \mathbb{B}) \times (Lab_\leftarrow \to \Sigma_\perp \cup \mathbb{B}) \times (Lab_* \to \Sigma))^\top$$

For some $\langle \rho, \phi, \psi \rangle \in Configuration$, $\rho[l]$ denotes the output value of the
operation with label l, $\phi[l']$ – the value set by adversary at operation with label l',
and $\psi[l'']$ – the value of the random coins generated by $rs^{l''}$. The value $\psi[secret]$
is the secret message being exchanged. The motivation behind putting all the
randomness used to one place is to be able to "replay" the run of the protocol in
"lock-step" with another, earlier completed run. Special configuration $\top$ denotes
that something inconsistent has happened during the computations.

Each operation with label l introduces a function from the dependencies used
as arguments to the operation to the result of the operation. This function has
type:

$$f^l : Configuration \rightarrow (\Sigma_\perp \cup \mathbb{B})^\top$$

For example, the operation $keypair^l(l_1, l_2)$, generating the key pair using random coins generated at l_2, and l_1 as the control dependency introduces the function:

$$f^l(\langle \rho, \phi, \psi \rangle) = \begin{cases} \mathcal{G}^{pe}(\rho[l_2]) & \text{if } \rho[l_1] = true \wedge \rho[l_2] \neq \perp \\ \perp & \text{otherwise} \end{cases}$$

where $\mathcal{G}^{pe}$ is the cryptographic function computing the public-secret key pair from the random coins. Semantics for the rest of the operations are defined in a similar way. The operations using the random source (rs, $secret$) or adversarial input (req, $receive$), use, instead of ρ, the configuration components ϕ (for accessing the adversarial input) or ψ (for getting the random source). The function for $mux_n^l(l^c, l_1^c, l_1^v, \ldots, l_n^c, l_n^v)$ is defined to return the value, the selector of which is $true$, and $\perp$ or $\top$ if less or more than one selector is $true$, respectively.

It can be verified that all the functions for evaluating operations' result are defined to be monotone. The graph evaluation function has the type

$$Eval : Configuration \rightarrow Configuration$$

and is defined as

$$Eval(\langle \rho, \phi, \psi \rangle) = \begin{cases} \top & \text{if } \exists l \in Lab.f^l(\langle \rho, \phi, \psi \rangle) = \top \\ \langle \rho', \phi, \psi \rangle & \text{where } \forall l \in Lab.\rho'[l] = f^l(\langle \rho, \phi, \psi \rangle) \text{ otherwise} \end{cases}$$
$$Eval(\top) = \top$$

The graph evaluation function is monotone, continuous and expanding ($\forall C.Eval(C) \geq C$).

The *execution* of a dependency graph, in parallel with the adversary $\mathcal{A}$, proceeds as follows:

1. ρ is set to map every dependency to $\perp$. ψ is initialized with the (uniformly generated) random coins used in the execution. ϕ (containing information on which of the protocol outputs are to be evaluated and the values to be fed to the graph from the network) is set to map every req operation to $false$ and every $receive$ operation to $\perp$.
2. The adversary produces a mapping $\phi' : Lab_{\leftarrow} \rightarrow \Sigma_\perp$ satisfying $\phi \leq \phi'$. The computational cost of outputting ϕ' is defined to be the number of labels l where $\phi(l) \neq \phi'(l)$.
3. The graph is evaluated — let $\langle \rho', \phi', \psi \rangle$ be the least fixed point of $Eval$ that is greater or equal to $\langle \rho, \phi', \psi \rangle$. The existence of such fixed point follows from the properties of $Eval$.
4. Let $Lab_{\rightarrow} \subseteq Lab_\bullet$ be the labels of all *send*-operations. The adversary is given the values of ρ on all points of $Lab_{\rightarrow}$.
5. The adversary decides whether the sequence should be repeated from the step 2 (putting $\phi := \phi'$, $\rho := \rho'$) or terminated.

4   Security Definition

Let the adversary be an algorithm operating in the Probabilistic Polynomial Time (PPT), relative to the security parameter n (of the encryption system used by the cryptographic operations in the graph). The same formal definition of the security parameter as in [18] is used. The running time of the adversary is its total running time for all iterations performed during the execution of the graph.

For a given dependency graph, random coins ψ and the adversary $\mathcal{A}$ let the *adversary's view* $\text{view}_\psi(\mathcal{A})$ be the distribution of $\alpha = \rho|_{Lab_\rightarrow}$ after computing the semantics of the graph with given random coins and adversary inputs. Let D be the distribution of ψ. In order to consider the protocol secure, we require that for all PPT adversaries, the adversary's view is independent from the secret message. Formally, the probability distribution of the pair of the secret message and the adversary's view produced while executing the protocol with this secret message should be indistinguishable from the probability distribution of the pair of the secret message and the adversary's view corresponding to a different secret message, taken according to the same distribution.

$$\{(\psi[secret], \alpha) \,:\, \alpha = Exec(\psi); \psi \leftarrow [\![D]\!]\} \approx$$
$$\approx \{(\psi'[secret], \alpha) \,:\, \alpha = Exec(\psi); \psi, \psi' \leftarrow [\![D]\!]\}$$

The exact meaning of indistinguishability between two *families* of probability distributions $D = \{D_n\}_{n \in \mathbb{N}}$ and $D' = \{D'_n\}_{n \in \mathbb{N}}$, denoted $D \approx D'$, is following: for all PPT algorithms $\mathcal{A}$, the difference of probabilities

$$\mathbf{P}[b = 1 \mid x \leftarrow D_n, b \leftarrow \mathcal{A}(1^n, x)] - \mathbf{P}[b = 1 \mid x \leftarrow D'_n, b \leftarrow \mathcal{A}(1^n, x)]$$

is a negligible function of n.

Theorem. The protocol which does not include the operation $secret^l$ (the only operation which returns the value of the $\psi[secret]$), is secure (as the generated value of the secret message is not used in it).

This theorem is the "very simple security analysis" mentioned in the abstract.

5   Dependency Graphs with Replication

Normally during the execution of the protocol some parts of it are executed repeatedly (for instance, the execution of the participant could take place more than once), and there is a possibility of data exchange between the different executions of the same operations (e.g. replay attacks, when the adversary records the data exchanged during one run of the protocol, and uses this data to produce values sent to the participants during the next run). To model multiple runs of the protocol, the dependency graph must contain a node for each operation in each possible run of the protocol.

For example, let us suppose that the inner part of the conditional statement of the example program from Sec. 3 could be executed at most two times, using the same value of the conditional test, secret message and the public key. The dependency graph corresponding to it is illustrated on the Fig. 2.a. As the same conditional statement, public key, and secret message are used in both runs, nodes, corresponding to them, are present in the dependency graph only once. The rest of operations are executed two times, which is represented by two copies of each node.

In general, each operation performed in the replicated part of the protocol is represented by a number (equal to the number of runs) of nodes in the dependency graph. The adversary can establish information exchange between the different runs of the program by using the value of the *send*-node corresponding to one run to calculate the value to set to *req* and *receive*-nodes corresponding to another run.

Now let us consider the case when the number of the protocol runs is not limited. Each operation in the replicated part of the program is still represented by a set of nodes, the cardinality of which is equal to the number of possible protocol runs; hence the dependency graph (built using the same principles as the example with two runs) becomes infinite. Despite the fact that the graph is infinite, the constraints put on the adversary's execution time mean that only a finite subset of the nodes of the graph are evaluated.

The structure of the (infinite) dependency graph with the replications is regular enough to be finitely represented. Fig. 2.b contains the representation of the dependency graph from Fig. 2.a., but with an infinite number of replications. Each node in the representation has an additional attribute (the rightmost part of the node), showing whether it is replicated or not – the number of replication dimensions. A replication dimension corresponds to a possibility to execute a part of the protocol countable number of times. In the current example, some nodes in the representation have zero dimensions and the rest have one dimension. A node in the representation having k dimensions corresponds to a set of nodes in the actual dependency graph, the nodes in this set have a natural one-to-one correspondence with the elements of the set $\mathbb{N}^k$. Hence a zero-dimensional node corresponds to a single node in the real graph, and a node with one or more dimensions corresponds to countably many nodes in the real graph.

In this example we only saw nodes with at most one replication dimension. Two- or more-dimensional nodes naturally arise if the protocol specification contains nested replications. We see another case giving rise to more-dimensional nodes in Sec. 6.2.

The representation also specifies the dependencies present in the replicated dependency graph. If the source and the sink of a dependency edge have the same number of dimensions, then this edge in the representation means that each instance of the sink node depends on the the corresponding instance of the source node (but if the number of dimensions is greater than one then the dependency may permute the coordinates). If the dependency sink has more coordinates than the source (it is the case with *pubenc* depending on *secret* in our example) then the value of (a single instance of) dependency source

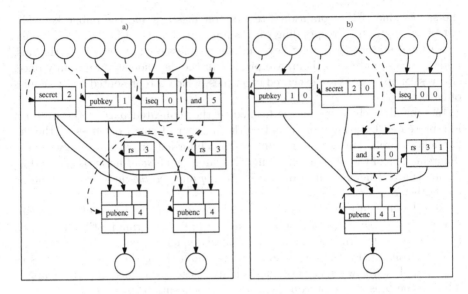

Fig. 2. Dependency graph with replications

is used in all the instances of the dependency sink. The third possible case – sink having less coordinates than the source – corresponds to each instance of the sink consuming an infinite number of arguments (a single argument from each instance of the source). In our dependency graph representations there are only two operations where this may happen — at logical *or*-s or at multiplexers.

6   Transformations

We use graph transformations to replace a potentially insecure graph with another graph, the adversary's view of which is computationally indistinguishable from the first. The meaning of the computational indistinguishability of two dependency graphs is analogous to the one specified in Sec. 4, with the difference that now the task is to distinguish two dependency graph with equal inputs (including secret value).

The transformations are designed in a way that each of them either reduces the complexity of the graph, makes the implicit result of some operations explicit, or eliminates data flows due to the properties to certain cryptographic operations. While performing possible transformations to the graph, it is gradually transformed to a form that makes more explicit which data flows really exist and which are "hidden" by the cryptographic operations. If at the end of the transformation sequence a secure graph is obtained, the very first graph is also secure.

The rest of the section contains the description of some of the transformations preserving the adversary's view on the graph.

6.1   Dead Code Removal

One special transformation is removal of dead code. Despite being trivial, it is important to consider, as it is the only transformation that makes the graph smaller (other transformations only add additional operations to the graph.)

A node in a dependency graph is *live* if it is a *send*-node or if the value produced by it is consumed by a live node. All nodes that are not live may be removed from the graph.

6.2   The Replacement of Encryptions

First, let us consider the asymmetric encryption operation. We require the encryption system to satisfy the IND-CCA2 property as defined in [6] – i.e. it should be impossible to distinguish two ciphertexts produced by the encryption oracle for two plaintexts given by the adversary with non-negligible probability in polynomial time even if the adversary is given the ability to decrypt everything except the challenge ciphertext. It means that encryption of the plaintext with the given public key could be replaced with the encryption of the string of zeroes (or any other constant) of equal length, and that latter ciphertext will be indistinguishable from the first for anyone, except for the one having the corresponding private key. On the decryption side we first check whether the ciphertext matches one of the ciphertexts already produced, and if it does, the corresponding plaintext is returned. If no match is found, the decryption operation is performed.

In terms of equivalent dependency graph fragments, it can be presented as follows. Suppose the graph contains the following operations.

$$rs^{l^{vrs}}(l^{crs}) \qquad keypair^{l^{vkp}}(l^{ckp}, l^{vrs}) \qquad pubkey^{l^{vpk}}(l^{cpk}, l^{vkp})$$

$$rs^{l_i^{vrs}}(l_i^{crs}) \qquad pubenc^{l_i^{vect}}(l_i^{ce}, l^{vpk}, l_i^{vept}, l_i^{vrs}) \qquad (\text{where } 1 \leq i \leq n)$$

$$pubdec^{l_j^{vdpt}}(l_j^{cd}, l^{vkp}, l_j^{vdct}) \qquad (\text{where } 1 \leq j \leq m)$$

The operations used are: rs is the generation of random coins, *keypair* and *pubkey* are the generation of the secret-public key pair and the extraction of the public key component from the pair, *pubenc* is the encryption of the given plain text using the given public key and random coins. All the operations have the control dependency as their first argument, and are evaluated only if it becomes *true*. The operation name is superscripted with the label of the operation (for instance, l^{vrs}). The abbreviations used in label names are: v stands for value, c for control, kp for key pair, pk for public key, rs for random seed, e for encryption, d for decryption, pt for plain text, and ct for cyphertext. The dependency is identified by the label of its source. We require that the dependencies l^{vrs}, l_i^{vrs} and l^{vkp} are not used in any operations except for the ones listed above.

By the definition of IND-CCA2, the semantics of the graph are indistinguishable from the semantics of the graph where all occurrences of the dependencies l_i^{vect} and l_j^{vdpt} in the graph are replaced with the $l_i'^{vect}$ and $l_j'^{vdpt}$, respectively. These new dependencies are defined as follows:

$$pubencz^{l'^{vect}_i}(l^{ce}_i, l^{vpk}, l^{vrs}_i) \qquad (\text{where } 1 \le i \le n)$$

$$iseq^{l^{cvar}_{ji}}(l^{vdct}_j, l^{vect}_i) \qquad isok^{l^{cdok}_j}(l^{vdpt}_j) \qquad (\text{where } 1 \le i \le n, 1 \le j \le m)$$

$$mux^{l'^{vdpt}_j}_{n+1}(l^{cd}_j, l^{cvar}_{j1}, l^{vept}_1, \dots, l^{cvar}_{jn}, l^{vept}_n, l^{cdok}_j, l^{vdpt}_j) \qquad (\text{where } 1 \le j \le m)$$

There are two operations that need to be clarified here: *pubencz* and *mux*. *pubencz* is the encryption of a special constant ("zero") that cannot be produced by any of the nodes in the graph. Decryption of the ciphertext produced by *pubencz* returns $\bot$. mux_n is the multiplexing operation. Beside the control dependency it takes n pairs of control and data dependencies as inputs. If the control dependency in exactly one of those pairs is true, the result of mux_n is the value of the data dependency. If none of the control dependencies are true, the result is $\bot$ (denoting error). If more than one of the control dependencies are true, the result is $\top$ (denoting inconsistency of the dependency graph; in this case the evaluation of the whole graph stops and this can be detected by the adversary). Note that among the above dependencies $l^{cvar}_{j1}, \dots, l^{cvar}_{jn}, l^{cdok}_j$ there can indeed be at most one that is true — if l^{cdok}_j is true then the ciphertext l^{vdct}_j cannot be created by a *pubencz*-operation and hence all comparisons $iseq(l^{vdct}_j, l^{vect}_i)$ return false. If one of these comparisons returns true then the ciphertext l^{vdct}_j was created by a *pubencz*-operation and its decryption l^{vdpt}_j will be false (by definition). Different *pubencz*-operations produce different values (the opposite event has negligible probability), hence at most one of $l^{cvar}_{j1}, \dots, l^{cvar}_{jn}$ can be true.

If infinite replications are present then we have to consider the dimensions of the operations as well. Namely, the set of dimensions of the *iseq*-operation labeled with l^{cvar}_{ji} is the union of the sets of dimensions of the i-th encryption and the j-th decryption operation. The representations of the dependencies to l^{cvar}_{ji} include coordinate mappings telling which dimensions of l^{vdct}_j and l^{vect}_i correspond to which dimensions of l^{cvar}_{ji}. The multiplexer labeled with l'^{vdpt}_j has just the same dimensions as the j-th decryption operation, hence it has to contract the rest of the dimensions of l^{cvar}_{ji}. In effect, the multiplexer will have an infinite number of inputs. The semantics stays the same — something different from $\bot$ or $\top$ is produced only if exactly one of (infinitely many) selectors is *true*.

Symmetric encryption is handled in a similar way. The requirements put on the symmetric encryption scheme are IND-CCA2, and ciphertext integrity (inability to generate a "valid" ciphertext without knowing the secret key) [7]. Similarly, based on these properties, the encryptions of the real text are replaced with the encryptions of the constant, and the decryptions are replaced with a set of comparisons with encrypted values. This can only be done if the encryption key is not used anywhere except as a key in encryption and decryption operations, and the random coins used in key generation and encryptions are used only there. The difference from the asymmetric decryption is that the decryption of the ciphertext does not have to be considered (due to the ciphertext integrity property). Formally, let the graph contain the following operations:

$$rs^{l^{vrs}}(l^{crs}) \qquad symkey^{l^{vsk}}(l^{csk}, l^{vrs})$$

$$rs^{l_i^{vrs}}(l_i^{crs}) \qquad symenc^{l_i^{vect}}(l_i^{ce}, l^{vsk}, l_i^{vept}, l_i^{vrs}) \qquad (\text{where } 1 \le i \le n)$$

$$symdec^{l_j^{vdpt}}(l_j^{cd}, l^{vsk}, l_j^{vdct}) \qquad (\text{where } 1 \le j \le m)$$

All occurrences of l_i^{vect} and l_j^{vdpt} in the rest of the graph are replaced with the l_i^{vect} and l_j^{dpt}, defined as following (*symencz* is defined in the same way as *pubencz*, but uses the symmetric encryption primitive):

$$symencz^{l_i^{vect}}(l_i^{ce}, l^{vsk}, l_i^{vrs}) \qquad (\text{where } 1 \le i \le n)$$

$$iseq^{l_{ji}^{cvar}}(l_j^{vdct}, l_i^{vect}) \qquad (\text{where } 1 \le i \le n, 1 \le j \le m)$$

$$mux_n^{l_j^{vdpt}}(l^{cd_j}, l_{j1}^{cvar}, l_1^{vept}, \dots, l_{jn}^{cvar}, l_n^{vept}) \qquad (\text{where } 1 \le j \le m)$$

6.3   The Movement of Multiplexers

After replacing the encryption and decryption operations with *mux*, it is usually possible to simplify the resulting graph. As the *mux* does not perform a computation on its input dependencies, an operation performed on the output of the *mux* can be "shifted" to all inputs. This movement may expose further simplification possibilities by putting next to each other the operations that cancel each other out. Formally if the graph contains the operations

$$mux_n^l(l^{cmux}, l_1^{cvar}, l_1^{vvar}, \dots, l_n^{cvar}, l_n^{vvar})$$

$$Op^{l^2}(\dots, l, \dots)$$

then all occurrences of the dependency l^2 in the graph may be replaced with l'^2 after we have added the following operations to the graph:

$$Op_i^{l'^{vvar}}(\dots, l_i^{vvar}, \dots) \qquad (\text{where } 1 \le i \le n)$$

$$mux_n^{l'^2}(l^{cmux}, l_1^{cvar}, l_1^{vvar}, \dots, l_n^{cvar}, l_n^{vvar})$$

If l'^2 is a control dependency (meaning that $l_1^{vvar}, \dots, l_n^{vvar}$ are control dependencies as well) then the resulting multiplexer can be replaced with a composition of boolean operations expressing the semantics of multiplexers.

Another possible simplification is the replacment of a *mux* with always selected option with that option. Suppose the graph has the operation:

$$mux_n^l(l^{cmux}, l_1^{cvar}, l_1^{vvar}, \dots, l_n^{cvar}, l_n^{vvar})$$

If it can be derived that $\rho[c_{mux}] = true$ implies for some i $\rho[l_i^{cvar}] = true$, $\forall j \ne i.\rho[l_j^{cvar}] = false$, then the only possible outcome of the *mux* is the i-th option (or *error* (always returning $\bot$), if the control dependency is not *true*). So, all the references to l can be replaced with l', defined as following: $id^{l'}(l^{cmux}, l_i^{vvar})$.

6.4   Other Transformations

Due to space requirements less principal transformations cannot be described in length – a brief overview on them is given instead.

Some of the transformations follow from the properties of the data operations. Projection of a component from just constructed tuple can be replaced with the dependency used in tuple construction; control dependency of that operation is a conjunction of tuple and the original projection operation control dependencies. The same simplification is also possible for other corresponding constructor-destructor pairs. But if a constructor is followed by an incompatible destructor (for example, projection from a ciphertext) then the destructor may be replaced with the *error*-operation — we assume that all values produced in the graph are tagged with their type, so the type confusion is impossible.

Most of the operations return $\perp$ if the control dependency is *false*, or any of the arguments is $\perp$. If it is statically known that either of these cases is always true, the corresponding operation could be replaced with the *error*.

Another set of transformations is based on the boolean logic: an and_1 or or_1 (operation with a single dependency) can be replaced with its input dependency; an *and* or *or* operation whose result is statically known (one of the dependencies is *true* in case of *or*, and *false* in case of *and*) can be replaced with that result; two sequential boolean operations of the same kind can be combined; if it can be derived that one dependency implies (in the boolean logic sense) another, then *or* and *and* of these two dependencies can be formulated using just one of the dependencies. If it is possible to derive that at most one of two control dependencies can be true at any time (for example, the results $iseq(l_1, l_2)$ and $iseq(l_1, l_3)$ where l_2 and l_3 can be equal only with negligible probability — they might be the results of different *pubencz*-operations) then their conjunction can be replaced with *false*.

As the semantics of the operation depend only on the incoming dependencies of the operation (except for the operations returning random coins or adversarial input), two operations of the same kind with the same dependencies return the same result, so in the graph the result of the second operation can be replaced with the result of the first. If the cardinality of the operation is greater than that of its input dependencies (except for the control dependency), then the same values of the input dependencies are copied to each of the instances of the operation; each instance returns the same result, so the "extra" dimensions could be removed from the operation, and the result can be copied the required number of times.

In some cases it is possible to explicitly reflect the result of the computation in the graph. If two dependencies must always be equal at the input to some operation, they are replaced (on the input to the operation in question) with the special operation *merge*. It either returns the value of the dependencies if they are equal or $\perp$ if not. Two *merge* operations going in sequence can be replaced with a single *merge* operation having the union of the original operations' inputs. The operation *isok* returns *true* if the value of the input dependency is different from $\perp$ and *false* otherwise. If the input to the *isok* is statically known, the result is also constant. Some operations (e.g. random coins generation) never fail. The success of some of the operations performing computations only depends on whether its arguments are valid (so *isok* of the result could be replaced with a conjunction of *isok* of each argument). Similarly, if the arguments to the comparison operation *iseq* are statically known, the results are also known and the operation could be replaced with a constant *true* or *false*.

7 Proving Integrity Properties

While the secrecy property we defined in Sec. 4 stated the independence of adversary's view from the secret messages, the integrity properties state that only runs satisfying a certain predicate are feasible (i.e. the probablity that a protocol run does not satisfy this predicate is negligible). *Correspondence assertions* are a well-known means for specifying integrity properties of protocols, and our approach turns out to be well-suited for arguing about them as well.

To state a correspondence assertion, one inserts statements of the form *begin*(E) and *end*(E) to the protocol text, where E is some expression. The execution of such a statement means finding the value v of E and recording that the statement *begin*(v) or *end*(v) has been executed. The correspondence is satisfied if each execution of *end*(v) is preceeded by an execution of *begin*(v) with the same value v. Moreover, the correspondence is *injective* if there is a separate *begin*(v) for each *end*(v) [20].

Similarly, we can insert nodes $begin^l(l^c, l^v)$ and $end^l(l^c, l^v)$ to our protocol. Here l^c is the control dependency and l^v carries the value that appears in the executed *begin*- or *end*-statement. An execution of the dependency graph also gives rise to a sequence of executed *begin*- and *end*-nodes (if several of those nodes are executed simultaneously then we assume that *begin*-s happened before the *end*-s), allowing us to define correspondence and injective correspondence in the same way. The protocol modifications do no change the order of execution of those statements, hence the original protocol satisfies the correspondence property iff the final protocol does.

Our experience shows that arguing about the order of executions of *begin*- and *end*-nodes in the final, modified protocol is quite feasible. To show correspondence we have to locate a node $begin^{l^b}(l^{cb}, l^{vb})$ for each node $end^{l^e}(l^{ce}, l^{ve})$, such that the values of dependencies l^{vb} and l^{ve} are equal whenever both are defined. If $l^{vb} = l^{ve}$ then the equality is trivial, but the dependency graph also enables us to straightforwardly check their equality if l^{ve} is defined as a *merge* of l^{vb} and something else (or other similar patterns). We also have to show that l^{ce} implies l^{cb}. We have devised an analysis for determining the implications between control dependencies (the results of this analysis are also used in transformations described in Sec. 6.4) and this analysis turns out to be precise enough for determining that $l^{ce} \Rightarrow l^{cb}$. The injective correspondence can be proved by showing that among several control dependencies, controlling several alternative *end*-statements, at most one can be true (the respective analysis of control dependencies was also hinted in Sec. 6.4).

8   Results Achieved

The dependency graphs-based approach, presented in this article, is a convenient tool for investigating the data flows taking place in the distributed computing systems. It is based on finding out the data and control flows on the protocol representation, and modifying the representation based on the semantics of the individual operations and connections between them.

The automatic protocol analyser has been implemented. The analyser has been applied to several protocols from the secure protocols open repository (http://www.lsv.ens-cachan.fr/spore/): Needham-Schroeder public key, Lowe's fixed version of Needham-Schroeder Public Key, Needham-Schroeder secret key, Kao-Chow Authentication, and TMN. TMN and Needham-Schroeder public key were not proved to be secure (corresponding graphs still contain secret message even after all the transformations applied); for both protocols there are known attacks. Graphs corresponding to Lowe's fixed version of Needham-Schroeder Public Key and Kao-Chow Authentication were transformed to a form not containing the secret message, thus indicating that secrecy property holds. The Needham-Schroeder secret key is considered secure under the condition that previously exchanged key is not compromised; the Denning-Sacco key freshness attack (if the adversary has obtained the key used in one of the previous sessions) was also successfully detected. Analysis of the Needham-Schroeder-Lowe public key protocol takes 10 minutes on Pentium M 1.60 GHz machine. The current implementation of the protocol analyser has some room for optimization (mostly – reusing the intermediate calculations between transformations), so the time of the analysis could be significantly reduced.

The difference with CryptoVerif [9,10,11] is that the transformations defined in our framework are not as sensitive to the order of applications as the CryptoVerif ones. The CryptoVerif, while being mechanized, is not automatic while operating on some protocols involving public key cryptography (e.g. Needham-Schroeder-Lowe public key). At some point in proof several transformations are "allowed", but only one of them leads to the successful proof. The human support is required to decide which transformation is the proper one. An example of transformations in question is *SArename* and the ones based on the properties of the cryptographic primitives . The *SArename* is performed to split the single variable defined multiple times (e.g. in different branches of *if*) into several separate definitions. Each use of such variable is then analysed in branches - one for each possible definition. Applying the transformation of the public key encryption "too early" in the analysis transforms the protocol to the form, where the *SArename* is no longer able to split the uses of the variable at the same fine granularity. Some of the information flows revealing the secret, present in the cases never executed, being combined with cases that are executed, are not removed from the further analysis, and the proof fails. When performed in the "right" order, same transformations separate the cases at sufficient granularity to produce a successful proof.

The analyser prototype we implemented is able to prove the secrecy of each secure protocol we tried it on by iterating the application of possible transformations until no more transformations are possible, without any hints from the user. So far we haven't observed the situation where the success of the proof depends on the order of transformations applied. We suspect the reason is in the usage of the "smaller-scale" transformations, and making all the conditions present at the point of definition (of each sub-case) explicit at the point of use, thus being able to delimit and remove the branches never executed with satisfactory precision without external hints. Another possible reason is that the multiplexer movement (described in sec. 6.3) is not present in CryptoVerif [9,10,11], nor seems there to be an easy way to add it. The information collection phase of CryptoVerif is able to compensate this omission to some extent, by propagating information about values through the multiplexer. This information can be used for validating certain simplifications, but not for doing cryptographic transformations.

The further research directions are quite "standard" — the application of the framework for determining other security properties, enriching the programming language with more cryptographic primitives, calculation of the exact (negligible) probability of distinguishing the semantics of the resulting graph from the initial one, and running the framework on more protocols. In particular, it would be interesting to verify protocols that are not so easily expressible in the Dolev-Yao model because of the cryptographic primitives they are using (e.g. verifyable secret sharing) and the security properties we are trying to prove. Voting schemes (for example, [14]) are obvious candidates for testing our framework.

Acknowledgement

We are thankful to the anonymous referees of TGC 2007 conference for their comments. They certainly have improved the readability of this paper.

This research has been supported by the Estonian Information Technology Foundation, the ESF Grants No. 6839 and 6944, and the EU FP6-IST project No. 15964 "AEOLUS".

References

1. Abadi, M., Rogaway, P.: Reconciling Two Views of Cryptography (The Computational Soundness of Formal Encryption). In: Watanabe, O., Hagiya, M., Ito, T., van Leeuwen, J., Mosses, P.D. (eds.) TCS 2000. LNCS, vol. 1872, pp. 3–22. Springer, Heidelberg (2000)
2. Abadi, M., Jürjens, J.: Formal Eavesdropping and its Computational Interpretation. In: Kobayashi, N., Pierce, B.C. (eds.) TACS 2001. LNCS, vol. 2215, pp. 82–94. Springer, Heidelberg (2001)
3. Adão, P., Bana, G., Herzog, J., Scedrov, A.: Soundness of formal encryption in the presence of key-cycles. In: di Vimercati, S.d.C., Syverson, P.F., Gollmann, D. (eds.) ESORICS 2005. LNCS, vol. 3679, pp. 374–396. Springer, Heidelberg (2005)
4. Backes, M., Pfitzmann, B., Waidner, M.: A Composable Cryptographic Library with Nested Operations. In: 10th ACM Conference on Computer and Communications Security (CCS 2003), October 2003, pp. 220–230 (2003)

5. Backes, M., Laud, P.: Computationally Sound Secrecy Proofs by Mechanized Flow Analysis. In: 13th ACM Conference on Computer and Communications Security (CCS 2006), pp. 370–379 (2006)
6. Bellare, M., Desai, A., Pointcheval, D., Rogaway, P.: Relations among Notions of Security for Public-Key Encryption Schemes. In: Krawczyk, H. (ed.) CRYPTO 1998. LNCS, vol. 1462, pp. 26–45. Springer, Heidelberg (1998)
7. Bellare, M., Namprempre, C.: Authenticated Encryption: Relations among notions and analysis of the generic composition paradigm. In: Okamoto, T. (ed.) ASIACRYPT 2000. LNCS, vol. 1976, pp. 531–545. Springer, Heidelberg (2000)
8. Bellare, M., Rogaway, P.: The Security of Triple Encryption and a Framework for Code-Based Game-Playing Proofs. In: Vaudenay, S. (ed.) EUROCRYPT 2006. LNCS, vol. 4004, pp. 409–426. Springer, Heidelberg (2006), http://eprint.iacr.org
9. Blanchet, B.: A computationally sound mechanized prover for security protocols. In: Proc. 27th IEEE Symposium on Security & Privacy (2006)
10. Blanchet, B., Pointcheval, D.: Automated Security Proofs with Sequences of Games. In: Dwork, C. (ed.) CRYPTO 2006. LNCS, vol. 4117, pp. 537–554. Springer, Heidelberg (2006)
11. Blanchet, B.: Computationally Sound Mechanized Proofs of Correspondence Assertions. In: Proc. 20th IEEE Computer Security Foundations Symposium (2007)
12. Canetti, R.: Universally Composable Security: A New Paradigm for Cryptographic Protocols. In: 42nd Annual Symposium on Foundations of Computer Science (FOCS 2001), October 2001, pp. 136–145 (2001)
13. Cortier, V., Warinschi, B.: Computationally Sound, Automated Proofs for Security Protocols. In: Sagiv, M. (ed.) ESOP 2005. LNCS, vol. 3444, pp. 157–171. Springer, Heidelberg (2005)
14. Cramer, R., Gennaro, R., Schoenmakers, B.: A Secure and Optimally Efficient Multi-Authority Election Scheme. In: Fumy, W. (ed.) EUROCRYPT 1997. LNCS, vol. 1233, pp. 103–118. Springer, Heidelberg (1997)
15. Dolev, D., Yao, A.C.: On the security of public key protocols. IEEE Transactions on Information Theory IT-29(12), 198–208 (1983)
16. Joshua, D., Guttman, F.: Javier Thayer, and Lenore D. Zuck. The Faithfulness of Abstract Protocol Analysis: Message Authentication. In: 8th ACM Conference on Computer and Communications Security (CCS 2001), November 2001, pp. 186–195 (2001)
17. Laud, P.: Handling Encryption in Analysis for Secure Information Flow. In: Degano, P. (ed.) ESOP 2003. LNCS, vol. 2618, pp. 159–173. Springer, Heidelberg (2003)
18. Laud, P.: Symmetric encryption in automatic analyses for confidentiality against active adversaries. In: 2004 IEEE Symposium on Security and Privacy, May 2004, pp. 71–85 (2004)
19. Laud, P.: Secrecy Types for a Simulatable Cryptographic Library. In: 12th ACM Conference on Computer and Communications Security (CCS 2005), pp. 26–35 (2005)
20. Lowe, G.: A Hierarchy of Authentication Specification. In: 10th Computer Security Foundations Workshop, pp. 31–44 (1997)
21. Janvier, R., Lakhnech, Y., Mazaré, L.: Completing the Picture: Soundness of Formal Encryption in the Presence of Active Adversaries. In: Sagiv, M. (ed.) ESOP 2005. LNCS, vol. 3444, pp. 172–185. Springer, Heidelberg (2005)
22. Micciancio, D., Panjwani, S.: Adaptive Security of Symbolic Encryption. In: Kilian, J. (ed.) TCC 2005. LNCS, vol. 3378, pp. 169–187. Springer, Heidelberg (2005)

23. Micciancio, D., Warinschi, B.: Completeness Theorems for the Abadi-Rogaway Logic of Encrypted Expressions. In: Workshop in Issues in the Theory of Security (WITS 2002), January 2002 (2002)
24. Riis Nielson, H., Nielson, F.: Semantics with Applications: A Formal Introduction. Wiley, Chichester (1992)
25. Pfitzmann, B., Waidner, M.: A Model for Asynchronous Reactive Systems and its Application to Secure Message Transmission. In: 2001 IEEE Symposium on Security and Privacy (IEEE S&P 2001), pp. 184–200 (2001)
26. Pingali, K., Beck, M., Johnson, R., Moudgill, M., Stodghill, P.: Dependence Flow Graphs: an Algebraic Approach to Program Dependencies. In: Advances in Languages and Compilers for Parallel Processing, pp. 445–467. MIT Press, Cambridge (1991)
27. Tšahhirov, I., Laud, P.: Digital Signature in Automatic Analyses for Confidentiality against Active Adversaries. In: Nordsec 2005 10th Nordic Workshop on Secure IT Systems, Tartu, Estonia, October 20-21, 2005, pp. 29–41 (2005)
28. Yao, A.C.: Theory and Applications of Trapdoor Functions (extended abstract). In: 23rd Annual Symposium on Foundations of Computer Science, November 1982, pp. 80–91 (1982)

Formal Proofs of Cryptographic Security of Diffie-Hellman-Based Protocols*

Arnab Roy[1], Anupam Datta[2], and John C. Mitchell[1]

[1] Stanford University, Stanford, CA
{arnab, mitchell}@cs.stanford.edu
[2] Carnegie Mellon University, Pittsburgh, PA
danupam@cmu.edu

Abstract. We present axioms and inference rules for reasoning about Diffie-Hellman-based key exchange protocols and use these rules to prove authentication and secrecy properties of two important protocol standards, the Diffie-Hellman variant of Kerberos, and IKEv2, the revised standard key management protocol for IPSEC. The new proof system is sound for an accepted semantics used in cryptographic studies. In the process of applying our system, we uncover a deficiency in Diffie-Hellman Kerberos that is easily repaired.

1 Introduction

Diffie-Hellman key exchange (DHKE) is one of the earliest public-key concepts [28]. It allows two parties without a prior shared secret to jointly create one that is independent of past and future keys, and is therefore widely used in many network security protocols. In this paper, we develop axioms for reasoning about protocols that use Diffie-Hellman key exchange, prove these axioms sound using cryptographic reduction arguments, and use the axiom system to formally prove authentication and secrecy theorems for two significant standardized protocols. The two protocols we consider are Diffie-Hellman Key Exchange for initial authentication in Kerberos V5 [43] (which we refer to as DHINIT) and IKEv2 [34], the IPSEC key exchange standard. Kerberos is widely used in Microsoft Windows networking and other applications, while IKEv2 is part of IPSEC which is widely used for virtual private networks. The authentication and secrecy theorems, for probabilistic polynomial-time execution and standard cryptographic protocol attacks, have not been proved before to the best of our knowledge. In analyzing DHINIT, we also discover that the KAS is *not* authenticated to the client after the first stage, but we are able to prove formally in our logic that authentication is nonetheless achieved at a later stage; we also suggest a change to the protocol to ensure authentication after the first stage. In analyzing IKEv2, which replaces the seriously flawed Internet Key Exchange

---

* This work was partially supported by the NSF Science and Technology Center TRUST and U.S. Army Research Office contract on Perpetually Available and Secure Information Systems (DAAD19-02-1-0389) to CMU's CyLab.

G. Barthe and C. Fournet (Eds.): TGC 2007, LNCS 4912, pp. 312–329, 2008.

(IKEv1) protocol using concepts from an intermediate protocol called Just Fast Keying (JFK) [3], we consider the IKEv2 mode in which signatures are used for authentication and Diffie-Hellman exponentials are never reused.

The axioms presented in this paper are used in Protocol Composition Logic (PCL) [24,26,41,25,39]. Our formalization uses the characterization of "good key" from [27], but improves on previous work in several respects: (i) we fix a bug in the **DH** axiom in [27] by using the "DHStrongSecretive" formulas developed in the paper, (ii) we present a general inductive method for proving secrecy conditions for Diffie-Hellman key exchange, and (iii) we present axioms for reasoning from ciphertext integrity assumptions. These three innovations are essential for the formal proofs for DHINIT and IKEv2, which could not be carried out in the system of [27]. In addition, the present soundness proofs are based on a new cryptographic definition and associated theorems about the joint security of multiple encryption schemes keyed using random or DHKE-keys. This paper complements [39] and completes the development of formal cryptographically sound proofs for three modes of Kerberos V5 ([42] contains technical details).

Most demonstrated approaches for proving security of complex network protocols, of the scale that appear in IEEE and IETF standards, use a simplified model of protocol execution based on symbolic computation and highly idealized cryptography [9,16,19,24]. However, proofs about symbolic computation do not provide the same level of assurance as proofs about probabilistic polynomial-time attacks. Several groups of researchers have therefore developed methods for deriving cryptographic meaning from properties of symbolic protocol execution [7,6,18,22,31,32,38]. These methods involve showing that the behavior of a symbolic abstraction, under symbolic attacks, yields the same significant failures as a finer-grained execution under finer-grained probabilistic polynomial-time attack. However, such equivalence theorems rely on strong cryptographic assumptions, and there are no known suitable symbolic abstractions of Diffie-Hellman exponentiation. In addition, there are theoretical negative results that suggest that correspondence theorems may be impossible for symmetric encryption if a protocol might reveal a secret key [17,23], or for hash functions or exclusive-or [5,8]. In contrast, computational PCL reasons directly about properties of probabilistic polynomial-time execution of protocols, under attack by a probabilistic polynomial-time adversary, without explicit formal reasoning about probability or complexity. In addition, different axioms depend on different cryptographic assumptions, allowing us to consider which assumptions are actually necessary for each property we establish. As currently formulated in the RFC, Kerberos requires a party to sign only its own Diffie-Hellman exponential. We prove this is sufficient, using axioms that depend on the *random oracle* assumption [12]. However, we are not able to give a formal proof using alternate axioms that do not depend on random oracles. On the other hand, the alternate axioms are sufficient to prove authentication if we modify the protocol slightly so that the KAS signs both the Diffie-Hellman exponentials, as is done in IKEv2 and JFK.

Two related studies are a symbolic proof for Kerberos (without DHKE) [4] and a cryptographic reduction proof for JFK [3]. In the Kerberos analysis, a correspondence between symbolic computation and cryptographic models [7] is used to draw cryptographic conclusions. This requires a separate verification that a "commitment problem" does not occur in the protocol (see [4]), and does not extend to Diffie-Hellman. The JFK proof is interesting and informative, with suggestions in [3] that "analysis based on formal methods would be a useful complement," but simpler than the proof of DHINIT since JFK digitally signs Diffie-Hellman values differently. More generally, Abadi and Rogaway [1] initiated computationally sound symbolic analysis of static equivalence, with extensions and completeness explored in [37,2]; a recent extension to Diffie-Hellman appears in [15], covering only *passive adversaries,* not the stronger active adversaries used in the present paper. Protocol Composition Logic [24] was used in a case study of 802.11i [29], has previous computational semantics [26], and was used to study protocol composition and key exchange [27]. In other studies of DHKE, [30] uses a symbolic model, while [36] imposes nonstandard protocol assumptions. The cryptographic primitives used in Kerberos are analyzed in [14].

Section 2 summarizes Protocol Composition Logic (PCL), with section 3 presenting the proof system and computational soundness theorem. Kerberos DHINIT and IKEv2 are analyzed in sections 4 and 5, respectively. Conclusions are in section 6.

2   Background

This section contains a brief summary of aspects of Protocol Composition Logic (PCL) used in the rest of this paper. Additional background appears in [24,26,41,25,39].

Modelling protocols. A protocol is given by a set of roles, each specifying a sequence of actions to be executed by an honest agent. Protocol roles may be written using a process language in which each role defines a sequential process, and concurrency arises as a consequence of concurrent execution of any number of instances of protocol roles. The set of role actions include generating a new nonce, signing or encrypting a messages, communicating over the network, and decrypting or verifying a signature through pattern matching. A role may depend on so-called input parameters, such as the intended recipient of messages sent by an instance of the role, or the recipient's public encryption key. An example protocol is presented in Section 4.

Protocol execution may be characterized using probabilistic polynomial-time oracle Turing machines [13]. In this approach, an initial configuration is defined by choosing a number of principals (agents), assigning one or more role instances to each principal, designating some subset of the principals as honest, and choosing encryption keys as needed. Protocol execution then proceeds by allowing a probabilistic polynomial-time adversary to control protocol execution by interacting with honest principals (as oracles). This gives the adversary complete control over the network, but keys and random nonces associated with honest parties are not given directly to the adversary unless they are revealed in the course of protocol execution.

Each protocol, initial configuration, and choice of probabilistic polynomial-time adversary gives rise to a probability distribution on polynomial-length executions. A *trace* records all actions executed by honest principals and the attacker during one execution (run) of the protocol. Since honest principals execute roles defined by symbolic programs, we may define traces so that they record symbolic descriptions of the actions of honest parties and a mapping of symbolic variables to bitstrings values manipulated by the associated Turing machine. Since an attacker is not given by a symbolic program, a trace only records the send-receive actions of the attacker, not its internal actions. Traces also include the random bits (used by the honest parties, the adversary and available to an additional probabilistic polynomial-time algorithm called the distinguisher), as well as a few other elements used in defining semantics of formulas over collections of traces [26].

Protocol logic, proof system, cryptographic soundness. The syntax of PCL and the informal descriptions of the principal predicates are given in [25,39]. Most protocol proofs use formulas of the form $\theta[P]_X\phi$, which are similar to Hoare triples. Informally, $\theta[P]_X\phi$ means that after actions P are executed by the thread X, starting from any state where formula θ is true, formula ϕ is true about the resulting state. Formulas θ and ϕ typically combine assertions about temporal order of actions (useful for stating authentication) and assertions about knowledge (useful for stating secrecy).

Intuitively, a formula is true about a protocol if, as we increase the security parameter and look at the resulting probability distributions on traces, the probability of the formula failing is negligible (i.e., bounded above by the reciprocal of any polynomial). We may define the meaning of a formula φ on a set T of equi-probable computational traces as a subset $T' \subseteq T$ that respects φ in some specific way. For example, an action predicate such as Send selects a set of traces in which a send occurs (by the indicated agent). More precisely, the semantics $[\![\varphi]\!]\,(T, D, \epsilon)$ of a formula φ is inductively defined on the set T of traces, with distinguisher D and tolerance ϵ. The distinguisher and tolerance are only used in the semantics of the secrecy predicates Indist and GoodKeyAgainst, where they determine whether the distinguisher has more than a negligible chance of distinguishing the given value from random or winning an IND-CCA game (standard in the cryptographic literature), respectively. We say a protocol Q satisfies a formula φ, written $Q \models \varphi$ if, for all adversaries and sufficiently large security parameters, the *probability* that φ "holds" is asymptotically overwhelming. A precise inductive semantics is given in [26].

Protocol proofs are written using a formal proof system, which includes axioms and proof rules that capture essential properties of cryptographic primitives such as signature and encryption schemes. In addition, the proof system incorporates axioms and rules for first-order reasoning, temporal reasoning, knowledge, and a form of inductive invariant rule called the "honesty" rule. The induction rule is essential for combining facts about one role with inferred actions of other roles. An axiom about a cryptographic primitive is generally proved sound by a cryptographic reduction argument that relies on some cryptographic assumption about that primitive. As a result, the mathematical import of a formal proof in

PCL may depend on a set of cryptographic assumptions, namely those assumptions required to prove soundness of the actual axioms and rules that are used in the proof. In some cases, there may be different ways to prove a single PCL formula, some relying on one set of cryptographic assumptions, and another proof relying on another set of cryptographic assumptions.

3   Proof System

Section 3.1 contains new axioms and rules for reasoning about Diffie-Hellman key exchange. Section 3.2 summarizes the concept of *secretive protocol* and proof rules taken from [39] that are used in this paper to establish secrecy properties. However, we give new soundness proofs for these axioms, based on an extension of standard multiparty encryption schemes [10] to allow for multiple public and symmetric encryption schemes keyed using random or Diffie-Hellman based keys. The associated cryptographic definitions and theorems are presented in Section 3.3.

3.1   Diffie-Hellman Axioms

In this section we formalize reasoning about how individual threads treat DH exponentials in an appropriate way. We introduce the predicate $\mathsf{DHGood}(X, m, x)$, where x is a nonce used to compute a DH exponential, to capture the notion that thread X only uses certain safe actions to compute m from values that it has generated or received over the network. For example, axioms **DH2** and **DH3** say that a message m is DHGood if it has just been received, or if it is just computed by exponentiating the known group generator g with the nonce x. Axiom **DH4** states that the pair of two DHGood terms is also DHGood.

Note that unlike the symbolic model, it is not well defined in the computational model to say "m contains x". That is why our proof systems for secrecy in the symbolic model [41] and computational model [39] are different - the computational system does induction on actions rather than structure of terms. The need to look at the structure of m is obviated by the way the reduction to games like IND-CCA works. The high level intuition is that a consistent simulation of the protocol can be performed while doing the reduction, if the terms to be sent to the adversary are "good".

DH0 $\mathsf{DHGood}(X, a, x)$, for a of any atomic type, except nonce, *viz.* name or key

DH1 $\mathsf{New}(Y, n) \wedge n \neq x \supset \mathsf{DHGood}(X, n, x)$

DH2 $[\texttt{receive } m;]_X \mathsf{DHGood}(X, m, x)$

DH3 $[m := \texttt{expg } x;]_X \mathsf{DHGood}(X, m, x)$

DH4 $\mathsf{DHGood}(X, m_0, x) \wedge \mathsf{DHGood}(X, m_1, x) [m := m_0.m_1;]_X \mathsf{DHGood}(X, m, x)$

DH5 $\mathsf{DHGood}(X, m, x) [m' := \texttt{symenc } m, k;]_X \mathsf{DHGood}(X, m', x)$

DH6 $\mathsf{DHGood}(X, m, x) [m' := \texttt{hash } m;]_X \mathsf{DHGood}(X, m', x)$

The formula $\mathsf{SendDHGood}(X, x)$ indicates that thread X sent out only "DH-Good" terms w.r.t. the nonce x. $\mathsf{DHSecretive}(X, Y, k)$ means that there exist nonces x, y such that threads X, Y respectively generated them, sent out "DH-Good" terms and X generated the key k from g^{xy}. DHStrongSecretive(X, Y, k) asserts a stronger condition - that threads X and Y only used each other's DH exponentials to generate the shared secret (The predicate Exp(X, gx, y) means thread X exponentiates gx to the power y). The formula SharedSecret(X, Y, k) means that the key k satisfies IND-CCA key usability against any thread other than X or Y, particularly against any adversary. Formally,

$$\text{SendDHGood}(X, x) \equiv \forall m. \text{ Send}(X, m) \supset \text{DHGood}(X, m, x)$$
$$\text{DHSecretive}(X, Y, k) \equiv \exists x, y. \text{ New}(X, x) \wedge \text{SendDHGood}(X, x) \wedge$$
$$\text{New}(Y, y) \wedge \text{SendDHGood}(Y, y) \wedge \text{KeyGen}(X, k, x, g^y)$$
$$\text{DHStrongSecretive}(X, Y, k) \equiv \exists x, y. \text{ New}(X, x) \wedge \text{SendDHGood}(X, x) \wedge$$
$$\text{New}(Y, y) \wedge \text{SendDHGood}(Y, y) \wedge \text{KeyGen}(X, k, x, g^y) \wedge$$
$$(\text{Exp}(X, gy, x) \supset gy = g^y) \wedge (\text{Exp}(Y, gx, y) \supset gx = g^x)$$
$$\text{SharedSecret}(X, Y, k) \equiv \forall Z. \text{ GoodKeyAgainst}(Z, k) \vee Z = X \vee Z = Y$$

The following axioms hold for the above definition of SendGood:

SDH0 Start$(X) \supset$ SendDHGood(X, x)

SDH1 SendDHGood(X, x) [a]$_X$ SendDHGood(X, x), where a is not a send action

SDH2 SendDHGood(X, x) [send $m;$]$_X$ DHGood$(X, m, x) \supset$ SendDHGood(X, x)

The following axioms relate the DHStrongSecretive property, which is trace based, to computational notions of security. The first axiom, which depends on the DDH (Decisional Diffie-Hellman) assumption and IND-CCA security of the encryption scheme, states a secrecy property - if threads X and Y are DHStrongSecretive w.r.t. the key k, then k satisfies IND-CCA key usability. The second axiom, which depends on the DDH assumption and INT-CTXT (ciphertext integrity [11,33]) security of the encryption scheme, states that with the same DHStrongSecretive property, if someone decrypts a term with the key k successfully, then it must have been encrypted with the key k by either X or Y. Both the axioms are proved sound by cryptographic reductions to the primitive security games.

DH   DHStrongSecretive$(X, Y, k) \Rightarrow$ SharedKey(X, Y, k)

CTXGS   DHStrongSecretive$(X, Y, k) \wedge$ SymDec$(Z, E_{sym}[k](m), k) \supset$
$$\text{SymEnc}(X, m, k) \vee \text{SymEnc}(Y, m, k)$$

If the weaker property DHSecretive(X, Y, k) holds then we can establish an axiom similar to **CTXGS**, but we have to model the key generation function as a random oracle and the soundness proof (presented in [42]) is very different. The intuition behind this requirement is that if the threads do not use each other's intended DH exponentials then there could, in general, be related key attacks; the random oracle obviates this possibility.

CTXG   DHSecretive$(X, Y, k) \wedge$ SymDec$(Z, E_{sym}[k](m), k) \supset$
$$\text{SymEnc}(X, m, k) \vee \text{SymEnc}(Y, m, k)$$

The earlier paper [27] overlooked the subtle difference between the DHStrongSecretive and DHSecretive predicates. Specifically, in order to prove the axiom **DH** sound without the random oracle model, it is necessary to ensure that both parties use only each other's DH exponentials to generate keys—a condition guaranteed by DHStrongSecretive, but not DHSecretive or the variant considered in [27].

To provide some sense of the soundness proofs, we sketch the proof for the **CTXGS** axiom. The axiom is sound if the set (given by the semantics) $[\, k) \supset$ SymEnc$(X, m, k) \vee$ SymEnc$(Y, m, k)]\!](T, D, \epsilon)$ includes almost all traces in the set T generated by any probabilistic poly-time adversary $\mathcal{A}$. Assume that this is not the case: Let E be the event that an honest principal decrypts a ciphertext c with the key k such that c was not produced by X or Y by encryption with the key k; there exists an adversary $\mathcal{A}$ who forces E to occur in a non-negligible number of traces. Using $\mathcal{A}$, we will construct an adversary $\mathcal{A}'$ who breaks DDH, thereby arriving at a contradiction.

Suppose $\mathcal{A}'$ is given a DDH instance (g^a, g^b, g^c). It has to determine whether $c = ab$. Let the DH nonces used by X, Y be x, y respectively. $\mathcal{A}'$ simulates execution of the protocol to $\mathcal{A}$ by using g^a, g^b as the computational representations of g^x, g^y respectively. Whenever a symbolic step ($k' :=$ dhkeygen $m, x;$) comes up, $\mathcal{A}'$ behaves in the following manner: since DHStrongSecretive(X, Y, k) holds, m has to be equal to g^b, then k' is assigned the value g^c; Likewise for the action ($k' :=$ dhkeygen $m, y;$). After the protocol simulation, if the event E has occurred then output "$c = ab$", otherwise output "$c \neq ab$". The advantage of $\mathcal{A}'$ in winning the DDH game is:

$$\mathbf{Adv}^{\mathrm{DDH}}(\mathcal{A}') = \Pr[E | c = ab] - \Pr[E | c \neq ab]$$

By the assumption about $\mathcal{A}$, the first probability is non-negligible. The second probability is negligible because the encryption scheme is INT-CTXT secure. Hence the advantage of $\mathcal{A}'$ in breaking DDH is non-negligible. The SendDHGood predicate that DHStrongSecretive implies, ensures that the protocol simulation can be carried out consistently. Intuitively, this is ensured as long as the protocol simulator has to manipulate received messages, g^x, g^y (but not x, y directly) and key messages with g^{xy} to construct messages to be sent out. Axioms **DH0 – 6** are used to formally establish that the protocol has this property.

3.2 Secretive Protocols

In this section, we adapt the concept of *secretive protocol*, a trace-based condition implying computational secrecy [40,39], to permit keys generated from DHKE. While the proof rules remain identical, the soundness proofs are significantly different and involve a reduction to a multi-scheme IND-CCA game that we introduce in Section 3.3 of this paper. This definition allows the use of multiple encryption schemes keyed using randomly generated keys or keys output from a DHKE. A secretive protocol with respect to a nonce s and set of keys $\mathcal{K}$ is a protocol which generates *secretive traces*, defined below, with overwhelming probability.

Definition 1 (Secretive Trace). *A trace is a* secretive trace *with respect to s and $\mathcal{K}$ if the following properties hold for every thread belonging to honest principals:*

- *a thread which generates nonce s, ensures that it is encrypted with a key k in the set $\mathcal{K}$ in any message sent out.*
- *whenever a thread decrypts a message with a key k in $\mathcal{K}$, which was produced by encryption with key k by an honest party, and parses the decryption, it ensures that the results are encrypted with some key k′ with k′ ∈ $\mathcal{K}$ in any message sent out.*

To account for DH keys in the set $\mathcal{K}$, we wish to establish that DH keys are used in a "safe" manner by the protocol, formally captured by the predicate DHStrongSecretive. Following [39], the predicate $\text{Good}(X, m, s, \mathcal{K})$ asserts that the thread X constructed the term m in accordance with the rules allowing a *secretive protocol* with respect to nonce s and set of keys $\mathcal{K}$ to send out m. The formula $\text{SendGood}(X, s, \mathcal{K})$ asserts that all messages that thread X sends out are good and $\text{Secretive}(s, \mathcal{K})$ asserts that all honest threads only send out good messages. The axioms characterizing these predicates are same as in [39] and are omitted here. The induction rule $\textbf{IND}_{GOOD}$ states that if all honest threads executing some basic sequence (i.e. a fragment of a role pausing before the next receive, denoted P) in the protocol (denoted $\mathcal{Q}$) locally construct good messages to be sent out, given that they earlier also did so, then we can conclude $\text{Secretive}(s, \mathcal{K})$. A set of basic sequences (BS) of a role is any partition of the sequence of actions in a role such that if any element sequence has a `receive` then its only at its begining.

$$\textbf{IND}_{GOOD} \quad \forall \rho \in \mathcal{Q}.\forall P \in BS(\rho).$$

$$\frac{\text{SendGood}(X, s, \mathcal{K})\ [P]_X\ \varPhi \supset \text{SendGood}(X, s, \mathcal{K})}{\mathcal{Q} \vdash \varPhi \supset \text{Secretive}(s, \mathcal{K})}\ (*)$$

(*): $[P]_X$ does not capture free variables in $\varPhi$, $\mathcal{K}$, s, and $\varPhi$ is a prefix closed trace formula.

Now we relate the concept of a secretive protocol, which is trace-based, to complexity theoretic notions of security. We define a level-0 key to be either a pre-shared secret, a public key or a DH Key. To apply the results here the DHStrongSecretive property has to hold for a DH key k for some pair of honest threads. A nonce is established to be a level-1 key when the protocol is proved to be a *secretive protocol* with respect to the nonce and a set of level-0 keys. This concept is extended further to define level-2 keys and so on.

For a set of keys $\mathcal{K}$ of levels ≤ 1, $\mathcal{C}(\mathcal{K})$ is the union of all the level-0 keys in $\mathcal{K}$ and the union of all the level-0 keys protecting the level-1 keys in $\mathcal{K}$. The formula $\text{InInitSet}(X, s, \mathcal{K})$ asserts X is either the generator of nonce s or a possessor of some key in $\mathcal{C}(\mathcal{K})$. $\text{GoodInit}(s, \mathcal{K})$ asserts that all such threads belong to honest principals. The formula GoodKeyFor lets us state that secrets established by secretive protocols, where possibly the secrets are also used as keys, are good keys against everybody except the set of principals who either generated the secret or are in possession of a key protecting the secret. For level-0 keys which we want to claim as being possessed only by honest principals we use the formula GoodKey. For protocols employing an IND-CCA secure encryption scheme, the following axiom is sound:

$$\textbf{GK} \quad \mathsf{Secretive}(s, \mathcal{K}) \wedge \mathsf{GoodInit}(s, \mathcal{K}) \Rightarrow \mathsf{GoodKeyFor}(s, \mathcal{K})$$

If the encryption scheme is both IND-CCA and INT-CTXT secure then following axioms are sound:

$$\textbf{CTX0} \quad \mathsf{GoodKey}(k) \wedge \mathsf{SymDec}(Z, E_{sym}[k](m), k) \supset$$
$$\exists X. \, \mathsf{SymEnc}(X, m, k), \text{ for level-0 key } k.$$
$$\textbf{CTXL} \quad \mathsf{Secretive}(s, \mathcal{K}) \wedge \mathsf{GoodInit}(s, \mathcal{K}) \wedge \mathsf{SymDec}(Z, E_{sym}[s](m), s) \supset$$
$$\exists X. \, \mathsf{SymEnc}(X, m, s)$$

The following axiom states that if a protocol is secretive with respect to s and $\mathcal{K}$, then the only keys, under which a message containing s openly is found encrypted in a "good" message, are in the set $\mathcal{K}$:

$$\textbf{SDEC} \quad \mathsf{Secretive}(s, \mathcal{K}) \wedge \mathsf{SymDec}(X, E_{sym}[k](m), k) \wedge$$
$$\mathsf{Good}(X, E_{sym}[k](m), s, \mathcal{K}) \wedge \mathsf{ContainsOpen}(m, s) \supset k \in \mathcal{K}$$

The predicate $\mathsf{ContainsOpen}(m, a)$ asserts that a can be obtained from m by a series of unpairings only.

The **soundness theorem** is proved by showing that every axiom is a valid formula and that all proof rules preserve validity. The soundness proofs for the four axioms above are sketched in [42]; they proceed by reduction to the multiple encryption scheme game defined in the next section.

Theorem 1 (Soundness). $\forall \mathcal{Q}, \varphi.$ if $\mathcal{Q} \vdash \varphi$ then $\mathcal{Q} \models \varphi$.

3.3 Joint Security of Multiple Encryption Schemes

A public-key encryption scheme $\mathcal{ES}$ is a triplet $(\mathcal{KG}, \mathcal{E}, \mathcal{D})$ such that $\mathcal{KG}(I)$ generates a pair of keys (ek, dk), where I is some initial information, ek is the public key and dk is the private key, and $\mathcal{E}$ and $\mathcal{D}$ are the encryption and decryption functions respectively. In [10], Bellare, Boldyreva and Micali analyzed the security of a single public-key encryption scheme in a setting where more than one independent keys are used. The security of an encryption scheme is defined in terms of a game between an adversary and a challenger. In the *chosen plaintext* (IND-CPA) setting, the adversary has access to a *left-or-right* encryption oracle $\mathcal{E}_{ek}(LR(\cdot, \cdot, b))$, which takes a pair of equal length messages m_0, m_1 from the adversary and returns the encryption of m_b with the key ek, the bit b being unknown to the adversary. In the *chosen ciphertext* (IND-CCA) setting, the adversary has, in addition, access to a decryption oracle $\mathcal{D}_{dk}(\cdot)$, with the caveat that it cannot query for the decryption of a ciphertext it received as an answer to a previous encryption oracle query.

In this section, we extend their definition to settings involving multiple encryption schemes. Consider a sequence of n, not necessarily distinct, encryption schemes $\langle \mathcal{ES}^i \mid 1 \leq i \leq n \rangle$, possibly consisting of public-key and symmetric-key encryption schemes with either pre-shared keys or setup by a Diffie-Hellman exchange. For notational uniformity we define $ek_i = dk_i$ for symmetric key schemes, both equal to the secret key. For Diffie-Hellman schemes, $ek_i = dk_i = keygen(g^{xy})$ where g^x and g^y are the public DH values. Let DH be the set of Diffie-Hellman public values (g^x, g^y) for those keys which are generated by a DH exchange and PK be the set of public-keys among the ek_i's. In the *multi-scheme* setting we let the adversary have access to n encryption and decryption oracles with their corresponding public informations (PK and DH), all using the *same* challenger bit b for encryption. Security in this setting is defined below.

Definition 2 (Multi Scheme Indistinguishability). *The experiment MS-IND-CCA, for adversary A, is defined as:*

$$\text{Experiment } \mathbf{Exp}_{\langle \mathcal{ES} \rangle, I}^{MS\text{-}IND\text{-}CCA}(A, b)$$

For $i = 1, \cdots, n$ do $(ek_i, dk_i) \leftarrow \mathcal{KG}^i(I)$ *EndFor*

$$d \leftarrow A^{\mathcal{E}_{ek_1}^1(LR(\cdot, \cdot, b)), \ldots, \mathcal{E}_{ek_n}^n(LR(\cdot, \cdot, b)), \mathcal{D}_{dk_1}^1(\cdot), \ldots, \mathcal{D}_{dk_n}^n(\cdot)}(I, PK, DH)$$

Return d

A query to any LR oracle consists of two messages of equal length and that for each $i = 1, \ldots, n$ adversary A does not query $\mathcal{D}_{dk_i}(\cdot)$ on an output of $\mathcal{E}_{ek_i}^i(LR(\cdot, \cdot, b))$. The advantage of A is defined as:

$$\mathbf{Adv}_{\langle \mathcal{ES} \rangle, I}^{MS\text{-}IND\text{-}CCA}(A) = \Pr[\mathbf{Exp}_{\langle \mathcal{ES} \rangle, I}^{MS\text{-}IND\text{-}CCA}(A, 0) = 0] - \Pr[\mathbf{Exp}_{\langle \mathcal{ES} \rangle, I}^{MS\text{-}IND\text{-}CCA}(A, 1) = 0]$$

The sequence of encryption schemes $\langle \mathcal{ES}^i \mid 1 \leq i \leq n \rangle$ is MS-IND-CCA secure if the advantage of any probabilistic poly-time adversary A is negligible in the security parameter.

The definition of MS-IND-CPA is similar, with the decryption oracles dropped. We prove that individual security of the encryption schemes implies joint security.

Theorem 2 (IND-CPA(CCA) $\rightarrow$ MS-IND-CPA(CCA)). *If encryption schemes $\mathcal{ES}_1$, $\mathcal{ES}_2$, ..., $\mathcal{ES}_n$ are individually IND-CPA(CCA)secure, then the sequence of schemes $\langle \mathcal{ES}_1, \mathcal{ES}_2, \ldots, \mathcal{ES}_n \rangle$ is MS-IND-CPA(CCA) secure.*

4   Kerberos with DHINIT

In this section, we formally model Kerberos with DHINIT and prove that it satisfies computational authentication and secrecy properties under standard assumptions about the cryptographic primitives. Authentication proofs for each stage of Kerberos rely on the secrecy guarantees of keys set up in earlier stages, while the secrecy proofs similarly rely on previously proved authentication guarantees, an alternation first pointed out in [20]. Since the later stages of DHINIT are the same as those of Basic Kerberos [35], we obtain proofs for the complete protocol by appealing to security proofs and composition theorems in a compatible setting [39].

We find, perhaps surprisingly, that the KAS is *not* authenticated to the client after the first stage and suggest a fix to the protocol to avoid this problem. Our counterexample is similar in flavor to the attack found on Kerberos V5 with public-key initialization by [19]. In addition, we use an axiom that relies on *random oracles* to complete the proof of the security properties. We also develop an alternative proof, using only axioms that hold in the standard model, for a variant of the protocol that requires the KAS to sign both the Diffie-Hellman exponentials. We leave open whether this discrepancy arises from a security flaw in DHINIT or a limitation of our current proof.

4.1   Modelling the Protocol

The Kerberos protocol involves four roles—the Client, the Kerberos Authentication Server (KAS), the Ticket Granting Server (TGS), and the application server. The KAS and the TGS share a long term symmetric key as do the TGS and the application server. Mutual authentication and key establishment between the client and the application server is achieved by using this chain of trust. We write $k_{X,Y}^{type}$ to refer to long term symmetric keys, where X and Y are the principals sharing the key and *type* indicates their roles, e.g. $t \rightarrow k$ for TGS and KAS and $s \rightarrow t$ for application server and TGS. Kerberos runs in three stages with the client role participating in all three. The client program for the first stage and the KAS program are given below but the complete formal description of the protocol is given in [42].

Client = $(C, \hat{K}, \hat{T}, \hat{S}, t)$ [
new n_1; new $\tilde{n}_1$;
new x; $gx :=$ expg x;
$chksum :=$ hash $\hat{C}.\hat{T}.n_1$;
$sigc :=$ sign "$Auth$".$chksum.\tilde{n}_1.gx, skc$;
send $Cert_C.sigc.\hat{C}.\hat{T}.n_1$;

receive $Cert_K.sigk.\hat{C}.tgt.enc_{kc}$;
verify $sigk$, "$DHKey$".$gy.\tilde{n}_1, vk_K$;
$k :=$ dhkeygen gy, x;
$text_{kc} :=$ symdec enc_{kc}, k;
match $text_{kc}$ as $AKey.n_1.\hat{T}$;
$\cdots$ stage boundary $\cdots$
]$_C$

KAS = (K) [
receive $Cert_C.sigc.\hat{C}.\hat{T}.n_1$;
verify $sigc$, "$Auth$".$chksum.\tilde{n}_1.gx, vk_C$;
$chk :=$ hash $\hat{C}.\hat{T}.n_1$;
match chk as $chksum$;
new $AKey$;
new y; $gy :=$ expg y;
$k :=$ dhkeygen gx, y;
$sigk :=$ sign "$DHKey$".$gy.\tilde{n}_1, sk_K$;
$tgt :=$ symenc $AKey.\hat{C}, k_{T,K}^{t \rightarrow k}$;
$enc_{kc} :=$ symenc $AKey.n_1.\hat{T}, k$;
send $Cert_K.sigk.\hat{C}.tgt.enc_{kc}$;
]$_K$

The client C and KAS K carry out a Diffie-Hellman key exchange protocol authenticated by digital signatures to set up a key $AKey$ to be used as a session key between the client and the TGS in the next stage. (In Basic Kerberos, this phase is simpler; it relies on a preshared key between C and K.) The first few actions of the client are explained as follows: it generates three random numbers $n_1, \tilde{n}_1, x$ using **new** actions. It then generates the Diffie-Hellman exponential gx and sends a message to the KAS K containing its signature over the exponential and a few other fields including the identities of the TGS $\hat{T}$ and itself. In the second stage, the client gets a new session key ($SKey$ - Service Key) and a service ticket (st) to converse with the application server S which takes place in the third stage. The control flow of Kerberos exhibits a staged architecture where once one stage has been completed successfully, the subsequent stages can be performed multiple times or aborted and started over for handling errors.

4.2 Security Properties and Proofs

Table 1 lists the authentication and secrecy properties of Kerberos with DHINIT that we want to prove. The authentication properties are of the form that a message of a certain format was indeed sent by some thread of the expected principal. The secrecy properties state that a putative secret is a good key for certain principals. For example, $AUTH_{kas}^{client}$ states that when C finishes executing the **Client** role, some thread of $\hat{K}$ indeed sent the expected message with probability asymptotically close to one; SEC_{akey}^{client} states that the authorization key is "good" after execution of the **Client** role by C. The other security properties are analogous. More specifically, GoodKeyAgainst(X, k) [27] intuitively means that if k were used instead of a random key to key an IND-CCA encryption scheme, then the advantage of X in the corresponding security game would be negligible. The motivation for using this definition is that stronger conditions such as key indistinguishability fail to hold as soon as the key is used; key indistinguishability is also not necessary to establish reasonable security properties of practical protocols (see [27] for further discussion). We abbreviate the honesty assumptions by defining $\mathsf{Hon}(\hat{X}_1, \hat{X}_2, \cdots, \hat{X}_n) \equiv \mathsf{Honest}(\hat{X}_1) \wedge \mathsf{Honest}(\hat{X}_2) \wedge \cdots \mathsf{Honest}(\hat{X}_n)$.

The following protocol execution demonstrates that $AUTH_{kas}^{client}$ does *not* hold after the first stage of the client role.

$$C \longrightarrow K(I) : Cert_C.SIG[sk_C](\text{``Auth''}.HASH(\hat{C}.\hat{T}.n_1).\tilde{n}_1.gx).\hat{C}.\hat{T}.n_1$$

$$I \longrightarrow K : Cert_I.SIG[sk_I](\text{``Auth''}.HASH(\hat{I}.\hat{T}.n_1).\tilde{n}_1.gx).\hat{I}.\hat{T}.n_1$$

$$K \longrightarrow I \longrightarrow C : Cert_K.SIG[sk_K](\text{``DHKey''}.gy.\tilde{n}_1).$$

$$E_{sym}[k_{T,K}^{t \rightarrow k}](AKey.\hat{I}).E_{sym}[k](AKey.n_1.\hat{T})$$

C cannot parse the incorrect tgt : $E_{sym}[k_{T,K}^{t \rightarrow k}](AKey.\hat{I})$, as it does not have the key $k_{T,K}^{t \rightarrow k}$. Consequently, after interacting with the KAS the client is not guaranteed that the KAS thinks it interacted with the client. This problem can be easily fixed by requiring the KAS to include the client's identity inside the signature. However, the subsequent interaction with the TGS does ensure that the KAS indeed intended communication with the given client.

Theorem 3 (KAS Authentication). *On execution of the* **Client** *role by a principal, it is guaranteed with asymptotically overwhelming probability that the*

Table 1. DHINIT Security Properties

SEC_k : $\mathsf{Hon}(\hat{C}, \hat{K}) \supset (\mathsf{GoodKeyAgainst}(X, k) \vee \hat{X} \in \{\hat{C}, \hat{K}\})$

SEC_{akey} : $\mathsf{Hon}(\hat{C}, \hat{K}, \hat{T}) \supset (\mathsf{GoodKeyAgainst}(X, AKey) \vee \hat{X} \in \{\hat{C}, \hat{K}, \hat{T}\})$

SEC_{skey} : $\mathsf{Hon}(\hat{C}, \hat{K}, \hat{T}, \hat{S}) \supset (\mathsf{GoodKeyAgainst}(X, SKey) \vee \hat{X} \in \{\hat{C}, \hat{K}, \hat{T}, \hat{S}\})$

$AUTH_{kas}$: $\exists \eta. \, \mathsf{Send}((\hat{K}, \eta), Cert_K.SIG[sk_K](\text{``DHKey''}.gy.\tilde{n}_1).E_{sym}[k_{T,K}^{t \to k}](AKey.\hat{C}).$

$\qquad\qquad E_{sym}[k](AKey.n_1.\hat{T}))$

$AUTH_{tgs}$: $\exists \eta. \, \mathsf{Send}((\hat{T}, \eta), \hat{C}.E_{sym}[k_{S,T}^{s \to t}](SKey.\hat{C}).E_{sym}[AKey](SKey.n_2.\hat{S}))$

SEC_k^{client} : $[\mathbf{Client}]_C \, SEC_k$ $\qquad\qquad\qquad$ SEC_k^{kas} : $[\mathbf{KAS}]_K \, SEC_k$

SEC_{akey}^{client} : $[\mathbf{Client}]_C \, SEC_{akey}$ $\qquad$ $AUTH_{kas}^{client}$: $[\mathbf{Client}]_C \, \mathsf{Hon}(\hat{C}, \hat{K}) \supset AUTH_{kas}$

SEC_{akey}^{kas} : $[\mathbf{KAS}]_K \, SEC_{akey}$ $\qquad\qquad$ $AUTH_{kas}^{tgs}$: $[\mathbf{TGS}]_T \, \mathsf{Hon}(\hat{T}, \hat{K})$

SEC_{akey}^{tgs} : $[\mathbf{TGS}]_T \, SEC_{akey}$ $\qquad\qquad\qquad\quad \supset \exists n_1, k, gy, \tilde{n}_1. \, AUTH_{kas}$

$\qquad\qquad\qquad\qquad\qquad\qquad\quad AUTH_{tgs}^{client}$: $[\mathbf{Client}]_C \, \mathsf{Hon}(\hat{C}, \hat{K}, \hat{T}) \supset AUTH_{tgs}$

SEC_{skey}^{client} : $[\mathbf{Client}]_C \, SEC_{skey}$ $\qquad$ $AUTH_{tgs}^{server}$: $[\mathbf{Server}]_S \, \mathsf{Hon}(\hat{S}, \hat{T})$

SEC_{skey}^{tgs} : $[\mathbf{TGS}]_T \, SEC_{skey}$ $\qquad\qquad\qquad\qquad\quad \supset \exists n_2, AKey. \, AUTH_{tgs}$

---

intended KAS indeed sent the expected response assuming that both the client and the KAS are honest, the signature scheme is CMA-secure, the encryption scheme is IND-CCA and INT-CTXT secure, and the Decisional Diffie-Hellman (DDH) assumption holds. A similar result also holds for a principal executing the **TGS** *role. Formally,* $KERBEROS \vdash AUTH_{kas}^{client}, AUTH_{kas}^{tgs}.$

The axiomatic proof is in [42]. The key steps of the proof are the following: (a) the client C verifies the KAS K's signature on its Diffie-Hellman public value (gy) and the client's nonce $(\tilde{n}_1)$ and infers using the **SIG** axiom that the KAS did produce the signature; (b) a program invariant (proved using the honesty rule **HON**) is used to infer that the KAS observed the client's nonce and produced the DH exponential gy by exponentiating some nonce y; (c) the next few proof steps establish that the Diffie-Hellman key k can be used as an encryption key only by C and K by proving that $\mathsf{DHSecretive}(X, Y, k)$ holds and then using the axiom **CTXG**; note that this step requires the use of the random oracle model since the soundness of **CTXG** depends on that; (d) since the client decrypted the ciphertext $E_{sym}[k](AKey.n_1.\hat{T})$ and the client did not produce it itself, we therefore infer that it must have been produced by the KAS. At this point, we are assured that the KAS agrees on $\hat{T}, gx, n$ and $AKey$. However, it still does not agree on the identity of the client. It turns out, as we will see in Theorem 4, that this partial authentication is sufficient to prove the secrecy of the authentication key $(AKey)$ from the client's perspective. Now, stronger authentication properties are proved from the second stage of the protocol once the client decrypts the message $E_{sym}[AKey] \, (SKey.n_2.\hat{S})$. We infer that some thread of $\hat{C}, \hat{K}$ or $\hat{T}$ must have produced the encryption because of ciphertext integrity. Using an invariant to reason about the special form of this ciphertext, we conclude that the encrypting thread must have received a *tgt* containing *AKey* and meant for itself. Since we have proved the secrecy of *AKey* already under the keys k and $k_{T,K}^{t\to k}$, we infer that this *tgt* must be keyed with one of k and $k_{T,K}^{t\to k}$ the holders of which—$\hat{C}$, $\hat{T}$ and $\hat{K}$—are honest. This reasoning is formally captured in the axiom **SDEC**. Now we use the honesty rule to infer that if an honest thread encrypted this message then it must have generated *AKey*; we know that thread is K. At this point, we conclude that the TGS agrees on the identity of the KAS. The proof that the TGS agrees on the identity of the client is similar.

Theorem 4 (Authentication Key Secrecy). *On execution of the* **Client** *role by a principal, the Authentication Key is guaranteed to be good, in the sense of IND-CCA security, assuming that the client, the KAS and the TGS are all honest, the signature scheme is CMA-secure, the encryption scheme is IND-CCA and INT-CTXT secure, and the DDH assumption holds. Similar results hold for principals executing the* **KAS** *and* **TGS** *roles. Formally, KERBEROS* $\vdash$ $SEC_{akey}^{client}, SEC_{akey}^{kas}, SEC_{akey}^{tgs}$.

The axiomatic proof is in [42]. The main idea is to prove by induction over the steps of the protocol that *AKey* occurs on the network only as an encryption key or as a payload protected by encryption with the Diffie-Hellman key k or the pre-shared key $k_{T,K}^{t\to k}$. Formally, this step is carried out using the secrecy induction rule IND_{GOOD}. We therefore infer that *AKey* is good for use as an encryption key using the axiom **GK**.

Since AKey is protected by both the DH key k and the symmetric key $k_{T,K}^{t\to k}$, therefore, we had to formulate a reduction to a multi party IND-CCA game where some of the keys can be symmetric, with either pre-shared keys or those generated by DHKE in section 3.3. Although not required for this paper, we considered the further generalization of also considering public keys, since that didn't involve additional innovation.

We prove additional authentication and secrecy properties about the later stages of the protocol. Since the later stages of DHINIT are the same as those in basic Kerberos, we leverage the composition theorems in prior work to reuse existing proofs [39].

Theorem 5 (TGS Authentication). *On execution of the* **Client** *role by a principal, it is guaranteed with asymptotically overwhelming probability that the intended TGS indeed sent the expected response assuming that the client, the KAS and the TGS are all honest, the signature scheme is CMA-secure, the encryption scheme is IND-CCA and INT-CTXT secure, and the DDH assumption holds. Similar result holds for a principal executing the* **Server** *role. Formally, KERBEROS* $\vdash$ $AUTH_{tgs}^{client}, AUTH_{tgs}^{server}$.

Theorem 6 (Service Key Secrecy). *On execution of the* **Client** *role by a principal, the Service Key is guaranteed to be good, in the sense of IND-CCA security, assuming that the client, the KAS, the TGS and the application server are all honest, the signature scheme is CMA-secure, the encryption scheme is*

Table 2. IKEv2 Security Properties

SEC_{sk}^{init} : $[\text{Init}]_A$ $\text{Hon}(\hat{A}, \hat{B}) \supset (\text{GoodKeyAgainst}(X, sk_i) \vee \hat{X} \in \{\hat{A}, \hat{B}\}) \wedge$
$\quad (\text{GoodKeyAgainst}(X, sk_r) \vee \hat{X} \in \{\hat{A}, \hat{B}\})$

SEC_{sk}^{resp} : $[\text{Resp}]_B$ $\text{Hon}(\hat{A}, \hat{B}) \supset (\text{GoodKeyAgainst}(X, sk_i) \vee \hat{X} \in \{\hat{A}, \hat{B}\}) \wedge$
$\quad (\text{GoodKeyAgainst}(X, sk_r) \vee \hat{X} \in \{\hat{A}, \hat{B}\})$

$AUTH_{resp}^{init}$: $[\text{Init}]_A$ $\exists \eta.\ B = (\hat{B}, \eta) \wedge \text{Receive}(B, \text{``}I\text{''}.info_{i1}.gx.n) <$
$\quad \text{Send}(B, \text{``}R\text{''}.info_{i2}.gy.m) < \text{Receive}(B, enc_i) < \text{Send}(B, enc_r)$

$AUTH_{init}^{resp}$: $[\text{Resp}]_B$ $\exists \eta.\ A = (\hat{A}, \eta) \wedge \text{Send}(A, \text{``}I\text{''}.info_{i1}.gx.n) <$
$\quad \text{Receive}(A, \text{``}R\text{''}.info_{i2}.gy.m) < \text{Send}(A, enc_i)$

IND-CCA and INT-CTXT secure, and the DDH assumption holds. Similar result holds for a principal executing the **TGS** *role. Formally, KERBEROS $\vdash$ $SEC_{skey}^{client}, SEC_{skey}^{tgs}$.*

5   IKEv2

IKEv2 [34] is a complex protocol used to negotiate a security association at the beginning of an IPSec session. We consider the mode in which Diffie-Hellman exponentials are never reused and signatures are used for authentication. We formally model this mode of IKEv2 and provide the first formal proof that it satisfies computational authentication and security guarantees in the standard model; full details are in [42]. A significant difference from DHINIT is that the IKEv2 proofs do not require the random oracle model. At a high-level, this difference arises because in IKEv2 honest parties authenticate their own as well as their peer's Diffie-Hellman exponential using signatures. This enables us to prove the DHStrongSecretive(X, Y, k) property and use the **CTXGS** axiom in our proofs. Recall that in the DHINIT proofs we could only prove the weaker DHSecretive(X, Y, k) property and hence had to use the **CTXG** axiom, which is sound only in the random oracle model. However, the key derivation function needs to satisfy certain properties (described in [42] based on issues identified in [21]).

The security properties of IKEv2, listed in Table 2, state that on completion of a thread executing one of the roles, the shared keys sk_i and sk_r satisfy the GoodKey property, i.e. they are suitable for use as encryption keys for an IND-CCA scheme. The authentication properties state that on completion of a thread executing either role, it is guaranteed with overwhelming probability that the intended peer indeed received and sent the corresponding messages.

Theorem 7 (IKEv2 Key Secrecy). *On execution of the* **Init** *role by a principal, the keys sk_i, sk_r are guaranteed to be good, in the sense of IND-CCA security, assuming that the Iniatiator and the Responder are both honest, the signature scheme is CMA-secure, the encryption scheme is IND-CCA and INT-CTXT secure, and the DDH assumption holds. Similar result holds for a principal executing the* **Resp** *role. Formally, IKEv2 $\vdash SEC_{sk}^{init}, SEC_{sk}^{resp}$.*

Theorem 8 (IKEv2 Authentication). *On execution of the* **Init** *role by a principal, it is guaranteed with asymptotically overwhelming probability that the intended Responder indeed received the intended messages and sent the expected responses assuming that both the Initiator and the Responder are honest, the signature scheme is CMA-secure, the encryption scheme is IND-CCA and INT-CTXT secure, and the DDH assumption holds. A similar result also holds for a principal executing the* **Resp** *role. Formally,* $IKEv2 \vdash AUTH_{resp}^{init}, AUTH_{init}^{resp}$.

6 Conclusion

We develop axioms and rules for proving authentication and secrecy properties of protocols that use Diffie-Hellman key exchange in combination with other mechanisms. The resulting reasoning method, which reflects intuitive informal direct arguments, is proved computationally sound by showing the existence of conventional cryptographic reductions.

We prove security of Kerberos with DHINIT, as defined in the RFC [43], in the *random oracle model,* and prove security in the standard model for a modification in which the KAS signs both the Diffie-Hellman exponentials. We also discover that the KAS is *not* authenticated to the client after the first stage and suggest a fix to the protocol to avoid this problem. While IKEv2 [34] provides for several cryptographic options, we focus on the mode in which Diffie-Hellman exponentials are never reused and signatures are used for authentication. We prove that IKEv2 satisfies computational authentication and secrecy guarantees in the standard model. Intuitively, we do not need the random oracle assumption because honest IKEv2 parties authenticate both their own and their peer's Diffie-Hellman exponentials, which we believe is a prudent engineering practice.

Acknowledgement. We thank the referees and Iliano Cervesato for helpful comments and suggestions.

References

1. Abadi, M., Rogaway, P.: Reconciling two views of cryptography (the computational soundness of formal encryption). Journal of Cryptology 15(2), 103–127 (2002)
2. Adão, P., Bana, G., Scedrov, A.: Computational and information-theoretic soundness and completeness of formal encryption. In: Proc. of the 18th IEEE Computer Security Foudnations Workshop, pp. 170–184 (2005)
3. Aiello, W., Bellovin, S.M., Blaze, M., Canetti, R., Ioannidis, J., Keromytis, A.D., Reingold, O.: Just Fast Keying: Key agreement in a hostile internet. ACM Trans. Inf. Syst. Security 7(4), 1–30 (2004)
4. Backes, M., Cervesato, I., Jaggard, A.D., Scedrov, A., Tsay, J.-K.: Cryptographically sound security proofs for basic and public-key Kerberos. In: Proceedings of 11th European Symposium on Research in Computer Security (to appear, 2006)
5. Backes, M., Pfitzmann, B.: Limits of the cryptographic realization of XOR. In: Proc. of the 10th European Symposium on Research in Computer Security, Springer, Heidelberg (2005)

6. Backes, M., Pfitzmann, B.: Relating symbolic and cryptographic secrecy. In: Proc. IEEE Symposium on Security and Privacy, pp. 171–182. IEEE Computer Society Press, Los Alamitos (2005)
7. Backes, M., Pfitzmann, B., Waidner, M.: A universally composable cryptographic library. Cryptology ePrint Archive, Report 2003/015 (2003)
8. Backes, M., Pfitzmann, B., Waidner, M.: Limits of the reactive simulatability/UC of Dolev-Yao models with hashes. In: Gollmann, D., Meier, J., Sabelfeld, A. (eds.) ESORICS 2006. LNCS, vol. 4189, pp. 404–423. Springer, Heidelberg (2006)
9. Bella, G., Paulson, L.C.: Kerberos version IV: Inductive analysis of the secrecy goals. In: Quisquater, J.-J., Deswarte, Y., Meadows, C., Gollmann, D. (eds.) ESORICS 1998. LNCS, vol. 1485, pp. 361–375. Springer, Heidelberg (1998)
10. Bellare, M., Boldyreva, A., Micali, S.: Public-key encryption in a multi-user setting: Security proofs and improvements. In: Preneel, B. (ed.) EUROCRYPT 2000. LNCS, vol. 1807, pp. 259–274. Springer, Heidelberg (2000)
11. Bellare, M., Namprempre, C.: Authenticated encryption: Relations among notions and analysis of the generic composition paradigm. In: Okamoto, T. (ed.) ASIACRYPT 2000. LNCS, vol. 1976, pp. 531–545. Springer, Heidelberg (2000)
12. Bellare, M., Rogaway, P.: Random oracles are practical: A paradigm for designing efficient protocols. In: ACM Conference on Computer and Communications Security, pp. 62–73 (1993)
13. Bellare, M., Rogaway, P.: Entity authentication and key distribution. In: Stinson, D.R. (ed.) CRYPTO 1993. LNCS, vol. 773, pp. 232–249. Springer, Heidelberg (1994)
14. Boldyreva, A., Kumar, V.: Provable-security analysis of authenticated encryption in Kerberos. In: Proc. IEEE Security and Privacy (2007)
15. Bresson, E., Lakhnech, Y., Mazare, L., Warinschi, B.: A Generalization of DDH with Applications to Protocol Analysis and Computational Soundness. In: Menezes, A. (ed.) CRYPTO 2007. LNCS, vol. 4622, Springer, Heidelberg (2007)
16. Butler, F., Cervesato, I., Jaggard, A.D., Scedrov, A.: Verifying confidentiality and authentication in Kerberos. In: ISSS, vol. 5, pp. 1–24 (2003)
17. Canetti, R., Fischlin, M.: Universally composable commitments. In: Kilian, J. (ed.) CRYPTO 2001. LNCS, vol. 2139, pp. 19–40. Springer, Heidelberg (2001)
18. Canetti, R., Herzog, J.: Universally composable symbolic analysis of mutual authentication and key-exchange protocols. In: Halevi, S., Rabin, T. (eds.) TCC 2006. LNCS, vol. 3876, pp. 380–403. Springer, Heidelberg (2006)
19. Cervesato, I., Jaggard, A., Scedrov, A., Tsay, J.-K., Walstad, C.: Breaking and fixing public-key Kerberos. In: Okada, M., Satoh, I. (eds.) ASIAN 2006. LNCS, vol. 4435, pp. 167–181. Springer, Heidelberg (2008)
20. Cervesato, I., Meadows, C., Pavlovic, D.: An encapsulated authentication logic for reasoning about key distribution protocols. In: CSFW, pp. 48–61 (2005)
21. Chevassut, O., Fouque, P.-A., Gaudry, P., Pointcheval, D.: Key derivation and randomness extraction. Cryptology ePrint Archive, Report 2005/061 (2005), http://eprint.iacr.org/
22. Cortier, V., Warinschi, B.: Computationally sound, automated proofs for security protocols. In: Sagiv, M. (ed.) ESOP 2005. LNCS, vol. 3444, pp. 157–171. Springer, Heidelberg (2005)
23. Datta, A., Derek, A., Mitchell, J., Ramanathan, A., Scedrov, A.: Games and the impossibility of realizable ideal functionality. In: TCC, pp. 360–379 (2006)
24. Datta, A., Derek, A., Mitchell, J.C., Pavlovic, D.: A derivation system and compositional logic for security protocols. Journal of Computer Security 13, 423–482 (2005)
25. Datta, A., Derek, A., Mitchell, J.C., Roy, A.: Protocol Composition Logic (PCL). Electronic Notes in Theoretical Computer Science 172, 311–358 (2007)

26. Datta, A., Derek, A., Mitchell, J.C., Shmatikov, V., Turuani, M.: Probabilistic polynomial-time semantics for a protocol security logic. In: Caires, L., Italiano, G.F., Monteiro, L., Palamidessi, C., Yung, M. (eds.) ICALP 2005. LNCS, vol. 3580, pp. 16–29. Springer, Heidelberg (2005)
27. Datta, A., Derek, A., Mitchell, J.C., Warinschi, B.: Computationally sound compositional logic for key exchange protocols. In: Proceedings of 19th IEEE Computer Security Foundations Workshop, pp. 321–334. IEEE Computer Society Press, Los Alamitos (2006)
28. Diffie, W., Hellman, M.E.: New directions in cryptography. IEEE Transactions on Information Theory IT-22(6), 644–654 (1976)
29. He, C., Sundararajan, M., Datta, A., Derek, A., Mitchell, J.C.: A modular correctness proof of IEEE 802.11i and TLS. In: ACM Conference on Computer and Communications Security, pp. 2–15 (2005)
30. Herzog, J.: The Diffie-Hellman key-agreement scheme in the strand-space model. In: Proceedings of 16th IEEE Computer Security Foundations Workshop, pp. 234–247. IEEE Computer Society Press, Los Alamitos (2003)
31. Herzog, J.: Computational Soundness for Standard Assumptions of Formal Cryptography. PhD thesis, MIT (2004)
32. Janvier, R., Mazare, L., Lakhnech, Y.: Completing the picture: Soundness of formal encryption in the presence of active adversaries. In: Sagiv, M. (ed.) ESOP 2005. LNCS, vol. 3444, pp. 172–185. Springer, Heidelberg (2005)
33. Katz, J., Yung, M.: Unforgeable encryption and chosen ciphertext secure modes of operation. In: Schneier, B. (ed.) FSE 2000. LNCS, vol. 1978, pp. 284–299. Springer, Heidelberg (2001)
34. Kaufman, C.: Internet Key Exchange (IKEv2) Protocol, RFC (2005)
35. Kohl, J., Neuman, B.: The kerberos network authentication service, RFC (1991)
36. Lakhnech, Y., Mazaré, L.: Computationally sound verifiation of security protocols using Diffie-Hellman exponentiation. Cryptology ePrint Archive: Report 2005/097 (2005)
37. Micciancio, D., Warinschi, B.: Completeness theorems for the Abadi-Rogaway logic of encrypted expressions. Journal of Computer Security 12(1), 99–129 (2004). Preliminary version in WITS 2002
38. Micciancio, D., Warinschi, B.: Soundness of formal encryption in the presence of active adversaries. In: Naor, M. (ed.) TCC 2004. LNCS, vol. 2951, pp. 133–151. Springer, Heidelberg (2004)
39. Roy, A., Datta, A., Derek, A., Mitchell, J.C.: Inductive proofs of computational secrecy. In: Biskup, J., López, J. (eds.) ESORICS 2007. LNCS, vol. 4734, pp. 219–234. Springer, Heidelberg (2007),
    http://www.stanford.edu/~arnab/rddm-InductiveProofs.pdf
40. Roy, A., Datta, A., Derek, A., Mitchell, J.C.: Inductive trace properties for computational security. In: WITS (2007),
    http://www.stanford.edu/~arnab/rddm-IndTraceProps.pdf
41. Roy, A., Datta, A., Derek, A., Mitchell, J.C., Seifert, J.-P.: Secrecy analysis in Protocol Composition Logic. In: Proceedings of 11th Annual Asian Computing Science Conference (to appear, 2006)
42. Roy, A., Datta, A., Mitchell, J.C.: Formal proofs of cryptographic security of Diffie-Hellman-based protocols. Manuscript (2007),
    http://www.stanford.edu/~arnab/rdm-DHProofs.pdf
43. Zhu, L., Tung, B.: Public Key Cryptography for Initial Authentication in Kerberos (PKINIT). RFC 4556 (Proposed Standard) (June 2006)

Anonymity Protocol with Identity Escrow and Analysis in the Applied π-Calculus

Aybek Mukhamedov and Mark D. Ryan

School of Computer Science
University of Birmingham
{A.Mukhamedov,M.D.Ryan}@cs.bham.ac.uk

Abstract. *Anonymity with identity escrow* attempts to allow users of a service to remain anonymous, while providing the possibility that the service owner can break the anonymity if the service is misused. We introduce a new protocol in which the user's identity is distributed among several token providers. Anonymity is assured provided at least one of the token providers is honest (and the misuse has not occurred). We analyse the protocol in the applied π-calculus.

1 Introduction

With the increasing sophistication and adoption of communication systems in businesses and personal use, privacy and anonymity has become a concern among users [2,7,1]. Service usages (such as usage of mobile phones, internet, financial payments) are routinely logged, and those logs will allow organisations to build sophisticated profiles of customers and their preferences and associates. Users fear that this information could be abused. But while users may wish for complete privacy and anonymity, the failure of digital cash to achieve widespread adoption shows that society as a whole also requires security and accountability. Digital cash failed because it would allow criminal behaviour to go undetected. An appropriate balance between unrestricted anonymity and totalitarian security needs to be found, and this is likely to be a major theme in security research for some years.

Identity escrow attempts to provide such a balance for some applications. It allows users to use services anonymously while guaranteeing that service providers can break the anonymity in special circumstances; for example, to assist in a criminal investigation. If Alice wishes to use the service from provider S, she first puts her identity in escrow with a *escrow agent* T, from whom she obtains a token. She presents the token to S as evidence that she has placed her identity in escrow. S allows her to use the service anonymously. In the event of service misuse, S can apply to T to obtain the identity of the user corresponding to the token.

Identity escrow systems were first introduced by Kilian and Petrank in [9], which was motivated by the ideas from *key escrow encryption systems* (e.g. [10,13]). *Group signature schemes* and *anonymous credential systems* are two

G. Barthe and C. Fournet (Eds.): TGC 2007, LNCS 4912, pp. 330–346, 2008.

mechanisms which can be used to offer identity escrow [4,5,6,8]. In both cases, a single agent (known as *group manager* or *issuer*) holds the escrowed identity. Clearly, the system breaks down if the escrow agent is dishonest, and reveals Alice's identity even if the agreed conditions for doing so have not been met. To address this problem Marshall and Molina-Jiminez [12] proposed a protocol in which the escrow agent is implemented as a *set* of agents called *token providers*. Neither S nor any token provider are supposed to know the identity behind an escrowed certificate, but if it is proved necessary, all token providers can cooperate in order to reveal it. This aims to provide a much stronger security property than group signatures or credential systems. Alice can choose the set of token providers she uses, and the idea is that her anonymity is preserved provided at least one of them is honest. Another advantage of Marshall and Molina-Jiminez's scheme is that it is based on standard cryptographic primitives (digital signatures and public-key encryption), which are better known than zero-knowledge proofs and more widely implemented in APIs.

In [14], we showed some fundamental flaws in Marshall and Molina-Jiminez's protocol, and presented a new protocol which fixes the problems. In this paper, we introduce a new protocol which is simpler and more efficient than the protocol in [14]: it has half the message complexity of the previous protocol and replaces half of the public key encryptions by symmetric key encryptions.

Our scheme offers several advantages over identity escrow schemes mentioned above. The esrowed identity is distributed among several token providers chosen by the user. Moreover, the user's list (except for the last token provider in the list) is not revealed when the user presents her token to the service provider. Lastly, our scheme uses standard cryptographic primitives, which can be chosen in a way as not to rely on esoteric hardness assumptions such as the strong RSA assumption or the Lysyanskaya, Rivest, Sahai, and Wolf (LRSW) assumption [11]. We model and analyze our protocol in the applied π-calculus, and show that it satisfies the anonymity property.

The remainder of the paper is structured as follows. In section 2, we present preliminaries, including our protocol from [14]. Section 3 presents the applied pi calculus model of the protocol, and section 4 details our analysis of the anonymity property. We conclude in section 5. Appendix A briefly summarises the applied pi calculus, for the benefit of readers not familiar with it. Appendix B contains the proofs of lemmas we rely upon for our analysis.

2 Preliminaries

2.1 Notation

The following labeling conventions are used throughout this paper:

- S denotes an anonymous service provider.
- $T = \{T_1, T_2, \ldots T_n\}$ is a set of *identity token providers*.
- Φ_i is an identity token issued by T_{a_i}. We also write Φ_A for the identity token obtained by A by using the protocol.

- A, B are service users.
- K_A is A's public key. $\{m\}_K$ is the message m deterministically encrypted with the public key K.
- $[m]_{K^-}$ is the message m signed with a signing key K^-.

2.2 The Protocol

The protocol consists of two parts. First, there is a *sign-up* protocol, which is the main protocol that is executed by A to receive a token from the members of T. The token permits A to use the service from S. Next, there is a *complaint resolution* protocol, which is executed by S upon a misuse of its service, in order to reveal the identity of the offending anonymous user.

Sign-up. Alice has a long-term certified public key K_A. A creates a temporary service public key $K_{[A]}$ which she will use to identify herself to S.

Alice starts by building up an onion Φ_n. At the end of this process (actions 1, 2 below), the onion consists of the service key $K_{[A]}$ in its centre, wrapped with encryptions and signatures by the token providers. This is then paired with Alice's identity A, and by engaging in the protocol with token providers, it is wrapped again by encryptions and signatures of the token providers. The formal definition follows; an illustration in the case $n = 4$ is given in Figure 1.

A choses a sequence of token providers $T_{a_1}, T_{a_2}, \ldots, T_{a_n}$ from T (possibly with duplications) and creates the following term:

$$1) \qquad \Phi_1 = \{\ \texttt{InitITKReq}, K_{[A]}, \mathsf{K}_{\mathsf{a}_1}\ \}_{K_{T_{a_1}}}$$

It is an encryption of a tag $\texttt{InitITKReq}$, public part of A's service key $K_{[A]}$ and the symmetric key $\mathsf{K}_{\mathsf{a}_1}$ by T_{a_1}'s public key, where $\mathsf{K}_{\mathsf{a}_1}$ is freshly generated by A. The goal of the protocol is to have the key $K_{[A]}$ associated with A's identity token in a way that does not reveal this link even if all but one T_{a_i} are dishonest.

Next A creates further terms from Φ_1:

$$2) \text{ for } i = 2 \text{ to } n-1 \quad : \qquad \Phi_i = \{\ \texttt{ITKReq}, \Phi_{i-1}, \mathsf{K}_{\mathsf{a}_i}\ \}_{K_{T_{a_i}}}$$

By the end of the sequence of encryptions (2) $(n - 2$ times), A will have obtained the token Φ_{n-1}:

$$\{\ \texttt{ITKReq}, \{\ \cdots$$
$$\{\ \texttt{ITKReq}, \{\texttt{InitITKReq}, K_{[A]}, \mathsf{K}_{\mathsf{a}_1}\}_{K_{T_{a_1}}}, \mathsf{K}_{\mathsf{a}_2}\}_{K_{T_{a_2}}}$$
$$\cdots\ \}_{K_{T_{a_{n-2}}}}, \mathsf{K}_{\mathsf{a}_{n-1}}\}_{K_{T_{a_{n-1}}}}$$

The token Φ_{n-1} serves as a disguise of the service key $K_{[A]}$. The symmetric keys $\mathsf{K}_{\mathsf{a}_i}$ generated by A in the above steps are used in order to randomise the ciphertexts and to encrypt messages from token providers in later stages.

Next, A signs the token Φ_{n-1} and sends it to T_{a_n}, and then contacts $T_{a_{n-1}}$, $T_{a_{n-2}}, \ldots, T_{a_1}$ anonymously as shown in Steps 3, 4, 3a, 4a. They reverse the sequence of encryptions, and at the same time build up the identity token $\widetilde{\Phi}_{n-1}$.

The notation $A \longmapsto B$ means that A anonymously sends a message to B. In this case, B does not know A's identity. Similarly, $A \longmapsfrom B$ means that B receives a message anonymously, from A; A does not know B's identity.

$$3) \quad A \quad \longmapsto \quad T_{a_n} \quad : \quad \{\,[\,\texttt{InitITKSig},\, \Phi_{n-1},\, A\,]_{K_A^-}\,\}_{K_{T_{a_n}}}$$

$$4) \quad T_{a_n} \quad \longmapsfrom \quad A \quad : \quad \widetilde{\Phi}_1$$
$$\text{where } \widetilde{\Phi}_1 = [\,\{\,[\,\texttt{InitITKSig},\, \Phi_{n-1},\, A\,]_{K_A^-}\,\}_{K_{T_{a_n}}},\, \Phi_{n-1}\,]_{K_{T_{a_n}}^-}$$

For $i = 1$ to $n - 2$:

$$*\quad\begin{cases} 3a) \quad A \quad \longmapsto \quad T_{a_{n-i}} \quad : \quad \{\,\texttt{ITKSig}, \widetilde{\Phi}_i, \mathsf{K}_{\mathsf{a}_{n-i}}\,\}_{K_{T_{a_{n-i}}}} \\[4pt] \qquad \text{where for } i > 1 \quad \widetilde{\Phi}_i = [\,\{\,\widetilde{\Phi}_{i-1}, \mathsf{K}_{\mathsf{a}_{n-i+1}}\,\}_{K_{T_{a_{n-i+1}}}},\ \Phi_{n-i}\,]_{K_{T_{a_{n+1-i}}}^-} \\[12pt] 4a) \quad T_{a_{n-i}} \quad \longmapsfrom \quad A \quad : \quad \{\,[\,\{\,\widetilde{\Phi}_i, \mathsf{K}_{\mathsf{a}_{n-i}}\,\}_{K_{T_{a_{n-i}}}},\, \Phi_{n-i-1}\,]_{K_{T_{a_{n-i}}}^-}\,\}_{\mathsf{K}_{\mathsf{a}_{n-i}}} \end{cases}$$

After step 3a, before sending out a response, the token provider $T_{a_{n-i}}$ checks that the session key $\mathsf{K}_{\mathsf{a}_{n-i}}$ supplied in the request matches the one embedded in Φ_{n-i} (cf. step 2 above). The same rule applies to T_{a_1} at step 5. In addition, both token providers also check that $\widetilde{\Phi}_i$ contained in the request was signed by a token provider.

$$5) \quad A \quad \longmapsto \quad T_{a_1} \quad : \quad \{\,\texttt{ITKSig}, \widetilde{\Phi}_{n-1}, \mathsf{K}_{\mathsf{a}_1}\,\}_{K_{T_{a_1}}}$$

$$6) \quad T_{a_1} \quad \longmapsfrom \quad A \quad : \quad \{\,\widetilde{\Phi}_A\,\}_{\mathsf{K}_{\mathsf{a}_1}},$$
$$\text{where } \widetilde{\Phi}_A = [\,\{\,\widetilde{\Phi}_{n-1}, \mathsf{K}_{\mathsf{a}_1}\,\}_{K_{T_{a_1}}}, K_{[A]}\,]_{K_{T_{a_1}}^-}$$

Upon reaching step 6, A has the following identity token:

$$\widetilde{\Phi}_A = [\,\{\, \ldots \,[\,\{\,\widetilde{\Phi}_1,\ \mathsf{K}_{\mathsf{a}_{n-1}}\,\}_{K_{T_{a_{n-1}}}}, \Phi_{n-2}\,]_{K_{T_{a_{n-1}}}^-} \ldots \mathsf{K}_{\mathsf{a}_1}\,\}_{K_{T_{a_1}}}, K_{[A]}\,]_{K_{T_{a_1}}^-}$$

The token $\widetilde{\Phi}_A$ associates the service key $K_{[A]}$ with A. He presents the token to S when requesting its service.

$$7) \quad A \quad \longmapsto \quad S \quad : \quad \{\,\widetilde{\Phi}_A,\, K_{[A]}\,\}_{K_S}$$

S checks that the token is signed by some token provider and the key $K_{[A]}$ is embedded in it. In case of service misuse the token may be delayered to reveal the identity of a user bound to it via the complaint resolution protocol.

Complaint Resolution. We assume that some misuse evidence $\widetilde{\Psi}_{K_{[A]}}$ is uniquely associated with A's service key $K_{[A]}$ and the service provider S. It must be verifiable by each token provider (or endorsed by a third party accepted by all token providers) and not forgeable by S.

The protocol is given as follows. As before, an illustration is given for the case $n = 4$ in Figure 2.

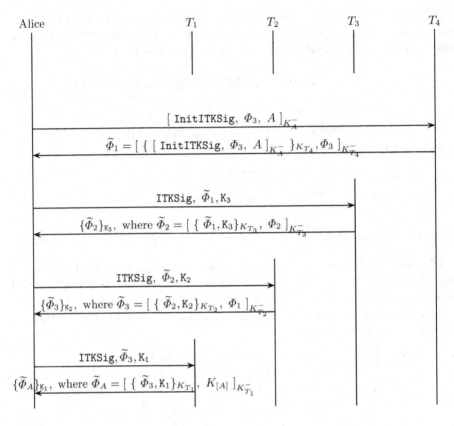

Fig. 1. Illustration of the sign-up protocol in the case $n = 4$. Messages from A are encrypted with the public key of the receiver (this encryption is not shown).

$$1) \quad S \longrightarrow T_{a_1} \quad : \quad \{\, \texttt{Reveal}, \widetilde{\Phi}_A, \widetilde{\Psi}_{K_{[A]}}, S \,\}_{K_{T_{a_1}}}$$

$$2) \quad T_{a_1} \longrightarrow S \quad : \quad \{\, [\widetilde{\Phi}_{n-1}, K_{a_1}, \widetilde{\Psi}_{K_{[A]}}]_{K^-_{T_{a_1}}} \,\}_{K_S}$$

For $i = 1$ to $n - 2$:

$$* \begin{cases} 3a) \quad S \longrightarrow T_{a_{i+1}} \quad : \quad \{\, \texttt{Reveal}, ((\widetilde{\Phi}_{n-i}, K_{a_i}), \ldots, (\widetilde{\Phi}_{n-1}, K_{a_1}), \widetilde{\Phi}_A), \\ \qquad\qquad\qquad\qquad\qquad\qquad\qquad\qquad \widetilde{\Psi}_{K_{[A]}}, S \,\}_{K_{T_{a_{i+1}}}} \\ 4a) \quad T_{a_{i+1}} \longrightarrow S \quad : \quad \{\, [\widetilde{\Phi}_{n-i-1}, K_{a_{i+1}}, \widetilde{\Psi}_{K_{[A]}}]_{K^-_{T_{a_{i+1}}}} \,\}_{K_S} \end{cases}$$

$$5) \quad S \longrightarrow T_{a_n} : \{\texttt{Reveal}, ((\widetilde{\Phi}_1, K_{a_{n-1}}), \ldots, (\widetilde{\Phi}_{n-1}, K_{a_1}), \widetilde{\Phi}_A), \widetilde{\Psi}_{K_{[A]}}, S \,\}_{K_{T_{a_n}}}$$

$$6) \quad T_{a_n} \longrightarrow S \quad : \quad \{\, [[\, \texttt{ITKSig}, \Phi_{n-1}, A\,]_{K^-_A}, \widetilde{\Psi}_{K_{[A]}}]_{K^-_{T_{a_n}}} \,\}_{K_S}$$

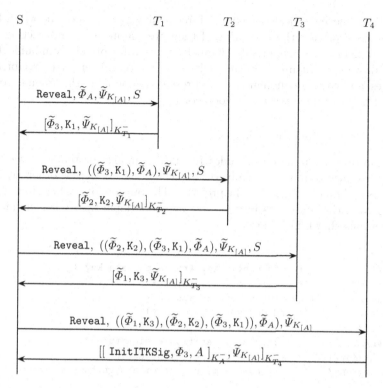

Fig. 2. Complaint resolution protocol for the case $n = 4$. All messages are encrypted with the public key of the recepient (to avoid clutter this encryption is not shown).

In message 3a, the tuple of $\widetilde{\Phi}_i$s serves to prevent complaint resolution messages in one session being used in another. Before sending a response each T_{a_i} checks that the sequence he receives is correct, i.e. $\{\widetilde{\Phi}_{n-i}, \mathsf{K}_{\mathsf{a}_i}\}_{K_{T_{a_{i-1}}}}$ equals to the second element in the signed tuple $\widetilde{\Phi}_{n-i+1}$, and $\{\widetilde{\Phi}_{n-i+1}, \mathsf{K}_{\mathsf{a}_{i-1}}\}_{K_{T_{a_{i-2}}}}$ equals to the second element in the signed tuple $\widetilde{\Phi}_{n-i+2}$, etc. , until $\widetilde{\Phi}_A$ is reached. This check ensures that T_{a_i} will not decrypt a token that is not related to $\widetilde{\Phi}_A$.

At the nth iteration S reveals the identity of the user when it receives $[\ \mathtt{ITKSig},\ \Phi_{n-1}, A\ ]_{K_A^-}$ from T_{a_n}. Importantly, in the sequence of unfoldings of $\widetilde{\Phi}_{a_i}$s, S also keeps track of Φ_{a_i}s inside them, using the session keys K_{a_i}, in order to make sure that Φ_{n-1} is formed from the session key she was given in the service request step. That is to avoid rogue token providers disrupting or misleading the identity recovery process.

3   Model in the Applied π

The protocol is modelled in the applied π-calculus. We do not put restrictions on the number of sessions, or agents, and assume an active adversary (aka

Dolev-Yao) that can inject as well as intercept messages from the network. Public channels represent the network and they are the means of interacting with the environment, whereas private channels are used for private communications among processes. Channels by themselves do not reveal sender or recipient of messages, and thus are anonymous. We present the model in the language of the ProVerif tool extended with a for-loop construct.

3.1   Signature and Equations

The signature of our model includes function symbols for public key cryptographic operations and universally verifiable signing, as well as other auxiliary constants and functions used in the protocol. The purpose of the functions should be clear from the comments in brackets. The equational theory is generated by the equations shown in Figure 3.

```
fun pk/1.          (* gets public key from a private key *)
fun enc/2.         (* public key encryption *)
fun senc/2.      (* symmetric key encryption *)
fun dec/2.         (* and decryption         *)
fun sdec/2.
fun sign/2.        (* universally verifiable signature *)
fun getSigKey/1.  (* retrieves public key of a signer  *)
fun getSigMess/1. (* retrieves a message from a signature *)

equation dec(enc(m,pk(sk)),sk) = m.
equation sdec(senc(m,k),k) = m.
equation getSigKey(sign(m,sk)) = pk(sk).
equation getSigMess(sign(m,sk)) = m.
```

Fig. 3. Signature and equational theory

3.2   The Protocol Process

The protocol is encoded in the processes as shown in Figure 4 and 5, where processT and processU denote token provider and user, respectively (defined below).

The fresh name skTh represents the private decryption key of the honest token provider. In our model signing keys are different from the private decryption keys and we allow intruder to access honest token providers signing key. In the last four lines we define the protocol as the parallel composition of an arbitrary number of users and honest token provider processes. The dishonest token providers are represented by the attacker that has an encryption key pk(skTd) and a signing key signTd.

The expression of the form new n; P corresponds to the restriction $\nu n.P$ of the applied-π calculus. A construct of the form (=N,y)=M pattern matches the left element of a tuple M against N, but assigns the right element of M to y.

```
free c.              (* public channel *)
free ITKReq, ITKSig, InitITKReq, InitITKSig.
free skTd,signTd. (* dishonest TP's decryption and signing keys *)
free signTh     (* honest TP's signing key *)

process
  new skTh; (* honest TP's decryption key *)
  out(c,pk(skTh)); new signA; new signB;
  let  (pkTh, pkTd) = (pk(skTh),pk(skTd)) in !processT |
  (out(c,(pk(signA),A))); let (signU,n,pU) = (signA,nA,pA) in processU |
  (out(c,(pk(signB),B))); let (signU,n,pU) = (signB,nB,pB) in processU)

let processU=
  (* pU is Th's position in U's request chain *)
  for 0<j<n+1, j<>pU:
      new sesK_j;
      let (upkT_j,signT_j) = (pkTd,signTd) in
  new sesK_pU;
  let (upkT_pU,signT_pU) = (pkTh,signTh) in
  new servK; out(c,pk(servK));

  (* Step 1 *)
  let phi_1=enc((InitITKReq,pk(servK),sesK_1),upkT_1) in
  (* Step 2 *)
  for 1<j<n:
    let phi_j=enc((ITKReq,phi_(j-1),sesK_j),upkT_j) in
  (* Step 3,4 *)
  let commit = sign((InitITKSig,phi_(n-1),pk(signU)),signU) in
  out(c,enc(commit,upkT_n));
  in(c,m3);
  let tphi_1=m3 in
  if getSigKey(tphi_1)=pk(signT_n) then
  let (x1, oldTphi) = getSigMess(tphi_1) in
  if oldTphi = enc((sign(((ITKSig,phi_(n-1),pk(signU)),signU)),upkT_n) then
  (* Step 3a,4a *)
  for 1<j<n:
      out(c,enc((ITKSig,tphi_j,sesK_(n-j+1)),upkT_(n-j+1)));
      in(c,m4);
      let tphi_(j+1)=dec(m4,sesK_(n-j+1)) in
      if getSigKey(tphi_(j+1))=pk(signT_(n-j+1)) then
  (* Step 5,6 *)
  out(c,enc((ITKSig,tphi_n,sesK_1),upkT_1));
  in(c,m);
  let token=dec(m,sesK_1) in
  if getSigKey(token)=pk(signT_1) then
  let (x2,key) = getSigMess(token) in
  if key = servK then out(c,token)
```

Fig. 4. The Main and the user processes. We have extended ProVerif syntax with a for-loop (used in steps 2 and 3a, 4a).

```
let processT=
  in(c,m);
  let req=dec(m,skTh) in

  let (=ITKSig,d4,k)=req in
  (
   let (x1,oldPhi) = getSigMess(d4) in
   (
   let (=InitITKReq,key,=k) = dec(oldPhi,skTh) in
   out(c,senc(sign((enc((d4,k),pkTh),key),signTh),k))
   else
   let (=ITKReq,oldPhi1,=k) = dec(oldPhi,skTh) in
   out(c,senc(sign((enc((d4,k),pkTh),oldPhi1),signTh),k))
   )
  )

  else let (=InitITKSig,d3,upk)=getSigMess(req) in
  (
   if upk=getSigKey(req) then
   out(c,sign((enc(req,pkTh),d3),signTh))
  ).
```

Fig. 5. The token provider process

4   Analysis of Anonymity Property

We prove that the protocol satisfies anonymity: the identity token produced by the user cannot be linked to its identity, even if all but one of the token providers are honest. We start with some general results which will be useful.

4.1   Auxiliary Results

In this section we present several results about the static equivalence of frames. We will use the lemmas in our analysis of the anonymity property in the next section. We omit proofs due to lack of space – the extended version of our paper [15] includes the proofs in Appendix B.

We assume that the equational theory used in the lemmas is convergent, which implies that all terms have a unique normal form. At any rate, most of our lemmas relate to the standard public key encryption equational theory Σ_{pk}, which known to be convergent. Σ_{pk} comprises standard public and symmetric key encryption and decryption operations, and message signing and tupling defined in Fig. 3.

Assumption 1. *Let E be an equational theory. We assume that the relation equality modulo E on terms is closed under substitutions of arbitrary terms for names and variables, and application of contexts.*

Definition 1. *We write $\{^M/_N\}$ for the syntactic substitution that replaces all occurrences of the term N by the term M. Note that $T_1 =_E T_2$ does not imply that $T_1\{^M/_N\} =_E T_2\{^M/_N\}$.*

Definition 2. *We say a frame $\nu\tilde{n}.\sigma$ is normalized if for all $\{^M/_x\}$ in σ, M is in normal form and $fv(M) \cap dom(\sigma) = \emptyset$.*

The first simple lemma shows that exporting nonces does not affect static equivalence on frames.

Lemma 1. *Let φ, φ' be frames, $\tilde{n}, \tilde{n}'$ be sets of names and k a name s.t. $k \notin fn(\varphi, \varphi') \cap (n \cup n')$. If $\nu\tilde{n}.\varphi \approx_s \nu\tilde{n}'.\varphi'$ then $\nu\tilde{n}, k.(\{^k/_x\} \mid \varphi) \approx_s \nu\tilde{n}', k.(\{^k/_x\} \mid \varphi')$, where $x \notin dom(\varphi)$.*

The following lemma establishes sufficient conditions under which parts of frames can be simplified (substituted by fresh names). All further lemmas make use of this result.

Lemma 2. *Given a convergent equational theory Σ, a closed term L in normal form, names $\tilde{n}, s$ and a frame φ in normal form such that $s \notin fn(\varphi)$, suppose:*

- *L does not occur in φ, and $\nu\tilde{n}.\varphi \not\vdash L$.*
- *for any $\tilde{m}, \sigma, M, N$ such that $\nu\tilde{n}.(\{^L/_x\}|\varphi) \equiv \nu\tilde{m}.\sigma$, $(fn(M) \cup fn(N)) \cap \tilde{m} = \emptyset$ and $M\sigma =_E N\sigma$ we have $M\sigma\{^z/_L\} =_E N\sigma\{^z/_L\}$.*

Then: $\nu\tilde{n}.(\{^L/_x\}|\varphi) \approx_s \nu\tilde{n}, s.(\{^s/_x\}|\varphi)$.

All subsequent lemmas are restricted to the equational theory with standard public and session key encryption, decryption and digital signing operations (Σ_{pk}) defined in Figure 3.

Lemma 3. *Let M, N and J be terms in normal form, s.t. M, N do not contain $\mathsf{dec}(x, J)$ and $M\{^{\{L\}_J}/_x\} =_E N\{^{\{L\}_J}/_x\}$, where L is in normal form. Then:*

$$(M\{^{\{L\}_J}/_x\})\{^z/_{\{L\}_J}\} =_E (N\{^{\{L\}_J}/_x\})\{^z/_{\{L\}_J}\}$$

Lemma 4. *Given a frame $\nu\tilde{n}.\sigma$ in normal form that does not contain $\mathsf{dec}(x, k)$ and $\nu\tilde{n}.\sigma \not\vdash k$, then for any M, s.t. $\tilde{n} \cap fn(M) = \emptyset$, $\mathsf{dec}(x, k)$ does not occur in $M\sigma\downarrow$.*

Lemma 5. *Given a frame $\nu\tilde{n}.\sigma$ in normal form, name $k \in \tilde{n}$, s.t. k occurs in σ only as an encryption key argument, for any M, s.t. $\tilde{n} \cap fn(M) = \emptyset$, $\mathsf{dec}(x, k)$ does not occur in $M\sigma\downarrow$.*

Lemma 6. *Given a closed term L in normal form names $\tilde{n}, s$ and a frame $\nu\tilde{n}.\sigma$ in normal form, suppose $\nu\tilde{n}.\sigma \not\vdash s$ and $\{s, L\}_{pk(k)}$ does not occur in σ. Then $\nu\tilde{n}.\sigma \not\vdash \{s, L\}_{pk(k)}$.*

Lemma 7. *Given a closed term L in normal form, names $\tilde{n}, s$ and a frame $\nu\tilde{n}.\sigma$ in normal form, suppose:*

1. *$\nu\tilde{n}.\sigma \nvdash k$, $\nu\tilde{n}.\sigma \nvdash \{s, L\}_{pk(k)}$ and $m \notin fn(\sigma)$*
2. *$\{s, L\}_{pk(k)}$ does not occur in σ.*
3. *$\text{dec}(x, k)$ does not occur in σ.*

Then $\nu\tilde{n}, s.(\{^{\{s,L\}_{pk(k)}}/_x\}|\sigma) \approx_s \nu\tilde{n}, m.(\{^m/_x\}|\sigma)$.

Lemma 8. *Given a closed term L in normal form, names $k, s \in \tilde{n}$ and a frame $\nu\tilde{n}.\sigma$ also in normal form, suppose:*

1. *k occurs in σ only as an encryption key argument.*
2. *L does not occur in σ and $s \notin fn(\sigma)$.*

Then: $\nu\tilde{n}.(\{^{\{L\}_k}/_x\}|\sigma) \approx_s \nu\tilde{n}, s.(\{^s/_x\}|\sigma)$.

Lemma 9. *Given a normalized frame $\nu\tilde{n}.\sigma$ and $s, k \in \tilde{n}$, where $\nu\tilde{n}.\sigma \nvdash k$, suppose for all occurences of s in σ:*

1. *either, there exists a term L such that $\{L\}_{pk(k)}$ occurs in σ and s is a subterm of L.*
2. *or s occurs in σ as an encryption key argument.*

Then $\nu\tilde{n}.\sigma \nvdash s$.

4.2   Proof of the Anonymity Property

Notation and set-up:

- Th is the honest token provider and Td is one of the dishonest ones. Our aim is to show the identity token produced by the user cannot be linked to its identity, even if all but one of the token providers are honest.
- The property is shown to hold even if Th's signing key is public. We model it as a free name that intruder can use.
- We don't model dishonest token providers Td, since they form part of the attacker. Their decryption and signing keys are free names.
- Honest users A, B are instantiations of the process processU in Figure 4.
- $\tilde{n}_A, \tilde{n}_B$ are sets of names that include A's, B's restricted values, i.e. signing keys, service keys, and session keys generated by A, B during the run of the protocol. $\tilde{n}_A = \{K_A^-, K_{[A]}\} \cup \{\text{KA}_1, \ldots, \text{KA}_{n_A-1}\}$ and $\tilde{n}_B = \{K_B^-, K_{[B]}\} \cup \{\text{KB}_1, \ldots, \text{KB}_{n_B-1}\}$.
- $\tilde{\Phi}(A)^j, \tilde{\Phi}(B)^j$ where $j \in \{l, r\}$ denote identity tokens output by A and B, respectively.
- A's *request chain* is a sequence of token providers that A uses when building a token for anonymous service usage. It is denoted by req_A with length n_A;

Th's position in the chain is p_A. Similarly, req_B, n_B, p_B refer to B's request chain.

- K_{Th} stands for a public encryption key corresponding to the decryption key sK_{Th}, i.e. $pk(sK_{Th}) = K_{Th}$.

We make the following important assumption that avoids attacks on anonymity based on simple traffic analysis:

Assumption 2. *We assume that Th processes requests in batches such that each batch contains at least two honest users. Hence, when Th receives a token request it waits for a certain number of other token requests (so that it has at least two requests from honest users) before responding. Furthermore, we assume that at least two honest users from the batch successfully receive token replies from Th.*

Let A^l, B^l be A's, B's processes, such that $A = \nu \tilde{n}_A.A^l$ and $B = \nu \tilde{n}_B.B^l$. We define A^r, B^r to be the same as A^l, B^l, except that in the former users swap their partial tokens over a private channel twice: i) during the construction of $\Phi(i)^r$, before application of encryption function with Th's public key, and ii) after receiving a reply with a token from Th. So, the process A^r stands for A's execution of the protocol, except that A commits to B's service key, and B^r stands for B's execution of the protocol, except that B commits to A's service key. We use this data swapping to express an indistinguishability test for unlinkability of user's identity with her token: if the attacker can establish the link than he can distinguish between A^l, B^l and A^r, B^r. We assume that A^l, B^l synchronize after receiving a reply from Th and similarly for A^r, B^r.

Theorem 1. *Suppose A and B are honest users of the protocol, and Th is an honest token provider and the above assumption holds. Under these hypotheses, the protocol guarantees user anonymity; that is,*

$$\nu \, sK_{Th}, \tilde{n}_A, \tilde{n}_B. \, (A^l; \mathsf{out}(ch, \widetilde{\Phi}(A)^l) \mid B^l; \mathsf{out}(ch, \widetilde{\Phi}(B)^l) \mid !Th)$$
$$\approx \nu \, sK_{Th}, \tilde{n}_A, \tilde{n}_B. \, (A^r; \mathsf{out}(ch, \widetilde{\Phi}(A)^r) \mid B^r; \mathsf{out}(ch, \widetilde{\Phi}(B)^r) \mid !Th)$$

where sK_{Th} is Th's private decryption key and ch is a public channel.

Proof. We prove labelled bisimilarity between our processes, since observational equivalence $\approx$ coincides with labelled bisimilarity $\approx_\ell$, and the latter relation is easier to reason about by hand. The definition of $\approx_\ell$ requires that every labelled and internal transitions of a process on one side of the equivalence are matched with those of a process on the other side. Furthermore, all the intermediate processes need to be statically equivalent.

In our case the matching of labelled transitions is straightforward, since we have essentially the same processes on both sides of the equivalence (only the data they manipulate are different): the OUT-ATOM transition only permits outputting terms by reference so we shall have the same such labels on both sides of the equivalence; and in case of IN rule, the same term M will be input on both sides. We match labelled transitions as follows: for A^l's, B^l's transitions on the lhs with pick those of A^r, B^r on the rhs, respectively (and vice versa);

and we match the rest with the transitions of the identical process on the other side of the equivalence. We just need to make sure that the lhs process blocks iff the rhs one blocks.

There are only two interesting points in the execution of the processes to consider for blocking. The first one is when Th tries to generate a reply that needs to be encrypted with a session key incorporated inside the $\Phi(i)$ token in the request – if it cannot extract the key then Th blocks. Since A^j and B^j check that replies from the token providers are of the expected format, Th does not block when replying to their requests. For all other terms M that attacker can input to Th we note that the lhs blocks iff the rhs blocks.

The second interesting scenario is when the rhs blocks due to not receiving an input on a private channel (used for exchanging tokens). That cannot happen during the token construction phase since A^j, B^j do not interact with the environment, but can occur during the token request phase if one of the processes does not receive an expected token reply. By our synchronization assumption, the lhs of the equivalence will also block. A further note, A^r's and B^r's token exchange via a private channel on the rhs of the equivalence is not captured by labelled transitions, but expressed by an internal reduction that we do not match to anything on the lhs.

Hence, the crux of the theorem is in proving the static equivalence of the lhs and the rhs at each step. In fact, it is sufficient to show that the largest possible frames are statically equivalent – then all subframes generated in the intermediate steps are also statically equivalent. So for our theorem we need to show the following holds:

$$
\begin{aligned}
&\nu \, sK_{Th}, \tilde{n}_A, \tilde{n}_B.(\phi_A^l \mid \{ {}^{\widetilde{\Phi}(A)^l}/_{z_a} \} \mid \phi_B^l \mid \{ {}^{\widetilde{\Phi}(B)^l}/_{z_b} \} \mid (\|_{i \in N} \, \phi_{Th_i}^l) \mid \\
&\quad \{ {}^{K_{[A]}}/_{a_{v_n}} \} \mid \{ {}^{K_{[B]}}/_{b_{v_n}} \} \mid \{ {}^{K_{Th}}/_{z_3} \}) \\
&\approx_s \\
&\nu \, sK_{Th}, \tilde{n}_A', \tilde{n}_B'.(\phi_A^r \mid \{ {}^{\widetilde{\Phi}(A)^r}/_{z_a} \} \mid \phi_B^r \mid \{ {}^{\widetilde{\Phi}(B)^r}/_{z_b} \} \mid (\|_{i \in N} \, \phi_{Th_i}^r) \mid \\
&\quad \{ {}^{K_{[A]}}/_{a_{v_n}} \} \mid \{ {}^{K_{[B]}}/_{b_{v_n}} \} \{ {}^{K_{Th}}/_{z_3} \})
\end{aligned}
\tag{1}
$$

where for $j \in \{l, r\}$, ϕ_A^j, ϕ_B^j are A's and B's frames respectively, and $\widetilde{\Phi}(A)^j$ and $\widetilde{\Phi}(B)^j$ represent the token output by A and by B respectively. We also have $sK_{[A]}, sK_{[B]}, K_A^-, K_B^- \in \tilde{n}_A \cup \tilde{n}_B$, and honest agents' session keys $\mathtt{KA}_i^j, \mathtt{KB}_i^j \in \tilde{n}_A \cup \tilde{n}_B$. N is a set of integers representing the number of times $!Th$ has been instantiated during the process evolution.

By inspection of the token provider process (Fig. 5), one sees that the frames it generates in response to $\mathtt{ITKSig}$ requests are of the form $\phi_{Th_i}^j = \{ {}^{\{[[M_i, L_i]_{K_{T_i}^-}, \kappa_1\}_{K_{Th}}, L_i']_{K_{Th}^-} \}_{\kappa_i}}/_{t_i} \}$, where $L_i' = \mathtt{snd}(\mathtt{dec}(L_i, sK_{Th}))$ and $K_i = \mathtt{thd}(\mathtt{dec}(L_i, sK_{Th}))$. From these equations, it follows that $L_i = [\{\mathtt{ITKReq}, L_i', K_i\}_{K_{Th}}]_{K_{Th}^-}$. The frames generated by Th in response to $\mathtt{InitITKSig}$ requests are $[\{x\}_{K_{Th}}, y]_{K_{Th}^-}$, where x and y are derived from the input; since the signing key K_{Th}^- is known to the attacker in this analysis, these frames can be formed by the attacker and we need not consider them.

Let ψ_{l1} be the left-hand and ψ_{r1} be the right-hand processes of the static equivalence (1), and suppose $C_1(j)[\_]$ is a context such that $C_1(j)[\|_{i \in N} \phi_{Th_i}^j)] = \psi_{j1}$ for $j \in \{l, r\}$. To prove (1), it is sufficient to prove

$$C_1(l)[(\ \|_{i \in N_1}\ \phi_{Th_i}^l)\ |\ (\ \|_{i \in N_2}\ dec\text{-}\phi_{Th_i})] \approx_s C_1(r)[(\ \|_{i \in N_1}\ \phi_{Th_i}^r)\ |\ (\ \|_{i \in N_2}\ dec\text{-}\phi_{Th_i})] \quad (2)$$

where $dec\text{-}\phi_{Th_i} = \{^{\texttt{dec}(L,K_{Th})}/_{t_{i_1}}\}$ and $N_1 = \{i \in N \mid L_i = \Phi(A)_{p_A}^j \vee L_i = \Phi(B)_{p_B}^j\}$ and $N_2 = N \setminus N_1$. To see this, note that (1) is obtained by applying the context $\nu t_{i_1}.\_\ |\ \{^{\{[\{[M,L]_{K_T^-},\texttt{thd}(t_{i_1})\}_{x_{t_3}},\texttt{snd}(t_{i_1})]_{K_{Th}^-}\}\texttt{thd}(t_{i_1})}/_{t_i}\}$ to each side of (2). A further step of this kind is also possible.

Let ψ_{l1} be the left-hand and ψ_{r1} be the right-hand processes of the static equivalence (2), and for $j \in \{l.r\}$ suppose $C_2(j)$ is a context such that $C_2(j)[\{^{\widetilde{\Phi}(A)^j}/_{z_a}\}\ |\ \{^{\widetilde{\Phi}(B)^j}/_{z_b}\}] = \psi_{j2}$. The terms $\widetilde{\Phi}(A)^j, \widetilde{\Phi}(B)^j$ have application of $\texttt{sign}$ (by some token provider T) at their outermost level. To prove (2), it is sufficient to prove

$$C_2(l)[\|_{x \in \{A,B\}}(\{^{\{\widetilde{\Phi}(x)_{n-1}^l,\texttt{Kx}_{n-1}^l\}K_T}/_{z_{x_1}}\}\ |\ \{^{K_{[x]}}/_{z_{x_n}}\})]$$
$$\approx_s C_2(r)[\|_{x \in \{A,B\}}(\{^{\{\widetilde{\Phi}(x)_{n-1}^r,\texttt{Kx}_{n-1}^r\}K_T}/_{z_{x_1}}\}\ |\ \{^{K_{[x]}}/_{z_{x_n}}\})] \quad (3)$$

We have (3)$\Rightarrow$(2), because (2) is obtained by applying the context $\nu z_{a_1}, z_{a_n}, z_{b_1}, z_{b_n}.(\_\ |\ \{^{[z_{a_1},z_{a_n}]K^-}/_{z_a}\}\ |\ \{^{[z_{b_1},z_{b_n}]K^-}/_{z_b}\}$, where K^- is a signing key, to each side of (3).

Intuitively, we *delayered* the term $\widetilde{\Phi}(x)^j$ by application of the closure property of the static equivalence. We recursively repeat such delayering of all non-atomic terms of the frames on both sides of the latter equivalence, except for the terms exported by the honest token provider's frames (we already dealt with Th's frames above). Delayering is performed until we reach either (i) atomic terms, or (ii) non-atomic terms which are the result of applying encryption or signing functions with a restricted name as the key argument (that intuitively represent a message encrypted with the honest token provider's public key, or A's, B's session key, or alternatively a message signed by A or B). For example, removing one layer from $\widetilde{\Phi}(A)_{n-k}^j$ for $n-2 > k > 0$ results in terms $\widetilde{\Phi}(A)_{n-k-1}^j, \Phi(A)_k^j, \texttt{KA}_{k+1}^j$ and delayering $\Phi(A)_k^j$ in turn results in terms $\Phi(A)_{k-1}^j, \texttt{KA}_k^j$. Here is the resulting equivalence, which assumes that the honest token provider Th is at the position p_x of a request chain req_x of length n_x:

$$C_3(l)[\|_{x \in \{A,B\}}\left((\|_{0<i<p_x}\{^{\texttt{Kx}_i^l}/_{x_{u_i}}\})\ |\ \{^{\Phi(x)_{p_x}^l}/_{x_{u_p}}\}\ |\ (\|_{p_x<i<n}\{^{\texttt{Kx}_i^l}/_{x_{u_i}}\})\ |\right.$$
$$\left.\{^{[\Phi(x)_{n-1}^l]K_x^-}/_{x_{u_n}}\}\ |\ \{^{\{\texttt{ITKSig},\texttt{Kx}_{p_x}^l,\widetilde{\Phi}(x)_{n-p_x-1}^l\}K_{Th}}/_{x_{t_5}}\}\ |\ \{^{\{\texttt{Kx}_{p_x}^l,\widetilde{\Phi}(x)_{n-p_x-1}^l\}K_{Th}}/_{x_{t_6}}\}\right)]$$

$$\approx_s$$

$$C_3(r)[\|_{x \in \{A,B\}}\left((\|_{0<i<p_x}\{^{\texttt{Kx}_i^r}/_{x_{u_i}}\})\ |\ \{^{\Phi(x)_{p_x}^r}/_{x_{u_p}}\}\ |\ (\|_{p_x<i<n}\{^{\texttt{Kx}_i^r}/_{x_{u_i}}\})\ |\right.$$
$$\left.\{^{[\Phi(x)_{n-1}^r]K_x^-}/_{x_{u_n}}\}\ |\ \{^{\{\texttt{ITKSig},\texttt{Kx}_{p_x}^r,\widetilde{\Phi}(x)_{n-p_x-1}^r\}K_{Th}}/_{x_{t_5}}\}\ |\ \{^{\{\texttt{Kx}_{p_x}^r,\widetilde{\Phi}(x)_{n-p_x-1}^r\}K_{Th}}/_{x_{t_6}}\}\right)]$$
$$(4)$$

where $C_3[\_]$ is the context $\nu s K_{Th}, \tilde{n}_A, \tilde{n}_B. (\|_{i \in N_1} \phi^r_{Th_i} \mid \|_{i \in N_2} dec\text{-}\phi_{Th_i} \mid \_).$

Remark. In the special case when $p_A = n_A$ or $p_B = n_B$ (i.e. when Th is the last one in A's or B's request chain) the resulting equivalence is slightly simpler and is dealt with in a similar way as below omitting non-applicable steps.

Next, we by Lemma 1 we eliminate all substitutions that export session keys. So, equivalence (4) holds if:

$$\nu s K_{Th}, \tilde{n}'_l \cdot (\|_{x \in \{A,B\}} \left(\{ {}^{[\Phi(x)^l_{n-1}]_{K_x^-}} / x_{u_n} \} \mid \{ {}^{\{ITKSig, Kx^l_{p_x}, \tilde{\Phi}(x)^l_{n-p_x-1}\}_{K_{Th}}} / x_{t_5} \} \mid \right.$$
$$\left. \{ {}^{\{ITKReq, Kx^l_{p_x}, \Phi(x)^l_{p_x-1}\}_{K_{Th}}} / x_{t_4} \} \mid \{ {}^{\{Kx^l_{p_x}, \tilde{\Phi}(x)^l_{n-p_x-1}\}_{K_{Th}}} / x_{t_6} \} \mid \{ {}^{K_{Th}} / x_{t_3} \} \right)) \mid$$
$$(\|_{i \in N_2} dec\text{-}\phi_{Th_i}) \mid (\|_{i \in N_1} \phi^l_{Th_i}) \mid \{ {}^{K_{[x]}} / x_{v_n} \}$$
$$\approx_s$$
$$\nu s K_{Th}, \tilde{n}'_r \cdot (\|_{x \in \{A,B\}} \left(\{ {}^{[\Phi(x)^r_{n-1}]_{K_x^-}} / x_{u_n} \} \mid \{ {}^{\{ITKSig, Kx^r_{p_x}, \tilde{\Phi}(x)^r_{n-p_x-1}\}_{K_{Th}}} / x_{t_5} \} \mid \right.$$
$$\left. \{ {}^{\{ITKReq, Kx^r_{p_x}, \Phi(x)^r_{p_x-1}\}_{K_{Th}}} / x_{t_4} \} \mid \{ {}^{\{Kx^r_{p_x}, \tilde{\Phi}(x)^r_{n-p_x-1}\}_{K_{Th}}} / x_{t_6} \} \right) \mid \{ {}^{K_{Th}} / x_{t_3} \} \mid$$
$$(\|_{i \in N_2} dec\text{-}\phi_{Th_i}) \mid (\|_{i \in N_1} \{ {}^{\{[\{Kx^j_{p_x}, \tilde{\Phi}(x)^j_{n-p_x-1}\}_{K_{Th}}, \Phi(x)^j_{p_x-1}]_{K^-_{Th}}\}_{Kx^j_{p_x}}} / t_{i_2} \}) \mid$$
$$\{ {}^{K_{[x]}} / x_{v_n} \}$$

$$(5)$$

We have unfolded $\Phi(x)^j_{p_x} = \{ITKReq, Kx^j_{p_x}, \Phi(x)^j_{p_x-1}\}_{K_{Th}}$ and $\phi^j_{Th_i} = \{[\{Kx^j_{p_x}, \tilde{\Phi}(x)^j_{n-p_x-1}\}_{K_{Th}}, \Phi(x)^j_{p_x-1}]_{K^-_{Th}}\}_{Kx^j_{p_x}}$, which appear in (4), to elucidate the difference between the lhs and the rhs frames.

Let ψ_{l_3}, ψ_{r_3} to be the lhs and the rhs of equivalence (5), respectively. We normalize those frames and consider each of the substitutions of the resulting equivalence in turn. In all of the cases, we start by replacing all occurrences of the exported term in question in other frames by a reference to the exporting variable:

- $\{ {}^{\{ITKReq, Kx^j_{Th}, \Phi(x)^j_{p_x-1}\}_{K_{Th}}} / x_{t_4} \}$. This term is the token $\Phi(x)^j_{p_x}$ that honest agents produce in the construction phase of the protocol. For $j \in \{l, r\}$, $\psi_{j_3} \not\vdash s K_{Th}$ and every occurence of $Kx^j_{p_x}$ in ψ_{j_3} either is an encryption key argument or is of the form $\{T, Kx^j_{p_x}, U\}_{pk(k)}$ for some T, U. Hence, by Lemma 9 we have $\psi_{j_3} \not\vdash Kx^j_{p_x}$. Since we replaced all occurences of the term in question in other substituions by a reference to x_{t_4} by Lemma 6 we have $\psi_{j_3} \not\vdash \{ITKReq, Kx^j_{p_x}, \Phi(x)^j_{p_x-1}\}_{K_{Th}}$. So now using Lemma 7, we can replace the substitution in question by a substitution of a fresh name on both sides of the equivalence. Similarly, we replace substitutions $\{ {}^{\{Kx^j_{p_x}, \tilde{\Phi}(x)^l_{n-p_x-1}\}_{K_{Th}}} / x_{t_6} \}$ with fresh names.

- $\{ {}^{\{ITKSig, Kx^j_{p_x}, \tilde{\Phi}(x)^j_{n-p_x-1}\}_{K_{Th}}} / x_{t_5} \}$. This substitution had resulted from delayering $\tilde{\Phi}(x)^j_{n-p_x}$, which is a token that Th issues to an honest participant. As above, for $j \in \{l, r\}$, $\psi_{j_3} \not\vdash s K_{Th}$ and every occurence of $Kx^j_{p_x}$ in ψ_{j_3} either is an encryption key argument or is of the form $\{T, Kx^j_{p_x}, U\}_{pk(k)}$ for some T, U. Hence, by Lemma 9 we have $\psi_{j_3} \not\vdash Kx^j_{p_x}$, and then by Lemma 6 we have $\psi_{j_3} \not\vdash \{\texttt{ITKReq}, \texttt{Kx}_{p_x}^j, \Phi(x)_{p_x-1}^j\}_{K_{Th}}$. Finally by Lemma 7, we replace the substitution in question by a substitution of a fresh name on both sides of the equivalence.

- $\|_{i \in N_1}\{\frac{\{[\{\texttt{Kx}_{p_x}^j, \widetilde{\Phi}(x)_{n-p_x-1}^j\}_{K_{Th}}, \Phi(x)_{p_x-1}^j]_{K_{Th}^-}\}_{\texttt{Kx}_{p_x}^j}}{t_{i_2}}\}$. These are replies from Th to an honest participant in the second stage of the protocol. For $j \in \{l, r\}$, we have $\texttt{Kx}_{p_x}$ occurs in ψ_{j_3} only as an encryption key argument after two transformations above, and the term encrypted by $\texttt{Kx}_{p_x}^j$ does not occur in the rest of ψ_{j_3}. Hence, by Lemma 8 we can replace the terms in question by fresh names on both sides of the equivalence.

After the above transformations we note that the lhs of the equivalence is α-equivalent to the rhs. Consequently, $\psi_{l_3} \approx_s \psi_{r_3}$.

5   Conclusions

We introduced a protocol which allows users of a service to remain anonymous, while providing the possibility that the service owner can break the anonymity if the service is misused. In the protocol, the user's identity is distributed among a set of token providers; this set is chosen by the user from a pool of available token providers. Anonymity is assured provided at least one of the chosen token providers is honest (and the misuse has not occurred).

We provided an analysis of the anonymity property in the applied pi calculus. The fact that the steps that the user takes is dependent on the number of token providers she has chosen makes the analysis complicated. Such *open-ended* protocols [3] are difficult to analyse in a formal setting. In future work, we intend to automate our analysis of the protocol using a software tool, such as Isabelle.

References

1. Harris interactive. In: IBM multi-national consumer privacy survey (October 1999)
2. Business Week/Harris poll: A growing threat. In: Business Week (March 2000)
3. Backes, M., Meadows, C., Mitchell, J.C.: Relating cryptography and formal methods: a panel. In: FMSE, pp. 61–66 (2003)
4. Camenisch, J., Lysyanskaya, A.: An identity escrow scheme with appointed verifiers. In: Kilian, J. (ed.) CRYPTO 2001. LNCS, vol. 2139, pp. 388–407. Springer, Heidelberg (2001)
5. Camenisch, J., Lysyanskaya, A.: Signature schemes and anonymous credentials from bilinear maps. In: Franklin, M. (ed.) CRYPTO 2004. LNCS, vol. 3152, pp. 56–72. Springer, Heidelberg (2004)
6. Camenisch, J., Shoup, V.: Practical verifiable encryption and decryption of discrete logarithms. In: Boneh, D. (ed.) CRYPTO 2003. LNCS, vol. 2729, pp. 126–144. Springer, Heidelberg (2003)
7. Cranor, L.F., Reagle, J., Ackerman, M.: Beyond concern: Understanding net users' attitudes about online privacy. Technical report, AT&T Labs-Research (1999)
8. Kiayias, A., Yung, M.: Group signatures: Provable security, efficient constructions and anonymity from trapdoor-holders. Cryptology ePrint Archive, Report 2004/076 (2004), http://eprint.iacr.org/

9. Kilian, J., Petrank, E.: Identity escrow. In: Krawczyk, H. (ed.) CRYPTO 1998. LNCS, vol. 1462, pp. 169–187. Springer, Heidelberg (1998)
10. Leighton, F.T.: Failsafe key escrow systems. Technical Memo 483, MIT Laboratory for Computer Science (1994)
11. Lysyanskaya, A., Rivest, R.L., Sahai, A., Wolf, S.: Pseudonym systems. In: Heys, H.M., Adams, C.M. (eds.) SAC 1999. LNCS, vol. 1758, pp. 184–199. Springer, Heidelberg (2000)
12. Marshall, L.F., Molina-Jiminez, C.: Anonymity with identity escrow. In: Dimitrakos, T., Martinelli, F. (eds.), Proceedings of the 1st International Workshop on Formal Aspects in Security and Trust, pp. 121–129, Istituto di Informatica e Telematica, Pisa (2003)
13. Micali, S.: Fair public-key cryptosystems. In: Brickell, E.F. (ed.) CRYPTO 1992. LNCS, vol. 740, Springer, Heidelberg (1993)
14. Mukhamedov, A., Ryan, M.D.: On anonymity with identity escrow. In: Dimitrakos, T., Martinelli, F., Ryan, P.Y.A., Schneider, S. (eds.) FAST 2005. LNCS, vol. 3866, Springer, Heidelberg (2006)
15. Aybek Mukhamedov and Mark D. Ryan. Anonymity protocol with identity escrow and analysis in the applied π-calculus (extended version) (2007), http://www.cs.bham.ac.uk/~{axm,mdr}

Formal Approaches to Information-Hiding
(Tutorial*)

Romain Beauxis[1], Konstantinos Chatzikokolakis[1], Catuscia Palamidessi[1],
and Prakash Panangaden[2]

[1] INRIA and LIX, École Polytechnique, Palaiseau, France
{beauxis,kostas,catuscia}@lix.polytechnique.fr
[2] Mc Gill University, Montreal, Canada
prakash@cs.mcgill.ca

Abstract. In this survey paper we consider the class of protocols for information-hiding which use randomization to obfuscate the link between the observables and the information to be protected. We focus on the problem of formalizing the notion of information hiding, and verifying that a given protocol achieves the intended degree of protection. Without the pretense of being omni-comprehensive, we review the main approaches that have been explored in literature: possibilistic, probabilistic, information-theoretic, and statistical.

1 Introduction

During the last decade, internet activities have become an important part of many people's lives. As the number of these activities increases, there is a growing amount of personal information about the users that is stored in electronic form and that is usually transferred using public electronic means. This makes it feasible and often easy to collect, transfer and process a huge amount of information about a person. As a consequence, the need for mechanisms to protect such information is compelling.

A recent example of such privacy concerns are the so-called "biometric" passports. These passports, used by many countries and required by all visa waiver travelers to the United States, include a RFID chip containing information about the passport's owner. These chips can be read wirelessly without any contact with the passport and without the owner even knowing that his passport is being read. It is clear that such devices need protection mechanisms to ensure that the contained information will not be revealed to any non-authorized person.

In general, privacy can be defined as the ability of users to stop information about themselves from becoming known to people other than those they choose to give the information to. We can further categorize privacy properties based on the nature of the hidden information. *Data protection* usually refers to confidential data like the credit card number. *Anonymity*, on the other hand, concerns the identity of the user who performed a certain action. *Unlinkability* refers to the link between the information and the user, and *unobservability* regards the actions of a user.

---

* This work has been partially supported by the INRIA DREI Équipe Associée PRINTEMPS and by the INRIA ARC project ProNoBiS.

G. Barthe and C. Fournet (Eds.): TGC 2007, LNCS 4912, pp. 347–362, 2008.

Information-hiding protocols aim at ensuring a privacy property during an electronic transaction. For example, the voting protocol Foo 92 ([1]) allows a user to cast a vote without revealing the link between the voter and the vote. The anonymity protocol Crowds ([2]) allows a user to send a message on a public network without revealing the identity of the sender.

Several anonymity protocols use randomized primitives to obtain the obfuscation of the information to be protected. This is the case, for instance, of the Dining Cryptographers [3], which use coin-flipping, Crowds [2] and Onion Routing [4], which select randomly another user of the network to forward the message to, and Freenet [5]. In this survey, we restrict our attention to the case in which the use of randomization is critical to achieve the intended security properties.

2   The Possibilistic Approaches

These are by far the approaches which have been explored the most in literature. Various formal definitions and frameworks for analyzing information-hiding have been developed. Some examples of these approaches are those based on epistemic logic ([6,7]), on "function views" ([8]), and on process-calculi ([9,10]). Here we focus on the last kind of approach.

Often possibilistic approaches rely on *nondeterminism*: a protocol provides protection if the set of possible observable outcomes is saturated with respect to the secrets. More precisely, if in one computation the instance of the secret to protect is s and the observable outcome is o, then for every other instance s' there must be a computation where, with secret s', the observable is still o. Formally:

$$f^{-1}(f(P)) \sim P$$

where P is the protocol, and f is a relabeling function that maps all the secrets into a dummy, and $\sim$ is a chosen equivalence relation [9].

A related approach is the one by [11,12], where the authors specify privacy in electronic voting (protection of the secrecy of the vote) as the property that if we swap the way in which two users, A and B, vote, then the resulting system is weakly bisimilar to the original one. Formally:

$$C[A[a/v]|B[b/v]] \approx C[A[a/v]|B[b/v]]$$

where a, b represent the votes of A and B respectively, and the context $C[\,]$ represents the rest of the protocol.

This kind of approach is reasonable, as long as the protocols of interest do not involve the use of randomization. In case they do, then we have a problem, because the pure possibilistic approach is unable to cope with probabilities. So, the choice is either to move to a probabilistic approach, or to try to abstract from probabilities. The second choice is explored in [9]: In that paper, the authors replace probabilistic choice by nondeterministic choice, and then apply the usual possibilistic definition.

We now illustrate the above idea on the example of the dining cryptographers.

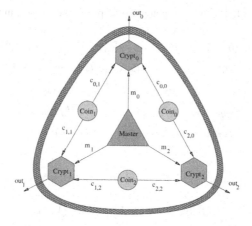

Fig. 1. Chaum's protocol for the dining cryptographers [3]

2.1 The Dining Cryptographers' Problem

This problem, described by Chaum in [3], involves a situation in which three cryptographers are dining together. At the end of the dinner, each of them is secretly informed by the master whether he should pay the bill or not. So, either the master will pay, or he will ask one of the cryptographers to pay. The cryptographers, or some external observer, would like to find out whether the payer is one of them or the master. However, if the payer is one of them, the cryptographers wish to maintain anonymity over the identity of the payer. Of course, we assume that the master himself will not reveal this information, and also we want the solution to be distributed, i.e. communication can be achieved only via message passing, and there is no central memory or central 'coordinator' which can be used to find out this information.

A possible solution to this problem, described in [3], is the following: Each cryptographer tosses a coin, which is visible to himself and to his neighbor to the right. Each cryptographer then observes the two coins that he can see, and announces *agree* or *disagree*. If a cryptographer is not paying, he will announce *agree* if the two sides are the same and *disagree* if they are not. However, if he is paying then he will say the opposite. It can be proved that if the number of *disagrees* is even, then the master is paying; otherwise, one of the cryptographers is paying. Furthermore, if one of the cryptographers is paying, then neither an external observer nor the other two cryptographers can identify, from their individual information, who exactly is paying.

In order to specify formally the protocol, we use a probabilistic version of the π-calculus, π_p, which is essentially the π-calculus enriched with a probabilistic choice operator $\oplus_p$. For a precise definition of the semantics of π_p we refer to [13].

The protocol can be described as the parallel composition of the master process *Master*, the cryptographers processes $Crypt_i$, of the coin processes $Coin_h$, and of a process *Collect*[1] whose purpose is to collect all the declarations of the cryptographers,

---

[1] The presence of the process *Collect* is due to technical reasons that have to do with the control of the power of the scheduler, and are out of the scope of this paper.

Table 1. The dining cryptographers protocol expressed in π_p

$$Master = \overline{m}_0\langle 0\rangle \,.\, \overline{m}_1\langle 0\rangle \,.\, \overline{m}_2\langle 0\rangle \,\oplus_p\, \bigoplus_0^2 p_i \overline{m}_{0+i}\langle 1\rangle \,.\, \overline{m}_{1+i}\langle 0\rangle \,.\, \overline{m}_{2+i}\langle 0\rangle$$

$$Crypt_i = c_{i,i}(x_0)\,.\,c_{i,i+1}(x_1)\,.\,m_i(x)\,.\,\overline{pay}_i\langle x\rangle\,.\,\overline{out}_i\langle x_0 + x_1 + x\rangle$$

$$Coin_h = \overline{c}_{h-1,h}\langle 0\rangle\,.\,\overline{c}_{h,h}\langle 0\rangle \,\oplus_{p_h}\, \overline{c}_{h-1,h}\langle 1\rangle\,.\,\overline{c}_{h,h}\langle 1\rangle$$

$$Collect = out_0(y_0)\,.\,out_1(y_1)\,.\,out_2(y_2)\,.\,\overline{outall}\langle y_0, y_1, y_2\rangle$$

$$DC = (\nu\vec{c})(\nu\vec{m})(\nu\vec{out})(Master \mid \prod_i Crypt_i \mid \prod_h Coin_h \mid Collect)$$

Table 2. The nondeterministic version of the dining cryptographers protocol expressed in π

$$Master = \overline{m}_0\langle 0\rangle \,.\, \overline{m}_1\langle 0\rangle \,.\, \overline{m}_2\langle 0\rangle \,+\, \sum_0^2 p_i \overline{m}_{0+i}\langle 1\rangle \,.\, \overline{m}_{1+i}\langle 0\rangle \,.\, \overline{m}_{2+i}\langle 0\rangle$$

$$Crypt_i = c_{i,i}(x_0)\,.\,c_{i,i+1}(x_1)\,.\,m_i(x)\,.\,\overline{pay}_i\langle x\rangle\,.\,\overline{out}_i\langle x_0 + x_1 + x\rangle$$

$$Coin_h = \overline{c}_{h-1,h}\langle 0\rangle\,.\,\overline{c}_{h,h}\langle 0\rangle \,\oplus_{p_h}\, \overline{c}_{h-1,h}\langle 1\rangle\,.\,\overline{c}_{h,h}\langle 1\rangle$$

$$Collect = out_0(y_0)\,.\,out_1(y_1)\,.\,out_2(y_2)\,.\,\overline{outall}\langle y_0, y_1, y_2\rangle$$

$$DC = (\nu\vec{c})(\nu\vec{m})(\nu\vec{out})(Master \mid \prod_i Crypt_i \mid \prod_h Coin_h \mid Collect)$$

and output them in the form of a tuple. See Table 1. In this protocol, the secret actions are $\overline{pay}_i\langle x\rangle$, and the observable actions are $\overline{outall}\langle y_0, y_1, y_2\rangle$.

2.2 Nondeterministic Version of the Dining Cryptographers

In the approach of [9] the dining cryptographers are formalized as a purely nondeterministic system: the coins are approximated by nondeterministic coins, and the choice on who pays the bill is also nondeterministic. The specification of the solution can be given in π-calculus as illustrated in Table 2 (in the original work [9] the authors used CSP [14]).

Let f be the function $f(\overline{pay}_i) = \overline{pay}$ and $f(\alpha) = \alpha$ for all the other actions. It is possible to check that $f^{-1}(f(DC)) \sim_T DC$, where we recall that $\sim_T$ stands for trace equivalence. Hence the nondeterministic notion of anonymity, as defined at the beginning of this section, is satisfied.

As a consequence of approximating the coins by nondeterministic coins, we cannot differentiate between a fair coin and a biased one. However, it is evident that the fairness of the coins is essential to ensure the anonymity property in the system, as illustrated by the following example.

Example 1. Assume that, whenever a cryptographer pays, an external observer obtains *almost always* one of the three outcomes represented in Figure 2, where a stands for *agree* and d for *disagree*. More precisely, assume that these three outcomes appear with a frequency of 33% each, while the missing configuration, d, a, a, appears with a frequency of only 1%. What can the observer deduce? By examining all possible cases, it is easy to see that the coins must be biased, and more precisely, $Coin_0$ and $Coin_1$

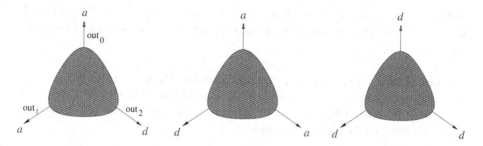

Fig. 2. Illustration of Example 1: The results that are observed with high frequency

must produce almost always *head*, and $Coin_2$ must produce almost always *tail* (or vice-versa). From this estimation, it is immediate to conclude that, in the first case, the payer is *almost for sure* $Crypt_1$, in the second case $Crypt_2$, and in the third case $Crypt_0$.

In the situation illustrated in the above example, clearly, the system does not provide anonymity. However the nondeterministic definition of anonymity is still satisfied (and it is satisfied in general, as long as "almost always" is not "always", i.e. the fourth configuration d, a, a also appears, from time to time). The problem is that the nondeterministic definition can only express whether or not it is possible to have a particular outcome, but cannot express whether one outcome is more likely than the other.

3   The Probabilistic Approaches

The probabilistic approaches have been investigated in particular in the field of anonymity, and almost exclusively in the strongest form, namely to express the property that the observables reveal no (quantitative) information about the secrets (*strong anonymity*).

There are essentially three probabilistic notions considered in literature: one based on the equality of the *a posteriori* probabilities, one based on the equality between the *a posteriori* probability and the *a priori* probability, and one based on the equality of the *likelyhoods*. All of them involve the notion of conditional probability $p(a|b)$, which represents the probability of the event a, given the event b. We recall the equality known as Bayes theorem:

$$p(a|b) \ = \ \frac{p(b|a)\,p(a)}{p(b)}$$

These probabilistic notions also require that the secrets are mutually exclusive events, and that $\sum_s p(s) = 1$. The same for the observables.

Equality of the *a posteriori* probabilities. The idea is to say that a system is strongly secure if, for any observable o, the *a posteriori* probability of a secret s (namely $p(s|o)$) is the same as the *a posteriori* probability of any other secret s'. Formally:

$$p(s|o) \ = \ p(s'|o) \qquad \text{for all observables } o, \text{ and secrets } s \text{ and } s' \tag{1}$$

This is similar to the definition of *strong anonymity* by Halpern and O'Neill [7], although their setting is different, being based on a probabilistic version of epistemic logic.

Equality of the *a posteriori* and *a priori* probabilities. The idea is to say that a system is strongly secure if, for any observable o, the *a posteriori* probability of a secret s is the same as its *a priori* one. In other words, the observation does not add anything to the expectation that the secret is s. Formally:

$$p(s|o) \;=\; p(s) \qquad \text{for all observables } o, \text{ and secrets } s \qquad (2)$$

This is the definition of *anonymity* adopted by Chaum in [3]. He also proved that the DC satisfies it if the coins are fair. Halpern and O'Neill also consider a similar property in their epistemological setting, and they call it *conditional anonymity* [7].

Equality of the likelihoods. The idea is to say that a system is strongly secure if, for any observable o, the likelihood of a secret s given o (namely $p(o|s)$) is the same as the same as the likelihood of any other secret s'. Formally:

$$p(o|s) \;=\; p(o|s') \qquad \text{for all observables } o, \text{ and secrets } s \text{ and } s' \qquad (3)$$

This was proposed as definition of *strong anonymity* by Bhargava and Palamidessi [15].

3.1   Comparison

It is easy to see that definitions (2) and (3) are equivalent. In fact:

(2) $\Rightarrow$ (3))

$$
\begin{aligned}
p(o|s) &= \frac{p(s|o)\,p(o)}{p(s)} && \text{by Bayes theorem} \\
&= p(o) && \text{by (2)} \\
&= \frac{p(s'|o)\,p(o)}{p(s')} && \text{by (2)} \\
&= p(o|s') && \text{by Bayes theorem}
\end{aligned}
$$

(2) $\Leftarrow$ (3)) We prove that $p(o|s) = p(o)$ for all observables o, and secrets s. From this it is immediate to derive (2) by applying Bayes theorem.

$$
\begin{aligned}
p(o) &= \sum_s p(o \text{ and } s) && \text{by the disjointness of the secrets} \\
&= \sum_s p(o|s)\,p(s) && \text{by definition of conditional probability} \\
&= p(o|s) \sum_s p(s) && \text{by (3)} \\
&= p(o|s) && \text{since } \sum_s p(s) = 1
\end{aligned}
$$

Definition (3) has the advantage that it makes clear that depends only on the protocol, not in the distribution on the secrets, and, more important, it does extend in a natural way to the case in which the choice of the secret is done nondeterministically. See [15] for more details.

Concerning definition (1), it probably looks at a first site the most natural, but it actually turns out to be too strong. that one is strictly stronger than (2) and (3). In fact it is equivalent to (2) and (3), *plus* the condition that the probability distribution of the secrets is uniform, namely

$$p(s) \; = \; p(s') \qquad \text{for all secrets } s \text{ and } s' \tag{4}$$

(1) ⇒ (4))

$$
\begin{aligned}
p(s) \; &= \; \sum_o p(s \text{ and } o) &&\text{by the disjointness of the secrets} \\
&= \; \sum_o p(s|o)\, p(o) &&\text{by definition of conditional probability} \\
&= \; \sum_o p(s'|o)\, p(o) &&\text{by (1)} \\
&= \; \sum_o p(s' \text{ and } o) \\
&= \; p(s')
\end{aligned}
$$

(1) ⇒ (3))

$$
\begin{aligned}
p(o|s) \; &= \; \frac{p(s|o)\, p(o)}{p(s)} &&\text{by Bayes theorem} \\
&= \; \frac{p(s'|o)\, p(o)}{p(s)} &&\text{by (1)} \\
&= \; \frac{p(s'|o)\, p(o)}{p(s')} &&\text{by (4)} \\
&= \; p(o|s') &&\text{by Bayes theorem}
\end{aligned}
$$

(1) ⇐ (3),(4))

$$
\begin{aligned}
p(s|o) \; &= \; \frac{p(o|s)\, p(s)}{p(o)} &&\text{by Bayes theorem} \\
&= \; \frac{p(o|s')\, p(s)}{p(o)} &&\text{by (3)} \\
&= \; \frac{p(o|s')\, p(s')}{p(o)} &&\text{by (4)} \\
&= \; p(s'|o) &&\text{by Bayes theorem}
\end{aligned}
$$

It is interesting to notice that (4) can be split in two orthogonal properties: one which depends only in the protocol ((3)), and one which depends only in the distribution on the secrets ((4)).

In our opinion condition (4) is not a suitable condition for defining the notion of protection provided by a protocol, because it only depends on the distribution on the secret data, which can be influenced by the users, but not by the protocol. We believe that a good notion of protection should abstract from such distribution. In this sense we consider (1) too strong.

There are also weaker notions of protection, still based on the comparison between conditional probabilities, which have been investigated in literature. In particular, Rubin and Reiter proposed the concepts of *possible innocence* and of *probable innocence* [2]. See also [16] for a generalization of the latter.

The need for formalizing weaker forms of protection comes from the fact that the strong properties discussed above are almost never achieved in practice. Hence the need to express in a quantitative way the *degree* of protection. Researchers have been exploring for suitable notions within the well-established fields of Information Theory and of Statistics.

4   Information Theory

Recently it has been observed that at an abstract level information-hiding protocols can be viewed as *channels* in the information-theoretic sense. A channel consists of a set of input values S, a set of output values O (the observables) and a transition matrix which gives the conditional probability $p(o|s)$ of producing o as the output when s is the input. In the case of protocols for information hiding, S contains the secret information that we want to protect and O the facts that the attacker can observe.

Let us revise some of the basic concepts of Information Theory: Let X be a random variable. The *entropy* $H(X)$ of X is defined as

$$H(X) = - \sum_{x \in \mathcal{X}} p(x) \log p(x)$$

The entropy measures the uncertainty of a random variable. It takes its maximum value $\log |\mathcal{X}|$ when X's distribution is uniform and its minimum value 0 when X is constant. We usually take the logarithm with a base 2 and measure entropy in *bits*. Roughly speaking, m bits of entropy means that we have 2^m values to choose from, assuming a uniform distribution.

The *relative entropy* or *Kullback–Leibler distance* between two probability distributions p, q on the same set $\mathcal{X}$ is defined as

$$D(p \parallel q) = \sum_{x \in \mathcal{X}} p(x) \log \frac{p(x)}{q(x)}$$

It is possible to prove that $D(p \parallel q)$ is always non-negative, and it is 0 if and only if $p = q$.

Now let X, Y be random variables. The *conditional entropy* $H(X|Y)$ is

$$H(X|Y) = - \sum_{y \in \mathcal{Y}} p(y) \sum_{x \in \mathcal{X}} p(x|y) \log p(x|y)$$

Conditional entropy measures the amount of uncertainty of X when Y is known. It can be shown that $0 \le H(X|Y) \le H(X)$. It takes its maximum value $H(X)$ when Y

reveals no information about X, and its minimum value 0 when Y completely determines the value of X.

Comparing $H(X)$ and $H(X|Y)$ gives us the concept of *mutual information* $I(X;Y)$, which is defined as

$$I(X;Y) = H(X) - H(X|Y)$$

Mutual information measures the amount of information that one random variable contains about another random variable. In other words, it measures the amount of uncertainty about X that we lose when observing Y. It can be shown that it is symmetric ($I(X;Y) = I(Y;X)$) and that $0 \leq I(X;Y) \leq H(X)$.

The maximum mutual information between X and Y over all possible distributions $p(x)$ is known as the channel's *capacity*:

$$C = \max_{p(x)} I(X;Y)$$

The capacity of a channel gives the maximum rate at which information can be transmitted using this channel.

In the following we recall some of the notions of protection, based on information-theoretic notions, which have been proposed in literature.

In [17,18] the authors propose a notion of anonymity based on the entropy of the users. The idea is to represent the lack of information that an attacker has about the secrets. Note that this is not in line with our point of view: in our opinion the interesting thing is to model the capability of the protocol to conceal the secret information despite of the observables that are made available to the attacker.

Zhu and Bettati propose in [19] a definition of anonymity based on mutual information.

In [20,21] the authors study the ability to have covert communication as a result of non-perfect anonymity. In [21] the authors suggest that the channel's capacity can be used as an asymptotic measure of the worst-case loss of anonymity.

In [22] we explore the implications of adopting the (converse of the) notion of capacity as measure of the degree of protection, and we introduce a more general concept that we call *conditional capacity*.

Note that the capacity is an abstraction of mutual information obtained by maximizing over the possible input distributions. As a consequence, we get a measure that depends only on the protocol and not on the input distribution, which is an advantage with respect to the mutual-information approach because in general we don't know the input distribution, and it also may change over time. Of course, in case we know the input distribution, then the mutual-information approach is more precise because it gives the exact loss of anonymity for the specific situation.

In [23] the authors use the Kullback-Leibler distance to perform a metric analysis of anonymity.

In [24] the authors define as information leakage the difference between the a priori accuracy of the guess of the attacker, and the a posteriori one, after the attacker has made his observation. The accuracy of the guess is defined as the Kullback-Leibler distance between the *belief* (which is a weight attributed by the attacker to each input hypothesis) and the true distribution on the hypotheses.

In the field of information flow and non-interference there is a line of research which is closely related. There have been various works [25,26,27,28,29,30] in which the *high information* and the *low information* are seen as the input and output respectively of a channel. From an abstract point of view, the setting is very similar; technically it does not matter what kind of information we are trying to conceal, what is relevant for the analysis is only the probabilistic relation between the input and the output information.

5   Hypothesis Testing

In information-hiding systems the attacker finds himself in the following scenario: he cannot directly detect the information of interest, namely the actual value of the random variable $S \in \mathcal{S}$, but he can discover the value of another random variable $O \in \mathcal{O}$ which depends on S according to a known conditional distribution. This kind of situation is quite common also in other disciplines, like medicine, biology, and experimental physics, to mention a few. The attempt to infer S from O is called *hypothesis testing* (the "hypothesis" to be validated is the actual value of S), and it has been widely investigated in statistics.

In this section we discuss possible methods by which an adversary can try to infer the secrets from the observables, and consider the corresponding probability of error, that it, the probability that the adversary draws the wrong conclusion. We regard the probability of error as a representative of the degree of protection provided by the protocol, and we study its properties with respect to the associated matrix.

We start by recalling the notion of *decision function*, which represent the guess the adversary makes about the secrets, for each observable: a decision function is simply any function $f : \mathcal{O} \rightarrow \mathcal{S}$.

The *probability of error* associated to a decision function f is the probability of guessing the wrong hypothesis by using f, averaged on all possible observables. In general the probability of error depends on the input distribution and on the channel's matrix. We will use the notation $\mathcal{P}(f, M, \vec{p})$ to represent the probability of error associated to the decision function f, the channel's matrix M, and the input distribution $\vec{p}$. The following characterization of $\mathcal{P}(f, M, \vec{p})$ is well-known in literature, see for instance [31].

$$\mathcal{P}(f, M, \vec{p}) = 1 - \sum_{\mathcal{O}} p(o|f(o))p_{f(o)} \qquad (5)$$

Given a channel $(\mathcal{S}, \mathcal{O}, M)$, the best decision function that the adversary can use, namely the one that minimizes the probability of error, is the one associated to the so-called MAP rule, which prescribes to choose the hypothesis s which has *Maximum Aposteriori Probability* (for a given $o \in \mathcal{O}$), namely the s for which $p(s|o)$ is maximum. The fact that the MAP rule represent the 'best bet' of the adversary is rather intuitive, and well known in literature. We refer to [31] for a formal proof.

The MAP rule is used in the so-called *Bayesian approach* to hypothesis testing, and the corresponding probability of error is also known as *Bayes risk*. We will denote it by $\mathcal{P}_{MAP}(M, \vec{p})$. The following characterization is an immediate consequence of (5) and of the Bayes theorem $p(s|o) = p(o|s)p_s/p(o)$.

$$\mathcal{P}_{MAP}(M, \vec{p}) = 1 - \sum_{\mathcal{O}} \max_s (p(o|s)p_s)$$

In [32] we have proposed to express the degree of protection Pt provided by a protocol T in terms of the probability of error of the corresponding matrix $M(T)$:

$$Pt_{MAP}(T, \vec{p}) = \mathcal{P}_{MAP}(M(T), \vec{p})$$

The problem with the MAP rule is that it assumes that the input distribution is known to the adversary. This is often not the case, so it is natural to try to approximate it with some other rule. One such rule is the so-called ML rule, which prescribes to choose the s which has *Maximum Likelihood* (for a given $o \in \mathcal{O}$), namely the s for which $p(o|s)$ is maximum. The name comes from the fact that $p(o|s)$ is called the *likelihood* of s given o. We will denote the corresponding probability of error by $\mathcal{P}_{ML}(M, \vec{p})$. The following characterization is an immediate consequence of (5).

$$\mathcal{P}_{ML}(M, \vec{p}) = 1 - \sum_{\mathcal{O}} \max_s (p(o|s))p_s$$

It has been shown (see for instance [22]) that under certain conditions on the matrix, the ML rule approximates indeed the MAP rule, in the sense that by repeating the protocol the adversary can make the probability of error arbitrarily close to 0, with either rule.

We have also explored, in [32], the possibility of defining the degree of protection provided by a term T under the ML rule as $\mathcal{P}_{ML}(M(T), \vec{p})$, but it did not seem reasonable to give a definition that depends on the input distribution, since the main reason to apply a non-Bayesian approach is that we do not know the input distribution. Instead, we have defined the degree of protection associated to a process term as the *average* probability of error with respect to all possible distributions $\vec{p}$:

$$Pt_{ML}(T) = (m - 1)! \int_{\vec{p}} \mathcal{P}_{ML}(M(T), \vec{p}) \, d\vec{p}$$

In previous definition, $(m - 1)!$ represents a normalization function: $\frac{1}{(m-1)!}$ is the hyper-volume of the domain of all possible distributions $\vec{p}$ on $\mathcal{S}$, namely the $(m - 1)$-dimensional space of points $\vec{p}$ such that $0 \leq p_s \leq 1$ and $0 \leq \sum_{s \in S} p_s = 1$ (where m is the cardinality of $\mathcal{S}$).

Fortunately, it turns out that this definition is equivalent to a much simpler one: the average value of the probability of error, under the Maximum Likelihood rule, can be obtained simply by computing $\mathcal{P}_{ML}$ on the uniform distribution $\vec{p}_u = (\frac{1}{m}, \frac{1}{m}, \dots, \frac{1}{m})$:

$$Pt_{ML}(T) = \min_{\zeta \in \mathcal{A}} \mathcal{P}_{ML}(M_\zeta(T), \vec{p}_u)$$

We believe that the probability of error is a central notion for information-hiding, and we expect that it will be thoroughly explored in the next future.

In [33] we have characterized the Bayes risk in terms of the solution of certain systems of equations derived from the matrix of the channel. This has lead to an algorithm to compute the maximum value of the Bayes risk. Furthermore, it has allowed us to improve functional bounds on the Bayes risk.

In [32] we have studied how the operators of π_p affect the probability of error. In particular, we have characterized constructs that have the property of not decreasing the degree of protection, and that can therefore be considered safe in the modular construction of protocols. As a case study, we apply these techniques to the Dining Cryptographers, and we are able to derive a generalization of Chaum's strong anonymity result for the Dining Criptographers. More precisely, we have shown that the Dining Cryptographers on an arbitrary graph (where the nodes are the cryptographers and the arcs are the coins) is strongly anonymous if and only there is a spanning tree formed entirely of fair coins.

6   Computing the Matrix Associated to a Protocol

In this section we show how to compute the matrix associated to a protocol specified in π_p, using our (very preliminary) π_p model checker VAMP (http://vamp.gforge.inria.fr/).

We consider the protocol for the DC represented in Table 1. Assume we want to compute $p(o|s_i)$, where s_i represents the fact that the cryptographer i is the payer, and o is of the form $\overline{outall}\langle y_o, y_1, y_2 \rangle$. We redefine the *Master* to be

$$\overline{m}_i \langle 1 \rangle \, . \, \overline{m}_{i+1} \langle 0 \rangle \, . \, \overline{m}_{i+2} \langle 0 \rangle$$

Then, we run the resulting process DC in VAMP, with query o. VAMP gives as result the (unconditional) probability of executing o in the new specification, which corresponds to the conditional probability $p(o|s_i)$ in the original specification.

We have computed various channel matrices, for different values of the probability p that a coin gives heads (we assume that each coin is biased in the same way). The results are shown in Fig. 3.

Finally, from the matrix, we can compute the capacity. This can be done, in general, by using the Arimoto-Blahut approximation algorithm, or, under certain symmetry conditions, we can apply a formula (see [22] for more details).

In this case we could apply the formula because the conditions are satisfied. The resulting graph is displayed in Fig. 4. As expected, when $p = 0.5$ the protocol is strongly anonymous and the relative loss of anonymity is 0. When p approaches 0 or 1, the attacker can deduce the identity of the payer with increasingly high probability, so the capacity increases. In the extreme case where the coins are totally biased the attacker can be sure about the payer, and the capacity takes its maximum value of $\log 3$.

	daa	ada	aad	ddd	aaa	dda	dad	add
c_1	0.25	0.25	0.25	0.25	0	0	0	0
c_2	0.25	0.25	0.25	0.25	0	0	0	0
c_3	0.25	0.25	0.25	0.25	0	0	0	0
m	0	0	0	0	0.25	0.25	0.25	0.25

	daa	ada	aad	ddd	aaa	dda	dad	add
c_1	0.28	0.24	0.24	0.24	0	0	0	0
c_2	0.24	0.28	0.24	0.24	0	0	0	0
c_3	0.24	0.24	0.28	0.24	0	0	0	0
m	0	0	0	0	0.28	0.24	0.24	0.24

	daa	ada	aad	ddd	aaa	dda	dad	add
c_1	0.37	0.21	0.21	0.21	0	0	0	0
c_2	0.21	0.37	0.21	0.21	0	0	0	0
c_3	0.21	0.21	0.37	0.21	0	0	0	0
m	0	0	0	0	0.37	0.21	0.21	0.21

	daa	ada	aad	ddd	aaa	dda	dad	add
c_1	0.52	0.16	0.16	0.16	0	0	0	0
c_2	0.16	0.52	0.16	0.16	0	0	0	0
c_3	0.16	0.16	0.52	0.16	0	0	0	0
m	0	0	0	0	0.52	0.16	0.16	0.16

	daa	ada	aad	ddd	aaa	dda	dad	add
c_1	0.73	0.09	0.09	0.09	0	0	0	0
c_2	0.09	0.73	0.09	0.09	0	0	0	0
c_3	0.09	0.09	0.73	0.09	0	0	0	0
m	0	0	0	0	0.73	0.09	0.09	0.09

Fig. 3. The channel matrices for probability of heads $p = 0.5$, $p = 0.6$, $p = 0.7$, $p = 0.8$, and $p = 0.9$

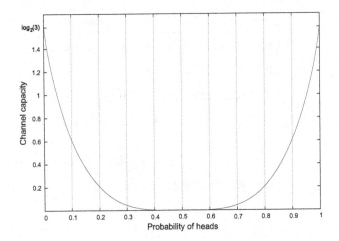

Fig. 4. The degree of anonymity in the Dining Cryptographers as a function of the coins' probability to yield heads

References

1. Fujioka, A., Okamoto, T., Ohta, K.: A practical secret voting scheme for large scale elections. In: ASIACRYPT 1992: Proceedings of the Workshop on the Theory and Application of Cryptographic Techniques, pp. 244–251. Springer, London, UK (1993)
2. Reiter, M.K., Rubin, A.D.: Crowds: anonymity for Web transactions. ACM Transactions on Information and System Security 1, 66–92 (1998)
3. Chaum, D.: The dining cryptographers problem: Unconditional sender and recipient untraceability. Journal of Cryptology 1, 65–75 (1988)
4. Syverson, P., Goldschlag, D., Reed, M.: Anonymous connections and onion routing. In: IEEE Symposium on Security and Privacy, Oakland, California, pp. 44–54 (1997)
5. Clarke, I., Sandberg, O., Wiley, B., Hong, T.W.: Freenet: A distributed anonymous information storage and retrieval system. In: Federrath, H. (ed.) Designing Privacy Enhancing Technologies. LNCS, vol. 2009, pp. 44–66. Springer, Heidelberg (2001)
6. Syverson, P.F., Stubblebine, S.G.: Group principals and the formalization of anonymity. World Congress on Formal Methods (1), 814–833 (1999)
7. Halpern, J.Y., O'Neill, K.R.: Anonymity and information hiding in multiagent systems. Journal of Computer Security 13, 483–512 (2005)
8. Hughes, D., Shmatikov, V.: Information hiding, anonymity and privacy: a modular approach. Journal of Computer Security 12, 3–36 (2004)
9. Schneider, S., Sidiropoulos, A.: CSP and anonymity. In: Martella, G., Kurth, H., Montolivo, E., Bertino, E. (eds.) ESORICS 1996. LNCS, vol. 1146, pp. 198–218. Springer, Heidelberg (1996)
10. Ryan, P.Y., Schneider, S.: Modelling and Analysis of Security Protocols. Addison-Wesley, Reading (2001)
11. Delaune, S., Kremer, S., Ryan, M.D.: Verifying properties of electronic voting protocols. In: Proceedings of the IAVoSS Workshop On Trustworthy Elections (WOTE 2006), Cambridge, UK, 45–52 (2006)

12. Delaune, S., Kremer, S., Ryan, M.: Coercion-resistance and receipt-freeness in electronic voting. In: Computer Security Foundations Workshop, pp. 28–42. IEEE Computer Society, Los Alamitos (2006)
13. Chatzikokolakis, K., Palamidessi, C.: A framework for analyzing probabilistic protocols and its application to the partial secrets exchange. Theoretical Computer Science (2005); In: De Nicola, R., Sangiorgi, D. (eds.) TGC 2005. LNCS, vol. 3705, pp. 146–162. Springer, Heidelberg (2005), http://www.lix.polytechnique.fr/~catuscia/papers/PartialSecrets/TCSreport.pdf
14. Hoare, C.A.R.: Communicating Sequential Processes. Prentice-Hall, Englewood Cliffs (1985)
15. Bhargava, M., Palamidessi, C.: Probabilistic anonymity. In: Abadi, M., de Alfaro, L. (eds.) CONCUR 2005. LNCS, vol. 3653, pp. 171–185. Springer, Heidelberg (2005), http://www.lix.polytechnique.fr/~catuscia/papers/Anonymity/concur.pdf
16. Chatzikokolakis, K., Palamidessi, C.: Probable innocence revisited. Theoretical Computer Science 367, 123–138 (2006), http://www.lix.polytechnique.fr/~catuscia/papers/Anonymity/tcsPI.pdf
17. Serjantov, A., Danezis, G.: Towards an information theoretic metric for anonymity. In: Dingledine, R., Syverson, P.F. (eds.) PET 2002. LNCS, vol. 2482, pp. 41–53. Springer, Heidelberg (2003)
18. Díaz, C., Seys, S., Claessens, J., Preneel, B.: Towards measuring anonymity. In: Dingledine, R., Syverson, P.F. (eds.) PET 2002. LNCS, vol. 2482, pp. 54–68. Springer, Heidelberg (2003)
19. Zhu, Y., Bettati, R.: Anonymity vs. information leakage in anonymity systems. In: Proc. of ICDCS, pp. 514–524. IEEE Computer Society, Los Alamitos (2005)
20. Moskowitz, I.S., Newman, R.E., Crepeau, D.P., Miller, A.R.: Covert channels and anonymizing networks. In: Jajodia, S., Samarati, P., Syverson, P.F. (eds.) WPES, ACM, pp. 79–88. ACM, New York (2003)
21. Moskowitz, I.S., Newman, R.E., Syverson, P.F.: Quasi-anonymous channels. In: IASTED CNIS, pp. 126–131 (2003)
22. Chatzikokolakis, K., Palamidessi, C., Panangaden, P.: Anonymity protocols as noisy channels. In: Information and Computation (to appear, 2007), http://www.lix.polytechnique.fr/~catuscia/papers/Anonymity/Channels/full.pdf
23. Deng, Y., Pang, J., Wu, P.: Measuring anonymity with relative entropy. In: Dimitrakos, T., Martinelli, F., Ryan, P.Y.A., Schneider, S. (eds.) FAST 2006. LNCS, vol. 4691, pp. 65–79. Springer, Heidelberg (2007)
24. Clarkson, M.R., Myers, A.C., Schneider, F.B.: Belief in information flow. Journal of Computer Security. Available as Cornell Computer Science Department Technical Report TR 2007-207 (to appear, 2008)
25. McLean, J.: Security models and information flow. In: IEEE Symposium on Security and Privacy, pp. 180–189 (1990)
26. Gray III, J.W.: Toward a mathematical foundation for information flow security. In: Proceedings of the 1991 IEEE Computer Society Symposium on Research in Security and Privacy (SSP 1991), pp. 21–35. IEEE, Washington - Brussels - Tokyo (1991)
27. Clark, D., Hunt, S., Malacaria, P.: Quantitative analysis of the leakage of confidential data. In: Proc. of QAPL 2001. Electr. Notes Theor. Comput. Sci, vol. 59 (3), pp. 238–251. Elsevier Science, Amsterdam (2001)
28. Clark, D., Hunt, S., Malacaria, P.: Quantified interference for a while language. In: Proc. of QAPL 2004. Electr. Notes Theor. Comput. Sci, vol. 112, pp. 149–166. Elsevier Science, Amsterdam (2005)

29. Lowe, G.: Quantifying information flow. In: Proc. of CSFW 2002, pp. 18–31. IEEE Computer Society Press, Los Alamitos (2002)
30. Boreale, M.: Quantifying information leakage in process calculi. In: Bugliesi, M., Preneel, B., Sassone, V., Wegener, I. (eds.) ICALP 2006. LNCS, vol. 4052, pp. 119–131. Springer, Heidelberg (2006)
31. Cover, T.M., Thomas, J.A.: Elements of Information Theory. John Wiley & Sons, Chichester (1991)
32. Compositional Methods for Information-Hiding. In: FOSSACS 2008, LNCS, vol. 4962, pp. 443–457, Springer, Heidelberg (to appear, 2008)
33. Chatzikokolakis, K., Palamidessi, C., Panangaden, P.: Probability of error in information-hiding protocols. In: Proceedings of the 20th IEEE Computer Security Foundations Symposium (CSF20), pp. 341–354. IEEE Computer Society, Los Alamitos (2007), http://www.lix.polytechnique.fr/~catuscia/papers/ ProbabilityError/full.pdf

Computational Soundness of Equational Theories*
(Tutorial)

Steve Kremer

LSV, ENS Cachan & CNRS & INRIA Futurs
`kremer@lsv.ens-cachan.fr`

Abstract. We study the link between formal and cryptographic models for security protocols in the presence of passive and adaptive adversaries. We first describe the seminal result by Abadi and Rogaway and shortly discuss some of its extensions. Then we describe a general model for reasoning about the soundness of implementations of equational theories. We illustrate this model on several examples of computationally sound implementations of equational theories.

1 Introduction

Security protocols have been deployed massively during the last years. However, their security is difficult to ensure and even small protocols are known to be error-prone. Two different approaches for proving such protocols correct have been developed. On the one hand, the *symbolic* or *formal* approach models messages and cryptographic primitives by a term algebra. The adversary manipulates the terms only according to a pre-defined set of rules. On the other hand, the *computational* approach considers a more detailed execution and adversary model. Protocol messages are modelled as bitstrings and cryptographic primitives as algorithms. The adversary is modelled to be any probabilistic polynomial time Turing machine and the security of a protocol is measured as the adversary's success probability.

A considerable advantage of the symbolic model is that proofs can be (at least partially) automated. Unfortunately, it is not clear whether the abstract symbolic model captures all possible attacks. While the computational model provides much stronger security guarantees, proofs are generally harder and difficult to automate. A recent trend tries to get the best of both worlds: an abstract model which provides strong computational guarantees. In their seminal paper, Abadi and Rogaway [4] have shown a first such *soundness result* in the presence of a passive attacker for a simple abstract algebra with symmetric encryption. However, many protocols rely on more complex cryptographic primitives which may have algebraic properties (see [15] for a survey on algebraic properties). Such properties are naturally modelled using equational theories.

In this tutorial paper, we first present the original Abadi and Rogaway result and briefly discuss some of its extensions. Then we present a general framework for reasoning about the soundness of the implementation of an equational theory [10,19]. The

---

* Work partly supported by ARA SSIA Formacrypt and ARTIST2 Network of Excellence.

G. Barthe and C. Fournet (Eds.): TGC 2007, LNCS 4912, pp. 363–382, 2008.

formal indistinguishability relation we consider is static equivalence, a well-established security notion coming from cryptographic pi calculi [3] whose verification can often be automated [2,11]. A soundness result for an equational theory proves that indeed "enough" equations have been considered in the symbolic model, with respect to a given implementation. We first consider soundness in the presence of a passive adversary and then extend the setting to an adaptive adversary. We present soundness results for several equational theories.

There do also exist soundness results in the presence of an active adversary, notably pioneered by Backes et al. [9] and Micciancio and Warinschi [23]. However, we are not aware of a framework for reasoning about soundness of equational theories with active adversaries which remains a challenging topic of research.

This tutorial is mainly based on joint work with Mathieu Baudet, Véronique Cortier and Laurent Mazaré [10,19].

2   Preliminaries

Let $f : \mathbb{N} \to \mathbb{R}$ be a function. We say that f is a *negligible* function of η if $f(\eta)$ remains eventually smaller than any η^{-n} $(n > 0)$ for sufficiently large η. Conversely, a function $f(\eta)$ is *overwhelming* if $1 - f(\eta)$ is negligible.

We denote by $\mathcal{A}^{\mathcal{O}}$ the Turing machine $\mathcal{A}$ which has access to the oracles $\mathcal{O}$.

$x \xleftarrow{R} \mathcal{D}$ denotes the random drawing of x from a distribution $\mathcal{D}$.

Let $\eta > 0$ be a complexity parameter and $(\mathcal{D}_\eta)$ a family of distributions, one for each η. A family of distributions $(\mathcal{D}_\eta)$ is *collision-free* iff the probability of collision between two random elements from D_η, that is, $\mathbb{P}[e_1, e_2 \xleftarrow{R} \mathcal{D}_\eta : e_1 = e_2]$, is a negligible function of η.

3   The Abadi-Rogaway Result

In this section we summarize the seminal result of Abadi and Rogaway [4,5]. They show the first soundness result for a simple equivalence on formal expressions. This paper has given raise to many extensions in the passive case and has inspired the generalization to the case of an adaptive and active adversary.

3.1   Formal Expressions and Equivalence

On the formal side, we consider a simple grammar of formal expressions or terms. The expressions consider two base types for keys and Booleans which are taken from two disjoint sets **Keys** and **Bool**. Keys and Booleans can be paired and encrypted.

$M, N ::=$	*expressions*
K	key ($K \in$ **Keys**)
i	bit ($i \in$ **Bool**)
$\langle M, N \rangle$	pair
$\{M\}_K$	encryption ($K \in$ **Keys**)

For example the formal expression $\langle K_1, \{\langle 0, K_2\rangle\}_{K_1}\rangle$ represents a pair: the first component of this pair is the key K_1, the second, the encryption with key K_1 of the pair consisting of the boolean constant 0 and the key K_2.

Before defining the equivalence relation between terms we first need to define the deducibility relation $\vdash$. Intuitively, $M \vdash N$, if the adversary can learn the expression N from the expression M. Formally, $\vdash$ is the smallest relation, such that

$$M \vdash M \qquad M \vdash 0 \qquad M \vdash 1$$
$$\text{if } M \vdash N_1 \text{ and } M \vdash N_2 \text{ then } M \vdash \langle N_1, N_2 \rangle$$
$$\text{if } M \vdash \langle N_1, N_2 \rangle \text{ then } M \vdash N_1 \text{ and } M \vdash N_2$$
$$\text{if } M \vdash \{N\}_K \text{ and } M \vdash K \text{ then } M \vdash N$$
$$\text{if } M \vdash N \text{ and } M \vdash K \text{ then } M \vdash \{N\}_K$$

For example, if $M = \langle K_1, \{\langle 0, K_2\rangle\}_{K_1}\rangle$, then we have that $M \vdash K_2$. Moreover, $M \vdash 1$, as the constants 0 and 1 are always known to the attacker.

The equivalence relation between terms is based on the equality of the *patterns* associated to each term. A pattern represents the *adversary's view* of a term. Patterns extend the grammar defining terms by the special symbol $\square$. The pattern of a term replaces encryptions for which the key cannot be deduced by $\square$. We define the function p, taking as arguments a term and a set T of keys, inductively as follows.

$$p(K, T) = K \quad (K \in \mathbf{Keys})$$
$$p(i, T) = i \quad (i \in \mathbf{Bool})$$
$$p(\langle M, N\rangle, T) = \langle p(M, T), p(N, T)\rangle$$
$$p(\{M\}_K, T) = \begin{cases} \{p(M, T)\}_K & \text{if } K \in T \\ \square & \text{else} \end{cases}$$

The pattern of an expression is defined as

$$pattern(M) = p(M, \{K \in \mathbf{Keys} \mid M \vdash K\}).$$

For instance $pattern(\langle K_1, \{\langle 0, \{1\}_{K_2}\rangle\}_{K_1}\rangle) = \langle K_1, \{\langle 0, \square\rangle\}_{K_1}\rangle$.

We say that M and N are formally indistinguishable, written $M \equiv N$ if and only if $pattern(M) = pattern(N)\sigma$, where σ is a bijection on keys (here interpreted as a substitution applied on $pattern(N)$). As an illustration, we have that $0 \not\equiv 1$, $K_0 \equiv K_1$, $\langle K_0, K_0 \rangle \not\equiv \langle K_0, K_1 \rangle$ and $\{0\}_{K_1} \equiv \{1\}_{K_0}$. Bijective renaming of keys reflects the intuition that two different randomly chosen keys are indistinguishable.

3.2 Computational Messages and Indistinguishability

In the computational setting, we reason on the level of bitstrings and algorithms executed on Turing Machines, rather than on abstract terms. An encryption scheme in this setting is a triple of polynomial time algorithms $\mathcal{SE} = (\mathcal{KG}, \mathcal{E}, \mathcal{D})$, which are the key-generation, encryption and decryption algorithms. The key generation algorithm is parametrized by a security, or complexity parameter $\eta \in 1^*$ and encryption is probabilistic. Intuitively, η defines the key length. As expected we require that $\mathcal{D}_k(\mathcal{E}_k(m, r)) = m$ for any $k \in \mathcal{KG}(\eta)$ and random bitstring r. Moreover, decryption fails and returns $\perp$ in all other cases.

We say that an encryption scheme $\mathcal{SE}$ is type-0 secure, following the terminology of [4], if for any security parameter η and any probabilistic polynomial time Turing machine $\mathcal{A}$ (the adversary) the advantage $\mathrm{Adv}^{\text{type-0}}(\mathcal{A}, \eta, \mathcal{SE}) =$

$$\mathbb{P}\left[k, k' \stackrel{R}{\leftarrow} \mathcal{KG}(\eta) : \mathcal{A}^{\mathcal{E}_k(\cdot), \mathcal{E}_{k'}(\cdot)} = 1\right] - \mathbb{P}\left[k \stackrel{R}{\leftarrow} \mathcal{KG}(\eta) : \mathcal{A}^{\mathcal{E}_k(0), \mathcal{E}_k(0)} = 1\right]$$

is a negligible function of η. By convention, we suppose that adversaries are given access implicitly to as many fresh random coins as needed, as well as the complexity parameter η.

Intuitively, we require that an adversary cannot distinguish the case where he is given two encryption oracles encrypting with two different keys from the case where he is given twice the same encryption oracle always encrypting the constant bitstring representing 0 with the same key. Note that the answers of the second pair of oracles will be distinct each time because encryption is probabilistic. Type-0 security is a message-length and which-key concealing version of the standard semantic security [18]. Message-length concealing means that the encryption hides the length of the plaintext. Which-key concealing means that the fact that two ciphertexts have been encrypted with the same key is hidden.

It is important to note that an encryption scheme respecting the above security definition may be insecure as soon as the adversary is given a *key cycle*. A key cycle is a sequence of keys $K_1, \ldots, K_n$ such that K_{i+1} encrypts (possibly indirectly) K_i and K_n encrypts K_1. An encryption of key K with itself, i.e., $\mathcal{E}_K(K)$ is a key cycle of length 1. An example of a key cycle of size 2 would be $\mathcal{E}_{K_1}(K_2), \mathcal{E}_{K_2}(K_1)$. In Abadi and Rogaway's main result, key cycles are therefore forbidden. This condition can be found in most soundness results[1]. To better understand the problem of key cycles suppose that $\mathcal{SE} = (\mathcal{KG}, \mathcal{E}, \mathcal{D})$ is a semantically secure encryption scheme and let $\mathcal{SE}' = (\mathcal{KG}', \mathcal{E}', \mathcal{D}')$ be defined as follows:

$$\mathcal{KG}' = \mathcal{KG}, \quad \mathcal{E}'_k(m, r) = \begin{cases} \mathcal{E}_k(m, r) & \text{if } m \neq k \\ \text{const} \cdot k & \text{if } m = k \end{cases}, \quad \mathcal{D}'_k(c) = \begin{cases} \mathcal{D}_k(c) & \text{if } c \neq \text{const} \cdot k \\ k & \text{if } c = \text{const} \cdot k \end{cases}$$

where const is a constant such that for any key k, the concatenation const $\cdot k$ does not belong to the set of possible ciphertexts obtained by $\mathcal{E}$. Obviously, if the attacker is given a key cycle of length 1, *e.g.*, $\mathcal{E}'_k(k, r)$, the attacker directly learns the key. It is also easy to see that $\mathcal{SE}'$ is a semantic secure encryption scheme as it behaves as $\mathcal{SE}$ in nearly all cases (in the security experiment the adversary could make a query for encrypting k with itself only with negligible probability).

The notion of computational indistinguishability requires that an adversary cannot distinguish two (families of) distributions, with better than negligible probability. Let $\mathcal{D} = \{\mathcal{D}_\eta\}$ and $\mathcal{D}' = \{\mathcal{D}'_\eta\}$ be two families of probability distributions, also called *ensembles*. $\mathcal{D}$ and $\mathcal{D}'$ are *compuationally indistinguishable*, written $\mathcal{D} \approx \mathcal{D}'$ if for any η and any probabilistic polynomial time Turing machine $\mathcal{A}$, the advantage

$$\mathrm{Adv}^{\text{IND}}(\mathcal{A}, \eta, \mathcal{D}_\eta, \mathcal{D}'_\eta) = \mathbb{P}\left[x \stackrel{R}{\leftarrow} \mathcal{D}_\eta : \mathcal{A}(x) = 1\right] - \mathbb{P}\left[x \stackrel{R}{\leftarrow} \mathcal{D}'_\eta : \mathcal{A}(x) = 1\right]$$

is a negligible function of η.

---

[1] A notable exception is [6] where a stronger definition is considered: Key Dependent Message (KDM) security.

3.3 Interpretation of Formal Expressions and Soundness Result

To state Abadi and Rogaway's soundness result we have to define an interpretation of formal terms as bitstrings. Bitstrings are tagged using types "key", "bool", "pair" and "ciphertext". The initialize procedure, first draws all the keys using the key generation algorithm $\mathcal{KG}$; $Keys(M)$ denotes the set of keys appearing in the term M. The convert procedure implements encryption using algorithm $\mathcal{E}$.

> **Initialize$_\eta(M)$**
> for $K \in Keys(M)$ do $\tau(K) \xleftarrow{R} \mathcal{KG}(\eta)$

> **Convert(M)**
> if $M = K$ $(K \in$ **Keys**$)$ then
>   return $(\tau(K),$"key"$)$
> if $M = b$ $(b \in$ **Bool**$)$ then
>   return $b,$"bool"$)$
> if $M = \langle M_1, M_2 \rangle$ then
>   return $(\textbf{Convert}(M_1), \textbf{Convert}(M_2),$ "pair"$)$
> if $M = \{M_1\}_K$ then
> $x \xleftarrow{R} \textbf{Convert}(M_1)$
> $y \xleftarrow{R} \mathcal{E}_{\tau(K)}(x)$
>   return$(y,$ "ciphertext"$)$

The initialize and convert procedures associate to a formal term M a family of probability distributions $[\![M]\!] = \{[\![M]\!]_\eta\}$, one for each η. Abadi and Rogaway's main result is the following.

Theorem 1. *For any formal expressions M and N that do not contain key cycles, whenever the computational interpretation of the terms uses a type-0 secure encryption scheme, then $M \equiv N$ implies that $[\![M]\!] \approx [\![N]\!]$.*

3.4 Extensions

The above result has known many extensions. We mention some of them here. Laud and Corin [20] allow the use of composed keys. Adão et al. [7] strengthen cryptographic assumptions to allow key cycles. In [8], Adão et al. consider different implementations of encryption allowing which-key and message-length revealing encryption and also consider the case of one-time pad encryption and information-theoretic security. Garcia and van Rossum [17] add (probabilistic) hash functions and Bresson et al. [12] consider modular exponentiation. However, these extensions require to re-define each time a new formal indistinguishability relation extending the classical notion of patterns.

Micciancio and Warinschi [22] also show a *completeness* result: whenever two families of distributions, resulting from the interpretation of two formal terms, are indistinguishable, then the two formal terms are formally inditinguishable. This result requires a stronger security requirement for encryption, which is *authenticated* encryption (see [22] for details). Such a completeness result ensures that no false attacks are reported by the formal model. Adão et al. [8] extend this result to different implementations of encryptions as for soundness.

4 Abstract and Computational Algebras

To avoid redefining a new model and a new indistinguishability relation for each extension, we define a general model [10,19] which relies on equational theories and static equivalence.

4.1 Abstract Algebras

In the Abadi-Rogaway model symbolic terms were given by a simple grammar modelling encryption with atomic keys, pairs and boolean constants. Here we introduce a more general model—called *abstract algebras*— which consists of term algebras defined over a many-sorted first-order signature and equipped with equational theories.

Specifically, a *signature* $(\mathcal{S}, \mathcal{F})$ is made of a set of *sorts* $\mathcal{S} = \{s, s_1 \ldots\}$ and a set of *symbols* $\mathcal{F} = \{f, f_1 \ldots\}$ together with arities of the form $\text{ar}(f) = s_1 \times \ldots \times s_k \to s$, $k \geq 0$. Symbols that take $k = 0$ arguments are called *constants*; their arity is simply written s. We fix a set of *names* $\mathcal{N} = \{a, b \ldots\}$ and a set of *variables* $\mathcal{X} = \{x, y \ldots\}$. We assume that names and variables are given with sorts. By default, we assume that an infinite number of names and variables are available for each sort. The set of *terms of sort s* is defined inductively by

$$
\begin{array}{lll}
t ::= & & \text{term of sort } s \\
\mid & x & \text{variable } x \text{ of sort s} \\
\mid & a & \text{name } a \text{ of sort s} \\
\mid & f(t_1, \ldots, t_k) & \text{application of symbol } f \in \mathcal{F}
\end{array}
$$

where for the last case, we further require that t_i is a term of some sort s_i and $\text{ar}(f) = s_1 \times \ldots \times s_k \to s$. We also allow subsorts: if s_2 is a subsort of s_1 we allow a term of sort s_2 whenever a term of sort s_1 is expected. We write $\text{var}(t)$ and $\text{names}(t)$ for the set of variables and names occurring in t, respectively. A term t is *ground* or *closed* iff $\text{var}(t) = \emptyset$.

Substitutions are written $\sigma = \{x_1 \mapsto t_1, \ldots, x_n \mapsto t_n\}$ with domain $\text{dom}(\sigma) = \{x_1, \ldots, x_n\}$. We only consider *well-sorted, cycle-free* substitutions. Such a σ is *closed* iff all of the t_i are closed. We let $\text{var}(\sigma) = \bigcup_i \text{var}(t_i)$, $\text{names}(\sigma) = \bigcup_i \text{names}(t_i)$, and extend the notations $\text{var}(.)$ and $\text{names}(.)$ to tuples and sets of terms and substitutions in the obvious way. The application of a substitution σ to a term t is written $\sigma(t) = t\sigma$ and is defined in the usual way.

Symbols in $\mathcal{F}$ are intended to model cryptographic primitives, whereas names in $\mathcal{N}$ are used to model secrets, that is, for example random numbers or keys. The abstract semantics of symbols is described by an equational theory E, *i.e*, an equivalence relation (also written $=_E$) which is stable by application of contexts and well-sorted substitutions of variables. For instance, symmetric encryption is modeled by the theory E_{enc} generated by the equation $E_{\text{enc}} = \{\text{dec}(\text{enc}(x, y), y) = x\}$.

4.2 Deducibility and Static Equivalence

We use frames [3,2] to represent sequences of messages observed by an attacker, for instance during the execution of a protocol. Formally, a *frame* is an expression $\varphi = \nu\tilde{a}.\{x_1 = t_1, \ldots, x_n = t_n\}$ where $\tilde{a}$ is a set of *bound (or restricted) names*, and for each i, t_i is a closed term of the same sort as x_i.

For simplicity, we only consider frames $\varphi = \nu\tilde{a}.\{x_1 = t_1, \ldots, x_n = t_n\}$ which restrict every name in use, that is $\tilde{a} = \text{names}(t_1, \ldots, t_n)$. A name a may still be disclosed explicitly by adding a mapping $x_a = a$ to the frame. Thus we tend to assimilate such frames φ to their *underlying substitutions* $\sigma = \{x_1 \mapsto t_1, \ldots, x_n \mapsto t_n\}$.

In the previous section, we introduced deducibility and formal indistinguishability for the simple term algebra of encryption and pairing. We now define similar notions with respect to an equational theory.

Definition 1 (Deducibility). *A (closed) term t is deducible from a frame φ in an equational theory E, written $\varphi \vdash_E t$, iff there exists a term M such that* $\text{var}(M) \subseteq \text{dom}(\varphi)$, $\text{names}(M) \cap \text{names}(\varphi) = \emptyset$, *and* $M\varphi =_E t$.

In what follows, again for simplicity, we only consider deducibility problems $\varphi \vdash_E t$ such that $\text{names}(t) \subseteq \text{names}(\varphi)$. Consider for instance the theory E_{enc} and the frame $\varphi_1 = \{x_1 \mapsto \text{enc}(k_1, k_2), x_2 \mapsto \text{enc}(k_4, k_3), x_3 \mapsto k_3\}$: the name k_4 is deducible from φ_1 since $\text{dec}(x_2, x_3)\varphi_1 =_{E_{\text{enc}}} k_4$ but neither are k_1 nor k_2. Deducibility is not always sufficient to account for the knowledge of an attacker. For instance, it lacks partial information on secrets. We refer the reader to [2] for additional details and examples. That is why another classical notion in formal methods is *static equivalence*, which will be our formal indistinguishability relation.

Definition 2 (Static equivalence). *Two frames φ_1 and φ_2 are statically equivalent in a theory E, written $\varphi_1 \approx_E \varphi_2$, iff* $\text{dom}(\varphi_1) = \text{dom}(\varphi_2)$, *and for all terms M and N such that* $\text{var}(M, N) \subseteq \text{dom}(\varphi_1)$ *and* $\text{names}(M, N) \cap \text{names}(\varphi_1, \varphi_2) = \emptyset$, $M\varphi_1 =_E N\varphi_1$ *is equivalent to* $M\varphi_2 =_E N\varphi_2$.

For instance, consider the equational theory E_{enc} of symmetric encryption. Let 0 and 1 be two constants (which are thus known by the attacker). Then the two frames $\{x \mapsto \text{enc}(0, k)\}$ and $\{x \mapsto \text{enc}(1, k)\}$ are statically equivalent with respect to E_{enc}. However $\varphi = \{x \mapsto \text{enc}(0, k), y \mapsto k\}$ and $\varphi' = \{x \mapsto \text{enc}(1, k), y \mapsto k\}$ are not statically equivalent for E_{enc}: let M be the term $\text{dec}(x, y)$ and N be the term 0. M and N use only variables defined by φ and φ' and do not use any names. Moreover $M\varphi =_{E_{\text{enc}}} N\varphi$ but $M\varphi' \neq_{E_{\text{enc}}} N\varphi'$. The test $M \overset{?}{=} N$ distinguishes φ from φ'.

4.3 Concrete Semantics

We now give terms and frames a concrete semantics, parameterized by an implementation of the primitives. Provided a set of sorts S and a set of symbols $\mathcal{F}$ as above, a $(S, \mathcal{F})$-*computational algebra A* consists of

- a non-empty set of bitstrings $[\![s]\!]_A \subseteq \{0,1\}^*$ for each sort $s \in S$; moreover, if s_2 is a subsort of s_1 we require that $[\![s_2]\!]_A \subseteq [\![s_1]\!]_A$;

- a computable function $[\![f]\!]_A : [\![s_1]\!]_A \times \ldots \times [\![s_k]\!]_A \to [\![s]\!]_A$ for each $f \in \mathcal{F}$ with $ar(f) = s_1 \times \ldots \times s_k \to s$;
- a computable congruence $=_{A,s}$ for each sort s, in order to check the equality of elements in $[\![s]\!]_A$ (the same element may be represented by different bitstrings); by congruence, we mean a reflexive, symmetric, transitive relation such that $e_1 =_{A,s_1} e'_1, \ldots, e_k =_{A,s_k} e'_k \Rightarrow [\![f]\!]_A(e_1, \ldots, e_k) =_{A,s} [\![f]\!]_A(e'_1, \ldots, e'_k)$ (in the remaining we often omit s and write $=_A$ for $=_{A,s}$);
- an effective procedure to draw random elements from $[\![s]\!]_A$; we denote such a drawing by $x \xleftarrow{R} [\![s]\!]_A$.

Assume a fixed $(\mathcal{S}, \mathcal{F})$-computational algebra A. We associate to each frame $\varphi = \{x_1 \mapsto t_1, \ldots, x_n \mapsto t_n\}$ a distribution $\psi = [\![\varphi]\!]_A$, of which the drawings $\widehat{\psi} \xleftarrow{R} \psi$ are computed as follows:

1. for each name a of sort s appearing in $t_1, \ldots, t_n$, draw a value $\widehat{a} \xleftarrow{R} [\![s]\!]_A$;
2. for each x_i ($1 \leq i \leq n$) of sort s_i, compute $\widehat{t_i} \in [\![s_i]\!]_A$ recursively on the structure of terms: $\widehat{f(t'_1, \ldots, t'_m)} = [\![f]\!]_A(\widehat{t'_1}, \ldots, \widehat{t'_m})$;
3. return the value $\widehat{\psi} = \{x_1 \mapsto \widehat{t_1}, \ldots, x_n \mapsto \widehat{t_n}\}$.

Such values $\phi = \{x_1 = e_1, \ldots, x_n = e_n\}$ with $e_i \in [\![s_i]\!]_A$ are called *concrete frames*. We extend the notation $[\![.]\!]_A$ to (tuples of) closed terms in the obvious way.

We focus on asymptotic notions of cryptographic security and consider families of computational algebra (A_n) indexed by a complexity parameter $\eta > 0$. As in previous section, the *concrete semantics* of a frame φ is a family of distributions over concrete frames $([\![\varphi]\!]_{A_n})$. We only consider families of computational algebras (A_n) such that each required operation on algebras is feasible by a (uniform, probabilistic) polynomial-time algorithm in the complexity parameter η. This ensures that the concrete semantics of terms and frames is efficiently computable (in the same sense).

5   Relating Abstract and Computational Algebras

In the previous section we have defined abstract and computational algebras. We now relate formal notions such as equality, (non-)deducibility and static equivalence to their computational counterparts, that is, equality, one-wayness and indistinguishability.

5.1   Soundness and Faithfulness

We introduce the notions of sound and faithful computational algebras with respect to the formal relations studied here: equality, static equivalence and deducibility.

Let E be an equational theory. A family of computational algebras (A_n) is

- $=_E$-*sound* iff for every closed terms T_1, T_2 of the same sort, $T_1 =_E T_2$ implies that $\mathbb{P}[e_1, e_2 \xleftarrow{R} [\![T_1, T_2]\!]_{A_n} : e_1 =_{A_n} e_2]$ is overwhelming;
- $=_E$-*faithful* iff for every closed terms T_1, T_2 of the same sort, $T_1 \neq_E T_2$ implies that $\mathbb{P}[e_1, e_2 \xleftarrow{R} [\![T_1, T_2]\!]_{A_n} : e_1 =_{A_n} e_2]$ is negligible;

- $\approx_E$-*sound* iff for every frames φ_1, φ_2 with the same domain, $\varphi_1 \approx_E \varphi_2$ implies that $(\llbracket \varphi_1 \rrbracket_{A_\eta}) \approx (\llbracket \varphi_2 \rrbracket_{A_\eta})$;
- $\approx_E$-*faithful* iff for every frames φ_1, φ_2 of the same domain, $\varphi_1 \not\approx_E \varphi_2$ implies that there exists a polynomial-time adversary $\mathcal{A}$ for distinguishing concrete frames, such that $\mathrm{Adv}^{\mathrm{IND}}(\mathcal{A}, \eta, \llbracket \varphi_1 \rrbracket_{A_\eta}, \llbracket \varphi_2 \rrbracket_{A_\eta})$ is overwhelming;
- $\nvdash_E$-*sound* iff for every frame φ and closed term T such that $\mathrm{names}(T) \subseteq \mathrm{names}(\varphi)$, $\varphi \nvdash_E T$ implies that for each polynomial-time adversary $\mathcal{A}$, we have that the probability $\mathbb{P}[\phi, e \xleftarrow{R} \llbracket \varphi, T \rrbracket_{A_\eta} : \mathcal{A}(\phi) =_{A_\eta} e]$ is negligible;
- $\nvdash_E$-*faithful* iff for every frame φ and closed term T such that $\mathrm{names}(T) \subseteq \mathrm{names}(\varphi)$, $\varphi \vdash_E T$ implies that there exists a polynomial-time adversary $\mathcal{A}$ such that the probability $\mathbb{P}[\phi, e \xleftarrow{R} \llbracket \varphi, T \rrbracket_{A_\eta} : \mathcal{A}(\phi) =_{A_\eta} e]$ is overwhelming.

We note that faithfullness is stronger than completeness as defined in [22]. It requires that whenever static equivalence does not hold distributions can be distinguished *efficiently*. Completeness could be defined by replacing "overwhelming" with "non-negligible". Sometimes, it is possible to prove stronger notions of soundness that hold without restriction on the computational power of adversaries. In particular, (A_η) is

- *unconditionally* $=_E$-*sound* iff for every closed terms T_1, T_2 of the same sort, $T_1 =_E T_2$ implies that $\mathbb{P}[e_1, e_2 \xleftarrow{R} \llbracket T_1, T_2 \rrbracket_{A_\eta} : e_1 =_{A_\eta} e_2] = 1$;
- *unconditionally* $\approx_E$-*sound* iff for every frames φ_1, φ_2 with the same domain, $\varphi_1 \approx_E \varphi_2$ implies $(\llbracket \varphi_1 \rrbracket_{A_\eta}) = (\llbracket \varphi_2 \rrbracket_{A_\eta})$;
- *unconditionally* $\nvdash_E$-*sound* iff for every frame φ and closed term T such that $\mathrm{names}(T) \subseteq \mathrm{names}(\varphi)$ and $\varphi \nvdash_E T$, the drawings for φ and T are independent: for all ϕ_0, e_0, $\mathbb{P}[\phi_0, e_0 \xleftarrow{R} \llbracket \varphi, T \rrbracket_{A_\eta}] = \mathbb{P}[\phi_0 \xleftarrow{R} \llbracket \varphi \rrbracket_{A_\eta}] \times \mathbb{P}[e_0 \xleftarrow{R} \llbracket T \rrbracket_{A_\eta}]$, and the drawing $(\xleftarrow{R} \llbracket T \rrbracket_{A_\eta})$ is collision-free.

Generally, (unconditional) $=_E$-soundness is given by construction. Indeed true formal equations correspond to the expected behavior of primitives and should hold in the concrete world with overwhelming probability. The other criteria are however more difficult to fulfill. Therefore it is often interesting to restrict frames to *well-formed* ones in order to achieve soundness or faithfulness: we have already encountered a typical example of such a restriction which was to forbid key cycles.

It is worth noting that the notions of soundness and faithfulness introduced above are not independent.

Proposition 1. *Let* (A_η) *be a* $=_E$-*sound family of computational algebras. Then*

1. (A_η) *is* $\nvdash_E$-*faithful;*
2. *if* (A_η) *is also* $=_E$-*faithful*, (A_η) *is* $\approx_E$-*faithful.*

For many theories, we have that $\approx_E$-soundness implies all the other notions of soundness and faithfulness. This emphasizes the importance of $\approx_E$-soundness and provides an additional motivation for its study. As an illustration, let us consider an arbitrary theory which includes keyed hash functions.

A symbol f is *free* with respect to an equational theory E iff there exists a set of equations F generating E such that f does not occur in F. A sort s is *degenerated* in E iff all terms of sort s are equal modulo E.

Proposition 2. *Let (A_η) be a family of $\approx_E$-sound computational algebras. Assume that free binary symbols $h_s : s \times Key \rightarrow Hash$ are available for every sort s, where the sort Key is not degenerated in E, and the drawing of random elements for the sort Hash, $(\xleftarrow{R} [\![Hash]\!]_{A_\eta})$, is collision-free. Then*

1. *(A_η) is $=_E$-faithful;*
2. *(A_η) is $\not\vdash_E$-sound;*
3. *Assume the implementations for the h_s collision-resistant in the sense that for all T_1, T_2 of sort s, given a fresh name k of sort Key, the quantity*

$$\mathbb{P}\left[e_1, e_2, e_1', e_2' \xleftarrow{R} [\![T_1, T_2, h_s(T_1, k), h_s(T_2, k)]\!]_{A_\eta} \ : \ e_1 \neq_{A_\eta} e_2, \ e_1' =_{A_\eta} e_2'\right]$$

is negligible. Then (A_η) is $=_E$-sound, $\not\vdash_E$-faithful and $\approx_E$-faithful.

6 Examples

We now illustrate the framework by several examples. Details and proofs can be found in [10,19].

6.1 Exclusive OR

We study the soundness and faithfulness problems for the natural theory and implementation of the exclusive OR (XOR), together with constants and (pure) random numbers.

The formal model consists of a single sort $Data_\oplus$, an infinite number of names, the infix symbol $\oplus : Data_\oplus \times Data_\oplus \rightarrow Data_\oplus$ and two constants $0, 1 : Data_\oplus$. Terms are equipped with the equational theory $E_\oplus$ generated by:

$$(x \oplus y) \oplus z = x \oplus (y \oplus z) \qquad x \oplus y = y \oplus x \qquad x \oplus x = 0 \qquad x \oplus 0 = x$$

As an implementation, we define the computational algebras $A_\eta, \eta \geq 0$:

- the concrete domain $[\![Data_\oplus]\!]_{A_\eta}$ is the set of bitstrings of length η, $\{0, 1\}^\eta$, equipped with the uniform distribution;
- $\oplus$ is interpreted by the usual XOR function over $\{0, 1\}^\eta$;
- $[\![0]\!]_{A_\eta} = 0^\eta$ and $[\![1]\!]_{A_\eta} = 1^\eta$.

Theorem 2. *The implementation of XOR for the considered signature, (A_η), is unconditionally $=_{E_\oplus}$-, $\approx_{E_\oplus}$- and $\not\vdash_{E_\oplus}$-sound. It is also $=_{E_\oplus}$-, $\approx_{E_\oplus}$- and $\not\vdash_{E_\oplus}$-faithful.*

6.2 Modular Exponentiation

As another application, we study soundness of modular exponentiation. The cryptographic assumption we make is that the *Decisional Diffie-Hellman* (DDH) problem is difficult: even when given g^x and g^y, it is difficult for any feasible computation to distinguish between g^{xy} and g^r, when x, y and r are selected at random. The original Diffie-Hellman protocol has been used as a building block for several key agreement protocols that are widely used in practice (e.g. SSL/TLS and Kerberos V5).

Symbolic model. The symbolic model consists of two sorts G (group elements) and R (ring elements), an infinite number of names for R, no name for sort G and the symbols:

$$+, \cdot : R \times R \to R \text{ add, mult} \qquad \exp : R \to G \qquad \text{exponentiation}$$
$$- : R \to R \qquad \text{inverse} \qquad * : G \times G \to G \text{ mult in } \mathbb{G}$$
$$0_R, 1_R : R \qquad \text{constants}$$

We consider the equational theory E_{DH} generated by:

$$x + y = y + x \qquad x \cdot y = y \cdot x \qquad (x + y) + z = x + (y + z)$$
$$x \cdot (y + z) = x \cdot y + x \cdot z \qquad (x \cdot y) \cdot z = x \cdot (y \cdot z) \qquad x + (-x) = 0_R$$
$$0_R + x = x \qquad 1_R \cdot x = x \qquad \exp(x) * \exp(y) = \exp(x + y)$$

There exists a direct correspondence between terms of sort R and the set of polynomials $\mathbb{Z}[\mathcal{N}_R]$ where $\mathcal{N}_R$ is the set of names of sort R. An integer i simply corresponds to $\underbrace{1_R + \ldots + 1_R}_{i \text{ times}}$ if $i > 0$, to $-(\underbrace{1_R + \ldots + 1_R}_{i \text{ times}})$ if $i < 0$ and to 0_R if $i = 0$.
We also write x^n for $\underbrace{x \cdot \ldots \cdot x}_{n \text{ times}}$. This correspondence can be exploited to decide static equivalence [19].

We put two restrictions on formal terms: products have to be *power-free*, i.e., x^n is forbidden for $n > 1$, and products must not contain more than l elements for some fixed bound l, i.e. $x_1 \cdot \ldots \cdot x_n$ is forbidden for $n > l$. Both restrictions come from the DDH assumption and seem difficult to avoid [12]. Furthermore we are only interested in frames using terms of sort G.

Concrete model. An Instance Generator IG is a polynomial-time (in η) algorithm that outputs a cyclic group $\mathbb{G}$ (defined by a generator g, an order q and a polynomial-time multiplication algorithm) of prime order q. The family of computational algebras (A_η) depends on an instance generator IG that generates a cyclic group $\mathbb{G}$ of generator g and of order q: the concrete domain $[\![R]\!]_{A_\eta}$ is $\mathbb{Z}_q$ with the uniform distribution. Symbols $+$ and $\cdot$ are the classical addition and multiplication over $\mathbb{Z}_q$, exp is interpreted as modular exponentiation of g. Constants 0_R and 1_R are respectively interpreted by integers 0 and 1 of $\mathbb{Z}_q$. The domain $[\![G]\!]_{A_\eta}$ contains all the bitstrings representation of elements of $\mathbb{G}$.

A family of computational algebras satisfies the DDH assumption if its instance generator satisfies the assumption, *i.e.* for every probabilistic polynomial-time adversary $\mathcal{A}$, we have that his advantage $\mathcal{A}$, $\mathrm{Adv}^{\mathsf{DDH}}(\mathcal{A}, \eta, IG)$, defined as

$$\mathbb{P}\left[(g, q) \leftarrow IG(\eta) : a, b \leftarrow \mathbb{Z}_q : \mathcal{A}(g^a, g^b, g^{ab}) = 1\right] -$$
$$\mathbb{P}\left[(g, q) \leftarrow IG(\eta) : a, b, c \leftarrow \mathbb{Z}_q : \mathcal{A}(g^a, g^b, g^c) = 1\right]$$

is negligible in η. We suppose that for any η there is a unique group given by IG. We show that the DDH assumption is necessary and sufficient to prove soundness of $\approx_{E_{\mathsf{DH}}}$.

Theorem 3. *Let (A_η) be a family of computational algebras. (A_η) is $\approx_{E_{\mathsf{DH}}}$-sound iff (A_η) satisfies the DDH assumption.*

6.3   Ciphers and Lists

We now detail the example of symmetric, deterministic and length-preserving encryption schemes. Such schemes, also known as *ciphers* [24], are widely used in practice, the most famous examples being DES and AES.

Symbolic model. Our formal model consists of a set of sorts $S = \{Data, List_0, List_1 \ldots List_n \ldots\}$, an infinite number of names for every sort $Data$ and $List_n$, and the following symbols (for every $n \geq 0$):

$$\begin{aligned}
enc_n, dec_n &: List_n \times Data \rightarrow List_n &&\text{encryption, decryption} \\
cons_n &: Data \times List_n \rightarrow List_{n+1} &&\text{list constructor} \\
head_n &: List_{n+1} \rightarrow Data &&\text{head of a list} \\
tail_n &: List_{n+1} \rightarrow List_n &&\text{tail of a list} \\
nil &: List_0 &&\text{empty list} \\
0, 1 &: Data &&\text{constants}
\end{aligned}$$

We consider the equational theory E_{cipher} generated by the following equations (for every $n \geq 0$ and for every name a_0 of sort $List_0$):

$$\begin{aligned}
dec_n(enc_n(x, y), y) &= x & enc_0(nil, x) &= nil \\
enc_n(dec_n(x, y), y) &= x & dec_0(nil, x) &= nil \\
head_n(cons_n(x, y)) &= x & tail_0(x) &= nil \\
tail_n(cons_n(x, y)) &= y & a_0 &= nil \\
cons_n(head_n(x), tail_n(x)) &= x
\end{aligned}$$

where x, y are variables of the appropriate sorts. The effect of the last four equations is that the sort $List_0$ is degenerated in E_{cipher} (all terms of sort $List_0$ are equal).

Notice that each well-sorted term has a unique sort. As the subscripts n of function symbols are redundant with sorts, we tend to omit them in terms. For instance, if $k, k' : Data$, we may write $enc(cons(k, nil), k')$ instead of $enc_1(cons_0(k, nil), k')$.

The concrete meaning of sorts and symbols is given by the computational algebras $A_\eta, \eta > 0$, defined as follows:

- the carrier sets are $[\![Data]\!]_{A_\eta} = \{0, 1\}^\eta$ and $[\![List_n]\!]_{A_\eta} = \{0, 1\}^{n\eta}$ equipped with the uniform distribution and the usual equality relation;
- enc_n, dec_n are implemented by a cipher for data of size $n\eta$ and keys of size η (we discuss the required cryptographic assumptions later). Since they are length-preserving they verify the equation $enc_n(dec_n(x, y), y) = x$;
- $[\![nil]\!]_{A_\eta}$ is the empty bitstring, $[\![cons_n]\!]_{A_\eta}$ is the usual concatenation, $[\![0]\!]_{A_\eta} = 0^\eta$, $[\![1]\!]_{A_\eta} = 1^\eta$, $[\![head_n]\!]_{A_\eta}$ returns the η first digits of bitstrings (of size $(n + 1)\eta$) whereas $[\![tail_n]\!]_{A_\eta}$ returns the last $n\eta$ digits.

For simplicity we assume without loss of generality that encryption keys have the same size η as blocks of data. We also assume that keys are generated according to the uniform distribution. It is not difficult to prove that the above implementation is unconditionally $=_{E_{\text{cipher}}}$-sound.

Concrete model. We now study the $\approx_{E_{\text{cipher}}}$-soundness problem under classical cryptographic assumptions. Standard assumptions on ciphers include the notions of super pseudo-random permutation (SPRP) and several notions of indistinguishability. In particular, IND-P1-C1 denotes the indistinguishability against lunchtime chosen-plaintext and chosen-ciphertext attacks. These notions and the relations between them have been studied notably in [24].

Initially, the SPRP and IND-P1-C1 assumptions apply to (block) ciphers specialized to plaintexts of a given size. Interestingly, this is not sufficient to imply $\approx_{E_{\text{cipher}}}$-soundness for frames which contain plaintexts of heterogeneous sizes, encrypted under the same key. Thus we introduce a strengthened version of IND-P1-C1, applying to a *collection* of ciphers $(\mathcal{E}_{\eta,n}, \mathcal{D}_{\eta,n})$, where η is the complexity parameter and $n \geq 0$ is the number of blocks of size η contained in plaintexts and ciphertexts.

We define the ω-IND-P1-C1 assumption by considering the following experiment $\mathcal{G}_\eta$ with a 2-stage adversary $\mathcal{A} = (\mathcal{A}_1, \mathcal{A}_2)$:

- first a key k is randomly chosen from $\{0,1\}^\eta$;
- (Stage 1) $\mathcal{A}_1$ is given access to the encryption oracles $\mathcal{E}_{\eta,n}(\cdot, k)$ and the decryption oracles $\mathcal{D}_{\eta,n}(\cdot, k)$; it outputs two plaintexts $m_0, m_1 \in \{0,1\}^{n_0 \eta}$ for some n_0, and possibly some data d;
- (Stage 2) a random bit $b \in \{0,1\}$ is drawn; $\mathcal{A}_2$ receives the data d, the *challenge ciphertext* $c = \mathcal{E}_{\eta,n_0}(m_b, k)$ and outputs a bit b';
- $\mathcal{A}$ is successful in $\mathcal{G}_\eta$ iff $b = b'$ and it has never submitted m_0 or m_1 to an encryption oracle, nor c to a decryption oracle.

Define the *advantage* of $\mathcal{A}$ as

$$\text{Adv}^{\omega\text{-IND-P1-C1}}(\mathcal{A}, \eta) = 2 \times \mathbb{P}\left[\mathcal{A} \text{ is successful in } \mathcal{G}_\eta\right] - 1 \qquad (1)$$

The ω-IND-P1-C1 assumption holds for $(\mathcal{E}_{\eta,n}, \mathcal{D}_{\eta,n})$ *iff the advantage of any probabilistic polynomial-time adversary is negligible. It holds for the* inverse *of the encryption scheme iff it holds for the collection of ciphers* $(\mathcal{D}_{\eta,n}, \mathcal{E}_{\eta,n})$.

We now state our $\approx_{E_{\text{cipher}}}$-soundness theorem. To define well-formed frames we orient the equations of E_{cipher} from left to right which forms a convergent rewriting system $\mathcal{R}$. A closed frame is *well-formed* iff its $\mathcal{R}$-normal form has only atomic keys, contains no encryption cycles and uses no head and tail symbols.

Theorem 4 ($\approx_{E_{\text{cipher}}}$-**soundness**). *Let φ_1 and φ_2 be two well-formed frames of the same domain. Assume that the concrete implementations for the encryption and its inverse satisfy both the ω-IND-P1-C1 assumption. If $\varphi_1 \approx_{E_{\text{cipher}}} \varphi_2$ then $(\llbracket \varphi_1 \rrbracket_{A_\eta}) \approx (\llbracket \varphi_2 \rrbracket_{A_\eta})$.*

Cryptographic assumptions of Theorem 4 may appear strong compared to existing work on passive adversaries [4,22]. This seems unavoidable when we allow frames to contain both encryption and decryption symbols.

6.4 A Theory for Guessing Attacks

In the context of password based protocols and guessing attacks, Abadi et al. [1] consider a complex equational theory: it accounts for symmetric and asymmetric encryption, as well as ciphers that can use passwords as keys. Security against guessing attacks can be elegantly modelled using static equivalence [14]. The main result is soundness of static equivalence for this equational theory. A direct corollary is soundness of security against guessing attacks. Because of lack of space we will not detail this result.

7 Adaptive Soundness

In [19], we extend soundness of static equivalence to the adaptive setting from [21]. In $\approx_E$-soundness the adversary observes the computational value of a fixed frame whereas in this setting the adversary sees the computational value of a sequence of adaptively chosen frames. Applications of this adaptive setting include the analysis of multicast key distribution protocols [21] and dynamic group key exchange protocols [19].

The adaptive setting is formalized through a cryptographic game. Let (A_η) be a family of computational algebras and $\mathcal{A}$ be an adversary. $\mathcal{A}$ has access to a left-right evaluation oracle $\mathcal{O}_{LR}$: given a pair of terms (t_0, t_1) it outputs either the implementation of t_0 or t_1. This oracle depends on a selection bit b and uses a local store to record values generated for the different names (these values are used when processing further queries). With a slight abuse of notation, we omit this store and write:

$$\mathcal{O}^b_{LR,A_\eta}(t_0, t_1) = [\![t_b]\!]_{A_\eta}$$

Adversary $\mathcal{A}$ plays an indistinguishability game and its objective is to find the value of b. Formally the advantage of $\mathcal{A}$ is defined by:

$$\mathrm{Adv}^{\mathsf{ADPT}}(\mathcal{A}, \eta, A_\eta) = \mathbb{P}\left[\mathcal{A}^{\mathcal{O}^1_{LR,A_\eta}} = 1\right] - \mathbb{P}\left[\mathcal{A}^{\mathcal{O}^0_{LR,A_\eta}} = 1\right]$$

Without further restrictions on the queries made by the adversary, having a non-negligible advantage is easy in most cases. For example the adversary could submit a pair $(0, 1)$ to his oracle. We therefore require the adversary to be *legal*.

Definition 3 (Adaptive soundness). *An adversary $\mathcal{A}$ is legal if for any sequence of queries $(t_0^i, t_1^i)_{1 \le i \le n}$ made by $\mathcal{A}$ to its left-right oracle, queries are statically equivalent:*

$$\left\{x_1 \mapsto t_0^1, \ldots, x_n \mapsto t_0^n\right\} \approx_E \left\{x_1 \mapsto t_1^1, \ldots, x_n \mapsto t_1^n\right\}$$

A family of computational algebras (A_η) is

- *$\approx_E$-ad-sound iff the advantage $\mathrm{Adv}^{\mathsf{ADPT}}(\mathcal{A}, \eta, A_\eta)$ of any polynomial-time legal adversary $\mathcal{A}$ is negligible.*
- *unconditionally $\approx_E$-ad-sound iff the advantage $\mathrm{Adv}^{\mathsf{ADPT}}(\mathcal{A}, \eta, A_\eta)$ of any legal adversary $\mathcal{A}$ is 0.*

Note that as variables are typed, any query (t_0^i, t_1^i) of a legal adversary to the oracle is such that t_0^i and t_1^i have the same sort. Adaptive soundness implies the original soundness notion for static equivalence.

Proposition 3. *Let (A_η) be a family of computational algebras. If A_η is $\approx_E$-ad-sound then A_η is also $\approx_E$-sound but the converse is false in general.*

Interestingly, in the case of unconditional soundness, adaptive and non-adaptive soundness coincide.

Proposition 4. *Let* (A_η) *be a family of computational algebras.* A_η *is unconditionally* $\approx_E$-*ad-sound iff* A_η *is unconditionally* $\approx_E$-*sound.*

A direct corollary of this proposition is the following.

Corollary 1. *The implementation of XOR for the signature considered in Section 6.1,* (A_η)*, is unconditionally* $\approx_{E_\oplus}$-*ad-sound.*

8 Adaptively Sound Theories

We have already seen that the theory of XOR is unconditionally adaptively sound. We now present additional adaptive soundness results for several equational theories: symmetric encryption (which is adaptively sound under IND-CPA) and modular exponentiation (adaptively sound under DDH). We also consider composed theories: symmetric encryption and modular exponentiation as well as symmetric encryption and XOR. For these theories we allow keys to be computed, using respectively modular exponentiation and XOR. Additional details and proofs can be found in [19].

8.1 Symmetric Encryption

We consider the case of probabilistic symmetric encryption which recasts the result of [21] in our framework and illustrates well the difference between a purely passive and an adaptive adversary.

Symbolic model. Our symbolic model consists of the set of sorts $\mathcal{S} = \{Data\}$, an infinite number of names for sort $Data$ called keys and the function symbols:

$$
\begin{array}{ll}
\text{enc}, \text{dec} : Data \times Data \to Data & \text{encrypt, decrypt} \\
\text{pair} : Data \times Data \to Data & \text{pair constructor} \\
\pi_l, \pi_r : Data \to Data & \text{projections} \\
\text{samekey} : Data \times Data \to Data & \text{key equalities test} \\
\text{tenc}, \text{tpair} : Data \to Data & \text{type testers} \\
0, 1 : Data & \text{constants}
\end{array}
$$

A name k is used at a key position in a term t if there exists a sub-term $\text{enc}(t', k)$ of t. Else k is used at a plaintext position. We consider the equational theory E_{sym} generated by:

$$
\begin{array}{ll}
\text{dec}(\text{enc}(x, y), y) = x & \pi_l(\text{pair}(x, y)) = x \\
\pi_r(\text{pair}(x, y)) = y & \text{samekey}(\text{enc}(x, y), \text{enc}(z, y)) = 1 \\
\text{tenc}(\text{enc}(x, y)) = 1 & \text{tpair}(\text{pair}(x, y)) = 1
\end{array}
$$

As usual $\text{enc}(t, k)$ is also written $\{t\}_k$ and $\text{pair}(t, t')$ is also written $\langle t, t' \rangle$.

Well-formed frames and adversaries. As usual we forbid the formal terms to contain such cycles. Let $\prec$ be a total order among keys. A *frame* φ *is acyclic for* $\prec$ if for any subterm $\{t\}_k$ of φ, if k' occurs in t then $k' \prec k$. Moreover as noted in [21], selective decommitment [16] can be a problem. The classical solution to this problem is to require keys to be sent *before* being used to encrypt a message or they must never appear as a plaintext. A *frame* $\varphi = \{x_1 \mapsto t_1, \ldots, x_n \mapsto t_n\}$ *is well-formed for* $\prec$ if

- φ is acyclic for $\prec$;
- the terms t_i only use symbols enc, pair, 0 and 1, and only names are used at key positions;
- if k is used as plaintext in t_i, then k cannot be used at a key position in t_j for $j < i$.

An *adversary is well-formed for* $\prec$ if the sequence of queries $(t_0^i, t_1^i)_{1 \leq i \leq n}$ that he makes to his oracle yields two well-formed frames $\{x_1 \mapsto t_0^1, \ldots, x_n \mapsto t_0^n\}$ and $\{x_1 \mapsto t_1^1, \ldots, x_n \mapsto t_1^n\}$ for $\prec$.

Concrete model. The family of computational algebras (A_η) giving the concrete semantics depends on a symmetric encryption scheme $\mathcal{SE} = (\mathcal{KG}, \mathcal{E}, \mathcal{D})$. The concrete domain $[\![Data]\!]_{A_\eta}$ contains all the possible bitstrings and is equipped with the distribution induced by $\mathcal{KG}$. Interpretation for constants 0 and 1 are respectively bitstrings 0^η and 1^η. The enc and dec function are respectively interpreted using algorithm $\mathcal{E}$ and $\mathcal{D}$. We assume the existence in the concrete model of a concatenation operation which is used to interpret the pair symbol. The corresponding left and right projections implement π_l and π_r. Finally, as we are only interested in well-formed frames, we do not provide any computational interpretation for tenc, tpair and samekey.

Semantic security. In this section we suppose a message-length, but not necessarily which-key concealing semantically secure encryption scheme. The definition that we recall below uses a left-right encryption oracle $LR_{\mathcal{SE}}^b$. This oracle first generates a key k using $\mathcal{KG}$. Then it answers queries of the form (bs_0, bs_1), where bs_0 and bs_1 are bitstrings. The oracle returns ciphertext $\mathcal{E}(bs_b, k)$. The goal of the adversary $\mathcal{A}$ is to guess the value of bit b. His advantage is defined as:

$$\text{Adv}^{cpa}(\mathcal{A}, \eta, \mathcal{SE}) = \mathbb{P}\left[\mathcal{A}^{LR_{\mathcal{SE}}^1} = 1\right] - \mathbb{P}\left[\mathcal{A}^{LR_{\mathcal{SE}}^0} = 1\right]$$

Encryption scheme $\mathcal{SE}$ is IND-CPA secure if the advantage of any adversary $\mathcal{A}$ is negligible in η. The standard definition of IND-CPA allows the scheme to be message-length revealing. By abuse of notation we call the above scheme also IND-CPA secure.

We also describe a variant of IND-CPA security, IND-CPA', which models non-adaptive adversaries. The left-right encryption oracle $LR_{\mathcal{SE}}'^b$ takes as input a list of pairs of bitstrings (bs_0^i, bs_1^i) for i in $[1, n]$ and returns the list of ciphertexts $\mathcal{E}(bs_b^i, k)$ for i in $[1, n]$. This oracle can only be queried once. The adversary can observe multiple encryptions but he is not allowed to chose them adaptively. The advantage of an adversary is defined in a similar way as above, replacing $LR_{\mathcal{SE}}^b$ by $LR_{\mathcal{SE}}'^b$. A symmetric encryption scheme is said to be IND-CPA' if the advantage of any polynomial time adversary $\mathcal{A}$ is negligible in η. These two notions of semantic security are related by the following proposition.

Proposition 5. *Let $\mathcal{SE}$ be a symmetric encryption scheme. If $\mathcal{SE}$ is* IND-CPA, *then $\mathcal{SE}$ is* IND-CPA$'$. *However $\mathcal{SE}$ can be* IND-CPA$'$ *without being* IND-CPA.

We now state the soundness theorem for symmetric encryption.

Theorem 5. *Let $\prec$ be a total order among keys. In the remainder of this proposition we only consider well-formed adversaries for $\prec$. Let (A_η) be a family of computational algebras based on a symmetric encryption scheme $\mathcal{SE}$.*

– (A_η) *is* $\approx_{E_{\text{sym}}}$*-ad-sound if $\mathcal{SE}$ is* IND-CPA *but the converse is false.*
– (A_η) *is* $\approx_{E_{\text{sym}}}$*-sound if $\mathcal{SE}$ is* IND-CPA$'$ *but the converse is false.*

The proof uses a similar hybrid argument as the one used by Micciancio and Panjwani in [21]. Results of this section are summed up in the following table. Note that the relations between adaptive and non-adaptive soundness have not been detailed formally.

$$\approx_{E_{\text{sym}}}\text{-ad-sound} \overset{\Leftarrow}{\nRightarrow} \text{IND-CPA}$$

$$\Uparrow \Downarrow \qquad\qquad \Uparrow \Downarrow$$

$$\approx_{E_{\text{sym}}}\text{-sound} \overset{\Leftarrow}{\nRightarrow} \text{IND-CPA}'$$

8.2 Modular Exponentiation

We suppose the same symbolic and concrete model as in Section 6.2. The DDH assumption is necessary and sufficient to prove adaptive soundness.

Theorem 6. *Let (A_η) be a family of computational algebras. (A_η) is $\approx_{E_{\text{DH}}}$-sound iff (A_η) satisfies the* DDH *assumption. (A_η) is $\approx_{E_{\text{DH}}}$-ad-sound iff (A_η) satisfies the* DDH *assumption.*

The proof of this result uses an adaptive variant of DDH called 3DH [12]: it generalizes several previously used variants of DDH. The main difficulty in this proof consists in relating DDH and 3DH.

Results for modular exponentiation are summed up in the following table. Note that while adaptive soundness and (classical) soundness are not equivalent for symmetric encryption, they coincide in this case.

$$\approx_{E_{\text{DH}}}\text{-ad-sound} \Longleftrightarrow \text{DDH} \Longleftrightarrow \approx_{E_{\text{DH}}}\text{-sound}$$

8.3 Composing Encryption with Exponentiation

Symbolic model. We consider an equational theory E containing both E_{DH} and E_{sym} and suppose that G is a subsort of $Data$.

Well-formed frames. Let $\prec$ be a total order between keys and exponentiations. A frame φ (on Σ) is well-formed for $\prec$ if:

- φ does not contain any dec, tenc, tpair, π_l, π_r or $*$ symbol, only names and exponentiations are used at key position.
- For any subterm $\exp(p)$ of φ used at a key position, p is linearly independent of other polynomials p' such that $\exp(p')$ is a subterm of φ.
- For any subterm $\{t\}_{t'}$ of φ, if t'' is a name of sort $Data$ or an exponentiation then $t'' \prec t'$.

The second condition is similar to the conditions on key cycles. The last condition is to avoid selective decommitment.

Concrete model. The concrete model is given by the models for symmetric encryption and modular exponentiation. However, exponentiations can be used as symmetric keys in our symbolic model. This needs to be reflected in the concrete model. The family of computational algebras (A_η) giving the concrete semantics is parameterized by a symmetric encryption scheme $\mathcal{SE}$ and an instance generator IG. We require the key generation algorithm of $\mathcal{SE}$ to randomly sample an element of $IG(\eta)$. Giving an IND-CPA encryption scheme $\mathcal{SE}'$, we build another IND-CPA encryption scheme $\mathcal{SE}$ which indeed uses such a key generation algorithm. This is achieved by using a *key extractor* algorithm Kex [13]. This algorithm (usually a universal hash function used with the entropy smoothing theorem) is used to transform group elements into valid keys for $\mathcal{SE}'$. Its main characteristic is that applying Kex to a randomly sampled element of a group created by IG produces the same distribution as the one given by the key generation algorithm of $\mathcal{SE}'$. Then the new encryption and decryption algorithms of $\mathcal{SE}$ apply the Kex algorithm to the group element which is used as key. This produces a symmetric key which can be used with the encryption and decryption algorithms of $\mathcal{SE}'$.

The family of computational algebras (A_η) implementing encryption with exponentiation is *EE-secure* if the encryption scheme $\mathcal{SE}$ is secure against IND-CPA and uses a key generation algorithm as described above and IG satisfies the DDH assumption.

Theorem 7. *Let $\prec$ be a total order between keys and exponentiations. Let (A_η) be an EE-secure family of computational algebras then (A_η) is $\approx_E$-ad-sound for well-formed frames for $\prec$.*

8.4   Composing Encryption with XOR

Symbolic model. We consider an equational theory E containing both $E_\oplus$ and E_{sym} and suppose that $Data_\oplus$ is a subsort of $Data$.

Well-formed frames. Let $\prec$ be a total order between keys and terms of sort $Data_\oplus$. A frame $\varphi = \{x_1 \mapsto t_1, \ldots x_n \mapsto t_n\}$ is well-formed for $\prec$ if the following conditions are verified. Let X be the set of maximal subterms of φ of sort $Data_\oplus{}^2$.

- φ does not contain function symbols dec, tenc, tpair, π_l or π_r and only terms of sort $Data_\oplus$ and names are used at key positions.

---

[2] Using standard definitions for manipulating terms X is formally defined as follows: $X = \bigcup_{1 \leq i \leq n} \{t_i|_p \mid p \in pos(t_i), sort(t_i|_p) = Data_\oplus, p = p' \cdot k \Rightarrow sort(t_i|_{p'}) \neq Data_\oplus\}$.

- For any $x \in X$ used at a key position, there does not exist a set $\{x_1, \ldots, x_i\} \subseteq X \cup \{1\}$, disjoint from $\{x\}$, such that $x =_{E_\oplus} x_1 \oplus \ldots \oplus x_i$.
- For any subterm $\{t\}_{t'}$ of φ, if t' is a subterm of t which is a name of sort $Data$ or an element of X then $t'' \prec t'$.

Concrete model. The concrete model is given by the models for symmetric encryption and exclusive OR. However, as in the combination of encryption with exponentiation, we need to reflect that nonces can be used as keys. The family of computational algebras (A_η) giving the concrete semantics is parameterized by a symmetric encryption scheme $\mathcal{SE}$. The XOR part uses the same implementation as in Section 6.1. We require that the key generation algorithm of $\mathcal{SE}$ consists in randomly sampling an element of $[0,1]^\eta$. The family of computational algebras (A_η) is said *EX-secure* if the encryption scheme $\mathcal{SE}$ is secure against IND-CPA and uses a key generation algorithm as described above.

Theorem 8. *Let $\prec$ be a total order between keys and terms of sort $Data_\oplus$. Let (A_η) be an EX-secure family of computational algebras then (A_η) is $\approx_E$-ad-sound for well-formed frames for $\prec$.*

9   Conclusion

In this paper we have described computationally soundness results for a model relying on equational theories and static equivalence. We consider the case of passive and adaptive adversaries and present several examples of sound equational theories to illustrate this framework. Whether this framework can be generalized to an active attacker is still a challenging research topic.

References

1. Abadi, M., Baudet, M., Warinschi, B.: Guessing attacks and the computational soundness of static equivalence. In: Aceto, L., Ingólfsdóttir, A. (eds.) FOSSACS 2006. LNCS, vol. 3921, Springer, Heidelberg (2006)
2. Abadi, M., Cortier, V.: Deciding knowledge in security protocols under equational theories. In: Díaz, J., Karhumäki, J., Lepistö, A., Sannella, D. (eds.) ICALP 2004. LNCS, vol. 3142, pp. 46–58. Springer, Heidelberg (2004)
3. Abadi, M., Fournet, C.: Mobile values, new names, and secure communications. In: Proc. 28th Annual ACM Symposium on Principles of Programming Languages (POPL 2001), pp. 104–115. ACM Press, New York (2001)
4. Abadi, M., Rogaway, P.: Reconciling two views of cryptography (the computational soundness of formal encryption). In: Watanabe, O., Hagiya, M., Ito, T., van Leeuwen, J., Mosses, P.D. (eds.) TCS 2000. LNCS, vol. 1872, pp. 3–22. Springer, Heidelberg (2000)
5. Abadi, M., Rogaway, P.: Reconciling two views of cryptography (the computational soundness of formal encryption). Journal of Cryptology 15(2), 103–127 (2002)
6. Adão, P., Bana, G., Herzog, J., Scedrov, A.: Soundness of formal encryption in the presence of key-cycles. In: di Vimercati, S.d.C., Syverson, P.F., Gollmann, D. (eds.) ESORICS 2005. LNCS, vol. 3679, pp. 374–396. Springer, Heidelberg (2005)

7. Adão, P., Bana, G., Herzog, J., Scedrov, A.: Soundness of formal encryption in the presence of key-cycles. In: di Vimercati, S.d.C., Syverson, P.F., Gollmann, D. (eds.) ESORICS 2005. LNCS, vol. 3679, pp. 374–396. Springer, Heidelberg (2005)
8. Adão, P., Bana, G., Scedrov, A.: Computational and information-theoretic soundness and completeness of formal encryption. In: Proc. 18th IEEE Computer Security Foundations Workshop (CSFW 2005), pp. 170–184 (2005)
9. Backes, M., Pfitzmann, B., Waidner, M.: A composable cryptographic library with nested operations. In: Proc. 10th ACM Conference on Computer and Communications Security (CCS 2003) (2003)
10. Baudet, M., Cortier, V., Kremer, S.: Computationally sound implementations of equational theories against passive adversaries. In: Caires, L., Italiano, G.F., Monteiro, L., Palamidessi, C., Yung, M. (eds.) ICALP 2005. LNCS, vol. 3580, pp. 652–663. Springer, Heidelberg (2005)
11. Blanchet, B.: Automatic proof of strong secrecy for security protocols. In: Proc. 25th IEEE Symposium on Security and Privacy (SSP 2004), pp. 86–100 (2004)
12. Bresson, E., Lakhnech, Y., Mazaré, L., Warinschi, B.: A generalization of ddh with applications to protocol analysis and computational soundness. In: Menezes, A. (ed.) CRYPTO 2007. LNCS, vol. 4622, pp. 482–499. Springer, Heidelberg (2007)
13. Chevassut, O., Fouque, P.-A., Gaudry, P., Pointcheval, D.: Key derivation and randomness extraction. Technical Report 2005/061, Cryptology ePrint Archive (2005),
    http://eprint.iacr.org/
14. Corin, R., Doumen, J., Etalle, S.: Analysing password protocol security against off-line dictionary attacks. ENTCS 121, 47–63 (2005)
15. Cortier, V., Delaune, S., Lafourcade, P.: A survey of algebraic properties used in cryptographic protocols. Journal of Computer Security 14(1), 1–43 (2006)
16. Dwork, C., Naor, M., Reingold, O., Stockmeyer, L.J.: Magic functions. J. ACM 50(6), 852–921 (2003)
17. Garcia, F.D., van Rossum, P.: Sound computational interpretation of symbolic hashes in the standard model. In: Yoshiura, H., Sakurai, K., Rannenberg, K., Murayama, Y., Kawamura, S.-i. (eds.) IWSEC 2006. LNCS, vol. 4266, pp. 33–47. Springer, Heidelberg (2006)
18. Goldwasser, S., Micali, S.: Probabilistic encryption. Journal of Computer and System Sciences 28(2), 270–299 (1984)
19. Kremer, S., Mazaré, L.: Adaptive soundness of static equivalence. In: Biskup, J., López, J. (eds.) ESORICS 2007. LNCS, vol. 4734, pp. 610–625. Springer, Heidelberg (2007)
20. Laud, P., Corin, R.: Sound computational interpretation of formal encryption with composed keys. In: Lim, J.-I., Lee, D.-H. (eds.) ICISC 2003. LNCS, vol. 2971, pp. 55–66. Springer, Heidelberg (2004)
21. Micciancio, D., Panjwani, S.: Adaptive security of symbolic encryption. In: Kilian, J. (ed.) TCC 2005. LNCS, vol. 3378, pp. 169–187. Springer, Heidelberg (2005)
22. Micciancio, D., Warinschi, B.: Completeness theorems for the Abadi-Rogaway logic of encrypted expressions. Journal of Computer Security 12(1), 99–129 (2004)
23. Micciancio, D., Warinschi, B.: Soundness of formal encryption in the presence of active adversaries. In: Naor, M. (ed.) TCC 2004. LNCS, vol. 2951, pp. 133–151. Springer, Heidelberg (2004)
24. Phan, D.H., Pointcheval, D.: About the security of ciphers (semantic security and pseudorandom permutations). In: Handschuh, H., Hasan, M.A. (eds.) SAC 2004. LNCS, vol. 3357, pp. 185–200. Springer, Heidelberg (2004)

Adversaries and Information Leaks
(Tutorial)

Geoffrey Smith

School of Computing and Information Sciences, Florida International University,
Miami, FL 33199, USA
`smithg@cis.fiu.edu`

Abstract. Secure information flow analysis aims to prevent programs
from leaking their H (high) inputs to their L (low) outputs. A major
challenge in this area is to relax the standard noninterference properties
to allow "small" leaks, while still preserving security. In this tutorial
paper, we consider three instances of this theme. First, we consider a
type system that enforces the usual Denning restrictions, except that it
specifies that encrypting a H plaintext yields a L ciphertext. We argue
that this type system ensures security, assuming strong encryption, by
giving a reduction that maps a noninterference adversary (which tries
to guess which of two H inputs was used, given the L outputs) to an
IND-CPA adversary (which tries to guess which of two plaintexts are
encrypted, given the ciphertext). Second, we explore termination leaks in
probabilistic programs when typed under the Denning restrictions. Using
a notion of probabilistic simulation, we show that such programs satisfy
an approximate noninterference property, provided that their probability
of nontermination is small. Third, we consider quantitative information
flow, which aims to measure the amount of information leaked. We argue
that the common information-theoretic measures in the literature are
unsuitable, because these measures fail to distinguish between programs
that are wildly different from the point of view of an adversary trying to
guess the H input.

1 Introduction

Suppose that a program c processes some sensitive information. How do we know
that c will not *leak* the information, either accidentally or maliciously? How can
we ensure that c is *trustworthy*?

The approach of *secure information flow analysis* is to classify c's variables
into different security levels, such as H (high) or L (low), and to do a *static
analysis*, often in the form of a *type system*, on c prior to executing it. The goal is
to prove that c conforms to some specified flow policy, which can encompass both
confidentiality and integrity concerns; in this paper, we will focus exclusively on
confidentiality. See [1] for a survey of this area.

It is important to recognize that the secure information flow problem involves
two adversaries: the *program* c itself, and also the *observer* $\mathcal{O}$ of c's public output.
These two adversaries have distinct capabilities:

G. Barthe and C. Fournet (Eds.): TGC 2007, LNCS 4912, pp. 383–400, 2008.

- The program c has *direct access* to the sensitive information (the initial values of H variables), but its behavior is *constrained* by the static analysis.
- The observer $\mathcal{O}$ has *direct access* only to c's public output (the final values of L variables, etc.), but its behavior is *unconstrained*, except for computational resource bounds.

The decision as to what constitutes c's public output is quite important, of course; in particular secure information flow becomes far more difficult if we consider c's *running time* to be a public output.

A classic approach to secure information flow in imperative programs is based on the *Denning restrictions* proposed in [2]:

- An expression is classified as H if it contains any H variables; otherwise, it is classified as L.
- To prevent *explicit flows*, a H expression cannot be assigned to a L variable.
- To prevent *implicit flows*, an **if** or **while** command whose guard is H may not make *any* assignments to L variables.

If c satisfies the Denning restrictions, then it can be proven [3] that c satisfies *noninterference*, which says (assuming that c always terminates) that the final values of the L variables are *independent* of the initial values of the H variables. Hence observer $\mathcal{O}$, seeing the final values of the L variables, can deduce *nothing* about the initial values of the H variables.

Unfortunately, noninterference is often too strong in practice. This leads to a major practical challenge: how can we relax noninterference to allow "small" information leaks, while still preserving security? In the next three sections, we consider three instances of this theme. In Sections 2 and 3, we consider secure information flow analyses that are permissive about leaks caused by *encryption* and *nontermination*, respectively; these sections summarize [4] and [5], where additional details can be found. In Section 4, we present some preliminary ideas about a general theory of *quantitative* information flow, which aims to measure the "amount" of information leaked.

2   Secure Information Flow for a Language with Encryption

Suppose that $\mathcal{E}$ and $\mathcal{D}$ denote encryption and decryption with a suitably-chosen shared key K. We allow program c to call $\mathcal{E}$ and $\mathcal{D}$, but we do not give it direct access to K. Intuitively, we would like to extend the Denning restrictions with the following rules:

- If expression e is H, then $\mathcal{E}(e)$ is L.
- If expression e is either L or H, then $\mathcal{D}(e)$ is H.

But are these rules *sound*? Note that they *violate* noninterference, since $\mathcal{E}(e)$ depends on e.

In fact these rules are *unsound* if encryption is *deterministic*. For example, suppose that *secret* is a H n-bit variable and that *leak* and *mask* are L variables. Consider the following program, in which "|" denotes bitwise-or, and "$\gg 1$" denotes right shift by one bit:

```
leak := 0;
mask := 2^{n-1};
while mask ≠ 0 do (
    if E(secret | mask) = E(secret) then
        leak := leak | mask;
    mask := mask ≫ 1
)
```

This program is allowed under the proposed rules. But if $\mathcal{E}$ is deterministic, then the program efficiently copies *secret* into *leak*, because then the test in the **if** command is true iff $secret \mid mask = secret$.

In fact it is well understood in the cryptographic community that deterministic encryption cannot give good security properties.[1] We recall the definitions of *symmetric encryption scheme* and *IND-CPA security* from [6]:

Definition 1. *A symmetric encryption scheme* $\mathcal{SE}$ *with security parameter k is a triple of algorithms* $(\mathcal{K}, \mathcal{E}, \mathcal{D})$, *where*

- $\mathcal{K}$ *is a randomized key-generation algorithm that generates a k-bit key; we write $K \xleftarrow{?} \mathcal{K}$*
- $\mathcal{E}$ *is a randomized encryption algorithm that takes a key and a plaintext and returns a ciphertext; we write $C \xleftarrow{?} \mathcal{E}_K(M)$.*
- $\mathcal{D}$ *is a deterministic decryption algorithm that takes a key and a ciphertext and returns the corresponding plaintext; we write $M := \mathcal{D}_K(C)$.*

We recall the notion of *IND-CPA security*, which stands for *indistinguishability under chosen-plaintext attack*. An adversary $\mathcal{A}$ is given an *LR oracle* of the form

$$\mathcal{E}_K(\mathrm{LR}(\cdot, \cdot, b)),$$

where K is a randomly generated key and b is an internal *selection bit*, which is either 0 or 1. When $\mathcal{A}$ sends a pair of equal-length messages (M_0, M_1) to the LR oracle, it selects either M_0 or M_1 according to the value of b, encrypts it using $\mathcal{E}_K$, and returns the ciphertext C to $\mathcal{A}$. Thus when $\mathcal{A}$ sends a sequence of pairs of messages to the LR oracle, it either gets back encryptions of the *left* messages (if $b = 0$) or else encryptions of the *right* messages (if $b = 1$). $\mathcal{A}$'s challenge is to guess which of these two "worlds" it is in.

---

[1] However, it is standard to *implement* strong encryption using a deterministic block cipher (modeled as a pseudo-random permutation) and random vectors, using techniques like cipher-block chaining with random initial vector [6]. Interestingly, Courant, Ene, and Lakhnech [7] have considered secure information flow in that lower implementation level, using an ingenious type system that tracks both the security level as well as the *randomness* of expressions.

Formally, $\mathcal{A}$ is executed in two different *experiments*, depending on the choice of the selection bit b:

Experiment $\mathbf{Exp}_{\mathcal{SE}}^{\text{ind-cpa-b}}(\mathcal{A})$

$K \overset{?}{\leftarrow} \mathcal{K}$;

$d \overset{?}{\leftarrow} \mathcal{A}^{\mathcal{E}_K(\text{LR}(\cdot,\cdot,b))}$;

return d

The *IND-CPA advantage* of $\mathcal{A}$ is defined as

$$\mathbf{Adv}_{\mathcal{SE}}^{\text{ind-cpa}}(\mathcal{A}) = \Pr[\mathbf{Exp}_{\mathcal{SE}}^{\text{ind-cpa-1}}(\mathcal{A}) = 1] - \Pr[\mathbf{Exp}_{\mathcal{SE}}^{\text{ind-cpa-0}}(\mathcal{A}) = 1].$$

Thus $\mathcal{A}$'s IND-CPA advantage is its probability of (correctly) guessing 1 in world 1, minus its probability of (wrongly) guessing 1 in world 0. Finally, $\mathcal{SE}$ is *IND-CPA secure* if no adversary $\mathcal{A}$ running in polynomial time in the security parameter k can achieve a non-negligible advantage. (As usual, $s(k)$ is *negligible* if for any positive polynomial $p(k)$, there exists k_0 such that $s(k) \leq \frac{1}{p(k)}$, for all $k \geq k_0$.)

Now we define the programming language that we will consider. We use a simple imperative language with the following syntax:

$$(expressions) \ e ::= x \mid m \mid e_1 + e_2 \mid \ldots \mid \mathcal{D}(e_1, e_2)$$

$$(commands) \ c ::= x := e \mid$$
$$x \overset{?}{\leftarrow} \mathcal{R} \mid$$
$$(x, y) \overset{?}{\leftarrow} \mathcal{E}(e) \mid$$
$$\mathbf{skip} \mid$$
$$\mathbf{if} \ e \ \mathbf{then} \ c_1 \ \mathbf{else} \ c_2 \mid$$
$$\mathbf{while} \ e \ \mathbf{do} \ c \mid$$
$$c_1; c_2$$

In the syntax, metavariables x and y range over identifiers and m over integer literals. Integers are the only values; we use 0 for false and nonzero for true. The command $x \overset{?}{\leftarrow} \mathcal{R}$ is a random assignment; here $\mathcal{R}$ ranges over some set of probability distributions on the integers.

The commands for encryption and decryption are slightly non-obvious. There are two issues: first, encryption cannot conceal the *length* of the plaintext; second, for IND-CPA security there must be *many* ciphertexts corresponding to a given plaintext, so ciphertexts must be *longer* than plaintexts. We deal with these issues in our language by assuming that all integer values are n bits long, for some n, and that encryption always takes an n-bit plaintext and produces a $2n$-bit ciphertext. Thus the encryption command has the form $(x, y) \overset{?}{\leftarrow} \mathcal{E}(e)$; it encrypts the n-bit value of expression e, putting the first n bits of the ciphertext into x and the second n bits into y. Symmetrically, the decryption expression $\mathcal{D}(e_1, e_2)$ takes two expressions, giving $2n$ bits of ciphertext, and produces the corresponding n-bit plaintext.

As shown in [3], the Denning restrictions can be enforced using a type system. We extend such a type system with rules for the new constructs; we do not show the rules here (they can be found in [4]), but they enforce the following rules:

- $\mathcal{E}(e)$ is L, even if e is H.
- $\mathcal{D}(e_1, e_2)$ is H, even if e_1 and e_2 are L.
- $\mathcal{R}$ (a random value) is L.

The reason for the last rule is that a random value is independent of the initial values of H variables.

We now wish to argue that our type system is sound. To do this, we introduce the idea of a *leaking adversary*. A leaking adversary $\mathcal{B}$ has a H variable h and a L variable l, and other variables typed arbitrarily. It is run with h initialized to either 0 or 1, each with probability $1/2$. It can call $\mathcal{E}()$ and $\mathcal{D}()$, and it tries to copy the initial value of h into l. Formally, $\mathcal{B}$ is executed in the following experiment:

Experiment $\mathbf{Exp}_{\mathcal{SE}}^{\text{leak}}(\mathcal{B})$
$K \xleftarrow{?} \mathcal{K};$
$h_0 \xleftarrow{?} \{0,1\};$
$h := h_0;$
initialize all other variables of $\mathcal{B}$ to 0;
run $\mathcal{B}^{\mathcal{E}_K(\cdot), \mathcal{D}_K(\cdot)};$
if $l = h_0$ **then return** 1 **else return** 0

Here $h_0 \xleftarrow{?} \{0,1\}$ assigns a random 1-bit integer to h_0. Variable h_0 must not occur in $\mathcal{B}$; it is used to record the initial value of h. Finally, the *leaking advantage* of $\mathcal{B}$ is defined as

$$\mathbf{Adv}_{\mathcal{SE}}^{\text{leak}}(\mathcal{B}) = 2 \cdot \Pr[\mathbf{Exp}_{\mathcal{SE}}^{\text{leak}}(\mathcal{B}) = 1] - 1.$$

The leaking advantage is defined in this way to reflect the fact that $\mathcal{B}$ can trivially succeed with probability $1/2$.

We argue the soundness of our type system via a *reduction*; for the moment, we drop decryption from our language:

Theorem 1. *Given a well-typed leaking adversary $\mathcal{B}$ that does not call $\mathcal{D}()$ and that runs in polynomial time $p(k)$, there exists an IND-CPA adversary $\mathcal{A}$ such that*

$$\mathbf{Adv}_{\mathcal{SE}}^{\text{ind-cpa}}(\mathcal{A}) \geq \frac{1}{2} \cdot \mathbf{Adv}_{\mathcal{SE}}^{\text{leak}}(\mathcal{B}).$$

Moreover, $\mathcal{A}$ runs in $O(p(k))$ time.

The theorem gives the following immediate corollary:

Corollary 1. *If $\mathcal{SE}$ is IND-CPA secure, then there is no polynomial-time, well-typed leaking adversary $\mathcal{B}$ that achieves a non-negligible advantage.*

The proof of Theorem 1 is by explicit construction. Given leaking adversary $\mathcal{B}$, we construct IND-CPA adversary $\mathcal{A}$ that runs $\mathcal{B}$ with a randomly-chosen 1-bit value of h. Whenever $\mathcal{B}$ calls $\mathcal{E}(e)$, $\mathcal{A}$ passes $(0^n, e)$ to its oracle $\mathcal{E}_K(LR(\cdot, \cdot, b))$ and returns the result to $\mathcal{B}$. If $\mathcal{B}$ terminates within $p(k)$ steps and succeeds in leaking h to l, then $\mathcal{A}$ guesses 1; otherwise $\mathcal{A}$ guesses 0.

To understand this construction, the first thing to notice is that if the selection bit b is 1, then $\mathcal{B}$ is run *faithfully*—whenever $\mathcal{B}$ calls $\mathcal{E}(e)$, it correctly receives in reply $\mathcal{E}_K(e)$. But if the selection bit b is 0, then $\mathcal{B}$ is run *unfaithfully*—now whenever $\mathcal{B}$ calls $\mathcal{E}(e)$, it receives in reply $\mathcal{E}_K(0^n)$, which is a *random value* that has nothing to do with e.

What is $\mathcal{A}$'s IND-CPA advantage? When the selection bit b is 1, then $\mathcal{B}$ is run faithfully and hence

$$\Pr[\mathbf{Exp}_{S\mathcal{E}}^{\text{ind-cpa-1}}(\mathcal{A}) = 1] = \Pr[\mathbf{Exp}_{S\mathcal{E}}^{\text{leak}}(\mathcal{B}) = 1] = \frac{1}{2} \cdot \mathbf{Adv}_{S\mathcal{E}}^{\text{leak}}(\mathcal{B}) + \frac{1}{2}.$$

When the selection bit b is 0, then $\mathcal{B}$ is run as a well-typed program in a language with random assignment but no encryption—in other words, $\mathcal{B}$ no longer can take advantage of the leak associated with the typing rule for encryption. Hence we would expect that standard noninterference results will prevent $\mathcal{B}$ from copying h to l with probability better than $1/2$. However, there is a subtlety here—when $\mathcal{B}$ is run unfaithfully, it might fail to *terminate*. (For example, $\mathcal{E}(h)$ and $\mathcal{E}(h+1)$ are always distinct if $\mathcal{B}$ is run faithfully, but they have a small probability of being equal if $\mathcal{B}$ is run unfaithfully.) To deal with this possibility, we need a careful analysis of the behavior of well-typed probabilistic programs that might not terminate. Such an analysis is described in Section 3 of this paper; it allows us to show that

$$\Pr[\mathbf{Exp}_{S\mathcal{E}}^{\text{ind-cpa-0}}(\mathcal{A}) \leq \frac{1}{2}$$

as expected. (Details are given in [4].) In conclusion we get

$$\mathbf{Adv}_{S\mathcal{E}}^{\text{ind-cpa}}(\mathcal{A}) = \Pr[\mathbf{Exp}_{S\mathcal{E}}^{\text{ind-cpa-1}}(\mathcal{A}) = 1] - \Pr[\mathbf{Exp}_{S\mathcal{E}}^{\text{ind-cpa-0}}(\mathcal{A}) = 1]$$
$$\geq \tfrac{1}{2} \cdot \mathbf{Adv}_{S\mathcal{E}}^{\text{leak}}(\mathcal{B})$$

as claimed.

We have shown that our type system rules out well-typed, efficient leaking adversaries. But can we get a result more like noninterference? To this end, let c be a well-typed, polynomial-time program in our language, and let μ and ν be memories that agree on L variables. Suppose we run c under either μ or ν, each with probability $1/2$, and show the final values of the L variables of c to observer $\mathcal{O}$, which we here refer to as a *noninterference adversary*. Could $\mathcal{O}$ guess which initial memory was used?

More formally, a noninterference adversary $\mathcal{O}$ for c, μ, and ν is a program that refers only to the L variables of c and outputs its guess into a new variable g. $\mathcal{O}$ is run in the following experiment, where h_0 is a new variable:

Experiment $\mathbf{Exp}^{NI}_{\mathcal{SE},c,\mu,\nu}(\mathcal{O})$

    $K \stackrel{?}{\leftarrow} \mathcal{K}$;

    $h_0 \stackrel{?}{\leftarrow} \{0,1\}$;

    if $h_0 = 0$ **then** initialize the variables of c to μ

        else initialize the variables of c to ν;

    c;

    $\mathcal{O}$;

    if $g = h_0$ **then return** 1 **else return** 0

The *noninterference advantage* of $\mathcal{O}$ is defined as

$$\mathbf{Adv}^{NI}_{\mathcal{SE},c,\mu,\nu}(\mathcal{O}) = 2 \cdot \Pr[\mathbf{Exp}^{NI}_{\mathcal{SE},c,\mu,\nu}(\mathcal{O}) = 1] - 1.$$

Now we have the following theorem:

Theorem 2. *If c is a well-typed, polynomial-time program and μ and ν are memories that agree on L variables, then no polynomial-time noninterference adversary $\mathcal{O}$ for c, μ, and ν can achieve a non-negligible noninterference advantage.*

As in Theorem 1, the proof is by explicit construction. Given noninterference adversary $\mathcal{O}$, we can construct a well-typed leaking adversary $\mathcal{B}$. An interesting point here is that $\mathcal{O}$ *cannot* be assumed to be well typed. But because $\mathcal{O}$ sees only the L variables of c, we can give all its variables type L, making $\mathcal{O}$ *automatically* well typed under our typing rules. Hence we can use $\mathcal{O}$ in constructing $\mathcal{B}$:

    Adversary $\mathcal{B}$

        initialize the L variables of c according to μ and ν;

        if $h = 0$ **then**

            initialize the H variables of c according to μ

        else

            initialize the H variables of c according to ν;

        c;

        $\mathcal{O}$;

        $l := g$

It is easy to see that $\mathcal{B}$ is well typed and that its leaking advantage is the same as $\mathcal{O}$'s noninterference advantage.

Thus we have shown that, on polynomial-time programs c, our type system ensures a property that is essentially as good as noninterference—a polynomial-time observer $\mathcal{O}$ is basically unable to determine *anything* about the initial values of the H variables from the final values of the L variables.

Finally, we remark that Theorem 1 can be generalized to the full language including decryption. A similar reduction can be done, except that from leaking adversary $\mathcal{B}$ we now construct an *IND-CCA adversary* $\mathcal{A}$ [6], which has a decryption oracle $\mathcal{D}_K(\cdot)$ in addition to its LR-oracle $\mathcal{E}_K(\mathrm{LR}(\cdot,\cdot,b))$. It is not clear to us whether this is strictly necessary—see [4] for more discussion.

We conclude this section by mentioning some related work. Peeter Laud has pioneered the area of secure information flow analysis in the presence of encryption; his works include [8,9,10]. The third of these papers treats a richer language with primitives for generating and manipulating keys directly, though not handling decryption explicitly, and necessitating more complex typing rules and proofs. Other recent work in this area includes [11,12,13,14]; a major goal of these works is to "scale up" the language to the point that practical applications can be built.

More distantly related is the large body of recent work aimed at proving computational security properties of cryptographic protocols; examples include the work of Backes and Pfitzmann [15] and Laud [16]. Such work has a quite different adversary model than what is used in secure information flow analysis—the focus is on distributed systems in the presence of an *active adversary* which can insert and modify messages without constraint by a type system, but which does not have direct access to secrets.[2] Also type systems for cryptographic protocols seem to offer less support for general-purpose programming—for example, the type system in [16] does not allow branching on secret data.

3   Termination Leaks in Probabilistic Programs

In Section 2, we assumed that all adversaries run in time polynomial in k, the key size. This might seem to be "without loss of generality" (practically speaking) since otherwise the adversary takes too long. But what if program c either terminates quickly or else goes into an infinite loop? In that case, observer $\mathcal{O}$ might quickly be able to observe whether c terminates.

Furthermore, the Denning restrictions allow H variables to appear in guards of loops, because disallowing them would seem too restrictive in practice. This means that H variables can affect termination, as in examples like

```
while secret = 0 do
    skip;
leak := 1
```

It is for this reason that the noninterference property discussed in Section 1 includes the assumption that program c *always terminates*.

In this section, we try to *quantify* such termination leaks. The setting we consider is probabilistic programs with random assignment, but no encryption or decryption. We use the same type system as in Section 2, except that we no longer need typing rules for encryption and decryption; thus we simply enforce the Denning restrictions, extended with a rule that says that random values are L. Semantically, our programs are modeled as *Markov chains* [17] of configurations (c, μ), where c is the command remaining to be executed and μ is the memory.

---

[2] However, a similar active adversary is considered in some recent work in secure information flow, such as [14], that addresses *integrity* in addition to confidentiality.

In this setting, perfect security is given by *probabilistic noninterference*, which says that the final *probability distribution* on L variables is independent of the initial values of the H variables.

Here is an example of a program that violates probabilistic noninterference:

$$t \xleftarrow{?} \{0, 1\};$$
$$\textbf{if } t = 0 \textbf{ then } ($$
$$\quad \textbf{while } h = 1 \textbf{ do skip};$$
$$\quad l := 0$$
$$)$$
$$\textbf{else } ($$
$$\quad \textbf{while } h = 0 \textbf{ do skip};$$
$$\quad l := 1$$
$$)$$

Note that $t \xleftarrow{?} \{0, 1\}$ is a *random assignment* that assigns either 0 or 1 to t, each with probability $1/2$. Assuming that h is H and t and l are L, this program satisfies the extended Denning restrictions. But if $h = 0$, it terminates with $l = 0$ with probability $1/2$ and loops with probability $1/2$. And if $h = 1$, then it terminates with $l = 1$ with probability $1/2$ and loops with probability $1/2$.

However we can argue an *approximate probabilistic noninterference* property:

Theorem 3. *If c satisfies the extended Denning restrictions and loops with probability at most p, then c's deviation from probabilistic noninterference is at most $2p$.*

In our example program, $p = 1/2$, and the deviation is $|1/2 - 0| + |0 - 1/2| = 1 = 2p$, achieving the bound specified by the theorem. (The first term compares the probability that $l = 0$ after $h = 0$ and after $h = 1$; the second compares the probability that $l = 1$ after $h = 0$ and after $h = 1$.)

To prove this theorem, we introduce the idea of a *stripped program*, denoted by $\lfloor c \rfloor$. We form $\lfloor c \rfloor$ from c by stripping out all subcommands that do not assign to L variables, replacing them with **skip**. (In terms of the type system, this is equivalent to stripping out all subcommands of type H *cmd*.) For example, the stripped version of our example program is the following:

$$t \xleftarrow{?} \{0, 1\};$$
$$\textbf{if } t = 0 \textbf{ then } ($$
$$\quad \textbf{skip};$$
$$\quad l := 0$$
$$)$$
$$\textbf{else } ($$
$$\quad \textbf{skip};$$
$$\quad l := 1$$
$$)$$

It turns out that if c satisfies the extended Denning restrictions, then $\lfloor c \rfloor$ contains no H variables. More interestingly, in this case c satisfies what we call the *Bucket Property*, which relates to behavior of c and $\lfloor c \rfloor$. To visualize this property, imagine that the result of running c is shown as a sequence of buckets, one for each possible final value of c's L variables; also, we have a bucket to represent looping. The probability of each outcome is indicated by the amount of water in each bucket. Suppose that c's buckets look like this:

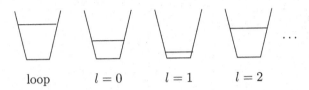

In other words, as we pass from c to $\lfloor c \rfloor$, the probabilities of L outcomes can only increase or stay the same; they cannot decrease.

Then the Bucket Property says that $\lfloor c \rfloor$'s buckets are gotten simply by pouring some of the water from c's loop bucket into some of the other buckets:

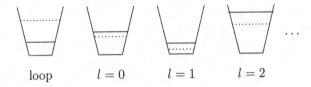

In other words, as we pass from c to $\lfloor c \rfloor$, the probabilities of L outcomes can only increase or stay the same; they cannot decrease.

In prior work on secure information flow, *probabilistic bisimulation* has often been a useful proof technique (see, for example, [18]). But in proving the Bucket Property, we use a non-symmetric *probabilistic simulation* [19] instead. Specifically, we define a *fast simulation*, which is a modification of the *weak simulation* considered by Baier, Katoen, Hermanns, and Wolf [20].

We develop the theory of fast simulation in the abstract setting of Markov chains. Intuitively, state t simulates state s if t can simulate whatever s can do. Thus if s can go to some state s' with probability p, then t should be able to match this by going to one or more states $t', t'', t''', \ldots$, each of which simulates s', with total probability at least p. However we must not "double count" t's probabilities—for example, if s goes to s' with probability $1/3$ and t goes to t' with probability $1/2$, then if we use t' to simulate the move to s' we must remember that $1/3$ of t''s probability is "used up", leaving just $1/6$ to be used in simulating other moves of s. These considerations lead to what is called a *weight function* Δ that specifies how the probabilities are matched up. A further consideration is that s might go to a state that is *already* simulated by t—in this case s has made an "insignificant" move, which t should not need to match. Thus in general we partition the states reachable in one step from s into two sets, U and V, corresponding to the "significant" and "insignificant" moves, respectively.

Formally, given a (discrete-time) Markov chain with state set S and transition probabilities $\mathbf{P}$, we define:

Definition 2. *Let R be a binary relation on S. R is a* fast simulation *if, whenever sRt, the states reachable in one step from s can be partitioned into two sets U and V such that*

1. *vRt for every $v \in V$, and*
2. *letting $K = \sum_{u \in U} \mathbf{P}(s, u)$, if $K > 0$ then there exists $\Delta : S \times S \to [0, 1]$ such that*
   (a) *$\Delta(u, w) > 0$ implies that uRw,*
   (b) *$\mathbf{P}(s, u)/K = \sum_{w \in S} \Delta(u, w)$ for all $u \in U$, and $\mathbf{P}(t, w) = \sum_{u \in U} \Delta(u, w)$ for all $w \in S$.*

We now describe the key theory associated with fast simulation. First, given binary relation R, we say that a set T of states is *upwards closed* if $s \in T$ and sRt implies that $t \in T$. Next, given state s, natural number n, and set T of states, let us write $\Pr(s, n, T)$ to denote the probability of reaching a state in T from s in at most n steps.

Now we have the key theorem, which says that if t fast simulates s, then t reaches any upwards closed set T with at least as great probability and at least as quickly as s does:

Theorem 4. *If R is a fast simulation, T is upwards closed, and sRt, then $\Pr(s, n, T) \leq \Pr(t, n, T)$ for every n.*

We remark that the *universal relation* $R_{\mathcal{U}} = S \times S$ is trivially a fast simulation. But under $R_{\mathcal{U}}$ the only upwards closed sets are $\emptyset$ and S itself, which means that Theorem 4 is uninteresting in that case.

We now apply the theory of fast simulation to the setting of probabilistic programs that satisfy the extended Denning restrictions. The key result is that we can define a fast simulation R_L such that $(c, \mu)R_L(\lfloor c \rfloor, \mu)$, for any well-typed command c.

Definition 3. *If c and d are well-typed commands, then we say that cR_Ld if this can be proved from the following six rules:*

1. *$c_1 R_L \mathbf{skip}$, if c_1 does not assign to L variables.*
2. *$(x := e)R_L(x := e)$.*
3. *$(x \xleftarrow{?} D)R_L(x \xleftarrow{?} D)$.*
4. *$(\mathbf{if}\ e\ \mathbf{then}\ c_1\ \mathbf{else}\ c_2)R_L(\mathbf{if}\ e\ \mathbf{then}\ d_1\ \mathbf{else}\ d_2)$, if $e : L$, $c_1 R_L d_1$, and $c_2 R_L d_2$.*
5. *$(\mathbf{while}\ e\ \mathbf{do}\ c_1)R_L(\mathbf{while}\ e\ \mathbf{do}\ d_1)$, if $e : L$ and $c_1 R_L d_1$.*
6. *$(c_1; c_2)R_L(d_1; d_2)$, if $c_1 R_L d_1$ and $c_2 R_L d_2$.*

We extend R_L to configurations with the following two rules:

1. *$\mu R_L \nu$, if μ and ν agree on L variables.*
2. *$(c, \mu)R_L(d, \nu)$, if $cR_L d$ and μ and ν agree on L variables.*

It can be proved that R_L is a fast simulation, and that for any well-typed c, $cR_L \lfloor c \rfloor$. This implies the Bucket Property. For given some L outcome (such as

$l = 17$), let T be the set of memories that satisfy that outcome (for example, $T = \{\nu \mid \nu(l) = 17\}$). Since T is upwards closed under R_L, we can apply Theorem 4 to deduce that $\Pr((c, \mu), n, T) \leq \Pr((\lfloor c \rfloor, \mu), n, T)$, for every n. Finally, we can extend to the probability of *eventually* terminating in T, since this is just $\lim_{n \to \infty} \Pr((c, \mu), n, T)$.

Given the Bucket Property, we can now prove the approximate probabilistic noninterference property. Recall that $\lfloor c \rfloor$ contains no H variables. Hence if memories μ and ν agree on L variables, then the behavior of $(\lfloor c \rfloor, \mu)$ must be *identical* to that of $(\lfloor c \rfloor, \nu)$. Thus we can build a "bridge" between (c, μ) and (c, ν):

$$(c, \mu) \xleftarrow{\text{Bucket Prop}} (\lfloor c \rfloor, \mu) \equiv (\lfloor c \rfloor, \nu) \xleftarrow{\text{Bucket Prop}} (c, \nu)$$

Since (c, μ)'s loop bucket contains at most p units of water, the sum of the absolute value of the differences between the L outcome buckets of (c, μ) and of $(\lfloor c \rfloor, \mu)$ is at most p. Similarly for (c, ν). Hence the sum of the absolute value of the differences between the L outcome buckets of (c, μ) and of (c, ν) is at most $2p$.

We conclude this section by remarking that observer $\mathcal{O}$, given the final values of c's L variables, could try to distinguish between initial memories μ and ν through statistical hypothesis testing. Assuming that the probability p of nontermination is small, then the approximate noninterference property gives us a way to bound $\mathcal{O}$'s ability to do this, as in the work of Di Pierro, Hankin, and Wiklicky [21]. Finally, we remark that the Bucket Property is used crucially in the proof of Theorem 1 in Section 2 of this paper, to bound the advantage of leaking adversary $\mathcal{B}$ when run unfaithfully.

4   Foundations for Quantitative Information Flow

In the two previous sections, we considered information leaks from H to L associated with encryption and with nontermination, showing that secure information flow analyses can be permissive about such flows, while still preserving security guarantees. More generally, it would be valuable to develop a theory of "small" information leaks that is independent of any particular programming mechanism. To this end, in this section we consider the foundations of a *quantitative* theory of information flows. Such a quantitative theory has long been recognized as an important generalization of the theory of noninterference, and there has been quite a lot of recent work in this area, including the works of Clark, Hunt, and Malacaria [22,23,24], Köpf and Basin [25], Clarkson, Myers, and Schneider [26], Lowe [27], and Di Pierro, Hankin, and Wiklicky [21]. Also related is work in quantitative *anonymity*, such as that of Chatzikokolakis, Palamidessi, and Panangaden [28].

We can identify four main research steps required to develop a useful theory of quantitative information flow:

1. Define a quantitative notion of information flow.
2. Show that the notion gives appropriate security guarantees.

3. Devise static analyses to enforce a given quantitative flow policy.
4. Prove the soundness of the analyses.

In this paper, we limit our discussion to Steps 1 and 2.

Moreover, rather than trying to tackle the problem in full generality, we will consider important *special cases* in the hopes of better understanding what is going on. We therefore adopt the following conceptual framework:

- We assume that there is a single secret h, which is chosen from some space S according to some a priori, *publicly-known* probability distribution.
- We assume that c is a program that has *only* h as input and (maybe) leaks information about h to its unique public output l.
- We assume that c is *deterministic* and *total*.

Having made these assumptions, we can now follow Köpf and Basin [25] and observe that the public output l is a *function* of the secret h; thus there exists a function f such that $l = f(h)$. Furthermore, f induces an *equivalence relation* $\sim$ on S:

$$h_1 \sim h_2 \text{ iff } f(h_1) = f(h_2).$$

(In set theory, $\sim$ is called the *kernel* of f.) Hence the program c *partitions* S into the equivalence classes of $\sim$.

So what information is leaked by c? The observer $\mathcal{O}$ sees the final value of l. This tells $\mathcal{O}$ which equivalence class h belonged to. How bad is that? We can first explore that question by considering two extreme situations:

Extreme 1. If f is a *constant* function, then there is just one equivalence class, and noninterference holds.

Extreme 2. If f is *one-to-one*, then the equivalence classes are singletons, and we have *total leakage* of h (in principle).

The reason that we say "in principle" in Extreme 2 is that $\mathcal{O}$ might be unable to *compute* the value of h efficiently from the value of l; our framework here is thus *information-theoretic* rather than *computational*.

To assess situations between the two extremes considered above, we need appropriate quantitative measures. Here we review two common information-theoretic measures. Let X be a discrete random variable whose values have probabilities $p_1, p_2, p_3, \ldots, p_n$, where we assume for convenience that $p_i \geq p_{i+1}$, for all i. The *Shannon entropy* of X is defined by

$$H(X) = \sum_{i=1}^{n} p_i \log \frac{1}{p_i}.$$

The Shannon entropy can be viewed informally as the "uncertainty" about X; more precisely it can be understood as the expected number of bits required to transmit X optimally. The *Guessing entropy* of X is defined by

$$G(X) = \sum_{i=1}^{n} i p_i.$$

The Guessing entropy can be understood as the expected number of guesses required to guess X optimally.

Let us now apply Shannon entropy to the partitions induced by program c. For simplicity, let us consider the case where h is *uniformly distributed* over space S, and $|S| = n$. Suppose that the partition induced by c consists of r equivalence classes $C_1, C_2, \ldots, C_r$, where $|C_i| = n_i$, for all i. Then the Shannon entropy of h is

$$H(h) = \sum_{i=1}^{n} \frac{1}{n} \log n = \log n.$$

This can be viewed as the "initial uncertainty about h". And the Shannon entropy of l is

$$H(l) = \sum_{i=1}^{r} \frac{n_i}{n} \log \frac{n}{n_i}.$$

Plausibly, this can be viewed as the "amount of information leaked". This view is supported by the two extreme cases discussed above. In Extreme 1, there is just one equivalence class, of size n, so

$$H(l) = \sum_{i=1}^{1} \frac{n}{n} \log \frac{n}{n} = 0$$

and in Extreme 2, there are n equivalence classes, each of size 1, so

$$H(l) = \sum_{i=1}^{n} \frac{1}{n} \log n = \log n.$$

We can also ask another question, which is more crucial from the point of view of security: how much uncertainty about h remains *after* the attack? This quantity can be calculated as a *conditional Shannon entropy*:

$$H(h|l) = \sum_{i=1}^{r} \frac{n_i}{n} H(C_i) = \sum_{i=1}^{r} \frac{n_i}{n} \log n_i.$$

Quite reasonably, in Extreme 1 we get $H(h|l) = \log n$ and in Extreme 2 we get $H(h|l) = 0$. Finally, there is a pretty equation relating these three quantities:

$$H(h) = H(l) + H(h|l)$$

which can be read as

"initial uncertainty = information leaked + remaining uncertainty".

So is Step 1 ("Define a quantitative notion of information flow") finished? In the restricted framework that we are considering, it certainly seems promising to *define* the amount of information leaked to be $H(l)$, and the remaining uncertainty to be $H(h|l)$. And in fact this seems to be the literature consensus: it is the approach taken by Clarke, Hunt, and Malacaria [22,23,24] and by Köpf and Basin [25] (although they also consider $G(l)$ and $G(h|l)$). The approach of Clarkson, Myers, and Schneider [26] is more general, because they consider the case when the observer $\mathcal{O}$ has (possibly mistaken) *beliefs* about the probability distribution of h. But in the special case when $\mathcal{O}$'s beliefs match the a priori distribution, and when the expected flow over all experiments is considered [26, Section 4.4], their approach then reduces to using $H(l)$ and $H(h|l)$.

So we might turn our attention next to Step 2 ("Show that the notion gives appropriate security guarantees"). A first step that can be taken here is to show that $H(l)$ ("the amount of information leaked") is 0 iff c satisfies noninterference. This is good, of course, but it is just a first step—it establishes only that the zero/nonzero distinction is meaningful. A more interesting result is the *Fano Inequality*, which gives lower bounds, in terms of $H(h|l)$, on the probability that observer $\mathcal{O}$ will *fail* to guess the value of h correctly, given l. Unfortunately these bounds are extremely weak in many cases.

Really the key question for Step 2 is whether the value of $H(h|l)$ ("the remaining uncertainty") accurately reflects the threat to h. Let us consider some example attacks to answer this question.

First consider a program c that simply copies $1/10$ of the bits of h into l; this could be done with a program like this:

```
l = h & 0177777;
```

Assuming as before that h is uniformly distributed over S, where $|S| = n$, this attack partitions S into $2^{0.1 \log n} = n^{0.1}$ equivalence classes, each of size $2^{0.9 \log n} = n^{0.9}$. Hence we get $H(l) = 0.1 \log n$ and $H(h|l) = 0.9 \log n$, which seems quite reasonable since $9/10$ of the bits of h are completely unknown to $\mathcal{O}$ after the attack.

But now suppose that the possible values of h range from 0 to $n - 1$ and consider the following program:

```
if (h < n/10)
    l = h;
else
    l = -1;
```

This program puts 90% of the possible values of h into one big equivalence class, and puts each of the remaining 10% into *singleton* classes. Hence we get

$$H(l) = 0.9 \log \frac{1}{0.9} + 0.1 \log n \approx 0.1 \log n + 0.14$$

and

$$H(h|l) = 0.9 \log(0.9n) \approx 0.9 \log n - 0.14$$

These quantities are essentially identical to those for the previous attack! But now observer $\mathcal{O}$ can guess h with probability $1/10$.

The conclusion is that if $H(h|l)$ is used as the measure of remaining uncertainty, then Step 2 cannot be done well, because $H(h|l)$ fails to distinguish between two attacks that are completely different from the point of view of their threat to the secrecy of h.

We might now revisit Step 1, in the hopes of finding a measure that works out better with respect to Step 2. But why not use Step 2 to guide Step 1? Why not define a measure of remaining uncertainty directly in terms of the desired security guarantees? Here is a very simple and basic measure that we can consider: let us define $V(h|l)$, the *vulnerability of h given l*, to be the probability that observer $\mathcal{O}$ can guess h correctly in one try, given l.

Let us now explore the value of $V(h|l)$ in the case when h is uniformly distributed, with n possible values. If the partition induced by c consists of r equivalence classes $C_1, C_2, \ldots, C_r$, where $|C_i| = n_i$ for all i, then the probability of ending in class C_i is n_i/n and the probability that $\mathcal{O}$ can guess h in one try, given that h is in C_i, is $1/n_i$. Remarkably, the n_i's cancel out and we get

$$V(h|l) = \sum_{i=1}^{r} \frac{n_i}{n} \frac{1}{n_i} = \frac{r}{n}.$$

So in this case all that matters is the *number* of equivalence classes, not their sizes!

Let us now consider some examples to assess the reasonableness of $V(h|l)$:

a. Noninterference case: $r = 1$, $V(h|l) = 1/n$
b. Total leakage case: $r = n$, $V(h|l) = 1$
c. Copy 1/10 of bits: $r = n^{0.1}$, $V(h|l) = 1/n^{0.9}$
d. Put 1/10 of h's values into singleton classes: $r = 1 + n/10$, $V(h|l) \approx 1/10$
e. Put h's values into classes, each of size 10: $r = n/10$, $V(h|l) = 1/10$
f. A password checker, that tests whether h is equal to some particular value:
   $r = 2$, $V(h|l) = 2/n$

All of these values seem reasonable, suggesting that maybe maybe $V(h|l)$ is a better foundation for quantitative information flow.

However it is clear that using a *single number* to represent a complex partition is necessarily crude. Compare examples **d** and **e**, which both have $V(h|l) \approx 1/10$. In example **d**, 1/10 of the time $\mathcal{O}$ will *know* the value of h, since it ends up in a singleton class, and 9/10 of the time $\mathcal{O}$ will have no idea about the value of h, since it ends up in the big equivalence class. In contrast, in example **e** we find that $\mathcal{O}$ never *knows* the exact value of h, but always knows it to within 10 possible values. Hence giving $\mathcal{O}$ a *second* guess would be essentially useless in example **d**, but would double $\mathcal{O}$'s chance of success in example **e**. Nevertheless, it seems that $V(h|l) \approx 1/10$ is a reasonable (though crude) measure of the threat to the secrecy of h in both of these examples.

We conclude by remarking that $V(h|l)$ is unfortunately not so good with respect to *compositionality*. This will be important when Steps 3 and 4 are considered—ideally, a static analysis should determine the threat associated with a sequential composition $c_1; c_2$ from the threats associated with c_1 and with c_2. But this does not seem possible for $V(h|l)$. Another challenging question is whether the information-theoretic approach of this section could somehow be integrated with the computational complexity approach of Section 2. These remain topics for future study.

Acknowledgments

I am grateful to Rafael Alpízar and Ziyuan Meng for helpful discussions of this work. This work was partially supported by the National Science Foundation under grant HRD-0317692.

References

1. Sabelfeld, A., Myers, A.C.: Language-based information flow security. IEEE Journal on Selected Areas in Communications 21(1), 5–19 (2003)
2. Denning, D., Denning, P.: Certification of programs for secure information flow. Communications of the ACM 20(7), 504–513 (1977)
3. Volpano, D., Smith, G., Irvine, C.: A sound type system for secure flow analysis. Journal of Computer Security 4(2,3), 167–187 (1996)
4. Smith, G., Alpízar, R.: Secure information flow with random assignment and encryption. In: Proc. 4th ACM Workshop on Formal Methods in Security Engineering, Fairfax, Virginia, pp. 33–43 (November 2006)
5. Smith, G., Alpízar, R.: Fast probabilistic simulation, nontermination, and secure information flow. In: Proc. 2007 ACM SIGPLAN Workshop on Programming Languages and Analysis for Security, San Diego, California, pp. 67–71 (June 2007)
6. Bellare, M., Rogaway, P.: Introduction to modern cryptography (2005), http://www-cse.ucsd.edu/users/mihir/cse207/classnotes.html
7. Courant, J., Ene, C., Lakhnech, Y.: Computationally sound typing for non-interference: The case of deterministic encryption. In: Arvind, V., Prasad, S. (eds.) FSTTCS 2007. LNCS, vol. 4855, pp. 364–375. Springer, Heidelberg (2007)
8. Laud, P.: Semantics and program analysis of computationally secure information flow. In: Sands, D. (ed.) ESOP 2001. LNCS, vol. 2028, pp. 77–91. Springer, Heidelberg (2001)
9. Laud, P.: Handling encryption in an analysis for secure information flow. In: Degano, P. (ed.) ESOP 2003. LNCS, vol. 2618, pp. 159–173. Springer, Heidelberg (2003)
10. Laud, P., Vene, V.: A type system for computationally secure information flow. In: Liśkiewicz, M., Reischuk, R. (eds.) FCT 2005. LNCS, vol. 3623, pp. 365–377. Springer, Heidelberg (2005)
11. Askarov, A., Hedin, D., Sabelfeld, A.: Cryptographically-masked flows. In: Proceedings of the 13th International Static Analysis Symposium, Seoul, Korea, pp. 353–369 (2006)
12. Laud, P.: On the computational soundness of cryptographically masked flows. In: Proceedings 35th Symposium on Principles of Programming Languages, San Francisco, California (January 2008)
13. Vaughan, J., Zdancewic, S.: A cryptographic decentralized label model. In: IEEE Symposium on Security and Privacy, Oakland, California, pp. 192–206 (2007)
14. Fournet, C., Rezk, T.: Cryptographically sound implementations for typed information-flow security. In: Proceedings 35th Symposium on Principles of Programming Languages, San Francisco, California (January 2008)

15. Backes, M., Pfitzmann, B.: Relating symbolic and cryptographic secrecy. In: Proceeding 26th IEEE Symposium on Security and Privacy, Oakland, California (2005)
16. Laud, P.: Secrecy types for a simulatable cryptographic library. In: Proceedings 12th CCS (ACM Conference on Computer and Communications Security), pp. 26–35 (2005)
17. Feller, W.: An Introduction to Probability Theory and Its Applications, 3rd edn., vol. I. John Wiley & Sons, Inc., Chichester (1968)
18. Sabelfeld, A., Sands, D.: Probabilistic noninterference for multi-threaded programs. In: Proceedings 13th IEEE Computer Security Foundations Workshop, Cambridge, UK, pp. 200–214 (July 2000)
19. Jonsson, B., Larsen, K.: Specification and refinement of probabilistic processes. In: Proc. 6th IEEE Symposium on Logic in Computer Science, pp. 266–277 (1991)
20. Baier, C., Katoen, J.-P., Hermanns, H., Wolf, V.: Comparative branching-time semantics for Markov chains. Information and Computation 200(2), 149–214 (2005)
21. Di Pierro, A., Hankin, C., Wiklicky, H.: Approximate non-interference. In: Proceedings 15th IEEE Computer Security Foundations Workshop, Cape Breton, Nova Scotia, Canada, pp. 1–17 (June 2002)
22. Clark, D., Hunt, S., Malacaria, P.: Quantitative analysis of the leakage of confidential data. Electronic Notes in Theoretical Computer Science 59(3) (2002)
23. Clark, D., Hunt, S., Malacaria, P.: Quantitative information flow, relations and polymorphic types. Journal of Logic and Computation 18(2), 181–199 (2005)
24. Malacaria, P.: Assessing security threats of looping constructs. In: Proceedings 34th Symposium on Principles of Programming Languages, Nice, France, pp. 225–235 (January 2007)
25. Köpf, B., Basin, D.: An information-theoretic model for adaptive side-channel attacks. In: Proceedings 14th ACM Conference on Computer and Communications Security, Alexandria, Virginia (2007)
26. Clarkson, M., Myers, A., Schneider, F.: Belief in information flow. In: Proceedings 18th IEEE Computer Security Foundations Workshop, Aix-en-Provence, France, pp. 31–45 (June 2005)
27. Lowe, G.: Quantifying information flow. In: Proceedings 15th IEEE Computer Security Foundations Workshop, Cape Breton, Nova Scotia, Canada, pp. 18–31 (June 2002)
28. Chatzikokolakis, K., Palamidessi, C., Panangaden, P.: Anonymity protocols as noisy channels. Information and Computation (to appear, 2008)

Author Index

Lecture Notes in Computer Science

Sublibrary 1: Theoretical Computer Science and General Issues

For information about Vols. 1–4618
please contact your bookseller or Springer